Perception

Perception
Essays After Frege

Charles Travis

OXFORD
UNIVERSITY PRESS

UNIVERSITY PRESS

Great Clarendon Street, Oxford, OX2 6DP,
United Kingdom

Oxford University Press is a department of the University of Oxford.
It furthers the University's objective of excellence in research, scholarship,
and education by publishing worldwide. Oxford is a registered trade mark of
Oxford University Press in the UK and in certain other countries

© in this volume Charles Travis 2013

The moral rights of the author have been asserted

First Edition published in 2013

Impression: 1

All rights reserved. No part of this publication may be reproduced, stored in
a retrieval system, or transmitted, in any form or by any means, without the
prior permission in writing of Oxford University Press, or as expressly permitted
by law, by licence or under terms agreed with the appropriate reprographics
rights organization. Enquiries concerning reproduction outside the scope of the
above should be sent to the Rights Department, Oxford University Press, at the
address above

You must not circulate this work in any other form
and you must impose this same condition on any acquirer

British Library Cataloguing in Publication Data

Data available

ISBN 978–0–19–967654–5

Printed and bound by CPI Group (UK) Ltd, Croydon, CR0 4YY

Links to third party websites are provided by Oxford in good faith and
for information only. Oxford disclaims any responsibility for the materials
contained in any third party website referenced in this work.

Contents

Introduction	1
1. The Silences of the Senses	23
2. Frege, Father of Disjunctivism	59
3. Viewing the Inner	90
4. Reason's Reach	118
5. The Inward Turn	144
6. Affording us the World	178
7. Is Seeing Intentional?	198
8. Unlocking the Outer World	223
9. Desperately Seeking Ψ	259
10. The Preserve of Thinkers	313
Appendix to The Preserve of Thinkers	352
11. That Object of Obscure Desire	364
12. While Under the Influence	391
Bibliography	413
Index	417

Introduction

What appears here is not a monograph but a connected series of essays, each succeeding one largely foreseen in what precedes it, and continuing one or two lines of thought already found there. The essays have two primary concerns. The first is to identify the most fundamental differences between perceptual and cognitive, or conceptual, awareness of the world we inhabit—a difference between awareness of the world, being as it is (or the world's being the way it is) and awareness of the world being some of the particular *ways* it is; a difference, too, at least on the whole, between awareness which is encountering, or witnessing, or being presented with things being as they are, and awareness which is bringing this under, or recognizing it as falling under, one or another generality. The second is to work out the ramifications, for perceptual experience, of that essential publicity, or shareability, of thought, correspondingly the publicity of its objects, on which Frege insisted. The first concern crystallizes, in one way, in issues as to whether perceptual experience has representational content. The second crystallizes, in one way, in issues over a view (or family of views) known as *disjunctivism*. But to work my way into these concerns, I begin with a story.

In the spring of 1966 Herbert Feigl came to UCLA to give a talk. Rudolf Carnap, then professor emeritus, was in the audience. Feigl's topic was 'central state materialism'. The gist of his talk was that, while he was sure central state materialism was correct, there was a residual problem he did not yet know how to deal with. This was the problem of 'raw feels', as they were then called. In the discussion that followed Carnap remarked that he thought he had a solution for Feigl's problem of raw feels. Feigl's interest was aroused. He asked Carnap, with some excitement, to tell him this solution. Carnap replied, 'Well, Herbert, I think the solution to your problem of raw feels is the a-factor'. Feigl appeared still more excited. 'Tell me, Carnap', he asked, 'What is the a-factor?' 'Well, Herbert', Carnap answered, 'You tell me what a raw feel is, and I'll tell you what the a-factor is'.

I was first provoked to write on perception, thirty-three years later, by the casual and widespread assumption that perception had representational content:

that perceptual experience(s) represent(s) the world as being 'a certain way'. Philosophy seemed to have taken a step backwards—a retreat from Austin, as I first thought of it, as I now see it also a retreat from, or simple rejection of, Frege. When it comes to perception, and its relation to thought, Frege was far ahead of his time (a time, perhaps, yet to come). He has inspired much in the lines of thought contained here. Hence the *double entendre* of a title here: essays post-Frege, essays following (so far as I can) in his footsteps.

In the beginning I did not appreciate that for many who saw perceptual experience as engaged in representing-as, the content thus assigned it was to be Carnap's *a*-factor. Representational content (harbouring somewhere in perceptual processing or states) was to replace, or just *be*, Feigl's raw feels—in current parlance, 'qualia'. Or anyway, a perceptual experience's having the 'phenomenal character' it did—looking, sounding, and so on, as it did to the experiencer—was to reduce to the (supposed) representational content of something or other (presumably sub-personal). Phenomenal character would at least then be no barrier to Feigl's 'central state materialism'.

I had not foreseen that Feigl's problem would fascinate so enduringly, or at this late date motivate much of anything. Subsequent essays in this series, notably 5 and 10, are aimed, *inter alia*, at correcting this initial oversight. The second, 'The Preserve of Thinkers', undertakes what most needs doing. If, in the case of perceptual experiences, the *a*-factor turns out to be some state of something sub-personal—perhaps a visual system or processing device—if it consists in that device, or its issue, representing things as being thus and so, there is no *obvious* reason why this should be recognizable to the *experiencer*, so no reason for a vehicle which makes this representing recognizable to him. One might then think that if there *is* such representing-as, this is for science to discover. *If* it is coherent to suppose what belongs to the sub-personal (for example, a visual system or processor) to engage in representing-as, this reflection might smooth the way to accepting that such actually occurs. The best prophylactic to this line of thought would be to show that the antecedent of this last conditional is false. The best way to do that would be to show, with as much generality as possible, just what the limits are on engaging in representing-as. Such is what Essay 11 undertakes. It aims to show that (and why) representing-as is an accomplishment available only to a thinker. If that is right, then the *a*-factor, whatever else it might turn out to be, could not be the bearing of representational content by one thing or another.

A felt need for Carnap's *a*-factor is not the only motive for holding perceptual experience to indulge in representing things *as* some way (or to 'contain' such representations). My initial concern was with another, prominent in some of the *most* important recent writings on perception and its links to thought.

Essays 1, 4, and 8 are aimed centrally at it. Before elaborating, though, I note that not every representationalist as per above is motivated, or at least clearly motivated, in either of the ways I mention, or certainly in the one way *rather than* the other. Some are simply unclear as to what, or where, the relevant representing is to be, or, notably, on whether it is representing *to* the perceiver, or simply *within* some internal processing or states. Some may simply be moved, wittingly or not, by the idea that all that processing must yield something *other* than the perceiver's surroundings for him to be aware of—a Lockean idea of objects of perception as representing, hence as other than, things in those surroundings. Such themes are also touched on in these essays. Still, I attach special importance to the motive I am about to mention.

The role assigned representation in the second motivation I will mention is to occupy a certain place in an answer to a question which I call *the fundamental question of perception*. That question is: How can perceptual experience make the world bear (rationally) *for the perceiver* on what he is to think and do? The answer in broad outline is, of course, by making recognizable to the perceiver what, in fact, bears on questions of what to think and do. In particular, if the question is whether to do such-and-such (for instance, to turn left *here*), then to make recognizable to the perceiver the obtaining of what are in fact determinate reasons to turn, or not to turn—for example, of the presence or absence of his destination to the left, or of a pride of lions straight ahead.

What a perceiver gains, for example, by looking, one would hope, is thus (*inter alia*) awareness of what stands in *rational* relations to the proposition that turning left is the thing for him to do—for example, of its being so that there is a pride of lions to his left. What burden does it put on perception to insist that *such* gains are what it must provide for? Such depends on what you think a *rational* relation is, or, again, on just what you think falls within reason's ambit. Here, I think, recent philosophy has encouraged some mythologies and misperceptions. For which, once again, Frege is the most effective antidote. Hence, again, the present title.

The key point in Frege for present purpose is a distinction he draws between what I have called the 'conceptual' and the 'non-conceptual', though I now favour the terms 'conceptual' and 'historical'. We can think of representing-as as a three-place relation: in the first place, a representer (some agent, or some item by which he represents, or, perhaps, some item which, in some other way, bears content); in the second place, what is represented *as* something or other; in the third place, a way for what occupies the second place to be represented as being. So thinking, the distinction I have in mind here is between what occupies the third place (the 'conceptual'), and what occupies the second (the 'historical').

A thought, to be that 'by which truth can come into question at all' (Frege 1918: p. 59), spans the last two terms of the relation. It fixes a way for one (or something) to occupy the first place—a way of representing something as something. It thus fixes—'contains'—both an occupier of the second and an occupier of the third place. (A thought *allows* truth to come into question. This is not to say that all representing-as is evaluable as true or false representing. As Frege stresses, representing-as may well stop short of representing something *to be so*—as in expressing a wish, or presenting the antecedent of a conditional.)

I begin with the third term of the relation, for a start the sort of term which a whole thought fixes. If the thought is true, then it is things being as they are which is (a case of) things being as represented. Things being such-and-such way is thus that third term which a whole thought fixes. Conversely, the thought is identified as the one it is in being *of* things being as they are (the second term it spans), and of this being things being the way in question (the third term it spans). 'Things' here bears what I call it's 'catholic' reading, one which blocks the question '*Which* things'. What thus occupies the second place in the representing-as relation (things, or their being as they are) is *history*, or historical—what encompasses such episodes as that bird chirping on the branch, the pig snuffling around the roots below. Things being as they are (history being as it is, or has been so far) is, or is not, things being such that a pig is snuffling. Such things are thus what occupy the second place in our relation.

A thought makes truth turn on whether things (catholic reading) are a certain way. What it thus does can be broken down, decomposed, into parts. If the thought makes truth turn on whether that pig is snuffling, it does this, in part, in making truth turn on who, or what, is snuffling, and in part in making truth turn on how that pig is. Something in the thought thus makes it about a way for *a* thing to be: such as to be snuffling. Such an element in a thought also represents something *as* something. It, too, is thus identified as the element it is by a second-place, as well as by a third-place occupier. What occupies the second place in this case? One *could* say: the relevant pig. To be sure, it is the pig which is snuffling or not. But pigs are the sorts of things to take up and leave off snuffling. Whether they now fall under that generality, *a thing being such as to be snuffling*, all depends on how they *now* are. It is that pig's being as it now is, or was last Tuesday at 10, or something else's being as it now is, which is, or is not, a case of something snuffling. Such are the particular cases which *instance* such generalities as a way *for a* thing to be. (Of course, the pig is not as it is unless things (catholic reading) are as *they* are. We could say: the pig reflects things in general from its own porcine point of view.)

A thought, if it is to bring truth into question, falls nowhere short of fixing the second-place occupier which it represents as thus and so. If we think of a way for *a* thing to be—such as to smoke, say—as independent of any thought which is (*inter alia*) about it, then a way for a thing to be (or what makes a thought about this) contrasts with a thought in this respect. For a way for a thing to be does not identify any individual in particular (nor any set of them) as that which *it* represents as such as to smoke. It is simply not in that line of work. It does not, as a thought does, represent anything in particular as anything. It may still be true *of* some things and not others. But it does not, as a thought does, engage in representing-as outright. (So nor does it identify any concept (*Begriff*) as Frege uses the term 'Begriff' after splitting off what he came to call *Bedeutung* from what he called *beurteilbare Inhalt* and then identifying concepts with functions.)

But we need to locate this contrast in the right place. It is not between what has, and what lacks, so to speak, 'empty places'—what Frege might have called 'unsaturated' and 'saturated' respectively. When we break a thought into elements, each element, being only a partial performance of the thought's task, calls for completion. One might thus view it as 'unsaturated'. But *all* the elements are in the same line of work as the thought itself. All relate a second-place occupier to a third-place one. If the thought makes truth turn on whether that pig is snuffling, then the element which makes it about snuffling stops nowhere short of representing *that* pig as snuffling. It is what it is—just as the thought is what it is—by virtue of its involvement with a given second-place, as well as a given third-place occupier. If we detach the relevant third-place occupier—a way for a thing to be, conceived as independent of any thought involving it—from the thought-element—that partial performance of the thought's whole task—then, of course, what we end up with is something not in the thought's line of work. But this comes from such detaching, and not from the circumstance of decomposing the thought into elements. One can, equally, detach from the whole thought a way to represent things in general as being, conceived independent of its role in any particular thought, as a mere third-place occupier for a thought to involve along with the second-place occupier it does. Such a thing would stand on equal footing (*in re* the envisioned contrast) with a way for *a* thing to be.

In the third place of the representing-as relation, then—*what* something is represented as being—we have a way for things, or a thing, to be. In the second place—what is thus represented as something or other—we have a fundamentally different sort of thing—things being as they are (or a thing as it is). The fundamental difference here is that, in a certain sense of 'generality', to be made out, it is essential to what occupies the third place to have a certain sort of generality which it is essential to what occupies the second to lack. Frege speaks of the relevant generality in remarking:

A thought always contains something reaching beyond the particular case, by means of which this is presented as falling under some general thing (*etwas Allgemein*).

(1882, *Kernsatz* 4)

A thought *contains* something by which it reaches beyond the particular case. In so reaching it presents that case as falling under some given generality. It represents that case *as* something or other. Part of its being the thought it is is thus its being *of* a particular occupier of the second place of our three-place relation. No less would make for something truth-evaluable. The thought that things are such-and-such represents *things* (or things being as they are) as something in particular. But its being the thought it is is also, intrinsically, its being of a particular occupier of the third place of the relation—of things (catholic reading) being such-and-such way in particular. It thus contains what makes it about this way. It is in its so relating to this third-place occupier that its intrinsic generality (of the sort of which Frege here speaks) resides. If we decompose a thought into elements out of which being about some way for things to be may be composed—say, being about some given way for *a* thing to be, and about some given individual—then we may speak of the thought, so decomposed, as containing those elements. Such is *one* use of 'contain'. If we think of the thought as fixed by (thus taking in) both a second-place and a third-place occupier, we reach another understanding of 'contain'. It is that understanding which is fundamental here.

The generality at issue emerges in the reflection that a way for things to be is, *eo ipso*, a way for truth to turn on how things are; a particular way for things to matter to a sort of representing-as. A way *for* things being as they are to matter to truth is, *per se*, fixed independent of things being as, in fact, they are. (Things might have been different while there was still *that* way for truth to matter.) Hence for truth to turn in that way on how things are cannot be for it to turn on *everything* as to how things in fact are. There is, then, what matters and what does not. For truth to turn on whether Sid smokes is, *inter alia*, for it not to count against truth that, for example, Pia smokes, or does not, or that Sid does, or does not, wear Bermuda shorts. So if things being as they are is a case of things being such that Sid smokes, such is *one* way for this to happen—one among indefinitely many ways. Nor is *this* feature peculiar to things being such that Sid smokes. It is built into the very idea of a way for things to be; a feature of *any* such way. In the terminology used in these essays, a way for things to be (or for *a* thing to be) *reaches to*, or is *instanced by*, indefinitely many distinct (possible) cases

Such generality is inherent in any way for things to be, thereby in *any* thought. It is missing in what instances, or is a case of, such a way. Things being as they are may be a case of things being such that penguins waddle. It is, anyway, what the thought that penguins waddle represents as instancing that way. Everything matters to things being as they are. It is thus one-off. But that is not the point. The point is rather that what instances a way for things to be is not itself what has a reach. What that pig is now doing is a case of snuffling. That pig's being (or doing) what it now is is a case of *something* snuffling. Its doings are an episode in world history. For something to have a reach is for it to be so of indefinitely many particular cases that they instance this thing, or do not. Something about the thing with reach must decide the status particular cases thus enjoy. The pig's doing, or being, what it now is does no such thing. Nor does anything about it. Nothing in what the pig is doing decides when (if ever) there would be another case of snuffling.

One might *witness* the pig's doing what it is, in which one witnesses a case of snuffling, equally, one of porcine snuffling. One cannot witness *for something to be a case of a thing snuffling*, or *what it would be for something to be a case of this*, or *what would count as a case*. Acquaintance with such things demands another source. As Frege notes, one gains such acquaintance, not through witnessing, but rather through *thinking*.

Generalizing, no proper part of the reach of some way for things to be determines anything about what the rest of that reach might be. (Thus a familiar point about ostensive definition: examples identify a way for things to be only given some adequate understanding of what it is they are to exemplify; of what makes them cases of that.) Conversely, a way for things to be does not (in general) depend for its existence on the existence of any particular case of it. Neither that pig nor its present doings need have been part of world history for there to be such a thing as snuffling. (This makes ways for things to be contrast with what Frege came to call concepts when these became *Bedeutungen* of predicative expressions.)

The interest of the conceptual/historical distinction for present matters—notably for the fundamental question—lies in the nature of instancing (being a case of). Two points are of note. First, if we view instancing as a relation, then its first term—a particular case—is not something to which a law of truth (logic) might speak. Things being as they are (or a thing as it is) is not the sort of thing which might, for example, *entail* something. It does not decompose into elements of a way for truth to *turn* on how things are. It is a *case* of things being thus and so (for literally countless 'thus and so's). But it does not entail that things are thus. Nor, again, is the relation between things being as they are and things being such that Sid smokes one between the *instancing* of one way for things to be and the instancing of others (the sort of thing which brings entailment into the picture). That Sid smokes may entail that Sid will die young. What instances (is a case of) someone being a smoker is at least likely to instance someone being such as to die young. But that things are as they are does not *entail* that Sid smokes. Things being as they are is just a case of it; an historical, filmable, episode of someone being a smoker. Things being as they are does not decide what things so being instances.

Second, there is no chance of an answer to the fundamental question unless instancing is the sort of thing a (perceiving) thinker can be *competent* to recognize. One may know a pig snuffling, or someone being a smoker, when he sees (or otherwise encounters) one. To see *that* the pig is snuffling in (or by) seeing the pig snuffling one must recognize what one thus sees (second occurrence) as a *case* of a pig snuffling. That first occurrence of 'see' is not a *perceptual* verb. Recognizing is a success. The success here consists in relating something to which the laws of truth do not apply to something to which they might. Seeing *that* A is F by seeing A F-ing requires acquaintance with both terms of the instancing relation—with what *does* the instancing, and with the way for things to be thus instanced. Nothing short of this could work the trick. Perception's mission is to provide *such* acquaintance. Loading perceptual experience with representational content can be no help with this. Again, the fundamental question *has* an answer only if there is such a thing as being *competent* to recognize where instancing obtains and where not. So it had better be possible to take in what does *not* belong to the conceptual—to be aware of things being as they are—other than by mediation of something which does so belong.

So, if there *is* any answer to the fundamental question, then things being as they are may certainly *bear* on whether for Sid to be a smoker is a way for things to be which is instanced. It is not something to which the laws of truth apply. But for all that it had better be something *i* regarding which reason may dictate what to hold. The right thing to say as to whether the way things are (or the goings on under that tree) counts as a case of a pig snuffling might just be that it does if anything does. We may thus sometimes *see* (non-perceptual use) what the historical *must* be counted as being.

By virtue of the first point above, one *might* refuse to count instancing as a rational relation. In which case, if perception *can* make the world bear for us on what to think, then it is not (because it cannot be) only through rational relations that it does this. Or, by virtue of the second point, one might count instancing as a rational relation. In which case, there is a distinction to be made between a rational relation—one for which reason may *dictate* to us what to hold—and a relation between what (perhaps modulo a grammatical transformation) can stand in relations to which logic speaks. Most notably among the essays here, 4 and 8 develop this idea.

I will eventually return to the conceptual/historical distinction, commenting a bit more on why it seems to some hard to buy. First, though, I turn to a second main theme of the essays here. Adapting a phrase of Spike Milligan's, once there was no talk of disjunctivism at all; now there is more of it than anyone might wish. Though the *term* is inspired (but not used) by J. M. Hinton, it is now understood in a variety of ways, many having little or nothing to do with this source. There is at least more agreement in use by those friendly to the term (or its supposed denotation) than those not. In any event, the most I can do is to say something about how *I* use it here.

First, a brief story agreed to by (nearly) all hands. I call it 'Stuff Happens'. It goes something like this. Light reflected from (or emitted by) things before the eyes arrives on retinas, there forming images. Those images generate (presumably electrochemical) signals which travel farther 'inward' along the optic nerve. Then stuff happens. Signals get processed—transformed into others, or into states of processors. As one might see things, the signals generated by retinas are impoverished in information about the scene before the eyes; the processing fills in, (fallibly) in line with what the source of this impoverished information is likely to be. (This part of the story is optional for present purpose.)

There are now two ways of understanding the Stuff Happens Model. On one, the upshot of the processing is (when things go well) awareness of the scene before him by the person whose processors they are; more specifically, *visual* awareness. On another, the upshot is (in the first instance) visual awareness of something else—an image, or picture, or anyway something created by the processing. Such an object of visual awareness is what *could* be available with or without the scene in question. If the image bears a certain relation to that scene, involving, perhaps, aetiology, perhaps correspondence with it, perhaps other factors, then the awareness of *it* is what is called (*visual*) awareness of the scene itself.

Disjunctivism understands the Stuff Happens story in the first way, and rejects the idea that seeing bears any such relation as the second understanding posits to visual awareness of something else, or that, in seeing, there *is* such a something else of which to be *visually* aware. This is not to deny that we *are* sometimes visually aware of things other than the scene before us, for example, of 'the room spinning' (inability to focus). (Not all anti-disjunctivists would agree that they are committed to visual awareness, in seeing, of *images*, as per above. Part of the point of the essays here is to argue that they are.)

One at home with labels might call the present essays *disjunctivist* and *anti-representationalist*. It might then be remarked that some noted disjunctivists are also representationalists. Are the positions then independent? It is anyway no surprise if one who wanted perception to make the *world* bear for the perceiver on what to think and do should also be a disjunctivist—certainly not if the role of perception in all this just is to provide acquaintance with, or (perceptual) awareness of, that which is thus to do the bearing. You can *call* visual awareness of an image visual awareness of the donkey standing impassively before me if you like. You can call anything anything if you like. But an image of a donkey—something there might be donkey or not—leaves it open, so far as *it* goes, what the thing for me to do would be if I am looking for a donkey ride, in a way that the presence of the donkey before me does not. Perception is not doing the job wanted here if it thus, inevitably, in the nature of the case, leaves me in the lurch. Conversely, a representationalist needs a *bearer* of content which—since it is content liable to be either true or false—must be a bearer which would be present whether I see a donkey or merely experience a ringer for doing so. Such a common element seems just what a disjunctivist denies. So one might think the two positions *not* independent. And so argue the essays here.

There is a general point about experience. I may tell you that I had an unusual, interesting, or perhaps excruciating, experience last night—or last month. The experience may have been one of listening to Sid drone on all night about football, or of viewing Mt Fuji from Lake Shojiko on a misty afternoon. Suppose you ask me what the experience was like. You *may* be asking either of several things. On one way of understanding the question I would answer by telling you what it was that I encountered—a reincarnation of Howard Cosell, say, or a snow-capped peak coming into and out of focus as mist swirled by; or, perhaps, what one undergoes—descending from a bus, one walks through a wood (the trees leafless at this time of year) until he arrives at a gravelly shore. Ahead, the mountain looms up as though rising out of the sea. Answering the question, so understood, is saying what *one* would experience—what is there to *be* experienced, what it is like for *one*.

So it is with visual experience. Asking what was seen is *one* way of asking what was experienced visually. *Seeing* just is seeing what is there for *one* to see. (Some think 'see' also has another sense. On this see especially Essay 7.) So an answer to *such* a question about visual experience fits the model just scouted. A first draft of such an answer would just tell us what was then (visibly) before the experiencer's eyes. It might mention, for example, the pig snuffling, the oak's rustling leaves. A refined draft would then delete whatever was missed, or for one reason or another, counts as *not* seen (by this viewer at this time). Sid did not see the robin on that branch, so focused was he on the search for truffles.

Some questions what was experienced (or what this was like) bear a different understanding. What Pia experienced listening to Hogo's talk on tropes and the sea battle was, for example, nausea welling up, or difficulty staying awake. Not that that is what is there for *one* to experience listening to Hogo. (Though *perhaps* it is.) It is just how things were for Pia, then. So it is with visual experience. Pia *saw* a flyspeck on the wall. In the throes of a vertigo attack, it was for her as though it was moving across the wall (without ever seeming to arrive anywhere). This last, too, may be an account of visual experience.

Disjunctivism lays stress on the idea that these two very different sorts of accounts of visual experience—answers to two very different sorts of questions about it—are answerable to (if anything) very different sorts of ingredients in things being as things are; so that it is not as though for Pia to have seen the flyspeck on the wall is for her to have experienced, visually, such-and-such, where that is an account of the second kind above (and, perhaps, for some further factors, other than her experiencing such-and-such, to obtain).

To what *is* the second sort of account of visual experience answerable? On what, if anything, does its truth turn? The present essays do not answer this question. (Not that any one answer need fit all cases.) But some of them—notably, 3, 5, 12—begin to explore one idea for an answer: that (a substantial part of) the work done in *seeing* by what there was to be seen (before the eyes) is taken over, where this is not what is to do the work, by the experiencer's *responses* (or responsiveness) to things being as they then were for him. (As, of what was there to be seen, it may be response which settles what was seen, what missed, so where we cannot speak of what was *there* to be experienced visually, still, response can fix what *is* to be fixed as to how things were then, visually, for that experiencer.)

Sight *affords* awareness of what is before the eyes (or as much of it as *can* be seen). If it thus puts opportunities on offer, *enjoying* awareness would be taking these up—something which, often, at least, we may or may not do. Searching the kitchen counter for my favourite knife, it might be 10 minutes before I finally see what was all along in plain view. Here seeing is registering. To do that I needed to look—direct attention—in the right way. I do not mean to suggest that, independent of this last step, visual processing all along *enabled* awareness of the knife. This may or may not be so. If Leibniz is right, it sometimes is. But attention *might* have its effects on visual processing (so far as the present point goes). Nor should 'sight affords awareness' be read: sight furnishes some object of visual awareness *other* than the scene before the eyes—an image of some sort—where a knife-image may, or may not have been, all along, part of what was thus furnished. I mean only that there is liable to be more there *to* be visually aware of—more that one could have been aware of if he noticed—than that of which a viewer actually enjoys visual awareness; *what* more there is determined by the scene itself.

Understanding affording in this way, there is, in seeing, always substantial distance between being afforded awareness and enjoying it—territory that may be occupied by cases, such as the knife. What distance, if any, is there between these two notions where to say what was experienced visually is to answer a question of our second kind—for example, its being for Pia as though the flyspeck is moving across the wall? Might she be failing to *enjoy* some awareness of how things were then for her visually—features, perhaps, of the path the flyspeck appeared to her as though it took—of which she was anyway *afforded* enjoyment; which were anyway there to *be* experienced (in this case, only by her?). Perhaps if Pia raised her eyes a bit she would see another flyspeck, and that, too, would appear to move. Perhaps if she continues watching, the one before her eyes will continue to move. But these are not things of which she is *now* afforded awareness. Such possibilities are irrelevant.

One might be tempted to either a positive or a negative answer. Neither, though, is free of cost (at least for those hostile to disjunctivism). Suppose we plump for the affirmative. Philosophical interest in visual experiences of the second kind is traditionally prompted, at least in part, by the following thought. Suppose that Pia sees the persimmon on the sideboard. Still, there are many ways things could look to someone who saw *just* what Pia thus did. The persimmon's colour might look different ways to different subjects. Or it might be more or less in focus for different subjects. And so on. So, the idea is, saying what Pia *saw* gives at most a partial answer to the question how things were then for her visually (or what she experienced visually). A full answer (the idea runs) calls for an answer to a question of the second kind. Further, there is some question of the second kind whose answer, added to the answer to our first question, would be such a full answer. (For an anti-disjunctivist, answers to a question of the first kind might then drop out as superfluous.) But an affirmative answer to our second question means that where, for example, Pia sees the persimmon there is that which there *is* to be experienced, independent of whether she actually *enjoys* awareness of it (in that sense, *does* experience it) or not; whether she recognizes, or registers, this as there to be experienced, or not. They are there to be *observed* or not. If there are such response-independent things *to be* experienced, then it is in the cards (at least the logical cards) that there should be different ways for one to experience them visually—different ways they may look, depending on the observer (or experiencer). In that case, saying what Pia experienced in her experience of the second sort is no more a *full* answer to the question how things were for her visually than is saying what she *saw*. The same issues arise for objects of experience of the second sort as do for objects of experience of the first.

But suppose we plump for a negative answer. Perception and thought generally divide along this line: perception provides us with awareness of things to respond to; thought (where such things are its object) *is* a response to this. For visual experience of the second kind, this distinction between presentation and response seems to collapse. For Pia to *enjoy* visual awareness of its being for here as though the flyspeck moved—for her to be responsive to this—and for there to be such a thing of which to enjoy visual awareness now coincide. Which, in turn, may seem to threaten to assimilate (perceptual) experience to thinking in incoherent ways. (Objects of thought cannot, as objects of perception can, literally grow on trees, or even appear to someone as though they were doing so.) Wittgenstein worried about such issues in his notebooks on aspects (among other places). Part of the work of the essays here is to do away with any such impression of a threat. But such (or as far as it gets here) is only part of understanding what needs understanding *in re* perceptual experience of the second kind.

If the robin on the branch was in plain view, Pia may unproblematically have been *afforded* awareness of it. Whether, in her fascination with the pig, she *enjoyed* such awareness depends on what sort of responsiveness to the robin might make for such enjoyment (or what sort of obliviousness might make for lack of it). There are different demands one might impose here, different understanding of what enjoyment might be. Still, though, what is in question is Pia's sensitivity to the *robin*, whose presence owes nothing to her awareness of it. Answers to questions of the second sort do not, or not obviously, put anything other than the robin (or other things before the eyes) in the role the robin here plays. If, eyes watering, Pia sees the robin in a blur, or (tricks of perspective) it seems smaller than it is, or if, somehow, the 'robin' is a mere mirage, it is not (or not obviously) as if there were a blur, or a smaller, or surrogate, robin, there independent of her awareness of it, for her to be *afforded* awareness of, option taken up or not. Such lack of independence, in experience of the second kind, of what there *is* to be experienced from responding to it, if such lack there is, gives *some* reason to suspect what the essays just mentioned consider: that work of what is independent of its experiencing in experience of the first kind is taken over by responses in experience of the second. In which case the disjunctivist's doubt becomes whether experience of what does not enjoy such independence can really *be* experience of what does, if only undergone in the right circumstances.

I return to the conceptual–historical distinction. This, along with the idea that a way for truth to turn on something is, *eo ipso*, a way for it to turn on a shared environment, and, correlatively, the idea that a thought is *intrinsically* what indefinitely many thinkers might think, forms Frege's core contribution to present work. It matters so much here that I am afraid I have introduced it often, and, perhaps, repetitively. I have explained it again above. I want now to scout some possible reasons why it has given some *very* good philosophers pause, or at least unease. *That* it does worries me greatly. I do not really understand this. But I will venture a few guesses.

For one thing, I have been accused of misappropriating Frege (misreading *Kernsatz* 4). Such is not yet to impugn the distinction itself, nor my use of it. Perhaps, though, we can work through this towards understanding the distinction's import better. To begin, *Kernsatz* 4 speaks of a thought *containing* (*enthalten*) something. On *one* understanding of containment, what a thought *contains* are its parts—those elements which make it up (on a decomposition). The thought's role is to make truth turn in a particular way on how things are. An element which made it up would make truth turn, in part, on something in particular. If the whole thought makes truth turn on whether Sid smokes, then an element might make truth turn, somehow or other, on who smokes—in terms of my distinction, on the career (of being instanced) of a certain way for a thing to be: such as to smoke. Reading *enthalten* in one way, the generality conferred on a thought by what it thus contains would be conferred on it by some element in particular—one might guess on what Frege might call a 'predicative element'.

I concede that text gives *some* support to this reading. In that same letter to Marty in which Frege insists that a thought is *not* built up out of elements, but rather decomposable into them, he *also* says what can be read as suggesting a somewhat different line. On the first score he says:

Now I do not believe that the formation of concepts can precede that of judgements, because this presupposes an independent existence of concepts, but I think that concepts arise through the decomposition of judgeable contents. I do not believe that for each judgeable content there is but one way it can be decomposed, or that one of the possible ways may always claim objective priority.

(1882: p. 118)

On the second this:

In this case, where the subject is an individual thing, the relation between subject and predicate is not a third thing added to both of these, but it belongs to the content of the predicate, through just which this (predicate) is unsaturated.

(1882: p. 118)

Here, where a thought *is* decomposed into an element which makes it singular, and a predicative element, the predicative element is given a kind of priority over the other one. There, it seems to be suggested, harbours what makes those parts into a whole thought. *There*, one might also think, harbours that which allows that whole thought to reach to particular cases so as to present them as instancing some given generality.

There is thus a *prima facie* tension in Frege, or at least in this letter. The reading just sketched is, for a start, certainly in tension with what Frege just said as to thoughts being multiply decomposable; and about putting whole thoughts first in approaching logic. But, having made my concession, I now put text aside. Anyway, the idea of a thought *containing* its elements is only one way of understanding the metaphor 'contain' here. A thought might also *contain* its generality (or what gives it its generality) in a way something like the way in which a letter may contain thinly-veiled contempt for its recipient. There is no particular element in the letter (understanding element as constituent—a given phrase or speech act) which is where the thinly-veiled contempt harbours. There is an aura about the whole. One *could* think of generality on this model: a thought contains something—namely, its particular way of making truth turn on how things are— to have which is to have a certain generality (as per my previous discussion of the distinction). If we decompose the thought so as to contain one main predicative element—as in that second quote above—then that element contains the same kind of generality as the whole thought. So does *every* element of a thought. Its generality lies in its contributing as it does to what the whole thought does (or, on another view of elements, to what whole ranges of whole thoughts do).

To privilege predicative elements as this first reading of containment does is most naturally to read particular cases—those things presented as falling under a generality—as *objects* which fall under concepts (on some understanding of concepts). It would then be *objects* which lack all generality (as, of course, they do), and concepts by means of which *these* are presented as falling under some given one. But, again, there is no compulsion to read things in this way. A particular case might just as well be things being as they are, or a thing as it is. One might also note here that Frege insists that where one *can* decompose a thought into an element which makes it singular with respect to some object, and then another which—so to speak—predicates something of that object, in place of that first element one can always just as well find a *predicative* element, predicating of something *being that very object* (such-and-such). Many cases of an object being as it is would be a case of an object being Frege, though, of course, ever so many others would not.

Michael Dummett (1981, 1991) has made a (to my mind) convincing case that '17 *Kernsätze*' is commentary on Hermann Lotze's *Logik*. This has been taken to suggest a different reading of *Kernsatz* 4 from mine. Lotze's primary sin here (or at least one) was to propose a distinction between 'true' and 'false' combinations of *Vorstellungen*. This makes combinations of *Vorstellungen* (or some range of them) truth-bearers, placing them in precisely the role which Frege assigns thoughts (and takes to explain what a thought, *au fond*, is). Of course, such is anathema to Frege. But why?

The term 'Vorstellung' seems to have been a primitive for Kant: he uses it to explain other terms, but uses it undefined (see 1781/1789: 19/33). Perhaps it is partly because of this that *Vorstellungen* were different things to different German philosophers in the nineteenth century. Frege gives his own explanation of what *he* means by a *Vorstellung* (see 1918: pp. 67–8.) The key thing here is that a *Vorstellung* belongs to the consciousness of a particular thinker; is co-existent with *his* awareness of it. Perhaps this makes Lotze's idea *particularly* objectionable. In any case, since Kant, *Vorstellungen* have often been conceived as objects of perceptual awareness. This in itself is objectionable to Frege, who insisted, 'A thought is something non-sensory, and all things observable by the senses are excluded from its domain' (1918: p. 61). Such is essential to his distinction between what is perceptually observable—things which can be represented as being one way or another—and that which belongs to thought—ways, or things, things of the first kind may be represented as being. One sees the flower's five petals, but—if 'see' remains a verb of perception—not *that* the flower has five of them (see 1897: 149).

Certainly Frege would find Lotze's idea objectionable—for a number of reasons. Seeing the *Kernsätze* as a commentary on Lotze, one might then think as follows. In the *Kernsätze*, Frege contrasts Lotze's *Vorstellungen* with concepts, which *are* the right sorts of things out of which to compose thoughts (or truth-bearers). Thus it is that he says, in *Kernsatz* 1,

The connections (*Verknüpfungen*) which constitute the essence of thinking are fundamentally different from the association of *Vorstellungen*.

Vorstellungen are the *wrong* sorts of things; concepts the right sort—a point emphasized by pointing, in *Kernsatz* 4, to concepts as the place where that generality harbours which allows thoughts to reach beyond the particular case—*if Kernsatz* 4 so points. The generality of a concept, the thought would be, consists in its being such as to make *objects* fall under it or not; and (the further thought) *here* is where a thought's generality resides, rather than, as I suggest, in its reaching to an indefinitely extendible range of particular cases. I will not speculate further on just *how* a thought's generality is to be conceived as residing here.

There is much more to be said about that second passage in the letter to Marty, and the idea in Frege it may seem to represent. But this is not the place for such exegesis. Instead, a different tack. The idea that *Vorstellungen*, in combinations or not, can be what brings *truth* into question is objectionable, and anathema to Frege, in several ways. One of these, though, seems particularly fundamental. In putting whole thoughts first as Frege does, he calls our attention to this point. To be an element of a thought—of that which brings truth into question—just is to make *truth* turn in part on something in particular (turn on how things are in part in a certain way). (Or, one *might* say, it is just making truth to turn in that way.) Such is something that *could* be done only in the context of a thought. So, to put it picturesquely, something could be an element in a thought—could make such a partial contribution to what a whole thought does—only if its life consisted in making such a contribution, that is, in being a part of some thought, or, perhaps, some range(s) of thoughts. Some other life that it might have had anyway (*for example*, being an object of perceptual awareness) could not confer on it fitness for life within a thought—the right sort of 'content' to function as a thought element were it then so inserted in a thought (whatever 'insert' might then mean). The problem is the idea that something else (other than belonging to the decomposition of a thought) could make *anything* such as to make truth turn in part on such-and-such. The point is not that it take a concept to *give* a thought its generality. (If anything, that idea has things backwards.)

There is, I think, a parallel here for *bearing* content: nothing could have a content by which it contributed to the expression of thoughts (so as to make these expressions of a thought with a certain thought element)—in shorthand, nothing could *express* a thought-element—except by virtue of having a life which consisted in contributing to the expressions of *thoughts*. Nothing *other than* this—for example, 'causal–nomological' relations with an environment—could confer on it the ability to lead such a life of thought-expression. Such can be seen as the core point of Essay 10.

Given this, of course, *Vorstellungen*, as Lotze seems to have conceived these (or as Frege did), could not be thought-elements, whether in combinations or not. Nor could many other things. The problem with *Vorstellungen* is not now merely that they are private (though this raises a different problem on its own). If the objects of perception were, instead, pigs and oaks, or Porsches, or clouds, mist, or snow-capped peaks, one could not build ways for truth to turn on things out of them either. Nor could one do this out of neural states or structures.

The problem is, put in a way Frege sometimes uses, you might find Venus in the night sky, but you will not find *being a heavenly body* there. Which is to say: the fundamental problem—what rules out both *Vorstellungen* and pigs and Porsches—concerns precisely what I have used *Kernsatz* 4 to introduce. You cannot build what lies on that side of the historical–conceptual distinction where thoughts reside (along with ways to represent something as being) out of what lies on the other side—things to represent as being one way or another (the historical). Nor, to put it in terms I have insisted on, out of cases of things being as thus represented.

In the scheme I have outlined, *instancing* is a relation between two absolutely disjoint domains: what stands on the first side of the relation (what belongs to the domain I have named 'historical') cannot belong to what stands on the second (what belongs to the domain I have named 'conceptual'), and *vice versa*. This mimics a feature Frege assigns to the relation he calls 'falling under': *objects* (in his broad sense of 'object') fall under *concepts*; what is an object cannot be a concept, and *vice versa*. But instancing is not falling under, ways for things to be are not concepts in Frege's sense, particular cases (things being as they are, something's being as it is) are not objects. One must not lose sight of the difference.

In 1882, Frege speaks of *concepts* as lacking independent existence—as understandable, and identifiable, only in terms of whole thoughts. This is the point I have just made, in expanded form. What Frege *means* by 'concept' is not quite what he will come to mean by it after separating off what he calls *Bedeutung* from 'judgeable content' and making a concept a *Bedeutung* of a certain kind of thought-element (or its expression). But the point stands and holds as well for objects. These, too, in a sense, lack independent existence and are identifiable only in terms of whole thoughts. Thought is not, of course, prior to Mount Blanc or the North Sea, or that snuffling pig. And objects can be 'presented to consciousness' either in the sense in which they are done so by a source, or in a channel, of information about them—as Dr Lauben's injured shin is presented to him as bleeding in his feeling the blood course down it—or in the sense in which Dr Lauben is presented in a thought as the one on whom its truth thus turns (for example, the one whose shin must be bleeding). But an object, for Frege's purpose, just is what truth can turn on in a particular way—what one arrives at as something a thought is about on a particular way of decomposing it. To *be* an object just is to be what functions in a certain decomposition of a thought in a certain way. The notion of a thought is thus prior to that of an object, just as it is prior to that of a generality under which an *object* might fall. Our intuitive notion of an object as a medium-sized piece of drygoods should not obscure this point. In this way, the particular cases of *Kernsatz* 4 are prior to objects.

Frege speaks of *objects* as falling under *concepts*. But if we think of a concept as *of* some given way for a thing to be—for example, of snuffling—then whether an object does this or not for a given concept depends on how that object is. In general (when we move away from mathematics) it is something an object does transiently, datedly. That pig is snuffling now; was not when it awoke this morning, will soon stop. It is the pig's being as it now is (and not, for example, its being as it was when it awoke) that is a case of snuffling. It is thus the pig's being as it now is that stands towards *something snuffling* as instancing it. (If (with Frege) we think of a concept as just a mapping of objects into truth values (or the taking on of given such values for given such arguments) then the point becomes: which concept *is snuffling* has as its *Bedeutung* is a matter of the ways things are at some time when this is to be determined.)

Objects do not fall on the historical side of the conceptual/historical distinction as drawn. They are, of course, in some sense historical. Like the world, they have careers (each the world's career as seen from that object's point of view). Rubens is an historical figure. The house he built with the proceeds of his success still stands in Antwerp. Place yourself suitably in its vicinity and rays reflected from it will form images on your retinas. They are things which can be *represented* as being thus and so; *not* ways to represent things being (or parts thereof). But it is their careers—their being as they are—which make those ways to represent them being ways to represent truly, or again, falsely. It is not the objects which do the instancing.

Some generality lies somewhere in an object's vicinity. Venus today, Venus tomorrow, Venus when we are all long gone. Indefinitely many cases of a thing's being as it is are cases of a thing being Venus. For an object to be Venus is thus a way for an object to be. It is here, in this way for things to be—and not in the planet, in its orbit in space—that the generality thus mentioned lies. Not that that way for a thing to be need always function in a thought-element in a predicative role. It also offers a way for a thought-element to make truth turn essentially, on how that particular object, Venus, is—on which ways for a thing to be its being as it is instances. But, as Frege points out (see, for example, 1882), whether it functions in one role or another in a given thought depends on how one decomposes that thought. The thought that Venus shines bright tonight is, on one way of seeing things, a thought of that planet in the sky that it is a certain way (namely, such as to shine bright). But on another way of seeing things—with equally respectable credentials, Frege insists—it is the thought that everything which is a certain given way—namely, such as to be that very thing Venus—is also another (see above). Again reason to be leery of the idea that the generality of a thought harbours in some *particular* element in it—or that Frege thought so.

A final note. Things being the *way* they are, which *ways* they are, still depends on a further factor: for each way for things to be, what would count as a case of things being that way (or, perhaps more modestly, whether things being as they are is something which would so count). In this sense, things being such that, for example, Pia is sipping Cava is something over and above things being as they are. Misreading the terms, 'further factor', 'over and above', or some other of that ilk, *might* give the misimpression that the way things are still needs to be transformed, somehow, into something else before we arrive at something which is genuinely Pia sipping Cava (transformed, perhaps, by something like some episode of representation). In a Kantian image (whether Kant's idea or not), in experience we enjoy perceptual awareness of manifold things, which, if the objects of perceptual experience are not to be utterly chaotic, must be transformed by something else into (as Kant puts it) an *image* (*Bild*)—one hopes a coherent one. In parallel, one might (try to) think of things being as they are as itself all chaos, transformed for us by something else into, for example, a pig snuffling beneath an oak.

A very bad idea about perception paired with perhaps an even worse idea about the world. The space between the historical and the conceptual in the present scheme of things makes no room for anything such imagery might fit. If Pia *is* sipping, then it is things being as they are, if anything, which is *one* way (among indefinitely many) for this to be so. Nothing this might be transformed into could possibly play this role. Pia's holding glass to lip in *just* the way this transpired *is* the historical which counts as a case of Pia sipping Cava—given what would so count. There is nothing in the historical–conceptual distinction to drive the objects of *our* thought out of the world we inhabit. Quite the contrary.

I have now scouted two main themes of the essays, and done a bit more than scout probably the most important idea deployed in developing them. The rest I leave to the essays themselves, with an apology for the repetitive introduction in them of that main idea (though the idea *has* evolved somewhat, and appears in somewhat improved form in this introduction). These essays, but for one, have all been previously published. Some are in new version here, as indicated. They appear here in roughly the order of their composition—not always corresponding to order of first appearance. Below I list the essays and their original place of publication.

1 'The Silence of the Senses', originally in *Mind*, 113, no. 449 (January 2004): 59–94. Here my perhaps idiosyncratic terminology provoked what I thought avoidable misreadings of the text. I revised the terminology accordingly. Revision is extensive.
2 'Frege, Father of Disjunctivism', originally in *Philosophical Topics*, 33, no. 1 (Spring 2005): 307–34.
3 'Viewing the Inner', originally in A. Hatzimoysis, ed., *Self-Knowledge*. Oxford: Oxford University Press, 2011: pp. 202–25. While this essay was being translated into French, I had considerable discussions with my translators on how to translate, or, more fundamentally, how to understand, certain sections. I benefitted from these enormously. I took the

opportunity to make substantial improvements. I thank Bruno Ambroise, Valérie Aucouturier, and Layla Raïd for this.

4 'Reason's Reach', originally in *The European Journal of Philosophy*, 15, no. 2 (August 2007): 204–24.

5 'The Inward Turn', originally in A. O'Hear, ed., *Conceptions of Philosophy: Royal Institute of Philosophy Lecture Series*, 2007/2008, appeared 2009.

6 'Affording Us The World', originally in *Reading Putnam*, M. Baghramian, ed. Routledge: 2012: pp. 322–40.

7 'Is Seeing Intentional?', *John L. Austin et la Philosophie du Langage Ordinaire*, C. Al-Saleh and S. Laugier, eds. Hildesheim: Georg Olms, 2011.

8 'Unlocking the Outer World'. This has not been published elsewhere.

9 'Desperately Seeking Ψ', originally in *Philosophical Issues*, 31 (2011): 505–57. This is revised from the original version. Here I saw a better way of putting a point *just* when it was too late for the original publication. Minor revision.

10 'The Preserve of Thinkers', originally in *Does Perception Have Content?*, B. Brogaard, ed. Oxford University Press: forthcoming. This is a general case against the view that things other than a *thinker* could engage in representing-as. For reasons of space I omitted some applications of that idea to particular cases. Here I append two such applications. They concern, respectively, Gareth Evans, and Jerry Fodor.

11 'That Object of Obscure Desire', forthcoming in a special issue of *The International Journal for the Study of Skepticism*, devoted to Thompson Clarke. The object of *obscure* desire is the sense datum. *If* there is *a* source of the desire, what it is remains obscure.

12 'While Under The Influence', originally in *Consciousness and Subjectivity*, S. Miguens and G. Preyer, eds. Frankfurt: Ontos, 2012: pp. 147–68. *Extensively* revised. This concerns Moore's paradox and its significance for understanding ideas of subjective character of perceptual experience (among other kinds).

For the most part these essays have been written in an exceptionally stimulating intellectual environment centred in London—all but the first while I lived in London, or half there and half in Porto. Of the many people from whom I thus profited, special thanks are due to Mike Martin, Mark Kalderon, and Paul Snowdon. Thanks, too, to Bill Brewer, Matt Soteriou, Naomi Eilan, Quassim Cassam, and the wonderfully helpful Warwick department. And thanks again to Bruno Ambroise, Jocelyn Benoist, Valérie Aucouturier, and Layla Raïd, who worked with me in Paris and in Lille. I am particularly thankful to Jocelyn for the inspiration for 'Unlocking the Outer World'. Peter Sullivan inspired the final discussion of the historical–conceptual distinction in the introduction. He also made me aware of the link of the *Kernsätze* with Lotze. For twenty years, and, for half of them through some long and memorable nights, Peter has been for me the point of resistance in responding to which my thought developed. Some of this material was written, and presented, in the context of projects at the universities of Port and of Santiago de Compostela, most especially within the framework of a project of Porto's MLAG (Mind, Language, and Action Group) called 'The Bounds of Judgement'. I would like to thank all there who commented on what was then *very* unfinished work. I would also like to thank my wife, Sofia Miguens, for help throughout, philosophical and otherwise.

1

The Silences of the Senses

Perhaps the most common view of perception today is that it is representational: that in perceptual experience—in our seeing, hearing, feeling, smelling, what we do—the world is represented to us as being thus and so. If we help ourselves to a far from innocent count noun, we may shorten the view's expression: a (given) perceptual experience has (given) representational content. In no case I am aware of is this view argued for. Rather, it is assumed from the outset. Some, perhaps, assume it *faute de mieux*, seeing representation as better material than 'qualia' for answering a very special question as to what an experience was like: a question whose answer would identify, precisely, and once and for all, what that experience was like (such as visually) *for the subject*, as thus experienced. That special question, as conceived, would demand an answer mentioning nothing there is *for one* to meet in his surroundings. What follows should suggest why *nothing* answers such a very special question. Some may be moved by the thought that perceptual experience, being mental, is intentional, and that intentionality just is that sort of *aiming* at the world which representation is. If intentionality is so construed, the present brief shows it to be but one form of the mental: perception, and experience, exemplify another. In any event, perception is not representational. What follows will show why.

1 The Position

The view at issue is advanced by such philosophers as Martin Davies, Christopher Peacocke, sometimes, of late, John McDowell; also by Gilbert Harman, John Searle, Michael Tye, and Colin McGinn, among many others. (See, for example, Harman 1990; Searle 1983: pp. 47–8, for example; Tye 1995: especially chapter 4; McGinn 1991: pp. 29–30; and McGinn 1982.)

Martin Davies expresses it as follows:

A subject's experiences represent the world to her as being a certain way. These experiences may be correct or incorrect... In short, experiences have representational or semantic properties; they have content.

(Davies 1992: p. 22)

Christopher Peacocke expresses it *en passant* as follows:

A perceptual experience represents the world as being a certain way. What is the nature of the content it represents as holding?

(Peacocke 1992: p. 61)

He later insists that it is crucial to distinguish 'perceptual experiences'

from states that do not represent the world as being a certain way to the subject.

(Peacocke 1992: p. 66)

The following four elements in the position will be in play here. All, I think, are non-controversially part of it. One aspect of the last, though, will emerge as optional. Nor, it will also then emerge, does present criticism turn on it.

1. **The representing in question is representing such-and-such as so.** 'Represent' and 'representation' have many uses. To represent may be to be an effect or trace of something. A ring on a tree trunk represents a year's growth. Its width may also represent the drought of 1923. Again, to represent may be, in various ways, to be a stand-in, or substitute, for what is represented. A bit of plastic may represent an infantry division in a game of strategy. A squiggle on a map may represent the Lot. None of these uses of 'represent' is relevant to the present case. The point about perceptual experience is to be that there is a way things are according to it, that it represents things as being thus and so—where, for all that, things need not be that way. So representationalists tell us. If certain neural states, say, represent certain distal stimuli in being their effects or traces, or those yielding our awareness of them, that would not be to the present point. It would not amount to *their* representing anything as so; as if that were something they might do without its being so. For if for them to represent involves their being traces, then where there is no such thing for them to be traces of, they simply do not represent that. (If, through some fluke, a tree gains two rings in one year, then a ring does not always represent a year's growth. It is not that a certain ring represents something—say, that there was one more year of growth—but falsely.) Similarly for the other cases here. The representing this essay is thus *not* about is, I suggest, enough to serve the purposes of serious psychology.

2. **Perceptual experience has a face value.** That idea is in Davies:

An experience may present the world to the subject as containing something square in front of her, and the subject may take that experience at face value and judge that there is something square in front of her.   (Davies 1992: p. 23)

McDowell also proposes it:

Minimally, it must be possible to decide whether or not to judge that things are as one's experience represents them to be. How one's experience represents things to be is not under one's control, but it is up to one whether one accepts the appearance or rejects it.
(McDowell 1994: p. 11)

That things are thus and so is the content of the experience, and it can also be the content of a judgement. It becomes the content of a judgement if the subject decides to take the experience at face value.
(McDowell 1994: p. 26)

The idea is that any perceptual experience has a face value, at which the perceiver may take, or refuse to take, it. To take an experience at face value is to take it that such-and-such is so (in the case of perception, that one's surroundings are thus and so). So the face value of an experience is that such-and-such is so. This just repeats point 1.

Where the face value of an experience is that things are thus and so, for all that things may, or may not, be that way. This just makes explicit a feature of representing things as so. Whatever does that *ipso facto* admits of correctness, or incorrectness, according as things are, or not, as represented—in present idiom, as one would take it in taking it at face value. *Such* correctness is what truth requires. So any such thing is truth-evaluable. If 'true' is not colloquial here, we might substitute the word '*veridical*'.

A second feature of face value is that whatever gives an experience its face value, and whatever makes that value recognizable, might be present in an experience, and might have been in *that* one, even if what, at that face value, is so in fact is not. So, for example, where the face value of an experience is that there is (visibly) a pig before one, what gives it that face value cannot be the presence of a pig. Nor can it be one's seeing that.

This makes room for a third point on which McDowell, for one, insists. The face value of an experience is, again, something the experiencer can accept or reject, believe or disbelieve. So I must be able to see my experience to have such-and-such face value—that P—without yet taking it that P. So whatever I recognize in grasping its face value must be something that could be present even if not P; recognizing merely *that* need not be to recognize P. (So if the face value is that there is a pig, what I grasp in grasping that fact cannot be that there is a pig.)

Discussion: McDowell speaks as if an experience's face value is a matter of how things appear, or what, or how, they appear to be. (To accept an experience at face value is to 'accept the appearance'—to take things to be as they appear.) Two preliminary points about that. First, we certainly do sometimes speak of things not being what they appear to be, or as, or what, they seem. Sid and Pia appear to be trysting; but they are only conspiring to throw a surprise party for Luc. The right explanation may make a host of small actions and signs look entirely different. But, as I will show in the next section, at least in a wide swathe of central cases, where things may be or not as they appear, their appearing as they do is an utterly different and distinct phenomenon from anything being represented as so. Second, though we are often enough confronted with appearances, that is not yet to say that the appearances, on a given occasion, add up to such a thing as 'the way things (then) appear to be'. It is a large assumption that there is, in general, such a thing as *the* way things appear to be. (For one thing, appearances are certainly not always a matter of things appearing *to be* some way at all.)

3. **Being represented to is not autorepresentation.** To take things to be thus and so just *is* to represent them to oneself as that way. Such representing is *all* in the attitude. It does not consist in producing, nor in awareness of, something which represents things as that way, and which one can, or does, then take as doing that (as a note held fast by a refrigerator magnet). Merely that would fall short of taking things to *be* as represented. Nor is it any part of representing things to oneself in this sense. I will call representing which just is a stance towards things being thus and so *autorepresenting*.

Autorepresentation contrasts with another phenomenon which is also representing things as a certain way. Where this is a way things are, or are not, representing things *to be* that way is representing truly, or falsely. One *might*, simply on that ground, hold the mere representing-as to be either true or false. What marks the second case of representing that I have in mind here is this: one (something) represents in this way only in, and by, making his (its) representing recognizable to *one* suitably *au fait* with its circumstances, and with the sort of project thus undertaken. Representing in this way requires producing something identifiable as present without prejudice to whether any representing is going on. On a different reading of the verb, what makes representing recognizable (what I will call a *vehicle*) may also be said to represent. (*Someone* asserts that pigs swim, thus representing things as that way; his words, 'pigs swim', may also be said so to represent things.) I will call such representing *allorepresenting*.

In a central case, allorepresenting represents such-and-such *to be* so. This it to represent things *as* a certain way, *with* a certain force. It is to *commit*, in some form, to things so being. To recognize such representing is to have it on *some* authority, however poor or dubious, that things *are* as represented. I will call this *committed* representing. It is such representing that can be accepted or rejected (where to accept it is to take to be so that which is so according to it).

Representing *as* may be merely representing things *being* thus and so. It thus ranges wider than representing *to be*. One might represent Pia *as* the darling of the silver screen (for example, by drawing her in an open-top Duesenberg, silk scarf fluttering, waving as to fans), without in the least suggesting that she *is* one. One might represent Sid being sick while representing him neither to be, nor to have been, so. One *ipso facto* represents things *as* (or *being*) a certain way in representing them to be that way—in doing so with such force. As Frege stresses, one can often represent things *as* some way, and do so with no such force—such as when one expresses some thoughts *in* (and as part of) expressing some others, as, for example, in expressing the antecedent, and the consequent, in expressing a conditional. Representing *as* need not be committed in the way one is *per se* in representing to be—what I here call *committed* representing.

Many declarative English sentences represent things *as* a certain way, on some reading of 'represent'. There are those who think such sentences are thereby truth-evaluable, as per the idea scouted above. This is a mistake, though I will not argue so here. (But see Travis 2008.) In any case, if they were, then, on the same reading of the verb on which they represent things *as* a certain way, they might be said also to represent things to *be* that way: that is something they are *for* doing, as a bread knife slices bread. Which might suggest them as an exemplar of another bad idea: that of a *vehicle* of truth-evaluable representing which could not be present without representing something to be so, thus without conferring such content on whatever they were present in. Again, that this is a bad idea I will not argue here. But whatever English sentences do, in recognizing one—say, 'pigs swim'—as representing as it does, one has it on no authority at all that things are as represented—for example, that pigs swim. *English* does not stand warrant for the things its sentences say. It would be crazy to hold *it* to such a motley of contradictory commitments. Nor, so far, is there anything other than English to do so. Nonetheless, by the second bad idea above, English sentences, viewed as truth-evaluable, may well encourage (in some) the idea that perceptual experience might represent truly or falsely.

Only committed representation can have a face value. Only with commitment is there something to accept or reject; something purportedly so. One cannot take the English sentence 'pigs swim' at face value. It has none. But it will make no difference to present arguments whether the representation that occurs in perception is committed or not.

The main point is now this. If we are represented to in perception, that cannot be autorepresentation. Further, it must be allorepresentation. For one thing, perception is, if anything, a source of information as to how things are in our surroundings. Autorepresentation is not a *source* of information at all. It *registers*, or pretends to. For another, our current autorepresenting does not leave us any option of taking it at face value or refusing to. To autorepresent something just is to accept it. Things will not count as having been represented to me as so merely because I autorepresent them—that is, take them to be so. *This* passive does not work that way.

Committed allorepresentation is a source of reasons of a certain distinctive sort for thinking things: a reason for thinking that things are thus and so *may* be that they were represented to one as that way. Current autorepresentation is no source of reasons for one to think things. Past autorepresentation may be. That I used to think that pigs swim may indicate that they do. Perhaps I used to know about such things. Uncommitted allorepresentation as such gives no reason for thinking things. The *occurrence*, or instancing, of a certain uncommitted allorepresentation at a certain time and place may give a reason for thinking something. For, like any other occurrence, it may *mean* something. The reason it gives will thus be of just the same sort as the reason those bald patches on the cat give for thinking it has mange.

4. **The relevant representing must be recognizable by us.** If we are going to be represented *to* in experience, then the relevant representing must be something we can appreciate for the representing that it is. If, in a perceptual experience, things are represented to us as being thus and so, then we must be able to appreciate the experience as representing as so what it thus does; to appreciate what it is that is so according to it. This need not mean that we can characterize such representational content accurately, or formulate it explicitly. But we should be able to recognize, where needed, of particular ways things may or may not be, whether that is what the experience represented to us as so—whether that is what one would take be so in taking the experience at face value—whether, for example, the experience is one according to which a certain stick is bent, or rather one according to which that stick is straight. The core idea is: you cannot represent things to people as so in a way they simply cannot recognize as doing that.

I suppose, for working purposes, that what would make the representational content of experience recognizable to the perceiver—*if* experience represented anything as so—would be, in some sense or other, the way things then look, or appear, or, again, their looking, or appearing, as they do. So, in some sense of 'looks' or 'appears', if things look, or appear, as they do on a given occasion, that should leave exactly one representational content for *that* particular experience to have. On that occasion, at least, a different content would have required things to look, or appear, different.

The relevant sense of 'looks', or 'appears', can be negotiated later. In fact, the representationalist can have more or less free choice. But I take it that it would be cheating if, say, 'looks like things are thus and so' turned out just to *mean* 'things are represented to the perceiver as being thus and so'. Looks in that sense might *be* representational content; but they could not be that by which an experience is recognizable as having the representational content that it does.

The idea here is that one could tell the representational content of an experience by the way, in it, things looked. I will call such content *looks-indexed*. I will, *pro tem*, take this to be part of the view in question, and, accordingly, use it. Eventually, I will be able to do without it, with no loss of results.

To sum up, then, the position on which in perception we are represented to, as I will construe it here, has four significant points.

1 The representation in question consists in representing things as so (thus, truly/veridically, or falsely/non-veridically).
2 It has, or gives perceptual experience, a face value, at which it can be taken or declined (or discounted).
3 It is not autorepresentation. (It is allorepresentation, though here, not crucially.)
4 Where we are thus represented to, we can recognize that, and how, this is so; most pertinently, we can appreciate what it is that is thus represented to us as so. Provisionally, I suppose it is (in some sense) the way things look that lets us do that.

2 Misleading

By perceiving I can learn things. Walking through a park near Lisbon, my nose tells me, and my eyes confirm, that there are eucalyptus. Seeing Luc and Pia touch hands at dinner makes all the pieces fall into place. By perceiving I can also be misled, at least because what I see (hear, feel, smell) may be misleading. A touch need not mean what it seemed to. An odour may be artificially produced. For *what* I perceive to be misleading, nothing need be *represented* as so. Perhaps *none* of the ways perception may mislead involves anything being represented to us as so. Perhaps in perception things are *not* represented to us as being thus and so. That was Austin's view. He put it this way:

Though the phrase 'deceived by our senses' is a common metaphor, it *is* a metaphor; and this is worth noting, for in what follows [in Ayer] the same metaphor is frequently taken up by the expression 'veridical' and taken very seriously. In fact, of course, our senses are dumb—though Descartes and others speak of 'the testimony of the senses', our senses do not *tell* us anything, true or false.

(Austin 1962: p. 11)

Austin's idea is that, rather than *representing* anything as so, our senses merely bring our surroundings into view; afford us some sort of awareness of them. It is then for us to make of what is in our view what we can, or do. Austin speaks as if he is taking issue with Descartes. There are, indeed, large differences between Austin and Descartes as to what it is we can see. (One main thing Austin saw and Descartes missed is, to label it, occasion-sensitivity, here—notably, the sensitivity to occasions for the counting, of what someone counts as having seen in some episode of viewing, and what awareness is mediated by the *visual* awareness he thus enjoys.) Prescinding from such issues, the two are allies on this particular point. Over a wider area which includes perception, Descartes said this:

By the mere intellect I do no more than perceive the ideas that are matters for judgement; and precisely so regarded the intellect contains, properly speaking, no error.
(Descartes 1954: p. 95, Fourth Meditation)

Whence, then, do my errors originate? Surely just from this: my will extends more widely than my understanding, and yet I do not restrain it within the same bounds, but apply it to what I do not understand.

(Descartes 1954: pp. 96–7)

Sensory experience is, for Descartes, one more case where I am simply confronted with 'ideas'. I cannot be confronted correctly or incorrectly, veridically or deceptively. I simply confront what is there. Perception leads me astray only where I *judge* erroneously, failing to make out what I confront for what it is. The possibility of error thus arises with, and only with, autorepresentation. If that is the only point at which such possibility arises, then there is no room for allorepresentation in perception; no place other than autorepresentation for what is liable to be veridical or not.

Part of the point here is that perception is, first and foremost, a source of *unmediated* awareness. I will call awareness of X *mediated* if it is hostage to awareness of something else: that further awareness is part of what entitles one to take it that X is so, or present; so part of what qualifies one as aware of that. In unmediated awareness, one's entitlement to take it that X is hostage to no more than some form of awareness of X itself (such as seeing it). Seeing your car in the *drive* makes me aware that you are home. That is mediated awareness that you are home; unmediated awareness that your car is in the drive.

Another part of the point is that *perception*, as such, simply places our surroundings in view; affords us awareness of them. There is no commitment to their *being* one way or another. It confronts us with what is there, so that, by attending, noting, recognizing, and otherwise exercising what capacities we have, *we* may, in some respect or other, make out what is there for what it is—or, again, fail to. It makes us aware, to some extent, of things (around us) being as they are. It is then up to us to make out, or try to, which particular ways that is. Perception cannot present things as being other than they are. It cannot present some way things are *not* as what is so. That would not be mere confrontation. So it cannot represent anything as so. Representing, by nature, is liable to be of what is not so.

Such is a view, and, so far, only that. On it, in perception things are *not* presented, or represented, to us as being thus and so. They are just presented to us, full stop. It is in making out, or trying to, what it is that we confront that we *take* things, rightly or wrongly, to be thus and so. Autorepresentation is the only representation in perceptual experience as such. Austin and the representationalist are thus at odds. The question who is right remains thus far open. The immediate point is that *misleading* perceptual experiences do not count in the representationalist's favour.

Perceptual experience *may* be misleading. Things may not be what they seem, or what they appear to be. On Austin's view, it is *what* is perceived, or experienced—what is actually presented to us—that may thus mislead. The form of misleading that is thus central is modelled in the following. Sid shows up for dinner drunk. That much we can all see. That he is drunk (at this hour) may mean that it will be a long and boring evening. Or, again, it may mean that, once again, he has lost his job. If it does mean that, then from what we see—that he is drunk—we may gain mediated awareness of those further facts. So far, perception is informative, not misleading.

What we see, hear, and so on, may be informative because it bears factive meaning. Factive meaning is, crucially, something utterly different from representation. The most obvious point is this: if A factively means B, then if (*since*) A, B. If Sid did not lose his job, then his drunkenness does not mean that. By contrast, if B is not so, that is no bar to something having represented it as so. Just this makes room for representing falsely, so for *any* representing things to be so.

There is a subtler, and at least equally important, difference. Suppose that there are various things one might understand by someone's being fired. On one understanding, but not another, perhaps, being riffed ('downsized') is being fired. Suppose that, on some understanding of being fired, Sid's drunkenness factively means that he was fired. On what understanding? That question is answered purely by how the world is, in fact, arranged. Just what would make Sid get drunk (at such an early hour)? By contrast, suppose Pia informs us that Sid has been fired. On what understanding of being fired has she thus represented this as so? That question is not answered by looking to the world. It is not a question of what, in Sid's history, would cause thus and so. It is rather a question of what Pia has committed herself to—that is, of for what she is rightly held responsible; of what ought to be expected of her by virtue of her representing as she did.

The contrast between factive meaning and representation also shows up in the structure of reasons. That A factively means B, once recognized, makes A proof of B. That B was represented as so leaves it open how good the reason is for thinking B. For all that, the issue may or may not be settled.

Misleading is not yet in the picture. To put it there, suppose that Sid is drunk, but was not fired. Then, perhaps, things are not what they appeared to be. Our experience may thus have been misleading. What would make it misleading is just this: given the way Sid is, one might have expected his drunkenness to mean that he was fired; such was to be expected. Similarly, seeing Luc and Pia's flat strewn with broken crockery, one might reasonably suppose there to have been a tiff. For all that, there may not have been one. Too much champagne at brunch may have led to an excess of exuberance. Where A might reasonably, or rightly, be expected factively to mean B, I will say that A indicates B. Indicating is no more representing something as so than factively meaning is. What one may expect things to mean depends as much as what they in fact mean on how world is arranged—here, on what *as a rule* co-occurs with what (though the relevant rule may vary with one's cognitive position).

A, in indicating B, may be misleading just by virtue of what it might have been expected to mean. What one *might* have expected might fail to be so. (Leaving work, Sid happened onto a vodka-tasting which, atypically, he failed to resist.) So something we perceive, or experience, may indicate what is not so. What it indicates is what there is reason to think, even when it is not, in fact, so. That is *one* way perceptual experience may be misleading, other than by representing something as so.

Our perceiving what means, or indicates, something is not the only way for perceptual experience to be informative. Meaning and indicating provide avenues of mediated awareness. Unmediated awareness may also be informative. There is such a thing as learning that there is a pig before one by seeing it. One might think that meaning and indicating similarly fail to exhaust the ways for perceptual experience to be misleading, or to misinform. But there is no parallel. Unmediated awareness is a way of being informed; not one of being misinformed, nor a further way to be misled. That there *is* such a thing is precisely no reason to think that perceptual experience is not only of what means or indicates, but also what *represents* things to be so.

It may be the pig's presence that makes me aware that there is a pig before me, thanks to my *seeing* it. I do not then *erroneously* take it to be there. If there is a pig to do any misleading, then that is one score on which I am not misled. Equally for my seeing one. If I am misled into taking a pig to be before me when there is none, I am misled by something else. The rear half of a pig, protruding from behind the barn, might do that if there is only a rear half there (perhaps mechanically animated). It *would* do so if I took it to mean there was a whole pig, thus inferring what, even if indicated, was not so. (If it is not just a rear half, perhaps one sees a *pig*, rear view.) Indications of a pig, or what I take for such, may lead me to conclusions. That is not for them, or anything, to *represent* something to me as so.

So far, there are no signs of something in perception to mislead other than by being taken to indicate what is not so. There are thus no signs yet that we are ever misled by, or in, having something *represented* to us as so. Visual illusions have been alleged to do this. Here is McDowell on that point:

> In the Müller-Lyer illusion, one's experience represents the two lines as being unequally long, but someone in the know will refrain from judging that that is how things are.
> (McDowell 1994: p. 11, footnote)

But is this so? In the Müller-Lyer, two lines are contrived (by means of accompanying wedges) to have a certain look. They do not just *seem* to have that look; they actually so look (as the illusion's robustness testifies). Two lines may well have that look because one *is* longer than the other. That is a familiar way for things to be. Depending on circumstances, that look may thus *indicate* that it is two lines of unequal length that one confronts. Or one might take it to. Unequal length *might* be what is to be expected; or at least what *is* expected. *Thus* may someone be misled by a Müller-Lyer. False expectations arise here in the wrong view of what something (a look) means, though perhaps a right view of what it *ought* to. What one gets wrong is the arrangement of the world: how the misleading seen thing in fact relates to other things. That mistake neither requires, nor suggests, that in this illusion one line is represented to us as being longer than the other, or that anything else is represented as so.

The phenomena of misleading experience do not suggest that in experience things are represented to us as so. That is no proof that they are not. We must examine that idea more closely.

3 Visual Appearance

If in perceptual experience things are represented to us as being so, that will be distinct from, and in addition to, things being indicated, or factively meant, by one or another thing we see (hear, and so on). It will be an additional way to be aware of our surroundings, giving different sorts of reasons for thinking things. If not-P, then *nothing* factively meant that P; though not-P cannot, by itself, rule out its having been represented as so that P. As for indicating, if P is to be expected, that is *per se* reason to think that P, whereas if P was *represented* as so, that may or may not be reason to think so, depending on the value of that representing. (Representation yields only mediated awareness of what it represents as so, though for the moment I will not press that point.) Being represented to in perception would also be utterly distinct from the autorepresentation that goes with making out, or noting, *what* one perceives. Does perception make room for such a further phenomenon? This section begins a case that it does not.

Someone to whom, in perceptual experience, things can be represented as so is someone who can take, and treat, his perceptual experiences as having the representational content they do; who can see, appreciate, what it is that is so according to them. If perception is representational, then we philosophers are, presumably, in that position. So where there is a question as to whether such-and-such is or is not so according to such-and-such experience, or was, or was not, represented as so in that experience, that is a question the answer to which should be, at least as a rule, or often, intuitively, or tolerably, clear, to us, among others—at least on suitable reflection.

One idea would be that it is looks-indexing that makes such facts available to us: the representational content of an experience can be read off of the way, in it, things looked. I will begin to examine that idea by distinguishing, and exploring, two different notions of looks. Neither, I will show, makes room for it. On the first, looks are something fit genuinely to make representational content recognizable. But they do not decide any particular representational content for any given experience to have. On the second, looks are not what might make content available to us. The most they might do would just be to *be* that content, In fact, though, they are a matter, not of representing, but rather of what is indicated. They do not point to any phenomenon in perception beyond that. Many expressions which speak of looks—though not all—*can* be used to express either notion. I will thus distinguish the notions simply in terms of when, on each, things would look thus and so. (There are, though, expressions reserved for the second notion only.)

On the first notion, something looks thus-and-so, or like such-and-such, where it looks the way such-and-such, or things which are (were) thus and so, does (would, might) look. (Caveat: Pia may look like her sister on a bad day, or so look in this light, or to Sid, without looking like her sister.) On this notion, Pia may look (rather, very much, exactly) like (the spitting image of) her sister. That man on the bench looks old. (He looks the way an old man would, or might.) The shirt looks blue (in this light)—as a blue shirt (so viewed) does, or might. The sun, at sunset, may look red. A van Meegeren may look (uncannily) like a Vermeer. A copy of a Vermeer, made by an amateur in the museum, may look (just like) the original. Or, perhaps, it may turn out looking more like a van Meegeren. Pia, having been dragged through the brambles by her dog, may look as though she had been in a fight. That is how one may well have looked had one been in a fight.

Pia looks like her sister. They resemble each other. For *that* to be true is not yet for either to look any particular way. But if she looks like her sister, there is a look, or are looks, both share. Pia *has* these looks, simply in looking as she does. Such a look may be identified by an exemplar—her sister, or, perhaps, herself. Given the example, what remains to be understood is in what way something must be like it in *visual* appearance for *that* thing's looking as it does to be another exemplar of the look in question. Whether something has the look is settled simply by its visual effect. It has the look, perhaps, only under given conditions for producing that effect—only when viewed *thus* (such as from a certain angle). The look may be detectable only by one with suitable visual equipment. But to have the look (viewed *thus*) is to have it *full stop*—independent of how its so looking bears on whether to take it to *be* any given thing it thus looks *like*. I will call looks on this understanding of a look *visual looks*, or, sometimes, because of the way they are fixed by exemplars, *visible* looks.

If Pia looks like her sister, there is a way she should be to be what she *thus* looks like: she should be her sister. If Pia's imitation of her sister nonplussed looks uncannily like her sister nonplussed, then, again, there is a way things should be to be what they *thus* look like: it should be her sister, nonplussed. How things should be to be the way they look, full stop, is another matter. Pia's looking even exactly like her sister does not yet mean that whenever one see *Pia*, things are not the way they look. Otherwise, *no* experience of seeing Pia, and, by parity, none of seeing her sister, would be one in which things were the way they looked. Seeing Pia, or her sister, to be present could *never* be taking experience at face value. No experience of seeing either one could be veridical. So it cannot be that what is required for Pia being what she looks like in looking like her sister is what is required for things being as they look where she is present, or where one sees her, full stop. The simple point is: how things should be to be the way they look (on a given occasion, or in a given experience) is not decided by how things should be to be the way they look in such-and-such looking thus and so. There are already intimations of why it cannot be so decided.

If perception is representational, then, for any perceptual experience, there must be a way things are according to it. If such content is looks-indexed, then things looking as they do on a given occasion must fix *what* representational content experience then has. Specific facts as to what things look like on this first notion of looks gain no purchase on what is thus required. How things must be to be what they *thus* look like does not decide how things must be to be the way they look; so nor, by that route, any way they must be to be as they (supposedly) are according to an experience in which things did so look. It is still open, perhaps, that things looking as they do points to some representational content for an experience to have; things looking thus and so does not. That is the first simple point.

Which ways things looked on an occasion and what they then looked like, is, in general, an occasion-sensitive matter: these are questions whose (true) answers vary with the occasion for posing them. (See Travis 2008 for more on occasion sensitivity.) For whether X looks like Y is very liable to depend on how comparisons are made. If Pia is blissfully asleep while her sister, bleary-eyed and insomniac, stares blankly at the flickering screen, they still look alike if you view the matter in one way, but not if you view it in another. Similarly, Pia will still look like Pia in ten year's time—when the matter is viewed in one way, but, sadly, not when it is viewed in another. Again, in the case of the Müller-Lyer, the two lines look like two lines of unequal length if you view the matter in one way (ignoring the wedges), but not if you view it in another. Given this, how comparisons *are* to be made for assessing the truth of a particular claim that X looks like Y will vary with precisely what was said in making it. On an occasion for describing a given perceptual experience, there may be definite things one *would* then say in saying X to look, or have looked, like Y—so, again, things one would not. But what one would say on some one such occasion does not decide, of that experience as such, how things looking as they then did relates to how things should be to be the way they then looked.

On an occasion for saying what, in an experience, things looked like, some comparisons may be natural, or right, or even possible, and others not. For all of what is thus sometimes so, in looking like Y, X also shares a look with many things. It looks as each of these does, or might, on some correct way of saying what things look like. If Pia looks like her sister, she also, on some understanding, looks the way she herself does, so might, or would, look. On some understanding or other, she looks (just) like any of indefinitely many different things. There is thus a substantial problem. Which facts as to Pia's looking (like) thus and so matter, and how, to how things should be to be the way they look simpliciter? Which looks, if any, matter to what is thus represented as so? And how? And why?

Our initial simple point now deepens. One cannot move from the various *ways* things should be to be the various *ways* they look to the *way* things should be to be the *way* they look. For those various ways move in mutually exclusive directions: things could be some of them only in not being others. For looks to identify a content, one needs a principled way of ignoring some of the specific ways things look, and attending only to others. That would be a policy for fixing, in terms of looks, what is so according to an experience, so when it would be deceptive, non-veridical, or misleading in the sought-for further way. If representational content is looks-indexed, the question becomes when looks—the *way* thinks look—would be deceptive, false, or misleading, so when a specific *way* things look would contribute to making them so. That question, posed of given (experienced) looks as such, clearly has no answer.

Looks on this first notion might make representational content recognizable, even bear it, were there any. They are *visible* features; not features of the content had (such as requiring such-and-such for truth). The trouble is that they are unfit to index content. For as to that they point in no one direction.

In looking like her sister Pia shares a look with countless other things—herself, a wax replica of herself in Madame Tussaud's, a good hologram, a body double, an actress made up to play the role of her, a Pia-clone, and so on *ad infinitum*. For each of these, there is a way things should be to be what they *thus* look like: Pia should be, respectively, herself, her sister, a wax dummy, a hologram, an actress, a clone, and so on. An experience that represented all that as so would be incoherent. Representation cannot fit into this picture unless something selects *which* facts as to what Pia looks like bear on it. It is no part of what perception is—of how it opens our surroundings to our view—that in perceiving one is to appreciate one set of facts as to what things look like, and ignore others. Looks, on this first notion of them, are thus not a route by which we might be represented to in perception.

Seeing Pia on terrasse may make us think any of many things—one for each of the things she then looks like. What it makes us think depends on our current proclivities to think things. Believing Pia is in foreign climes may raise the odds that we will take her for her sister. But it can hardly be that what perception represents to us as so is a matter of what we are anyway prone to believe or conclude. If you represent Pia to me as in Greece, I cannot turn that into your representing her as in Athens merely by so concluding. For us to take Pia for her sister is for us to autorepresent. It is a matter of what we *think* we see; of taking what we see for something else. Being represented to has no role in the aetiology of such mistakes. They involve nothing purporting falsely to inform. Nor can autorepresentation be conjured into being represented to.

What goes for Pia goes for peccaries. What goes for peccaries goes for something's being blue. A peccary, confronted in the right way, may look exactly like a pig (or it may do to us novices). It also, of course, looks just the way a peccary might look (so confronted). It may also look like a tapir, a clever dummy pig, a wax imitation peccary, and so on. Experience cannot coherently represent it to us as both a peccary and wax (and a pig, and so on). Similarly, a shirt may look like a blue shirt. In looking as it does, it will also look the way a white shirt would when illuminated in certain ways, or when in certain conditions. It may also look like countless other things. Some such fact might index the representational content of things so looking. But only on condition that the other such facts do not. The problem now is: *what* decides that it is some one such fact, and no other, which plays that role.

Suppose that, in looking blue, some shirt looks a way one can exhibit by exhibiting a certain colour—say, by holding up a blue paint chip. Is it, in that case, represented to us as being blue? It looks the way a blue shirt does, or might, illuminated in a certain way. But that is not decisive. We are not on the track of representation here unless there is (as there clearly is) such a thing as a shirt merely looking, but not actually being blue. Choose a way for that to happen. Perhaps the shirt has been dipped in rapidly disappearing ink. Perhaps (like certain sculptures) it constantly changes colour, depending on exact conditions of viewing. Or perhaps, up close, it is a pointilliste motley. Insofar as these are ways of failing to be blue, they provide us with further things the shirt looks like. It looks just the way some pointilliste motley would (viewed from a distance), and so on. So our problem rearises: which of these facts matter (and how) to what was represented to us as so?

The point generalizes. Take any way things may be said to look. Now take any way that things may fail to be what they would need to be to be what they *thus* look like. That is *another* way things may be said then to look: they look just the way they would if *that*, rather than the first thing, were the way things are. So this second way for things to be—for them not to be that first thing they may be said to look like—could, if it in fact obtained, make it the case that things were not the way they looked only if something decided that only the first thing things looked like, and not the second, mattered to things being as they looked full stop. By the same token, the obtaining of this second thing, or of anything else that made things fail to be that first thing, would make for misrepresentation in perception only if something decided that it was only the first fact about looks, and not the second, or any other such, that indexed representational content. Perception does not do such selecting for us.

The conclusion so far is that *on our first notion of looks*, looking like such-and-such cannot contribute to determining how things should be to be the way they look *simpliciter*. For, so far as it goes, there is no particular way things should be to be the way they look *simpliciter*. For that reason, things looking like such-and-such, or looking such-and-such ways, on this first notion of looks, cannot index anything as represented to us as being so.

A wax lemon may be so artfully done that it is only with great difficulty, if at all, that it can be told, by sight, from the real thing. For most purposes, it can thus be said to look (just like) a (real) lemon. It is enough for it to look that way that it is sufficiently similar in looks to the real thing; that there is a suitable visually decidable resemblance. The look in question is visual; shared by anything looking suitably the same way as an exemplar. Precisely because the look *is* visual in this sense, it would be rash in general to conclude from something's *thus* looking (just) like a lemon that it is one—unless one may suppose that, in the case at hand, such looks have a certain factive meaning. Nor, for that reason, can we conclude from the mere fact of the wax looking like a lemon in this sense that it should be one for *things* to be the way they look. Its lemon-like look suggests no such thing. So the fact of its looking like a lemon does not help make it so that it is represented to us as being one.

We *do* sometimes say, 'It looks like it is a lemon', the 'it' referring to the lemon, or functioning as dummy subject, where the item must be a lemon for *things* to be the way they thus look. What that shows is that there is another notion of looking like. I turn to that notion next.

4 Thinkable Appearance

Consider, first, words like these: 'It looks like (looks as if, looks as though) Pia will sink the putt/that painting is a Vermeer/Pia's sister is in town'. Here what the grammatical object speaks of which is said to enjoy a certain status. Here 'looks like' takes a sentential object. Grammatically, its subject might be viewed as a dummy. One might also think of the subject here as just *things*, in that catholic sense of 'things' in which it is a *bêtise* to ask which ones. Things being as they are, or simply the way things are, is what makes it look as if Pia will sink the putt, or the painting is a Vermeer. Or, more exactly, it is what is in evidence, made known, as to how things are—what, from the relevant position, has been, or can be, recognized as to this, which makes things look this way.

I will take the central case to be one in which the speaker, in saying this, represents himself as subscribing to a view as to how things are: while the mentioned proposition (for example, that the painting is a Vermeer), has not quite been established, nevertheless it is the thing for one to suppose, at least *pro tem*, given what is known, or revealed, of how things are. Going only on what is known (or revealed), such is what one *would* suppose. If that is the central case, there are, of course, derivatives. Van Meegeren's task was to fool the Nazis into buying fake Vermeers. Complimenting him on his success at that, I might say, 'It looks just as if that painting is a Vermeer', knowing full well that it is not: there is a position from which things would so look—the position we hope the Nazis to occupy. From that position—the position of one not in the know as Van Meegeren and I are—that it is a Vermeer would be the thing to think. (Now we need only hope that the Nazis are rational about this.)

What matters here is not how cases are divided into primary and derivative, but rather the general sort of thing that is said on such a use of 'looks like' or 'looks as if'. It is a remark about the thing to think, or at least what the speaker finds the thing to think. Now the central point is this: awareness that something is the thing to think (or, on some qualification, the qualified thing to think) is not *visual* awareness. So wherever 'looks like' has anything like the suggested readings, awareness of it looking like P will not be visual, or perceptual awareness. The point holds wherever 'looks like' takes a sentential complement, or at least where that complement is to be understood as what does the mentioned looking. For there is nothing which that Pia will sink the putt, or that the painting is a Vermeeer, looks like. *That such-and-such* is not the sort of thing to have a look. Unlike, say, the lemon on the counter, it is not the sort of thing to form images—a point of Frege's, who thus says of 'see' what might be said of 'looks like' on such uses: that it really speaks of a form of thought, or judgement. (See 1897: p. 153.)

I will call the looks spoken of on such uses of 'looks like', 'looks as if', and so on, *thinkable looks*. They are not looks to be achieved simply by assuming the right shape, colouration, and so on. They are not possessed by what *is* shaped and coloured as such; not instanced in the world simply in objects, or scenes, looking as they do, being such as to form the visual images they would. They are rather what is to be made of things by a thinker relevantly *au fait* with the world, and knowing enough of what to make of what he is thus aware of.

Suppose that, beginning with 'It looks like Pia will sink the putt', we substitute for 'Pia will sink the putt', 'it is a lemon', the 'it' referring, say, to a very lifelike wax lemon. Then the first 'it' remains 'dummy'. That is, we get: *things look as if that thing is a lemon*. We thus get the use just discussed. But in 'It looks as if it is a lemon', the two 'it's may be coreferential. This *may* just be an idiomatic variant of the locution already discussed (as when one says, 'that putt here looks as if it will be sunk'). But it may also bear a different understanding. What remains so, on this understanding, is that it is a way of attributing a certain status to (the proposition) that that thing is a lemon; one having to do with its credibility, or likelihood. What may change here is what is represented as conferring that status: it is what the lemon, in looking as it does, makes evident as to how things are which gives the proposition that status. Where 'looks like' is so read, all the above points hold, most crucially that awareness of the object looking like a lemon (where that is its looking to be one, or its making things look as if it were) is not *perceptual* awareness—Frege's point applied again.

The second notion of *look* I mean to present here is thus one on which looking is a matter of some proposition enjoying some status or other *in re* being the thing to think. Looking like, on this notion, is a matter of things, or something, having a certain rational force regarding some given proposition; a certain bearing on the thing to think. Such looks, thinkable looks, are not visual looks in the present sense. The *locution*, 'It looks like (it is) a lemon' (coreferential 'it's) and its kin may sometimes speak of visual looks—of it looking (in some respect or degree, to be understood from context) as a lemon would. A visual look is a look exemplified, *per se*, in a given thing looking as it does—a thing, that is, liable to have a look, liable to form images. However one understands *looking like a lemon*, or *looking pockmarked*, or *looking waxy*, or any other look a wax lemon might have—however waxy, or pitted, something must look to count as looking waxy, or pitted, in the meaning of the act—whether a given object has (or given doings have) that look is decided solely by (or in) its (their) looking as it does (they do). It is a matter of *visual* comparisons. Whereas whether, for example, some object looks like (it is) a lemon, where this speaks of thinkable looks, is never decided simply by its looking as it does. To adapt a point of Austin's, when wax lemons get good enough, and are widely enough distributed, it will cease to be true that you can tell by looking whether something is a lemon, so that what now makes things look that way, so makes there be a certain thinkable look, may cease to do so. Things will no longer so thinkably-look.

All of this is just for the sake of ensuring that visual looks and thinkable looks are not conflated. Holding them safely apart, we may ask which sort of look might give either reason, or means, for taking perceptual experience to have representational, truth-evaluable, content. *Visual* looks are the sort of thing to be decided just by looking. Any given such look is such as to be exhibited in some given range of cases, where what members of the range need to share in common is some identifiable *visual* resemblance. On this notion of *look*, something looking waxy, or pitted, or like a lemon, or a Vermeer, need carry no suggestion that it *is* waxy, pitted, a lemon, or a Vermeer. Its right to membership in the given class is in no way compromised by absence of such suggestion. The trouble now, as discussed already, is that there are too many things something would look *like* in looking the way it thus does—all the things, in fact, which belong to the class of things which so look. It might as well *be* any of these as any other, purely so far as its *visual* looks go. Nothing in its visual looks distinguishes any of these as what it ought to *be* to be as represented, if for it to look visually as it does were for anything to be represented as so. Visual looks, properly wielded, might be the *vehicle* of some representing; but *they*, on their own, hardly identify what that representing would be.

So we might look to the second notion for means to identify such content. This notion, thinkable looks, *is* a matter of what can be gathered from, or what is suggested by, the facts at hand, or those visibly (audibly, and so on) on hand. So it cannot look as if X on this notion where it is perfectly plain that X is not so. Further, it look as if X only where one has not actually seen, or observed (for himself) that X is so; in which case there would be nothing to gather.

On this second notion, if it looks as if Pia's sister is approaching, or as if the painting is a Vermeer, then there is a way things should be, *simpliciter*, for things to be the way they thus look: Pia's sister should be approaching; the painting should actually be a Vermeer. For all that, it may not be Pia's sister approaching. It may be Pia's sister, but retreating, or no-one at all, mere light and shadows. In that case, *something* is deceptive (whereas Pia looking, on the first notion, like her sister without being her does not yet make anything deceptive). It is perhaps just this feature of looks on this second notion that makes perception appear (to some) to represent things as so. But all depends here on what it is that is deceptive.

If perception represented things to us as thus and so, there would have to be, for any instance of it, a way things were according to it. Looks, on this second notion, where, or insofar as, there are any, identify something such a way *might* be. So far, that is all to the good for the representationalist. They are not, on the other hand, what might serve as *vehicles* of content—the sort of thing that might make representing recognizable to one. There is no particular visual look present in, or by, things looking like/as if X where this is a thinkable look. Things look like X in this sense *wherever* X is how things should be to be the way they look. Such is not a further fact made recognizable by things so looking. Nor, if the way things should be to be the way they look were the way they should be to be as represented, would looks in this sense be some perceptible cue to *that* fact. If perception were representational, looks in this second sense might *be* its representational content; but they could not be what made that content recognizable for us.

But for it to look such-and-such way, where this is a thinkable look, cannot be for it to be represented *to the perceiver* that such-and-such is so. *Perhaps* for it so to look to *me* is for me so to (auto)represent things to *myself* (though not for me to be represented to from any other source). For it so to look full stop might be (roughly) for it to be the thing for *one* to autorepresent (unless specially in the know), going on what there is here for *one* to go one. But it is certainly not for *me* to be represented to, either by myself, or from some other source.

Suppose I say 'It looks to Sid as if the painting is a Vermeer', or again, 'as if Pia will win the tournament (will sink the putt)'. I thus credit Sid with a certain view of a certain matter. I say him to take it, perhaps tentatively, hesitantly, with some uncertainty, that, for example, Pia will win the tournament. (I will not speak correctly if Sid knows full well that Pia will win the tournament, or that the painting is a Vermeer. But it will be safe to waive that point here. I will not speak *truly* if Sid does not think the painting is (even probably) a Vermeer, or so on.)

Suppose, now, that I say simply 'It looks as if Pia will sink the putt' (or whatever). To begin with, that is properly understood as (*inter alia*, perhaps) an expression of my own—perhaps tentative and hesitant—view of the matter: I think, or am inclined to think, going on the facts in hand, that she will sink it. I may have done no more than say how things thus seem to me; in which case I could have spoken more explicitly by saying 'It looks *to me* as if Pia will sink the putt'. Here, speaking of looks indicates explicitly that I am going by what I take it can be gathered from the facts in hand, or from things looking as they do. (Thus my view is about what I have not actually observed.)

But there may be more to an 'It looks as if P' than that. If I say 'It looks as if this car has been repainted', I may be saying that, again going by the looks—by what is observable, or perhaps more generally, by all the facts in hand—*one can conclude* with some, though perhaps not complete, certainty, that the car has been repainted. That, according to me, is what the looks, or the facts in hand, indicate. I am mistaken if they do not indicate that: I mistake a bit of undercoat for the original colour, say. Whether I am right or wrong depends on what things (factively) mean (or ought to)—a crucial feature of this second notion.

It may look to Sid as if the painting is a Vermeer when, in fact, it does not at all look as if it is a Vermeer; it has all the characteristics of a van Meegeren— a subject matter and style of dress, say, never found in Vermeer. There are observer-independent facts as to what looks to be the case, however occasion-sensitive a matter it is what counts as such a fact. When would a painting not, in fact, look like a Vermeer? When, for example, the woman sweeping the courtyard is using a type of broom not made until the eughteenth century, or is wearing a hat never worn in Holland; or when the brush strokes are a bit too broad to be Vermeer's, or feather in the wrong way, or the pigments are a little off. When does it not look as if Pia will sink the putt? When, for example, the ball is on a straight course for the hole, where it would have to be off to the right to catch the roll nearer the cup. When would it not look as if there are fresh roses in the vase? When, for example, the petals (if you look closely) are a bit too waxy to be real; or, again, when one is in an artificial flower shop. When would it not look as if Pia (marked as she is) had been in a fight? When, for example, her dog often drags her through brambles, so that you cannot tell by looking whether she has been in a fight or not.

We are now on familiar ground. The thing about the broom is that it *means* (factively) that the painting was not done by Vermeer. Or if, unaccountably, Vermeer painted such a broom, then, though it does not mean that, one might have expected it to. Conversely, if, on inspection, the looks (first notion) really are distinctively the looks of a Vermeer—if that is the way he painted—then that *indicates* that it is a Vermeer. In which case, on this second use of 'look', it looks, so far, like (as if) it is a Vermeer. One may so conclude. Again, the course of the ball means that it will catch the lie wrong, and hence miss the cup. If it does not miss—there is a freak guest of wind, or the earth moves—then, though that course did not mean that she would miss, one might rightly have expected so.

What things look like on this use of 'looks' is thus a matter of what things mean factively, or indicate; of how the world is contingently arranged. That is precisely not a matter of things being represented as so. Representation simply does not work that way. Whether it was represented to us as so that Pia will sink the putt is never a matter of whether her sinking it was indicated. Nor, by contrast with factive meaning, can it be decided by whether she did in fact sink it, so that if not, then, *ipso facto*, no such thing was represented as so.

So we have two notions of looks, neither of which allows looks to decide what was *represented* as so. Things looking (visual looks) as they do fixes no way things should be to be the way they look full stop; nor, *a fortiori*, to be as represented. Things just have too many visual looks in looking visually as they do. It/things looking like/as if what it does/they do (thinkable looks) fixes a way things should be to be the way they look full stop. But to take that to fix what was *represented* as so would collapse representation into indicating, or factive meaning, and thus to lose it altogether.

I have now distinguished two notions *looks*—a distinction Frege drew (see 1897, 1918). There are *visual* looks, objects of *visual* awareness. And there are *thinkable* looks—objects of judgement, or thought. There are two main sorts of statements of visual looks: one ascribing some such look in particular; the other merely noting a resemblance between the looks of one thing and that of another. 'Pia looks just like her sister' may be used for either thing: one may identify a look in citing her sister as instancing it (so that things are as said only if Pia looks *thus*, for something 'thus' may thus refer to); or one may merely say Pia and her sister to resemble one another visually. Statements about thinkable looks also come in two notable varieties: so to speak, committed or not. 'That painting looks just like (looks to be) a Vermeer' may express a judgement as to what is probably so, or ought to be supposed so, given the speaker's exposure to how things are. Or it may express no such commitment on the speaker's part, merely say what *someone* would suppose, on given available grounds, if not further in the know. For example, an accomplice might say this to van Meegeren, knowing the painting to be a van Meegeren. This variety in statements does not disturb the underlying taxonomy of looks.

5 Hybrids

Neither notion suits the representationalist. He might thus seek a third. Both the temptation and its execution are visible in McDowell's effort to explain a notion of 'ostensibly seeing'. Ostensibly seeing is to be either of two cases. One disjunct is simply seeing something to be so—say, there to be a pig before one. One has the pig manifestly in view. In terms McDowell favours, its presence stands revealed. The other disjunct is a class of ringers for the first. It is not obvious just which class McDowell means to capture. In any case, he appeals to *some* notion of looks for doing so. As he explains things,

> Ostensible seeings are experiences in which it looks to their subject as if things are a certain way.

He then says this about the relevant notion of looks:

> Even if one does judge that things are as they look, having them look that way to one is not the same as judging that they are that way. In some cases, perhaps, one does judge that things are a certain way when they look that way. But ... unless there are grounds for suspicion, such as odd lighting conditions, having it look to one as if things are a certain way—ostensibly seeing things to be that way—*becomes* accepting that things are that way by a sort of default.
>
> (McDowell 1998: pp. 438–9, my italics)

McDowell clearly cannot mean 'looks as if (indicative)' in its normal English sense. So read, for it to look to one as if X *is* is for one to take it that X; for one's mind to be made up. It is not to keep the option of accepting, or rejecting, 'at face value', that things are that way. Nor is it to be in a condition that may *evolve* into judgement. It *is* to judge. This fits with the first disjunct of what McDowell means to capture. Where I *see* the pig to be before me, my mind *is* made up. Nothing remains (on that score) for me to take at face value or not. The world has already drawn credence from me. To see that such-and-such is so is to take it to be so.

So reading it may not fit well with what McDowell means to capture in the other disjunct. What unites the ringers in the cases where it looks to me as if there is a pig before me is nothing other than the fact that I so take it—that I am, thus, fooled. No visual look, for example, is present in all these cases. There need not even be any such thing as a visual look in every such case—certainly not a porcine one. This class would not be the same as the class in which things look as they would were there a pig before me (however exactly one identifies that class). What all its members would share in common with all instances of the first disjunct is only a bit of autorepresentation, not a visual likeness. Looking as if X is meant to be a feature shared by all instances of either disjunct. But autorepresentation is implausibly the right feature.

It is clear to some extent what notion McDowell wants. First, it should be possible, on it, for it to look (to N) as if X, while, for all that, *not* X (so that there may be a face value). Second, it should be possible for it to look to N as if X, on this notion, even when N is entirely agnostic as to whether X (so that looks may be taken or left at face value). So, too, it should be possible for it to look as if X, on the notion, even though X is not to be concluded, even tentatively, from— is not indicated at all by—the facts in hand, or placed by the experience in hand. It looks as if it is a Vermeer; we *know* it is a van Meegeren.

The relevant sense must make this attitude coherent, 'That, anyway, is how things look (to me); as to what there is reason to think, that is quite another matter'. For that, the way things (first sense) look (to N)—what is fixed by their visual looks, so viewed—must fix how, in the relevant sense, they look to N.

There is nothing wrong with a notion that works in that way. Though there are ordinary means of expressing it, McDowell may choose whatever means he likes. It is the next step that makes everything go wrong. For McDowell also wants a look in his sense to carry as such a given import: for it to be present is, as such, for such-and-such thereby (at least) to be suggested; so for there to be a way things should be to be the way they look full stop. Only then could there be such a thing as judging (all the more refusing to judge) that things are as they look. Only then could there be any such thing to judge; such a thing as things being, or not, as they look.

This feature of McDowell's notion makes looking in his sense contrast with having a visual look. A visual look, like any other visible thing, may sometimes indicate something. But that is a contingent matter. A porcine look sometimes indicates a pig, but need not. All that visual looks fix as to how things look fixes *no* particular way things should be to be the way they look full stop. (Nor would fixing what is indicated fix what *representation* requires.) But, in meeting the first desideratum, what is thus fixed *would* fix how things look to N in McDowell's sense. So how things look to N in that sense cannot fix what way things should be to be the way they look. The two desiderata cannot consistently be fulfilled by *any* notion of looks.

McDowell wants to mix two immiscible notions. Looking as if X is to be what unites the two disjuncts of McDowell's 'ostensibly seeing'. It is to be what is in common to a pig being visibly before me, and the relevant cases of the mere appearance of that. For that he needs a look in his sense to be identified (as present or absent in any given case) as looks in our first sense are: there will be a ringer wherever things (as seen by me) look suitably as they would were there a pig before me. Just so is the occurrence of a ringer independent of what is indicated by, or what I make of, things (as viewed by me) looking as they do. Just that holds looks in his sense apart both from autorepresentation and from indicating. McDowell must draw on our first notion of a look to block that collapse. Such looks are just what *is* independent of indicating, and of autorepresentation.

McDowell thus needs looks in our first sense, so visual looks, to have intrinsic import: for such a look to do what a thinkable look does: to make, *per se*, for a way things should be to be the way they look full stop. Only that would give an appearance the right shape to evolve into a judgement—would allow one to *judge*, or take it, that X where, or in, not doubting that things are as they look. There must already be a *that* X in the way things thus look for there to be something to doubt or not.

The problem with this combination—a feature from one notion, a feature from the other—is that no visual look, nor any look in our first sense, *has* any intrinsic import. Its presence *cannot* mean as such that there is some way things should be to be the way they look *simpliciter*. The reasons for that have already been rehearsed. In brief, depending on exactly how one individuates such looks, either a given such look is the look of things being countless different rival ways—Pia approaching, her sister approaching, and so on—or it inevitably cohabits with the looks of things being those ways, where, again, there is nothing to choose from among these looks those which show how things should be to be the way they look *simpliciter*.

There is, and can be, no notion of look to serve McDowell's purpose. It is the purpose that is at fault. McDowell's bind here is just the representationalist's. Looks that allowed us to appreciate that it was being represented to us as so that such-and-such would be identifiable as visual looks are, and not simply by what would be so if things were as they looked. If their mere presence fixed *how* things were represented to us as being then, in doing that, they would fix a way things should be to be the way they look full stop. Such looks would combine features of our first and second notion. But those features do not combine. The representationalist, like McDowell, places an impossible set of demands on looks.

6 Responses

It is hard to say (since they themselves do not) why representationalists are unimpressed by the above points. Perhaps they disown some of the position I ascribed to them (those four points by which, at the start, I fixed the representationalism here at issue). Perhaps they think of representation as occurring in perception otherwise than as portrayed above. I will explore these possibilities by considering Gilbert Harman's version of the view (Harman 1990). That version illustrates as well as any what might tempt one down representationalism's primrose path. Discussing an undefended position, though, inevitably involves guesswork.

Of those four points, the first two—that the relevant representing is of such-and-such as so, and that it gives perceptual experience a face value—are taken from the mouths of representationalists. Anyone who renounces these points is not my target. As for the third point, the crucial part is that the relevant representing not be autorepresenting. Perceptual experience is a form of awareness of our surroundings. Perhaps we cannot have such awareness without registering at least some of what is around us. Perhaps to do that just is to autorepresent things as so. I take no stand here. If a representationalist wants to say no more than this, I will not cavil. McDowell, for one, insists that it is not all he wants to say. (Being represented to, though not yet, may *become*, a judgement.) And it is not all one does say in insisting that in perception we are represented to.

Not all representationalists speak explicitly of things being represented *to* (or *for*) *the perceiver* as so. But they are my target if they maintain the following: first, that a perceptual experience has a particular representational content (its content), namely, that such-and-such is so; second, that the perceiver can recognize this feature of it (as he would in grasping when the experience would be veridical, when not); third, that this is a content the perceiver may accept or reject (where accepting would be taking, or coming to take, what is thus represented as so to be so). To abbreviate, you are my target if you think experiences have a face value. This places at least all cited authors within my target range.

There is no more than the above in the idea that the relevant representation is allorepresentation, though the point need not be pressed. Allorepresentation requires something to do the representing. But that something can just be the perceptual experience itself, or else (the fact of) things looking as they did. A representationalist need not balk at that.

As for point 4, a representationalist *could*, I think, disown the idea that content is looks-indexed. That is suggested by something Harman says. I thus drop the requirement, retaining only the requirement that this content is recognizable. That will prove not to help the representationalist's case.

I will focus on four points in Harman's view. Three are in this passage:

> Eloise is aware of the tree as a tree that she is now seeing. So, we can suppose, she is aware of some features of her current visual experience. In particular, she is aware that her visual experience has the feature of being an experience of seeing a tree. That is to be aware of an intentional feature of her experience; she is aware that her experience has a certain content.
>
> (Harman 1990: p. 38)

Harman speaks of Eloise's awareness of the tree as a tree that she is now seeing. Of course, she may *see* the tree without any such awareness. She may mistake it for a power pole, or a mastodon leg, or be unable to make out *what* it is. If she *is* aware of the 'intentional' feature Harman claims she is (whatever he means by 'intentional'), this is, to repeat a point, not *visual* awareness. Insofar as her *visual* experience consists of (the objects of her) visual awareness, it includes awareness of no such feature. She may *know* what she sees for what it is. This is for *her* to represent things to *herself* as a certain way. So far, there is no other source of representational content *for* her to be aware of.

In any case, Harman's take on the situation suggests the following points:

A. When we are aware of something being so, or present, that is *represented* to us as so, or present. We are aware of seeing a tree, its brown trunk, its partly occluding other trees, and so on. It is accordingly represented to us as so that there is a tree, it has a brown trunk, and so on.

B. We are aware of being represented to (of the experience's (supposed) face value). (Harman 1990: p. 46.) We are aware of our experience having the representational content that it does; of what is so according to it.

C. To be aware that one's experience is an experience of such-and-such (or simply to be aware of experiencing such-and-such) is to be aware of its being represented to one that such-and-such. Experiencing seeing a tree is, *per se*, experiencing being represented to.

In all these cases, by Frege's point, the relevant form of awareness could not be *perceptual* (such as visual) awareness. One may, of course, be visually aware of the tree. But not that one's experience has the feature of being of seeing a tree.

Harman also says this:

> Look at a tree and try to turn your attention to intrinsic features of your visual experience. I predict you will find that the only features there to turn your attention to will be features of the presented tree, including relational features of the tree 'from here'.
>
> (Harman 1990: p. 39)

Neither a tree nor its features (being, looking, perhaps seeming, certain ways) does any representing. But that there is a tree which is, looks, and so on, thus and so is what is represented as so. So the point here is to be:

D. We are not aware of anything, other than, perhaps, the experience itself, which does the relevant representing, or bears the relevant content. We are aware of the familiar objects of perception, and of no further vehicle which contains a representation of them as present.

Points B and D suggest how a representationalist might reject my initial point 4. They at least suggest that when I see a tree before me, it need not be that I have noted some looks on grounds of which I take that to be so. Nor *need* it be some look, or looks, from which I can see that I am so represented to. It is unclear that Harman would actually deny that the relevant content is looks-indexed. But anyway, if, in this case, it need not be gathered from (awareness of) something else that such-and-such is represented as so, then someone might deny it.

Recognition capacities may be of different sorts. In some cases, we can recognize a such-and-such, or its presence, and there is a story to be told about how we do that: certain observable features of the environment, to which we are perceptually sensitive (whether we note them or not) are a mark, for us, of the presence, or absence, of the relevant thing. Psychologists, I think, hope that facial recognition works like that. I suppose that my ability to tell a pig when I see one (such as it is) normally does too. In other cases, though, perhaps there is no such story. We can tell, as a rule, when the thing is present. But there is no describable function from other observable features of a situation to the cases in which we would recognize its presence. That idea, I think, is not absurd. If not, and if we are represented to in experience, then perhaps our ability to detect the content of such representing works like that. Point 4 can thus be weakened to allow this possibility. What remains is that the relevant being represented to is recognizable.

If we are represented to in perception, perhaps we can just tell how things are thus represented to us; there is no saying precisely how we can tell. It is still so, on Harman's view, that we *can* tell; that we are aware of being represented to, and appreciate how things are thus represented. That raises two questions. First, *what* is it that we thus tell? When would an experience have given representational content? Or, for a given experience, just what content does it have? Second, in cases where we do see things, how does our being represented to relate to our seeing what we do?

I begin with the first question. I have already said why I think it has no answer. There is, I have argued, nothing in a perceptual experience to make it count as having some one representational content as opposed to countless others. Harman, though, says something that may *sound* like an answer. It is important to see why it is not one. But first we must face a peculiarity in Harman's speech. I thus turn to his point D.

Harman insists that when Eloise is aware of seeing a tree, she is thereby aware that her experience has a certain *intentional* feature; namely, one of having such-and-such content. Exactly not, one would have thought. Intentionality, as usually conceived, is world-directedness. It is being hostage to the world's favour for some success which the intentional item, as such, aims at. Whereas seeing is, per se, a success. For one to see a tree is for there to be one. There is nothing seeing as such aims at that has not already been achieved if it occurs at all. Which would make seeing a tree precisely *not* an intentional feature of experience.

Harman, though, rejects this view of seeing. Following Miss Anscombe, he believes that he can see things that are not there. So when he says Eloise to see a tree, he does not mean it to follow that there is one. If there is one, the seeing was a success. But she might have seen one anyway, on his proprietary use, even if there were not. That may well make seeing intentional. In due course we will see good reason (aside from the obvious ones) not to talk that way. For the moment, though, I will need to put the relevant point in two ways. First, I will use 'see' to mean what it does; thus, as a success verb. Then I will try to speak in Harman's way.

So, what representational content does a given perceptual experience have? What might make any answer to this question right of a given case? Harman tells us that if Eloise sees a tree before her, then it is represented to her as so that there is a tree before her. Taking 'see' to mean *see*, one naturally thinks of the case where there *is* a tree before her. Harman's dictum then applies equally whether she takes what she sees for a tree, or it so much as looks, or appears to her much like a tree, or whether, in fact, it *does* look like one, or this can even be told by looking. (The tree may be obscured, in haze, or in disguise.) Taking 'see' for *see*, we now know that her experience represents a tree to be before her when there *is* one, and she sees it. But it is characteristic of representing that something may be *represented* to be so when it is not—a possibility allowed by Harman in using 'see a tree' to speak of something Eloise may do when there *is* none. A question thus arise for Harman. In which cases in which there is none would it be represented to Eloise that there was? More generally, where she sees a tree, what *else* does her experience represent to her as so? In particular, when, and why, would it be representing things that were in fact false? Where *part* of the content of Eloise's experience is that there is a tree before her, what more content, if any, is there? More pointedly, what makes the correct answer here correct?

There are familiar constraints on a reply. The cases where it is falsely represented as so to Eloise that such-and-such had better not just be those where she takes that such-and-such to be so—for example, where she falsely takes there to be a pig before her. That would reduce representation in perception to autorepresentation. That is not the view in question. Similarly, they had better not just be the cases where porcine presence is *indicated*: where a pig was to be expected, going by the looks. Nor, equally, should they just be cases where the perceiver *did* expect a pig going by the looks. For, as has been made clear, indicating is not representing. If representing merely echoed everything already indicated, it would be a (very annoying) wheel idling.

If how an experience represents things is fixed, somehow, by what the experience was like, one will not find the material for fixing this in visual looks, for reasons already given. If looks matter at all—whether in specifiable ways or not—one is forced to the other side of the divide: to looks for which there is, *per se*, a way things should be to be the way they look, that is, *thinkable* looks, the *import* of things looking as they do. That move gets one nowhere. For one thing, it only moves us into the domain of indicating. But should looks, or what an experience is like, matter at all to its representational content? Again, that we are represented to in experience is meant to be a familiar phenomenon; something we can tell is happening. It is not just events occurring in visual processing mechanisms of which we are all ignorant. It should not come as a complete surprise some day, to be sprung on us by future neurophysiologists, that we are thus represented to (uselessly, of course, since we were all ignorant of it). So yes. But, for reasons covered, there is just nothing in what perceptual experience is like to make the representational content of a given one some given thing as opposed to indefinitely many rivals.

Let us now try to use 'see' in Harman's way. I will write this 'see★'. The idea is to be: I see★ a pig before me just in case either there is a pig before me and I see it (and, perhaps, some further condition as to my seeing it as, or to be, a pig), or... What should follow this 'or'? The familiar problems arise. Is it a condition on this disjunct of seeing★ a pig that I see what looks like a pig? Or that things look as they would, or might, if I were seeing a pig? Or, anyway, that they so look *to me*? In all of this, seeing★ would be very different from seeing. And it would do no more to bring representing into the picture than such looks do—a matter already discussed. Are the relevant cases just those in which I take myself to see a pig before me? Is autorepresentation the crucial feature here? If Harman wants to speak that peculiarly, fine. But now there is no plausibility in the idea that a pig is represented to me as there every time I see★ one. *Must* I be so represented to in order to autorepresent? Can I not sometimes just take a pig to be *indicated* when it is not? In any case, since being represented to is one thing, and autorepresentation another, it still remains to say *in general* where the former phenomenon would occur. (To make the phenomena *necessarily* coextensive would just remove being represented to from the scene altogether.)

Perhaps, then, the relevant cases are just those in which the way things look suggests, or indicates, that there is a pig before me. (From the way that snout is twitching, I would say that it is a pig.) Again, a very strange use of 'see'—to cover precisely what I cannot see, but must infer. But let that pass. For, again, suggesting, or indicating, is not representing. If these are supposed to be the cases in which it is represented to me as so that there is a pig before me, then such representation is entirely otiose; a mere re-rehearsing of what experience has otherwise made plain.

Or perhaps the relevant cases are just those where things look as the presence of a pig does, or might. (Without further explanation, this picks out no definite class of cases. But that does not matter to the present point.) There will then be *many* diverse cases where on sees★ a pig. It cannot be that in all of these it is represented to one as so that there is a pig before one. That idea, applied to *all* the things one would thus see★ in any given case of *seeing* (such as a pig), would make representation in perception incoherent, thus not intelligibly representation. Too many things would thereby be represented as so at once. There are just too many things things look like.

Follow the 'or' with whatever you like, and it cannot be so that to see★ a pig is to have it represented to one as so that there is one. The problems in filling the blank are just one reason among many why it is, as a rule, a bad idea to claim to see things that are not there. Just what are we to understand you to be doing? Harman's problems in answering our first question, and, more particularly, in saying just what seeing★ is supposed to be, are just McDowell's in trying to make sense of ostensibly seeing. Ostensible seeing could, no doubt, just serve as seeing★ if only we knew what it was.

I turn now to the second major question. Suppose there is a pig before me, and I see it. That is one case in which, according to Harman, it is represented to me as so that there is a pig before me. Just what is the relation supposed to be between these two things—my seeing the pig, and my being thus represented to? There are two ways of conceiving the matter. On the one, I have two separate sources of information. I am aware of two different things: first, the pig; second, being represented to. Awareness of neither carries with it, *ipso facto*, awareness of the other. I see the pig; it is otherwise intimated to me, redundantly, that there is one. On the other, there is but one source. I am represented to, and cognisant of that. To be aware of all that I thus am just *is* my seeing a pig—where there is one that I see. My awareness of being represented to then constitutes that awareness which seeing a pig (to be) before me is.

On the two-source view, I experience, in the relevant cases, its being represented to me as so that there is a pig before me. I am unmediatedly aware of that. Sometimes, when there *is* a pig before me, I am also unmediatedly aware of something else: the pig before me. I see it, *and*, in addition, it is represented to me as so. I thus have, twice over, reason to take it that there is a pig, each reason different in kind, each independent of the other. Perhaps whenever I see a pig, this other experience, being represented to, tags along. But it is never my sole source of awareness of the pig. It is an extra intimation or porcine presence. Sanity would be hard won if representation in experience were thus both inescapable and redundant—like a relative at the movies, reciting what you have just seen. Where I see a pig, that further intimation of one is gratuitous. Where I do not, and no pig is indicated, it carries no conviction. But experience is obviously not that way. No-one thinks it is.

What remains is the one-source model. On it, on a given occasion of its being represented by my experience as so that there is a pig before me, there is whatever I would then *ipso facto* experience simply in experiencing that to be represented to me—something which, on the model, I might experience with or without pig before me. Then (since I do experience seeing a pig) there is whatever it is I then experience in seeing a pig before me. The idea is: though the first could occur, or could have, without the second, where both occur this is simply because, under those circumstances, experiencing the first just counts as experiencing the second. Under those circumstances, where I experience the first, I could not also count as failing to experience the second.

In experiencing the first thing, I am aware, in a certain way, of certain things. *Mutatis mutandis* for my experiencing the second thing. By hypothesis, all there is for me to be aware of in the second instance is what there is for me to be aware of in the first, plus whatever experiencing that much then makes for me experiencing. So I am aware of no more than whatever I am in my experiencing the first, plus whatever that awareness then amounts to awareness of. So what I am aware of in seeing a pig (to be before me) is no more than that.

How may awareness of X amount to awareness of Y? It may just be that; or it may make for that—be all or part of what makes one count as aware of Y. I may experience all I do just in its being represented to me that there is a pig before me without a pig before me. So for me to be aware of what I am precisely in experiencing that cannot just *be* for me to be aware as I am of (seeing) a pig before me. What it might do, sometimes, where there is a pig before me, is make for awareness of that. It, and surrounding conditions, may make me count as aware of that. The hope must be that the awareness this delivers is that which I have in seeing a pig to be before me.

As a rule, awareness of something else plus satisfaction of surrounding conditions cannot add up to that awareness of porcine presence which we have in seeing one (to be there)—in my terms, unmediated awareness. Or, more exactly, if X is something there might be even without Y, then awareness of X (and whatever accompanies it *per se* in a particular case) cannot qualify as unmediated awareness of Y—the sort one might have in seeing Y. The rule holds where X is its being represented to one that Y is so (or present), where representation takes any of the forms we are familiar with. It holds equally, in familiar cases, where X is whatever is a part of the being represented to as such—uttering some words, say.

For example, Pia may learn there are pigs about by being told. She might, that is, if she is, or was, aware of being told. Being told, in that case, may qualify her as aware that there are pigs about. It might do that; but only sometimes. Not, for one thing, if she refuses, or omits, to *take* there to be pigs about. Not, for another, if she was not told because it was so—if that telling did not mean that there were pigs about. And not, for a third, if she was not entitled to rely on that. All these are things that sometimes happen. So her being told qualifies her as aware that there are pigs only given certain quite substantial contingencies.

These features make for mediated awareness, if any. They distinguish mediated from unmediated awareness. With the unmediated awareness one has in seeing there to be pigs (in seeing pigs), Pia cannot refuse, or omit, to take pigs to be present. The limitation is grammatical, not psychological. To see there to be pigs about is, *inter alia*, to be aware of their presence, thus of seeing *pigs*. One's stance on that score is thus set; one's mind made up. Further, if what she is thus aware of—the presence of pigs—*means* that there are pigs, that is not something it might or might not do all depending. So no substantial entitlement is needed, where one goes on that, to take there to be pigs.

The difference between seeing pigs and merely having it represented to one that there are pigs is not exhausted by such marks. In that unmediated awareness of a pig which is seeing it to be there, it is the pig itself whose presence forms my cognitive responses to it. It is its doings themselves which make me privy to them. I need not follow at one remove, by following the career of something else, and taking the pig's career to be what it then must be. I need not, in particular, keep track of how I am being represented to, or of whatever it is (surely not the pig) that does the representing. Its being represented to me as so that there are pigs about *may* make me aware that there are; but (in familiar cases) it cannot deliver awareness of that sort—awareness in which no more than the relevant porcine doings is required for keeping me *au fait* with the changing, or changeable, porcine state of affairs; in which I need follow nothing else to keep abreast of its continuation or extinction.

I have so far spoken of a *familiar* form of being represented to: being told. What it delivers is at best mediated awareness of what is told. That should be undisputed. Why might one think that representation could work differently where it is in, or as part of, a perceptual experience that something is represented as so? Here is a line of thought. In your representing it to me as so that there are pigs about, there is both more and less for me to be aware of than there is when there are pigs about. There must be more; for even if you produce a virtual reality pig simulation, there must be something to indicate that this is to be taken as representing what is so, rather than, say, as representing what it would be like if it were so. There will also be less: the pig itself is no part of your representing; and, typically, your representing will look and sound nothing like a pig before me. By contrast, the line goes, where, in a visual experience, it is represented to me as so that there is a pig before me, such differences, or any that are phenomenological, are all erased. There need be, in such an experience, no more for me to be aware of than there might be where I saw a pig to be before me. There need not be quite as much for me to be aware of as there is where there is a pig before me, since there need be no pig (such representation can be false). But such an experience will be just like one of seeing a pig before me in this sense: in it things will look, or seem, just as a pig before me would, or might. There need be nothing further it is like for an experience to be one in which I am so represented to; and nothing less will do. So I have such an experience *just* where things look, or seem, that way.

The idea does not work. On the one-source model, I need be aware of nothing more in my experience than I am in my awareness of being represented to for it to be (made) so that I see a pig before me—that I am aware of its so being as I thus would be. Nor could I be aware of less—it is not as if I have some other way of being, or qualifying as, aware that a pig is present. But all I am thus aware of is what might be there for me to be aware of even if there were no pig. That leaves room for me, fully recognizing all that, to refuse to take it that there is a pig there; room for all that not to mean that there is a pig there (even if, in fact, there is one); and so on. The marks of mediated awareness of a pig before me thus remain. And that would not be seeing one to be there. Perhaps I may sometimes count as having been aware, in a given experience, of the presence of a pig, and sometimes count merely as having been aware of things looking that way. It would be a mistake to take that to mean that my awareness of things looking that way could ever count as awareness of a pig before me, or could make for more than mediated awareness of that.

The idea is anyway a non-starter, for familiar reasons. On it, a visual experience is to be one in which it is represented to me as so that there is a pig before me just where in it things look as they would, or might, were there a pig before me. One could draw the look in question. It is, if anything, a visual look; thus equally a way things would, or might look if any of countless other things were so—for example, if there were a peccary before me. So, on the idea, this would also be an experience in which it was represented to me as so—for example, that there was a peccary before me. Nor would that be a matter of representing two different things as before me. The idea thus gives visual experiences incoherent content.

There is a fundamental problem. On the idea, an experience is identified as one in which it is represented to me as so that there is a pig before me by the way, in it, things look or seem, or by their looking, or seeming, as they do. As we have seen, there is nothing in things looking as they do to make anything the way things should be for an experience to be veridical—if it did represent, for things to be as represented. The one-source model requires our being represented to in perceptual experience to be representation of an extraordinary kind. But the idea of such extraordinary representation is bankrupt. The postulated representing is to be found neither in *what* we experience, nor in our responses to it, where one finds but autorepresenting. The one-source model thus fails. That leaves no room in perceptual experience for things to be represented to us as so. Autorepresentation aside, perceiving what we do *has* no representational content.

Harman writes,

Perceptual experience represents a particular environment of the perceiver... The content of perceptual representation is functionally defined in part by the ways in which this representation normally arises in perception and in part by the ways in which the representation is normally used to guide actions.

(Harman 1990: p. 46)

Perhaps it is experience's sources, and not its looks, that give it content. But that idea leads nowhere. Issues of normalcy arise for repeatably enjoyable experience types. Whereas what we need to fix content for are particular experiences, such as the visual experience I am having now, say, with a pig before me. Any particular experience instances countless types. Which of these matter to its content? Certain types obviously cannot. My experience belongs to the type *seeing a pig*. But that I do, in fact, see one cannot make that represented to me as so. On Harman's account, a tree is represented to Eloise as before her just where, in his proprietary sense, she sees one. Whether she does that is meant to be a matter of how things look (to her)—on *some* notion of looking. So perhaps it is looks that, somehow, type experiences relevantly. These had better be visual looks on pain of misreading autorepresentation as being represented to.

We may, perhaps, ask how experiences so typed 'normally' arise—in my life, in human existence, or whatever. Perhaps some one such type is thus due to porcine presence. (Which?) Its action-guiding force might, for all that, be almost anything, depending on how one autorepresents an instance of it. One who takes himself to see a peccary in some one instance will be guided differently from one who thus takes himself to see a pig. But autorepresenting cannot fix how one was represented to. The proposal is thus left with nothing other than such a type—and thus with no particular action-guiding force—as that by which content is to be fixed. So any experience of this type, so mine, will be one in which a pig was represented to the perceiver to be before him—even where he plainly saw a peccary.

But do visual looks identify types that thus matter to content? Do *they* matter to content in some determinate way? We have seen why they do not. If they did, they would give an experience a face value. Where things were not, in fact, as they are according to that face value, the experience would be, *ipso facto*, deceptive, or non-veridical. To trust the experience would be to take it at face value. If looks fix, or identify, face value, that would be to take things to be as they look. But visual looks do not make *any* way the way things should be to be the way they look; nor do we suppose they do; nor is it them as such in which we trust. So they cannot type experiences that fix content. Nor does anything else. (Not, for example, what they indicate.)

The fundamental problem is this. Being represented to in experience was meant to be a familiar phenomenon. That an experience would be deceptive, or non-veridical, unless such-and-such were so is something an experiencer was supposed to recognize about it. There is no such familiar phenomenon. There is thus no such work for sources of experience to do. Perception is not the stuff of which things might be represented to us as so. It is, in a crucial way, not an intentional phenomenon.[1]

---

[1] I am deeply grateful to the (then) editor of *Mind*, Mike Martin, for his patient, insightful, and no doubt time-consuming efforts, for which this essay is vastly better than it might have been. He is not thereby accountable for any views expressed.

2

Frege, Father of Disjunctivism

> The concept of the 'inner picture' is misleading, for this concept uses the 'outer picture' as a model; and yet the uses of the words for these concepts are no more like one another than those of 'numeral' and 'number'.
>
> Wittgenstein, *Philosophical Investigations*, IIxi: p. 196

Why disjunctivism, its seeming complexities and quirks? In the case of perception, Frege has a compelling answer. It gains him claim to fatherhood. (Cook Wilson is the natural parent in the case of knowledge. For singular thought, Russell will do as inspiration. The case of (reasons for) action remains to be explored.) My main aim here is to make Frege's case. A subsidiary aim is to begin to sketch some of its wider implications for the nature of our 'inner lives'.

Disjunctivism about perception and disjunctivism about knowledge oppose a common form of target. The target posits an ingredient in seeing, say, a lemon, or knowing there to be one, which could also be present in some range of cases where there was no such thing to see, or to know. For seeing, the ingredient is something of which the experience affords awareness. For knowing, it is an attitude one could hold anyway. The target (often) also holds that for one to see, or know, the thing in question is for this further ingredient to be present under suitable conditions, of whose obtaining one need not be aware.

But there is a disanalogy. Disjunctivism about perception concerns what experience provides *to be responded to*—if appearances, then *things* appearing (as experienced) thus and so, not one's holding of an attitude. Disjunctivism about knowledge concerns our *responses*—the idea of a response which may, or may not, be knowledge. For knowing P, there does *seem* to be an attitude one could hold anyway even were there no such thing to know, namely, thinking that P. Current disjunctivists—as opposed to Cook Wilson—tend to grant that point. Their brief is then that there are no surrounding conditions which could make mere thinking so into knowledge. In the case of perception, it is nothing like apparent that there *is* the ingredient the target posits. Disjunctivism's brief, as presented here, will be that there is not. In which case, the further question whether seeing could be a hybrid of this ingredient and surrounding conditions lapses. Of course, something may look yellow, as encountered by an observer, where nothing *is* yellow. But such banal facts do not make for the ingredient the target wants there to be.

I will begin here by developing Frege's master point, with no further concern, for the moment, for what disjunctivism might be. I will then apply the point, first to a special form of disjunctivism's target, and then, generalizing the target, to a different case. This last case will be a form of intentionalism about perception. Some intentionalists believe that the supposedly recognized evils of sense datum theory are avoided simply by eschewing qualia, or special unworldly objects with visual, or other, perceptual properties. Frege's lesson is that this simply is not so. To reorder one idea of Frege's: to judge is to expose oneself to error; there is something to judge to be one way or another only where something affords the opportunity so to expose oneself; such opportunities occur only in an environment. Intentionalism shares with sense datum theory a difficulty in respecting this idea.

1 Judgement

Let us think of *the environment* as home to all things to be met with. That subjectless passive is meant to signal two things. First, if something is to be met with, then there is no-one one must be to meet with it. Second, if something is to be met with, then, for any meeting with it, there could have been another. I leave the idea of a meeting unexplicated except by example. Seeing, hearing, smelling, tasting, are each a form of awareness of things to be met with. One, say, smells the violets. The awareness thus afforded is a meeting with them. A proof that there is no largest prime is something one meets with, *inter alia*, in grasping it. The thought that tapirs are porcine may be met with in speculating about tapirs—in entertaining it. Perception being of what is to be met with, smelling the violets is a kind of meeting with them available to anyone suitably placed, and perceptually equipped. There is no-one one must be for this.

Perception thus models occasion for a very special kind of attitude. I see a lemon only where there is one to be met with. I may respond to the experience with an attitude correct or not precisely according to whether there is a lemon *to be met with*. What correctness would be here points to a certain notion of correctness. The attitude thus correct or not exemplifies the special sort at issue here. Frege was concerned with a general case thus exemplified: attitudes whose correctness (of the indicated sort) is decided solely by things being as they are. He termed these 'judging'. So will I. The general case transcends attitudes towards the perceivable. Our problem is: does it also transcend attitudes towards what is to be met with?

What is it for correctness to be decided exclusively, and precisely, by how things are? For one thing, whatever it is that decides this correctness should do such deciding as it does regardless of any thinkers' attitudes towards its so doing; so it should be there to do the deciding it does regardless of any thinkers' attitudes towards *that*. How are we to understand this? One thing we will need is: such an attitude *may* be correct, or incorrect; and if it is (in)correct on any taking of it, then it is correct on all. This leaves out craving duck's tongues; also, quite likely, finding them delicious. It also makes the correctness at issue here contrast with being justified: in my Proustian bedroom, I may be unjustified in thinking it is snowing (the thought resting on nothing but intrinsic pessimism), while you, looking out the window, may be entirely justified in thinking so. But you are correct in the present sense if I am.

One might want more. But to get this much we also need more. To make sense of an attitude being correct on any taking of it, we need to be able to separate what is to be correct or incorrect—a certain attitude available to take—from any taking of it. Where there is a judging, there must thus be that which is thus judged (a judgement). For us to be able to detach a particular attitude taken from a given case of someone standing towards things as he does, it must be determinate enough when, in someone's standing towards things as he does, it would be *that* attitude (*inter alia*) which he was taking. Which will be determinate enough if, but only if, it is sufficiently determinate *how* someone would stand towards the world (or things being as they are) in taking it.

One might plausibly think it also a requirement on detaching an attitude from some holding of attitude that the attitude detached be to be met with (in thought)—in grasping, or entertaining, it. Which means: there is no-one one need be to take the attitude; and that for any taking of it there might have been another. Here, though, this calls for argument. Frege's concern in what follows is with whether, in someone's standing as he does towards things being as they are, there are detachable attitudes *for him* to take—that things are thus and so—which are available only for him to take, or, more generally, meet with. These will be attitudes towards what there is only for him to meet with—if not necessarily such-and-such items, in any case such-and-such ways for things to be. For there to be such attitudes is for the extent of how things are to transcend that of how things to be met with are. What Frege aims to show is that it does not.

Perhaps there is *a* way of counting thoughts on which the thought *I* think and the one you do, where we both think that I am cold are different ones. It all hangs on special modes of presentation of oneself. But then there is another.

For in such a case each of us is right or wrong according to something in particular as to how things are: whether I am cold. One of us will be wrong as to that just where the other is. Which identifies an attitude we share, specifically, a judgement, we both judge. That there are also ways of distinguishing our attitudes is, for the present, beside the point.

In ordinary speech, the verb 'judge' has connotations of confronting something and sizing it up. I may, inspecting him, judge the man looking at me in the bar to be dangerous. But if I merely think, in my cork-lined room, that it is snowing (manifesting my pessimism), that is not judging. So we ordinarily speak. But not here. To be a judgement is, here, and for Frege, just to be truth-evaluable. To judge is to hold a truth-evaluable attitude.

To judge a pig to be wallowing is to be exposed to being right or wrong as to what is to be met with. What might it be to expose oneself to error, as one *ipso facto* does in judging, as to what is *not* to be met with?

2 Inner Confrontations

I now start an extended argument. Frege presents it in terms of an analogy. This section concerns the first term of that comparison. It does not draw the conclusion of the argument. For that the whole analogy is needed. So, in particular, it does not decide whether the realm of things for *me* to judge extends beyond that of judgements as to what is to be met with. It is but a first step towards such decision.

If there is something it is for a rubber ball, or towel, or sunset, to be red, it does not follow that there is something it is for the E flat above middle C, or the rate of recidivism in Ohio, to be red. Those ideas may yet lack sense. There is, Frege tells us, another sort of case where new sense would be called for. He says:

> The word 'red', if it does not indicate a property of things, but is meant to indicate marks of sense-impressions which are part of my consciousness, is applicable only in the domain of my consciousness.
>
> (1918: p. 67)

If I used 'red' to speak of things there for only me to meet with, I would not thus be speaking of a way for environmental things to be. So if I do use 'red' to speak of a way for environmental things to be, I cannot be speaking of a way for non-environmental things to be. 'Red' has a sense in which it speaks of environmental things—balls, towels, and such. For it to speak of non-environmental matters it would need new sense. For in its environmental sense it does not speak of a way there is for a non-environmental thing to be. If I encounter, say, looks, or patches, or visual sensations, to be met with only by me, then these can be *red* only on a new understanding of what something being red would be. So Frege tells us.

Why should this be? The answer must turn on the absence, in the non-environmental case, of certain materials present in the environmental one; materials which, when present, constitute, in whole or part, what it is for something to be red—what it is we say of something in so saying. Conspicuously, there are those two features the notion *to be met with* brings on board: there is no-one one must be to encounter the thing which is red, or its being red; for any encounter with this, there might have been another. I will call these features *recurrability*. Recurring need not take time. I may later encounter what I now do. But someone else might encounter what I now do. To be re-encountered is just to be encountered at least twice.

The notion *recognize* fits what can recur. One may register new encounters with the already met. One may also register what one encounters as instancing a certain way for things to be. Both these notions are of cognitive achievement: one goes right, where one *might* have gone wrong. One will go wrong on the second notion of success where *one* would not meet the supposed instancing in *a* meeting with what was meant to do it. One may similarly go wrong as to what would count as something being thus and so, where such is demonstrated by other occasions of having being *that* in mind.

Recurrability allows making particular sense of 'would'. That peccary has a porcine look. Which means: there is a way it *would* look. When? On an encounter with it (barring reasons for it then not to). For it to have the look is for that to be met with by anyone suitably placed and perceptually equipped. A grasp of 'suitably' will be a grasp of when there would be such an encounter. Peccaries are dangerous in rut. This one would have been if in rut. Peccaries, and something being in rut, are both recurrent parts of the environment. A grasp of which parts is a grasp of when *this* peccary would have been *in rut*.

A ball's being red, as we conceive such things, is something with an aetiology and with effects. (Being red has effects, which is why stop signs are red.) If a ball is red, its so being so would be encountered on any meeting with it, barring happenings to change its colour. There are facts as to what would, or might, and what might not, do this. (Depending on the aetiology of its being red, the sun might, or might not, fade the red out.) If you encountered a red thing in blue light it might look purple. If you encountered it in the dark, you could not detect its redness by looking. Each of these banal remarks make sense only given that a suitable 'would' also does. If the ball is red, then there is a way it would look in blue light. Recurrability gives us such a 'would'. Such facts as to what would be are part of what it *is* for a ball to be red. Recurrability is thus essential to the environmental sense of 'red'.

Something is red just when its so being is to be met with. So, whatever it would be to meet with something being red, if it is red, then there is that to meet with on an indefinite range of occasions. If, say, being red is the sort of thing one can normally tell by looking (as one might expect if to be red is to have a certain look), then if the ball is red, that is something one could tell by looking on indefinitely many (actual or possible) occasions.

A ball's being red *matters* in a certain way to what there is to encounter in the environment. Nature has a large voice in just how. Nature's being granted such a voice is part of what something *environmental* being red *is*. Nature *could* so function only where a suitable 'would' fits. If the shirt is red, it need not be so that there would still be that look to be encountered on meeting with it after it was washed. But if not, that is because of what, nature being what it is, washing it *would* do. The key point: for something environmental to be red is for nature thus to matter to what would be met with in meeting the item. That is part of what it is, here, for something to be red.

So what being red is to be understood to be, and nature, decide jointly, in understandable ways, what there would be to be met with if such-and-such were red. The role of what is to count as something being red stands out clearly where there are contrasting understandings. This setting sun in Hackney is red on one understanding of its being so, not on another. How do these understandings differ? On the one, the sun need not then look red observed from Bristol. On the other it had better. The understandings differ precisely in what would be met with if, on each, the setting Hackney sun were red.

One should not expect, in general, to be able to tease apart the work of nature from that of what one understands by *being red*. What mattters is that the whole joint enterprise gets off the ground in the environmental case only thanks to what recurrence puts in place. That such a joint enterprise *is* off the ground is part of what it is for something to be red in the usual environmental sense.

Something's being red matters in determinate ways. For the environmental, what this mattering is *to* is what is to be met with. In the non-environmental case there can be no *such* mattering. When such mattering is stripped away, what *would* it be for something to be red? What it would be for an environmental item to be red does not yet answer this question. That is why 'red' needs new sense to apply in the non-environmental case.

What *might* it be for things non-environmental to be red? One might envision the following route to an answer. Delete from our usual notion of being red all the ways in which something's being red (or not) is liable to be a matter of what is to be met with. Then look at what is left. What *is* left? One suggestion: for something to be red is for it to have a certain look; having that look is a matter of what is to be met with in the environmental case.

But perhaps there is still something it would be for something non-environmental to have that look: it is to be, or look, just the same colour as environmental red things. The idea clearly will not do. For it helps itself to the notion of *looking* thus and so. We know what it is for something environmental to look a certain way: there is something one would meet on meeting with it. But that idea does not fit the non-environmental case. So how are we to understand *looking* here? This notion, too, needs new sense (or an explanation of why not). There is so far no progress.

To be the same colour *might* be to be indistinguishable in colour. But what indistinguishability of environmental items comes to does not show what indistinguishability of the colours of an environmental and a non-environmental item might be. I may aim to make a soap, visually indistinguishable from a certain lemon. I succeed or fail according to whether there is a visually detectable feature of the lemon not to be met with in the soap (or *vice versa*). A detectable feature is one which *could* be met with, and registered, in an indefinitely extensive range of encounters. It is what a suitably equipped observer would detect. If there is such a feature, then the suitably equipped could distinguish the lemon and the soap in indefinitely many encounters with them. There are, anyway, such encounters to be had. None of these ideas makes sense in the non-environmental case. For we have not made sense of the idea of what *would* be so on a meeting with something not to be met with. So, equally, nor of someone being able to detect something on a meeting. Someone with an ability is someone who would get things right on suitable occasions for its exercise. We do not yet know what it would be to get things right as to how things stand with something not to be met with. Surely not the same thing that it would be to get things right as to what *is* to be met with.

It is thus not obvious *what* remains of the notion of being red when its anchoring in what is to be met with is stripped away, or how anything left could, all by itself, allow us to make sense of something non-environmental being red. If there is no core understanding that could do this on its own, there is, equally, no core understanding which, on its own, determines what the right new understanding of being red is to be.

Any way for things to be has an intrinsic generality. Not *everything* in things being as they are would be required for things, or something, to be (or not to be) that way. There is what matters to being the way in question, and what does not. There is, accordingly, the range of cases in which things being as they were would be things, being the way in question. The range is always extendible: for any given members there could always be another. For something in my inner world to be red would be for my inner world to be a certain way. It would be for something to be met with only by me, perhaps, only on the occasion, to be a certain way. The remarks about *any* way for things to be apply. In my inner world's being as it is there would be what mattered to whether things, or something, was that way, and what did not so matter. There would, accordingly, be the range of cases in which my inner world's being as it was *would* be things, or something, in it being the way in question. What is 'would' to mean here? And what should *mattering* in a determinate way amount to? We have, so far, no answers to these questions. *Perhaps* they have answers. This is but the first stage of an extended argument.

If one judged things, or something, non-environmental, to be, or appear, 'red', *what* way one thus judged things to be would not be fixed by what it is for something to be *red*. That is Frege's point. So it remains to be said what one *would* thus judge. That such-and-such is red is something *one* might judge. It is *to be met with* in thinking, just as something's being red is to be met with in seeing. One meets with it in meeting with something to which the environment matters in a certain way. Someone's so judging is, again, something to be met with. It is to be met with in the environment's mattering as it does to the way he *thus* guides his dealings with it. In identifying something to be judged of a non-environment (correlatively, ways it may, or may not, thinkably be), we cannot appeal to such ways of mattering. For they are intrinsically environmental. Whether there are things to be judged of a non-environment at all, and by what such things might be identified, thus remain open questions.

3 Background

Pausing between the two legs of Frege's argument, let us ask how to make sense of the idea of there being such-and-such, in particular, there to be judged—of someone judging *thus and so* in his current holding of the attitude he does. When would such a thing be present in someone's holding the posture he does towards things? Its presence would be that of something available to judge, even if only for this person then—available whether it had been judged or not; thus, if judged, then separable from the circumstance of its having been; identifiable anyway without that circumstance to refer to. It would represent a particular way for a thinker to expose himself to error; to stake his cognitive success on how things are. That particular way for things to matter to success would be a particular way for things to be. When may we sensibly suppose someone's attitude towards things to contain as elements such discriminable attitudes?

A judgement would be available, even where not taken. An attitude an open sentence expresses—taking something to be red, say—is available to take on different occasions and towards different things, including ones towards which it is not. An attitude expressed in a closed sentence—say, that this scarf is red—might have been taken even had things—even that scarf—been different.

We may speak of an attitude as there to take on various occasions only with an adequate notion of *same attitude* in place. Where the attitude is judging, we need an adequate notion of *same way to judge things to be*. The notion *same*, on its own, does not supply what we need here. Nor does the notion *judgement*, added to it. The usual applies here. Whether my violet singlet is the same colour as my purple shorts is not settled by what the same is, nor by that plus what a colour is. There are various ways of thinking of colours; room for various notions of same colour. Similarly for attitudes. Whether Sid and Pia think the same thing as to the colour of my shorts depends on what that thing might be. Find a sense in which they do think the same, and you *ipso facto* find something to judge in judging shorts a certain colour; something Sid and Pia did each judge. Fixing what judging the same thing might be and fixing a way to judge things come as a package.

Here, now, is an analogy (not Frege's). For its first term, suppose it were said of a given proposition—say, that that pig is wallowing—that it articulates into certain elements: being about that pig (or a feature that makes it so); and being about something wallowing. What could it mean to call these *elements*? Wittgenstein, in January 1930 (see Waismann 1979: p. 90), had this to say. An element of a proposition is simply an identifiable respect in which that proposition is *the same as* some range of other propositions (that pig is grunting, that pig is snuffling, and so on): they are all *thus* alike. So it makes sense to speak of an element of a proposition only insofar as that proposition is part of such a range. If there were no such contrasting propositions, and if one could still represent that pig as wallowing, that representation would be unstructured, without elements. Its 'logical form' would be *pigwallow*.

The analogy's second term starts from a thinker at a time. There is his posture towards things: all his sensitivities, affinities, aversions, propensities to disappointment, deception, gratification, triumph, and to set, change, or hold course—his engaging with things as he does. For him to judge such-and-such is for this posture to articulate; to contain this judging as an element. Perhaps one discriminable feature of his posture is his judging that that pig is snuffling. Now the analogy. Just as it makes sense to speak of an element in a judgement only where it is present in an identifiable range of judgements, so it makes sense to speak of an element in a posture—here the posture-holder's judging thus and so—only where there is a range of postures it is (or would be) part of; a certain range of otherwise-different postures all alike in being, *inter alia*, ones of judging *this*.

An attitude thus just is a common element in postures. There are those cases of someone standing towards things which are alike in that they are all cases of taking this pig to wallow. That is one identifiable way for postures to be alike. A posture may *recognizably* contain *this* element. To judge that pig to wallow is to be exposed to a certain form of error as to *what is to be met with*. One might, say, misjudge the viscosity of the ground beneath the pig. One can (sometimes) *see* people to be wrong about such things. Their being so is to be met with. Such identifiable samenesses in exposure to disappointment or surprise can unite a range of postures. They may thus identify something one might judge. Conversely, where there *is* something someone might judge, there are such samenesses in postures. *This* much must be so even if those samenesses are not in ways of standing towards what is to be met with; even if a posture could not *recognizably* contain them. The general point applies even for postures towards a non-environment. The question is what, there, a sameness between different postures might be.

Someone's engagement with the environment can itself be part of the environment. His liability to (in)corrrectness in his cognitive ventures can be to be met with—as is Pia's and Sid's discomfiture as, arriving for a talk on tropes, they find the doors locked. (The talk must have been on Thursday.) Their discomfiture is to be met with: there is no-one one must be to meet it. So can its cause: the locked doors, as is its being caused. Pia and Sid are guiding their environmental dealings as it would take open doors, or, better, a talk on tropes, to put right. Such things show themselves, as does a ball's being red, in what is to be met with in experience of the environment. One could, here, share something in common with Pia and Sid; be guiding one's transactions in ways it would take the same to put right. Such an understanding of *the same*, in terms of what would be to be met with, is itself to be met with—shared—in thought.

Where it is the environmental towards which Pia guides her dealings, rightly or wrongly, we gain right to a now-familiar 'would'. Here guidance is as to what is to be met with, and is on or off target accordingly. The would we need—when things would be as Pia and Sid suppose—is already in that 'is to be met with', referring as it does to no particular meeting. They *are* right if a talk on tropes would be to be met with by anyone suitably placed at 3. They would be right where this was to be met with. Someone else's posture would contain this element in theirs if he were liable to be right or wrong accordingly. For Pia and Sid both to think thus and so is for 'the same' in 'think the same thing' to have a particular sense. We have just fixed (roughly, perhaps) such a sense

What needs fixing is that range of circumstances in which someone would be holding such-and-such attitude which Pia does; that range of postures of which it *would* be part. We have just seen, in outline, how the environment can make such projects unproblematic. This fixing must be done somehow in the non-environmental case as well on pain of there being *no* thinking-so in a posture towards a non-environment. For any given way someone might judge his non-environment to be, sense must be made at least of when *he* would be judging that; of when that would be an element in his posture towards his non-environment. We must still think in terms of a range of postures towards a (perhaps his) non-environment, of which *this* judgement would be an element.

Engagement with a non-environment is itself part of a non-environment. A thought that a non-environment is thus and so cannot be identified by when it would misguide, or rightly guide, environmental dealings. For then it would be right or wrong according to how the environment was, thus a judgement as to how the environment was. Rather, it must be identified in terms of transactions with what (at most) only one thinker could be aware of, so transactions of which (at most) only one thinker could be aware. So that a thinker stood in the same way twice towards his non-environment—that, say, he once, then, took, and now, again, takes, it to be thus and so, or that he would now take it to be thus and so if he were now thinking in such-and-such way could be something at most he could ever recognize. How what he thus thought might serve aims would be again for him alone to recognize. It would be unlike identifying an element in postures by its rightness or wrongness in guiding one to lecture rooms at certain times.

But recognizing is an ability. To recognize the same thing to have been present twice is not just to take it to have been. It is registering a circumstance which could still have obtained unregistered. The problem here is in what such a circumstance might consist.

What there is to recognize, in present matters, is when, on a certain understanding of *the same*, the same had occurred twice. In the environmental case a thinker might go wrong in taking this to have happened in either of two ways. He might be wrong as to *what* had occurred in the one case or the other. Or he might go wrong as to whether what did occurr counts as the same thing twice. In the second case he would mistake what was to count as the same— here, as thinking such-and-such. What is to count, here, is graspable by indefinitely many. He may be shown wrong by what indefinitely many would thus see. In the non-environmental case, going wrong in this second way cannot be like that. Someone cannot, in that way, have the *wrong* understanding of *the same* as it occurs in some particular idea of his having the same posture twice towards his non-environment. For only he can have *any* such understanding: only he can get in mind those things that might, or might not, so count. Perhaps, then, there *is* no such second way for him to be wrong here: the right understanding of *same attitude* is just the one he does have; a matter of what *he* would, thus of what he *does*, recognize. But it cannot be like that. He was meant to *grasp* what his holding the same attitude twice would be. That he *says* such-and-such cannot constitute grasp of anything. Which prepares us for the second leg of Frege's argument.

The idea *judge that P* has sense only where someone so judging is liable to recur. What it would be for so judging to recur (occur twice) in postures towards a non-environment cannot be what it would be for it to recur in the environmental case. Just as we saw with being red, the notion *same attitude* and with it the notion *judge that P* require new sense here. I have not yet said that no such sense could be supplied. Whether it could is the topic to be considered next.

4 Truth★

Frege's treatment of *red* is the first term of an analogy. Here is the second:

> I said that the word 'red' would only be applicable in the domain of my consciousness if it did not cite a property of things, but only indicated certain features of my sense impressions. So, too, if the words 'true' and 'false', as I understand them, didn't concern something I am not the bearer of, but were fixed so as to characterize, somehow or other, contents of my consciousness, they would be applicable only in the domain of my consciousness. Thus would truth be limited to the contents of my consciousness, and it would remain doubtful whether anything similar occurred in the consciousness of another.
>
> (1918: pp. 68–9)

Frege tells us here that if a thought needed a bearer, then the sense (if any) in which 'true' and 'false' applied to it would not be one on which they apply to the thoughts it is open to *one* to think about environmental matters. By argument parallel to that in the case of 'red', this means that for 'true' to apply to a thought that needed a bearer, 'true' would need new sense—a sense not fixed by its sense on its environmental applications.

For a thought to need a bearer would be for it not *to be met with* in thought, but only to be met with (on suitable occasions) in so-and-so's thought. Meeting a thought in thought would be thinking it, or entertaining it (considering whether things are that way), or thinking of things being as they are according to that thought, in thinking something more complex, or just grasping it— seeing what it would be for things to be as that thought has them. To think the thought would be to expose oneself to error in a certain way. For a thought not to be met with, only one thinker could expose himself in that way. 'To be met with' here has its (presently) usual subjectless sense. A thought to be met with is one *one* might meet with in thinking in the right way.

Truth began life as part of a package. It was a particular kind of correctness (contrasting, for example, with being justified), where explaining what kind of correctness that is and explaining what special sort of attitude *judgement* is are one and the same enterprise. To be a judgement just is to be subject to that sort of correctness. Frege tells us here that to speak of thoughts which require bearers is to sunder this package. Such thoughts would be 'true' only in a new sense of the word. Which is to say that the sort of correctness to which they are liable is *not* the sort which makes for *judgement*. *What* it is is not fixed by what *truth* is. For something to be *red* is for its being as it is to matter in a certain way to what is to be met with. Correspondingly, for there to be a question as to whether it is red—for it to be what is liable to be red—is for what is to be met with to matter in a certain way to that question's answer. Similarly, for a given judgement to be true is for its standing as it does towards things to matter in a certain way to what is to be met with. And for it to be liable to truth—for the question of its truth to arise—is for what is to be met with to matter in a certain way to that question's answer. A thought needing a bearer is not liable to be true. No such question arises. Things being as they are cannot matter to *its* answer. If it is liable to any sort of correctness, things being as they are must matter in a determinate way to whether it is correct in that sense. But such liability would not make for *judgement*. Whereas what we needed to find room for was precisely *judgements* about a non-environment. One might envision a new package: truth★ and judgement★, each explained in terms of the other. The old package does not tell us how such explanation might go. Nor is it clear what interest such a new package might have. So we may see Frege as a bit laconic here, as if, seeing the Ching vase smash on the slate floor, one opines that it will never be quite the same again.

But we need worry only if a thought about a non-environment would be a thought that needs a bearer. The case for that starts here: to be a thought is to have a certain generality. It is not just that things being as they are is, or is not, things being as that thought has them. If things were, or had been *thus*, or, again, *so*, that would be things being the way they are thus thought to be. So, as already noted, for any thought there is an indefinitely extensive range of cases in which things being as they were would be things being the way they are thus thought to be. For a thought about the environment, a case within the range is one of to be met with being *thus*. For a thought about my non-environment, a case within the range would be, in at least indefinitely many instances, something only I could meet with. Only I could be acquainted with it. So only I could think of it that *this* is a case of things being the way in question. To grasp what it is that is so according to the thought would be, *inter alia*, to grasp, or be able to grasp, of what would be things being that way (and of what would not) that *this* is being the way in question, *this* not. Such singular thoughts (turning precisely on the status of things being *thus*) are ones available only to me. Only I could be acquainted with their being *thus*. So only I could grasp what the generality of this thought was. So only I could grasp it. Which is just to say that such a thought would require me as its bearer. It could not be to be met with.

The initial hope was that what I encounter in my inner world may be things being some very same ways that what is to be encountered in the environment may be. I could thus judge things to be, or not, those ways. Such thoughts, the idea was, would not need a bearer. Though you can never see that which I judge to be this or that way, you could at least grasp *what* I judge of it—that, say, it is *red*. The first leg of Frege's argument dashed such hopes. To grasp what it is I was thinking in thinking something environmental 'red', you would have to grasp that new sense which I attached to 'red'. But grasping the range of cases in which things would be red in this new sense is beyond your reach. So these hopes are dashed.

If there were a way which both environmental things and objects of my non-environmental encounters might be, there would be a range of cases in which things being as they are would be their being that way, where you could think these to be such cases—the environmental ones—and a range such cases which you could not think to be such cases—the ones where objects of my non-environmental encounters were the relevant way. The range of which you could think would not determine what the range of which you cannot think should be. What you can grasp as to what the generality of such a thought would be leaves undetermined what its generality in fact would be. So you cannot grasp the thought. This is a way of appreciating just how right Frege was about 'red'. It now means: thoughts about a non-environment do need a bearer.

Frege tells us: what it would be for a thought about what is to be met with to be true does not fix what it would be for a thought that needs a bearer to be true. A thought *about* what is not to be met with (in our present sense) would be one case of a thought which needs a bearer. So a thought about a thought about what is not to be met with, since a thought about what is not to be met with (in thought) would need a bearer. So a thought about such a thought that it was correct, in some form in which it might be—call that being true★—would need a bearer. It would not be a thought that *we* could think or grasp. A thought about a non-environment would still need to be a common element in some range of postures towards that non-environment. But as to which range of postures this was, only the bearer of the thought could so much as have, or grasp, a view. A thought about a non-environment could not be *true*. Which is to say that *true*, like *red*, is an environmental notion. I will return to defending this idea. But suppose, for a moment, it is right.

If truth is an environmental notion, then one may *judge* one's inner world to be thus and so only on a new notion of judging, call it judging★. What one judges—that such-and-such—is a *judgement* only on a new notion of judgement, judgement★. A judgement was to be what is liable to a certain kind of correctness: truth. But now correctness can be truth only on a new notion of it, truth★. It would be decided by how things are only on a new understanding of being decided by how things are. Can we introduce such notions?

To make sense of any notion is to fix (adequately) what it would be for it to be *true* of something, or when it would be. For it to make sense is for there to be such a thing as when it would be true. So one thing that needs fixing here is what it would be for *true*★ to be true of something—specifically, of something not to be met with in thought, neither thinkable, nor graspable, except, at most, by one thinker. Which, as we have seen, is what a judgement about a thinker's non-environment would be. 'True', if an environmental notion, would not apply to what 'true★' thus did. So nor would it apply to such things being true★, nor to a thought (if there were one) that something was true★, neither of which would be something to be met with. There is nothing it *could* be for it to be true that such a thing was true★. There is no such thing as 'when true★ would be true of something'. So there can be no fixing this. There is, accordingly, no such thing as making sense of any of the family of required new notions just listed above. There can be no such thing as truth★. Truth admits no substitutes. There is, accordingly, nothing to be judged in a would-be thought that needed a bearer. There are no such thoughts. The idea of merely 'judging★' them cannot help here. There are, thus, no thinkable ways for a non-environment to be.

Must the notion *true* figure in making sense of any notion? Suppose we want to make sense of something being red★. Would it not do just to say what it would be for something to be red★, or when something would be that? Truth need not be mentioned. But truth need not be *mentioned* to figure in thought. It is what thought aims at. There is such a thing as something's being red★ just where there is such a thing as the range of cases in which something's being as it was would be its being red★. That is just the range of cases in which something would be as judged in judging it red★; thus, in which the correctness of such a judgement would be decided solely by things being as they are. Correctness here, to belabour the familiar, is *truth*. So where we can make the right sense of *being red★*—of something's being as it was being what was needed for its being red★—we can make equal sense of the idea of its being *true* that the thing is red★; and *vice versa*. For 'red★' we may substitute any way for things to be, notably, the supposed *true*★. We cannot make sense of its being *true* that something is true★. So we cannot make sense of something being true★, full stop.

What it would be for something to be red is fixed just so far as it is fixed in what range of cases something's being as it is would be its being red. An *understanding* of what it would be for something to be red is formed in part by what one is prepared to recognize as to what, specifically, would, and what would not, count as something's being red; so (in part) by thoughts, of particular cases of things being as they are, that *this* would so count (or not)—thoughts tied to a particular circumstance as a singular thought is tied to an object. An understanding available to someone stretches only so far as there *could* be something he was prepared to recognize in such matters, so only so far as the singular thoughts, of the above sort, he *could* intelligibly be credited with thinking. So the understandings available to us jointly of what it would be for something to be red—those understandings to be met with—extend only so far as what it would be for things to be met with to be red. That is why 'red's usual sense does not make it applicable in a non-environment. What belongs to *that* range of cases of something's being red leaves it open what would belong to some other range, notably, one including cases of a non-environment being as it is, or its inhabitants being as they are. For all the shareable understanding fixes, *any* such range would do as well as any other. *Red* is not something something non-environmental might be.

Mutatis mutandis for *being true*. Our understanding of being true extends no farther than cases where what is true, and its being so, are to be met with—cases in which *one* could think, of what is true, that *that* is true. Such a range stops short of thoughts not to be met with. Nor does *it* fix what range of *such* thoughts would be the true ones. By the above, then, there is nothing it would be for a thought not to be met with to be true. Nor does truth admit of substitutes. There is no way to introduce one. Things count as a certain way just where it counts as true that they are that way. So nor is there such a thing as when a non-environment (or what belongs to it) would be such-and-such way. My inner world being what it is (if that is anything) cannot consist in its being such-and-such ways. The last leg of Frege's argument brings us to this point.

I have so far supposed that truth is an environmental notion. It applies only to thoughts which do not need a bearer: if that thought is that such-and-such, one need not be so-and-so to think that so. This combines with the idea that a thought about something non-environmental would need a bearer to deliver this result: the idea of a *judgement* about the non-environmental has no sense. But one might resist the idea that truth *is* an environmental notion. Frege tells us:

The meaning (*Bedeutung*) of the word 'true' is unfolded in the laws of being true.

(1918: p. 59)

Being true is what those laws (the laws of standard logic) thus unfold. Such laws are purely formal. If they *exhaust* truth's content, then one might suppose that so is truth. A purely formal notion, on might think, cannot require only environmental applications.

But this idea is true neither to Frege nor to truth. Frege's laws of being true chart (mirror) connections between thoughts; specifically, inferential, notably truth-preserving ones. But the idea of truth begins with a thought about the relation of an attitude to its object—of a *representation* to that which it represents as some way or another. Such relations, though part of truth, are not the inferential ones those laws mirror; not relations between *judgements* (or their contents). Judgement was to be that attitude liable to a certain kind of correctness, a kind settled solely, by things being as they are. Such correctness of a judgement that the wind is howling is settled solely by the presence, or absence, of howling wind—by meteorological conditions. The way in which reigning conditions settle it is one way in which a question of truth may be settled. That its truth is so settled by things being as they are is thus a *very* small partial unfolding of the notion *true*: here is *one* way to be liable to truth and falsity.

To think that P is to be exposed, in a particular way, to error or vindication. In the environmental case *error* has a certain sense. An attitude towards the encounterable is in error, if at all, as to how things re-encounterably are. For someone so in error, that which he is wrong (or right) about is to be encountered in an indefinitely extensive range of meetings. Its being an error matters systematically, in the usual ways, to what one *would* encounter. Here we are entitled to a 'would' which makes sense of these ideas—as, too, the idea, *when someone would be making* this *error*. If circumstances were *thus*, one would still be making it; if they were *so*, then not. So this 'would' which comes along with re-encounterability, allows identifying a specific generality for a representation of something as so to have: that particular generality which goes with the issue whether P. Only with such a generality in place can there be talk of thinking something so.

A stance towards what was not to be met with, if it were liable to a correctness conferred or withheld by how things not to be met with are, would not be an attitude to be met with in thought. Still, were there such a stance, there would be that range of cases in which to hold it would be to be in error, and that in which holding it would be being right. Here, though, the usual notions of error and vindication do not fit. Nor can we understand the 'would' in 'would be in error (right)' as we do where error (correctness) is to be met with. To make sense of the idea of judgement here we would need new sense for 'error' and for 'would'. The point of the above argument is that there can be no such thing as the senses we thus need.

Eligibility for truth goes with eligibility for error. My grasp of the generality of a particular thought—of what range of cases would be ones of its error, what cases would be its correctness—extends no farther than my ability to think, of a case in the range, that it is such a case. So our grasp of a particular thought's generality, so of its being true, extends no farther than re-encounterable postures towards the re-encounterable. The range of *such* cases of something being an error, and of something being true, leaves it open what range of cases would be ones of stances towards a non-environment being in error, or true. What error comes to where it is re-encounterable does not tell us what it would come to where it is not. So, too, for truth. Thus it is that truth is an environmental notion.

Frege's target here is the idea of ways a non-environment may be *judged* to be; an idea of judgements true or not according to how *it* is. That idea aims to hold two things together. First, what one encounters in a non-environment is to be part of how things are. So to judge of it is to be correct or not according to how things (there) are. Second, how things there are is not integrated with how things otherwise are. It is independent of what one would meet with in meeting what is to be met with. The project is, perhaps, not absurd on its face. But it is unsurprising that it should founder.

'How things to be met with are' is pleonastic. 'How things are' would speak of just the same. For something to be true is for it to be vindicated by things being as they are. Nothing else could decide truth. Pleonastically put, for something to be true is for it to be vindicated by things to be met with being as they are. This is what Frege proved.

5 A Simple Disjunctivism

Seeing is a kind of awareness of (some of) one's surroundings. It furnishes occasion for responding—in attitude, affect, or action—to what one is thus aware of, or to its experiencing. Here is an intuition. I see the lemon on the sideboard; there is a way things then look. Things could be for me, visually, just as they thus are even were there no such lemon to be seen. This would not (just) consist in my being delusional—convinced of many things which simply were not so. Rather, for things to be visually for me just as they thus were would be for there to be something in the experience for me to be visually sensitive to, which I *was* thus sensitive to. For there to be just that for me to be aware of would be for things to be visually for me just as they were where I saw the lemon. This supposed ingredient in an experience of seeing a lemon and all those in which things would be just the same for me I will call a *common factor*, or CF.

So where I see the lemon, there is also a certain CF for me to be aware of. Another intuition: that CF could be there no matter how my surroundings were, and no matter what other experiences were to be had, 'could' here meaning there is such a thing as that. Things *could* be that way without my being simply delusional. Being delusional is a matter of one's (would-be) *responses* to what is going on. A CF is something there is for one to respond to.

Where the CF is present, either I see the lemon or I am having a perfect (visual) ringer for that experience. There are, the idea is, no visual clues, registering which would be a way of telling that I am was not seeing the lemon. There is no other way things ought then to look. The thought, again, is that things could be thus no matter how things not then experienced were arranged.

Disjunctivism is a negative thesis. It rejects the idea of a CF, present where I see the lemon. Perhaps where I see the lemon there is a way things visually are for me. But the idea of a CF is not a way of making sense of that. Nor, in general, for seeing, hearing, smelling, and so on. A simple disjunctivism chooses a simple target. In this version the CF in seeing the lemon is itself an object of *visual* awareness, such as things ((as) experienced) *looking* such-and-such a way.

The crucial idea here is: *things* look a certain way. It need not be that some *thing* does. On some versions of the simple version there will be such a thing—a sense datum. But there need not be for something to qualify as the present target. The lemon is, and, moreover looks, yellow and pebble-grained. Those are both features *it* has. If I see it, I take in its having them. So one might posit an *ersatz*-lemon, eligible to be present, and an object of visual awareness, no matter how the environment is in fact arranged, and postulate that it, too, looks yellow and pebble-grained. But also, when the lemon is present *things* look a certain way. Here 'things' picks out the scene in view: the lemon, the sideboard, the tiled floor. If the CF is *things* looking thus and so, 'things' cannot be that. For there need be no scene before me. Still, it might be held, things appear (look) as would a scene which looked a certain way. An experience may be like that; which, the idea is, imposes another good reading on 'things'.

On this story, when the CF is present, things appear as if yellow and ovoid, or as if something yellow and ovoid were there. Now Frege's point has application. We must be careful to apply the whole, and not just the first half, of his argument. Here is a particular way things, on the present use of 'things', appear. 'Yellow and ovoid' we are told. I may judge (take) them so to appear. I may thus *register* things appearing the way they in fact do. (Or, if mistakes are in the cards here, get things all wrong.) But things appearing as they thus do is not something to be met with. For their so appearing is, by hypothesis, independent of what would be met with in any other meeting with anything.

(The motivation is: no matter how all that may be, things *could* still be the same for me in the particular experience I am then having. I could still have that much cause for taking myself to see a lemon.) So, by the first leg of Frege's argument, 'yellow' and 'ovoid', in their above deployment, cannot have their usual sense (by which I mean all and only the sense they have on their environmental applications). (Being ovoid, for example, cannot here be the sort of thing one might establish, or disprove, by *measurement*. It is not what a 'primary quality' was meant to be.) If they are to apply at all here, they call for new sense. Their usual (environmental) sense does not decide what this new sense is to be. 'Yellow and ovoid'? When would things, on the current use of things, appear (as if) that way? When would one be *taking* things, on this use, to be just that way? These questions as yet have no answer. None is to be derived from the environmental uses of 'yellow' and 'ovoid'.

Perhaps, then, 'yellow' and 'ovoid' *have* some other sense, which they bear in such applications. The modifier 'phenomenal' might be (perhaps has been) meant to signal it. But just what are these senses? For there to *be* an answer to this question (forget whether anyone could ever give it), there would have to be an answer to the question when it was *true* of things (on the present use of 'things') that they were phenomenally yellow (or ovoid). There could be no answer to that precise question, because 'true' could not apply to judgements that things were phenomenally yellow. That is the first stage in the second leg of Frege's argument. So one might try to tell the needed story here by appeal to some substitute notion, 'true★'. But the second leg of Frege's argument shows that there can be no such substitute notion. So there can be no such thing as 'things being phenomenally yellow'. And so on in general. This completes the application of Frege's argument to this simple case of disjunctivism's target.

6 A Wider Target

Vorstellung is a usual translation of the word 'idea' as it occurs in eighteenth-century British philosophy. Related uses may carry visual, or other perceptual, connotations. But such connotations are not essential to Frege's use of the term. When Frege asks whether a thought can be a *Vorstellung*, he does not suppose that his question is already answered by what he has previously stressed:

A thought is something non-sensory, and all perceptually observable things are excluded from the domain in which truth can come into question at all.

(1918: p. 61)

Rather, what makes something an idea, or Vorstellung, in Frege's terms, is the way in which it attaches to a particular bearer; in present terms, its belonging to an inner, or a non-environment. This suggests that we may now widen the target susceptible to Frege's core point.

The target: In the version of disjunctivism's target on the table so far, the common factor—present where I see the lemon, also eligible to be present where I do not—is something of which, whenever present in my experience, I am, or can be, visually aware. There is something it is visually like. Common factors in the wider target need not be objects of *perceptual* awareness, nor need there be anything they are perceptually (such as visually) like. The target's more general form can be this. When I see the lemon I am in a certain conscious state which I *could* be in where there is no lemon to see; more generally, no matter how things yet unexperienced stood. I would be in this state when seeing the lemon and whenever having a perfect illusion thereof. Optionally, if I am in it then either I see the lemon or I am having a perfect illusion thereof (it is for me just as though I were seeing the lemon).

It remains to say what the common factor is wherever one is in such a state—what is present whether or not I see the lemon. We might try this. For me (or one) to be in that state is for my (or one's) experience to have a certain intentional content—that is, a representational content: its being represented as so that things are a certain way. Where I do see the lemon (and surrounding scene), things are as thus represented. On the view in question, that is meant to fix what the relevant representational content is. For things to be like *that* is for them to be the relevant way. But my experience might have that content where I did not see the lemon, and, in fact, no matter what there was to see, or to experience, in my environment. (Byrne and Logue (forthcoming; Section 5) present and defend this version of disjunctivism's target.)

Experience furnishes things for us to respond to. (At least it does when it involves witnessing, and is not mere undergoing (see Hinton 1973: especially pp. 5–21)). It is occasion to respond to them. One may so respond in responding to one's experiencing (such as seeing) them. The intentionalism just described is present disjunctivism's target on two conditions. First, the representing just posited must lie on the side of what there is to respond to, and not just on the side of a response to it. It will do for this, for my purpose, if the representation in question does not consist in the subject representing things to himself as so—taking, thinking, supposing, noticing them to be so, and so on.

Second, in having the experience the subject must be afforded awareness of things being so represented, in the sense that this is something he is thereby prepared, or equipped, to recognize about the experience: if things prove *thus*—for example, there proves to be no lemon—then the experience was not right; things are not as they were according to it; if things prove *so*, then they are as the experience had them. For there to be representing here is for there to be a way things would be if the experience were right; the experiencer can recognize when things are that way. Preparedness to recognize such things where they are so is all I want of the idea that the subject is aware of how, in the experience, things were represented to be.

The relevant representing thus cannot be entirely inaccessible to the experiencer, *merely* a feature of some sub-doxastic state, though this says little about what access to it might be like. Such access might just be things appearing to be, or as though, a certain way. Anyway, the idea here is that experience can be true, or untrue to how things are; and that the subject can grasp what being true or untrue would come to in the case at hand; when the experience would be true, when untrue. I see no reason to think that things are represented as so in sub-doxastic states. But that is another story.

How things are represented to be, while the subject is in the postulated conscious state, is, in this sense, recognizable by him. So if things were represented differently, or not at all, that, too, would be recognizable. For the subject to be in that state is for things to be represented to be a certain way. So if he were not in that state, but rather some other, this, too, would be recognizable. For then things would not have been represented as they in fact were.

John McDowell's version of representationalism (for example) meets both conditions. He tells us:

Minimally, it must be possible to decide whether or not to judge that things are as one's experience represents them to be. How one's experience represents things to be is not under one's control, but it is up to one whether one accepts the appearance or rejects it.
(McDowell 1994: p. 11)

A subject, confronted with a pig in plain view before him, may represent it as so to himself that there is a pig before him—that is, take there to be one. It is not then up to him whether to accept that things are as thus represented. He *has* accepted it: that is what taking-to-be is. Nor can one decide to accept or reject what one cannot be aware of. (Moreover, if there is any *sensible* question as to whether to accept or reject that things are as represented, then there is such a thing as their *not* being, though, also, they might be that way. So the representing is a common factor in cases of perception and *some* range of others, though McDowell does not here say that this common factor could be present no matter *how* the environment were arranged.) Thus, McDowell locates the representing he posits so as to meet both of my conditions.

These conditions are motivated by a role which, as I understand things, representational content was meant to play. Suppose that, looking at a wax ringer-lemon I take myself to see a lemon. That is understandable, reasonable: so one might well do, experiencing what I did. Something about the experience speaks in favour of it. Nor is it merely, for instance, that I cannot tell a lemon from a lime. Sight furnished no clues that things were otherwise. Representational content is one way to *explain* what here is understandable: one might well take oneself to see a lemon because things were so represented. There is that much reason for me so to take things. Such content is reason for *me* so to suppose only if recognizably present in the experience in the minimal sense set out; not, for example, as an undetectabe part of a sub-doxastic state (which could at most cause my responses). More generally, such explanation *works* only be appeal to something to respond to, not to a response, especially not one thus to be explained.

Does such representing admit of ringers? For a conscious state in which things are represented as being F, could there be a different one in which things are not represented as that way (but, perhaps, as some other way), but where, for one in this different state, this would be unrecognizable? The ringer state would be one in which things were represented as being, not F, but, say, G. But the consciousness enjoyed by one in the state would provide no means for him to tell that. I think I see a lemon, say. But it is wax. So I am wrong on that count. I think that if there is no lemon, then my experience presented things to me as they are not. But wrong again, though undetectably. What was in fact represented as so is that there was either a lemon or a replica before me. Does this idea make sense?

One well might take a wax ringer for a lemon. They look just the same. *That* makes this error understandable. Intentionalism is meant to relieve us of need for *such* explanation. It provides a substitute: representational content. Such content is apt to be available where ringers are not, such as in an hallucination. So if it is represented as so that there is a lemon, that makes it understandable that one should think so, just as a ringer's looking like a lemon would.

For it to be represented that there is a lemon is not for me to think there is. I *can* distrust representations. But if there is a ringer for things being so represented, then it is similarly understandable that I should think things were so represented—that I should blame my experience for being untrue to how things are. Something must explain *this* being understandable. If intentionalism is to the rescue here, then that thing will be its being represented as so in this experience that things were so represented.

Such would be detectable (recognizable) in the current minimal sense. Since nothing *recognizable* in this ringer state marks it as a ringer (by definition), this further detectable feature would be shared by the ringer state, by the state in which it was represented as so that there was a lemon, and by some range of others in which, also, it was not represented as so that there was a lemon—but *was* represented as so that this was represented as so. There would be a conscious state I am in where I see the lemon, also where it is merely represented as so that I do, and also in a range of cases in which neither of these things is so. Such a state would have two explanatory burdens. First, where I neither see the lemon nor is this represented as so, it explains why I might think it was represented as so that there was a lemon. Second, it thereby explains why I might think I saw a lemon. That things were so represented cannot do the job in this case. For things were *not* so represented.

The idea of ringer-representing now collides with what called for representing in the first place. The idea was: where I see a lemon, I also experience a common factor, present there, and also in all experiences which provide no ways of telling, perceptually, that they are not ones of seeing the lemon—all ringers for doing so. In any such range of cases *something* speaks in favour of my taking myself to see a lemon; something makes it understandable for me to do so. That something is to be the common factor. With ringer-representing, the common factor is not its being represented that there is a lemon, but rather its being represented that things were so represented. So this last must do the explaining in all ringer cases. Nor could we rest there, or with any other determinate iteration of 'It was represented that' once ringer representing is in the cards. Whereas if it is disallowed, then the range of ringer cases extends no farther than those in which it was represented that there was a lemon. *Such* representing can then be what makes things understandable.

If a third state were called for, there is anyway a problem as to what it ought to be. For then there are two states (the initial one and a ringer for it) which would in no way differ in what was recognizable to me about my experience if I were in them. In one, things are represented as a way they are not if there is no lemon. In the other they are represented as a way this still may be—for example, if there is a wax replica. Which of these states should the third state represent me as in? And why? I do not think this question could have an answer. I also think it points to a problem with the very idea of representation in experience. But I drop the point, and turn instead to Frege.

Frege's point: The representations posited above can just be of the *environment* as being thus and so. The features they ascribe to it are ones for environmental things to have—being red, say, in the usual sense of 'red'. Problems raised by non-environmental ways for things to be do not arise yet. But our suspicions should be aroused. We have a perfectly adequate understanding of what it is for something to be red. If we help ourselves to the idea that something non-environmental might be red on that understanding of so being, our straightforward version of disjunctivism's target becomes unproblematic.

But it is problematic. We may not help ourselves to that idea. That is Frege's point. Similarly, we have a perfectly adequate understanding of what it is for it to have been represented as so that such-and-such where this is an environmental matter (as where it says so in the Times). If we help ourselves to the idea that in a non-environment it might have been represented as so that such-and-such, on *that* understanding of something being represented as so, then, again, all the rest is unproblematic. But may we help ourselves to this? Would not Frege's point apply?

For a lemon to be on the sideboard is for the environment to be a certain way. For it to have been represented as so that a lemon is on the sideboard is for the *environment* to be a certain way only if that representing (its occurring, or its production) is to be met with. An instance of the presently postulated representing is to be met with *by me*, say, by my being in a certain conscious state. It is to be met with then by me in what my being in the state makes recognizable to me about it—what I am thus positioned to tell, in the above minimal sense, as to when things would be as, in it, things were presented. That things were so represented can be available only to me, then. For, conversely, *that* representing could have occurred no matter what was *to be met with*; no matter how things were of which I was not conscious in (or while) being in that conscious state.

So the postulated representing of something as so is not something to be met with. Which places us in familiar territory. We know what it is for it to be represented as so that P, for example, in talk. Here things having so been represented—the talk's being so to be taken—is something to be met with. One may make mistakes about such things. One may misunderstand. There are familiar ways to learn of this. Facts about the circumstances of the talk, about the familiar usage of the words used, about the use made of them in this case, may all emerge in further encounters, such as with the words used, and with those presumed to be familiar with them. There are things with the recognizable shape of a demonstration that things were actually represented this way, rather than that—that, say, Sid was not really to be taken to have been speaking of dinner when he said, 'Pia had a little lamb'. None of this could be part of what it would be for things to have been represented as thus and so in one of the postulated conscious states. Which is to say that, in this case, the expression 'represent it as so that P' requires new sense. The phenomenon it speaks of as instanced, such as in talk, simply does not fix *what* phenomenon it would be speaking of in the case of these conscious states. That is for the new sense to do.

That in such a state it was represented as so that P is meant to be the content of a *judgement*. So there is meant to be something in things being as they are on which the *truth* of such a judgement might turn; something which, if present, would make the judgement true, and if absent would make it false. Something thus to judge about; something for its thus being represented as so to be. But the question now is on *what* the truth of such a judgement might turn. That is a question only new sense for the notion *represent as so* could answer. Which again places us on familiar ground.

If there is such a thing as representing it as so, in such a state, that P, then there is a range of cases in which, in such a state, *that* is how things would be represented. But the particular cases in which things were so represented in *my* states of the postulated sort would be ones which only I could get in mind. Only I could be acquainted with the representing thus occurring; only I could have thoughts of *it* (in a given case) that *it* was thus and so. Only I could see what the relevant generality was to be here—that belonging to the notion *represent as so that P*, on its application to my (relevant) conscious states. So only I could grasp the thought, of some such state that I was in, that in it what was going on was its being represented as so that P. Again, the trouble is not with the notion *that P*, but rather with the notion of *representing as so*, applied in this domain. Thoughts to the effect that *this* is the way things are according to (the representing going on in) *this* state would be thoughts that needed a bearer. But that means, as we have seen, that it could be 'true' only in some new sense of true. And, as we have also seen, there can be no such new sense. Which answers the question what there could be for a judgement that in such a state it was represented as so that P to answer to: nothing. In what way could it be beholden for correctness to things being as they are? In no way.

The present intentionalist version of disjunctivism's target thus ends up in just the same boat as our initial more straightforward version. For the straightforward version it turned out in the end that there was nothing it could be to be confronting non-environmental *red*, no range of cases which were the ones of things being that way—not even in a new sense of 'red', for, in the non-environmental case there is no such sense to be introduced. In the intentionalist case it turns out in the end that there is nothing it could be to confront (what turns out to be) non-environmental representing of it as so that P, no range of cases which would be ones of confronting that—not even in some new sense of 'represent'. For, in the desired case there is no such sense to be had. The root trouble with sense-datum theory was not that it required non-environmental bearers of properties like being yellow, or ovoid, or pebble-grained. It was rather the prior idea of ways things non-environmentally are.

Faced with this trouble, an intentionalist might try to make his postulated representing something environmental—perhaps something neurological. But an environmental anchor, of that sort, or of any other, would reinstate the possibility of ringer-states, with ringers for given representing. Which, as we have seen, would sabotage the intentionalist project in a different way. If we were to waive this point, I might then need to unbracket the points I have so far waived, about the intelligibility, anyway, of the idea of representing without an agent. But that would be another project.

Disjunctivism's target walks a narrow line. On the one hand, in all its forms, it posits something in (an) experience distanced enough from the experiencer to be something there to respond to, and, specifically, something to judge about: something one can take to be one way or another, rightly or wrongly according to how it anyway is—thus, something fit to decide that correctness to which judgement is peculiarly liable. On the other, this something is to be so closely tied to the experiencer that it would not be there at all but for the experience it is part of. Frege's point is: this trick cannot be turned. In targeting idealism, Frege targeted—most strikingly, perhaps, but not exclusively—the idea of non-environmental sensory objects of judgement. It is noteworthy that intentionalism falls within his target's scope.

7 Varieties of Attitude

We do have inner lives. There is something it is like to be me, something it is like to experience what I do (on an occasion). I frequently respond to my inner life. Such responses may be part of what is to be met with, as when I say 'Everything is spinning'. What is thus to be met with may be important—without, for all that, being a *judgement* as to how things are for me alone. *If* they are responses to what I alone could be aware of—towards something otherwise inaccessible being as it is—then their standing as they do towards what they do is not something to be met with. They cannot, thus, be judgements. So much for disjunctivism's target. In an experience of perceiving (such as seeing) things, we do not encounter what, on the one hand, there could be to be encountered anyway, regardless of the layout of the scene in view (thus, something not to be met with) and something which is, or not, determinate ways it may be judged to be. Perception is an encounter with the environment, in which we are more or less sensitive, more or less accurately, to *its* being as it is. It is occasion for responding to just *that*. It supplies sensory awareness of nothing else to judge about.

Using 'inner sense' for a mode of awareness whose objects are non-environmental, John McDowell has said:

> If we can make out that judgements of 'inner sense' are about anything, it has to be that they are about impressions of 'inner sense' themselves, not about something independent of which the impressions constitute awareness.

This is a very difficult area. Wittgenstein himself sometimes seems to betray an understandable wish to duck the difficulties. What I have in mind here is the fact that he sometimes seems to toy with denying that self-ascriptions of sensations are assertions, articulation of judgements about states of affairs at all.

(1994: p. 22)

For judgements of 'inner sense' to be about impressions of inner sense is for them to turn, for correctness, on how those impressions are; namely, whether they are thus and so. I have denied that judgement could be like that—that there are such things for it to turn on. McDowell seems to suggest that this is 'ducking difficulties' and a cop-out. But it is not. We have feelings, which sometimes matter deeply to us, to which we respond in ways which matter to what we thus feel. And, perhaps, sometimes *vice versa*. It is just that what we respond to does not matter to our responses *in the way* a judgement as to an impression's being thus and so would.

McDowell is *nearly* right when, crediting Miles Burnyeat, he says:

In ancient scepticism, the notion of truth is restricted to how things are ... in the world about us, so that how things seem to us is not envisaged as something there might be truth about ... whereas Descartes extends the range of truth and knowability to the appearances on the basis of which we naively think we know about the ordinary world. In effect, Descartes recognizes how things seem to a subject as a case of how things are; and the ancient sceptics' concession that appearances are not open to question is transmuted into the idea of a range of facts infallibly knowable by the subject involved in them.

(1986/1998: p. 239)

Descartes, McDowell tells us, misconstrues Pyrrhonian appearances as judgements—a first step on his road to ruin. But appearances may be any of several things. (Conflating these can make one impose the shape of an attitude on what is not one.) The appearances *on the basis of which* we naively think we know about the world are appearances which the world, and its denizens, *have*. These are not attitudes. For Descartes to go wrong in the cited way would be for him to make an attitude of something that is not; whereas Pyrrhonian appearances are to be precisely non-truth-evaluable *attitudes*. Something may appear to me to be thus and so not in my detecting its so appearing (which would bring back into the picture just what the Pyrrhonians wanted to eliminate: to detect is, *inter alia*, to take something to be so), but rather in my holding a certain view. The Pyrrhonian suggestion was that this may be a non-truth-evaluable view—not judgement: no matter how things are, for all that, things so appeared to me. Such appearances, they held, may substitute for *thinking*-so in guiding action. I may, not unreasonably, move out of the cart's path because of how things seem to me. So what the Pyrrhonians meant to point to was precisely a way for an attitude to matter (*inter alia* to conduct) without being a judgement.

In a way, then, ancient sceptics were one with Frege. There is not always room for judgement, nor need there be. A judgement is beholden to how things are in a way for which there is not always room. The ancient's seemings-to-one-to-be are not so beholden. They are attitudes available anyway, even where judgement is not. If a seeming to be cannot be false, this does not mean that there is *judging* which is immune to error. To understand inner life we need to see the various ways in which such attitudes may be important.

For this we can again turn to Frege. Describing a patient in pain, Frege says:

> The patient who has a pain is the bearer of this pain ... the doctor who treats him, who thinks about the cause of this pain, is not a bearer of the pain ... The patient's pain *may* correspond to an image in the doctor's consciousness; but this is not the pain, and not that which the doctor is concerned to remove. Perhaps the doctor consults another. Then we need to distinguish: first, the pain, whose bearer is the patient; second, the first doctor's image of it, third the second doctor's image of it. This image belongs, of course, to the contents of the second doctor's consciousness, but is not the object of his thought, though perhaps an aid to that thought, as a symbol might be. Both doctors have as common object [of thought] the patient's pain, whose bearer they are not. One can see from this that not only a thing, but also an idea, can be the common object of thought of people who do not have that idea.
>
> (1918: p. 73)

The patient is the one in pain. Only he has the pain. Only he *undergoes* his experience. But (Frege's point is) his *having* the pain may be part of the environment: something to be met with (in space), for example, by the two doctors; something thus, and thereby, to be judged about. His being in pain is to be met with in space; judgements as to his pain are thus to be met with in thought. The patient's attitudes towards his pain may be to be met with. But they need not be *judgements* as to the features of that which is not to be met with, and which *he* encounters in being in pain. There are other ways for these attitudes of his to relate to his being in pain. They need not be judgements at all.

The point generalizes. Wherever someone is, psychologically, a certain way, his so being is a feature of the environment. It is something *to be met with*, not merely something to be met with by the subject. It is the sort of thing that *may* be observable, or ascertainable, where these are environmental notions. Frege shows us why this must be right. Someone's attitudes towards how it is for him—towards his undergoing, or feeling, sensing, and so on, what he does— may be an important part of what is to be met with in his being, psychologically, thus and so. The sort of role such reactions play in his so being depends very much on the case in hand. But there is a wide range of roles those reactions could not play if they were *judgements* as to how things were with him. It is important that there are other things for such attitudes to be.

Where someone's being thus and so is part of the environment, his being so *may* be something he encounters in a way no-one else can. Insofar as it is his so being—something environmental—which he thus encounters, he encounters something he can *judge* about. Some of our attitudes towards ourselves may sometimes correctly be so understood. I may encounter myself sitting, or speeding up as I walk across the quad (late again). I thus encounter something there is for me to judge: I have started to walk very fast. I do not mean here to set limits to what *can* be so understood. I merely point to the importance of understanding some of our attitudes towards ourselves otherwise—an importance I can here no more than gesture at.

There is, notably, the case of pain. Pain is, notoriously, the sort of thing one minds (even if one would welcome it, administered by a lover), the sort of thing which, if severe enough, one would find awful. How one minds one's pain may be integral to its being the sort of pain it is. When the patient says 'It is becoming unbearable', that may express, or manifest, not canniness, nor acuity in observation, but rather a response in which its being unbearable pain he experiences (in part) consists.

Again, walking home, I say to you, 'I think there is enough beer at home to last the match'. I express an attitude towards my refrigerator, which is, unproblematically, judgement. In saying what I think, I *may* also, sometimes, for some purposes, be viewable as manifesting an attitude towards *my* being as I am. My response towards my standing towards the world as I do may express acknowledgement of the world's, or experience's, power over me; my lack of choice as to what to think. To take there to be beer at home is precisely to lack such choice. My acknowledgement, or acquiescence in the world's power here may thus just be part of what it is for me to think so.

Or, again, something tasting not at all like chocolate may, just for a moment, taste of (hints of) chocolate to me. It *seemed* to me to have such hints. Is this seeming an attitude, or a matter of its *tasting*, momentarily, a certain way? Well, perhaps, *inter alia*, an attitude (in which case not one of judging). But then, perhaps also, something's tasting thus and so to me. Perhaps, so responding, in the right surroundings, just is part of things so tasting.

Frege set himself consciously and with determination against a view of perception which was pervasive in the nineteenth century, and much of the last, and which, I have tried to show, is still operative in the view the rejection of which just is disjunctivism. In its full traditional form it has a very odd feature. It begins with the question what we *see* (hear, and so on), and ends with, as answer, objects of awareness which could not possibly be objects of sight (or so on). As Frege puts it,

> Ideas cannot be seen, or felt, neither smelled nor tasted, nor heard. I take a walk with a companion. I see a green meadow; I have thereby a sense-impression of green. I have it, I do not see it. (1918: p. 67)

Frege saw that he needed an environment, and thus perception, and not merely sensation, if there was to be something for logic to be about. Not that logic applies only to environmental thoughts. but rather, only given an environment for thinkers can the notion of judgement gain a foothold. The position disjunctivism opposes need not go so far as to propose as objects of perception what could not be that—what does not belong to an environment. But in positing perceptual experiences outside an environment it strays beyond the bounds of judgement. The oddity it thus collapses into entirely parallels that strange idea of seeing what could not be in sight.[1]

---

[1] Those without whom not are, this time, as not unusually, Mike Martin and Joan Weiner. Thanks also to Alex Byrne, Charles Parsons, Sharon Berry, and Eylam Ozultun.

3

Viewing the Inner

> It exhibits a fundamental misunderstanding if I am inclined to study my current headache in order to get clear about the philosophical problem of sensation.
>
> Wittgenstein, *Philosophical Investigations*, §314

> Surely $\sqrt{-1}$ must mean just the same in relation to -1 as $\sqrt{1}$ means in relation to 1! This means nothing at all.
>
> Wittgenstein, *Philosophical Investigations*, IIx

Frege discerned bounds to what he called, and I will, judgement. *I* can judge only what there is for *one* to judge. What there is for one to judge *of* is that of which *one* can think that *it* is thus and so. There is no list one must appear on to be within the scope of these 'one's: for any thinkers who had, or grasped, a given thought, there could be (or have been) others.

To judge is essentially, as Frege put it, to expose oneself to risk of error. It is thus to stand towards the world in a certain posture. So Frege's judging is not an *act*. Nor need it involve sizing up, or evaluating. Nor, judging being the special thing it thus is, is its scope as wide as attitudes to the effect that things are thus and so—a thought that will be crucial to what follows.

To judge *something* is to incur a *particular* exposure; to risk a particular error. A way for things to be identifies such a risk; a particular error one is in or not, entirely according as things, in being as they are, are, or are not, that way. Thus the initial point in material mode: there is a way things may be *judged* to be, or not, just where that things are that way is something *one* might judge (of things being as they are).

So, too, for mental life. There is a way for someone's mental life to be—for *anyone* to think it—only where *one* may think that life to be that way; so only where *one* can think of the one whose life it is that his being as he is is his being that way; so only where *one* can get in mind what *is* that person being that way. What, then, might mental life be? Specifically, what might visual experience be? That is our topic.

1 Frege's Constraint

Frege begins on his constraint this way:

For if the word 'red' is not to indicate a property of things, but rather marks of a sense impression belonging to my consciousness, it is applicable only in the domain of my consciousness.

(1918: p. 67)

'Red' *could* not say the same of what belonged to my consciousness—of what Frege calls a *Vorstellung* (idea)—as it said of what surrounds us. *One* reason is this. If something in our surroundings is red, this situates it within networks of factive meaning. Being appropriately so situated is part of what it is for such a thing to be red. One may (and may need to) take a towel into daylight to see its colour. If it is red, there is a way it will thus look (exactly what way depending on the daylight). I cannot carry a content of my consciousness into daylight. So there is no such thing as how it *would* look if so carried. There is no such would.

Frege lists four marks of a content of consciousness—an *idea* in present parlance (1918: pp. 67–8). Two matter most here. First, an idea needs a bearer. It must be the content of someone's consciousness—what he is (or can be) conscious of. Second, no idea has two bearers. So my idea is an object of my consciousness, and could not be an object of yours. *Could not*: there is no such thing as that. For sensory (as opposed, for example, to mathematical) experience, ideas contrast with what belongs to our surroundings—what is spatially related to us, so literally to be met with (by getting to the place it occupies), and, for thinkers, something for *one* to be aware of, for example, to perceive, on our current use of 'one'. For any thinkers aware of my new hat, there could have been another; whereas to be aware, or conscious, of my idea, you would need to be me. Ideas are an idea for conceiving mental life. We may conceive it as rife with them. But the mere idea of an idea, as just set out, is so far without prejudice to whether there are any. Denying that there are would be, I will urge, overreaction, but not absurdity.

I may be aware of there being an elephant in the garage, or I may be aware of the elephant itself, perched on my Peugeot. In the first case, I know *one* way things are. In the second, I have access to indefinitely many. For awareness of the elephant itself is (in some degree) awareness, not just of some way it is, but of the way (how) it is; of its career in the unfolding. It is awareness by which to follow this. It is what thus permits *recognizing*, of that which is this elephant's now being wrinkled, or puzzled, that it *is* that. One recognizes, in the elephant's being as it is, it being the particular ways it thereby is. Awareness of an idea, where one could get it, would be like awareness of the elephant, and not just of its being in the garage. It would position one to recognize that idea's being as it is as whatever this might intelligibly be.

One 'would', at least, has no sensible application to an idea. Ideas are systematically infected with such lack of *woulds*. A central case. If the towel is red, there is something for *one* to recognize about it. One may recognize of its being coloured as it is that *this* is being red. One *would* recognize this if suitably aware of (acquainted with) how the towel is, and sufficient master of what (being) red is. Whereas there is no such thing as what *one* would recognize of my idea's being coloured as it is. There is, accordingly, a problem as to how there could be such a thing as what my idea would have been, whether I had been aware of this or not. This, in turn, makes problems for how there could be *ways* for an idea to be at all. I will not unpack these problems now. I merely note how absence of woulds may spread.

Frege moves to this conclusion: a thought that only I could grasp, so think, would be no thought at all. Where only I could see what it would be for things to be as they are according to a thought, there is nothing this would be. It is part of what judging is that *only* things being as they are can decide whether one escapes or succumbs to the risk thus incurred. For Frege, this idea makes (the right) sense only where the risk I expose myself to is one for *one* to to run in judging. *One* must be able to grasp a thought if anyone can, so if I can. There can be nothing for me to judge which is not for others to judge, so grasp, as well.

A thought, to be a thought at all, must be one which *one* can grasp. It must be shareable. Grasping a thought means knowing when it would be true (false): what would be things being as they are according to it (or being otherwise). The idea now is: such grasp is (at least in part) ability to recognize what is (or at least what would be) things being as they are according to the thought *as* that. Such a recognition ability must be sharable. Only I could be aware of my idea itself. As with awareness of the elephant itself, this would be *one* form of awareness of how the idea was. *ipso facto* one form of awareness of *things* being as they are. Suppose, for some thought that my idea is F, one needed just *this* form of awareness to be aware of that which *was* things being this way (or, again, their not). So one would need this to recognize what was things being that way as things so being. So one would need to be me to do this. Then, by the line of thought just traced, the thought that my idea is F would be *no* thought; there would be *nothing* it would be for my idea to be that way.

I will not set out Frege's argument (for which, see Essay 2), but we can expand his intuition by fitting two of his ideas together. These are:

The fundamental logical relation is that of an object falling under a concept. All relations between concepts can be reduced to it.

(1892–1895: 25)

The thought always contains something which reaches out beyond the particular case, by which this is brought to consciousness as falling under something general.

(1882: 23, *Kernsatz* 4)

To begin, what bears the fundamental relation to what? Does my cup, for example, (now) bear it to the concept *being empty*? This depends on how my cup now is.

Being empty is a way for an object, such as a cup, to be; *being fuller* than a way for a pair of them to be, and so on. We might speak of a *concept* as *of* some way for things to be, and such that to be that concept is to be of that way. We might then use 'satisfy' so that what satisfied the concept would be what was that way. This is not Frege's way with concepts. For him, a concept is a function from objects to truth values. Which such function maps just the empty things onto the value true depends on how things are—such as on how my cup is. A way for things to be—concept on suggested usage—fixes *how* it depends on this. My cup is now empty, so the right function would map it onto the value false. A moment ago it was full, and might have remained so. The right function would then have mapped it onto the value true. A concept (suggested usage) may identify some such function (Frege's *concept*), *given* how things are. In Frege's parlance, what speaks of such a way refers to (*bedeutet*) one. But what it refers to depends on how things are, just as what 'The last one to reach the bar' does in 'The last one to reach the bar pays the round'.

I will adopt the un-Fregean usage. As I will speak, a one-place concept is of a way for an item to be, a two-place concept a way for an ordered pair of objects to be (say, the first emptier than the second), and so on. I will also speak of a zero-place concept; for example, my cup (now) being empty. This is not a way for an n-tuple of objects to be, for any positive n. It is rather a way for *things* to be. Here 'things' has its catholic sense, as in 'Things have been slow around here lately'. 'Things', so used, does not admit the question, 'Which ones?' If we think of a thought as, for example, the thought of my cup being empty, then a zero-place concept is a thought. If a thought is, for example, *that* my cup is empty, then it is what presents some zero-place concept as satisfied.

Speaking in this way neatly captures Frege's second insight. Whether my cup satisfies the concept being empty—whether being empty is a way it is—and hence (Frege's usage) which concept *is* the concept being empty—depends on how my cup is. Whether things (catholic sense) satisfy the concept *my cup (now) being empty* depends on how things are, specifically on whether the way things are—things being as they are—is my cup now being empty. Such captures a thought's role in judging. To judge something is to expose oneself to risk of a particular error. Things (catholic sense), and things alone, are qualified to speak as to whether one succumbs to, or escapes, the error risked. The thought identifies the particular risk incurred. It thus fixes how it is that things are to do their speaking. If there is genuine exposure to a genuine risk—equally, if the thought is of a genuine way *for* things to be—then not everything in things being as they are matters to whether one who so judged would succumb or escape. There is what matters to whether my cup is empty and what does not. The thought separates what matters from what does not. If my cup is empty, some ways for things to be other than they are would leave that much untouched; others would not. The thought identifies where deviations from the way things are would do the one thing, where the other.

In this way the thought reaches beyond the particular case—things being as they are—to other ways things could have been. It identifies that range of cases which would be ones of things being such that my cup was empty (and that range which would be things being such that my cup was not). If the thought that my cup is empty plays this role, we can identify in it something which plays a subrole: on present usage, the concept of being empty. If something in that thought makes the way *my cup* is what matters, there is something else which makes the way my cup is matter in a particular way. This is something shared by a range of thoughts: something in common to the way all those thoughts make things being as they are matter to whether things are as thus judged. (This is Frege's context principle.) The thought reaches beyond the particular case in having parts (players of sub-roles) which do so—in Frege's terms, by what, in it, is unsaturated.

Such is the point of talk of zero-place concepts: a way of assimilating what is distinctive of the thought to what is distinctive of that in in it in which its generality is found. A thought reaches beyond the particular case. What it represents as thus and so—the particular case, things being as they are—does not. Nor do Frege's *concepts* reach as thoughts—what *he* calls thoughts—do.

I will say that things being as they are *instances* a zero-place concept just in case it *is* that which the concept is a concept of. A *thing* being as it is instances a one-place concept just in case its so being is it being what that concept is a concept of, and so on. Thus, things being as they are is my cup now being empty. It instances the zero-place concept *my cup now being empty*. My cup's being as it is is *something* being empty. Its being as it is thus instances the one-place concept *something being empty* (present usage). My cup, *in* being as it is, *falls under* the concept *being empty* (Frege's usage).

Whether my cup falls under that concept which in fact is *being empty* (Frege's usage) depends on whether its being as it is *instances* something being empty. Its instancing this or not fixes, in part, which function the concept *being empty* (Frege's usage) in fact is. A different function might have played that role had only my cup been full. Falling under presupposes instancing.

What instances what? What is instanced (zero-place case) is a way for things (catholic sense) to be (or concept (present use) thereof). Such things reach beyond the particular case to a range of cases. I will call what does this (the) *conceptual*. What does the instancing does not itself admit of instances. Nothing about things being as they are makes it reach to *any* further cases; reach in any way rather than any other. A further case would be a *further* case; not one of things being as they are. Things being as they are identifies no range for further cases to belong to. *It* presents nothing to consciousness at all; *a fortiori* not as falling under some generality.

I return to Frege's constraint. What would be needed for there to be a way for an idea of mine to be—call it being F—and a thought, of some idea of mine—call it V—that V is F? For one thing, that *one* could think this thought, could expose himself to error in this way. This does not mean that *everyone* could. It means exactly what it was said to at the start: for any list of eligible entertainers of this thought, there might have been another. A thought—any thought—reaches out beyond the particular case. It has that generality which marks the conceptual. Grasping the thought means grasping how it does this. It is thus grasping how a certain zero-place concept, here V being F, engages with the non-conceptual: which cases of things being as they were would instance things being that way. So it is possessing an ability: one to recognize that which would count as V's being F as so counting. Exercising such an ability requires adequate acquaintance with the non-conceptual. If what was thus needed were acquaintance with my *idea's* being as it is, the ability would be one only I could have. So the (supposed) thought that V is F would be one only I could grasp, or entertain. So, by Frege's constraint, it would not be a thought.

The problem is not that you would need to be me to *tell* whether some idea of mine was F. It is rather that you would need to be me to be aware of an idea of mine doing (being) that which was an idea (of mine) being F. The problem can be put thus: to grasp what being F was, you would need to grasp what being F was; which would be to grasp how being F reached to particular cases, so to *what* particular cases it would reach. For that you would need to be able at least to think of what *was,* or was not, a case of something being F—of what would so count, or not, depending on *how* it is—that *this* is a case to which being F reaches (or counter-reaches). Thinking such a thing is like thinking of *that* man there that he looks *louche*, a thought available only to one suitably acquainted with that man. By present hypothesis, you would need to be me to be acquainted with a case of an idea of mine being the *right* way, or the *wrong* way, for it to count as being F. For only I encounter—say, in perceptual awareness—that (or all of that) which is an idea of mine so being. So you cannot see what reach to particular cases being F has. For that you would need to be me. Which transcends the bounds of Frege's constraint on judgement. Why this constraint? Why could I not, on my own, give enough sense to the notion of (an idea of mine) being F to make room for (my) judging that some idea of mine was F? *One* answer might be: here we lose the needed material for making sense out of the idea of judgement as making one's fate turn precisely and only on the *world's* being as it is. Frege's answer in 1918 turns on the impossibility of giving truth an application in such a case. But, as said, that is a story told elsewhere.

Conceiving ideas as contents of consciousness there *are* no ways for them to be, no thoughts about them. But there is the *way* things are, and the *ways* things are: two different notions of *way* as different from each other as *things* (catholic sense) is different from *things* (plural of thing). The *ways* things are are just those *instanced* by the way things are. The way things are is none of these, nor some logical sum of them. If there is such a thing as the way things are for me, where only *I* could see how that was, then, by Frege's constraint, *this*, on its own, would not be articulable into identifiable *ways* things thus are for me. Which is not quite to say there is no such thing as how things are for me, nor, certainly, as that which you would have to be me to experience. The question is *how* such things might enter into thought. Not, anyway, on their own. We come next to Frege's approach to this question.

2 Grammatical Manoeuvres

Frege, having made his case, goes on to say this:

The ill person, who has a pain, is the bearer of this pain, but the doctor who treats him, who reflects on the cause of this pain, is not its bearer... Perhaps the doctor consults a second doctor. Then one must distinguish: First, the pain, whose bearer is the ill person, second, the first doctor's idea (*Vorstellung*) of this pain, third, the second doctor's idea of this pain. This idea belongs, to be sure, to the contents of consciousness of the second doctor, but is not the object of his reflections... Both doctors have as common object the pain of the ill person, whose bearer they are not. One can see from this that not only a thing, but also an idea, can be the common object of thought of those who do not have this idea.

(1918: p. 73)

Any object of any thought is the common object of the thoughts of many. Thoughts are intrinsically sharrable. How can an *idea* fit this bill? How can *it* be the object of anyone's thought—its owner included?

Grammar shows the way. When I have a headache, only I am (thus) pained. But my experiencing the headache is, *ipso facto*, my experiencing having a headache; which is, in turn, my experiencing *my* having a headache. Not that my feeling the pain is the *only* way for me to experience my having a splitting headache. Noticing my present short fuse, or my inability to concentrate, or experiencing the boredom of the doctor's waiting room, are also ways for me to experience my having the headache. Feeling the pain, though, is *one* way.

What I thus experience in feeling the pain—my having a headache—is something for others to experience as well. You may be the unhappy victim of my transitory short fuse, or my lack of focus. Or you may see, or hear, me suffering. Doctors, presumably, learn other ways of witnessing this.

If you can experience my having a headache, then you can—on one condition—think things of this, for example, that I am having (so that it is) a *splitting* headache. So *I* can think that too. The condition is: what *one* experiences in experiencing my having a headache is no less than what *is* my having it. Things being as *one* can experience them being is what counts as—instances—my having a headache. My having a headache (or, again, a splitting one) is, on this condition, a way for *things* to be, where *one* may see when things being as they are would be things being that way.

For my having a headache to be my having a *splitting* headache (on the condition, something *one*—so I—may judge) *is* for my headache to be a splitting one. So if you can grasp the thought that I am having a splitting headache—which, on the condition you can—then you can, equally, grasp the thought that my headache is a splitting one. So now there is something for you and the doctors—so for *me*, you and the doctors—all to think about.

The doctors may think that my headache calls for ibuprofen. For that to be so is for no more than what *one* may be acquainted with to be (instantiate) my having a headache which calls for ibuprofen; for it to be *one* within the range of diverse particular cases of which this would be so. My headache thus calls for ibuprofen (if they are right) in one of the literally countless ways that a headache (that is, someone's having a headache) may do so.

My cup's being as it is is *a* cup, or, again, *something*, being empty. It instances a certain one-place concept (present usage): *a cup* (or *something*) *being empty*. It thus falls under the Fregean concept *being empty*. Headaches *can* follow suit. Things being as they are is (say) my headache throbbing. If one likes, one may say: my headache throbbing is *something* throbbing, namely, my headache. But only I experience having the headache. In that sense, only I experience it. Only I feel it. You would need to be me to do that. So, it seems, my headache is a (my) idea in Frege's sense. In which case, an idea can be particular ways there are for an idea to be, and to be judged to be. Which may seem to violate Frege's constraint.

Only I have the headache. If we allow such a thing as what it is like to have precisely *this* headache, that will be, it seems, what it is like for *me*. You would have to be me to see just how things were in being precisely like *that*. Or, more perspicuously, you would have to be me to experience that episode of things being like that. Things being like that is, presumably, contemporaneous with their being like that for *me*, so, presumably, with my experiencing this. It is things being like that, one would think, which *is* my headache throbbing. So, it would seem, only I could be acquainted with that of the non-conceptual which is my headache throbbing. So if just that *is* my headache throbbing, then Frege's constraint seems violated.

But Frege suggests a finesse. Suppose there is a way things are for me in having precisely this headache: things being as they then are for me. Suppose you would have to be me to see, appreciate, *how* things thus are. Still, things being that way (for me) can be things being thus and so—my having a throbbing headache, say—*provided* that the above condition is respected: for that to be so—for an idea of mine, in Frege's sense, to be a throbbing headache—is for no more to be so than is so in my having a headache being my having a throbbing headache, where when things would be such as to count as my having a throbbing headache is something for *one* to see (appreciate). Frege's constraint does not mean there are *no* ideas—something of the non-conceptual which one would need to be so-and-so to be conscious, or aware of—as one is aware of the elephant on the Peugeot. It is just that an idea's being as it is cannot, of itself, be something being thus and so. It can be that if, but only if, *things* being as they are, exclusive of ideas, just *is* that idea's being that way. Frege's constraint, finesse included, is, I claim, a substantial constraint on how we view the mental.

So what I feel now is a throbbing headache only if the non-conceptual *one* could be aware of—what is not an idea—instances a certain way for *things* to be: my having a throbbing headache. This may seem behaviourism. But is not. The point is only that *one* may see, be acquainted with, what it is that counts as my now having a throbbing headache. It might be, for example, that (in favourable circumstances) someone may *visibly* have a throbbing headache. But the requirement itself leaves open just how it may be satisfied in one case or another.

If Frege's constraint were violated by headaches, then while *my* reason for taking myself to have a throbbing headache might be my actually suffering it, *your* reasons would have to be less telling. They could only be what you *could* recognize as present in the way things are, given your ability to see when there would be a case of things being as they are being things being thus and so. Which would exclude my having a headache. You could not take me to have a throbbing headache on grounds of my having one. That would give a certain meaning to the expression 'privileged access'. It would also raise insuperable barriers to our understanding of the mind.

Headaches are ideas if each requires a bearer—someone aware of it—and does not admit of two. So, one would think, they are ideas. And so we may regard them. Frege's finesse shows how to do that within the bounds of Frege's constraint. I want now to consider applying that finesse to visual experience.

3 Subjectivity

I stand in the square before the temple of Diana. I *see* what I do of the scene before me. There is that which I see and that which I fail to. Perhaps it is obscured; perhaps I am oblivious. Seeing something enables attitudes towards it. Seeing that pitted pillar third from left enables me to think of it that it is the worse for wear; and of its being as it (visibly) is that *that* is a pillar being pitted.

Thinking what I thus can of the pillar, or its presence, demands acquaintance. So, too, for my thoughts of its being as it is. Visual awareness offers this. To take up this offer is to stand towards the pillar in a certain way: to register its presence; to guide one's thought and deed accordingly. It is to respond to what vision puts on offer with an attitude towards this (in a suitably broad sense of attitude).

I could not think as I thus can of the pillar but for my seeing it. The scene before me fixes what there *is* for one, so for me, to see. My responses, or responsiveness, decides, by and large, what of this I do see. (Though given the work the scene thus does we may sometimes allow that I saw what was on offer to respond to where that offer was not taken up. More on this in section 5.)

There is another sort of case, which does not work this way. Wittgenstein points to it as follows:

> If someone looking at the schema of a cube [a Necker] were to express himself this way: 'Now I see a cube in *this* position—now one in *this*'—he could mean two very different things. Something subjective; or something objective. His words alone do not reveal which.
>
> (1982, §447)

One vocabulary; two different sorts of use. What is subjective use here? To begin with, *any* description *for* the way things are *ipso facto* has many other uses. The description, 'A pig is in the tulips' is for describing a pig as in the tulips. Used for what it is thus for, it would be used to say a pig *to be* in the tulips. But, as such, it speaks merely of a pig being in the tulips—that is, as a certain way for things to be: such that a pig is in the tulips. So speaking, it may be used to assign many other roles to that way for things to be. For example, it may be used to say what someone is imagining, or how things are in a story he is telling. 'I'm imagining arriving at my holiday bungalow in Tavira'. 'And what do you see?' 'A pig standing in the tulips'. When words *for* describing (or saying) how things are are used for some such other purpose—to assign some status to the way for things to be they speak of *other than* being a way things are, I will speak of them having (a) *shifted use*.

Words, 'N sees A', are *for* describing someone, N, as standing in a certain way towards something or other in his environment. The way is: enjoying that sort of awareness of A which one does in *seeing* it. The A is (I claim, following Frege) something which can form images on retinas. Such is those words' unshifted use. But, again, if that is what such words are for, then, *ipso facto*, they also have other uses; a multitude of shifted ones. On those shifted uses, they are not used as a description of how someone in fact stands towards his environment. They do not say N, or anyone, to have that sort of awareness 'see' speaks of of whatever it is in the environment 'A' would speak of if there is any such thing. Where 'see' is not used to say someone to have such awareness, 'A' need not be used to to describe something to be found in the environment. Its contribution to what is said in that whole 'N sees A' need not be *via* that route. In a wide class of cases it does not speak, or even purport to speak, of such a thing. In some of these, though, the whole 'N sees A' is used to say something as to what N experiences visually—how *he* is in that respect (which, by Frege's strictures, is itself an environmental circumstance).

Suppose, for example, that the third pillar from the left in the temple of Diana was purposely built to look bulgy. A *trompe-l'oeil* pillar. Then I may say, 'It bulges (when you stand there)' to describe how the pillar *looks*. What I say, on this use, is not false on grounds that the pillar in fact does not bulge. So this is shifted use of 'It bulges'. Or, if I stand in the right place, I may describe my own experience by saying, 'Now I see it bulging'. If this expresses truth, as it might, then here we have shifted use of 'N sees A'. (The first person is incidental here.) What I am describing, in the first case, is how the pillar *looks*. *Bulgy* is the way it looks (according to me). What I am describing in the second is my seeing, or experiencing visually, what I do of how it looks: my taking in its bulgy look, or again, its looking bulgy. One can *thus* say when things would be as I said: when

I saw, was visually aware of, the pillar looking bulgy (or its bulgy look). Here talk of the pillar's bulgy look, or my seeing, or noticing that look (or, more naturally, my seeing how it looks bulgy, or seems to bulge) is all in unshifted use. The pillar, in fact, *does* look bulgy. That is a feature of the environment, there to be reported on. Talk of looks, or seeming, here just reports it. So here is a route from shifted to unshifted use. One can say what I said in 'I see it bulge' in shifted use by saying, 'He saw its bulgy look', in unshifted use.

Not every case is like this. Suppose that, having had too much sun, or too many *bagaços*, I stand before, not the *trompe-l'oeil* pillar, but another perfectly ordinary one. My head swimming, I suddenly notice it starting to look bulgy to me. Complaining of my condition, I say, 'I see it bulging', or 'Now it's bulging', or 'It's starting to bulge'. I am not so far gone as to think that is what the pillar is really doing. I speak on shifted use. I *could* have said instead, 'Now the pillar looks bulgy'. But I would not thus escape shifted use. For what I say could be right, let alone capture what I said the first time, only if 'looks' occurs here on shifted use. The *ordinary* pillar does not look bulgy. There is no *such* thing to be aware of, let alone *visually* aware of. (Which is why it is difficult to describe my situation by saying, 'I see the pillar looking bulgy'. If I could do that, all that would have to be on shifted use as well.) So here something else is needed before we can say, in words used on unshifted use, how I said things to be in those initial words of mine on shifted use. I can at least indicate this here with a 'me': now the pillar looks bulgy *to me*. We *could* view this as unshifted use of a locution, 'looks to me'. For what else should this describe in unshifted use but a situation of the present sort? I will refer to such a use of 'see'—one not replaceable by unshifted use of 'looks'—as *double-shifted*.

Shifted use is not *per se* Wittgenstein's 'use for saying something subjective'. There is nothing subjective about taking in, or seeing, or noticing, the *trompe-l'oeil* pillar's bulgy look, or no more than there is in seeing the apple on the desk. That bulgy look is there to be seen. There *is* (plausibly) something *per se* subjective about double-shifted use. Wittgenstein is concerned with seeing the Necker in one way rather than another. 'I see a thus-cube', one says, where a thus-cube is one in such-and-such position. The Necker looks like a thus cube, but only on shifted use of 'looks'. The Necker as such no more looks like a thus-cube than it looks like a so-cube (the other way of seeing it). This is *one* kind of case of saying something subjective in saying what you 'see' (shifted use). The case of the *bagacos* is of a different sort. Even though the Necker does not, as such, look like a thus-cube, a thus-cube is something there is *for one* to see in looking at it; something some can *make* themselves see with practice. There are ways of getting oneself to do this. Drinking more *bagaço* is not a way of seeing the pillar's bulgy look. The *pillar* has no such look. *Bagaço* just does strange things. If the *trompe-l'oeil* pillar looks bulgy, that is not a fact about me. If the Necker looks like a thus-cube to me now, that is largely, but not entirely, about me. If the normal pillar looks bulgy to me now, that is *very largely* a fact about me. By Frege's strictures, if it is a fact at all, then it is an environmental one. What sort of environmental fact might it be? Frege's finesse points the way.

Some philosophers, among whom A. J. Ayer (1940: p. 23) and Elizabeth Anscombe (1965: p. 13), have taken shifted use to show two different phenomena *seeing* may be; one captured on unshifted, one on shifted use (for Anscombe, 'material' and 'intentional' descriptions of what is seen). But no such thing is indicated. Shifted use provides *no* reason for thinking that *seeing* may be something other than awareness of one's surroundings. Pia reclines, imagining her fantasy summer. Sid asks of the imagining, 'What are you doing now?' She replies, truly, 'I am strolling down the beach, arm in arm with Leonardo'. It would be rash to conclude that there is something strolling down the beach may be such that one can do this lying on a sofa, a thousand miles from any beach. 'I am strolling down the beach' is simply *not* used here for identifying some way things *are*. It is an account of how things are *imagined*. If strolling down a beach *can* be done lying on a sofa far from water, it is not that which Pia is imagining. If seeing a pillar bulge could be done without a pillar, it would not be *that* which my *bagaço*-induced visual experience is like.

There is, *sometimes*, a way the pillar looks to me which is not any way it looks (unshifted use of 'look'). *How* it thus looks to me may sometimes be said in shifted use of 'see'. It does not follow that whenever I see some of my surroundings, there is that, or even something, which I 'see' (shifted use). Shifted use is designed for a particular sort of unusual case. It need have no application in others, certainly no routine one. Where things look as they do, there is not always, further, the way they look to me—unless this is just my *seeing* some of how things look, failing to see some of this. In any event, 'seeing' (shifted use) such-and-such need not be, on any understanding of what seeing might be, *seeing* anything at all.

4 Limits

Shifted use, with 'see', is a way of saying how things look to someone; especially apt where things so looking is not his registering how things *look*. Not that there are *always* such things to report, whenever someone experiences visually. That perfectly straight pillar can, perhaps, look bulgy on occasion to one who has been hitting the *bagaço*. Where it does not, 'It looks perfectly straight to him' does not automatically state a truth. Where looking to me is not my taking in a look there is for *one* to see—as it may be where I see the thus-cube in a Necker—what is it? What would shifted use then report?

'It looks to me' *can* simply express an attitude: it looks to me as if the university is doomed. That is my take on things. It is not for me to experience visually the university being doomed (even if such be possible). Our concern is not with this use of 'looks to me', but with its use to describe how I experience things visually.

That pillar may look bulgy. It may be built to do that. It may also look bulgy from *here*: what *one* may see by standing there. It may look bulgy to me, too, just in my seeing what there thus is for one to see. The case of the *bagaços* works differently. Drinking *bagaço* is not a way of coming to be able to see a look a pillar *has*, not even from a certain vantage point; nor even of coming to see a look the pillar *can* have, though it can be difficult to get oneself to see it, as the Necker harbours the look of a thus-cube. Downing *bagaços* is not working oneself into a position from which the pillar does look bulgy (pleonastically to *one*). Insofar as this is so, the case calls for different treatment.

Here is one suggestion. That bulgy pillar is, and looks, bulgy. *It* so looks, full stop. That *trompe-l'oeil* pillar looks bulgy only when you stand *there*. *It* so looks; but only when you stand there; only when you view it in a certain way. Let us call a particular way of viewing something a *viewing*, and the view on offer when one views it in that way a *view*. One views in a certain viewing and thus enjoys a view. If the pillar looks bulgy, there is no *one* way you must view it to see it so looking. But you must stand *here* to see its looking as it does (so see *how* it looks) from here. More generally, you must view it in such-and-such a way to see it looking as it does viewed in that way.

Seeing the pillar looking as it does from here is (visual) contact with the non-conceptual; a particular refinement of *things* looking as they do. Its looking as it thus does may also be its looking thus and so. This it, or other pillars, may also do in other viewings. Looking *that* way would then be instanced by different things. There is *that* good sense to be made of seeing the same thing in (from) different viewings. There is also that sense to be made of the idea that one sees what one does in a given viewing (things looking as the thus do) only in that viewing.

A sequence of viewings may demand progressively more for the taking. One may view the pillar without viewing it from *here*, view it from *here* without viewing it in a mist; view it in a mist without viewing it in an early morning mist; and so on. All these are ways for *one* to view it. *Looking A to N* may be N's seeing, taking in, what is on view from such a viewing. Our present interest is in cases (if any) where it is not that. So we might try suspending that condition on viewings which makes it that. We can suppose a limit of demandingness, belonging to demandingness itself. At this limit, you would need to be me now to be viewing things (the pillar, say) in the way I am now. Such is part of what the way in question is. And we can try to reckon this way of viewing things among viewings in our present sense. We can call it a *limit viewing*. Now the idea is: things looking to me as they do—and their looking to me such-and-such way—where these are not my taking in the looks of things from some non-limit viewing, is things so looking from my current limit (viewing).

I take no stand here as to in what cases—if any—*looking to N* needs to be, or can correctly be, construed as looking from a limit viewing. I will return to that point below. What is of interest at the moment is that looking from a limit is subject to Frege's constraint. If you have to be me to encounter (visually) things looking as they do from my limit—to encounter *that* much of the non-conceptual—then things so looking is an idea in Frege's sense. What is *on* view from a non-limit would be on view whether viewed by me or not. Things would look, from that non-limit, as they look anyway. How would things look from my limit if I were not aware of this? There is no such would—once again that absence ideas are prone to. It is not what, so far, just in being what it is, may *be* (instance) things looking thus and so. So if it is to be so that things looking as they do to me (viewed in my limit viewing) *is* things looking thus and so, then we need to apply Frege's finesse. We have seen that finesse applied to headaches. How might it apply here?

In *seeing* labour is divided between scene and subject. The scene in view decides what there is to be seen; the stance in which the subject responds to his visually experiencing it decides what of that he does see. In a viewing, the scene's work in this enterprise drops out. If we think of something as *on* view at a limit, that can only be things looking as they do so viewed. Which (by Frege's constraint) is not, so far, things looking thus and so. So what is on view does not, so far, provide looks for the viewer to take in or not. Exactly not. If it did, then things looking thus and so to the subject would here be just another case of registering. But this does not *per se* cancel out the second half of the enterprise. I cannot judge of what does not admit of judging. If an idea's being as it is cannot be, *per se*, its being thus and so, then (barring Frege's finesse) I cannot think of an idea that it is thus and so and thereby think truly or falsely, according to how it is. But this is no bar to my having attitudes, or stances, to things being as they are for me, even where, by the above, those attitudes could not be judging.

I may find my headache awful. My headache's being as it is need not be called on to decide the truth of that (though with Frege's finesse in play, you, seeing me, may, with some justice, accuse me of over-dramatizing.) *Perhaps* 'It's awful!' never expresses a judgement. But what may sometimes be judged so *may* also, sometimes, be apt for an object of other attitudes. Seeing that the sun has risen is, Frege tells us (1918: p. 61), recognizing something in what one sees: its instancing a certain general way for things to be, the sun's having risen. Here recognizing is *Erkennung*, a cognitive achievement. But there is also recognizing, *Anerkennung*: acknowledging, accepting, counting as, giving faith and credit. (Stating is, for Frege, *Anerkennung* of the truth of something.) In awarding a doctorate, we recognize the student as a *bona fide* philosopher—a mistake, perhaps, but not just on grounds that he is not one. (It is for us to set the bar.) For what is on view at a limit, *Erkennung* is not in the cards. *Anerkennung*, or something like it, still might be. My stance towards that pillar may be that it seems to bulge (looks bulgy). Such a stance, we are supposing, cannot be made true or false simply by what is on view from my limit viewing of the pillar. Still, that can be how it is for me in my limit viewing. And that stance towards things looking to me as they do may be wrung from me—in one respect at least—just as judging is: as to this, here I stand, I can do no other.

Now a key point. If things looking as they do in my limit viewing is an idea in Frege's sense, it does not follow that my stances towards this are ideas, at least not where those stances are not judging. If I find my headache awful, my responding as I thus do to what is happening to me, whatever that may be, is something *one* may experience, even if one cannot think, of the non-conceptual to which I am responding, that *it* merits, or not, such a response. (Even if you would need to be me to be aware of *its* being as it is.) If I respond to my visual experience, under the influence, with an attitude of its being, for me, just as though the pillar bulged, then, again, my response is for *one* to encounter even if one cannot encounter, nor get in mind, that which *is* for me a pillar bulging.

For a pillar to look bulgy to me, on any understanding of this, is for *things* to be a certain way, where *one* could get in mind that which would be things being (or not being) that way. It is for *me* to be a way for *one* to be; a way *one* may understand someone to be. Someone's standing towards his experience—what is happening with him—with, or in, given attitudes—is that which remains of a cooperative enterprise of determining what is seen, in a case where *seeing* is in question, even where there is no scene (nor substitute for it) to decide what there is, anyway, to *be* seen. It is such an environmental circumstance—part of the surroundings we all cohabit. *It* may be, wholly, or substantially, that circumstance which is, say, the pillar looking bulgy to me where that is not my registering a look the pillar *has* when viewed in such-and-such way. (Not that things could look just *any* way to me and it still be the *pillar* that was looking thus and so, nor that just *any* stance towards what is happening to me could be, on just any occasion, a part of things *looking* one way or another to me. Delusions, perhaps some hallucinations, need not be *that*.)

An attitude which played this role, while in that role, could not be a *judgement* to the effect that things looked thus and so, though it might 'have the form' of a judgement—be, say, that the pillar seems to bulge. It could not be taking my *idea*—things being visually as they are for me—to be thus and so (Frege's constraint). It is too involved in the only judgeable (environmental) circumstance there is here—my being one to whom the pillar seems to bulge—to be *judging* that *that* obtains. On the other hand, if there *is* such a judgeable circumstance, there are circumstances in which *I* might judge it to obtain. What expressed such a judgement might sound just like what expressed what was not one. Nor need it be that any expression of an attitude is per se, and full stop, either an expression of a judgement or not. I return to this below.

Attitudes are optional. Correspondingly, while there is a way the pockmarks in that third pillar look viewed in the setting sun, there may well be *no* way they look to *me*, where that is not my registering their look. For I need hold no stance in this respect. Things looking to me thus and so (in looking to me as they do) thus has the sparseness of fiction—the sort exhibited in the fact that, while every man is a particular height, every tie a particular colour, Maigret, though a man of average height, was N centimetres tall, and, on an occasion, wore a *red* tie only if that is, in one way or another, part of the story Simenon told. The sparseness of looks, on this notion of looks manifests the role of attitudes in fixing facts about them.

I take no stand here on which cases of visual experience need treatment as per above, nor even as to whether a given case of things looking to me thus and so must, per se, be viewed either as a case of my registering something or as per above. (Though it would be rash to assume that *whenever* something looks thus and so to someone, there is a way to view it such that *so* viewed it so looks to one.) There may sometimes be options.

Consider, for example, seeing spots before your eyes ('seeing stars'). Such sometimes happens to people. Low blood sugar, standing up too fast, a smart blow to the head. *It*, so far as that goes, is something for *one* to experience. Perhaps, in one of the above ways, I could arrange for you to experience it. If you did so, say, in an encounter with a door, this could be viewed as your experiencing something there is for *one* to experience (though, on the present view, you could not have done that without registering it, thus standing towards it in a certain way). What you *thus* experienced is no more than what there is for *one* to experience in 'seeing stars'. Spots, 'stars', to be sure. And just how did the spots look? There is, so far, an answer to that only insofar as there is such a thing as how 'stars' look to one.

So far, two people who have seen stars have thus seen the *same* thing, just as two people who have seen the third pillar from the left have seen the same thing. If—as may be on occasion—there is some particular way things looked to you, then the question *what* way this was must be asked from a different stand point. Here, I have suggested, we need to think of you as involved in a limit viewing. The above model then applies.

Similarly for the Necker. One *can* view this as like seeing the sailboat among the dots in the puzzle painting. So viewing things, seeing the thus-cube is (finally) coming to make out something there for *one* to see. What one thus sees, as with the sailboat, is the particular *thus* cube of that particular Necker: if there is a slight irregularity, or discolouration, in a line in that Necker, there is that irregularity, or discolouration, in the corresponding line in the thus-cube that you see.

Such visual experiences *can* be viewed as registering something. Then the story told above does not apply. *So* seen, they leave room for a further question. What you *view* in seeing that thus-cube in that Necker, or those 'stars', is just what is on view for *one*. There is thus the thus-cube with the brown spot just *there*. The further question there is room for is: and how did *this* thus cube, or those 'stars', look to *you*? One cannot *always* make such questions arise (so as to have an intelligible answer). Sometimes, though, one can. Such a question, where there is one, may well be as to how things are in a limit viewing; so, ineluctably (since it *is* a limit) how *you* are, specifically, how you *stand* towards what is happening with you in so viewing things. How things *look* so viewed— if we are to speak of that at all—leaves *no* room for a further question how, in so looking, they look to you. Just that can, on occasion, give the idea of a limit view point.

Frege's constraint brings in question whether there *can* be anything on view in a limit viewing; then, further, whether, in such a limit things can look to the viewer thus and so. On the first point, if there is something on view at a limit, it belongs to the non-conceptual. It is things looking, so viewed, as they do. Frege's constraint concerns the bounds of *judgement*; the possibility of standing towards the non-conceptual so as to wring from it a verdict as to whether one thus takes things to be as they are—*that* way for things to be, as opposed to others. The constraint itself does not touch on the question whether we may think of a limit as a point from which there is non-conceptual on view. For the further question, Frege's finesse, worked out as above, shows how sometimes, at the limit, things looking as they do to me can be their looking thus and so. *My* standing towards things as I do can make this so.

5 Apperception

Where the idea of limit views applies, my stance towards my experience *forms*, in part, the environmental circumstance of things looking to me thus and so. So there is no *such* looking without my stances (attitudes). Looking to me, in that sense, lies in my *Anerkennung*, or acknowledgement, or some close kin; anyway in some form of recognition of things so looking. Such is the present idea. Freud held that consciousness was an incidental feature of a mental phenomenon: whatever could occur consciously could also occur unconsciously. Which *might* seem to conflict with this idea. But in the sense in which I think Freud very likely right it does not. It is perhaps worth explaining.

Leibniz defended unconscious *perception*—in his terms, perception without apperception. But he conflated two quite different things. One is, indeed, something unconscious perception might be. The other is at best only dubiously perception. Only the second is at odds with the present view. Here is the first:

> We do not notice the moving of a mill or a waterfall, when we have lived around it for some time. It is not that this movement does not strike our organs... but these impressions... devoid of the attractions of novelty, are not strong enough to attract our attention and our memory, occupied with more urgent matters... But if someone alerts us to it just afterwards, and causes us to note for example some noise which we come to hear, we remember and we are aware of having had some sensation of it.
>
> (1765/1966: p. 38)

If I can remember the sound of the mill, then I heard it, even if it did not command my attention at the time. So, plausibly—an innocuously—sometimes I hear what I do not note.

I *registered* the mill's sound, or what I later did was not *recalling*. Was I, at the time, *aware* of it? Neither 'Yes', nor 'No', can be *the* right answer to that question. For awareness admits of understandings. My standing towards the mill's sound as I did is *one* thing awareness of it can be understood to be. What awareness is as such allows for this. But awareness *can* also, sometimes, be understood to be something which my so standing was not. Understanding it in the first way, I was aware, though unconsciously, of the mill's sound. Understanding it in the second I was not. It is on the first understanding that there was a sound for me to *recall*. Leibniz, understandably, did not see awareness as admitting of competing understandings. Just that leads to his conflation.

Leibniz' second phenomenon is meant to be sub-doxastic perception. He describes it as follows:

> At every moment there are an infinity of perceptions in us, but without apperception, and without reflection, that is, changes in the soul itself which we do not apperceive

because the impressions are either too small and numerous, or too unified, so that nothing sufficiently distinguishes them on their own, but, joined with others, they do not fail to have their effect.

(1765/1966: p. 38)

It is these small perceptions which determine our course in many encounters without one realizing it, and which fool the vulgar with the appearance of an indifferent equilibrium, as if we were entirely indifferent as to whether, for example, to turn right or left.

(1765/1966: p. 40)

An imperceptible bulge in the pillar may leave its mark on my retinas, thereby on my visual system, and, thereby, awaken in me, say, disquiet, or a dry mouth, or raised blood pressure. It need not so work through my awareness of it. So nor need vision even permit such awareness. There need be nothing her I could recall. The bulge may be beyond the reach of human visual acuity.

Retinal stimulation, so some distal object, or configuration, might produce, say, dry mouth, or an urge to turn right, while remaining beyond the reach of human visual acuity. Would this be *seeing* the distal stimulus? *Can* the imperceptible (in principle) look, visibly, thus and so? There is a nice set of questions here. But we can bracket them. Our concern is with what happens at a limit. Here *such* interactions are not in the cards.

What is on view only at a limit cannot produce retinal patterns. It is not for *sight* to grant awareness of it; not *thus* work for a visual system. It is not part of our environment. Nor could it produce patterns in some *inner* organ of sense, conceiving this as something which grants awareness of one's body. My body is just another part of my (*our*) environment, in the meaning of the present act. What is on view at a limit cannot operate sub-doxastically—for one thing— because it is not *located* (pleonastically, in our environment).

There is a more fundamental barrier. What is on view (only) at a limit belongs to the contents of my consciousness, is an idea, in Frege's sense. Just that forestalls, in principle, further questions as to how things looked to *me* in *it* looking as it did. Which means there are no woulds to support talk of what it *would* do, were I aware of it or not. So it drops out of causal networks. The notion *cause* has no application here. The idea of *it* working sub-doxastically is thus without sense. Frege's finesse permits thinking of ideas as being given ways there are for a thing to be—if, and when, there is cause to. But one must accept the consequences. The non-conceptual on view in *seeing* is what it is, seen or not—thus its role in a cooperative enterprise. It is an instance of things being (*inter alia* looking) thus and so just where it is what *one* would count as such an instance. If we allow ourselves to speak of the non-conceptual on view in a limit viewing, we can precisely not say of it that it is what it is whether viewed or not. Among the things we thus cannot say is that it would, anyway, have such-and-such sub-doxastic workings.

My stance towards things looking as they do to me may make for an environmental circumstance, which, then, may have its workings, *inter alia*, on me, known or unknown to me. The idea that what is on view at a limit may so work, whether or not I stand towards it in *any* way—in a Leibnizian sub-doxastic case, whether I even *could* so stand—is one we simply cannot understand.

6 Self-access

What *general* morals are there here for our access to ourselves? In *The Blue Book*, Wittgenstein claims two different uses for words containing 'I' or 'my'—that is, for words *for* saying oneself to be thus and so. He illustrates the first use with (*inter alia*) 'My arm is broken' and 'The wind blows my hair about'. Some examples of the second: 'I see so-and-so', 'I think it will rain', 'I have toothache'. (See 1958: pp. 66–7.) One suggestion may be that there are (here) two different sorts of access to how things are with oneself. One *might* also see a second: that for any given way for one to be (or any within the indicated ranges), there is the one of these which is that form in which one accesses being *that* way. Frege's finesse, as developed here, bears on both of these.

'The wind blows my hair about' is, here, relatively unproblematic. I can *observe* the wind blowing my hair—in a mirror, for one thing; for another, I can *feel* my hair being blown. You, too, can observe *that very thing*—in a mirror, though you hardly need to; usually you can just see it straight on. I can observe this in a way you cannot. You cannot feel *my* hair being blown about—except by feeling it being blown in your face (hardly relevant here). But you can observe this in a way I cannot. I cannot see the blowing hair straight on. This last might be seen as a contingency of human visual apparatus—we might have had eyes on stalks. Perhaps *all* of the above might be seen in that way. In any case, my hair being blown about—that very thing—is, unproblematically, something for *one* to see, so observe. It is nothing like a part of the contents of my consciousness.

What, then, should we say of 'I have toothache', or 'I see the pillar bulge'—or 'I think it will rain', thought of as about me rather than the weather? Here, it seems, my access to myself is, somehow, by a more intimate route. Take 'My head is throbbing' (describing my headache, not the physical contours of my head), or 'Now the pillar looks as though it bulged' (saying how it looks *to me*). Do I *observe* things being thus to me?

On the one hand, perhaps we should say 'No'. For what *is* there for me to observe? If anything, it seems, the throbbing pain, the bulgy look. But *this* could not be the very same thing there is for *you* to observe (if there is anything for you to observe) in observing my head throbbing (my having a throbbing headache), or the pillar looking bulgy to me. And if there *is* that to be observed, then, it can seem, it must be just *that* which is reported in my 'My head is throbbing'. So the case would be quite unlike 'The wind is blowing my hair'. It would not be, in such cases, that you and I could observe the very same thing about me, though each in our own way. That which was my head throbbing, or the pillar seeming to bulge as *I* viewed it would be nothing for you to observe at all. For good Fregean reasons, we might think there could be no such thing as that.

On the other hand, one might be inclined to say 'Yes'. I *feel* my throbbing headache. If that is not observing my having one, what is it? Moreover, it has at least seemed that, in certain cases, I *can* be wrong as to whether I believe such-and-such. And if Austin is right (I think he is), there is also room for being wrong as to how things looked to *you*. You *say* the patch looked magenta. Could it not have really looked burgundy? And what could being wrong be here except failing to have observed (noted, registered) something there was to be observed?

What might it be for, say, the pillar looking bulgy to me *not* to be something I did, or might, observe? One might think it part of the notion *observation* that what one observes is what there is, anyway, to be observed. (Cf. *Investigations* IIix.) (Quantum mechanics may challenge this on some understandings of it, but not, I think, in ways here relevant.) Which may give some reason for holding that I cannot observe things looking as they do to me; for it is not as if there would have been *that* to be observed whether observed by me or not. What I do towards what is on view at a limit, the thought is, is not quite *observing* things looking as they do. Whatever one thinks of that idea, Frege's constraint imposes another: I cannot observe things looking to be *thus and so* in looking as they do. At least certainly not just in observing things looking as they do. For their looking as they do is *not* their looking thus and so unless for some environmental circumstance to obtain just is for things thus to look thus and so to me. Such an environmental circumstance must be made of other stuff—on the present account, *inter alia*, of my stance towards things being for me as they are.

All of which is good reason to think that my access to the pillar's looking bulgy to me (for example) *can* be something other than *observing* this (the pillar's so looking). Frege's finesse gives us something else for this to be. It can be a stance on my part towards things looking as they do to me; one which is not judging, but is, nonetheless commitment on my part—here to its being, for me, visually, as though the pillar bulged. (There is, of course, much more to be said as to what it is to hold such a stance. Seeing the shape of Frege's finesse is only a first step.) There is, anyway, no reason to think one needs to observe oneself having a stance towards things in order to have it. A stance is present in how one so standing is prepared to treat things. And now we see what the second use of words with 'I' or 'me'—words for saying how one is—would be: it would be for the expression of such a stance.

Finally, then, for the second *seeming* suggestion in Wittgenstein's discussion. It is that for a given way for me to be, words for me to speak of my being that way would, per se, be to be employed either on the first, or on the second, of the above uses. Wittgenstein *need* not be read this way. Even if *The Blue Book* should be, it is a suggestion explicitly rejected later on. (Again see *Investigations*, IIix.) The suggestion anyway cannot be right. If there may be an environmental circumstance of me being such as for things to look thus and so to me—one which requires, or is thanks to, some stance by me towards things so looking—then that that circumstance obtains is something there is for *one* to judge. There is no reason in principle why I am excluded from those eligible so to judge, though *what* I thus judge may well depend on the circumstances calling for this. Where there is that for me to judge, one form of words which would express the judgement is that very form in which I may also express that stance which is not a judgement, but which contributes to the obtaining of the circumstance thus judged. So given the two uses Wittgenstein points to—for reporting, for expressing a stance which is not judging—the *same* expression can have either use in speaking of the same way for one to be.

Thus we (begin to) see how Frege's case against idealism, as presented in 'Der Gedanke', gives shape to our understanding of the mind (and minds). It fixes a framework into which any attempt to make sense of our by no means transparent ways of speaking of our mental lives must fit if they are to make sense. It thus helps us make sense of the forms of our access to ourselves.

7 Neutrality

Ayer, we saw, posits two extant senses of 'see'. In one, one sees what is there to be seen, but may be other than it looks. In the supposed second sense, one sees what need not be there at all (exist), but cannot be other than it seems (or looks). (See 1940: p. 23.) This second sense corresponds to 'see' in double-shifted (Wittgenstein's subjective) use. I cannot, in that use, 'see' what *looks* like (the presence of) a bulgy pillar, but is really otherwise. He then proposes to coin a third sense. In it, what one sees cannot be other than it seems (looks), but also, necessarily, exists. What one saw in this sense would not be in the environment. But, Ayer supposes, we can arrange, *by fiat* for such things to see. Where things look to me, or you, as though a pillar bulged, we create by fiat an item of which we are visually aware, which bulges.

No further comment on Ayer's faith in the power of fiat. Anyway, he thinks his neologistic sense has a point, though availing oneself of it is optional. It allows us to identify a visual experience—say what it was that was experienced—in a way that preserves a certain neutrality. Here is Ayer:

Since ... our main object is to analyse the relationship of our sense-experiences to the propositions we put forward concerning material things, it is useful for us to have a terminology that enables us to refer to the contents of our experiences independently of the material things that they are taken to present.

(1940: p. 26)

The idea is this. Whenever I view a scene before me (or it is for me as though I did), there is, anyway, a story to be told as to what I saw in Ayer's third sense of 'see'. In that sense, anyway, I saw such-and-such. What I thus saw will be what I saw in his second sense (on double-shifted use). For things to have looked to me as they did (limit viewing) is, on the idea, for there to be that much story to tell. My experiencing things so looking *may* also be for me to have seen something in Ayer's first sense. It may have been for me to be aware, visually, of the presence of some things in the scene before me—which then may or may not be as they looked to me. But to take any stands on such issues would be to stick one's neck out considerably beyond its extension in saying what I saw in Ayer's third sense. There is *that* story to tell anyway. For all of things being as per it, the scene before me may have been any of many ways, so that in the awareness the story ascribes to me I may have *seen* (first sense) any of many things; or even nothing.

What price neutrality? Imagine this. I note the shifted use of 'stroll'. I take this to speak of *strolling* in some second sense. *Such* strolling requires no beaches to stroll on, nor any actual ambulatory motion. I take this second sense to preserve a certain neutrality: whenever someone is strolling, in either sense, there is, anyway, the strolling he is doing in this second sense. This, plus the obtaining of further conditions (yet to be discovered) may, but need not, add up to, in addition, some strolling in the first sense. So given strolling in the first sense is always given (or suitable) strolling in the second sense, plus further factors to be specified.

What is wrong with this? In brief, to stroll in this supposed second sense is to imagine strolling. When I stroll along a beach I need not be imagining anything; certainly not the strolling I am doing. Turning the idea around, when I am strolling, first sense, I may or may not be doing any strolling second sense. If I am, that will involve the obtaining of further conditions. Not that imagining strolling is actually strolling plus something else. Those conditions must, on their own, add up to me imagining what I thus am. Equally, if I am strolling, second sense—that is, imagining strolling—then the extra conditions which must obtain for me also to be strolling first sense are no less than what, on their own, would add up to my strolling, first sense.

Strolling involves ambulatory motion. But it is motion produced in a certain frame of mind—for example, with a certain interest in, and attention to, what one is doing. Imagining strolling is being in a certain frame of mind. But it is the wrong one for this role. Imagining myself strolling along the beach in Donostia while ambulating there is the wrong sort of thing to make those ambulations strolling. Similarly, imagining myself stepping over a sunbather while actually doing so is not minding where I put my feet. Conversely, for my frame of mind to make my ambulations strolling, my imagining things (particularly strolling) is beside the point.

If my proposal were a good one, one could say (or grasp) what strolling (first sense) was in saying (grasping) that it was strolling (second-sense) while such-and-such else. But one cannot grasp what strolling (second-sense) is except in grasping strolling (first sense). For strolling (second sense) is imagining strolling (first sense). So on the above recipe for saying what strolling (first sense) is, it would be: imagining (in the presence of such-and-such else) strolling first sense. So the recipe cannot be a way of saying what strolling (first sense) is—unless one has some way of saying what it is to imagine strolling (first sense) without reference to strolling (first sense).

Is Ayer's proposal for understanding seeing (his first sense) any better? A key point is: how things look in my limit viewing—what I 'see' on double-shifted use, so see in Ayer's supposed second sense of 'see'—is a story which remains to be told *after* we have fixed to just what, on view from non-limits, I am visually sensitive enough to qualify as seeing it. I may *see* the pillar bulging (shifted use), while, if there *is* such a further story to tell, it may be one on which the pillar looks to me shaped just as it thus is, or the pillar looks to me otherwise. If you stand *here*, the pillar seems to bulge. I stand there. I see, spot, its so looking. But now, how did it look *to me* (in my limit viewing)? Did it look as it does thus look—did it look to me to have the bulge it looks, from there, to have? Or did it look otherwise? Only sometimes is there something it would be for the answer to this to be one thing rather than another; something it would be for that bulgy look, registered by me, to, moreover, *look* to me as it did rather than otherwise, or *vice versa*. A special case of the more general point that there never *need* be such a thing as how things looked from my limit viewing; what is thus *on* view is liable to share the sparseness of fiction. So my *seeing* what I do (of my surroundings) is not inevitably my seeing such-and-such (double-shifted use) plus further circumstances.

Conversely, suppose the pillar did seem to me to bulge *thus*. What else must be added for this to be a case of my seeing how (from here) the pillar seems to bulge? Whatever it took to make my experiencing visually as, or what, I am visual awareness of the pillar's seeming, as it does (from here), to bulge. Add this, and now you can subtract the pillar's looking as it did to *me* (in my limit viewing). It may have done this, or not, for all we care. So it is here as with strolling: throw in enough to make for a case of me strolling (first sense), and you may, *ad lib*, add or delete my strolling (second sense).

There is a further parallel between seeing/'seeing' and strolling/'strolling'. For me to see the pillar bulge (double-shifted use) is for it to be for me just like/as though seeing a pillar bulge. One can grasp what that is only in grasping what it would be to see a pillar bulge. Appeal to seeing (double-shifted route) is not a route towards an understanding of what seeing (one's surroundings) might be. On that question, at least, Ayer's strategy is anything but neutral. Nor, on reflection, does it recommend itself.

8 *Vorstellungen*

The English 'idea' in seventeenth- and eighteenth-century philosophy came, through translation, to be '*Vorstellung*' in subsequent German philosophy, and then, through translation back, (often) 'representation'—not the first word that recommends itself for the ordinary German '*Vorstellung*'.

Ideas, as in Locke and Berkeley, are usually thought of as objects of sensory awareness. They are also generally thought of, as Frege did, as contents of someone's consciousness (in his sense). Descartes' equivalent, *cogitatione*, is meant to be representational in some sense—not necessarily (and *not*, for Descartes, or Locke) representing anything to be *so*. (The difference between representing Gonçalo Mendes on horseback and representing him to have gone on a crusade.)

A sense-datum, conceived as in Ayer, picks up the first two strands in the idea of an idea. It thus misconstrues the nature of the inner, in violation, as it is, of Frege's constraint. Whether a sense-datum is conceived as representational depends on the theorist. Sense-data are, nowadays, in well-earned disrepute. There remains the third strand in the (Cartesian) idea of an idea: the idea that it is representational.

Reading 'representation' here as representation of such-and-such as so, ideas in this sense are now much in vogue. It is widely thought to be patent, that is, that perceptual experience has representational content in this sense.

Not all who think this unite in motives. One idea, though, is that the idea of an idea, so construed, does justice to something called 'the phenomenal character of experience', while steering clear of the ills besetting the idea of a sense-datum. Bracketing the claim of justice, does this idea really avoid the ills? One might approach this through another question. As I now gaze idly, in the rough direction of outwards, my visual experience, the idea is, has a certain content: it represents it as so that such-and-such, for some suitable substitution for that dummy. In the circumstances, at least, that content is meant to be identified by things looking as they then do, on some understanding of *looking*: different content would have required different looks. If that content is meant to do justice to 'phenomenal character', then, conversely, to have that content is to have those looks. The question now concerns that sense of 'looks'. Is it to be looking in a limit viewing, or in a non-limit viewing, that does the work here?

Here our representationalist faces a quandary. Suppose it is some non-limit view that does the work. Then it is the *scene's* being as it is that determines how things are represented in an experience of viewing it. It is the pillar's being, or looking, bulgy, or its being such as to look bulgy when viewed from *here* that does this work. Grasping how one's experience represented things would be taking in the representational import of the scene itself. But (bracketing signage, and so on) a scene *has* no representational import. The pillar does not represent anything as so. Nor does its being pock-marked. Moreover, since a scene might look any of many ways to *someone* while looking as it does, this appears *not* to capture the 'phenomenal character' of experience (though who knows what that may be).

But suppose the looks which do the work are looks in a limit viewing. *Their* being as they are cannot as such (without working Frege's finesse) be things being *any* way there is for things to be. So, in particular, it cannot be things being such that the experience represents things as being thus and so (or in it things are so represented); nor such as to decide this. On this option, a representational content for experience would violate Frege's constraint. So, though such may *seem* to be necesssary if representation is to capture phenomenal character, it is also ruled out. If it *seems* to be called for, something is being conceived wrongly. So much, on either option, for representationalism.

You would have to be me to experience things *now* looking as they now do to me; how they look on *this* viewing of them. Frege's finesse shows how we need not balk at this idea, even though the looking things thus do would belong to the contents of my consciousness. Perhaps we need the idea to make sense of the idea of things thus looking to me a way there is for things to look to *one*, so, perhaps, a way they now also look to you. For such is an idea of some non-conceptual instancing some particular bit of the conceptual. And where within the non-conceptual might that be? But here the non-conceptual can engage with the conceptual only via Frege's finesse; only thanks to the engagement of something which does not belong to the contents of my consciousness with some suitably related bit of the conceptual: for my headache throbbing, my being one whose headache throbs; for the pillar's bulging, my being one for whom it is as though I saw a bulging pillar (on a suitable understanding of 'as though'). Such linked engagements rest on one's attitudes towards how things are for him—ones whose content is that things are thus and so, but, for all of which, are not *judgements*. Such are Frege's lessons for philosophy of mind.

4

Reason's Reach

Experience (notably perception), one would have thought, makes our surroundings bear on what we are to think. In it, we are aware of some of how these surroundings are, or what is in them. We are thus aware of what bears on what is so: what settles the question whether P, or makes P likely, or is evidence for P, or is, or would (*ceteris paribus*) be reason to think P. Sometimes we are aware of such bearing, in which case some of *our* questions what to think are settled. If we are aware that what we are aware of settles, say, affirmatively, whether Sid is sitting, then that Sid is sitting is the thing for us to think.

But all this has been challenged. The skeletal thought is this. There is a certain condition on standing in a rational relation, that is, on bearing, as per above, on what is so; so being capable of bearing in the above way on what we are to think. What I experience, notably perceive, fails this condition. So it does not bear on what is so of, or in, my surroundings, so nor on what I am to think of them. For the moment I will use 'The Condition' as a placeholder for this supposedly failed condition. The first section will discuss what it might be.

A thought of so-and-so that he drives is about Sid just in case its truth turns suitably on how Sid is. A thought (that such-and-such is so) is about our environment just in case its truth turns on how that environment is. If our surroundings do not bear on whether P, then P is not about them. Suppose our surroundings could not bear on whether to think P so. Experience could not make them. So, no matter how things went, one might just as well either think P or think not. So if one thought P, there would be nothing it would be to treat the world accordingly, or to shape one's thought and agency accordingly. There would be no identifiable shape that thinking P would give to thought, which threatens the idea that P is really something one could think so or not at all. (Nor would one *be* thinking that P, or that not, while seeing how nothing does, or ever could, make this what you *ought* to think (to think what is so).)

If the skeleton is right, this is how it is for everything we might have thought we thought as to how things are around us. That red meat on the white rug, for example, cannot settle for me, in my seeing it, whether there is red meat on the white rug. The skeleton merits no more allegiance than that idea about the meat. It would be bad faith to mouth what states it, claiming for our words some special sense. *That* it is mistaken can thus be clear enough without our seeing *how* it is.

John McDowell's *Mind and World* (1994, 1996) is a response to some fleshings of the skeleton. Appealing to a Sellarsian distinction between a 'logical space of nature' and a 'logical space of reasons', he describes one fleshing out as follows:

> Whatever the relations are that constitute the logical space of nature, they are *different in kind* from the normative relations that constitute the logical space of reasons. The relations that constitute the logical space of nature, on the relevant conception, do not include relations such as one thing's being warranted, or—for the general case—correct, in the light of another... Suppose we want to conceive the course of a subject's experience as made up of impressions, impingements by the world on a possessor of sensory capacities. Surely such talk of impingements by the world is 'empirical description'; or, to put the point in the variant terms I have introduced, the idea of receiving an impression is the idea of a transaction in nature... On these principles, the logical space in which talk of impressions belongs is not one in which things are connected by relations such as one thing's being warranted or correct in the light of another. So if we conceive experience as made up of impressions, on these principles it cannot serve as... something to which empirical thinking is answerable.
> (1996: xv)

In sensory experience the world impinges. That it so impinged is a fact of nature. So, the idea is, it belongs to 'the logical space of nature', hence *not* to 'the logical space of reasons'. Normative relations belong to 'the logical space of reasons'. Hence the world's impingements cannot stand in rational relations; so nor bear on what to think. What one *is* to think is a normative question. The world's impingements, natural occurrence, leave *such* questions open. This sketches one way with the skeleton.

If there is a problem here, it is, for McDowell, only an apparent one. *Mind and World* will show why no fleshing out of the skeleton, so not this one, could be right. But there are two tacks one might take in so aiming. One would be to accept The Condition and show how (some of) experiential intake meets it. That is McDowell's tack. The other is to reject The Condition. That is mine. So I will aim to identify objects of experience—things in our surroundings, and in their being as they are—which fail The Condition, but all the same bear, in specific ways, on what one is to think. I will, in fact, argue that The Condition is incompatible with genuine thought full stop. All of which remains programmatic until, in Section 1, The Condition is identified.

1 The Condition

What might The Condition be? McDowell tells us,

A normative context is necessary for the idea of being in touch with the world at all, whether knowledgeably or not.

(1996: xiv)

The relations that constitute the logical space of nature, on this conception, do not include relations such as one thing's being warranted, or—for the general case—correct, in the light of another.

(1996: xv)

If we are to speak of two spaces as Sellars does, and if we locate the relations between perceiver and what is perceived (perceiver and the world's impingements on him) in the logical space of nature, then (the idea is) such relations will not include *warranting* thinking such-and-such, or making so thinking correct. For *such* relations normativity is needed. Perceptual experience so viewed has no room for perceiving what *bears* on what to think. Thus the apparent problem.

Nothing *warrants* red meat being on a white rug. It just happens when you toss a steak around. Something may warrant your putting the meat there—if, say, your family honour called for it. What did so would stand in a rational relation to your so doing. So it would satisfy The Condition (if valid). So, too, for whatever made it called for for you to *think* such-and-such. Thinking something so engages with normativity: one may thus think truly or falsely. *Perhaps* liability to that sort of correctness is what engagement with normativity requires. *Representing* is what is liable to be true or false. If The Condition demands such liability, then there had better be representing in what we experience of things if the skeleton is to prove wrong.

McDowell speaks of experiences as such that in them things appear to be, and thus are represented as, a certain way. (See, for example, 1996, 11.) But he does not think anything along the lines just outlined. On the contrary, he assures me emphatically that he could drop all such mention of representing as so without changing his defusing of the apparent problem. So far as I can see, he is right in this. So I will not pause to explain why the notion of representing as so does not fit perceptual experience. (But see my 2004a.)

In any case, being liable to correctness of some sort (being, say, truth-evaluable) is not, and cannot be, the only way of engaging with normativity. For where there is such liability there is also such a thing as bearing on it—for example, making for the relevant correctness in a given case. There is the thought that the meat is on the rug. *That* the meat is on the rug is things being precisely such as to make that thought correct. It is *so* that there is precisely where it is true to think so. Meat's being on the rug is neither true nor false. But it is a way things count as being just where a certain thing counts as true to think. If the latter is something normative (whatever that comes to), then so is the former. One can say: the meat's being on the rug is such that for things to be that way is for a certain thought to be true. *Thus* do the meat's being on the rug, its being so that it is, and so on, also engage with normativity. There are at least two routes to engagement. I will call this The Clue (to reason's reach).

McDowell says, 'the space of reasons does not extend further than the space of concepts' (1996: 14). Perhaps this is another clue to The Condition: a term of a rational relation must belong to the space of concepts. What might it be to do that? Perhaps to be conceptually *structured*. But that idea, in turn, admits of understandings. A strong version of it is suggested by this:

> Consider, say, judging that there is a red cube in front of one. There is a conceptual capacity that would be exercised both in making that judgement and in judging that there is a red pyramid in front of one, and another conceptual capacity that would be exercised both in judging that there is a red cube in front of one and in judging that there is a blue cube in front of one. In judging that there is a red cube in front of one, one would be exercising (at least) these two capacities together. What does 'together' mean here? Not just that one would be exercising the two capacities in a single act of judgement; that would not distinguish judging that there is a red cube in front of one from judging, say that there is a red pyramid and a blue cube in front one. In a judgement that there is a red cube in front of one, the two conceptual capacities I have singled out would have to be exercised with a specific mode of togetherness: a togetherness that is a counterpart to the 'logical' or semantical togetherness of the words 'red' and 'cube' in the verbal expression of the judgement, 'There is a red cube in front of me'. Here we see the point of the idea that non-overt conceptual episodes are to be understood on analogy with linguistic acts...
>
> ...Now we can say that in an ostensible seeing that there is a red cube in front of one—an experience in which it looks to one as if there is a red cube in front of one—the same conceptual capacities would be actualized with the same mode of togetherness.
>
> (1998: 438–40)

A statement that there is meat on the rug is in particular words, and thereby deploys particular concepts in a particular structured way ('mode of togetherness'). The *suggestion* here is that thoughts, one's awareness of the environment in a perceptual experience, and thus the object(s) of such awareness follow this model. To belong to the conceptual, on this idea, would be to be conceptually structured in this sense.

The idea here is Tractarian. (For one of Wittgenstein's expression of it see Waismann 1979, 89–90.) A representation-as-so, the idea is, has one particular structure. The elements of such a structure are some definite battery of concepts, or atomic representaional devices (names). The structure deploys each in a particular logical role within the whole it forms. Within the structure each element bears a particular structural relation to the others. It is essential to the thought, or representation, to be precisely *so* structured. For its structure determines what it represents as so: that the elements *its* elements represent are structured in precisely the way its elements are in it. A different structure would thus represent a different thing as so. In which case what a representation represents as so *must* share its structure. That it takes just *that* structure to represent just *that* as so just is a sense in which what would thus be so has that structure. So to be aware, in experience, of things being so is, *ipso facto*, to be aware of conceptually structured things. An ostensible seeing is then at least seeming such awareness. On this idea, it is not, *pace* Frege (1892), just *Aussagen*, but equally *Gedanken,* that are each built in a particular way of particular concepts.

Suppose that things being as they are did not articulate into conceptually articulated *ways* things are as per the Tractarian idea. Then a given way things were—a given thing so—would not require a given structuring of concepts to say it to be so. It might be reported in words which structured concepts in any of many ways. In that sense it would be *structurable* in many ways. Would *this* block experience making the world bear on what to think, where the Tractarian idea would allow it? Or in making what we see bear on what to think would we simply be spoiled for choice? I defer the question.

For McDowell does not, he assures me, avow the Tractarian idea. The Condition, as he reads it, asks conceptual structure only in the weaker sense of being of the form *That things are thus and so* (or perhaps its grammatical cousin, *things being thus and so*). McDowell's response to the skeleton is thus that we perceive (see, hear, feel, and so on) things of the form *that such-and-such. Perhaps* he thinks all we perceive to have that form. ('In a particular experience in which one is not misled, what one takes in is *that things are thus and so.*' (1996: 26)) What matters here is that, in any event, *such* things are what make the world bear on what to think.

McDowell tells us,

Any impingements across...a...boundary [between the conceptual and something else] could only be causal, and not rational; that is Davidson's perfectly correct point.

So if there *is* rational bearing, thought experience, on what to think, then

The facts that are made manifest to us in [impressions on our senses] ... are not beyond an outer boundary that encloses the conceptual ... and the impingements of the world on our sensibility are not inward crossings of such a boundary.

(1996: 34)

Something non-conceptual, the idea is, *could not* impinge rationally on what one is to think. It *could* not stand in a rational relation. Hence the condition. But, though facts *that* belong, truistically, to the conceptual, and though there is *a* notion of perceiving on which one can sometimes see a fact (to be one), there precisely *must* be rational relations between the conceptual (what satisfies the condition) and something *else* if we are to make sense of experience bearing on what one is to think. Or so I am about to argue.

2 Frege's Line

Frege writes:

But don't we see that the sun has risen? And don't we thus also see that this is true? That the sun has risen is no object which sends out rays that reach my eyes, no visible thing as the sun itself is. That the sun has risen is recognized on the basis of sensory impressions. For all that, being true is not a perceptually observable property.

(1918: 61)

The remark occurs within a discussion of Frege's insistence that only what lacks perceivable features can make questions of truth arise. *Very* briefly, what is perceivable—a sentence, say—admits interpretation; so *it* does not raise some *one* question of truth. There is an objection to what Frege here insists on. We see that the sun has set. We thus see that this is true. So we can see the truth of at least some things. So truth *can* be, a perceivable feature of a perceivable thing. In response to this objection, Frege draws a distinction. Things like the sun (*inter alia*, things which, like it, reflect or emit light into one's eyes) fall on one side of it. Things like *that the sun has set* fall on the other. I will call the distinction *Frege's line*, and the first side of it the *left* side, the second the *right*. To draw the distinction will also be to provide a sense in which things to the right (so things which make questions of truth arise) are not perceivable.

What has visual, auditory, or spatial, properties, Frege tells us, can represent as so only insofar as an intention attaches to it. (Frege 1918, 59) That is, only insofar as it *is to be taken* as representing in a particular way (as opposed to others in which, for all its perceivable features, it might). If that painting represented Chartres cathedral as looking thus and so, that is in part because that blue patch in it, on the image of a wall, is to be taken as mattering in a certain way to what one would see in viewing the cathedral if it were as represented (whether, say, the wall would be coloured, or merely in shadow). We need a *way of taking* what is perceivable for the way things are (the world) to matter in some determinate way to whether things are as it represents them. An intention's function here would be to make the world matter in one definite way rather than others. For a question of truth to arise just is for the world to matter in some such way. What *raises* such a question, in the case of perceivable representing (such as words or pictures) is how the perceivable is to be taken. That something is to be taken in such-and-such way (so as to make the world matter *thusly*) is not itself perceivable, where this means: something with perceivable, or spatial, features.

It is in this sense that what is perceivable is excluded from 'the domain of things for which truth can come into question at all.' (1918: 61) The Clue suggests a converse point. The roast needs no *intention* attaching to it for it to be so that it is on the rug. But for it to be so that the roast is on the rug is for a particular question of truth to have an affirmative answer; for representing to which the world mattered in a particular way to be true. The relevant representing would be just that which is to be taken in a certain way: as representing things as thus and so. If for the roast to be as it is is for it to be on the rug, then its being as it is is one thing which ought to count as *being as thus represented*; one thing which *belongs* within the range of what would count as being as thus represented. That its being as it is *ought* so to count, that this belongs within a certain range of cases, those of being the way in question, is no more perceivable—no more an item with perceivable, or spatial, features—than that a representation *is to be taken* in such-and-such way. This points to a sense in which *that the sun has set*, along with *that it is true that it has* are not perceivable things. To work out this converse will be to see what distinction Frege's line draws.

Seeing the sun, or its trajectory, or the roast on the rug, or the dog carrying it off, or its oxidized condition, is seeing what is *in* one's surroundings. One sees what is at a particular location. One sees that location in the condition it is in. That the sun has set (in Rostock) may be, in some sense, *about* a location. But *it* has none. The sun, perhaps, is in the sky. That it has set is not. So, it seems, what lies to the right of Frege's line has no location. But location is not the crucial point.

I will now assign a sense to *conceptual*. A concept, as I will speak, is always *of* (being) such-and-such. As such it has a certain sort of generality. There is a generality it need not have. It may be, necessarily, of just one thing. There may even be one thing it is necessarily of. Still, there is a sort of generality it has. Suppose a concept were of being Frege. To fit that concept one could stop nowhere short of being him. But suppose (if you can) Frege had taken to wearing a beret, or had devoted his life to sailing. He would have been different than he was. Still, he would have fit that concept. Suppose, again, that Brahms had not visited Breslau, or that Bismarck had not resigned. Still, Frege would have fit that concept. So there is a variety of circumstances which would count as someone's fitting that concept (and here a variety of circumstances which would not so count). There being at least one such range of cases is one thing one might mean by generality. It is what I will mean here by the generality of the conceptual.

The concept of being red meat is general in a sense in which a concept of being Frege is not. It might have fit other than what it does, were the world but different. But it is also general in the present sense. What fits the concept *red meat* might still have done had it had a bit more gristle, or, while older, were not overly oxidized, and even if Texans were all vegetarians.

The key feature of the conceptual, on its present understanding, is that for anything conceptual there is a specific form of generality intrinsic to it. There is then a range which is the range of cases, or circumstances, which would be ones of something instancing that generality (or, again, a range of things not instancing it). The range is indefinitely extensive: for any list of things belonging to it, there are (one can find) more. So for given circumstances to belong is not just for them to be as they are, but for them to satisfy some intelligible demand on membership.

In particular, a representation as so is conceptual in this sense. Sid might represent it to Pia as so that he has been driving. Perhaps he has: things being as they are counts as things being as he said. But suppose they were not quite as they are. Suppose he lacked the lipstick on his collar, or he drove the Fiat and not the Lexus. For all that, they might still have been as he represented them. So there is a range of cases which are the ones in which things would be as Sid represented them. Which is to say there is a specific form of that sort of generality which marks the conceptual in the present sense.

Now we can apply The Clue. If a representation of it as so that Sid has been driving is conceptual, then so, equally, for its being so that he has. For it is so that he has precisely where things are such as to make that representation true. So there is an indefinitely extendible range of cases which would be ones of Sid's having been driving. It is just those cases which would make the corresponding representation true. Its being so that Sid has been driving thus has a specific form of that generality which marks the conceptual. Representation does not exhaust the conceptual. A role for the conceptual—say, in experience—is not per se a role for representations. A need for the conceptual—say, so as to bear on what to think—is not *per se* a need for representing.

To the right of Frege's line is the conceptual. What is there to the left? What *instances* (first-order) conceptual generalities. Such as that piece of meat. A piece of meat is not in the business of being instanced. So treating it would be bad grammar. *A fortiori* there is no range of cases which instance it. It is not conceptual. Of course, for any given piece of meat, there is a concept of being it. Being a concept, this does have its range of instances: the meat in the butcher's case, the meat in butcher paper, the meat on the rug, and so on. If we so think, then, entering the salon, seeing the meat on the rug, what one sees is one instance of that range: the meat as it there, and then, is. At least in sublunary affairs, it is the meat, in being as it is, that instances one generality or another—oxidizing, staining the rug. Its being as it is is, *inter alia*, its bleeding rapidly into the rug. So the meat in being as it is, and, if we like, its being as it is, instance generalities. (The latter instances the generality of the zero-place predicate *the meat being on the rug*.) Nor is the meat's being as it is in the business of being instanced, any more than the meat is. Correspondingly, there is no range of cases of the meat being as it is. Nor to be as it is need it satisfy some demand on being a certain way. It is the way it is *however* that may be. What did all that was required for being the meat as it is would simply be the meat, as it is—one way for something to be that piece of meat, but the only way for something to be that meat as it now is. That for which there is thus no range of cases I will call the *non-conceptual*.

It is the non-conceptual that occupies the left of Frege's line. We can now work out Frege's point. To see the meat on the rug is just to be suitably sensitive, or responsive, to it as it then is—to the non-conceptual. Similarly for seeing its condition (how it is), or its movement or changing. Sensitivity to the presence or absence, coming or going, of what is there, literally before me, is enough. To see that the meat is on the rug I must register something else: the instancing by things being as they are of a certain way for things to be, meat being on a rug. I must recognize things being as they are as belonging to a certain range of cases, as what *such* cases would be. The range in which I thus fit things being as they are is not something visible, nor (present case aside) is what would fit in it. My access to these things is not by sight. For a range, on present use, to be the one it is is for it to *require* what it does for membership; for it to make such-and-such matter, other things not, to this (as there is what matters, and what not, to being meat). (As for Frege (1904) it is what matters to being the value of a function for a given argument that identifies the function.) One does not *see* (observe) a range *requiring* one thing or another, any more than one literally *sees* being meat requiring something for so being.

Some have spoken of something called 'non-conceptual (representational) content'. On the present idea of the conceptual, that idea makes no sense.

Representing as so is essentially conceptual. One represents *something* as so where there is something it would be for things to be as represented, so what matters to so being, so a range of cases of what would *be* things so being. With no such range there could be no *question* of truth without things being as they are, but then no way for such a question to turn on *how* they are. This is Frege's point in saying,

> A thought always contains something reaching out beyond the particular case, by which this is presented to consciousness as falling under something general.
> (Frege 1906/1983: 189)

A representation may be arbitrarily *specific*—arbitrarily definite, say, as to just how something must be coloured where. But specificity is not the particularity, the concreteness, of the non-conceptual. The concreteness of perceptual experience cannot be located to the right of Frege's line. But we can find it if we follow Frege. McDowell speaks of such things as *that the meat is on the rug* as part of 'the layout of reality'—to which experience is, he tells us, openness (1996: 26). But there are various conceptions of *layout*. Here, too, there are echoes of the *Tractatus*. There is the layout of the furniture in my room: chairs *there*, sofa *there*, and so on—a geometrical arrangement. Such a layout is something visible, and also non-conceptual, just as the roast is. Some such conception of a layout *may* have inspired Wittgenstein's idea that a proposition represents its structure as the structure of reality. But if the meat's being on the rug is part of the layout of reality, that would have to be in things being as they are instancing meat being on a rug; in the meat being on the rug being *one* of the ways things are in being as they are. The layout of reality would consist in all such instancing there is. That would be a very different notion of layout.

Conflating one sort of layout with the other, one might try to model seeing that on seeing the arrangement of a room. So modelled, seeing that would show up as seeing what is *in* one's surroundings, things being as they are at the various locations in them. That might seem to allow our surroundings, when (suitably) experienced, to bear on what to think merely by virtue of relations between what belongs to the conceptual. But if seeing that were seeing an item visible as meat is, one could say: 'Sid saw *that there was meat on the rug*, though clueless as to what it was he saw', 'Sid saw that there was meat on the rug, but mistook it for that the Lexus was in the garage'; and if Sid were asked 'What are *you* looking at?', an intelligible (though perhaps not advisable) response would be: 'I haven't the faintest idea. Perhaps it's that there's red meat on the rug. But it may be that I have been driving'. Such things make no sense. Reason to be wary of the idea that 'perceptual intake' is, *per se*, conceptually structured in so much as McDowell's weak sense.

3 Expertise

The meat, in being as it is, instances being meat. Its so being is *one* thing, among indefinitely many, that would so count; one way of so counting. The meat *fits* within a certain range of cases. If you judged it not to fit (it being as it is), you would be wrong. Its being as it is *dictates* that verdict. (So that it can be *judging* that you thus did.) Following Frege, one *recognizes*, on the basis of what one sees of the meat, that it is meat. 'Recognize' here is '*erkennen*', not '*anerkennen*'. It is registering what is so; what is *shown* so by what one sees *in* one's surroundings. So there is a *rational* relation between the meat's being as it is and its being meat. The first *bears* on the second. Its bearing is a matter about which one can *judge*. The Condition is thus mistaken.

To judge is to be liable to a particular kind of error, over which things being as they are holds sole sway. Judging that there is a roast on the rug incurs a particular form of such liability: things being as they are decides correctness precisely in deciding whether there is a roast on the rug. One thus judges truly precisely where the surroundings, in all their particularity, instance that generality. If rational relations held only between generalities (bits of the conceptual); if what instanced those generalities (what is non-conceptual, such as some bit of the surroundings being as it is) bore no such relations to those generalities, then things being as they are could not render verdicts as to when one had succumbed to, when escaped, the sort of error liability to which makes judging *judging*. There would then be no judgement.

But the non-conceptual—things being as they are, or a thing being as it is—can settle *our* questions what to think only if we can appreciate, grasp, its bearing on what is so. Where it is the non-conceptual that bears on the conceptual, grasp of bearing *can* consist in knowing a generalization. The meat on the rug bears on Pia's mood this way: if there is meat on the rug, she will be furious. Knowing this and seeing that there is meat on the rug, one has reason to think she will be furious. One might also think: where one thing means another, for it to bear as it thus does on what is so is for some such generalization to hold. For that lipstick to mean that Sid has been driving, say, is for it to be so that if there is lipstick on Sid's collar then he has been driving. Austin (1946) explained why this is wrong. If that beast's snout is too *retroussé* for a peccary, it is not *that* it is *retroussé* that means it is not a peccary. If *that* barking means the dog will not bite, this is hardly because barking dogs do not bite. If that grunting means the boar are in the wild yams, well, you just have to know the right grunting.

Telling a peccary's snout, innocuous barking, when grunting means the boar are in the wild yams, admits of expertise. One can learn, and be recognizably able, to tell such things. One can tell how given barking, or grunting, bears on what is so. Its so bearing lies within the scope of reason—is a rational relation to what is so—insofar as it actually settles questions, or provides evidence, and so on. Barking, to one who can tell when it is threatening, a snout to one who can tell when it is a pig's, does bear, when he hears, or sees, it, on what he is to think. Where one so skilled takes it to be the bark of a dog about to bite, that the dog will bite just is what it is rational for him to think. He *can* think no other; nor should he. Such is one thing rationality is like.

Ti-Jean hears the grunting and can tell the boar are in the wild yams. He sees how the grunting bears on that. That he can tell reduces his options. It is not as if, despite what he hears, he might decide to believe the boar have all gone south. His position is Lutheran: he sees how things are; he can think no other. But his lack of options does not make it less rational for him to think the boar are in the yams. It does not change the bearing of the grunts on what *he* is to think; so nor the rational relation in which they stand to, first, the boar being in the yams, and, second, his so thinking.

Seeing the bearing of the non-conceptual on the conceptual cannot consist in seeing that when things are such-and-such way they are also such-and-such other. That would be seeing a relation between the conceptual and the conceptual. But one can be expert as to the bearing of the non-conceptual on the conceptual in given matters—even if 'expert' may be a rather grandiose term. One can know red meat, or meat on a rug, when one sees it, or a peccary when one sees one. Or one can know when to say that meat is red, or on a rug, or that something is a peccary. 'I know a peccary when I see one' may *answer* the question, 'How do you know that's a peccary?'

Correspondingly, if, knowing a peccary when you see one, you now say of the beast before you, 'That's a peccary', you have (though it sounds grandiose) exercised expertise. You take it to be a peccary in grasping how its being as it is bears (thus far) on *what* it is. You grasp—can tell—how it does bear. That is what expertise here is. You thus take it to bear as it does. The beast's being as it is thus bears, for *you*, on what to think—on the right thing to think in this matter. Thus may the non-conceptual bear a rational relation to what one is to think.

Knowing a peccary at sight, or when to say that something is one, is the kind of expertise we can acquire through experience. It is the kind we may *recognizably* have. As Frege also taught us, that such expertise can be shared, and recognized by one thinker in another, underlies there being such a thing as judging, along with rational relations between the non-conceptual and the conceptual (here see Essay 2), For this reason too, The Condition is simply a mistake.

Where we see that the meat is on the rug—whether in seeing it there, or otherwise (in Pia's face, in the dog's behaviour)—that the meat is on the rug thereby bears, for us, on what to think. That is not in doubt. But nor does it account for the world's bearing as it does, through experience, on what we are to think. What cannot be right is that it bears only through relations within the space of the conceptual. Nor can it be that experiential intake is conceptually structured. Passivity makes a more than notionally separable contribution to spontaneity. The Condition must be disallowed.

4 Occasion Sensitivity

I have so far followed Frege. I now go where he may not care to. But *he* made the space I will now occupy. My aim is to work out what is really wrong with thinking of *that such-and-such* as visibly before us—in view—as, say. the meat is. Or, again, what that 'as the meat is' might mean.

The core idea so far is: for it to be so that such-and-such is for things being as they are to belong to a particular range of cases. Frege speaks of recognizing such belonging: *here* is a case of being (one way to be) thus and so. German marks two notions of recognition: *erkennen* and *anerkennen*. On the first notion, one registers how things anyway are. On the second, one accepts, or accredits, something as something, lends one's authority to its so being. In the citation Frege speaks of *Erkennung*—the first notion. But belonging, above, is a normative notion. So there is sense to be made of the second as well in the present context.

To you Sid is a great striker. I agree he has moments, but would not call him great. One of us may be demonstrably wrong. You cannot, perhaps, score *that* many own goals and be called great. But perhaps not. There is room to be impressed differently by a given style of play. Sid is what you call great, not what I do. You recognize him as first class; I do not. That is recognition in something like the sense of *Anerkennung*. If one of us were demonstrably wrong, there would be no room for it. Insisting that Sid is a great striker if he could not score on an empty pitch is a bit much. But if it is all a matter of what style of play impresses you—what you think proper football should be like—then there is such room. When it comes to the greatness of a striker, there are two ways one might reasonably think.

Handing you a packet from the butcher's I say, 'Here's the meat I bought for dinner'. You open it and find the kidneys. 'I don't call that meat', you say. 'Meat, for me, is muscle'. 'Well, I do', I say helpfully. Again one of us may be demonstrably wrong. Lamb's kidneys are no more meat than wool is, to one who knows what meat is. But perhaps not. In fact, there are various understandings one might have of being meat, consistent with what being meat is as such. In that sense, being meat admits of understandings. We sometimes distinguish (such as in good markets) between meat and offal. Then if the kidneys wound up in the meat section they are in the wrong place. On the other hand, one would not (usually) serve kidneys to a vegetarian with the remark, 'I made sure there would be no meat at dinner'. Similarly, brains or spinal column, however delicious fried, gristle, however tasty stewed, would count as meat on some occasions for so counting, but not on others. There are various ways being meat *admits of* being thought of.

The point so far: if for things to be thus and so is for them to *belong* to a certain range of cases, there may be two or more (sometimes) reasonable ways of sorting cases into those which do belong and those which do not, with different results for things as they are. Implicit in the making of that point is this: where a notion admits of understandings, as that of being meat does, a particular occasion for deploying it may impose some given one. Where we are planning a vegetarian meal, kidneys are likely to count as meat on the understanding on which we would then speak of (something) being meat. In the market you may just misunderstand the sign if you look on the meat counter for offal. Conversely, where you have promised to spare me Pia's ubiquitous tofu, I will be thankful indeed for the stewed gristle, will consider your promise kept. If, perchance, I am ungrateful, issues of *Anerkennung* again arise: 'For the purpose, this ought to count as meat'. 'No', I reply, removing the steak from my inner pocket, '*This* is what ought to count'.

Where a notion admits of understandings, and, as above, would bear different ones on different occasions for deploying it, I will say that it is *occasion-sensitive*.

How might occasion-sensitivity matter? For one thing, to this question: Does the world—the *way* things are—articulate absolutely into one particular range of *ways* things are? Or again, does things being as they are partition all the ways there are for things to be into those ways things in fact are and all the others?

Compare: Does colour articulate absolutely into some one range of colours: *the* colours? In a sense not. There are various possibilities for dividing up colour space. But none *excludes* any other. Let shmurple be a colour that (only) some shades of purple, and some shades of blue, are. Then something may both be blue and be shmurple.

But I mean something else here by 'absolutely'. There are things (such as those kidneys) which, in things being as they are, are meat on some ways of thinking of being meat, but not on others. If we do count them as meat, then, so thinking, one of the ways things are in being as they are is: there is meat on the rug. If we do not, then this is *not* among the ways things are. Neither way of factoring the way things are into ways things are is right *tout court*, though either may be right on some occasions for the factoring. Nor is there any occasion on which it counts as so that there is meat on the rug, and (moreover) there is not. ('There is and there isn't' normally says something else entirely.) In that sense, the way things are factors differently (and in mutually incompatible ways) into *ways* things are on different occasions for the factoring.

Donald Davidson has taken Hilary Putnam to task:

> My form of realism...is not internal realism because internal realism makes truth relative to a scheme, and this is an idea I do not think is intelligible. A major reason, in fact, for accepting a coherence theory is the unintelligibility of the dualism of a conceptual scheme and a 'world' waiting to be coped with.
>
> (1986: 309)

Putnam now rejects 'internal realism'. But explicitly not all of its elements. (See his 1993.) Specifically *not* the present idea: that there are competing, mutually exclusive, *correct* ways of dividing things up into ways things are. The history of science, I think, led Putnam to that view. Mundane considerations show it correct. This is the idea that makes no sense to Davidson. Such different articulations would, for him, deploy (or be) different conceptual schemes, each capturing a way things were anyway, independent of either. That would be Davidson's 'dualism of scheme and content'. And he cannot see what that might come to.

But we only need Frege to show us what this might be. Conceptual schemes (of course) belong to the conceptual. What they capture—what falls under, or fits, them—belongs to the non-conceptual. If they are adequate, what they are adequate to is things being as they are, which *admits* of being articulated in the way they call for. The idea of occasion-sensitivity exploits Frege's insight in one way it admits of. I have suggested that the insight, and with it a dualism of scheme and content, is a good idea, without which we can make no real sense of thought. It just comes with the dualism of the left and the right of Frege's line. McDowell subscribes to Davidson's rejection of such dualisms. Perhaps it is this which makes his response to the skeleton too late.

5 Seeing That

Where one sees the meat, what one is thus aware *of* is the meat. Where one sees that there is meat on the rug, what one is *thus* aware of is its being so that there is meat on the rug (or there being meat on the rug). So if we parse 'see that there is meat on the rug' into 'see' and 'that there is meat on the rug', then the object of the verb is not the object of awareness, as it is in 'see the meat'. (We speak of being aware of the fact that such-and-such, but then not of seeing the fact that such-and-such. 'See' in such a construction would call for an object that the fact that such-and-such could not be—something, like the roast, to the left of Frege's line.) What is grammar trying to tell us here?

For one thing, this. The meat is *in* the surroundings. To see it, look where it is. Look there, too, to see the condition it is in. You can watch the meat— watch it change (in condition or position), watch *for* changes. To see that the meat is on the rug, you *might* look where the *meat* is. You might also look elsewhere—in Pia's face, say (the horrified look). You cannot look 'where that the meat is on the rug is'. There is no such place. You cannot *watch* that the meat is on the rug, nor watch for, nor see, changes in it. It is not eligible for such changes. (You can watch only what you can look for changes in.) Vision affords sensitivity to the goings on in one's surroundings, and to what undergoes them. What one is *thus* sensitive to is not that such-and-such is so. One's visual sensitivity to what is going on may gain one sensitivity to things being thus and so. Such depends on your sensitivities to things before you being, or not, particular ways they may be. (What sensitivities, and how it so depends, remain to be explored.) This was Frege's point in disallowing *that the meat is on the rug* as an object of visual awareness.

Wittgenstein describes thinking otherwise:

The idea of a general concept being a common property of its particular instances connects up with other primitive, too simple, ideas of the structure of language. It is comparable to the idea that *properties* are *ingredients* of the things which have the properties; e.g., that beauty is an ingredient of all beautiful things as alcohol is of beer and wine...

(1958: 17)

Alcohol, if in fact odourless, *might* smell. One can feel it in the nose, or in the gut, or see it burning blue, or evaporating, or freezing. It is the sort of thing one might watch, or perceptually keep track of. Along with the meat (or the wine) it is *in* our surroundings, what we may recognize to instance generalities. To think of properties on the model of alcohol in wine would be to take being alcoholic (or that wine was) for alcohol. One could see being alcoholic, or that wine was, where seeing was occasion for watching, keeping track of, what was seen. There is a red glow in the sky just after sunset. *It* is not the property of being coloured red, nor that something is so coloured. One can watch it fade, as those other things cannot.

If one conflated properties with ingredients, it would be pointless to insist that for something to be red is for it to fit within a certain range of cases. One could say so. But an item's so fitting would be observable, something one saw before him, just as its red colouration is. There would be nothing normative about it. Seeing it would not be a matter of grasping what belongs where (with what range of cases), or when to say that something was a case of something—just as one sees a peccary if it is, in fact, a peccary before him, independent of any grasp of when it would be a *peccary* that was there. This erases Frege's line. That the sky is red now has all the features of what falls on either side of it. Which erases the need for rational relations between the conceptual and the non-conceptual. That things are thus and so is now both (perhaps visibly) *in* the surroundings, literally before us, and part of how they are. Nothing *else*, not in the surroundings—no range of cases, no requirement—need bear on whether things are a given way, or be part of their so being. But what allows this is patent nonsense. Wittgenstein was not concerned with this solecism as such. His interest, in the *Blue Book*, was in a sense in which *our* concepts leave it open what their proper applications would be—what ought to count as fitting them. His point was: the *same* way things were might be counted as fitting a certain concept—as things being thus and so—or as not, for all the concept dictated as such. It might so count on some occasions for, or ways of, applying the concept, but not on others. His concern, thus, was with occasion-sensitivity.

But occasion-sensitivity just is the idea that things being as they are—something to the left of Frege's line—might be taken to bear in different ways on whether things were thus and so—for each way, *correctly* so taken on some occasion for the taking. Things to the left must bear on—stand in rational relations to—*distinct* things on the right. It needs Frege's distinction. Erasing that distinction, as above, erases room for occasion-sensitivity; for the idea that the same thing may sometimes count, and sometimes not, as things being thus and so.

How, then, does occasion-sensitivity bear on seeing that? In the salon, plainly visible, on the white rug, is the raw meat. Pia enters. What is there for her to see? For one thing, that meat. That would be a right answer on any occasion for giving one. It is a relative fixed point across occasions for answering that question. I referred to the meat in speaking of it as meat. There is no guarantee that one could always do that across all such occasions. If I am speaking now of kidneys, then there are occasions on which one could do that and ones on which one could not. But one could always speak of *it*. Across a *very* broad range of occasions, what one thus spoke of would count as something there to be seen in that scene.

Suppose we decided to restrict rational relations to the conceptual. Then, for one to see what bore on what he was to think, he would have to see things that belonged to the conceptual. So there would have to be such things to be seen; things which became visible to one, say, on entering the salon and looking at the rug. One would see these things on a different notion of seeing than the one on which one sees a piece of meat. One might, for example, see that the meat was on the rug. What one thus saw would not be literally *in* the surroundings. It could not have a location. But (in the present case, at least) we might settle for the fact that it becomes visible (to one suitably qualified to see it) when he looks where the meat is. (It is an accident of the example that this one place seems privileged as it does. To see that Sid has left the room one *might* look at the room, or equally at Sid, outside it. Either might work if, or only if, one knew to make the right thing of what one thus saw.)

Occasion-sensitivity makes for a contrast here between that there is meat on the rug and the meat. Suppose we ask the question just asked for seeing on the notion on which Pia saw the meat. *What* of the conceptual is visible in the scene in the salon? A prior question: what of it is *present* in things being as they (there) are? Here we lose the stability there was for what is present, and visible, of the non-conceptual. That that meat is present is relatively insensitive to occasions for saying so; that it (or some facing part) is visible roughly equally so. Not so with such things as *that there is meat on the rug*. For what is on the rug is liable to count as meat on some understandings of being meat, but not on others (for example, if it is kidneys). In which case it will sometimes count as so, and sometimes not, that there is meat on the rug. It will so count on, but only on, occasions where, in speaking of meat one speaks on a suitable understanding of being it. So it will inevitably be for the scene's relation to at least many bits of the conceptual. So what would be, on some occasions, a true, if only partial, answer to the question 'What is there to see?', 'see' taking as objects conceptual items, would, on other occasions, be not so much as true. Which conceptual items are so much as part of the scene being as it is varies with occasions for saying which. There is not in this case such a thing as 'that which is to be seen', where what this is remains stable across occasions as what is to be seen of the non-conceptual (such as the meat) remains stable across occasions. What is to be seen *of the conceptual*, in viewing a scene, is not what is to be seen simply in the scene being as it is.

Here we run up against the difference in grammar between the two sides of Frege's line. Occasion-sensitivity belongs to the conceptual. It concerns the leeway there is *intrinsically* in sorting cases under rubrics. For any way there *is* for things to be, things being as they are *may*, in point of grammar, count as that way on some understandings of so being, and as not that way on others. It is just bad grammar to speak of the meat, as it is on an occasion, as counting as it thus is on some, but not other, understandings of it so being. Its being in the condition it is does not (so far) call for understandings. They are not to the point. (Again, it might be *that* meat in any of many further conditions. What it would be for something to be *that* does call for understandings. (Is it *that* meat as mince?))

The scene in view articulates (so good as) absolutely into items literally in it. It may thus articulate in many ways; but where one way does not exclude another (as being shmurple does not exclude being purple). The scene does not thus articulate (even nearly) absolutely into ways things were in being as they were in it. Not just that there are many such articulations. Whether something *is* an articulation—which is to say, *which* ways for things to be things are in that scene—has no right answer independent of an occasion for asking.

How does the stability which thus goes missing matter? Pia enters the salon and sees what she does. What she sees in fact bears on what it would be right to think, both in ways she appreciates and in ways she does not. Insofar as she does appreciate how it bears, it bears on what she is to think. So, for example, if she knows meat on a rug when she sees it, then what she sees bears on what she is to think as to whether there is meat on the rug. How her experience thus bears on what she is to think does not seem to vary with occasions for saying how it bears, or at least not in the way it would vary if how it bore depended on whether or not she saw that there was meat on the rug. The bearing remains (relatively) stable across occasions for describing it. I mean by this that it remains constant across occasions which vary, the one from the other, in what there was in the scene, by way of the conceptual, that might be seen—which vary, for example, as to whether that there was meat on the rug was part of how things were, thus part of what someone might see. But if the bearing is indifferent to that kind of variation, then for there to have been the bearing there was cannot be just for it to have been visible that P, that Q, and so on, for fixed substitutes for those place-holders. It cannot be for there to have been such-and-such things to be seen, or that Pia did in fact see, where those things are that things are such-and-such way, or things being some such way. This can be right neither for the bearing there in fact was on what it would be right for one to think, nor for the bearing there was for Pia, present in her experience, on what she was to think. For her experience to have made the world bear on what she was to think as it did cannot be for her to relate, either in seeing them, or in any other way, to such-andsuch conceptual items so conceived.

Might the wanted stability be found while reason reaches no farther than the conceptual? Pia, entering the salon, sees what she does as to how things are there. She appreciates what she does as to how what she thus sees bears on what to think. If one spoke on a suitable understanding of meat being on the rug, one could, perhaps, capture some of this in saying her to see that there is meat on the rug. One could, for one thing, if she were sufficiently sensitive to how things being as they are bore on whether there was meat there; on how it could be right, or wrong, to say so, given things as they were. So far as her appreciation so extends, thus far does what she sees as to how thing are in fact bear on what she is to think (and will). If rational relations start with the conceptual, perhaps her seeing what she did of how things were was her seeing things to be a certain way (such-and-such way), where that belongs the conceptual. What way? On different occasions there will be different ways of naming it. What names it on one may not do so on another. Perhaps nothing names it full stop. Sometimes one might name it in mentioning *being meat*, and *being on a rug*. Sometimes one may need to mention (say) *being edible animal parts* in place of *being meat*. And so on. *Being meat*, for example, works when, but only when, one speaks on the right understanding of things so being. The posited way for things to be which so relates to names for it, we hope, will be stably present in the way things are (in the scene Pia views) in just the way the meat is.

If the scene in view does bear stably on what it would be true to think (that there is meat on the rug on the understandings on which there is, that there is not on the understandings on which there is not, and so on), and if it bears as stably as it does on what Pia is to think, occasion-sensitivity calls for a story on these lines. To what does it commit us? On it, the scene came to bear on what Pia was to think in her seeing it to be a certain way. One might ask: What would name it when? When, for example, would one name it in speaking of meat as being on the rug? When one spoke on a suitable understanding of meat being on a rug. Different understandings of meat being on a rug are different understandings as to how particular cases of things to the left of Frege's line sort into those belonging to that range of cases and those not. An understanding would be *suitable* where the cases which count as meat being on a rug on that understanding are those which would instance the generality of that supposed occasion-invariant way Pia saw things to be. Which would be just when things being as they *thus* were (in that particular case) would bear on what Pia was to think in just the way she saw things being as they were (in the scene before her) to bear on what she was to think. With these observations we see that to answer the question which arise on the present story we need to recognize rational relations between things to the left and things to the right of Frege's line. For answers rest on the facts as to when particular cases of things being as they are *are rightly taken* to instance this or that generality (for example, that of meat being on a rug), and on what Pia can recognize about this. In which case the story has failed of its purpose—if that purpose was to confine rational relations to the realm of the conceptual.

In which case we do not need the story. Pia seeing what she did as to how things were need not be her seeing things to be such-and-such way. We may simply think of her experience as follows. Pia saw what she did of things being as they were, in the scene before her; thus saw what she did as to how they were (notably, though possibly not only, how the scene before her was). She was thus enabled to recognize the instancing of an indefinite variety of bits of the conceptual, within the limits of her grasp of what instancing them requires; and to treat the world accordingly within the limits of her appreciation of what difference it would then make that such-and-such generality was instanced. What she saw of how things were need no more (nor less) be that there was meat on the rug than that there were edible animal parts there—even though for things to be the one way is not in general for them, *ipso facto*, to be the other. There need be no particular repertoire of conceptual items which, in the scene's being as it was, just were those present and (all going right) visible—not even an infinite repertoire—nor any such repertoire which just were, as such, the ones Pia saw. A grasp of what meat being on a rug is, for thinkers like us, includes, as a rule, an ability to see how various particular cases might, or might not, count as that. If Pia has such a grasp, then she will be sensitive to the various understandings on which one might speak of meat being on a rug, thus to those on which that is how things were (when occasion for having those understandings arises). But that there was meat on the rug is not (independent of some particular such understanding) either a way she saw things to be, or not one. Nor need there be any other way for things to be—for example, one tied to no particular name for it—which does play that role in the shaping of her thought by her experience of that scene.

Pia, like most of us, can adjust her way of saying what she saw to fit the occasion for saying it, so that, in the words she chooses, she will say the right thing. She may speak of meat as on a rug, when so doing would be saying the right thing. When it would not, then, seeing that, she can speak of something else—say, edible animal parts. What she saw is no more what she speaks of in some one such way than what she speaks of in another. Her experience is no more of any one such structuring of concepts than of any other.

How *can* she thus fit what she says to her audience, always saying what, in fact, she saw? One answer might be: for each two such different ways of (sometimes) saying what she saw, there are two different things she in fact saw *tout court*; two different items visible in viewing the scene, each seen, and registered, independent of the other. Another would be that some one thing which is what she *really* saw—that things were *F*; where speaking of being F is at most sometimes, perhaps never, a way of *saying* what she saw. She translates from talk of F to other renderings (for example, that there was meat), each adequate to its occasion, conforming to the (supposed) correct canons of saying the same.

Neither of these views is plausible—especially if, for the second answer, canons of correct translation (of the sort envisioned) must refer only to relations which hold between different bits of the conceptual *as such*, and not to any rational relations between what belongs to the conceptual and what does not. No relation that holds *per se* between being meat and being an edible animal part makes speaking of the one a good way of saying what one says in speaking of the other. What *may* make for this is a relation that holds between speaking of one *on one occasion* and speaking of the other on another which holds by virtue of what would count, on each occasion, as instancing the generality thus spoken of. There is no escaping reason reaching beyond the scope of the conceptual. Without our seeing how it thus reaches, experience could not rationally shape our thought.

If the non-conceptual lies without the reach of reason, we are not entitled to the idea of occasion-sensitivity. For it cannot then be that instances—items to the left of Frege's line—are *rightly* placed in ranges differently, on different occasions and for different purposes; that they in fact *belong* where they are thus placed. We must then conceive seeing what is before you as visually confronting some given battery of conceptual structures, in the present sense of that term. To see that such-and-such is to see some one of these; which, in turn, is to make it out for what it is. One confronts these things not in being literally before them (or *vice versa*); but in *some* other way they are available as objects of sight. To see what one does of how things are is thus to see *that* they are such-and-such ways. Conversely, with the idea of occasion-sensitivity in play we may conceive seeing that as seeing what is literally in view (the non-conceptual) and grasping some of its bearing on the conceptual. Crediting someone with seeing *that* such-and-such would then be part of a particular way of articulating his visual awareness of how things were into awareness of particular aspects of their so being—just as saying that things are thus and so is part of a particular way of articulating the *way* they are into *ways* they are.

6 Givens

Is the 'Myth of the Given' a myth? *Not* if the Given is nothing but the non-conceptual—such familiar bits of our surroundings as a roast and a rug. But for sure if it is certain other things it is sometimes said to be. It is then a quite familiar myth.

McDowell says this about it:

> The idea of the Given is the idea that the space of reasons, the space of justifications, or warrants, extends more widely than the conceptual sphere... The extra extent of the space of reasons is supposed to allow it to incorporate non-conceptual impacts from outside the realm of thought. But we cannot really understand the relations in virtue of which a judgement is warranted except as relations within the space of concepts: relations such as implications or probabilification, which hold between potential exercises of conceptual capacities. The attempt to extend the scope of justificatory relations outside the conceptual sphere cannot do what it is supposed to do.
>
> (1996: 7)

> We must not picture an outer boundary around the sphere of the conceptual, with a reality outside the boundary impinging inward on the system. Any impingements across such an outer boundary could only be causal, and not rational; that is Davidson's perfectly correct point...
>
> (1996: 34)

> According to the Myth of the Given, the obligation to be responsibly alive to the dictates of reason lapses when we come to the ultimate points of contact between thinking and reality; the Given is a brute effect of the world, not something justified by it.
>
> (1996: 42)

The Given as first portrayed (1996: 7) need only be the non-conceptual. We have seen how reason reaches that far. McDowell tells us that we cannot conceive of relevant rational relations—such things as warranting or making correct—except as between what belongs to the conceptual. As we have seen, this is simply not so. In the second passage McDowell endorses Davidson's view that the non-conceptual, since it could not stand in a rational relation to anything, must only bear causally on what we in fact happen to think. The last passage (1996: 42) again depends on the claim that the non-conceptual cannot stand in rational relations to things. If not, then in dealing with *it* obligation to be rational (alive to the dictates of reason) trivially lapses: there are no such dictates. But if so, there is no lapse, nor cause to think there is.

So innocuous becomes myth on an assumption: reason is confined to the conceptual. Why make it? One *could* be led to it in misunderstanding Frege's idea that laws of logic unfold the concept truth. (1918: 59) Laws of logic of course concern *thoughts* and their relations. As Frege saw them, they reflect the most general structure of any system of thoughts. Nor could one think *counter* to them. There is no *such* exemption. It is not as if they touch on only *some* thoughts. If they were the full unfolding of the concept truth, questions of truth could arise only for what they governed. So, too, for rational relations.

But there is another half to Frege's story. Judging is exposure to error (so, too, correctness) decidable *solely* by things being as they are. For Frege, laws of logic arise out of this feature of that rather special attitude, and, correspondingly, apply precisely to it. For a given judging, things being as they are may *be* their being as judged, or, again, their being otherwise. When they would be which must be decided by the particular nature of the judgement—the particular way in which, in so judging, one exposes oneself to error. But what matters here is that such things *are* (sometimes) decided. It can be, and sometimes is, that things being as they are *settles* that a given judgement is correct (or, again, incorrect). It can be that this would remain (or cease to be) so if such-and-such changes were worked on how things are. Where there were no such facts there would simply be no judgement. There is a determinate way in which things being as they are thus matters to a judgement's truth. That truth *can* depend on how things are in that way—in the way how things are settles whether there is meat on the rug, for example—is also part of the unfolding of the concept truth: of what it is and may be. Yet it is not laws of logic which settle that, or when, this is so. Nor do they touch on the relevant relata. Things being such as to make it true to say that there is meat on the rug is *not* a relation between one conceptual item and another—though, of course, if they are such, then it is so that there is meat on the rug. This is just, once again, the lesson of Frege's line.

So reason's reach is not the same as logic's reach; and could not be if logic is to have any reach at all. The assumption crucial to the idea of a *myth* is not *so* justified. Something *else* in Davidson makes for an entirely different myth. Davidson excludes *perception* entirely from his picture. The Given, conceived merely as the non-conceptual, is such things as roasts and rugs. By contrast, The Given in Davidson's picture could not be something we *perceived*—saw, heard, and so on. (As Frege noted, it would be something one *had*.) A roast could not be a bit of it. If there are any roasts, they are *visible* items, what *one* would see by looking in the right place. Here is Davidson on what our senses deliver:

> We have been trying to see it this way: a person has all his beliefs about the world... How can he tell if they are true...? Only, we have been assuming, by connecting certain of his beliefs with the deliverances of the senses one by one, or perhaps confronting the totality of his beliefs with the tribunal of experience. No such confrontation makes sense, for of course we can't get outside our skins to find out what is causing the internal happenings of which we are aware.
>
> (1984: 312)

So the objects of sensory awareness—the deliverances of our senses—become *internal happenings*—in the best case sensations, but not (like a muscle cramping) what one might *perceive*. It is internal happenings, so conceived, which he holds cannot stand in logical relations—which, succumbing to the confusion just scouted, he equates with standing in *rational* relations.

> The relation between a sensation and a belief cannot be logical, since sensations are not beliefs or other propositional attitudes. What then is the relation? The answer is, I think, obvious: the relation is causal.
>
> (1984: 311)

I bracket the question whether a sensation could bear rationally on *anything*, since that lies outside present concerns. Anyway, having a sensation as of falling over backwards, or as of being bloated, is not yet feeling oneself falling over or being bloated, even if one also feels sensations. Feeling oneself falling over is enjoying awareness of a going on in one's surroundings—of one's body moving floorwards. Feeling (having) a sensation as of falling over is feeling nothing but the sensation. A sensation is not *of* the objects, or events, around one. My body's moving bears on what is so of my surroundings as a sensation could not.

Perception just *is* of one's surroundings; of what is in them, of how they are. Of, for example, the meat perching on the plinth. Which bears on whether there is meat perching on the plinth. Sensation is not of one's surroundings; not of what stands to there being meat on the plinth as the meat on the plinth does. If the senses delivered only sensations, and not perception, they would supply no awareness of that in our surroundings which bears on what to think of them. If the Given were what was thus delivered, it would be a myth that *that* was *any* grounding for our beliefs about the world.

McDowell accuses Quine, correctly, of leaving no room in his official view of experience for us to experience what bears on what to think, or even for us to respond to experience with so much as a *belief* 'about the empirical world—something correctly or incorrectly adopted according to how things are' there (1996: 138–9). He adds, 'The point does not turn on the detail of Quine's conception of experience, as stimulation of sensory surfaces. There can be less resolutely anti-mentalistic conceptions of experience that nevertheless match Quine's conception at a more abstract level, in that they take experiences to be deliverances of receptivity, (McDowell 1996, footnote p. 138).

Conceiving experiences as 'deliverances of receptivity', as that idea is meant here, would be conceiving them as *of* what lay 'outside the bounds of the conceptual'. That would leave no room for experience to bear on what one is to think, so no room for belief at all—*if*, but only if, the conceptual were co-extensive with reason's reach. But, we have seen, it is not. Which makes 'stimulation of sensory surfaces' more central to the predicament. The root of Quine's problem is that his official view abolishes *perception*. On it, *any* experience is compatible with the truth or falsity of any proposition. (See my 2004) 'Stimulations', or 'irritations', *might* preserve that idea. Ideas (*Vorstellungen*), as explained by Frege (1918: 67–8) would. Just Frege's point (see Essay 2). It is another matter if what Pia experiences is meat on the rug. Such an experience is incompatible with the truth of the proposition that there is no meat on the rug. One can recognize this of the experience, in having it, in seeing the bearing of something outside the conceptual—the meat, as it is—on something there is to think—that there is meat on the rug. The point holds more generally if there are things *in* the environment which we sometimes *perceive*. *That* is the right answer to Davidson's claim that experience, 'understood as what receptivity provides us' is *eo ipso* removed from the space of reasons.

If we do not so much as experience our surroundings, then thoughts about what we do experience (if such thoughts there be) are not thoughts about our surroundings. Nor could our experience reveal how those surroundings were. All that is orthogonal to the question whether there are rational relations between the non-conceptual and the conceptual. I have argued that reason reaches, and had better reach, that far.[1]

---

[1] The person I am far and away the most indebted to in this essay is John McDowell. He has been incredibly generous with his time, and has shown infinite patience trying to get me to see what it is that matters. We have spent many hours in discussion, over an extended period of time. The result, of course, is my responsibility. I am also very thankful to Guy Longworth, Dawn Phillips, and M. G. F. Martin.

5

The Inward Turn

> Philosophers constantly see the method of science before their eyes, and are irresistibly tempted to ask and answer questions in the way science does. This tendency is the real source of metaphysics, and leads the philosopher into complete darkness.
>
> Wittgenstein, The Blue Book (1958: 18)

Seeing is, or affords, a certain sort of awareness—visual—of one's surroundings. The obvious strategy for saying *what* one sees, or what would *count* as seeing something would be to ask what sort of sensitivity to one's *surroundings*—such as the *pig* before me—would so qualify. Alas, for more than three centuries—*at least* from Descartes to VE day—it was not so. Philosophers were moved by arguments, rarely stated, which concluded that one could not, or never did, see what was before his eyes. So much for the obvious strategy. It occurred to almost no-one to object that this *could* not be right. Frege did, but no-one noticed. Austin, finally, did away with that conception of good faith in philosophy which had allowed such a thing to pass, and then with those arguments themselves. Until then, philosophy was deformed. Robbed of the obvious approach, a *Drang* set in to gaze inward, hoping to find what it *really* is to see in what *enabled* sensitivity to pigs, or in its byproducts. Gazing inward *can* be science, but often merely poses as it. It can be difficult to disentangle actual science (or at least empirical fact) from mere preconception pretending to its rigour. Most nowadays *feel* rid of the grip of those barriers to the obvious approach. But, as we shall see, many so feel wrongly. The *Drang* still misshapes their thought. I aim here to identify the *Drang* at work; thereby, I hope, to rid us of it.

1 Seeing

One sees, one would have thought, such things as mangoes, sloths, the setting sun, the sun setting, the blackened condition of the toast. An account which said otherwise would, one would have thought, thereby be shown mistaken. As noted, for more than three centuries the nearly universal, and unquestioned, view was: 'Not so'. What one *really* saw, it was supposed without a blush, were, in Frege's terms (pointing to the solecism here) *contents of one's consciousness*: objects of awareness such that, first, there is someone one would need to be to be aware of them, and, second, their career as something *to* be aware of was coeval with that person's awareness of them. (See Frege 1918, 67) One saw things in one's surroundings, if at all, only insofar as seeing these other things might pass for seeing that.

H. A. Prichard—an otherwise admirable philosopher—exemplifies the frame of mind. He begins a pre-war essay, 'Perception', by admitting that in the 'everyday attitude of mind' of philosophers and others, one counts 'chairs and tables, boats going downstream, and so forth' as the sorts of things one sees and touches (1950: 52), then commenting,

It need hardly be said that this view, much as we should all like to be able to vindicate it, will not stand examination.

(1950: 53)

It will not stand examination because of a principle which Prichard expresses in the following ways:

If we really see a body...as...from a certain point in space...it must present the appearance to us which any body of the kind in question seen as from this point must present.

(1950: 53)

A body, if it be really seen and seen along with other bodies, can only present to us just that appearance which its relations to the other bodies really requires.

(1950: 53)

This raises the question...how if we see a body it can...look other than what it is, and if we press this question home to ourselves we can only answer, as before, that it cannot.

(1950: 54)

Given the principle, the idea that we see such things as boats, or walls, is refuted by such ordinary facts as that the moon (roughly spherical) sometimes looks flat, or that if you look at a wall in a mirror, left and right reverse.

Many of us have, at one time or another, failed to see a wall (in time). But, one might think, if a principle entails that one can *never* see a wall, then, in point of good faith, it is, *ceteris paribus*, false. Prichard offers a reason for thinking otherwise. He reminds us that we are 'concerned simply with the nature of what we see in the proper "mental" sense of see' and not 'with what we see in the physical sense of what affects our eyes' (1950: 53). So our idea that we see such things as sloths and walls comes from our thinking of some 'physical sense' of 'see', whereas Prichard, and any philosopher of perception, means to speak of another. It is not clear what either of these senses is; nor even that there *are* different senses of 'see'.

All the same, Prichard's talk of physical and mental seeing is suggestive. No-one, I think, thinks there is *any* sense of 'see' in which merely to have something 'affect your eyes'—say, form retinal images—is to see it. Why not? A natural, though not inevitable, idea is: before one saw anything, more stuff would have to happen. (Not inevitable: to have images on one's retinas would not be to see something whether or not more stuff needed to happen.) A further natural idea might then be: at a certain point the relevant stuff, or enough of it, *has* happened. At that point, the perceiver goes into a certain 'internal' state, the upshot of the stuff, where this is one of a specified range of states into which a particular device, 'that which enables vision', might go. In such a state, the idea is, one enjoys visual awareness (or experience). One sees only in enjoying visual awareness. The state decides *what* visually awareness one thus enjoys; thus, at least, what it is in which one might be seeing something.

The nature of the state is to be fixed (causally) by that of which it is an upshot. Any retinal state might unleash any of various sequences of stuff happening. Retinal states thus underdetermine what such internal state one arrives in. So, accordingly, for whatever one has in view; whatever formed images on one's retinas. Viewing *that* might place one in any of various internal states, each differing from the others in what one is thereby visually aware of. Conversely, for any such terminal internal state one, what was actually in view before one might be any of many things—*perhaps* even nothing.

A crucial idea here is that such an internal state furnishes all the visual awareness one enjoys. It thereby furnishes *an* answer to the question just what one is then visually aware *of*. So, for one to be in it is for there to be a determinate way one experiences things being (or seeming) visually. For there to be a *determinate way*, as this is usually understood, is for such-and-such to be the way; thus for one to experience things being, or seeming, visually (arranged) thus and so. *Perhaps* being visually aware of what it thus decides you are, while, in fact, viewing given things—say, a pig—is what it *is* to see (so be visually aware of) something in one's surroundings—say, the pig. If so, then *that* much as to what one is visually aware of, the internal state would *not* determine. Modulo that possibility, the internal state you are in at the time answers the question of what you are then visually aware of.

I will call the whole of the above the *SH model* ('SH' for 'stuff happens'.) The mere idea that we are enabled to see by some identifiable states, the products of happenings unleashed by retinal images, *may* be science, or something it presupposes. The rest is not. It is a *picture* of what awareness must be. I will next begin to trace the current career of the SH model. I hope to show a few reasons why that picture will not suffice.

2 Perceptual Experience

Gareth Evans is concerned with visual experience, a wider notion than seeing; still more widely, with perceptual experience in general. He writes: 'In general we may regard a perceptual experience as an informational state of the subject...' (1982: 226)—as he insists repeatedly, an *internal* state. Such is an odd start. An experience, where one can speak of one, is, one would have thought, an *episode*, in which one experiences something or other there *is* to experience—in the case of *perceptual* experience, typically, though perhaps not always, something impinging from without—the warm summer breezes, perhaps, the patterns of sunlight on the wall. To regard all that as an *internal* state is, for one thing, to leave *what* is experienced out of the picture altogether. Such an internal state—the terminus of that stuff which in fact happened—might be what it is while what it is that was experienced was any of many things, and *vice versa*. *If* experience is to be an internal state, the SH model provides ones for this to be. Could Evans' talk of experiences as states of a subject be symptomatic (or more) of allegiance to that model?

The informational states in question are not themselves objects of their owner's perceptual awareness. In experiencing, say, the barnyard, I am (visually) aware of that pig in the sty, not of any *internal* state of mine. But, Evans tells us, I *can* be aware of features of such a state, specifically of the information it contains. For experiencing the barnyard *is* experiencing being in the state: being in it, I experience. One can, Evans tells us, exploit this way of experiencing the state 'by reusing precisely those skills of conceptualization that he uses to make judgements about the world' (1982: 227).

He goes through exactly the same procedure as he would go through if he were trying to make a judgement about how it is at this place now, but excluding any knowledge he has of an extraneous kind. (That is, he seeks to determine what he would judge if he did not have such extraneous information.) The result will necessarily be closely correlated with the content of the informational state which he is in at that time. Now he may prefix this result with the operator 'It seems to me as though...'

So, for example, it seems to me as though that pig is spotted; *ceteris paribus* the relevant state contains the information that that pig is spotted. I thus *can* be aware of the state containing information it does. *Just* so, for Evans, can perception perform its most central task in a *thinker's* life: allowing how things are to bear, according to their bearing, on how to *think* they are; thereby on how to act.

A state which *thus* contains information is also liable to contain *mis*information. It may seem to me as though that pig is spotted when it is not. (Just the shadows of the branches of that spreading chestnut.) One *could* appropriate 'information' to include that. It will avoid confusion not to. Information, here, will be as to what is *so*.

But there are two uses of 'seems'. On one it seems as though Sid did it if, based on how we see things are, such is most probable. On the other, that pig, standing under those branches, in the filtered sunlight, looks as though it were spotted. It looks (just, or rather) like a spotted pig. It may so look even if we *know* it is just the light and shadow. It would be a further claim that it does not just *seem* that way, but seems to *be* so.

These two readings of 'seem' point to two different ways for something to contain information. The scene before me may, in the first way, contain the information that there is a *bísaro* before me: it makes this recognizable (to one who knows his *bísaros*). It may contain the information that *this* pig has swine flu: a decent veterinarian could tell that at sight. That road sign contains information in the second way. It contains the information that Santiago is 48 km hence: it says so. The information contained in this second way consists of just those things which what contains it represents, truly, as *so*.

The scene before me, in being as it is, instances literally countless ways there are for a scene, and thus countless ways for *things*, to be. It is *recognizably* countless such ways. So any scene contains indefinitely much information in the first way. Which is not a way of containing *mis*information: information contained in this way is available through the exercise of *recognition* capacities; a capacity being, *per se*, one to get things *right*. Thus it is that scenes—signposts and billboards aside—are not liable to contain misinformation. If there is something in perceptual experience that *is* so liable, it will have to be something other than the scene in view, or its inhabitants, again signposts and the like aside. There will have to be something about *it*, not present in a scene, which allows it to do so.

By contrast, the second way of containing information is by *representing* something as so. The signpost contains just that information (misinformation) which it represents truly (falsely) to be so. That something was represented as so never means as such that it *is* so. There is always that much room for representing falsely. So this second way of containing information is a way of containing misinformation.

Frege shows why, if perception is going to make the world bear, for us, on what to think, then it had better do so in affording us awareness of what contains information in the first of these two ways. It had better afford opportunity for exercising, on what we are thus aware of, capacities for *thus* extracting information. For, to begin with,

The fundamental logical relation is that of an object falling under a concept: all relations between concepts reduce to this.

(1892–1895: 25)

In Frege's working of the point, concepts are satisfied, or not, by objects—items not themselves eligible for being satisfied, or not, by anything. A given concept 'reaches to' a range of objects which are those things which satisfy it (and identifies a range which are those things which do not). Relations purely between some concepts and others cannot *on their own* tell us to what range of cases a given concept reaches (though, given to which ranges certain concepts reach, relations internal to the domain of concepts might tell us to what some further one reaches). To grasp a concept is to grasp both how it relates to other concepts, and—a different matter—how it relates to what are *not* concepts—in Frege's working of the point, to objects: what satisfy, but are not, themselves, satisfied. One must be able to tell, of *such* things, when they would be such as to satisfy the concept. Such capacities are just the sort one would exercise in extracting information contained in something in the first way. Without such capacities, one would have no concepts, so would not be a thinker at all. There would be nothing on which the world *could* bear for you. So the possession and exercise of such capacities *must* be fundamental in any story of how perception makes this bear on what to think.

The point is worth reworking. Frege also says,

A thought always contains something reaching out beyond the particular case, by which this is presented to consciousness as falling under something general.

(1882, *Kernsatz* 4)

The thought is of things being a certain way. The generality of a thought, in the present sense, consists in the fact that there are various ways things being as they are might instance things being that way. If the thought is that that pig is a *bísaro*, things might be that way while the pig is in a sty, or in open range, while it eats acorns or yams, in a good or mediocre vintage year, and so on. The thought reaches to a range of cases in which things being as they were would be their being that way. Doing so is intrinsic to being a thought at all. What it reaches to is the particular case, which is: things being as they are. Such a thing *has* no reach to anything.

The generality of a thought is shared by a way for things to be, a way for *something* to be, and by whatever would make a thought *about* a way for something to be (call that a concept). It is lacked by what such (first-order) things reach to.

I will call what has it (*the*) *conceptual*, and what lacks it (*the*) *non-conceptual*. The point is now: one is not engaging in thought at all; one is certainly not in a position in which there is *any* way perception could make the world bear for him on what to think, unless he has, and exercises, capacities to see how the conceptual reaches to the non-conceptual: when things being as they are would be things being thus and so; something's being as it is it being thus and so. Without such capacities for extracting information in the first way, one would not be a thinker at all.

This idea appears in Frege's view of *seeing that*. Here are two expressions of it:

But do I not see that this flower has five petals? We can say this, but if we do, the word 'see' is not being used in the sense of having a mere visual experience: what we mean by it is bound up with thinking and judging.

(1897/1983: 149)

But don't we see that the sun has risen? And don't we thereby see that this is true? That the sun has risen is no object which emits rays which arrive in my eyes, is no visible thing like the sun itself. That the sun has risen is recognized as true on the basis of sensory input.

(1918: 61)

Sight affords visual awareness of a scene, and of things, happenings, and conditions obtaining in it: that sloth, the waving of the branches, the blackness of the toast. It thus affords opportunity for exercising certain sorts of capacities: I can recognize, of the scene being visibly as it is, that that is that sloth sleeping, or that toast being burnt. Such is a fundamentally important way for perceptual experience to make the world bear, for me, on what to think.

I return to Evans. In what way does he think one of his internal states contains (retrievable) information? Is it in the first way, so that it would be the pig's *looking* spotted (to me) which is necessarily closely connected with the state containing the information that it is spotted, or in the second, so that it is my *thinking* (in the right way) that the pig is spotted which is thus connected with the state containing the information that it is? The first idea excludes misinformation; which would exclude representing as so. Evans is attached to the idea of misinformation (what an internal state would be intrinsically liable to provide); but *also* to the idea that perception is occasion for exercising capacities of *conceptualization*; thus ones belonging to the first idea. So he is ambivalent. On the one hand, he insists,

The informational states which a subject acquires through perception are *non-conceptual*, or *non-conceptualized*. Judgements *based upon* such states necessarily involve conceptualization: in moving from a perceptual experience to a judgement about the world (usually expressible in some verbal form), one will be exercising basic conceptual skills.

(1982: 227)

Which looks, so far, like the first idea. But on the other, he insists that a perceptual state

> has a certain *content*—the world is represented as a certain way—and hence it permits of a non-derivative classification as *true* or *false*.
>
> (1982: 226)

Perceptual states are truth-evaluable. Only containing information in the second way could make something so evaluable. Only the second way makes room for misinformation—something *representation* is *intrinsically* liable to provide. In fact, Evans seems to want the best (for him) of both worlds: representation, but representation with non-conceptual content. Representation necessarily reaches beyond the particular case which it represents as a certain way. So it belongs to the conceptual. If we draw a conceptual–non-conceptual distinction as above, 'non-conceptual representational content' is senseless. *Perhaps* Evans understands these notions in some other way. I do not think so. I think he simply fails to choose where one must. I will return to that presently. First, how does Evans' story reflect the *Drang* in general, and the SH model in particular?

3 The Inner

Visual experiences, for Evans, *are* certain inner states. These float free of what lies within the subject's view. For all that in that scene there is a pig beneath the oak, that inner state which is the subject's experience of this may or may not contain the information that this is so. For all that it contains the (*mis*)information that there is a pig beneath the oak, there may or may not be one. If the visual experience is one of *seeing* a scene, then that inner state it is is, presumably, the upshot of interactions with the environment; presumably involving, somehow, retinas. So Evans' account just *is* the SH model. The first thing to note is that it is a *necessary* condition for *visual* experience to represent things as so; to be truth-evaluable. For that, experiencing visually must contain something floating free of the scene in view, as per above. There is nothing in visual experience which could do that except, if it exists, something the *subject* puts there; something *inner*, independent, in principle, of what surrounds him.

Scenes do not represent things as so. Nor do their constituents. There is no way things are according to that pig before the oak (unless it talks). There is no way things are according to its being beneath the oak, or according to the spreading of those branches. None of these things is truth-evaluable. A pig is not. *Nothing*'s being thus and so is. Correlatively, neither the scene nor the pig nor the spreading contains *mis*information. Perceptual experience would need some other ingredient for *it* to represent anything as *so*. The spreading of those branches no doubt *means* various things. Perhaps it tells us something about the average hours of sunlight per year in that place. But there is no such thing as it telling us this *falsely*; which highlights the point that such meaning (the factive sort) is not *representing* anything as so. (See my 2004.)

There are more notions of representing than are found in representing as so. The state of Sid's liver represents years of hard drinking; the state of those rocks, aeons of water erosion. Sid's liver thus contains the information that he indulged in years of hard drinking, the rocks the information that this was once a river bed. Which makes neither Sid's liver, nor its state, truth-evaluable. These do not represent years of hard drinking if there were none. The spreading branches may represent something—say, careful pruning—in this sense. But something else is needed before anything in an experience of seeing them could represent anything as so: *commitment*. *Something* in the experience must make itself hostage to whether something is some given way. (Hostage, that is, for *correctness*. Which *might* mean harbouring *ambitions*—as judging is a posture one aims to hold only in a particular sort of world.) The spreading of the branches is not thus *hostage* to their being pruned; if they were not, it simply does not mean they were.

Representationism—the view that experience represents as so—thus requires the SH model. Does the model otherwise invite it? Adepts of it *have* tended to see visual experience as representing in *some* sense. But not always as representing things to be *so*. Descartes is a good representative of the alternative. For him, all '*cogitationes*' (ideas) represent. But he also holds,

Ideas, considered in themselves, and not referred to something else, cannot strictly speaking be false.

(1954/1641: 78, Third Meditation)

The mind finds within itself ideas of many things; and so long as it merely contemplates these, and neither asserts nor denies the existence of something like them outside itself, it cannot be in error.

(1954/1644: 184, Principles XIII)

A room in the Louvre is filled with sycophantic paintings, by Rubens, of Cathérine de Medicis, for example, astride a horse, in battle armour, leading grateful troops. That painting represents her so doing. Basing one's judgement on the painting, you *could* take it *that* Cathérine once, on horseback, led troops. That would be a mistake, which the painting, rightly understood, in no way encourages. The painting does not represent it as *so* that Cathérine ever did such a thing. The mistake would be all yours. So it is, for Descartes, with perceptual experience in general. My visual experience, as I view the scene, represents a pig in the (or a) sty. I may take it that there is a pig in the sty. But in this I am on my own. No such thing is so according to the experience. It does not represent it as *so* that any pig is in any sty. *Nothing*, on Descartes' view, is so according to an experience as such. (*Thus* far Descartes and Austin are one. See Austin 1962, 11.)

An Evansian inner state, where one *saw* a pig in the sty, would represent a pig in the sty in the way that the state of Sid's liver represents hard drinking. It could not represent in that Rubensesque way above. For that it would need something which functioned as a canvas does: (some of) *its* visual features, themselves objects of the subject's visual awareness, would carry representational import, thanks to something paralleling an *intention* that they should be taken in a certain way. Evans explicitly rejects any such thing. Might these states still represent things as *so*? What function, within the SH model, would such representing serve?

Perception's *essential* task in the life of a thinker is to allow the world—specifically his surroundings—to bear for him on what he is to think (and do) according as it bears on what is *so*. If *cogitationes* were, as it were, a mere play of shape and colour, they would play no such role; would make for no such bearing. For that, they must, for a start, carry information as to how those surroundings are. There are two ways for an object of (perceptual) awareness to carry information. It (our its presence) may *mean*, factively, or indicate something; or it may represent things as some way (on some notion of representing as). Suppose that the play of shape and colour *meant* things (as well it might if there is such a play at all). A particular visual arrangement in the play might mean, say, that there is a pig before me. Then, if I appreciate its meaning, I can *conclude* from what I am visually aware of that there is a pig before me.

Frege's point about the conceptual–non-conceptual distinction is *one* reason why factive meaning, so far as it goes, cannot allow perception to do its job. Some display of shape and colour may *mean* there is a pig before me (my porcine warning system), just as some grunting sound, or Aunt Ida's shrieks, might. If I appreciate its meaning, any of these, if taken in, may be reason for me to think there is a pig before me. But that of the *world* which in fact bears on whether there is a pig before me is, in first instance, things before me being as they are. It is *that* which *is*, or is not, a pig being before me. Perception's job is not done unless it makes available to me (at least sometimes) *that* for me then to evaluate, or recognize, as a pig being before me or not. Perception must afford me opportunities to exercise my abilities to link the non-conceptual to the conceptual as it in fact links, by that fundamental relation of falling under, or instance, or just being, as per above. If I am cut off from such possibilities, then, as per above, I cannot so much as get the right bits of the conceptual in mind—a pig being before me, say. Then factive meaning, for all that it may still be there in the world, is no use to me when it comes to what I am to think. To appreciate it, I would need to recognize the bearing of something I *do* experience on... *what?* Anyway, on something of which, so far, nothing furnishes me awareness.

The only alternative, then, is to take *cogitationes* to provide information by, or in, representing things. Descartes wisely resists supposing *cogitationes* to represent things *to be so*. So they represent, roughly, Rubensesquely. But this clearly makes no progress. I will put this by harping on a point. A *cogitatione* is the content of someone's consciousness, in Frege's sense. The scene before me, and its contents—that pig staring at me from the sty—are things for *one* to experience, to witness, to observe, where, crucially, there is no-one one must be to be the one. It is precisely *not* a content of consciousness. As Frege insists (1918: 67), it would be a solecism to speak of *seeing* a *cogitatione*, precisely not solecistic to speak of seeing the pig, or the scene. So my *cogitationes* of the moment being as they are is one thing; the scene before me being as it is another. Accordingly, my being *aware* of my *cogitationes* being as they are is one thing; my being aware of the scene being as it is another. Just maybe, I could be (visually) aware of a scene being as it is *in* being (visually) aware of my *cogitationes* being as they are (though I doubt it). But awareness of my *cogitationes* being as they are is *not* awareness of the scene being as it is. My *cogitationes* being as they are *may* be (though Frege, I think, showed not) their being thus and so—such as their representing a scene with a pig front and centre. My awareness of their being as they are may make this recognizable to me (if the notion recognition (*Erkennung*) fits here). But *this* is not what representation needs to deliver here. What is needed is that my visual awareness of the *scene* being as it is can make it recognizable to me that *that* is a pig being before me. No such thing is in the cards. Representation is hopeless for its appointed role here.

Representing makes no progress over factive meaning here. Neither offers awareness of what would be, so could be recognized, as things (before us) being thus and so. Such should have been obvious from the moment *cogitationes* came on the scene. Whatever *they* do, awareness of them doing it could not be awareness of a scene doing its thing. But Evans will have no truck with *cogitationes*. For *them* to represent would be for their visual features to have representational significance. To take in their representing what they do would be to take in those visual features and appreciate their representational significance. (Anyway, as Frege stressed (1918: 59), *such* things would need (very roughly) an intention attaching to them for *them* to represent. Where would *that* come from?) Whereas Evans explicitly denies that we are aware how experience represents by being aware of some *vehicle* whose visible features bear representational significance. Those internal states which represent, for him, are not objects of perceptual awareness; which leaves him with nothing that could represent Rubensesquely. Which is fine with him, since, anyway, in his view, doing the job right—making the world bear as perception must—requires representing things *as so*.

So is the representing Evans posits any more fit for its task than Descartes'? Descartes is driven to posit representing because, given what he thinks perceiving is, it is the only hope for perception to give the *world* bearing on what we are to think. Once *cogitationes* are in the picture, they must *somehow* carry information about the world; nothing *else* could make them do so. Evans' hand is similarly forced. Not that he posits sensory *vehicles* of representing. But he holds a version of the SH model. On it, an *internal* state decides what I am visually aware of in experiencing visually: something I might be aware of no matter what the scene before my eyes (visibly) provided. Awareness of *that* must, somehow, make the *scene's* being as it is bear on what I am to think— allow me so much as to think, and then to judge, of the *scene's* being as it (visibly) is that *that* is a scene being thus and so. What else but representing to connect me with that of which I am thus to judge?

Now the *same* considerations that defeated *cogitationes* for this purpose do in as well what such an inner state makes one visually aware of. For awareness of *that* is not, and could not be, awareness of the *scene before me* being as it is. (It is another matter whether *in* visual awareness of the one sort I might sometimes enjoy some awareness of the other.) I am not so far offered so much as the chance to get in mind that which I must judge to be thus and so. All remains just as for Descartes.

If anything, Evans is in a worse position. For representing as so mismatches the conceptual with the non-conceptual. It provides, at best, only bits of the conceptual to bear on other bits of the conceptual; where what is needed is the *non-conceptual*—the scene before me being as it is—to bear for me on what I am to think as to how various bits of the conceptual reach to *it*. Experience, on Evans' view, makes available to me, to bear on how I should think of things, at best the fact that the pig is in the sty, where what I need is acquaintance with things being as they are, so that *this* may bear on whether to think that such is the (or a) pig being in a sty.

Some have thought that experience, to do its job, *must* supply one with things shaped like (truth-evaluable) *thoughts*. Christopher Peacocke, for example, tells us,

By perceiving the world, we frequently learn whether a judgement with a given conceptual content is true or not. This is possible only because a perceptual experience has a correctness condition whose holding may itself exclude, or require, the truth of a conceptual content.

(1992: 66)

Only what was shaped as a proposition could bear on the truth of a proposition. Such reflects one conception of rational bearing. But Frege shows how so conceiving bearing gets things exactly backwards, at least when it comes to performing perception's task. Experience must provide that on which I can exercise my capacities to recognize connections between the conceptual and the non-conceptual. Only then can it provide me with that by which I can judge, non-inferentially, that, say, a pig is in the sty. Representing things as so is hopeless for that task. Leibniz on being (so thinking about) an individual is *à propos*: for no proper sub-set of an individual's properties (closed under strict entailment) is *having them* being *it*.

Experience representing things as so could not be what places us in contact with the world. Such representing would present *our surroundings* to us as falling under a certain generality. It would thus reach to a range of cases of surroundings being as they were, or a scene as it was—just those instancing the relevant generality. *Thus* would it represent things as being a certain way. To grasp such representing we would need to grasp when what does (or fails to do) such instancing would do so or not; so get in mind its doing so. If our only route to getting in mind the particular things which do such instancing is through having it represented to us that they do, or do not, instance this or that, how could we so much as think such thoughts? In which case, what would make *these* the ways our experience represents things to be? (Frege saw the point (1918: 67–9). John McDowell made it well (see 1986). See also Essay 2.) The SH model cuts us off from the world in our visual experiencing—as we must be cut off for representation by, or in, experience to so much as gain a foothold. Once so cut off from the world, it is a nice question how we are ever able again to get in touch with it.

4 Non-Conceptual Content

So the SH model ends in an impasse. Such are the wages, for perception, of an inward gaze. It can be understandably tempting to fasten on representation for effecting an escape. But it is hopeless for that task. The idea of representing in or by experience—at least as means for experience to bring the world to bear on its subject's thought—positively requires something with just those features of the SH model which condemn it to failure—reason enough to give up on that idea.

But it can be hard to abandon the SH model, especially when it masquerades as mere science.

There is, *inter alia*, this tempting picture. On Evans' account (as on the SH model), in a visual experience there is a way things appear, or seem, visually, to us. Call that, if you like, things appearing, or seeming, a certain way (namely, the way they do). It is just this (through the procedure Evans describes) which makes *how* our experience represents things recognizable to us. So we are in contact with *something* belonging to the non-conceptual (things appearing as they do), which we can thus recognize as falling under various generalities—instancing appearing as though a pig were spotted, say. Why cannot *that* opportunity for exercising conceptual capacities on the non-conceptual be all that is needed for the *world's* being as it is to be made to bear on what we are to think? After all, the right sorts of capacities are in the picture *somehow*. Well, it cannot because what is needed is opportunity for exercise of those capacities on the non-conceptual *our surroundings* supply (or bring into view). But, conflating awareness of A *in* awareness of B with awareness of B just *being* awareness of A, that point goes missing.

The very pull of such manoeuvres shows the tension between the SH model's untenability and seeming inevitability. Such tension is, perhaps, reflected in the strange idea of non-conceptual content. Here *content* is to be the content of what is truth-evaluable; what represents as so (or, again, potential components thereof—what may be true *of* something). The content of a given item fixes, or is fixed by, what is so according to it; on *what* its truth turns. To represent as so is to represent things as a certain way. For (such a) representation to have non-conceptual content would be for there to be a way for things to be which was (or was in part) non-conceptual. If we draw the conceptual–non-conceptual distinction as it has been drawn here, this is patent nonsense. A way for things to be, so, too, representation (of things as a certain way)—in Frege's terms, a thought—is *essentially* what reaches to the non-conceptual in a particular way so as for a thought to present the particular case (things being as they are) as falling under some particular generality. Representational content belongs *essentially* to the conceptual, on this deployment of terms.

Evans, and his intellectual heir, Christopher Peacocke, are two among many who think that the representational content of experience is 'non-conceptual' (or, in Evans, non-conceptualized). Peacocke (soon to be centre stage) begins his treatment of perception with the remark (for him mere truism) that 'a perceptual experience represents the world as being a certain way' (1992: 61). That way, he further holds, may be in whole or part 'non-conceptual'. If they are not just talking nonsense, they must mean something else by 'non-conceptual' than the use it has been given here. It can illuminate distortions in the SH model to ask what this can be. (This *may* oversimplify. Perhaps Evans, or Peacocke, simply gives in, simultaneously, to the pull of both poles of that above tension.)

It might seem less pressing to say what 'non-conceptual content' might mean if it seemed absolutely *mandatory* that experience represent as so. If, for one or another reason, the content of such representation could not be straightforwardly conceptual, well, we can leave it to later to work out just what else it might be. *Pro tem* 'non-conceptual' will do as a placeholder. But, we have seen, it is a mistake (or two) to think any such thing mandatory. So what *might* Peacocke mean by non-conceptual? It is none too easy to say. 'Conceptual content', he tells us, 'is content of a kind that can be the content of judgement and belief' (2001: 243). If we suppose that non-conceptual content is content which is *not* conceptual, it follows that non-conceptual content is of a sort which cannot be the content of a judgement. I take this to mean: either of things (catholic reading), or of some thing(s) that they are (it is) thus and so. So that the concept *being a crisp* is not non-conceptual merely because one cannot 'judge that a crisp'. But, for both Evans and Peacocke, an experience was to represent things as a certain way; where that is to be read as a way *there is* for things to be. Just so does Peacocke hope to finesse the 'problem' of how experience can provide something which *bears* on what to think, from which we may *learn* that such-and-such. Experience represents things as thus and so (on their story); the subject then takes experience's word for it—acquiesces in the representing, so judges—or, if ornery, or suspicious, resists—declines so to judge. On Peacocke's own account of conceptual content, it seems, there could be no non-conceptual content.

In such binds one might try relativizing. What, for Peacocke, points towards non-conceptual content suggests he has some such thing in mind. For example, he says,

> Some of the non-conceptual content of our experience can be identical with the representational content of the experience of creatures that either possess no concepts, or possess only a set of concepts far more rudimentary than our own.
>
> (2001: 242)

We, perhaps, could judge things to be as represented—just *that* way. But other creatures, whose experience could still represent things as that way, could not so judge. So goes the thought. If my experience represents Sid just to have grunted, that is a way I, but not these other creatures, might judge things to be. But in this case (the idea seems to be) those other creatures could not so much as have experiences which represented things as that way. For that, they would need the concept *grunt*. (I blush at such thoughts. But such are issues for other occasions. Anyway, I suppose something like this must be what Peacocke thinks.) So, the thought is, *conceptual* content would be content an experience could not have unless its subject had the relevant concepts; non-conceptual content is what could be the content of experiences *both* of those who could judge things that way and of those who could not.

Non-conceptual content in this sense would still be conceptual in the sense of having that generality which, for Frege, is the mark of a thought. It would reach in a particular way to a range of cases, so as to present the particular case—what is experienced—as falling under a certain generality. Only then could it so much as be something *we* could judge. The main question, to follow, is how *any* experience could arrange for anything to do *that*. But, again, necessity is the mother of bracketing such issues. This done, Peacocke's idea above is, I think, just another manifestation of the original tension: representation *must*, but cannot, make the SH model work. I will call those other creatures, who cannot judge what we can, 'cats'. Why think their experience *has* this content, which they cannot recognize, or so much as take it to have (on pain of being able to judge so)? The idea is (details of cat eyes, and so on, aside): if I am looking at a sparrow in a bush, and a cat is looking at a sparrow in a bush, we *might* see, and experience visually, the same thing. It is not as if the cat must be *blind* to some region of the scene where I can see what is going on. But representational content, if there is to be some, must be a function of the character of the experience—what it was like (visually). Accordingly, that sameness in what I and the cat experience visually must be reflected in a shared representational content of our respective experiences. Unfortunately for the cat, that content could not be the content of feline judgement.

So it would be if the sameness here must emerge in a sameness of representational content. And *this* must be so if the information about my surroundings which my experience makes available to me must be made available through things being represented as so. For what it would take non-conceptual content (in Peacocke's sense) to represent as so *is* what I might recognize to be so of my surroundings, given what I see of them—that the blood from the T-bone has made just *that* pattern in the rug, say. But we are not so shackled. I and the cat both see how things are in and about that bush. We *thus* see, and experience, the same thing. We may both, say, be responsive—each in his own way—to those avian movements in the branches. I can recognize things being *that* way as their being thus and so, for various values of 'thus and so'. The cat cannot do all I thus can. But sameness of experience here need not lie in sameness of how anything is represented in our shared awareness of the scene before us looking as it does. Without the SH model, it can just consist in the awareness afforded both of us of the scene being, visibly, as it is.

Which, on reflection, is no doubt a good thing. The scene before the cat and me is, in being as it is, literally innumerable ways there are for a scene to be—one for each way of reaching to a range of cases which reaches this one. I cannot grasp all the ways (condemned as I am to the *human* condition). It is hard to see how my experience could *represent* things as all these ways. So there are our friends the martians, graspers of many ways beyond our grasp, failing to grasp others within ours. With them in view, it appears that *all* content of *all* our judgements is non-conceptual in the sense suggested by Peacocke's remark above.

Still, there is an underlying picture here which needs to be addressed. It is clearer in Evans than in Peacocke. Their shared idea was: in visual experience, things appear to me a certain way. In Evans, things so appearing makes it recognizable to me what way, or ways, my experience represents things to be: those ways it is as though things are in things appearing as they thus do. Now a thought might be: Why not cut out the middle men? If things appear to me a certain way, let my experience represent things to me as *that* way. Things appear as though *blah*; my experience represents them as *blah*. Here original tension emerges in a new way. Things appearing to me a certain way can just be things appearing to me as they then do—a denizen of the non-conceptual. So we have here something non-conceptual in the Frege-inspired sense I have given that term. The way my experience represents things is (something like) *as they appear*. If their so appearing is their appearing as they do, so something non-conceptual, then, it seems, so to represent them is to represent them as a certain way, where things being that way also belongs to the non-conceptual.

But the 'certain way' in 'represent as a certain way' cannot be read in the same way as that in 'things appear a certain way', where this is to be read just as things appearing as they do. It must be read as *such-and-such way there is for things to be*, otherwise we have no representation at all. If anything is *represented* as so here—if there is anything truth-evaluable—then things need not be *just* as they in fact are for things to *be* as thus represented; nor for them to be so represented. The particular case is represented as what it would be in doing something (determinate) less than just being all it is; so in what might be done in a *range* of cases. The idea is things appearing as they do, just in being what *it* is—a certain particular case of things appearing—is to determine *how* this representation is to reach; just what it would be for things being as they are to be all they *need* to be to be as represented. But particular cases have no reach, determine as such no reach for anything conceptual to have. So the idea makes no sense.

What could give the impression that merely things appearing as they do, in itself, while remaining non-conceptual, could, for all that, determine something it would be for things to be as they were *according* to it—a bit of the conceptual? Evans suggests one thing. An ordinary photograph *registers* (digitally, on film, in a print) the scene before the lens. It thus contains information about that scene in our now familiar first way. There is that photograph of Pia on the boardwalk. It shows the way she was back then. Her hair was bobbed then, her chin-line firmer. In her eyes was that sparkle, now lost. There is much the photograph does not show: Sid's sideburns and bellbottoms (he *took* the photograph, was not in it); his then-addiction to chicken nuggets; the lovers *under* the boardwalk. Nor whether Pia was suffering indigestion, or her obscured arm was then freckled. So things would have been as shown in the photograph while the world at large was—things were—any of various ways. In a range of cases things would have been as shown—perhaps the range some bit of the conceptual might reach.

So the photograph shows Pia to look a way she could have looked while various things were going on. Someone might take that to mean that it *represents* her to be that way—that there is a way things are *according to* it. If photographs can do this, it does not seem to require conceptual capacities so to represent things; which *may* want to make us label representation so achieved as 'non-conceptual' (though the achievement would remain presenting the particular case as falling under some given generality).

One tempted by such thoughts should attend to *what* answers questions as to when things being as they were would be their being as shown. Would Pia's hair have been bobbed then if things were as shown? One might consult the photograph to see how it presents her. But is what it shows hair being *bobbed*? A photograph cannot answer that. What lies in, or behind, what a photograph thus cannot do?

If the photograph represents things as so, the most it could do is represent it to be so that Pia then was (*inter alia* looked) *thus*—as shown. If being *thus* counts as having one's hair bobbed, then her being as she was according to the photograph is, in fact, her having her hair then bobbed. When it comes to which concepts under which to bring Pia's being as thus represented, just *how* being as shown reaches beyond the particular case, and to what, what the photograph shows, its photographic image, so far as that goes, leaves us entirely on our own. Someone *might* think of this as just giving further content to the idea of *non-conceptual* content. The thought would be: perceptual experience is just like that. It, too, represents a scene as *thus*—as it thus appears. But we need to look more closely at whether this is really *representing* at all.

We began with the idea that a photograph contains information as the non-conceptual does. This has been worked into the idea that it, so experience, too, can do that while representing as so. It contains information *retrievable* in the first way, but in representing things to be such as for that to be retrievable *information*. What, then, decides *what* information the photograph thus contains? The photograph contains information as to how Pia looked back then, or at least that day on the boardwalk. Obvious first questions: Back when? What day? What answers these is when the photograph was taken; *not*, at first blush, information the *photograph* contains. Perhaps the information is written on the back (if a print is in question). Otherwise, there is an historical fact, to be sought as such facts are. For example, ask Sid. By contrast, suppose I *say*, 'Pia wore her hair bobbed then', saying Pia's hair to have been bobbed at a certain time (or in a certain period). When was her hair bobbed according to me? That depends on how my words are to be understood. For all of my uttering them when I did, I may have said, or not said, her to have had bobbed hair at any of an indefinite variety of periods, or moments.

The crucial point has been made. In a court of law we would speak of the photograph *meaning* (factively) that, say, Pia wore her hair bobbed when she was 17 (so, further, that she was not then in the cult). Which is just what it might do, depending on the facts: when it was taken, how constant Pia was in her coiffure in that period, whether she might have been wearing a wig. A *caricature* of Pia with bobbed hair, or a photograph of her (or a body-double) with bobbed hair, as one frame in a photograph-BD titled, 'Pia at 17' *might* mean something as to her coiffure at 17, or her coiffure at 35 (if, say, her flowing tresses then would have made the caricaturist depict hair as bobbed). But it *represents* her hair as bobbed at a time decided by how it is to be understood. For the BD, produced when she was 35, using a body-double, the title is a clue to that. These are all things a photograph as such could not do. There is nothing wrong with the idea that that caricature *means* that Pia's hair was bobbed at 35, but *represents* her as with bobbed hair at 17, or that it represents her as with bobbed hair at 17, but does not represent her *to have had* such hair. All things beyond the reach of a photograph. Moreover, that frame of Pia in the BD might represent her as with bobbed hair even if she is wearing a wig. If I said, 'Pia had bobbed hair', the fact that she might have worn a wig in those days takes nothing away from the fact that I *represented* her as having bobbed hair; it merely means that what I said might be wrong. Again, if the photograph happens to be of a body-double, then all it shows is the body-double having bobbed hair, and all it means (pending further facts) is that the body-double's hair was bobbed. Such are some of the differences between representing as so and factive meaning.

The differences are manifest throughout. In the photograph, Pia's skin is smooth and pale. Her eyes seem preternaturally wide. Does the photograph show her as having such skin, or eyes? It depends on how the photography worked. Perhaps the film (or programme) is not true to skin colour, the lens not true to eye dimensions. The camera produced a certain image; now the question is what, given the apparatus, such an image *means*; what we can conclude from it, what *information* is retrievable. If the film is not true to skin colour, then it is not as though the photograph *represents* Pia to have skin of some colour other than she did. Rather, to that extent, it contains no information as to her true skin colour. It cannot represent falsely; by the same token it cannot *represent* at all.

Factive meaning is a relation borne, sometimes by the conceptual, sometimes not, to bits of the conceptual. So there is, as a rule, a range of cases in which things would be as meant. But what factively means cannot, in doing *that, reach* in any particular way to any particular range, as is intrinsic to what belongs to the conceptual. Photographs mean, but cannot represent (though, like anything, they can be *used* to do so, as in the BD). They are no model for how anything could represent non-conceptually.

5 Filling Out Space

The SH model cannot allow perception to bring the world to bear on what to think as perception would do. Representation cannot allow it to. So the SH model of perception is wrong. Representing in or by perceptual experience—notably things as so—requires the SH model. So there is no room for representation in or by perceptual experience. The next question is: if the SH model fails, what is the *right* way to conceive perception? But temptations to think that perceptual experience represents things run so deep, and touch on things so fundamental, that it will help in addressing that question first to consider, from some other angles, why this is something perceptual experience could not do.

Peacocke's idea of how visual experience represents things is, seemingly, inspired by that photographic (mis)conception of how something belonging to the non-conceptual can be conjured into a bit of the conceptual; perhaps by a conception of how a photograph can be digitalized. Accordingly, he postulates a kind of content of such experience which he calls *scenario content*. This is content of a visual experience, identified by a scenario. A scenario is a three-dimensional space with labelled origin and axes, and with each point in the space assigned some set of properties drawn from a stock out of which scenarios are generated. A positioned scenario is assigned a viewer at a time. For example, if the origin is *right between the eyes*, and the axes *right–left* and *up–down*, then to position the scenario for Sid now is to take the origin to be right between Sid's eyes, where he is now, the right–left axis to run from Sid's right to his left, facing as he is now, and so on. Sid's present visual experience has the content thus identified just in case things are as they are according to the experience only if each point in the space around Sid has the properties assigned that point in the scenario. One might, in that case, call the scenario *true*, or true relative to that positioning. 'Only if' because scenario content is only one sort that Peacocke thinks visual experience might have. One might say: on this condition, Sid's experience is true *so far*. A wrinkle: Actually, Peacocke tells us, the content of Sid's experience is identifed by a *family* of positioned scenarios. His experience is true so far just in case *one* of them is true. The family is to reflect Sid's inability, for example, to distinguish fine shades of colour. I will ignore these complications except where they demand attention. (For all this see 1992: 61–2.)

So *if* a given positioned scenario fits Sid's current experience, then that experience is true so far if that positioned scenario is true: for that scenario to fit is for there to be a certain way things are according to the experience; for it to be true (so positioned) is for things to be that way (though this may not be the *whole* way things are according to the experience). Indeed, this *is* what it is for a scenario to fit. If Sid's experience represents things as they are according to the scenario, it fits. There need not be a unique scenario which thus fits. Perhaps there is a unique one generated from some given stock of properties. But there may be others generated from other stocks. If a scenario which fits assigns to a given point being blue, and part of a solid surface, that is *one* way of capturing how things are according to Sid's experience. But there may be others. (This is part of the inspiration for *non-conceptual* content.) The question now is: Which scenarios *would* fit Sid's experience, given that it was as it was? About this, Peacocke says,

Of course, I still owe a philosophical account of what it is for one scenario, with one set of labelled axes and origin rather than another, to be the content of an experience. But once we recognize the level of the scenario, there is nothing to make this problem insoluble.

(1992: 73)

Really? Let us see. First, though, for some ground rules. Little in them should be controversial here.

First, how *much* should a visual experience represent as so? Suppose Pia can just *see* Sid's inebriated look, the red meat on the carpet, the blood seeping into the white fibres. Then, *perhaps*, that visual experience should represent it as so that Sid looks, or is, inebriated, and so on. But suppose she only learns he is inebriated later, by seeing the bottle of Old Codswallop he has been at. She may deduce, or infer, from that, correctly, that he is inebriated. But this is not part of what she is, or is made, aware of in, or by, seeing Sid staring sheepishly at the red meat on the rug. So it is more than *that* experience should represent as so. A visual experience should not represent as so what one would need to deduce from other things one had taken in. It would thus proffer more information than vision, or mere seeing, then makes available. (With rules to come, this should mean that Pia's present visual experience should not represent *more* as so than she could, or *might*, see to be so if her experience is in fact one of seeing a scene before her.)

Plausibly, for Peacocke or Evans, some form of converse point should hold. If Pia just sees Sid going at the Old Codswallop, and can thereby see that he is going at it, then her experience should represent this as so. For, though seeing that *need* not be based on visual input, here it is. Here there is nothing else from which Pia must, or could, *infer* that Sid is so engaged. *Inference* is not in the cards here. Pia can just recognize of what she sees—the scene being as it is—that *this* is Sid going at the Old Codswallop. Peacocke tells us (and I think Evans agrees) that experience representing things as so is *the* way in which it allows us to learn things from it as to how things are. This, we know, is false. But if it were true, then, since Pia's current visual experience allows her to learn, just from *it*, that Sid is so engaged, *it* would have to represent this as so. Given its *ad hominem* character, I will treat this as plausible, but not mandatory. But if experience representing things as so is *not* the only way for it to make the world bear on what to think, what is the point of its doing so at all? Such would just be making the same information available in two ways at once—as where Pia, *really, really*, not wanting Sid to forget their anniversary, sows the place with both wedding pictures and notes.

Second rule. It should be recognizable to the subject *what* way his *visual* experience represents things to be. Something in what he is, or can be, thus visually aware of should *make* this recognizable to him. I am not here disputing Evans' claim that perceptual experiences cannot themselves be objects of perceptual awareness. Nor am I supposing that perceptual experiences bear their content in anything like the way a sentence does. But I recall something Evans himself relies on: enjoying a perceptual experience *is* a way of experiencing being in whatever state enjoying that experience is—being in one of Evans' internal states, if such there be. What I am insisting on is: experiencing what one *thus* does—something one thus experiences—makes it recognizable to one which way one's experience represents things to be. What one experiences can just be things looking to him as they then do. Recognition need come to no more than this: confronted with the way things relevantly *are* (or prove to be), one is able to say (see) that *this* is not, or, again, is, things being as they were according to that experience: the experience was *wrong*, or *right*. And one can recognize, sufficiently often, of sufficiently detailed concrete examples, what *would* be, or not, things being as represented. For only *recognizable* representing (in the present attenuated sense) could make the world bear, for the subject, on what to think and do; which was to be the point of representing in experience.

Third, it cannot follow merely from the fact that the scene before me is *not* a certain way that my experience did not represent it as that way; nor, conversely, merely from the fact that my experience did represent things as such-and-such way that they *are* that way. For experience, as elsewhere, truth must not be a requirement on representing at all. For suppose that my experience could not so much as *say* that there was a sloth in that tree unless there was one. Then it could not recognizably so claim where it was doubtful that a sloth was present, or where this was something one still needed to *learn*. So experience could represent *only* what there were other ways of ascertaining, or being certain of. Experience would thus reduce to a fillip on what fares well without it.

Fourth, if experience may represent falsely, it cannot lie blatantly. Suppose I plainly see the snake moving in the grass. Then my experience cannot represent it as so that nothing is moving in the grass. Which means: if my experience represents it as so that the snake is moving, I cannot tell just by looking (at the snake) that it is not. My visual experience cannot represent it as so that the snake is moving if things look to me (so far as I can tell how things look) just like a snake lying still. I omit a general formula, but suppose we can recognize instances.

6 Commitment

The curious idea that perception represents overlooks many obstacles. This section sets out one; the next another. The first obstacle is pervasive. It arises wherever there are two ways for things to look the way they do. Suppose I face an effigy of São Mamede. It looks blue. *Suppose* there are three ways for it to look just the way it does: it may be made of blue plaster; it may be painted blue; it may be neutral-coloured, coloured blue by lasers. (The example, inspired by laser-coloured effigies at Amiens, is *not* far-fetched.) Perhaps things would not look just as they do all three ways: you could tell if the effigy were made of blue plaster, rather than being painted. In that case, representing is *de trop*: its looking as it does *means* that it is painted. But suppose things might look just the same one way or the other. By our rules, what I experience visually must make it recognizable to me how things are represented. But how could things being *visually* as they are for me make it recognizable to me that *visual* experience represented things as one of these ways (blue plaster *there*), rather than any of the others?

The effigy looks just like a blue-plaster effigy—as one would or might. It must *be* a blue plaster effigy to be as it thus looks. It looks just like a blue-painted effigy. It must be blue-painted to look as it thus looks. It looks like a blue-laser-illuminated effigy. It must be *that* to look as it thus looks. But none of this so much as speaks to the question how *things* must be to be the way they look ('things' here bearing its catholic reading, on which one cannot ask 'Which ones?'). Yet, it seems, visual experience provides nothing beyond things looking as they do to tip me off as to how it represents things to be. So it seems that such experience could *not* represent things as any of these ways. Of course, I may be in a situation in which there could not be lasers, or, perhaps, blue plaster. In that case, things looking as they do might *mean* that there is blue paint there—but then, no representing needed.

A natural reaction here would be some form of minimalism. Let us retreat to it by steps. First, perhaps my visual experience just represents that region as occupied by something *blue*, no commitment to *how* blue. But if the effigy is neutral-coloured, the blue due to lasers, there is an understanding of something being blue on which it does count as something blue, and a contrasting one on which it does not; on which something blue only in the laser light is not something blue. Similarly for paint. So on what understanding of being blue does my experience represent that region as occupied by something blue? The above form of argument can be repeated here.

Second, perhaps my experience merely represents it as so that things *look* blue in that region of space. But this cannot help. What makes it recognizable to me how my experience represents things (when to say it was *false*) is things looking as they do to *me*. There are two ways for that to happen: they may so look; or it may just be me. Now the above argument repeats itself again.

Third, perhaps my experience merely represents it as so that things look blue now to me. There are several problems with this idea. But one will do for the moment. I am already authoritative as to how things look to me. (Or if I have lost track of that, it is obscure how representation can help me.) Of what is representation supposed to be informing me here? Or is it, again, just a wheel idling? (Aunt Ida as I stand before the donkey: 'That's a donkey'.) Perhaps it informs me that *that* (things looking as they do) is something looking *blue*. But then how am I to understand it? It would be nice if my visual experience could represent it as so that *that* colour is *heliotrope, that* one burnt umber, and so on, I being bad at recognizing those colours. It would then be a sort of cognitive prosthetic. But, though, taking that '*that*' to refer to a region of my surroundings, it may be *so* that that is burnt umber, it is hard to see how experience could commit itself to any such thing. Recall our first rule: visual experience should not represent any more as so than is retrievable from what is visually experienced. If I do not know burnt umber when I see it, then that *that* is burnt umber is not information so retrievable.

So, it seems, there is just nothing visual experience could legitimately represent as so.

7 Status

Using the strategy of the last section, I now develop a second obstacle. I begin, it will seem to some, off target. I then hone my aim. Here the problem is squaring experience's representing with our first rule (and its converse). If I oversimplify epistemology, the main point will be seen, I hope, to withstand the complications. I draw it from Thompson Clarke (1965). It would not touch a view that visual experience represents, not the scene before one as such-and-such ways, but merely (in suitable cases) itself as revealing—as an experience of *seeing*—how things are. *That* idea was disposed of in the last section.

To begin, then, a fresh baguette is on the kitchen table, on a breadboard, facing Sid (seated). What does Sid see? One answer: 'The baguette'. If so, then perhaps, by 1's converse, his experience should represent it as so that there is a baguette before him. So, too, for any ringer for a baguette-seeing experience—say, one of seeing a play-dough 'baguette'—what *visual* experience would not reveal as *not* one of seeing a baguette. Suppose, though, that the right answer is, 'The front surface of a baguette'. Then, by the first rule, Sid's experience should *not* represent it as so that there is a baguette before him. That would be something for him to *infer* from the information *perception* made available. Such is the shape of seeing's bearing on what visual experience might represent as so.

Here Clarke's point: *no* answer is the right one as such to 'the' question what Sid (actually) saw. Rather, different answers would be the right ones on different occasions for *saying* what Sid saw. What counted, on some such occasions, as what he saw would not do so on others. *And there is no further occasion-independent fact as to what he 'really' saw.* Similarly, an undyed cotton shirt, coloured blue by lasers, counts as then blue on some understandings of what its being blue would be, as not blue on others. There is no further fact as to what its colour 'really' is. Besides those occasional ways of drawing a blue–non-blue distinction, there is no other.

The Clarke point, as I will call it, is that there is no one right answer to the question of what Sid saw. So there is no one right answer to the question what he would need to infer. So there can be no one right answer to the question of how, by our first rule, his experience is to represent things. Neither the samples above, nor any other answer, could be right *as such*. Which means that there can be no right answer at all. If Sid's experience is to represent, for him recognizably, then *how* it represented in a given case cannot vary from occasion to occasion of the asking, according to what Sid would *then* count as needing to infer.

One could argue for Clarke's point by cases. If the little imps have been attaching front surfaces of baguettes to play-dough and leaving them in hopes of their muzzy elders preparing play-dough *tartines*; if such impishness may have struck, then, while Sid may *say* he saw a baguette on the breakfast table, we might count him as really having seen only a front surface. Once the children have all been packed off to military school, we can go back to talking about seeing baguettes. What Sid saw is not decided merely by the presence of the baguette, nor by his alertness being as it was to the occupation of that region, nor by whether the children have in fact been packed off. The circumstances of discussing his situation matter.

But there is a better way to see the point. If perception's job is to make the world bear on one's thought, then to see something is to enjoy a certain epistemic status. That thought, worked out, imposes occasion-sensitivity. I start with *perhaps* slight oversimplification. An experience of seeing a baguette before one is one which allows the world to bear on his thought as a baguette's presence before him bears on what is so. Which means: it makes available, to its subject, the information that there is a baguette before him: given adequate, and functioning, recognition capacities, he can recognize the scene before him as one in which there is a baguette before him; so he can *judge* that there is one there on grounds that he *sees* it. Seeing *can* be, for him, *proof*. There is no gap between seeing a baguette and there being one through which absence might slip. But if one only sees the front surface of a baguette, then no more is made available to him than that there is a front surface: judgements as to baguettes must be conclusions drawn.

Deciding what someone saw is thus deciding how the world has been brought to bear on his thought; what about it has been made available. Cases like the above bring out the need for such decisions to take account of the uses to which such information is to be put. Telling whether there is a baguette or play-dough on the table may be one such use. For Sid to be *thus* enabled would be for him, then, to be able to tell baguettes from play-dough at sight. Where *clever* imps are an issue, he cannot. Ordinary recognition capacities—say, knowing a pig at sight—are inherently dependent on hospitable environments for being that. If there is a tapir which looks just like a pig, or a pot-bellied pig which looks very unlike one, and if the gentlemen farmers of Oxfordshire are stocking their farms with these, then, though, usually, I *do* know my pigs when I see them, I cannot tell a pig by sight in Oxfordshire. It is not the *actual* oneupmanships of Oxfordshire gentry which cost me the capacity. False rumours in Chelsea may cost me it, on some occasions for the reckoning, if Chelsea somehow relies on me. Whether I have lost my capacity on arrival in Kingston Bagpuize all depends on who is asking, and when and why. *Knowlege* would not be in the picture otherwise. All the rest follows from seeing's role in making one knowledgeable.

Such is a simple thought. Perception allows information to bear on what one is to think—given his ability to extract it from a scene by his capacities to identify *what* counts as being *what*. Sid sees that goldfinch with its distinctive goldfinch head. He cannot tell it is a goldfinch: he does not know them by their heads. Seeing may well (though need not) make the information available (on one good understanding of *available*). Perhaps Sid could describe the head so that an expert knew at once it was a goldfinch. Still, that there is a goldfinch on the branch is not something that may yet bear, for Sid, on what he is to think. In the bread case, the problem is not *knowing* what distinguishes a baguette; nor with what distinguishes one from play-dough. It is that in impish surroundings the marks of a baguette are not on its facing crust. So it is not that perception makes available to Sid information he cannot use. It is rather that it does *not* make available to him information he perfectly well could use if he had it. It thus does not make available to him the information that a baguette is before him—not even as it did that there was a finch on that branch. So he cannot have seen the baguette. Now the question is: for purposes of saying what he saw, *what* count as the circumstances he was in—impish or not? The answer to that question can only be an occasion-sensitive matter.

Can this be right? If I have checked that it was, in fact, a baguette on the table, I might describe Sid (truly) as having seen a baguette, though all he could tell was that there was a facing surface. On the other hand, in impish surroundings, if Sid claimed to see a baguette, we could confront him with the impish possibilities and force the admission that all he really saw was the facing surface. All of which is just what one would expect if it is an occasion-sensitive matter what circumstances Sid counted as being in. When I establish that it was a baguette, I establish that Sid was not in (relevantly) impish circumstances. I now speak of what he saw accordingly—as it is to be spoken of on an occasion where his circumstances so count. This no more shows that what he 'really' saw was the baguette than finding an occasion on which one would not say a shirt was blue shows that it 'really' is not blue. It does not, for one thing, because it no more shows this than confronting him where he counts as in impish circumstances shows that what he 'really' saw was a facing crust. What one sees, so what one's experience *could*, or should, represent as so, depends on the circumstances one is in. What these are depends on when, and why, you are asking; which destroys the idea that there could be such a thing as a way things are according to an experience of seeing.

Which may tempt a representationist to minimalism. The rough idea would be: what an experience of seeing represents as so is just the *least* one would ever count as seeing (if one is). If there is a least Sid would ever count as having seen viewing the baguette, this would have to be a facing surface, or region of space. Beyond that, the environment drops out and it is seeing no longer. But the Clarke point applies to surfaces and regions. Suppose Sid, lost in reverie, is but dimly aware of the baguette. On the crust is a dark spot which some say resembles São Mamede. Here cracks, there what *might* be an impish thumbprint. Such details are lost on Sid. Did he see the crust? Or only part, or parts, of it? If the last, then which one(s)? Just which surfaces before Sid's eyes are ones he could judge to be present, or thus and so, which regions thus and so, on grounds of seeing their presence, or being that way—that is, non-inferentially?

Suppose we (mentally) place a grid over the facing crust, one square, for example, taken up with the São-Mamedeish spot, and ask, for each square, whether Sid saw what is in it. Could Sid really judge, of square R6, that that was occupied by crust—on grounds of seeing it so occupied? Suppose imps may have been cutting bits out of crusts, hoping we will suspect mice. Does what Sid sees allow him to say whether R6 is occupied (or even base a judgement on how he has seen R6 to be)? One would, at least, sometimes, suppose not. But this device, if it can be worked at all, can be worked for each region of the grid (not necessarily simultaneously). (Things become worse if, to oblige Peacocke, we try for answers for each *point* on the crust.) If we add up these results, we would seem to get the result that Sid sees *none* of the facing surface (or at least not much, or much of it not), which would be not to see *it* at all.

But suppose we now ask whether Sid, as he then was, was enabled, by sight, to base a judgement that there is a front surface before him on the presence of that surface—whether he might be able to judge such a thing non-inferentially. For each bit of grid, or most, we can build a story within which it would be wrong to say that Sid could judge non-inferentially that there was crust in that region, simply, by his seeing it, on grounds of there being crust there. But this does not seem to preclude a positive answer to the question. Seeing what he did may make Sid authoritative as to the presence of the crust, while being liable for any, or even many, regions of the grid, to leave him not authoritative as to whether there was crust there. It may be liable to grant such authority over a region even where, if there were no crust in that region, then there would be no facing crust present (but only, at best, a part of one). Which forces some form of occasion-sensitivity: Sid may count as authoritative as to whether there is a crust; basing judgement on the presence of a crust, even where we recognize that, on certain occasions for asking, he would not count as authoritative as to the presence of a crust in region R, and if there is no crust in region R, then there is no facing crust for him to see. He counts as authoritative as to the crust just where his circumstances do not count as ones in which he is not authoritative as to region R (which need not be for them to count as ones in which he *is* so authoritative). Now we need only remember: that kind of occasion-sensitivity is incompatible with squaring experience's representing with the demands of rule 1.

Minimalism is more familiarly worked in a slightly different area. Sid may wrongly, but understandably, take himself to see a baguette where there is only a facing crust. All he really saw was the crust. But it seemed that there was a baguette: so far as he could tell by looking there was. Similarly (it seems), Sid may wrongly, but understandably, take himself to see a facing crust where it is just a facing image, or just all in his head; but where there is nothing he experiences visually to tip him off. (It is none too easy to say *how* it might be all in his head. But let that pass.) Where there is only the facing crust, it seems that he is seeing something he would, or might, also have been seeing where there a baguette. By parallel, it may seem that where there is no facing crust, he experiences visually (seeing now having dropped out) something which he would also experience visually if there were a crust, or still better, a baguette. This something-visually-experienced, whatever it is, would be the minimal ingredient in an experience of seeing, present independent of the occasion for the asking. The rest can all then be seen as mere seeing-by-courtesy.

The manoeuvre can be made to lose its charm. Sid sees the baguette. *What* is it that he would see whether there was a baguette or not? *One* answer is: the facing crust. But does Sid see that *whole* crust, or only part of it? That is an occasion-sensitive matter. What was it like visually to see what Sid did? One answer to that would be by holding up the crust. Things—what he saw—looked like *that*. Here, one needs to fix an understanding of looking like. There are understandings on which the crust, when I hold it up, no matter how carefully, does *not* look as it did when Sid saw it. (Light and shadows, for one thing.) But anyway, if we aim to find a minimal feature in visual experience by looking inward to, say, the features of some internal state, something belonging to Sid's consciousness, as per the SH model, then holding up the crust does not even address the question we mean to ask. What we what to know is how things were visually *for Sid*. How, then, was it visually for Sid if there was a São-Mamedeish spot on the crust he saw? If pointing to the spot on the crust is not an answer, then there is *no* answer to this until something fixes what it would be for things to be one way or the other in this respect. That would be work of an occasion for the asking. Without that—unless, perhaps, the spot was, for Sid, particularly striking—there is no such thing as 'how that region looked to Sid'. In general, there is no such thing as *the* way things looked to someone in his seeing what he did, unless that way is simply: the way they did. So this way of moving inward moves nowhere. It is crucial, if experience is to represent, that it lead somewhere. For, to repeat a now familiar theme, only determinate objects of visual awareness *other than* what is seen could possibly make room for experience to represent.

8 Gazing Out

It is not for a philosopher to deny that retinal images unleash chains of happenings. Personally, I am inclined to believe this. Nor is it for a philosopher to deny that such chains terminate in states of some characteristic sort. I am officially neutral. Nor is it for a philosopher to deny that without such happenings and states *we* would see nothing. Some such things no doubt *enable* seeing. This settles little as to what it is that they enable. It does not settle *what* someone sees on an occasion, or when someone would count as seeing such-and-such. Nor does it help much to insist that the things he sees must be ones whose images on the retinas unleash things. Nor can we suppose that those terminal states in the enabling story just envisioned, in having the features they do, might *ipso facto* settle something which was *the* way things (then) looked to their possessor. Nor, correlatively, should we suppose that they settle something which, with the presence of given further factors, not themselves seeing, or even visual awareness of anything—pre-retinal aetiology, say—might add up to seeing whatever their possessor happens to see on the occasion—as if seeing were a hybrid of appearings and a friendly world.

How, then, to conceive visual experience? It has taken too long to get this far for me to say very much about this here. But what has been said so far provokes a few suggestions. First, some visual experience is seeing, some is not. Seeing is what is enabled when all goes well—as all is liable not to. If we do not conceive seeing as a hybrid, with an underlying 'way things look to the perceiver', present whether things are going well or not, we might then treat these cases separately. Which, I suggest, would be helpful.

I begin, then, with seeing. One striking difference between seeing (perceiving in general) and testimony is that seeing is, and remains for its duration, *au courant*. If Sid is told, reliably, that his ribeye has just gone on the grill, he may then know how things were *then*. So long as he has the testifier's word for it, he, perhaps, continues to know how things were then. If, meanwhile, the ribeye has been carbonized into inedibility, it takes a new piece of testimony to make him *au fait* with that. If, by contrast, Sid *sees* his ribeye going on the grill, he is thereby afforded, for so long as the experience lasts, constantly *au courant* awareness of the ribeye's career. He can suffer agonies as, helpless, he watches it carbonize, or, a little less feckless, flip it himself. Seeing is dynamic. (So, perhaps, are enablings, though again my philosophic business is not to claim or hypothesize.)

Seeing things is thus following them. Sid, before the baguette, shifts his attention, his eyes, his head; fidgets, swivels, rolls the chair around (it is one of those). Whatever we say as to his seeing the baguette, we do not normally conceive of seeing such that the right answer to that question changes from moment to moment—unless there is some special reason for it to change, as, when Sid swivels all the way around, the baguette goes, momentarily, out of sight. So seeing the baguette is something one qualifies, or not, as doing over an *interval*. It is relevant intervals—whatever counts, on an occasion, as Sid's experience of seeing, or failing to see, the baguette—which are evaluable as ones in which he saw it, or, again, did not. More reason not to suppose such a thing as 'the' way things looked to Sid in seeing the baguette, or that the momentary features of some internal state could fix what this was. Here, too, we find reason for conceiving seeing sometimes as *affording* awareness, if also sometimes as actually conferring it (Sid may see (still) the baguette at a moment at which his attention is fixed on that dark spot)—but, in either case, as a matter of what Sid holds onto throughout the interval.

A second central feature of seeing (and perceiving generally) is that it is occasion for exercise of our capacities for recognizing the reach of various bits of the conceptual to various cases of the non-conceptual. Being carbonized to reach to the non-conceptual as it does may be for it to reach to Sid's ribeye's being as it is: Sid's ribeye's so being is a ribeye being carbonized. The very thought that *that* is a ribeye being carbonized is not one which Sid, or anyone, could so much as entertain without acquaintance with *that*—the particular case (any more than I can now think, of a certain man in Ulan Bator, that *he* is now drinking tea). Seeing the ribeye is an exemplary way of making that thought available. Such is a most central role of sight—tied up, too, with the idea, discussed above, that seeing has really not made the world bear on what to think as it ought if it falls short of providing acquaintance with the particular case— the ribeye being as it is.

More generally, seeing makes thoughts, and, more generally, attitudes available to a subject which are otherwise liable, sometimes bound, not to be. No doubt these extend beyond those involved in seeing the reach of the conceptual to the non-conceptual. So we now have two measures for what it is that someone saw: what one sees must stay in step with one's epistemic status, as per the last section. It must also stay in step with the attitudes one might count as holding. Seeing the man in Ulan Bator allows me (*ceteris paribus*) to think of *him* that he is drinking tea. Conversely, the right thing to say as to whether I *can* so think may bear on what to say as to whether I saw him. These two constraints may allow one to look at a subject, and what is before him, and, without looking *inside* him, say, on occasion, what it is he saw.

Now for visual experiences which are *not* seeing. I confine attention to cases where enabling processes and states have gone wrong, as where, in special conditions of illumination, convex and concave, for example, on that house across the road, may reverse. I begin with a problem. We can think of seeing as affording, as well as as conferring, awareness—awareness one might enjoy, where one might also have failed to; awareness of what there is anyway to be aware of. We can do that precisely because seeing is a relation to an environment, whose denizens are for *one* to encounter, broadly speaking, in experience. It is just this—that awareness is of what one *might* be unaware of—which calls for enabling, such as might be provided for *seeing* by chains of happenings unleashed by the retinas, and so on.

The task of those chains of happenings unleashed by retinas was to be to enable visual awareness of one's *surroundings*. The SH model assigns them another role: to issue in states *affording* awareness of something else: how things are visually for—how they look, or seem, to—the subject, where this is independent of how *things* (pleonastically, in the environment) are visually, or look, or seem. This goes inevitably with the idea of such a state as with other features (physiological, perhaps) which impose a unique answer to the question how things are visually for one in it. If such a state thus *affords* awareness, as distinct from conferring it, then this is awareness one might enjoy or not (as, for example, Evans insists). So it is something which calls for enabling, just like seeing itself. And, to borrow a term from Frege (1918: 60), the game can begin anew. (Nor could the enabling here be self-enabling, accomplished by those very processes and states which provide such further things to be aware of: such would not be for us to be *afforded* awareness of them.) It is not quite *incoherent* to suppose that an enabling internal state produces something its subject must, but may, be enabled to be aware of. But it *is* incoherent to suppose it an intrinsic feature of enabling stories that they involve states which *do* produce such things.

It would at least eliminate promissory notes if the story of what enabled seeing did not posit any such thing.

Suppose that what enables seeing also, on occasion, provides something else of which to be aware visually—say, things looking as they then do to someone. Suppose that this something else belongs to the contents of that person's consciousness, in Frege's sense. Then Frege's lesson applies: such contents of consciousness could not be objects of a *judgement*; there is no sense in the idea that they, just in being as they are, might be thus and so—might thus relate to some given bit of the conceptual (see Frege 1918, 67–9, and Essay 2); which does in the idea that one might be *afforded* awareness of such things—as if that is awareness one might enjoy or miss out on.

The idea of seeing as dynamic suggests a way of reading Frege's lesson. On that idea, a stream of impressions on, so chains unleashed by, retinas, over an interval, goes with a certain responsiveness to the scene before the viewer's eyes, stable over that interval—stable opportunities for attitudes, or affordings of them. What one sees is then some sort of resultant of such responsiveness and what there is for it to be responsiveness to. If, say, what enables seeing sometimes provides further things to experience visually, which are *not* things of which to be afforded awareness in the present sense, then that role of the scene in the above cooperative enterprise drops out. Nothing performs it. What may remain is a subject's responsiveness (through intervals) to things being visually as they are for him; where here awareness may be *conferred*, but not (merely) afforded. Responsiveness to *this* could not take the form of *judging* that (in being as it is) it is thus and so. It could still take the form of seeing things being visually as they are *for* their being thus and so (*auffassen*, perhaps *anerkennen*; not *erkennen*). In any event, responsiveness could now take over the role of making such a circumstance one which, in being as it is, is a subject experiencing things being for him visually thus and so—for example, as though he were seeing a cantilevered upper floor.

But suppose we think of what enabling-gone-wrong provides, not as contents of consciousness, but rather as determined by, say, features of some neural configuration, or, otherwise, facts as to how the visual system reverses convex and concave when it does. Now we can think of enabling as providing something of which to be afforded awareness. For now I am (so far) aware visually of what I am where, say, concave and convex reverse, in and by being a way there is for *one* to be. By the same token, now enabling is called for for me to be aware of what I thus am. Now, too, there is room for enabling to go awry, and in that way among others room for things thus to look *to me* one way or another in being afforded awareness of what I thus am. Again, the game *can* begin anew. But something must allow the chain of enablings to stop. The previous idea shows how it can.

All this is at best the bare beginnings of understanding perceptual experience. The main aim here was to clear away a picture of such experience which positively blocks understanding. It is a picture widely at work even in those who disclaim it. It is (most often) engendered by a false impression of what it would be to ask after perceptual experience in a scientific manner, or while giving science its due. As Wittgenstein predicted, that impression leads only into darkness.[1]

---

[1] I am thankful to Mark Kalderon, and to Mike Martin, for their patient and painstaking efforts to make me see things better. The usual disclaimers apply.

6

Affording us the World

> 'While I was speaking to him I did not know what was going on in his head'. In saying this one is not thinking of brain-processes, but of thought processes. The picture should be taken seriously. We would really like to see into his head. And yet we only mean what elsewhere we would mean in saying we would like to know what he is thinking.
>
> Wittgenstein, *Philosophical Investigations*, §427

In *The Threefold Cord*, in describing the faulty underpinnings of the bad side of internal realism, Hilary Putnam says he once thought of

> perceptual inputs [as] the outer limit of our cognitive processing: everything that lies beyond those inputs is connected to our mental processes only causally, not cognitively.
>
> (1999: 16)

In which case there is this problem:

> What my 'model theoretic argument' showed is that interpretations of our language—even ones that make true the very sentences that are 'really true', true from a 'God's eye view' (assuming [this] makes sense)—can agree on what these inputs are while disagreeing wildly on what our terms actually refer to.
>
> (1999: 16)

On the idea that there was some sort of problem here he now comments,

> How could the question 'How does language hook onto the world?' even appear to pose a difficulty unless the retort: 'How can there be a problem about talking about, say, houses and trees when we see them all the time?' had not already been rejected in advance as question-begging or 'hopelessly naïve'?
>
> (1999: 12)

This need one can feel to construct our relations to windfall cherries, or bowls of them, or peccaries on our path, out of something inside a boundary of the sort Putnam mentions, with perceptual inputs stationed along them, sentinels looking out at something beyond, is an expression of a difficulty Wittgenstein expresses in another context like this:

It is so difficult to find the *beginning*. Or, better: it is difficult to begin at the beginning. And not try to go further back.

(1999, §471)

Here the felt need to start too far back manifests itself as a compulsion to look inside the head for what is to be found in the world around us; specifically, to look there for what it is we (*really*) respond to in—as we call it—seeing some cherries. The *Drang* (henceforth 'The *Drang*') runs very deep through much of philosophy of mind. It has various tributaries. It is easy enough to cut off one or several while leaving The *Drang* in place. What makes for it is not yet well understood.

I

Seeing is a form—visual—of awareness of one's (spatial) surroundings. Sight *affords* awareness of some of what is there, or there happening. Seeing that dirty cup on the counter, just after having started the dishwasher, is enjoying some of what vision places on offer. Seeing it to be a cup, or even an object (an integral piece of dry goods) is a further achievement, tied, as Frege says, to thinking and judging (1897: 149). Following the cup's career is yet another. Seeing places all this in reach. It remains *au courant*, as testimony does not.

The question what it is to see a bowl of cherries thus asks us to fasten on *that* item, and ask how we are privileged with access to how *it* is when, and in, seeing it. *What* we see would then be no more than is in our surroundings, and in view. What sensitivity to *that* would we enjoy in seeing it? That would be the question.

It is thus remarkable that from about the time Montaigne read Sextus to soon after VE day—three centuries plus—almost no-one thought that strategy worth a glance. When, for example, in the late 1930s H. A. Prichard wrote 'Perception', one was entitled to take for granted that this approach was wrong. Prichard begins,

I assume that 'perception' is a word used for the genus of which what we call seeing, hearing, smelling, tasting, and feeling or touching are the species

(1950: 52)

All well so far. He then remarks that in the 'everyday attitude of mind' of both philosophers and non-philosophers, one counts 'chairs and tables, boats going downstream, and so forth' as the sorts of things one sees. But, he announces, and only barely argues, this obviously will not do:

It need hardly be said that this view, much as we should all like to be able to vindicate it, will not stand examination.

(1950: 53)

Argument is sparse and shaky. Prichard was unusual among philosophers of perception in several respects. But not in this one. What we need to do, on the research strategy he is determined to follow, is not to ask, of the cherries before me, how I am sensitive to *them* in seeing *them*, but rather to ask what *else* it is to which visual experience might allow me to be sensitive. To Prichard's credit, he realized that such a something else would have to be available to my awareness only, and hence could not be an object of judgement. Cook Wilson had at least that much good effect.

2

There are various perception-specific roots of Prichard's amazing research strategy—the argument from illusion, in various forms, among them. There is failure to see how *special* the uses of language on which 'N saw O' does not imply O's presence in the scene. There is also a general attitude towards philosophical good faith expressed in finding it unremarkable that we could all, pre-philosophically, be *that* wrong as to what we *saw*. But The *Drang* is not confined to perception. It surfaces in views of thinking things so. Michael Dummett expresses it. In his 'inadvertent' book on Frege, in a chapter really more about Kripke, he writes:

The content of a belief appears to depend, not on the mode of presentation as determined by commonly agreed linguistic convention, together with the relevant circumstances, but on the connection which the individual subject makes between the expression and its referent...

An accurate characterization of a speaker's belief requires an account of his personal understanding of the words by means of which he expresses it... When we follow our usual procedure of characterizing someone's belief by means of a sentence considered as having the meaning that it does in the language to which it belongs, we are very often giving only an approximate statement of the content of that belief.

(1981: 115–6)

Parallel to the obvious strategy for studying what it is to see a bowl of cherries, the obvious strategy for studying what it is to think something would be first to ask what there *is* to think or not, and then, of some given thinker, which of *these* things he does think. First ask: 'What is it that might *be* so or not?', then, 'Of that, what does N *think* so?' I mention something to be thought, and say someone to think *that*; as a rule there is no issue of approximation. (Frege gives us excellent reasons for thinking of thinking in this way. I leave them unexplored here.)

Again, though, there is something that makes that obvious strategy seem— and not just to Dummett—hardly worth a second look. Instead, to see what someone thinks we need to look inside his head. It is not the world he thinks about, but views of it from a vantage point you would have to be him to enjoy, which determines what he 'really' thinks—now not a matter of his answer to the question whether there are cherries.

Jerry Fodor (1998, 2008, for example) feels The *Drang*. On his view, for me to think there is a peccary on the path is for me to bear a certain relation to something *literally* in the head. In the (English) sentence 'There is a peccary on the path', there is a string of letters beginning with 'T' and ending with 'h'. (The obvious one.) That string is the string it is independent of any considerations of how it is to be understood. If a given instance of that string is also an instance of the sentence 'There is a peccary on the path', then, as an instance of that sentence (but not just as that string) it is to be understood in a certain way. Similarly, on Fodor's view to think something is to relate to something with an identity entirely independent of anything to do with representing; which thing also, as it happens, is to be taken in a certain way—does, in fact, have some representational properties. That something has whatever representational features that subject's contact with the world has happened to bestow on it. Its having the features it does is very much a part of that subject's particular vicissitudes. At the same time, that something belongs to a language—a systematically structured collection of such somethings—and, as such, represents as it does by virtue of its place in that system. The remarkable thing is now that that system of such somethings just happens to draw just those distinctions which are drawn by the distinctions there are between one Fregean sense and another. Here there really are the problems Putnam pointed to in his development of Skolem's thought.

Fodor is, of course, moved by proprietary factors—notably by a misguided sense of naturalism. That is why I began here with Dummett, who is certainly not in thrall to any *such* compulsion. Though they may understand 'in the head' differently, Dummett and Fodor share a view of the work what is in the head would have to do. There must be deeper roots. My candidate is the idea that there is such a thing as '*the* distinctions there are between one Fregean sense and another'. For the moment I merely point out the parallel.

3

Hilary is sometimes too modest. In *Cord* he records having learned from Austin how to resist one sort of temptation to look inside the head (for what in fact is located outside it). Austin did much, I think, to show us how there is no need to look anywhere but in the environment to find what it is that we see (more generally, encounter, are made aware of, in perception). But even before discovering Austin, Hilary taught us some very valuable lessons in how to resist temptations to look elsewhere. I will now introduce a particular such temptation, and then say briefly how Hilary defuses it. I will appeal to an idea which, in *Cord*, he presents as 'the face of perception'. But the idea is much deeper, and longer standing, in his thought than that title for it.

One can introduce the temptation by asking how we differ from cats. There is the business of the tails, and so on. But when we are done with that, it seems we may need a look inside. Cats do not see the world as we do. Let us grant, for the moment, that there is a sense in which they are not thinkers (*rational animals*) at all. (As usual in philosophy, 'rational' now takes on a special meaning. You cannot reason with my cat. You cannot reason with Aunt Ida either. Aunt Ida is just not rational; but not in the sense in which, here, a cat is meant not to be.) The point about cats can be put this way: cats are Pyrrhonian. Things may seem to them certain ways. Feline constitution naturally inclines them to respond to seemings in certain ways. Seemingly something large approaches. The cat dives beneath a hedge. Natural inclinations thus guide the cat. But here 'guide' can only mean *cause* it to do things. For that is all a natural inclination can accomplish. We, by contrast, are thinkers, that is, judgers in Frege's sense: we take truth-evaluable attitudes towards things. To judge is to hold true (or so). It is just when I stand in that way towards something being so that its being so bears, for me, on what to think and do as its being so in fact bears on what is to be done and what it is right to think (insofar as I grasp this bearing). That there is a peccary on the path may be good reason for me to think I am in Oxfordshire, given its bearing on the excess wealth of the local landed. But it is reason for *me* so to think only insofar as I take the fact in.

So we have this situation. In fact there is a peccary on the path. In fact, this means I am in Oxfordshire. I judge there to be a peccary on the path. I know that peccaries about means I am in Oxfordshire. But we need a link between the first fact about the peccary, and the first fact about me. That there is a peccary on the path must make this the thing for me to think. Seeing is to forge that link. I see the peccary; in my seeing it, that there is one becomes the thing for me to think.

The core difference between myself and a cat (on present assumptions) is that the cat is Pyrrhonian, while I am a judger. But now this can seem to call for a further difference in the nature of our experience. For, in thinking of the link just mentioned, one might think like this. What *really* makes it rational for me to judge there to be a peccary is *the fact* that there is a peccary. If my visual experience is to make that fact bear for me on what to think, then it must provide—make me aware of—something shaped as that fact is for me to respond to with that attitude. For, the thought would be, it is hard to see how anything not so shaped could bear a *rational* relation to whether to think there to be a peccary. So, it may seem, in seeing the scene before me I gain something to respond to that the cat does not—am made aware of something that the cat is not. Such an object of awareness is shaped just as my thoughts are. So, the thought goes, it is shaped by what shapes my thoughts.

So that I am a judger and the cat not now seems to entail a further difference: what I experience in seeing the scene is other than what the cat does—*in experiencing the same scene*. This forces us to look inward for the difference. The difference, we have decided already, is the upshot of conceptual capacities I, but not the cat, enjoy. Now, of course, if the cat and I are watching an approaching game warden, I may experience an uneasiness the cat does not—despite the bird in its mouth. The shiver going up my spine, but not the cat's, would be a difference in what we experience. The cat may thank its lack of conceptual capacities for its aplomb. But if the difference in what we experience is conceived as a difference in what we experience *visually*—how we (thus) experience things *being* visually—my conceptual capacities are responsible for differences in the cat's, and my, objects of *perception*—in this case, sight. And then it seems—there being only one *scene* for the cat and me to gaze at—those differences will have to be found by looking inside. My conceptual capacities certainly do not shape the peccary. If they shape any object of perception, it will have to be one found where no peccary can tread. We are now adrift, cut off from the world.

4

Hilary is, in a number of ways, an antidote to any such drive to look inward to find what is experienced. I begin with what seems most important for the present purpose. Grant that cats are Pyrrhonian, we judgers, and not *vice versa*. By the preceding line, it is meant to follow that visual experience must provide us different things to respond to than it provides the cat. Hilary shows why it does not.

Cats do not judge, and we do, the thought is, because they lack certain capacities we have: *conceptual* capacities. So it takes conceptual capacities to judge. The idea, in brief, is: to judge is to commit to things being a certain way; to do that one must grasp what it would be for things to be that way—when, that is, they would so count. Hilary shows what is contained in such a grasp; hence what judging requires. Now, one good idea about judging is that we could not *judge* as to how (which ways) our surroundings are—so much as make intelligible *commitments* as to this—unless experience were able to make the way those surroundings bear, for us, on how to think them; bear for us, that is, according as *what* we experience bears on what is *so*. And the idea, of which Hilary will help disabuse us, is that in order to do that experience must provide us *objects* of experience differing from those feline experience supplies a cat. Any such idea, I have suggested, is disastrous.

In *Cord* Hilary makes the right point with an image borrowed from Cora Diamond (see her 1981). Long before that, though, he made the point without that image. Seeing this will help see how he matters to present matters. The image is of a *face* of a concept (or of a way for things, or for something, to be). Applying that image (before developing it), a conceptual capacity would be one to see the *face* of being such-and-such way in its indefinite potential manifestations in things, or some thing, being as they are/it is. Following Wittgenstein, Hilary develops the image, in *Cord*, in terms of games. When would a game be a form of poker? Is there a recipe for this? There need not be. If I invent a game, like central cases of poker in some respects, but which one can play by oneself, to a *Spielkenner's* eye—the eye of someone with a proper sense for what *matters* in poker—my invention might just be recognizable as another form of poker, or as not that. What ways for things to be we have in mind when we ask whether something would count as (being) such-and-such, which particular cases are cases of these things, does not float independent of what the *Kenner*—the person with a proper sense for things—would find. This is one crucial point.

To see how central this idea has always been to Hilary, consider another example. Newtonian mechanics speaks of a physical quantity called kinetic energy. Relativistic mechanics speaks of a quantity called *energy*. Are both these theories thus speaking of *energy*? We can recognize the face of a concept, *energy*, in what both speak of. That *is* an answer. There is no other. (On this, see my *Objectivity and the Parochial* essay 'The Shape of the Conceptual') This should make the centrality of the idea apparent.

On the points so far Hilary is one with Wittgenstein, though not Wittgenstein as read when Hilary first made them. And, I suppose, he is one with all at this round table. In *Cord*, Hilary uses the point against Michael Dummett's conception of how a concept stands to its applications. But for technical details which do not matter here (the difference between rules and axioms), he might equally well be making it against Paul Feyerabend, or against any of many other people. On Dummett's account a concept is fixed by (given, identifiable) rules for its introduction and elimination. Any different rules would *ipso facto* govern a different concept. If we think of a concept, as we may, as intrinsically of a given way for things to be—of being round, say—then, equally, a way for things to be is fixed by such rules. It is the way things would be just in case those rules licensed counting things being as they are as things being that way. Again, different rules *ipso facto* speak of a different way for things to be. If this is so, then if Newton spoke of energy, Einstein did not, and *vice versa*. To which Hilary says in *Cord*:

The difference between Dummett's Wittgenstein and Diamond's Wittgenstein parallels the difference we saw earlier between Dummett and myself. Dummett wants to say that the rules for the application of expressions such as 'too small to see' change with the invention of the microscope, and therefore the meanings of the expressions change, or rather they are given new meanings in their new contexts of use. I want to say that the question is not one of distinguishing between the 'rules' of the activity of using words and components of the activity that are not 'rules', and that here too the question is one of our ways of 'seeing the face' of one activity in another.

(1999: 64)

A concept is not identified by any given set of principles, or rules, in the way Dummett (along with many others) supposes. It may be that it applies (is satisfied) according to such-and-such principles, given the occasion there in fact will be (or in fact can be) for applying it. But its applications are not bound by any such principles in the sense that whatever applied differently simply would not be that concept, no matter what. Different occasions for applying it are liable to require different principles of application. Or at least the concept being, and being of, what it is always leaves room for that.

I will make Hilary's point in several ways before I am done—just now by asking after how *recognition* capacities relate to conceptual capacities. The image, *face of* . . . , appeals to resemblances with the phenomenon of facial recognition. One can recognize a human face, or, again, a similarity between faces within a given family, or between Pia's face and, say, Nicole Kidman's. One can recognize Pia's face across the span of a lifetime, and through a wide range of distortions life, or beauticians, may inflict on it. Just at this point, there is an idea which can spoil the comparison sought for. Facial recognition is a topic for psychologists. It is not obvious what allows us to see right away that that is David Soul at the next table, twenty years after his last appearance. But a psychologist might find out. The idea is precisely to look for features, to which we are sensitive, and which remain constant across the years. It is no mean intellectual achievement to find them; but they can be found. One *might* try to conceive the concepts, to which Hilary applies the image, on this model: what features remain constant across all the cases of what would fit the concept is not evident. It would be a considerable intellectual achievement to find them; but they are there, and may be found.

This would spoil the image, which was to be one of there being, in some sense, *no* features in common to all the cases where a concept applies—except that they are all ones of being that which the concept is a concept of—a way for things, or for something, to be—and are all recognizable as one by a *Kenner*— one with a proper sense for such things. But the image is not spoiled if we attend to what success for the psychologist would be. The psychologist identifies features which *do* allow us to recognize a face, as encountered in the circumstances in which we might encounter it. It would be good enough, perhaps more than that, if he could do that much. Working according to our sensitivity to those features, we can count as having a *capacity* to tell a face. For *most* things there are to recognize, any *such* capacity is liable to stop being that in a hostile environment. Perhaps you can recognize Pia by her face. But perhaps not if everyone has plastic surgery so as to look just like her; or if she has radical enough plastic surgery so as not to. The surgery would not detract from the psychologist's achievement. That the capacity he seeks is one liable to fail is what makes that achievement possible in the first place.

A *conceptual* capacity positions us to do something a recognition capacity, as just conceived, would not. It positions us to recognize when a given recognition capacity—an ability to tell peccaries, say, when you see one—has ceased to be that. It allows us to make sense of the idea that, while it would be a peccary if this were decided by those features to which the some-time recognition capacity is sensitive, for all that it is not one. I have described a cognitive achievement to which a psychologist might aspire, *in re* recognizing someone's face. We need not suppose that a parallel achievement is in the cards when it comes to recognizing when a recognition capacity like that for faces would have failed—what it might be for something to have *those* features, but not be a peccary, or Pia's face. There may be all sorts of things that could make a situation count as one which was that way. And now we have the wanted image. Someone—the *Kenner*—may *have* the capacity to recognize what our *conceptual* capacities position us to see, to make the right sense, on the right occasion, of those situations these capacities allow us to understand; but there need be nothing external to his sense for such things, standing towards *what* he is prepared to recognize as those very abstract features of faces stand towards an instance of the face, to which a *Kenner's* sense could be held accountable. This is a form of an idea which, I think, has informed much of what is most exciting in John McDowell's philosophy.

How, if this is right, would a conceptual capacity relate to a recognition capacity, construed, as above, as a proper subject for psychology? Such a recognition capacity would be exhausted by some set of principles governing its operations; the conceptual capacity would not. What this need not mean, though, is that a conceptual capacity is, intrinsically, sensitive to things of a very different shape than a recognition capacity might be. We tell pigs by their looks. We are sensitive to the presence of a certain look. We can thus tell pigs when we see them, at sight. When we tell, of a particular case, that it is what would be, or not, a case of things being such-and-such way, we need not be telling by, or sensitive to, anything very different in kind. Experience—say, visual experience—cannot make the world bear on what we are to think unless it engages with our conceptual capacities. It must provide that to which such capacities are sensitive; that by which we can *see* the reason there is to think that, say, there is a pig before us—perhaps just that there is one. But such capacities need not be different in kind from those which allow us to tell a pig when we see one. And, I will suggest, for that they need not bring any more into view than *might* be in view for a cat too when confronted by a pig (abstracting from here-boring details of feline optics). This is *one* way to spell out Hilary's point. Now for another. (Some, I am afraid, are about to leave the boat.)

5

The above point about conceptual capacities, and their relation to recognition capacities, conceived as subjects for the psychologist, is so important that I am going to put it in another form. Frege found something *intrinsically* general about a thought—a particular way for a posture towards the world to make *its* correctness, independent of any taking of it, turning *entirely* on how things are. Frege expressed the point thus:

A thought always contains something which reaches out beyond the particular case, by which it presents this to consciousness as falling under a certain generality.

(1882: *Kernsatz* 4)

A thought *demands* something of the particular case for its being as represented. It cannot, the idea is, demand *everything*; that is, that the particular case be *just* the way it is. One can put this by saying that, for principled reasons, it must be so that things *could have* been represented as any given thought represents them without their *being* precisely as they are. Not *everything* in how things are matters to whether one could represent them as any given thought does; not everything, thus, matters to whether they *are* as represented. This is to say that if the particular case *is* as represented, if it is the way it was represented to be, then it instances (realizes) things being that way in only one of an indefinite variety of ways this could be done. If the pig is in the sty while Pia prepares a daube, then there is also a way for the pig to be in the sty while Pia suns herself in the *chaise longue*. There is a *range* of cases in which things being as they were would be their being such that the pig is in the sty. There is a generality—something for a particular case to be—which reaches just to that range. Such is the generality under which the thought that the pig is in the sty brings the particular case. Such is the intrinsic generality of thoughts.

The particular case is that which the thought represents as a certain way. Which is just: things being as they are. Things being as they are, so far as that goes, does not bring anything under any given generality; or present anything to consciousness as so falling. If it presented anything to consciousness, that could only be itself. It cannot be instanced in an indefinite *variety* of ways. If we were to speak of it as instanced at all, that would have to be only by itself. But that would be at best a degenerate use of 'instance'. In fact, it is not *instanced* by anything. For it makes itself hostage to nothing for correctness. It is neither correct nor incorrect (except in the sense that it is just *so* wrong for Bush to be president). All of which is to say: it reaches to no range of cases; it has no reach. The generality of a thought consists its representing things as some way that might be instanced in an indefinite variety of ways. What does the instancing *has* no such generality. If we call what has this generality *(the) conceptual*, we might call what lacks it *(the) non-conceptual*.

Frege further tells us,

The fundamental logical relation is that of an object falling under a concept. All relations between concepts are reducible to this.

(1892–1895: 25)

Frege's notion of a concept is of something at the level of reference, not sense (in his sense)—the level at which, for him, a thought belongs. He does not quite manage to invest his notion with that generality which marks a thought. But, as he does insist, a thought, on any decomposition of it, has some element—some proper contribution to the thought's doing what it does—which shares the generality of a thought (in fact, whose generality the thought restricts in some way), which is being about a way there is for *something* to be, so under which those objects which are that way may be said to fall. Such elements identify one thing we might call, and what I here will call, a concept.

If an object is that way for something to be which identifies the concept—the way it, or that element in thoughts which identifies it, represents things—we may speak of that object as falling under the concept. For an object to fall under a concept in this sense is for its being as it is to be it being the way that concept represents a thing; or, equally, for things being as they are to be this object being that way. The object's being as it is thus *instances* what the concept is a concept of, or, in shorthand, simply the concept.

An object's being as it is belongs to the non-conceptual. So the fundamental relation Frege speaks of can be read as, or as mirroring, an at least equally fundamental relation between the conceptual and the non-conceptual. This relation is fundamental, *inter alia*, in this way: if we are to be thinkers on whose thinking the world may bear *rationally*—so if we are to be thinkers at all—then we had better be able to recognize instances of its holding. One could not so much as have the conceptual in view (or in mind) without such competence. Perhaps being a crisp entails being greasy. But one does not grasp *that* fact (or thought) without an adequate grasp on what an instance of a crisp, or being greasy, would be. Absent any grasp of how these concepts reach, what would make it being a *crisp* and *greasy* that one is thinking of? This is another point Hilary has made unmistakeable for us. Take any structure of internal relations, such as entailments, between concepts, divorced from any identification of the reach of these concepts to the non-conceptual, and the 'concepts' remain mere tags: *nothing* in such a structure can make the tags reach to some one set of cases—bring things under some one generality—rather than indefinitely many others. Such is the message of 'Models and Reality' (1977).

A recognition capacity in the present sense—an ability to recognize a pig at sight, say—would be a capacity to recognize the reach of the conceptual to the non-conceptual. One sees, and recognizes, instances of something being a pig. By the same token, so would a conceptual capacity in the present sense. As it had better be to be a *conceptual* capacity at all. For it is, *inter alia*, an ability to recognize the limits of any given recognition capacity. So if we have recognition capacities, and their corresponding conceptual capacities, we are in shape to be thinkers; to think things of the world we inhabit. And, I think, only if that. I further think we can feel safe here.

Perception's *essential* role in the life of a *thinker* is to allow the world to bear, for him, on what he is to think according to the bearing of what that thinker is aware of on what is so. It thus does such things as allowing the presence of the pig before me to bear, for me, on whether to think *that* there is a pig there. For it to serve this role requires nothing less than for it to bring the non-conceptual—that which the world provides—within reach of our recognition (so conceptual) capacities. Perhaps an easy way to see this is this. Perhaps that a pig is in the sty means that the farmer is home. Perhaps perception—vision, in this case—allows me to see that a pig is in the sty. If it accomplishes this much, then it has brought that fact about the world to bear on what I am to think: if I also see enough of factive meaning, the thing for me to think is that the farmer is home. But if that were *all* perception accomplished, or the only accomplishment to its credit, it would not have fulfilled its appointed role. For (see the discussion above) if the pig is in the sty, this is so in just *one* particular way of the indefinitely many ways there are for it to be so—such as the pig sleeping in the mud, or standing by the railings. What perception must make available to me, to make the world bear on my thinking as it is perception's job to make it bear, is *the way* in which that general way for things to be, a pig being in the sty, is instanced by things being as they are. This it can only do by bringing the non-conceptual in view; making it available for exercise by me of my recognition, and conceptual capacities.

Such is needed, for one thing, if perception is to allow me to see how *this case* of a pig being in the sty bears on what else is so. Perhaps, often, a pig in the sty is black pudding on the way; but not when it is this prize pig, or the neighbour's pig—the sort of sizing up I must be positioned for if that pig in the sty is to get its full bearing, for me, on what to think and do—for example, whether to gather apples for the *geitespek*. More crucially, it is the pig's presence in the sty that bears on whether there is a pig before me. If I am to take it, fully rationally, simply on grounds of what I see, that there is a pig before me, seeing must confront me with nothing less than the pig's presence, in its full glory, as it were: things being as they are, at least at that place where the pig is present. I must be able to see, for example, just what sort of thing it is that is the pig in the sty here; just *how* it is. One reason is this: suppose it is a piglet, or a pot-bellied pig, or a tusked wild boar that is in the sty; or, again, a pig carcass, or just the hind quarters of the pig, the rest of it in that crib of corn, or the baby's crib. *Is* the way things are the pig being in the sty? That depends on what you understand by a pig being in a sty. Such is one sort of question over which it is perception's job to allow me to exercise my *savoir faire*, or cultivated sensibility.

So perception makes—and must make—the way things bear, for me, on how to think things are through positioning me, *inter alia*, to exercise my abilities, such as they are, to recognize instances of (the image of) what Frege calls the fundamental logical relation—that between the non-conceptual and the conceptual where the first instances the last. Now for Putnam's point. Conceptual capacities need not reduce to recipes; to recognition capacities insofar as these are tractable problems for psychology, as conceived above. It need not always be that for a concept to fit is for what it fits to have a certain constellation of (perhaps highly abstract) features. Conceptual capacities are liable to rely, at least for some purposes, on an irreducible sense for how the non-conceptual would connect to some given bit of the conceptual. It will do for the exercise of such capacities to have access, notably perceptual access, to the non-conceptual which is to be related to one or another bit of the conceptual. Indeed, as we have just seen, often nothing less than such access will do for full exercise of such *irreducible* capacities.

Indeed, as we have seen, conceptual capacities *cannot* always reduce to recipes. Just maybe, a conceptual capacity *in re* being a bachelor reduces to capacities to recognize when something's being as it is would count as its being male, and when it would count as its being married. But then, what of these capacities? If *all* our conceptual capacities were thus reducible, we would be in that position which 'Models and Reality' showed to be impossible: a position in which all there was to bring the conceptual within our view was internal relations between bits of it—a structure identified independent of how anything it structures reaches to the non-conceptual. In that position, thought vanishes entirely from our lives.

If conceptual capacities were all reducible, it might do for perception merely to bring bits of the conceptual to bear on our thought; merely to afford us awareness of them (if we can even really make sense of this idea). But our conceptual capacities do not work like that, which is another reason that perception cannot have done its job if it falls short of bringing the non-conceptual in view. Conversely, it would be fine for it to do just that. Exercising our capacities to recognize what would count as things being one or another given way, we can then supply relevant bits of the conceptual ourselves. This is what Frege had in mind when he wrote:

> Although a law of nature obtains quite independently of whether we think of it or not, it does not emit light or sound waves by which our visual or auditory nerves could be affected. But don't I see that this flower has five petals? One can say that; but then uses the word 'see' not in the sense of mere perception by means of light, but something involving thought and judgement.
>
> (1897: 149)

The pig before me, when I see it, is what allows me to see—recognize, register—that there is a pig before me. Perception need only bring the pig in view. The rest lies in my capacities for knowing what it is I see—when perception has brought a pig in view; when it thus makes that there is a pig before me the thing for me to judge.

6

Which expressions, on which faces, are ones of grief? Which circumstances would be ones in which Newton and Einstein spoke of the same physical quantity (one truly, one falsely) in speaking of 'energy'? Answers to such questions are not provided simply by things being as they are. It takes a *Kenner* to see them. Just for this reason, experience must supply us with something for a *Kenner's* capacities to work on. Just for that reason, perception must do no less, and need do no more, than bring the non-conceptual into view. Some philosophers, such as Gareth Evans and Christopher Peacocke, have missed this point. For them, perception could make the world bear on what we are to think *only* by presenting us with recognizable bits of the conceptual. Peacocke puts it this way:

By perceiving the world, we frequently learn whether a judgement with a given conceptual content is true or not. This is possible only because a perceptual experience has a correctness condition whose holding may itself exclude, or require, the truth of a conceptual content.

(1992: 66)

It is thus for experience to make something conceptual do the *world's* bearing on what we are to think—a hopeless assignment. For Evans and Peacocke, that assignment is to be carried out in experience representing things as so—for reasons we have seen, again a hopeless project.

Such a view inevitably sends us searching inward looking for the *real*, or first, objects of visual awareness. Why? Suppose that visual experience provided (visual) awareness merely of what was before one's eyes—a scene. Bracketing billboards and the like, scenes do not represent anything as so. For a scene to do that, it, just in being as it is, would have to fix some generality under which it presented things—presumably just itself—as falling. It would have to reach in a particular way to what were to be instances of things being as it represented them. As we saw in setting out the conceptual–non-conceptual distinction, such a thing is just not on. On the other hand, if experience representing things as so is to be the route by which it makes the world (or anything) bear *for me* on what I am to think, then it must be recognizable to me just *what* way my experience represents things to be—in a fairly minimal sense: I must be able to say of the way I find things, and perhaps of ways I might, that, given this, my experience was *right* (*casu quo* wrong) as to how things were. My experiencing, visually, what I do must make this so recognizable. My experiencing, visually, the *scene* will not turn the trick. So I must experience, visually, something else— just what Evans provides, or tries to, in making perceptual experience an *internal state*, whose content we get at by asking ourselves certain questions as to how, in it, things seem to us—answers to which float entirely free (in principle) of how the scene in view *is*, or how *it* seems.

Evans and Peacocke are on a hopeless, though as we have also seen, needless, search. A search for what distinguishes us from cats (more generally, Pyrrhonian creatures) *can* send us on a similar and, I think, similarly doomed search. The idea would be: for non-Pyrrhonian creatures like us, conceptual capacities would have to shape *something* in experience. Kant thought they shaped reality itself, taking reality to be just what there is to experience, and to judge of—things being as they are. (Kant thought they shaped only a special tract of reality. But I bracket that.) So, for Kant, they shaped precisely the only objects of (our) perception there are or could be. But suppose that while holding the general view you reject the idea that conceptual capacities can shape a peccary. So they do not shape reality in this sense. So, if there *is* any perception, they do not shape its objects—what is perceived, such as the scene before you. Now you are on your way inward, I have suggested, looking for what they do shape.

Of course, with Putnam and Frege on board, conceptual capacities are still located *somewhere* in experience. Frege put things rightly. They are located in our responses to what we experience (perceptually): in our recognizing what we do *in* that which we experience, such as visually, that of which *sight* affords awareness—such things as a case of a pig in a sty. But now, suppose we do not want to locate conceptual capacities merely there. One insists on their shaping the very things which, by means of our senses, or at least in perceiving perceptually, we experience. Then we are, inevitably, on our way inward. We must end up in something like Evans' position, in which perceptual experiences are internal states.

I want to end, then, by posing a question to John McDowell. It is a question, not an accusation: I am not at all confident I understand him on the relevant point. But the question is whether John is not committed to (a very subtle version, to be sure) of that same gaze inward that I located in Evans. A text which raises this question—and which I think I do not understand—is a response to Hubert Dreyfus, entitled 'What Myth?' (McDowell, 2009a). In it, John takes up the question what distinguishes us from cats. (I take bits of this out of order.) He writes:

My experience might disclose to me that an opening in a wall is big enough for me to go through. A cat might see that an opening in a wall is big enough for it to go through. My experience would be world-disclosing and so conceptual in form in the sense I have introduced. The cat's perceptual intake would not be world-disclosing and so, in the relevant sense, not conceptual in form. It is irrelevant to this difference between the cases that there is that match in what the cat and I would be getting to know through the exercise of our perceptual capacities.

(2009: 321)

The match between the cat and John is: both would come to know that an opening in the wall is big enough. The difference is that John's experience would be 'world-disclosing', the cat's not. For the moment, let 'world-disclosing' be a place-holder for what distinguishes feline from human experience. Anyway, John tells us, that difference has a consequence. John's perceptual intake is, in a certain sense, 'conceptual in form'. Not the cat's. So John takes in, perceptually, something the cat does not. He thus experiences, *perceptually*, such as visually, something the cat does not. I do not think John means something like, the cat experiences things being all bright and shiny, John their being all dull and matte-finished, or that, where John sees a hole in the wall, the cat draws a blank, or sees what looks as though it is bricked up. I note that if what John takes in, perceptually, is just what he sees, or what is before his eyes, then, since it is the same *scene* John and the cat see, their perceptual intake is so far the same. I note too that that the hole in the wall is big enough for a philosopher to pass through, or just that there is a hole, is not *in* the scene, as the whole itself is. (See Frege on petals.)

It *looks* as if other passages give a clue to what John has in mind. Here are two:

Granting that belief-formation, on the part of a rational animal, is an exercise of the animal's rationality, why should we suppose rationality must be operative also in the constitution of that to which perceptual belief-formation is rationally responsive?... Perceptual experiencing, on the part of a rational animal, is not just something that can elicit rational responses in the shape of perceptual beliefs... the perceptual experiencing of rational animals is itself rational openness to the world—which includes openness to affordances, as I have been insisting. So capacities that belong to a subject's rationality must be operative in the subject's experiencing itself, not just in responses to it.

(2009: 316–7)

What is important is this: if an experience is world-disclosing... all its content is present in a form in which... it is suitable to constitute contents of conceptual capacities.

(2009: 319)

So perceptual experiencing of rational animals—us and not cats—is 'rational openness to the world'. This is, presumably, another form of the distinction John is getting at with the term 'world-disclosing'. This requires, he tells us, that a subject's rationality must be operative in his experiencing itself, not just in responses to it. Which means, on the above line of thought, that it is operative in *constituting* 'that to which perceptual belief formation is rationally responsive'.

I take it that perceptual belief formation is belief formation on the basis of what is experienced; so that what it is responsive to is that which is perceptually experienced.

Why should one seem to see such connections? Suppose that *what* I experience perceptually—by sight—is just the trail before me, that peccary glaring at me, half turned in my direction. I might respond to that in recognizing what I thus see as a case of a peccary being on the (or a) trail before me. *That* is a rational response to what I see, as I—I claim Hilary and I—insist. It exercises my ability to link up the non-conceptual with the conceptual, to register instances of Frege's fundamental logical relation (or its mirror, as constructed above). So far, my conceptual capacities have no role in constituting *what* I respond to. For them to do that, they would have to constitute, in part, the peccary, or its glare, or something of this sort.

But John thinks—or *seems* to think (this is a question)—that my perceptual intake, what I respond to, what I apply my capacities to in forming beliefs based on it, must be 'conceptual in form', or 'in a form suitable to constitute the content of conceptual capacities'. So it could not just be the peccary, poised as it is, or its pawing of the path, and so on. It is tempting, I confess, to read this as an idea that what I, but not the cat, *perceive*, that of which I am afforded visual awareness, or some of it, belongs to the *conceptual*, rather than the non-conceptual, as if it were such things as *being on a path*, a way there *is* for something to be. Behind which it is also tempting, I confess, to find a picture on which, for my benefit, but not the cat's, the world is presented articulated into those particular ways for *things* to be (catholic sense—do not ask which ones), or for something to be, which things *are*, or something is, in things (in the scene before me) being as they are. What would make such an idea attractive (to the extent that it can be) would be the idea that only something of conceptual form could bear *rationally* on questions of what to think (or of what is *so*)—the very idea which moves Evans and Peacocke to their own form of cutting us off irretrievably from the world.

I hope, and expect, that I am reading John wrongly. In any event, there is this to say about the above ideas. First, as Frege saw, the idea of encountering the conceptual *perceptually* makes no sense. This is what Frege is getting at when he observes that while the sun, or a flower, is a visible thing, emitting rays arriving in our eyes, that the sun has set, or that the flower has five petals, is not. It is not before us to be seen. Neither are ways there are for a thing to be. They are something else entirely. Second, the world, or that part of it, the scene before me, does not articulate in any particular way just in being as it is; nor in any unique way full stop. Nor does what perception provides for me to respond to commit me to any one particular way of articulating it. This is related to the conceptual not being literally *in* the scene. Third, if the world is really going to bear, for me, *rationally* on what I am to think—with bearing of the sort it has on what is so—then perception had better provide me opportunity for exercising my capacities to link the non-conceptual with the conceptual—to recognizing those particular instancings, each in its own way, of those ways for things to be which are in fact instanced. Hence, fourth, if I am equipped with capacities for making the world so bear—capacities which acts may well lack—there is no need for those capacities to shape that which I experience perceptually (visually). That would not just be *de trop*; it would spoil everything.

Finally (see point 1), if we needed to make bits of the *conceptual* objects of perceptual awareness, we would have to look elsewhere than the scene in view, where they are not to be found. We would have to look elsewhere, too, to find things that our conceptual capacities could shape. Where the peccaries are is, as noted, the wrong place to look. So it would be no surprise if here, just as with Evans and Peacocke, though in a different form, the wholly mistaken idea that only the conceptual can bear rationally on what to think *so*—that *rational* relations hold only *inside* the conceptual—drives us to posit inner objects of perceptual awareness, parts of every experience in which—if we are lucky—the world is revealed to us. But I neither know nor expect that John holds that wholly mistaken idea.

7

Hilary speaks of a face of the conceptual. He also speaks of a face of perception. He models both on facial expressions. Here he endorses Diamond, who explains that when we say two faces have the same expression,

This is not like saying the mouths are the same length, the eyes the same distance apart; it is not that kind of description. But it is not a description of *something else*, the expression, distinct from that curved line, the dots, and so on.

(Diamond 1981: 249)

And he goes on to say:

Seeing an expression in a picture face is not just a matter of seeing the lines and dots; rather it is a matter of seeing something *in* the lines and dots—but this is not to say that it is a matter of seeing something *besides* the lines and dots.

(1999: 63)

What I have been trying to bring out above is that to see things which are present in this sort of way, one needs to have the non-conceptual in view;

something on which to exercise capacities to link that of a sort to fall under given generalities with the generalities it in fact falls under. With that in view, there is no need for any other sort of experiential intake on which to base, rationally, judgements as to how things are in our environment. The best of John's work stresses the presence, in precisely this way, of a wide range of phenomena which have seemed intractable to philosophers who failed to recognize this form of presence—such things as virtues, or understanding, or personal persistence through time. He, if anyone, should have a hold on what this means for the nature of experience.

A recognition routine might settle whether a peccary is yonder by presence or absence of those distinctive stiff bristles. The routine would work only in amenable environments. If custom were to shave peccaries, or some other beast had the same bristles, it would not work. A conceptual capacity addresses the very different question what it is for something to be a peccary—what would and would not count (when). Is a butchered peccary in the shop window a peccary? Conceptual capacities are engaged in moving from routine to routine; from one way of recognizing something to another. They get us from Newton's account of how to tell how much energy an object has to Einstein's, revealing one thing each would be right of in favourable circumstances. *Such* achievements may be beyond the reach of non-linguistic creatures. For all of which (modulo differences in visual equipment), what these creatures see remains what we do: none other than what may come as well before their, as before our, eyes.

7

Is Seeing Intentional?

1 Taking Aim

Intentionality, we have been told, is the mark of the mental; which is little use in marking off the mental until we know what intentionality is. Perhaps the interesting project is to find some sense for 'intentional' which makes the slogan true. But perhaps the slogan rests on a misconception of the mental. This essay will explore those possibilities.

'Intentional' in its usual sense marks much less than all the mental. I may, perhaps, intentionally place myself so as to see what goes on across the street. But when it happens, I do not *intentionally* (nor unintentionally) *see* it. Just so is perception standardly classed a passion.

So 'intentional' is not to have its ordinary sense. What then? Metaphors are on offer. One main one is that of aiming, or being aimed, or directed, at an object: 'object' in some sense corresponding to *accusative*; or object, the sort of thing that falls under concepts, but is not fallen under—a bearer of (first-order) properties; or, perhaps, what Frege called 'the particular case'—things (catholic sense, admitting no 'Which?') being as they are (or some thing being as it is). (See 1882, *Kernsatz* 4.)

What, then, is aiming at an object? First, is there always, *per se*, an object aimed at? (It would be cheating to say, 'Yes, but perhaps a non-existent one'.) Taking 'aim' literally, I can aim at a deer in the copse, but not at a deer that is not there (though I may *think* I am aiming without a deer to aim at). So, perhaps, yes. But it *seems* I may want to meet the winner of the race, though it was called off, or ended in a tie. In which case 'Yes' would *seem* to make wanting non-intentional. We do not want that. So, perhaps, 'No'.

There is a parallel issue about Frege's notion of a mode of presentation of an object (bearer of properties). Some hold that a way of presenting *A* (a contribution to expressing a *singular* thought about A) requires *A* for there to be *that* way of presenting anything at all. Others hold that a way of presenting *A* (as above) may be that in a kind world, but in an unkind one, a way of presenting something which presents nothing. There are powerful reasons (given by

McDowell 1984, 1986, 1991) and present in Russell (1918)) why this last could not be right. I mention this only to signal that construing aiming in the one way or the other, and then holding some wide class of conditions, episodes, postures, or whatever, thus to aim, may be taking sides on quite substantive matters.

There are other issues as to what understanding 'aim' or 'directed at' is to bear. Aiming, on its ordinary meaning, is intentional in involving *intention*. I may shoot Bill unintentionally, aiming at the apple above his head, or intentionally, aiming at him. If I aim, I do at least something intentionally. So reading 'aim', seeing does not aim. So it is not intentional if such aiming marks the intentional. But aiming, sometimes, may be mere harbouring ambition, apart from doing anything to realize it.

Postures towards the world, such as judging (taking something to be so), or wanting, may be seen as harbouring ambitions: for judging, to be held in a world (suitably) right for it—thus, for judging such-and-such, a world of a certain sort, namely, where *that*; for wanting, that the world become (or remain) one of a certain sort—where I want an alembic (or still want mine), one in which I have one (or it). In such ways, understanding *intentional* as aiming for some object, and aiming as mere harbouring ambition, may bring attitudes within intentionality's ambit.

Seeing, however, still remains without it. On its face, it harbours no ambitions, has no pretensions. In aiming as it does, a judgement imposes a requirement for its success—that requirement identified by (or identifying) what was judged. As Frege noted, it is intrinsic to this that there be a range of cases in which that requirement would be satisfied (where it is satisfiable at all). If I judge that a *bísaro* is beneath the spreading *castanheiro*, there are a variety of ways for me to be right. Another *bísaro* might replace the one in fact there, or that one may be sleeping or awake, rooting for truffles, or pawing the ground; all the while, Pia may be engrossed in her novel, or painting her toes. For to judge is to bring 'the particular case' under some given generality (*Kernsatz* 4). By contrast, for me to see what I do is just for *that* to be what is before my eyes (and for me to be suitably sensitive to it). My judging there to be a *bísaro* points to a range of cases in which things would be as I judged. My seeing what I did points to no range of cases in which things would be what I saw. If things before me being as they were *was*, in fact, there being a *bísaro* before me, then I saw, *inter alia*, a *bísaro*. There is a range of cases in which one would have seen a *bísaro*. But to see what *I* did, you would have to have seen *this* one, being just as *it* is. Nothing in my seeing what I did points to some range of cases of things being as they are being their being *that*. There is no such range. So nothing in seeing does anything paralleling what is done by those ambitions an attitude may harbour. So nothing in it points to its having any such ambition. Or so, on their face, things seem.

Judging, Frege suggests, is, *intrinsically,* exposing oneself to risk of error. Wanting is, similarly, intrinsic exposure to risk of disappointment. *Judging*, or wanting, that P does nothing, so far as it goes, to remove such risks. By contrast, seeing the *bísaro* before me, or knowing there to be one, are not ways of exposing oneself to such risks. There are risks where one *asks* something of the world. But not *all* mental phenomena do that. Some are simply ways of taking up its offers. So such asking cannot be the mark of the mental, nor of a notion of intentionality that marks it. Unless, perhaps, such things as seeing, or knowing, factor into a 'purely mental' component, which does some asking, and the further fact of the world obliging. But such is not something to be supposed lightly.

So images of aiming, or being directed, at do not seem to capture seeing in their net. Suppose, still attracted to those images, and convinced that seeing *is* intentional, we supposed they *must*. Then we would need to find something seeing asks of the world; so, accordingly, something it pretends, or aims, to be. This would naturally force seeing into the mould of judging. So forcing it, we would, perhaps, insist on seeing as pretending, first, to be revealing of how things are (visually, visibly) in the scene before me, and then revealing of their being thus and so (some way there is for (visible) scenes to be). Many have taken that route. But that way darkness lies. (See Essay 1, this volume.) Better to give up either on these metaphors as means for capturing what we shall mean by 'intentional', or on the idea that seeing *is* intentional.

A linguistic notion may promise a new idea of what intentionality might be. It is the notion of an *intensional* (or *opaque*) *context* (or *open sentence*). Start with a sentence of some language—'Sid ate all of Pia's pizza', say. Find in it some term whose function, on a use, is to identify some object (faller under concepts) which the sentence, so used, would then say to be some given way. Erase the term, leaving a blank for future filling in. The result is a *context* (or *open sentence*). For example, 'Sid ate all of__'s pizza'. Do this repeatedly if you can and like, leaving multiple blanks (a multiply open sentence). For a context to be intensional (with respect to a given blank) is for it to have two features. First, having filled each other blank, filling that blank with two different ways of referring to the same thing is liable to yield two different truth values. Call this failure of substitution. Second, where filling the blank with a name of some object yields a truth, filling it instead by existential quantification may not. So, if '__grunts' had this feature, then 'Sid grunts' might be true where 'There is someone who grunts' was not. Call this failure of existential generalization.

Where an open sentence is intensional, what fills it so as to express a thought fixes more as to what thought that is than merely what object (or individual) is thereby thought of. The notion of intensionality says nothing as to what that more might be. Perhaps quite different things in different cases. If so, the notion of intensionality, as such, offers no taxonomy.

Intensionality is a linguistic notion, *intentionality* not. How might the two connect? Here is one simple idea. One *might* call a (sort of) condition, or episode, or process, or whatever, intentional just in case, first, there is a context which speaks of someone (so-and-so) as in (some particular version of) that condition, or engaged in (some particular version of) that episode, and so on, which is intensional with respect to some blank, and, second, it contains no proper context which is also intensional with respect to that blank. (This would need refinement, but will do as an approximation.) Thus, thinking something so would be intentional, on this notion, if, say, 'Sid thinks that__ate the last piece' is intensional. ('__ate the last piece' is a proper part of that whole, but, presumably, not intensional.)

I am not proposing this. It is just one way to forge a link. In fact, formulating questions about intentionality in linguistic terms may easily yield illusions. I will mention them next in discussing a certain proposal. I have so far spoken as if seeing a *bísaro* requires, at the least, a *bísaro*. Some have claimed this to be so of one, but not another, notion of seeing. I will argue that there is no such other notion. Even if there were, this would make, not *seeing*, but at best only one notion of it, intentional. But there is not.

2 Ayer and Anscombe

A. J. Ayer and G. E. M. Anscombe are two of the many who thought they saw two notions of seeing, one intentional. Ayer puts this straightforwardly in terms of *senses* of 'see'. In one, he tells us,

it is necessary that what is seen should really exist, but not necessary that it should have the qualities that it appears to have.

(1940: 23)

In the other,

it is not possible that anything [seen?] should seem to have qualities that it does not really have, but also not necessary that what is seen should really exist.

(1940: 23)

In Ayer's second sense one may see what is not there. Seeing, so read, might be seen as aiming for what it *misses*, there—promise of catching this notion within intentionality's net. Further, what one sees, in this sense, cannot differ from, and perhaps not outrun, what it seems. One use of 'seem' is tied to attitudes: 'It seems that I will never catch up'. Such is what the facts suggest (to me). Another is perceptual: that *bísaro* beneath the *castanheiro* seems as though spotted (in the dappled sunlight). It would be adding something to say, 'and the *bísaro* actually seems to *be* spotted (thus making the first use of 'seem'). Ayer is not clear which he means. If perceptual 'seem', then his last stricture yields a doubtfully coherent notion. If the first, coherence depends on what necessity there is for a subject to take, or be ascribed, only coherent attitudes. Anyway, Ayer's second sense of 'see', though not his first, is, *if* coherent, a ripe candidate for the intentional.

Anscombe identifies her two notions in terms of different 'uses' of 'see'; different ways of employing it. First, there is

> what I shall call the material use of verbs of sense... The material use of 'see' is a use which demands a *material* object of the verb. 'You can't have seen a unicorn, unicorns don't exist'. 'You can't have seen a lion, there wasn't any lion there to see'.
>
> (1965: 13)

For all of which,

> Verbs of sense-perception... are intentional or essentially have an intentional aspect.
>
> (1965: 11)

On the intentional use,

> object phrases are used giving objects which are, wholly or in part, merely intentional. This comes out in two features: neither possible non-existence (in the situation), nor indeterminacy, of the object is an objection to the truth of what is said.
>
> (1965: 13)

> 'Ordinary language' views and 'sense-datum' views make the same mistake, that of failing to recognize the intentionality of sensation... This failure comes out clearly on the part of an ordinary-language philosopher if he insists that what I say I see must really be there if I am not lying, mistaken, or using language in a 'queer', extended (and therefore discountable) way.
>
> (1965: 13)

Ayer's second sense of 'see' and Anscombe's intentional use are thus much alike. Both allow for the non-existence of what is seen, allowing for which, as we have seen, is a mark of intentionality on some, though perhaps not all, conceptions of it. The 'indeterminacy' of the object in Anscombe's intentional use corresponds, in Ayer, to the impossibility of the object differing from (for

Anscombe, outrunning) what it seems. It is indeterminacy akin to that of fiction. Perhaps Maigret was a man of average height. But unless Simenon said so, or what entails so, it is neither so that Maigret was a metre 80, nor that he was a metre 78, nor that he was a metre 77, and so on. Unless such were allowed for, Simenon (if alive) would still be working on his first novel. Similarly, on Anscombe's second use, I may have seen a (non-existent) robin, but it need neither be so that I saw a red-breasted one nor that I saw an orange-breasted one (assuming there are those two types), unless things so impressed me. For I see, on this use, no more than I am responsive to. Just so, except by losing track of what he was about, or getting caught up in inconsistency, it cannot merely *seem* to Simenon that Maigret was of average height. Just so, too, except in over-haste, or something of the sort, one cannot merely *seem* to see (on Anscombe's second use) a bird in the nest (while, in fact, it was perched on the branch).

Between the time of Ayer's two senses and that of Anscombe's two uses, J. L. Austin expressed a contrary view:

> The fact that an exceptional situation may thus induce me to use words primarily appropriate for a different, normal situation is nothing like enough to establish that there are, in general, two different ('correct and familiar') *senses* of the words I use, or of any one of them... It is not, as Ayer says, that 'there is no problem so long as one keeps the two usages distinct'; there is no reason to say that there *are* two usages; there is no problem so long as one is aware of the *special circumstances*.
>
> I might say, while visiting the zoo, 'That is a lion', pointing to one of the animals. I might also say, pointing to a photograph in my album, 'That is a lion'. Does this show that the word 'lion' has *two senses*—one meaning an animal, the other a picture of an animal? Plainly not.
>
> (1962: 91)

Austin puts his point—since directed against Ayer—in terms of senses. But the real point is: there is no notion of *seeing* on which it is intentional in Anscombe's sense, or on which either Anscombe's second use, nor Ayer's second sense, are ways of saying someone to *see* things. The different usages of 'see' here are different usages for *any* words; ones other than for describing what those words normally do. The temptation to think otherwise corresponds to a misunderstanding of intensionality, and thereby of intentionality. I turn to that misunderstanding.

3 The Non-Existent

Intensionality is a *linguistic* phenomenon. Intentionality is a property of conditions, episodes, and so on. Trying to capture it linguistically invites confusions.

We have just seen one example. Suppose that 'see' has certain linguistic properties—a second sense, say. Before it were shown that a certain perceptual phenomenon, seeing, sometimes has corresponding properties, it would need to be shown that, in that second sense, 'see' speaks of that phenomenon.

A mark of intentionality, it is sometimes said, is something called 'intentional in-existence'. This is sometimes read: what an intentional phenomenon relates one to is there anyway in thought (or in the phenomenon), and has no further need actually to be there. So an intentional phenomenon which relates one to an object (faller under concepts) somehow has the power to relate one to a non-existent one. It *might* also be read: what an intentional phenomenon relates one to, whatever that may be, is there (exists), full stop. No further question of it failing, in any sense, 'really to be there'. But something like the first reading—instanced in the idea that one may see what is not there—is encouraged by a misunderstanding of *intensionality*, plus some notion of its relation to intentionality. So let us help that misunderstanding out of the world.

The intensionality of a context (at a given blank) consists in two features: failure of substitution; failure of existential generalization. Quine correctly argued that the first entails the second. The second is: if '__F' is intensional, then 'A F' can express a truth while 'There is something which is F' does not. Which is sometimes understood as: 'A F' can express a truth while 'A', in it, refers to nothing. But this reading is wrong.

One can—*perhaps*—see *that* the cow is clearing Hesperus without seeing *that* it is clearing Phosphorous, or that Pia is with Nick without seeing that she is with The Thin Man. One would not think it followed that one might see that 'Pia's brother, Sol, was with Nick' if Pia does not have a brother. One can see that Pia is with Nick in seeing her with Nick. One cannot see 'Sol' with Nick if there is no 'Sol'. In *any* case of seeing that, you cannot see what is not so. It is not the case that Pia's brother is with Nick if she does not have one.

What, then, did Quine prove in proving that failure of substitution entails failure of existential generalization? One can see that by asking why intensionality is essentially linguistic. Let us try to define it for a concept—say, that of being greasy. Starting with substitution, if this *concept* is intensional, then **a** might satisfy it while **b** does not, even if **a** is **b**. This would violate Leibniz's law. So there is no such possibility. Now for existential generalization. Suppose that **a** satisfies *greasy*( ). For existential generalization to fail here would be for there to be nothing which satisfied the concept. But we just supposed that something did; namely, **a**. Which is to suppose that existential generalization does not fail. As Frege put it, the existential quantifier is a second-order concept, predicating being satisfied of a first-order concept. We supposed *greasy* to be satisfied in supposing **a** to satisfy it. *Fertig*. (A concept, Frege also tells us, is a *function* mapping objects into truth-values; which is just to say that it cannot map one object (**a**, aka **b**) onto two values, nor nothing onto anything.)

A thought is the content of a judgement. Its task is to fix when that judgement would be correct (true). That task can be apportioned into sub-tasks. A concept is (or is identified by) what would perform a certain sort of sub-task. But this is a task performable at all only in the context of the performance of those other sub-tasks on the apportionment. Choose an object, and a concept may make truth turn on whether *that* one satisfies it. Choose no object, and there is (bracketing quantifying) as yet no work for a concept to do; no sub-task within a thought to be performed by anything.

A one-place first-order concept just *is* of a way for an object to be. What we have just seen is that an intensional context does not (as such) express a concept; speaks, on its own, of *no* way for an object to be. We may now recall that it was precisely ways for a subject to be that were to be caught in intentionality's net. An intensional context speaks of no such candidate. Consider, for example, '__ is so-called because of his consumer habits'. 'John is so-called because of his consumer habits' may express truth, while, though John is also known as Fats, 'Fats is so-called because of his consumer habits' does not. But that just reflects the fact that there is no such thing as 'being so-called because of one's consumer habits'. So 'Someone is so-called because of his consumer habits' (where 'someone' is a quantifier) says nothing. It is not false. It is not even well-formed. It is just nonsense.

This is what Quine proved. Where substitution fails, you simply cannot generalize. You are not yet speaking of any way for something, or things, to be; so generalizing can only yield nonsense. (*Not falsehood*.) An intensional context is *no* source of truths about nothing—a bizarre idea anyway, come to think of it. A *context*, so an intensional one, has, by definition, blanks to be filled by reference to *objects* (bearers of properties). Otherwise, talk of failure of substitution, and so on, makes no sense. Fill a blank with what does *not* refer to an object (one that there *is*, to wax pleonastic), and you fail to say *anything* to be so, either truly or falsely. Fats, perhaps, is called John because of his consumer habits. The same could not be so of 'Pia's brother' if she has none.

'John is so-called because of his consumer habits' is true because he is called *John* because of his consumer habits; 'Fats is so-called . . .' is false because he is not called *Fats* because of his consumer habits. This points to a linguistic problem. Only when an intensional context has its blanks filled does it speak of a way for something to be, which it can then, truly or falsely, say someone to be. The problem is to say what contribution the fillers—terms which normally contribute only in identifying an object—make to determining *what* way for something to be is thus spoken of.

But it is ways for things to be which are meant to be *intentional* or not. An *intensional* context speaks of no such way. *Such* a context needs to be filled before we can so much as detect, in the filled result, any way for a thing to be, thus anything which might be intentional or not. Being called 'John' because of one's consumer habits is, perhaps, an intentional condition (though presumably it is not). 'Being so-called because of one's consumer habits' is (without anaphoric reference for that 'so-called' to pick up) simply ill-formed, not (mention of) a way for one to be.

Though Nick Charles is fictional, might there not be truth in some claim that he smoked Melachrinos, not Murads? So it seems. The questions are: What sorts of claims? What sorts of truths? Does Nick Charles show that smoking is something one can do without existing? The point so far is that whatever one says to this in the case of smoking, there is so far no reason to say any different for intentional phenomena, whatever these may be; certainly not for seeing.

4 Seeing Things

'See that' seems as intensional as 'think that', however intensional that is. What of 'See (NP)'—for such NPs as 'Sid', 'the sun setting', 'the carbonized condition of the toast'? To start with, what you see (unless you miss it) is what is there. If I see Sid staggering, and Sid is the regional representative of Duvel, then I see the regional representative of Duvel staggering, whether or not I know that, or can even entertain the thought. So, it seems, 'See (NP)' cannot fail substitutivity *salva veritate*; which means it does not form intensional contexts. There is so far no cause for thinking you can see what is not there.

Ayer's second sense of 'see', and Anscombe's 'material use', are not, on their face, uses on which substitutivity fails—though there may be a poverty of things to substitute. If, on these uses, I see a bird in a nest, or a bird with a red head, and *if* the bird is a grouse, or red is Almodóvar's favourite colour, then I see a grouse in the nest, and a bird with a head in Almodóvar's favourite colour. If they are right, though, then on these uses I may see what is not there. There is no reason why this need entail failure of substitutivity, any more than failure of substitutivity entails it.

It is widely thought that it may be true that Pia thinks Nick Charles smokes Melachrinos; it is nothing against the truth of this that there is no such person as Nick Charles. (Though it *might* matter if there were no such fictional character.) Which has encouraged some to think that it is possible to *think* something to be so in thinking of *no-one* that *he* smokes Melachrinos. We have seen there to be no such consequence. (I can tell you what the square of some integer is; but not what the square of nothing is.) Perhaps we can see, in another way, why one should not be so encouraged. There are, to be sure, occasions on which one could express a truth—some truth or other—in saying, 'Pia thinks Nick Charles smokes Melachrinos'. But those are very likely to be occasions on which one could continue the monologue, truly, along lines like these: 'But he doesn't. He smokes Murads'. Where 'He smokes Murads' may express truth in speaking of no-one, so might anything. Which signals something: on those occasions on which one would thus speak truth, some special sort of discourse is afoot. (Another signal is the occasions on which one could not thus speak truth. The question is whether, as generally supposed, only Anabaptists smoke Melachrinos. 'Nick Charles smokes Melachrinos and he is no Anabaptist', Zoë helpfully suggests. 'There's no such person' is a fair response.)

If I am telling you how The Thin Man stories go, I am free to relate anything occurring in them, in straight assertoric form—'The mayor shucked an oyster at midnight with a switchblade', if so the story goes. What is required for truth is not that the mayor shucked, for example, but that so the (Thin Man) story goes. An utterance of a sentence such as 'The mayor shucked...' *can* be an assertion as to how things are around us. But it can also be other things; in this case, a commitment to how a certain story goes; how things are in *it*. 'The mayor shucked...' provides a description for the way things are. But it need not be *used* for describing how things are. If it has that use, it inevitably has others. Describing how things would be if as per the story, or just how they are in the story, is one such.

One cannot think things so in thinking of no-one that he is thus and so. One does not do it by thinking things of a character in a story. One simply mentions ways for things, or some thing, to be as a means of recounting the story—saying how things are *in it*. There is something one might think in thinking the story to be one in which a certain character, Nick Charles, smoked Melachrinos. One can sometimes be *said* to think this in words, 'He thinks Nick Charles smoked Melachrinos'. There is nothing one might think in thinking someone non-existent to have smoked Melachrinos. There *are* no non-existent someones. A non-existent someone being a way there is for *someone* to be is not a way for things to be: there is no such thing as that. There is no such way to think things. Name someone, say him to have smoked Melachrinos, and you have described a way for things to be. You may *use* such a description for saying how things are: as thus described. You may also use it for countless other ends, for example, in saying how a story goes. Such other uses do not suggest the absurdity that the description, 'smoked Melachrinos', may be true of someone there is not. What goes here for smoking Melachrinos goes, too, for thinking someone did. So, too, for seeing the Murad in the ashtray when there is no Murad to be seen (even if, in some sense, it is for someone as though there were).

So far, then (unsurprisingly), we have found no cause for thinking that a context with a space for a reference to *something* can be made true, or even so much as true or false, by filling it up with something which refers to nothing; or, in non-linguistic terms. that there could be a thought which is, *inter alia*, about being such-and-such way for an object to be, but not about any object, or some range of them, *being* that way. Such would violate what Frege called the context principle: constituents of a thought (on a decomposition) are so only *en masse*. Frege need not yet fear.

Yet another use for descriptions for the way things are. Pia is in her *chaise longue* daydreaming of touring Spain. 'What are you doing now?', Sid asks. 'Running with the bulls', she replies. In a *chaise longue*? But no. Pia is not telling blatant falsehood. She is simply saying what she is daydreaming—imagining. She is right if, when Sid asks, *that* is what she is picturing doing. Running with the bulls is the way her daydream runs. There need be no further running in Pamplona.

Vocabulary *for* describing what is happening in Pamplona is used here for another purpose: describing what Pia is imagining happening—how things *would* be if as imagined. Such talk has two features. First, Pia has a sort of authority over what happens in her daydream which resembles the authority we normally have over what we mean by our words. If I think 'tenuous' means *tenable*, I may be correspondingly confused as to what I *mean* when I call a position 'tenuous'; as to how I am using my words. Barring such confusion, how I mean to be using them is, within wide latitude, up to me to say. It takes special circumstances for me to be mistaken as to whether I meant 'bank' to mean riverside. Similarly, if Pia says that in her daydream she is running in Pamplona, and then, describing her (imagined) surroundings, gives a perfect description of Burgos, *perhaps* she is daydreaming about Burgos. Generally speaking, though, when someone, describing her daydream, says she is running along a beach, it is hard to make sense of a reply, 'No, you are not. You are swinging in a hammock'. Second, as Anscombe claims for her 'intentional use' of 'see', daydreaming is sketchy as fiction. As Pia passes the cathedral (in her daydream), there need be no answer to questions as to where the shadows fell, or what colour the stone was, or even whether the bells tolled.

Now we turn to 'see (NP)'. Here is the sort of case which inspired Anscombe's intentional use of 'see'. Looking at the sheet of paper, tired and emotional, I see two sheets. (See 'How many fingers?') I feel pressure on my leg (though it has been amputated). I see rails rushing ahead. The psychologist works his magic with the successions of lights and I see, now clockwise, now counterclockwise, motion where there is none. Fiddling with the card of the bird and the card of the nest in the opthamologist's machine, I arrange for me to see the bird in the nest. (Anscombe's example. She is impressed by the fact that the opthamologist does not need first to teach me a nonce-sense for 'see' and only then to pose his question (1965: 12–13).)

Suppose that 'N sees O' were a form of description for a subject's relation to some object (or occurrences) in his surroundings—as on Anscombe's supposedly contrasting 'material use' of 'see'. Would it then, *ipso facto*, or at least reasonably, acquire additional uses on the model of 'Pia is running with the bulls', used, say, for describing how things are daydreamed to be, how imagined, for example? Might it be useable for describing how things looked to N—like, as though, such-and-such? Plausibly, yes. If I am trying to describe my tired and emotional (or, again, hypoglycaemic) state, I may, staring at the sheet of paper, say 'I see two sheets', using that description for a relation to *surroundings* to describe things looking as they do *to me*. If you want to know how things look to me, it is as though there were two sheets of paper. Similarly for rails rushing, and similarly for all the other cases above. It is no wonder that I need learn no nonce-sense of 'see' before grasping the opthamologist's question. I grasp, effortlessly, that a description *for* one sort of thing can be used to describe another sort by the above sort of connection.

'I am running through Pamplona' speaks of doing something with one's legs in a certain Spanish city; something which could *not* be done anywhere else; something which could not be done while lying still in a *chaise longue*. But if you know what it would be for someone to be doing that, you can also know what it would be to be daydreaming doing it. You would know this in knowing what would be happening (on some suitable occasion) if things were as in the daydream. Similarly, 'I see two sheets of paper' speaks of my standing in a certain way towards *two* sheets of paper. But if you understand what it would be for me to be doing that, you may also know how things look to me, or are for me, visually, now, in the grip of my hypoglycaemia. If you have ever felt pressure on your leg, you can know how things feel to me, now literally legless, at this moment, if you understand that it is, for me, the way things feel when there is pressure on one's leg—and know, as you might, how *that* feels.

Anscombe asks only for an intentional *use* of 'see'. Has that not just been provided? Is it not right that with 'see' working as thus described, one can see two sheets of paper when there is only one? First, note that if this *is* an intentional use, then there is, equally well, an intentional use of 'run with the bulls', on which this can be done without benefit of bulls, or need to run.

Equally well for 'is sitting in a *chaise longue*', or virtually any other context (open sentence) you choose. But no-one ever thought running with bulls, or sitting in a *chaise longue*, is intentional. And if everything is, the distinction disappears.

Second, this points to the dangers of sliding from a linguistic phenomenon to a a phenomenon language might describe. 'Sid sees two sheets' might express a truth without benefit of two sheets. Since 'two sheets' is not a referring expression here, we cannot move directly to an *intensional* context by deleting it. But there *is* a context, 'Sid sees___', where the blank is to be filled up by a reference to something—what functions as a name. I doubt that this can be filled with a (would-be) name, which fails to refer to anything, so as to express a truth even on the above special use. Fiction, again, is beside the point.

But which forms of words might or might not express truth of Sid's situation is not really to the point. The question was whether there is a notion of *seeing* on which this is intentional. Is *seeing*, on one understanding *it* admits of, something one can do *in re* what does not exist, or is not there within one's sight? Where 'Pia is running with the bulls' is so used as to express a truth while Pia is sitting in her *chaise longue*, far from any bulls, it is precisely *not* used to describe what Pia is doing, or at least not to describe that as running with some bulls. It is used to describe what she is *imagining* doing. Just so that it does not follow from its truth, so used, that one may run with bulls by sitting in a chair, no bulls present. Similarly, when, on the above account, 'Sid sees two sheets of paper' expresses a truth though there are no two sheets of paper, it is not being used to describe what Sid is doing, or at least not what he is doing as seeing two sheets of paper. It is being used to describe what, for him, it is as though he were doing. It accordingly fails to follow from the truth of the description *so* used that seeing a sheet of paper is something one can do without benefit of paper.

Not all uses of 'see' which may give the appearance of intentionality in Anscombe's sense are to be accounted for in the above way. Austin points to examples like these: 'I see a silver speck on the horizon', while on the horizon is only the daily flight form Rio. This is a Boeing 747—a very large airplane, hardly a speck. So the speck I see, the thought is, is a speck that is not there. But this, as Austin points out, is thinking wrongly. There are various things there being a speck on the horizon might be understood to be. One thing this might be understood to be is for there to be something on the horizon which, viewed from here, and at this distance, appears as a speck. On such an understanding, an airplane on the horizon would be there being a speck on the horizon. The speck you see, on this understanding of there being one, just *is* the airplane. Here truth comes from a particular understanding of 'speck', not a particular understanding of 'see'. No special use of that verb is at work.

A minimal conclusion. Examples of the sort Anscombe gives, or of the sort illustrated above, give no reason to think that there is any intentional notion of seeing. When Anscombe marks out her intentional use of 'see', she is concerned centrally with issues of non-existence—orthogonal at least to *intensionality*—little, or less, with substitutivity—a mark identifying that phenomenon. There is no case for failure of substitutivity in contexts formed from 'see (NP)', even on Anscombe's supposed use. Failure would, anyway, not bear on her issues of non-existence. Nor do issues of non-existence clearly bear on substitutivity. It remains open how either issue links to a notion of intentionality on which this might be the mark of the mental.

5 Beyond Judging

A feature of Ayer's second sense of 'see' is that, in this sense, 'it is not possible that anything should seem to have qualities it does not really have'. (1940: 23) His example of something we can 'see' in this sense is: 'a silvery speck no bigger than a sixpence'. This is to make the objects of seeing, in this sense, very special sorts of things—*not*, notably, objects of *sight*: sight involves the *eyes*; anything *they* afforded awareness of would be inherently liable to be other than, through them, it seemed. In fact, such a thing could not have any of the visible properties things in our surroundings are liable to have (or at least liable to have or lack). Nor could it have any other properties which visual awareness might reveal. One could not intelligibly *judge* it to have or lack any such property, thus making one's correctness turn how *it* is. So if such a thing seemed to be red or square, say, it would thus be seeming to have properties it could not have. If it could not seem to have properties it lacked, this would just mean that it could not so much as *seem* to be red or square. It would be irrelevant to this if, as Ayer suggests, what is seen in this sense might be non-existent.

Frege maps the bounds here (1918; see Essay 2). I condense the case. If the tomato on my plate, or my beach towel, is red, this locates them within webs of factive meaning. It means, say, that my towel will enrage bulls, or sticklebacks, or that it has certain reflectance properties, or that others will be impressed by my taste, or lack of it, in towel colours, or that it will be the same colour as certain other towels. Which means, *ipso facto*, that if, on a certain occasion, based on my exposure to the towel, I judge it to be red, I am inherently liable to be wrong: what lies on those other nodes within these webs in which my towel's being red would find itself (if it is red) may just *mean* that the towel is not, in fact, red. Such could not happen for any way something I saw in Ayer's second sense seemed, as seen, to be. So *such* a thing's being red, if it could accomplish this, could not lie within such webs of meaning. Which is just to say that whatever way such a thing might be, it would not be being *red*. So it could not seem red, because then it would seem to be what it was not, violating Ayer's dictum.

Those supposed objects of seeing in Ayer's second sense would need not to be denizens of our shared environment. So if they had *observable* properties, these would be of a very different sort from any had by such denizens. Ayer's items would belong to what Frege calls 'contents of someone's consciousness': there is someone one would have to be to be aware of, or acquainted, with them; they coexist with that person's awareness of them. So only that person could be aware, for example, visually, of such an item's having such a property. Which means, as Frege argues, that only that person could so much as entertain the thought, of any such item, that it had any such property. Which, for Frege, means that there are really no such thoughts—so no such facts—at all. Again, in brief, such a thought, if there were one, could be *true* only in a new sense of 'true'; not in the same sense in which it is true that I have just eaten the last crisp. But it would be up to the only person who could entertain that thought to give 'true' such a new sense. Which proves an unintelligible project.

Frege wrote,

With the step by which I win myself an environment I expose myself to risk of error.
(1918: 73)

But the environment is all there is to judge of. He could have said: With the step by which I win myself the possibility of judging *anything* I expose myself to risk of error. So there is no such thing as judging truly (or perhaps truly, perhaps falsely) of something that it is F, where seeming so would make it so. So there is no such thing as something *being* what it could not but be if it so seems. So the objects (accusatives) of 'see' in Ayer's second sense cannot be *objects*: things which *are* a multitude of ways, and which might intelligibly be *thought* to be one way or another.

What, then, might we see in Ayer's second sense? A silvery speck, he suggests. But grammar might mislead less if we change examples. Perhaps Dick Cheney standing on his head is the sort of thing one might see in this sense. Unfortunately, Cheney exists. But perhaps no headstands by him do. Which will do *here*. Now, 'things', in 'things being as they are, may—typically does—bear a catholic sense, a mark of which is that one cannot ask 'Which things?' It is things being as they are which is things being, or not being, those ways there are for things to be—such that sloths sleep, or such that Cheney is standing on his head. Cheney standing on his head is a way for things to be.

Cheney standing on his head is something which (from the perspective of logical space) might occur, or at least might fail to.

One cannot see a way for things to be (though one might see, or witness, things being that way, if so they are). Equally, one cannot see something which might occur or not, though one might see it occurring, or happening. If Cheney stands on his head, you might see him doing so. Seeing Cheney standing on his head is also, presumably, something one might do in Ayer's second sense of 'see'. Cheney would have to stand on his head—things would have to be *that* way—for you to witness him—take in his—doing so. But, presumably, you might see him standing on his head in Ayer's second sense of 'see' without his doing so. *What* you saw, in this sense, would not be (as what you *see* would be) part of things being as they are.

Things being as they are, in the normal catholic sense of 'things', is the extent of what there is to judge of. *Just this* is what would be things being some way there is for things to be; what may make a judgement true or false. Although Cheney standing on his head, *if* it occurs, is part of things being as they are, what you 'see' in Ayer's second sense when you see Cheney standing on his head is not. If 'seeing' (second sense) Cheney standing on his head is a visual experience, it is (by contrast with seeing some actual headstand) not of what, in being as it is, *shows* one thus to have experienced such-and-such (for example, some *headstand*-facsimile). What one *thus* experiences does not support a judgement. *Its* being as it is could not be Cheney standing on his head, no matter *what* things being that way was understood to come to. If Ayer 'sees' (second sense) Cheney standing on his head, it may seem (look) *to Ayer* as though Cheney were so standing. But this cannot be a matter of Ayer's visual awareness of something which instances things so seeming—as Jack Black's impression of Cheney so standing might.

Ayer's insistence that what you 'see' (second sense) cannot diverge in how it is from how it seems now comes to this. It cannot *seem* that you thus 'see' Cheney standing on his head, whereas you are actually 'seeing' Rove standing on his hands, or Bush standing on his own feet; nor that you see a star above Emerson Hall which *seems* to flicker, but really does not. There is no more *to* what you see, in this sense, than you are prepared to tell; no way for it to merely *seem* to you that you see things being this way rather than that. One might resist at this point. Suppose, instead, we agree: this is what seeing (second sense) is to be.

Frege's point then gets new grip. Suppose it cannot merely seem to me that I see (second sense) A, while what I really see (second sense) is in fact B. Then any posture I take to the effect that my experience is one of seeing (second sense) such-and-such does not expose me to risk of error. So it is not a *judgement* to that effect. An attitude towards whether I am seeing (second sense) Cheney standing on his head cannot, so far, be a way for me to make the fate of a posture turn on how *things* are. Perhaps with such a posture by me present, someone else could judge something to the effect that I saw (second sense) Cheney standing on his head. Perhaps there is *then* something for *someone* to judge. Perhaps in the right circumstances that someone could be me. But then there would be, for me, risk of error as to what it was I thus experienced—room, say, for confusing Cheney and Tamberlane. And what made me right or wrong—decided the fate of *this* posture—would not be merely what I experienced in seeing what I did (second sense) being as it was. If I think I see Cheney smirking, I am right or wrong according as what I have in view is or is not (an instance of) Cheney smirking. Its seeming so to me hardly makes this so. This is entirely a matter of how *things* are. It would not be like that where I perceived my seeing what I did (Ayer's second sense) as my seeing Cheney smirking.

That idea of intentionality which Ayer expresses as above, and which, so expressed, points to loss of judgement, Anscombe expresses in terms of the poverty of facts about accusatives of what speaks of the intentional—the sort of poverty of fiction. No *more* is so of what I see on Anscombe's intentional use than I *recognize* as so, or am prepared to. Here, too, there is no question of the *facts* as to what I see outrunning this. The word I just used—'recognize'—may speak of two quite different phenomena—a distinction marked in German by 'anerkennen' and 'erkennen'. *Erkennung* is pure cognitive achievement, *Anerkennung* not. *Anerkennung* is acknowledging, or crediting, counting, or perhaps endowing with a status—as, say, certifying a plumber. For Frege, stating is the *Anerkennung* of the truth of what is stated—commitment. (1918: 65) There is something to *erkennen* just where there is something to judge. There may be, anyway, things to *anerkennen*. One may, anyway, *anerkennen* what one sees (Ayer's second sense) as Cheney on his head, even if there is no question of one's *judging* this. Similarly, one may *anerkennen* seeing the hen in the nest, even if, minus such stances, *Erkennung* is not yet in the cards. (On this point only, see seeing figures in a Pollock.) For Anscombe, where there is no prospect of such *Anerkennung*—for example, of the hen's seeming to have 1,013 feathers—there is no question of something to *erkennen* either. Thus far, her position fits within Frege's bounds. The mistake, if she makes it, is just to think that what is in question here is *seeing*. It is, essentially, of things to judge about.

For judgement to come into question, Frege teaches us, one must win oneself an environment. It is not an *environment* one describes in describing what one experienced visually as the hen being in the nest. Here, too, judgement is not yet in the picture. This is not yet to say that there is *no* way for it to enter. If I *anerkennen* the hen being in the nest, *that* is a feature of *our* shared environment. It is thus a possible judgement that I did this or not. Which is enough to show that there *can* be truth, or falsehood, to be told in saying me now to see the hen in the nest, or two sheets of paper, on *some* use of 'see'—perhaps that use I suggested above. The question here is just what sort of truth it is. That it was for me as though the hen were in the nest may be part of how things are. Things being, visually, thus and so, where one could not witness this without *being* me, is not part of things being as they are. A stance that I saw the hen in the nest cannot have its correctness decided by how what only I *could* witness was. Such is Frege's lesson.

Suppose seeing the hen in the nest were being in a certain neural state. Now there is something for *one* to do, seeing the hen in the nest, which *one* can do by getting into the right state (practicalities aside). The situation is comparable to seeing the hen in the nest, hidden in the mass of dots in a puzzle picture: the image is *there*, it may take a lot of work to get it into focus. When, after days of staring at the painting, I finally spot the hen, what I do hardly fits Anscombe's intentional use of 'see'. Of course there is no real hen clucking away on, and heating up, the canvas. Nor is there a real horse attached to Rubens' canvas of Cathérine de Medici seated on one. When we talk of seeing vapours coming from the horse's nostrils, of course we are speaking of seeing an *image* of that—yet another use of 'see'. What we are *not* doing is speaking of seeing something not there to be seen. Similarly, I suggest, where seeing A is being in a certain neural state. There *is* something to be seen by getting in that neural state. Not that there are chickens in your brain. But nor are there any on a canvas.

So far, then, Ayer's sense, and Anscombe's use, fit well into the picture I have drawn. Consider once again daydreaming. When Sid asks, of Pia's daydream, what she is doing now, and she answers 'Running with the bulls', it would be quite unnatural to think that what has happened is that Pia has observed something being as it is, and recognized *that* as its being such that she is running with some bulls—not even as one may observe a canvas, or a photograph, being as it is and recognize that *that* is Pia running with the bulls (an image of it, of course). Rather, the daydream is a playing-out, in Pia's head, of a certain story; Pia gets to tell the story (modulo such things as confusing Pamplona with Burgos). Pia's answer to Sid is thus not very naturally read as a *judgement* as to what she is experiencing in daydreaming as she is. It is something at least akin to *Anerkennung*. It is, anyway, a form of story-telling. Such things as 'I see two sheets of paper' (as above) are, anyway, akin to story-telling: there is that characteristic poverty of fact about the paper seen. It is not *pure* story-telling: I do not get to say just whatever I want. But *Anerkennung* plays a like role in it.

Again, the question is not whether some form of words—say, 'I see a hen in a nest'—can say what is true where no hen is in any nest. No doubt such forms *can* state such truths. The question is *what* truths these are. Ones to make of *seeing*, on one understanding of *it*, an intentional phenomenon? Nothing yet so indicates. And there are counter-indications. The central task of seeing, along with other forms of perceiving—hearing, feeling (with your fingers), for example—in a thinker's life is to allow the world to bear, for that thinker, on what he is to think (and do) according as it bears on what is *so* (*inter alia*, as to the thing to do). The world: things being as they are; that is, the environment we all inhabit being as it is.

If I adjust the handles *so* and see the hen in the nest, this may mean—and I may thus learn from the experience—that I am astigmatic. What I thus experience—my 'seeing' the hen in the nest just *then*—bears on what is so; my experiencing it bears for me on what to think. But it is not like that with seeing. *Seeing* the lion before me makes the lion's presence bear on what I am to think as to there being a lion before me: I may, properly, judge that there is on grounds of the lion's presence. The lion's presence may *thereby* bear, for me, on what else to think—for example, that I am glad I made my will—according to what it *means* (as a lion's presence before you means that it would be good to have made a will).

What bears on whether I am astigmatic is *my seeing* (Anscombe's use) the hen in the nest with the handles adjusted *so*. It is my being affected as I am. It is not that there is, independent of that, a hen in a nest to so affect me; nor something which looks like one; nor an image of one. Such would be something there was for *one* to see (from a suitable vantage point). The hen in the nest is none other than how things look to *me*; something present only with my stance towards my experiencing visually as I do. Things being as they *visibly* are in the Sahara before me is, recognizably, a lion being present. *I* can tell it is that; *one* can tell. For things to be as they thus are just is for there to be a lion. This model does not fit the hen in the nest. It is not that things looking *thus* is the hen looking as though in the nest (so that my taking in things so looking is, in other words, my 'seeing' the hen in the nest). It is not as though things so looking is what *one* might be visually aware of. There is no looking here other than looking to *me*; and there is no looking to *me* here apart from my being so impressed. My being so impressed is not here my responding to what is so *recognizable*, so nor my *recognizing* (*erkennen*). That notion of recognizing does not fit here.

There is no cause to think that seeing (Anscombe's intentional use, Ayer's second sense) is *visual* awareness of what bears on *what* it is I thus experience as seeing what I do in the veldt is visual awareness of what bears on whether I confront a male or female lion. Males have a certain look, females a certain other. I may or may not see the difference. It is anyway there for *one* to see. Whereas what bears on whether I see a hen in a nest, or hovering above it, is not whether I confront, visually, what has the one look, or what has the other (whether I can tell or not).

6 Looking and Watching

Perhaps one trouble here is that intensionality—a linguistic phenomenon—is not so much as a clue to what intentionality—a supposed mark of the mental—might be. If some once thought it was, they misread failure of existential generalization. What, then, *is* intentionality? Does it have anything to do with being *about*, without being about anything? Wittgenstein remarked: you can look for someone when he is not there, but not hang him when he is not there. Looking for, along with wanting and hoping, are clear cases of intentionality if anything is. Perhaps there is a clue in Wittgenstein's distinction. First, though, does it bear on being about the non-existent?

'A fountain of youth', in 'look for a fountain of youth', is not a name. Nor need 'the fountain of youth nearest to Miami' be one. 'Look for__' can be completed by a name. But these other completions show nothing about what happens then. So far, *intensionality* is not touched on. Might 'Sid wants N' be true, N functioning in that context as a *name*, but naming nothing? The idea seems absurd. To be a name just *is* to make the whole it is a part of about some individual—have its truth turn essentially on how *that* individual is. A name which names nothing cannot do this. Consider cases. 'Sid wants to meet King Edward IX', or 'Syd wants to eat a Mars Bar' ('Syd' naming Sid's sixteenth-century ancestor). (Where Sid has in mind a series of organized mishaps resulting in an Edward IX next week, 'Edward IX' does not function as a name in saying what he wants.) 'Sid wants . . .' should answer some question what it is that Sid wants. There is no such thing as 'meeting King Edward IX'. There is no such person to meet. So saying, or trying to say, Sid to want to do *that* is not providing such an answer. It is not identifying anything to be done; hence not anything Sid could want to do. Put 'meet Edward IX' in scare-quotes, and let there be a story about what Sid mistakenly thinks is such a thing to do, and matters may change. If 'wants to do X' is for identifying something there *is* to do as something someone wants to do, it inevitably has further uses in identifying what someone *imagines* there is to do as something he *imagines* he wants to do. Again, Syd could not have wanted to eat a Mars Bar, since there was, then, no such thing (even in the planning). At best he could have dreamed of some future confection to be called 'Mars Bar'. Wanting to eat such a thing is not wanting to eat a Mars Bar. Syd could only then have wanted things he could then have got in mind.

So far, no signs that 'Sid wants__' is intensional. What about substitutivity? If Nicole is really Mom, can Sid want Nicole, but not Mom? He can, I suppose, if he can *think* that Nicole, but not Mom, makes *churros* just right. It is not at all clear that he can do that either. If he could, it would not help him want, or think of, things (individuals) there are not. Nothing would, though derivative uses of 'wants...' (like derivative uses of 'smokes...') may make it *sound* that way. Nor is it clear how any of this links to *intentionality*.

Intensionality does not require that a context could be filled so as to yield truth, where the filler referred to nothing. If it did, it would be questionable to say the least. The role of a name is to make the whole it is part of express a singular thought: a thought whose truth turns precisely on how *such-and-such* (so-and-so) is. Whereas a general thought may be that there is someone who is *blah*, for a singular thought, there is someone such that the thought is that *he* is *blah*. A name which referred to nothing could not effect this. For it to be a *name* would be for it to play the role a name does without identifying an individual— an absurd idea anyway, and one which collapses singular thoughts into general ones. I omit further discussion.

One thing suggested so far is that there are two uses of 'looking for', or 'wants', for example, paralleling those two uses of 'see' and of 'run'—for saying what someone *saw*; for saying what it is for him as though he saw; for saying where someone ran, for saying where he imagined running. The first use of 'is looking for' is for saying what it is that someone is looking for; of 'wants' for saying what it is someone wants. The second sort of use of 'look for' occurs where there is a name which names nothing, or nothing the searcher could have had in mind— 'Edward IX', 'Mars Bar'. It is for saying what it is someone imagines there is to look for, or to do. 'Looking for a fountain of youth' can be the first sort. 'A fountain of youth', again, is not a name. How to understand *this* sort of case?

Wanting and looking for are, on their face, relational. If one can look for what is not there—a fountain of youth—what this suggests is that the relation is not to an *object*. So a relation to what? There is a way for someone to be: having found a fountain of youth. It is a perfectly good way for someone to be, even if it will never be instanced by anyone being as he is. It is not intensional (since not an open sentence), and, I will suggest, not plausibly intentional either, even if one cannot find what one was not looking for, or at least what one does not register, and looking for *is*, or registering should prove, intentional. Looking for can be a relation to a way for things to be. It can be, roughly, *aiming* for things to be that way; trying to achieve that. Like any relation, it is not one something can bear, but bear to nothing. Which is why it is not one one can bear to 'meeting Edward IX'. So, again, if 'Sid wants to meet/is looking for Edward IX' might sometimes express a truth, this will not be one as to what it is that Sid is looking for, or who he wants to meet, but rather, say, one about what he *imagines* he is looking for, or wants to meet.

There may be intentionality about. But the only relating to nothing is not relating to anything. This goes for aiming at and being directed toward. What, then, might intentionality be? Looking for and wanting, I have suggested, are relations to ways for things to be. For there to be a given way for things to be, there may or may not need to be given objects. You cannot *literally* be older than Methuselah without Methuselah. You can hope to meet an honest man some day without there being any. If a given way for things to be thus requires such-and-such object, there is no such way for one to relate to unless there is that object. A relation to a way for things to be might hold independent of whether that way is instanced. Such a relation need not be intentional. My *diospireiro* bears a relation to this way for things to be: it bearing persimmons. The relation is: it fails at this. My *diospireiro* doe not, presumably, enjoy intentionality.

To capture this difference we might return to the idea of being directed towards, or aiming at. Looking for, I said, aims at (the instancing of) a certain way for things to be. Wanting (to be rich, say) is directed towards this. And so on. Where there is aiming, there is success or failure. Wants may be realized, or frustrated, looking for may be successful or not. The state, or circumstance, of N looking for, or wanting, such-and-such, imposes a condition on such success, much as what expresses a thought may thereby impose a condition on its own truth. My *diospireiro* does not *aim* to produce persimmons. It just does its thing. Its doing whatever that may be identifies no range of cases in which it would be a *success*, or *correct*, in doing what it does. Perhaps here we find the marks of intentionality.

But is this right? Why not say that my *diospireiro* aims at producing persimmons, and that an unhealthy *diospireiro*, which does not produce, is not a success at what it aims at? One answer runs on these lines. If you are looking for a fountain of youth, or want to find one, then, so long as you remain in that condition, you have reason to carry on with certain courses of action, which, once the success has been achieved, you thereby have reason to stop. You need to know when to stop looking. Part of that is knowing when to give up; but part is knowing when *looking* is no longer in the cards: the goal has been reached. Looking for is thus connected, by its aims, to reasons in a way that being such as to bear persimmons if healthy is not. If my *diospireiro* becomes healthy and bears, that gives it no *reason* to do anything. It is not the sort of thing to have reasons. Perhaps that is fundamental. Those for whom things can be reasons are intentional creatures; intentional states are essentially such as to impose them. Such is *one* notion of intentionality.

If we think of intentionality along such lines, is intentionality the mark of the mental? Perhaps those creatures with mental lives just are those apt for intentional states. But is a *state* (circumstance, process, for example) mental just in case it is intentional? Tim Crane, in a recent defence of Brentano's thesis ('Intentionality, the mind's "direction upon its objects" is what is distinctive of mental phenomena' (Crane, 1998: 1)) remarked,

> If perception were the only mental state under discussion, intentionalism [Brentano's thesis] would not be a controversial thesis.
>
> (1998: 4)

Exactly not so, one would have thought. There are mental phenomena, like looking for something, which aim at something, have a goal, are directed. And there are others which, to speak loosely, aim at nothing, but rest where they have arrived—ones which are, in some sense, factive, purely relations to the way things *are*. Perception—seeing, for example—would seem to be a central example of that second sort of case. Knowing would be another. In some sense of 'should', there is a way things should be according to a subject who is looking for someone. By contrast, one simply sees what is before him (modulo acuity, attention, for example). My seeing the lion in the grass (or the rabbit) neither realizes nor harbours any aim *I* have. It does not even require taking the lion for a lion (and not a rabbit). (Seeing *that* is different in this last respect. But this does not seem to make *it* intentional either.)

Why might Crane think perception was a clear case of intentionality? I only proposed *a* notion of intentionality—on which perception is, *prima facie*, not intentional. Perhaps there are others on which it is intentional. Perhaps he has some such notion in mind. Crane considers two elucidations of intentionality. The first is Brentano's, which Crane renders,

> Every intentional act 'includes something as an object within itself'... the object on which the mind is directed exists *in* the mental act itself. For example, in hearing a sound, the sound... a physical phenomenon—is contained within the act of hearing the sound—a mental phenomenon.
>
> (1998: 3–4)

Here Crane speaks of direction at an *object*, rather than, as here, at a way for things to be. This is an important difference in how one conceives intentionality. I have explained my choice already. 'Is contained in' is a metaphor. I take it to mean something like this: it would not be *that* act (hearing that sound) without that sound. So the object contained is something essential to the identity of the mental phenomenon. In any case, I see no way of construing this idea so that it does not cast much too wide a net for identifying the intentional. The act of washing the dinner plates contains within it those plates, even when done by a machine. Perhaps the net seems narrower if we think of the object of the act as what need have no existence independent of the act. But we have now disposed of that idea.

Crane casts a perhaps narrower net later in identifying 'two main elements of the concept of intentionality'. These are 'the apparent relational structure of intentionality', and 'the perspectival, or fine-grained nature of intentionality' (1998: 12). The relevant relational structure relates a subject (thinker) and the object of the state (episode, for example). Relational structure on its own does little to identify the intentional. There is a relational structure—via the *being stained by* relation—between a thinker and that bowl of soup which stained his trousers. A lot hangs here, I think, on the word 'apparent'. The idea, I think, is that the *phenomenon* may still be instanced, the condition still obtain, even though the relevant relation *only* appears to, but does not, hold: there is no second term for a subject to relate to. I cannot be stained by non-existent soup. But I can look for soup when there is none. Merely apparent relational structure, so understood, is, I have argued, an illusion: what I relate, and appear to relate, to in looking for something is a way for things to be, which I would like to be helping to be instanced. Where that way requires some object to exist (I am 'looking for that diamond as big as the Ritz'), and it does not, there is nothing I am looking for; which is to say: I am only under the illusion of looking for something; *true* descriptions of me as so looking are descriptions of how things are in my illusion.

As for fine-grainedness, there are two ways of understanding this. The first idea is: whenever I bear a fine-grained relation to something, I always do so from some perspective, or vantage point, on it. If I am looking for an honest man, I do that with a certain picture of what it is to be an honest man. If I see the lion in the grass, I do that from a certain perspective on the lion. If I am stained with soup, I do that from a particular perspective: me below the soup, the waiter hovering with it above. This idea is not much help. The second idea is: my perspective actually enters, somehow, as, in effect, a further term in the relation. So I am not just looking for an honest man *full stop*. Rather, I may be looking for one under one 'mode of presentation' of *being an honest man*, not under some other. *If* looking for is really like that, 'N is looking for__' may be intensional.

So reading Crane's two main elements, seeing, at least seeing what is before you, remains non-intentional. I do not see the lion under some modes of presentation, not under others. I see it, or not. Of course, seeing it from different perspectives (angles) makes different information about it available to me. That is another matter. And seeing is not liable to be merely apparently relational. We could keep looking for other notions of intentionality on which seeing would be intentional. But should we?

Thinking of perception as intentional has, in fact, distorted thought about it. It has, for one thing, engendered a feeling that one needs to find something for it to be directed towards; something like a 'correctness condition' for seeing what one does on an occasion. Which moves some to find in perception something simply not there: representational content, that is, representing such-and-such as so. Knowing, like seeing, is not an intentional phenomenon, if we conceive intentionality as above. But it is related to what, if anything, is intentional: *thinking* something so. It is related, for one thing, by a rational retreat: I *thought* I knew, but now I see I only thought so. Suppose knowing were a hybrid, an amalgam of *thinking* something so, and some further conditions, of the obtaining of which a subject need not be aware. Then one could so conceive intentionality that knowing simply inherits its intentionality from that thinking-so which is a component of it. We need not look for it to pass, on its own, any further tests. So if you think knowing just *has* to be intentional, you have motive to try to make it out to be a hybrid. Similarly, some have thought, for seeing. I *thought* I saw a rabbit in the grass. But now I see that it only *appeared* that way. On the model of knowing, perhaps seeing is a hybrid of things appearing such-and-such way, and further conditions obtaining of which visual awareness is not needed, nor, perhaps, possible. Then seeing can be intentional in the same way as knowing on the above plan. (Crane sees the connection here. His defence of Brentano's thesis rests, explicitly, on seeing (experiences of) seeing as representing things as so, hence as hybrid.) But there are serious objections to the idea that either knowing or perceiving is a hybrid. (Frege showed why seeing cannot be so conceived.) In which case, insofar as there is any point to the idea of directedness, the best course will be just to acknowledge that some mental phenomena are intentional, and some are not.[1]

---

[1] I want to thank Mark Kalderon for invaluable help in getting these ideas in focus.

8

Unlocking the Outer World

> The same function which gives unity to the various ideas (*Vorstellungen*) in a judgement also gives unity to the mere synthesis of various ideas in an intuition (*Anschauung*).
>
> Kant 1781/1789: A79–80/B105–106

> What distinguishes my conception of logic is first of all recognizable by the fact that I place the content of the word 'true' to the fore, and then by the fact that I immediately proceed to *thoughts* as the things by which truth can come into question at all. Thus I do not begin from concepts, and build up thoughts, or judgements, out of these, but I obtain parts of thoughts by decomposing thoughts.
>
> Frege 1919b: p. 273

In advancing his view of judgement, Frege also advanced a view of perception and of experience more widely. In both instances, he advanced our understanding. The advance begins to show itself in the contrast between Frege and Kant above. Kant draws a parallel between one supposed task to be performed—forming the unity of a judgement out of 'the ideas' of which it is formed—and another—forming a particular sort of unity out of those elements which form an *Anschauung*—for example, a visual experience, or experiencing. If we follow Frege, the comparison breaks down before it starts. For there is no such thing as unifying elements into a judgement; no such work to be done. Thoughts, judgements, are not built out of building blocks which somehow require something else to hold them together. Rather, the existence of their elements—such things as concepts, or as he later put things, their counterparts in the realm of *Sinn*—presupposes whole thoughts, only by decomposition which are concepts (and so on) arrived at. Nor, as he further expands his view of judgements, is the sort of awareness we enjoy, for example, in seeing the things around us, that in which capacities of *thought* have a role to play. I take none of this to be either self-explanatory or apodictic. In what follows I will try to explain what Frege's advance is, and why it is an advance. My story will touch on Kant, and, considerably, on John McDowell, the most astute wielder of Kant's slogan above (henceforth The Slogan).

Frege's advance is in answering what I will call the fundamental question of perception: How does perception make the world bear (rationally) for the perceiver on what he is to think and do? How does it thus open up the world to his view? How, for example, could seeing a pig snuffling beneath that oak make that a pig is snuffling there the thing for someone to think? How recognizably a way things are? Frege's 'Der Gedanke' (1918) contains a satisfying answer.

The Slogan suggests a line of attack (whether Kant's or not) on a problem he sees as fundamental. I will call this *Kant's Problem*. Schematically, for the world to bear on the truth of things *we* think, there must be, Kant thinks, a certain match, or agreement, between the most general shapes of those things and the most general shape of what we think *about*—what we represent as being thus and so. If, but only if, there is the required match, things being as they are can *be* things being as we judge them, thus make our judgements true or false. For there to be such match is, *inter alia*, for certain very general propositions to be true. *That* they are true is, for Kant, a substantial matter, needing *proof*. Absent proof, it is doubtful whether our seeming judgements are really that, or merely masqueraders; still more doubtful whether anything, so anything experienced, really *could* bear rationally for us on what the thing to think would be.

In Frege's terms, a thought is what brings truth into question at all. To bring truth into question is to raise, or identify, a particular question of it—for example, whether there are apples in Sid's basket. What questions of truth there are is in general a contingent matter. But for a highly contingent episode in around February 1848, there would be no questions as to *Frege's* being thus and so. Things could conceivably have been that way. So, conceivably, what we *take* for such questions could turn out to be mere 'questions', masqueraders. Similarly, as Kant seems to view things, there would be no questions (with *true* answers) as to, for example, whether an *object* was thus and so, or whether one thing *caused* another (whether, for example, Sid tripped or was pushed) unless certain very general propositions were true (however generality is here measured). While these propositions are not quite *contingent*, they are, he seems to suppose, things for which there must at least *be* proof.

The slogan *can* suggest a key to the desired proof. Abstractly, if the same rational capacities are responsible for organizing for us both our thoughts about the world, and that of it which we experience, then it would be unsurprising if, at the required level of generality, at least, they organized each in the same way. Which would be (again at some level of generality) to impose the same form on each. Such, the thought would be, can just be the required match. Such application for the slogan is obviously problematic.

McDowell's problem is not Kant's Problem, but rather the fundamental problem of perception. So his application of the slogan is not this one. It calls for independent treatment. In preparation for this I will first discuss some issues Kant faces, then introduce Frege's picture of perceptual experience.

1 Unities

We *are* thinking (judging) only if there is, at a general enough level, a suitable match between the shapes of our thoughts and the shape of the world. Such is the idea. In one stretch of the *Tractatus* (around 6.32–6.34) Wittgenstein tried out the opposite idea. The most general (proprietary) structure of our thoughts in any given region makes *no* commitment to how the world is, or is shaped; so is impervious *punkt* to foundering on how the world is. Wittgenstein's sample case was physics, the sample impervious structure there being Newtonian laws. Wittgenstein was wrong. Kant's Problem is not dissolved in that way.

Kant's Problem arises because we are, plausibly, thinkers of a particular sort. We are endowed with a *parochial* capacity for thought. The same put less optimistically: we are *saddled* by our nature with thought of a particular kind. Now who is to say that this is really thought at all? To us it is, but we *would* say so, would we not? Kant's slogan, applied as suggested, *might* seem to reassure (whether it so reassured *Kant* or not). The application would run on these lines. Our capacities of mind saddle us with thought of a certain discernible most general shape. But, not coincidentally, our capacities for perceptual experience saddle us with experiences of that same shape, in some interesting sense of 'same'. So, of course, our experiences and thoughts match up. They were made for each other. (See Kant A114.) But this rough idea is useless for its purpose.

The rough idea rests on two assumptions. First, what we *judge* to be one way or another, at least where we judge how things stand in the sub-lunary world, must be found among those objects of sensory awareness which are unified by the capacities in question. If, say, we judge chipmunks to eat acorns, then chipmunks and the circumstance of their eating acorns must be among the things we encounter in perceptual experiences so formed.

Second, what the mind thus shapes must lie within the power of the mind to shape. The relevant capacities may give us chipmunks and their careers to think about. But if shaping is called for to guarantee the needed match—between our representations and what they would then represent as such-and-such—such does guarantee this only if these capacities shape how chipmunks and acorns *are*, so as to make the ways they are ways of which our would-be judgements are either true or false. On the 'promising' idea, it is the work of our capacities which is to guarantee that it is really *judging* that we do of chipmunks (supposing these to be sorts of things of which we might judge). So it had better be chipmunks and acorns, or their being as they are, which these capacities shape (and offer us for delectation). If not, then however our minds shapes our *experiences* of them for our benefit, how things actually stand with them is another matter.

As the slogan has it, capacities of mind are to shape our sensory *experience* of that of which we judge. There, perhaps, is something a mind *could* shape. But our minds cannot just shape our *experience* of chipmunks so that we *experience* them as, for example, fit to form conga lines or not, so long as whether they are really thus fit, or categorizable, remains another matter. The slogan, in present application, works only where the truth of our judgements turns on no more than what the mind's work assures there *is* for truth to turn on, thus in forming that *of* which there is for us to judge. The truth of a judgement turns on how things are. How chipmunks must *appear* to us in sensory experience guarantees nothing where it leaves this open. If what is shaped is only how chipmunks *appear*, then the only questions of truth there are for us to raise must turn solely on how they appear.

The only thing the mind could shape to be fit for judgement of some given form (were such shaping called for) is something the mind could shape full stop; that is, something mind-dependent. It could shape this into something such judgements might be true or false of only by shaping it into something some such judgement would be true of (if not that it is an acorn, then that it is not). Such shaping of things *of which* to judge is not what the mind does in presenting the way things are as falling under generalities of particular shapes, or in shaping our thinking so as for us to entertain generalities of just those shapes. *Such* mind's work does not touch that which is to oblige by instancing, or not, those generalities; by being or not the ways in question. It would do nothing to shape how things are into cases of things being, or not, such ways, were any such shaping called for. Exactly not: otherwise there could not be Kant's problem. Just here lies the rub.

In 1918 Frege identified a vicious form of mind-dependence. It turns on *his* notion of a 'Vorstellung'. There are two key things about a *Vorstellung*. First, for it to be is for it to have a bearer—in Frege's term, to belong to someone's consciousness. Second, it brooks no two bearers. If you are conscious of a *Vorstellung*, and I am conscious of one, then, *ipso facto*, these are two. The key point about a *Vorstellung* is that it cannot be an object of judgement. In Frege's terms there cannot be a thought—a question of truth—which decomposes as singular into a part which presents a certain *Vorstellung*—which makes the thought's truth turn on how that *Vorstellung* is—and a part which presents a way for a *Vorstellung* to be—which makes truth turn on which *Vorstellungen* are that way.

Here I omit most of Frege's argument. But I do think he was right. (See Essay 2 and Travis 2011.) So if the kind of mind-dependence this application of the slogan needs means that what we experience, shaped by our minds, are *Vorstellungen* in Frege's sense, then rather than winning some match between judgement and what is judged of, we will have eliminated (sub-lunary) judgement altogether.

But perhaps all it needs is some more benign form of mind-dependence? I think not. Suppose I experience (as it were) a bit of some chipmunk's career: it (so to speak) scales a tree, acorn in mouth. Suppose, now, that *you* similarly experience some part of a chipmunk's career. Suppose one would need to be me to experience what my experience was thus of—as it were, 'that chipmunk climbing'—and ditto for you. *So* far, so good, at least for seeming to make the slogan apply as wished. But suppose not. Suppose you *might* have experienced the same 'chipmunk'—there is such a thing as that. Now there is room for the chipmunk to *have* a career, or bits of one, unobserved by either of us, or for that matter by anyone. Now the chipmunk is fully part of a world which is what it is independent of how we stand towards it. Judgements about chipmunks are now in good standing. But now where is the guarantee that this career, which would be what it was independent of what it (inevitably) would look to be to our sensory awareness, in fact matches up in the needed way with what were, for Kant, the most general forms of our judgements? There is none. So, it seems, the application requires chipmunks to be *Vorstellungen* in Frege's sense.

H. A. Prichard, in *Kant's Theory of Knowledge* (1909), wrote:

Kant . . . renders the elucidation of his meaning difficult by combining with this view of the distinction [between perception and thought] an incompatible and unwarranted theory of perception. He supposes, without ever questioning the supposition, that perception is due to the operation of things outside the mind, which act upon our sensibility and thereby produce sensations. On this supposition, what we perceive is not . . . the thing itself, but a sensation produced by it. Consequently a problem arises as to the meaning on this supposition of the statements 'by the sensibility objects are given to us' and 'by the understanding they are thought'.

(1909: p. 30)

Kant, Prichard tells us, correctly and properly distinguishes between (what belongs to) perception and (what belongs to) thought; but then obscures his good idea with (as Prichard sees it) a bad theory of perception—or, as one might see it, an infelicitous deployment of terminology. What is bad in the bad theory (or what obscures the good point) is the combination of two ideas: first, that perception involves the operation on us of 'things without the mind'; and, second, that what these things do is to provoke, or produce, awareness of something other than themselves, and, to boot, something *not* outside the mind.

Prichard speaks of things outside the *mind*, not outside the *skin*. That *these* provoke perceptual awareness cannot in itself be a bad idea. Things outside the mind are just things whose existence, and whose conditions, are independent of us—as Frege argues, just a precondition for being things one can judge about at all: things about which there *are* questions of truth, answers to which—for example, that Sid *is* snoring—perception can place one in a position to *recognize*. But perception can so place us only insofar as these things, and their conditions are objects of our perceptual awareness. Just this comes into question with the second term of the combination. For what things without the mind provoke, on the 'bad theory' is awareness of sensations, and sensations, as ordinarily conceived, are *not* things without the mind; certainly not those things which provoke them. They are, as Prichard puts it, 'not the thing itself'. I may, for example, have an itching sensation in the back of my throat (of the sort honeydew melon produces), but at most only a sensation *as* of ants crawling over my back, even if 'ants crawling over my back' may sometimes work to identify it. Whether I have the sensation is a different and independent question from that of whether there are ants. Perhaps what Kant meant by *Empfindung* is something other than what we now mean by sensation. In any case, if this is the 'bad theory', then on it the object of perceptual awareness is not what we may *judge* to be thus and so, not what the *truth* of a judgement might turn on—at least if a judgement (so what it is of) cannot be a (Fregean) *Vorstellung*. Such really is a 'bad theory', especially *in re* perception's fundamental problem.

My present concern is not to decide whether Kant really held the bad theory. It is merely to identify some ideas to avoid. But where in Kant is there what might suggest to someone what Prichard thinks is suggested? Prichard himself refers to the opening of the 'Transcendental Logic' (B74–75, A50–51). Here Kant speaks of the first of two 'fundamental wellsprings of the mind' as the ability 'to receive *Vorstellungen* (receptivity to impressions)', and he says that 'through this first an object is given to us'. 'Vorstellung' is, for Kant, an undefined term (with a broad use, itself partly responsible for obscuring Kant's good point). The term at least suggests something not outside the mind. In any case, at the start of the *Kritik,* where Kant introduces his terminology (B33–34, A19–20) he tells us that *our* ability to 'relate (cognitively) to objects directly' rests on an ability to be affected by objects in a certain way, namely, to get (*bekommen*) *Vorstellungen* through being affected by objects; and that this is the *only* way we are provided with *Anschauungen* (cases of 'directly' relating to an object). He then tells us that 'the effects of an object on the capacity for *Vorstellungen*, insofar as we are affected by it, is sensation', and that an 'empirical' *Anschauung* (presumably the kind at issue in perception) is a case of relating to an object directly through (by means of) sensation (*Empfindung*). At B74 (the passage to which Prichard refers) he puts it this way:

> *Anschauungen* [perceptions, viewings] and concepts thus constitute the two elements of all our knowledge...Both are either pure or empirical. Empirical if they contain sensation (which presupposes the actual presence of the object).
> (B74)

So, it seems, if by 'Empfindung' Kant does mean *sensation*, then it is certainly at least suggested that the relevant *Vorstellungen* (those occurring in sensation) are not 'things outside the mind'.

So the picture is: we relate 'directly' to objects in perception in experiencing those sensations (getting those *Vorstellungen*) by which those objects affect us; that is, on the above suggestions, by, and in, experiencing things not outside the mind. Kant does not ever say—at least not in any passage so far—that the objects we thus relate to are themselves outside the mind. But one can see how Prichard might read that into the idea that these are objects which *affect* us, and which *produce* sensations (or sensation). Such talk is causal talk. And if Frege is right about things which are *not* outside the mind, then causal talk, as we ordinarily understand it, simply has no application to what is not outside the mind. On the other hand, it is a strange notion of 'direct' on which we relate directly to an object in perceptual (such as visual) awareness of something else which it produced 'in us'. *Perhaps* Kant had neither idea in mind.

If we buy the bad picture so far (bracketing the issue whether it is Kant's), we are then in a position to extract two more suggestions from his (perhaps unfortunate) deployment of terminology. For the first we need the term 'Erscheinung', which Kant introduces thus: 'The undetermined object of an empirical *Anschauung* is called *Erscheinung*' (B34/A20). He then says:

> In an appearance (*Erscheinung*), I call what corresponds to the sensation its matter, but that which assure that the multiplicity of the appearance *can be* structured in certain relations, the form of the appearance. For that by which sensations alone arrange themselves, and can be placed in a certain form, cannot itself be more sensation. Thus, despite the fact that the matter of all appearances is only given *a posteriori*, the form of these must lie ready in the mind *a priori* for them collectively, and thus can be considered apart from all sensation.
> (B34/A20)

There are two suggestions here. First, that what is produced in us by objects relating us to them directly—by their affecting our capacity to get *Vorstellungen*—is a multiplicity, or mass, of *Vorstellungen*—in the case at hand, sensations—which it is then open to our minds, or capacities of mind, to arrange for us in various ways, where the arrangement is done according to *a priori* principles, thus in ways *not* deriving from, nor achieved by, things without the mind.

This first idea, whether Kant's or not, can be fitted together with the use he actually makes of the slogan from which this work starts:

Thus this same understanding, and, to be sure, by just the same transactions by means of which, in the case of concepts, through analytical unity, it created the logical form of a judgement, also, by means of the synthetic unity it brings overall to an *Anschauung's* multiplicity, brings a transcendental unity to its *Vorstellungen*, which, accordingly, are called *pure concepts of the understanding*, and which apply *a priori* to objects, as cannot be established by general logic.

(B105/A79)

Putting all so far together, objects (or those in question here) are what we relate to directly through *Erscheinungen,* whose multiplicity (or, perhaps, inchoate mass) of sensation is unified by *a priori* powers of the mind, yielding the result that a certain set of concepts (pure concepts of the understanding) apply to these objects (to which we thus relate directly) *a priori*. Really?

There is the obvious problem. What are these objects to which certain concepts apply *a priori* (so of which certain very general things are true)? Are they those objects which, working on our sensibility, generate things other than themselves (*Vorstellung*, sensation) for us to be aware of? Then how can the way (or ways) those other things are formed by our minds into objects of our sensory (thereby other) awareness (ways the 'matter' of an *Erscheinung* admits of being organized), *a priori* or not, assure anything about what concepts do, or do not, apply to *those* objects, distinct as they are from what is thus organized? Or is it that the objects in question here—now objects of our sensory awareness—just *are* the results of such constructions, or impositions of form? So they are constructs out of the products of what Kant calls 'Sinnlichkeit'—our capacity for sensation. In which case, presumably, they are *not* objects without the mind. In which case Frege's point applies. They generate no questions of truth; no questions of some one of them as to whether it is thus and so. So the question what *concepts* apply to them simply does not arise.

Several ideas may mask the problem here. First, there is the idea that studying the work of the mind on input generated by, but distinct from, objects without the mind (and generally without the skin) is a perfectly respectable, in fact fruitful, branch of empirical psychology. So it must be an enterprise in good standing. Light forms images on retinas. These generate signals which are processed in given ways. The upshot is: we see what we do. This much is, by now, at least, a commonplace. Call the whole thing—such generation and processing of signals—the visual system. Science studies the visual system, and with good result. The workings of the mind which Kant posits here, the idea is, are formally, functionally, just like that. But this idea is wrong. The commonplace, and its expression in the empirical study of visual systems, is entirely compatible with this idea: what the visual system does is to furnish, or afford, us awareness of various features of what (generally) lies beyond our skin—such as colour boundaries, edges, angles, depth, animate things (spots and cows). There is no warrant in the commonplace for the idea that objects outside the mind (such as those beyond our skins) produce in us awareness of *something else*. And even if, on occasion, they did this (as, for example, when our eyes water) there is still less warrant for the idea that our awareness of these extradermal objects (now 'direct' only by courtesy) is via and through awareness of such other things.

The dilemma would not worry someone who, rejecting, or just deaf to, Frege, was an unapologetic idealist, an idealist *sans phrase*. For such a one there is another idea: embrace the dilemma's second horn. One could then take a Berkeleyan tack. Given that the objects of our perceptual awareness, so of our empirical judgements, are *not* without the mind, we can, nonetheless, separate a category within them, objects 'without our skins', extradermal objects, where 'extradermal' is now understood in terms of 'as though's— what is, for example, as though one could touch it with which what is as though his hand. This could be contrasted with, for example, a sensation as of ants crawling across one's back, which, though at first blush as though there are ants is, on examination, independent of whether there are or not. Still the sensation, even if the right visual impressions do not ensue. It has been suggested that Kant's 'empirical realism' is like that. But it is said that this incensed Kant. And indeed we might expect better of him. Anyway, though I *have* omitted his argument here, one turns a deaf ear to Frege at one's peril.

There is a further idea. Its image is: reality (the world without the mind) is a sort of seamless, flowing, mass out of which a mind is free to carve shapes *ad libitum*. It is, so to speak, like a sheet of '*stsie*' (*hostie*) before the wafers are stamped out. One might stamp out wafers. Or one might stamp out *bolachos de São Gonçalo*, depending on the stamps on board. Other issues aside, the idea here will not serve Kant's purpose. One can stamp wafers out of sheets of *stsie*. These will stand in spatial relations to each other. These relations will be governed by certain general principles. But all that is only because the sheet itself is already an object in space, standing in spatial relations, and so on, and so forth. Nothing new is won, certainly no new guarantees, by the carving. The truths whose status Kant is out to secure are meant to be among the most general ones governing those objects we (think we) think about. It is obscure how the carving image helps here. At this level of abstraction, carving cannot conjure new sorts of objects, or anyway new sorts of guarantees, into existence.

But perhaps we are looking for truth, or guarantees of it, in the wrong place here. Suppose we distinguish between generalities and things which instance them: on the one side, the sort of generality intrinsic to a thought, so to a concept where, as with Kant, this is an element in a thought (though not where it is what it is for Frege); on the other, for example, instances of things being as they are according to some thought. Then one might think: the truth of the sorts of truths which interest Kant really turns on relations between things on the first side of this distinction, generalities; whereas what perception, or *Sinnlichkeit*, furnishes us is awareness of what falls on the second side—things which instance generalities. On the side of the generalities, there is, plausibly, *some* room for the mind, or its capacities, to furnish us with a particular range of these to engage with in thought—a particular range, not the only one there is—and that there is, accordingly, some room for the mind, in its operations, to provide, among the things there thus are for us to think, things whose truth is guaranteed by their very nature. There is something in this idea, though not enough, I think, to give us what Kant might want. (Again, it is in general a contingent matter what generalities there are. There is, so far as we know, no level of generality, or other dividing line, beyond which a would-be way for things to be is *absolutely* immune to potential slings and arrows of what there may be to instance it—just *could* not fail to be genuine.) But *such* issues need Frege on hand.

Kant says just the right thing (nearly) when, working his way towards the transcendental deduction (A-version) he writes:

> ... Receptivity can only make knowledge possible when combined with spontaneity. This is now the basis of a threefold synthesis, which necessarily occurs in all knowledge: namely, *apprehension* of *Vorstellungen*, as modification of the mind in an *Anschauung*, *Reproduction* of this same thing in the imagination, and its *Recognition* in a concept.
>
> (A97)

What matters here is the distinction between apprehension and recognition. The first, apprehension, is awareness of what falls on the second side of the distinction I have just drawn—what *instances* (or fails to) various generalities. Such *of course* is not yet knowledge, or anyway, knowledge-that. Recognition is (or ought to be) recognition of *such* a thing's falling under, or instancing, some generality—something which only a concept (in Kant's sense), or, more properly (if we follow Frege) a whole thought, could bring into the picture. Only with that do we get something which *might* be instanced. With this distinction all is going well enough. It is just this which Prichard wished not to be obscured by Kant's further deployment of terminology. Unfortunately the seeds of obscurity are already sown here by Kant's use of the term 'Vorstellung', both for what is generated by *Sinnlichkeit* in furnishing us with *Anschauungen* (cases of 'directly' relating to an object) and for *Begriffe* (concepts). (It is an *Anschauung's Vorstellungen* which, in B105, are called 'pure concepts of the understanding'.) The suggestion (Kant may not have meant) is: one material, two sorts of operations on it. (Frege, too, gives 'Vorstellung' a wide reach. But for him *Vorstellungen* are what judgements are neither made of nor about.) To become clearer on what Kant's terminology leaves unclear, I turn to Frege.

2 Unlocking

Thus far I have been dealing with *suggestions* one might find in Kant. Perhaps Prichard is right: these arise merely from an unfortunate deployment of terminology, obscuring those good ideas which are really Kant's. Or perhaps the suggestions *are* Kant's (though not necessarily unequivocally so). Be such things as they may, my purpose here has merely been, using Kant, to set out some bad ideas about perception—without yet fully unfolding what is bad about them. Frege offers a much better picture of perception than anything on offer so far. It is a good framework within which to see what is wrong with what I have labelled 'bad ideas'. To develop his picture I begin near the end of 'Der Gedanke', where he writes:

> Sense impressions are certainly a necessary ingredient of sensory observation, and these are part of the inner world... These alone do not open the outer world for us. Perhaps there is a being that only has sense impressions, without seeing or feeling things [by touch]. Having sense impressions is not yet seeing things. How is it that I see the tree just where I see it?... Someone else sees the tree in the same place. He, too, has two retinal images, which, however, differ from mine... And still, we move about in the same outer world. Having sense impressions is, to be sure, necessary for seeing, but not sufficient. What still must be added is nothing sensory. And it is just this which unlocks the outer world for us; for without this non-sensory thing each of us remains shut up in his inner world. Since the difference thus lies in what is non-sensory, a non-sensory thing could also, where no sensory thing helps, lead us out of the inner world and let us grasp thought.
>
> (1918: p. 75)

Frege mentions two things here: first, being shut up in an inner world, and second, having this unlocked for us by capacities of a certain sort. What would we experience if shut up? What is added to experience when the outer world is unlocked? First question first.

A creature with senses locked in an inner world (we, if we were so locked) would get from his senses nothing but sense impressions. For (Prichard's) Kant, objects without the mind impress themselves on us. They generate sense impressions. The way that works is this: they stimulate a faculty of mind which, accordingly, generates objects of sensory (such as visual) awareness *other than* the objects which stimulated it. For Prichard's Kant, as later for Donald Davidson (1983, for example), these are sensations. For Frege, too, objects without the mind generate impressions—for us as things stand, for the creature locked in an inner world (for us if so locked). But Frege's story does not require these impressions to be of anything other than the objects which generate them. Our experience can be awareness of *these*, and of nothing else. There need be no *other* objects of visual, or other sensory, awareness. There need be nothing like sensations. What changes when the outer world is unlocked need not be, and for Frege is not, what our sensory experience is *of*, of *what* we enjoy sensory awareness. Being locked in an inner world is not a matter of being furnished with the wrong things to experience.

For Kant the capacity which is stimulated by objects without the mind is a capacity to produce *Vorstellungen*. For Frege, too, an inner world is made of *Vorstellungen*. For someone locked in an inner world, life consists, so far as he can tell, of, *so to speak*, just one *Vorstellung* after another. (Even that 'after another' goes too far.) But Kant's use of 'Vorstellung' and Frege's are quite different. For Kant (so far as I can tell) 'Vorstellung' is an undefined term, a primitive. It *seems* to embrace both objects of sensory awareness and 'concepts', whatever Kant thinks concepts are. Frege *explains* exactly what *he* means by 'Vorstellung'. In synopsis, the key features of a (Fregean) *Vorstellung* are these. First, a *Vorstellung* requires a bearer. It belongs to the contents of someone's consciousness. For it to be is for it to be in someone's consciousness—in some sense, something *he* is conscious of. Second, a *Vorstellung* brooks no two bearers. Imagistically, suppose you now have a *Vorstellung*, and I have one. Then *ipso facto* two *Vorstellungen* are in play. Nothing in Frege's notion of a *Vorstellung* requires this to be an object of sensory awareness. (The same, one hopes, holds for Kant.) Frege's examples of *Vorstellungen* span a wide space, including, besides sense-impressions, fantasies (creations of the power of imagination), sensations, feelings, moods, inclinations, wishes—but not decisions. (See 1918: p. 66)

Before me is a pig munching petunias (or snuffling beneath an oak). There is an object without the mind, generating in me impressions (for Frege as I read him, of itself). I see the pig. I enjoy visual awareness of it, and its munching, or snuffling, and so on. The pig is something for *one* to experience. It brooks awareness by many. It is no *Vorstellung*. My current visual awareness of the pig—that episode of experiencing what I now do of the pig's being as it is, that particular glimpsing of the pig—is another matter. For experiencing *that* glimpsing, for undergoing that particular case of pig-viewing, you would need to be me, then. So here, in the particular case—here one of a sensory experiencing—we can isolate a *Vorstellung* in Frege's sense. I had that *Vorstellung*: to have it was just to undergo that episode of experiencing I then underwent. If I were locked in an inner world, such would be all that was left for me, all life would consist of *for me*—not that what would be *left* in such a case need have any substantial role to play where the outer world *is* unlocked.

What is going on here is related closely to a fundamental difference between arguments for scepticism and arguments for sense-data. Both may appeal to the possibility of ringers—perfect illusions of, for example, a pig snuffling, things which, if experienced, simply could not be told apart from that by sight. But the appeal must be substantially different in each case. As for knowledge, what I cannot *tell* is liable to bear straightaway on what I know. If I cannot tell Pia from her twin, that may well impeach my claim to know that I saw her passing arm in arm with Vic. By contrast, the possibility of ringers does not bear (directly) on what I saw. If that pig is what was before me, then that pig is what I saw. It matters not at all that things would have looked the same had there been a ringer. For that reason, in arguments for sense data, appeal to ringers must be supplemented by some (usually easily resistible) assumption as to what seeing must be (for example, something such that I *see* something red, even if no red thing is before me). Locked in an inner world, whether it is a pig or a pig-ringer means nothing to me. Such is not a difference I am equipped to be responsive to. But none of that bears on whether my visual awareness was, in fact, of a pig. What matters to *that* is only what was before me, what there then was for me to have visual experience of. Or at least what does *not* matter is whether I am locked in or not.

Such is the beginning of an answer to our next question. What goes missing for a creature locked in? Or, conversely, what is added if the outer world is unlocked? What is missing is that, while he experiences the world around him, how it is is not thereby *revealed* to him. He sees (or hears, or feels, and so on) things being as they are. But he does not thereby see *how* things are—not if that involves seeing what *ways* things are. For a start, he cannot recognize, or see, what he is doing as what there is for *one* to do. He sees, for example, the pig snuffling. But while this *is* what he experiences, he cannot see what he experiences (a pig) as something there is to be experienced, by an experiencer which need not be him. Though he *does* such a thing, he cannot take in his so doing.

What, then, is changed when the outer world is unlocked? *Not* what he experiences visually. It is not as if one sort of object of visual experience is conjured into, or exchanged for, another. In Frege's picture, at least, there is no room for that. Rather, Frege tells us, what effects the unlocking is something non-sensory (a *Nichtsinnliche*). And its products are not objects of sensory awareness. To understand this properly we need to introduce another idea of Frege's, perhaps the most fundamental distinction that he draws. Frege writes:

A thought always contains something which reaches beyond the particular case, by means of which it presents this to consciousness as falling under some given generality.
(*c*. 1882: p. 189, *Kernsatz* 4)

Two things are in play here: first, 'the particular case', or particular cases; second, generalities under which these fall (and are brought, or presented as falling, by a thought). I start with the generalities. There is, the idea is, a kind of generality intrinsic to a thought. It is intrinsic to *any* thought, not what distinguishes one kind of thought, the general ones, from others. It consists in its relation to a particular generality, that under which it presents, or represents, *the* particular case as falling. In philosophy we typically think of a thought as the thought *that* such-and-such. But we can also think of it as a thought *of* a (given) way for things to be. It is a (or the) thought *of*, say, it being so that Sid is eating peanuts. As the thought *that* Sid is doing this, it presents this way in a certain way—as enjoying a certain status: being a way things are; as realized by things. We can then think of that way for things to be as the generality under which a thought presents the particular case as falling. The generality Frege has in mind lies here.

Frege explains a thought as what brings truth into question at all. Such is done only in bringing it into question in some determinate way, by raising, or speaking to, some particular question of truth—for example, the question whether Sid is eating peanuts. Now the idea is: whether a thought is *true*—what the *answer* is to the question of truth it raises—depends on how things are. But, the idea continues, in the nature of the case it cannot depend on *everything* in how things are. Not *everything* can matter to its truth. It would (or might) still be a case of Sid eating peanuts if Pia's Porsche were not in the shop, or if *A Tasquinha* were closed, and Sid were doing what he was doing somewhere else—say, at *La Bellota Hermosa*. Or even (*just* possibly) if Sid's shirt were tucked in, or he had changed out of his flip-flops. Things being such as for Sid to be eating peanuts is tolerant enough to allow for all that and more. *That* it is is not just an accident of the example I happened to pick. For this purpose any other would have done as well. So we can say: for any way for things to be, there is an indefinitely extendible *range* of cases which would be ones of things being that way. Or, if not that, then an indefinitely extendible range of cases which would be ones of things *not* being that way. Or, often, both. Such is the generality of ways for things to be. Accordingly, it is the generality of that 'something' in any thought.

I turn to the particular case. This is that which a thought presents as *falling under* some generality. So, then, what must be a case of the relevant generality if things are to be as the thought presents them? One good answer is: the way things are, or, in different mode, things being as they are. Sometimes we can be more specific. In the above example, *Sid's* doing what he now is, or, if you like, peanuts being subjected to the treatment they now are. Things being as they now are, of course, comes only once. Now, in fact, time passing, it is gone. But then, in ten minutes things will be as they then are. That will be another particular case. *It* must be a case of Sid eating peanuts if things are to be as the thought that he is then eating them presents them. A thought's generality may also be seen as a restriction on generalities of other sorts—for example, on Sid being something or other, and on something/some things eating peanuts.

A particular case may instance things being such that Sid is eating. A way for things to be is instanced by—or, in active voice, reaches to—a range of particular cases. There is no such thing as instancing a particular case. Each generality has its *way* of reaching; there is what it would be to be reached by it. No such thing holds of particular cases. What would be a case of the sun setting over the *foz* is not to be decided by, or found in, any particular case of the sun's so doing. The point here is perhaps reflected in the absolute gulf Frege finds between objects and concepts. But the present distinction is prior to, more basic, than that.

If we thought of generalities as forming a domain, a natural name for it would be 'the conceptual'. If we thought of particular cases as forming a domain, they might then be called, 'the non-conceptual'. I will so speak. Things conceptual—ways for things to be, or for *a* thing to be—participate in two sorts of relations. First, there are relations between them; for example, one, or several such things may *entail* another. Or, short of that, a given such thing may *bear* on another in some given way. Second, there are relations between the conceptual and the non-conceptual, the most fundamental and important of these being that of instancing, or its converse, reaching. Something non-conceptual—a particular case—may be a case of, instance, something conceptual, for example, things being such that that pig is snuffling. About a different but related pair of contrasting sorts of thing Frege wrote,

The fundamental logical relation is that of an object falling under a concept. All relations between concepts can be reduced to this.

(1892–1895: p. 128)

The conceptual–non-conceptual distinction is not that between concepts and objects. (It is more like that between *Sinn* and *Bedeutung*.) But one might also, plausibly, see instancing as the fundamental relation on which all relations within the conceptual rest. Or at least it is fundamental to this: to what identifies any given conceptual item as the thing it is. One is reminded of this in the mere fact that for, for example, snuffling to entail having a nose (if this is so) just is for whatever instanced (was a case of) something snuffling *ipso facto* to instance, be a case of, something having a nose. Suppose we know, for example, that being red excludes being green. (Suppose, for working purposes, that it does.) That such a relation holds between these two ways for a thing to be does not in itself identify either of them either as *being red* (for a thing to be red), or as *being green*—or not independent of the reach of at least one of these items. Being red excludes many things. As does being green. *Being red* is identified by its reach, and by nothing short of this. For it to be the way for a thing to be it is is for it to reach as it does, thus *to* what it does: to what it in fact does, and—since it might have reached to more had there been one more pig or peony—to what it *would*. *Mutatis mutandis* for *grasping* ways for *things* to be. Grasping *what* way for a thing (or for *things*) to be any given way (being red, say) is is, minimally, grasping how it participates in the instancing relation—to what it would reach.

Frege draws on (or perhaps elaborates) the conceptual–non-conceptual distinction in distinguishing seeing an object (or bit of history)—henceforth 'O-seeing'—from seeing-that—henceforth 'T-seeing'. There is, on the first side of the distinction, such things as seeing the pig, seeing the pig snuffling, the pig's snuffling, the pig's muddiness, the pig tiring. On the other side of the distinction is seeing *that* the pig is snuffling, so seeing it *to be* snuffling, or muddy, and so on. Seeing, on the first side of the distinction, is a *perceptual* accomplishment, *visual* awareness of something historical—of the world without the mind, and, in the case of seeing, generally without the skin, engaged in being as it is. Seeing, on the far side, is *not* perceptual. One might see that the pig is snuffling either in seeing the pig snuffling or in seeing (truffle-hunting) Pia's happy little schottische. Different capacities no doubt are drawn on in each sort of case. But in each case the seeing involves *recognition* of something which need not be recognized for O-seeing. The object of T-seeing involves an ingredient which does not occur at all in O-seeing. To T-see is to relate to (*inter alia*) something which is not the sort of thing to be visible, tangible, and so on—not a possible object of sensory awareness.

In 1918 Frege explains the difference thus:

But don't we see that the sun has risen? And don't we thereby see that this is true? That the sun has risen is no object which emits light rays which arrive in my eyes, is no visible thing like the sun itself. That the sun has risen is recognized as true on the basis of sensory experience.

(1918: p. 61)

In 1897 he explains it this way:

But don't I see that this flower has five petals? One can say that, but then uses the word 'see' not in the sense of mere sensing things via light, but one means a thought or judgement connected with that.

(1897: p. 149)

In 1918 the stress is on the fact that the object of T-seeing, for example, that the sun has risen, is not an object of sensory awareness. It cannot be before one's eyes, since it is not the sort of thing to have location at all. *It* does not rise from the east as the sun does. Nor was it already beyond the horizon waiting for the sun—in contrast to the pig, which *is* to be seen beneath the oak. In 1897 the stress is on the fact that T-seeing involves a relation to a thought—a thought, of course, being *just* the sort of thing which, as Frege rightly insists, is neither visible nor tangible, and so on.

But in both years the key notion is that of recognition. Pia sees the pig before her eyes. She recognizes what she thus sees as a case of—as instancing—a pig snuffling beneath the oak—a certain generality, a way *for* things to be. Such recognition is what draws on what might rightly be called a conceptual capacity: familiarity with what belongs to the conceptual, with that whose instancing one takes in—grasping what it is, for example, for a pig to be snuffling; what makes it recognizable that *this* is a case of it.

What Pia O-sees is precisely what *does* instance a pig being beneath the oak—nothing short of the pig, as it is, beneath the oak, as *it* is. Such is what is *there* to be seen. Suppose she lacked, or failed to draw on, the conceptual capacities just mentioned. She would still O-see what was there to *be* seen, what in fact instances the generality in question. She would just fail to recognize its doing so. The capacity to recognize a pig as a pig—being *au fait* with so much of the conceptual—can hardly be the capacity to transform something else into something which is then recognizable as a pig. Such would not be a capacity to recognize pigs at all. The capacity had better be one applicable to what was anyway, recognized or not, a pig, and to appreciate how *just that* relates to that certain bit of the conceptual, *for something to be a pig*.

Recognizing pigs typically involves capacities of two different sorts: a capacity to tell a pig at sight; and a capacity to recognize what counts as something being a pig as so counting. As we ordinarily conceive the first sort of capacity, and as empirical psychology might study it, it depends on a hospitable environment for being a capacity at all. Those features of the porcine it is responsive to are ones no-one would suppose capture what would count as something being a pig. My capacity to tell a pig when I see one ends when I enter the land of uncannily pig-like marsupials. And if (known to me or not) I tell a pig by its unmistakeably porcine snout, I would never suppose that to be a pig just is to have such a snout. Plastic surgery might sever that connection in either direction. A capacity to tell a pig by sight is responsiveness to *visible*, and, quite likely, to *visual*, features of the beasts among us. So it might, with *some* justice, be reckoned a visual capacity—though not one to *generate* objects of visual awareness, as in Prichard's Kant's bad theory. Still, one cannot recognize a pig *to be* a pig without thereby entering into transactions with the conceptual; without exercising mastery of what the instancing relation relates—so without engaging with thoughts, or drawing on conceptual capacities in the present sense.

What is operative in seeing-T, then—what distinguishes it from O-seeing as not a *perceptual* accomplishment—is a non-sensory (*nichtsinnliche*) ingredient—just the sort of ingredient which, he tells us, unlocks an outer world for us. For Frege, it is *one* such ingredient which plays both roles. Indeed, they are not really two roles: being fit to engage in T-seeing *is* having the outer world unlocked for one. Without this *Nichtsinnliche*, one might still experience visually. At various moments, things might be for one visually as they thus are. *What* one is experiencing visually could be—might as well be—(some of) the world around him, such as a pig snuffling beneath an oak. Then this is what he O-sees. But *that* this is so is nothing to him. He sees things being as they are. In one sense, perhaps, this is seeing *how* things are. But it is not seeing *what* ways things in fact are. Such is a matter of recognizing generalities as instanced. That would be T-seeing, beyond reach to one missing this *nichtsinnliche* ingredient. T-seeing is on offer only to one who knows his way around within the conceptual, who is at home there with its inhabitants. *Such* familiarity is not for the senses to supply.

Someone who sees that pig snuffling does something there is for *one*, not just himself, to do. His being as he is is thus a case of something there is for one to do. He, or his being as he is, instances a certain generality. But without Frege's missing ingredient—conceptual capacities, ones to to see the *nichtsinnliche* for what it is—this would be nothing *he* could recognize. Not that it is not there *to be* recognized. Not that he does not see the pig. But the fact of his doing so is something he is blind to. He is equally blind to the facts of *what* he sees—the pig, and nothing less—instancing the generalities it does, among which *a thing being a pig*. Awareness of the world around him is not what goes missing here. What goes missing is rather recognition of its being this.

If what the ingredient-less creature experiences visually is, in fact, a pig snuffling beneath an oak, then he is experiencing not just what others might, but also what has a worldly career, a career of interactions with the rest of our shared environment, which is independent of its being experienced, either by this creature or by others, and which is liable to continue (and much of which does continue) without being observed. It is the career of a continuant, with an historical start and end. It is an animate career, a porcine career. One might go on. To do so is just to continue the indefinitely extendible litany of all that which this creature is blind to. Such blindness just is, at least within Frege's picture, confinement in an inner world.

Honeydew melon is wont to produce a certain itch in the upper throat: call this 'honeydew itch'. It is a sensation. It thus contrasts with pigs and snuffling. Like experiencing *a* pig, or *some* snuffling, honeydew itch can be experienced by *someone*, not necessarily so-and-so, not necessarily now. It contrasts with pigs thus: if I now experience a pig beneath the oak, that particular case of a pig's presence might be experienced by *one*, not necessarily me (though, discounting film, and so on, necessarily then). Whereas this instance of itchiness—the one I am now experiencing—can be experienced (felt) only by me, now. Experiencing honeydew itch is still, like experiencing a snuffling pig, falling under a generality, being a way for one to be. But absent the *nichtsinnliche* ingredient there would be no difference *to me* between experiencing a case of the itch and experiencing a case of a pig snuffling. To me, it is all experiencing things being as they are, *fertig*. It might as well all just be sensation—so far as I am concerned, I lacking the ingredient. But it had better not all just *be* experiencing sensation. Sensations are not recognizable as pigs, because they are *not* pigs. *No* ingredient could make what I experience recognizable as a pig if it is *not* a pig. No ingredient could conjure what is *not* a pig—some sensations—into a pig, whether one which I thereby experience or not. If any ingredient is to be *any* help, it had better be a pig I experience all along.

Perception's role is to provide awareness of the non-conceptual, or the particular case. Without such awareness there is no seeing, or even taking, the instancing relation to hold between anything and anything (just as there is no taking it to hold without having the conceptual in view). If perception is to perform this role, it must confine itself to it. Conceptual capacities come into the picture only with our operations in thought on what perception has anyway provided; only with our ability to see when what we have O-seen (heard, felt, tasted) of how things are reveals it as what counts as things being thus and so.

3 The Given

John McDowell applies Kant's slogan, not to Kant's Problem, but to another. For his purpose he reads the slogan thus:

> The unity of intuitional content reflects an operation of the same unifying function that is operative in the unity of judgements, in that case actively exercised. That is why it is right to say the content unified in intuitions is of the same kind as the content unified in judgements: that is, conceptual content. We could not have intuitions, with their specific forms of unity, if we could not make judgements, with their corresponding forms of unity.
>
> (2008: 7; 2009b: 264)

For Frege there *is* no 'unifying function' operative in the unity of judgements. Whole thoughts, or judgements, come first. A judgement decomposes (non-uniquely) into elements. If such elements do not already jointly form a judgement, they are no elements at all. No unifying work is called for. No unifying work could form a judgement of what were not already elements in this sense. Frege's point, of course, is about *being* true, not *holding* true. There is no *logical* work of unifying. Perhaps there is still *psychological* work. Such work would lie somewhere in forming particular things which *contain*, or *express* thoughts. It would be work of allowing us to have thoughts in mind, or stand psychologically otherwise towards them. It remains to say just what such 'unifying work' McDowell may have in mind. First, though, what work does he want the slogan to do?

The central question, help for which McDowell hopes to find in the slogan as he reads it, is, I think, a better one than Kant's Problem. It is how perception can make the world bear *for us* on the thing to think. I call this 'the fundamental problem of perception'. There is the world, populated by such things as pigs snuffling, their snuffling, the aged and still ageing oaks under which they stand, their standing there, and so on. And there are the things for us to think: that a pig is snuffling, that there may be truffles at that oak's roots, and so on. The snuffling is audible, the pigs visible, but *that* that pig is snuffling is, logically, conceptually, a very different sort of thing. So how can sensitivity to the first sort of thing, in whatever form it is granted, reveal to *us* how we are to stand towards things of the second sort? A good question. But now, McDowell thinks that there is a certain sort of condition on any adequate answer to that question: it must avoid 'The Myth of The Given'. So *McDowell's* problem is to find an answer to the fundamental problem which avoids this 'Myth'—which satisfies both desiderata at once.

THE GIVEN   243

In 1991 McDowell spoke of an answer which did not avoid this 'myth' as

a vain appeal to the Given, in the sense of bare presences that are supposed to constitute the ultimate grounds of empirical judgement

(1994: p. 24)

An appeal to the Given thus succumbs to this 'myth', which in 2008 McDowell explains this way:

Givenness in the sense of the Myth would be an availability for cognition to subjects whose getting what is supposedly Given to them does not draw on capacities required for the sort of cognition in question.

(2008: 1/2009b: 256)

Of course, no-one could get what was given him (so nor be given it) without the capacity to get it. But 'getting it', in McDowell's sense here, would, in relevant cases, draw on capacities for cognition—capacities suitable to the thing given. So getting it presumably means coming to stand towards what was given in a suitable cognitive way.

We now need to ask what, for McDowell's purpose, the suitable way of standing is, and what suitable capacities for so standing would be. I think we get a clue to this in what McDowell takes to be just another form of the Myth:

... to think sensibility by itself, without involvement of capacities that belong to our rationality, can make things available for our cognition.

(2008: 2; 2009b: 258)

Which, in turn, he takes to mean:

The rational faculty that distinguishes us from non-rational animals must also be operative in our being perceptually given things to know.

(2008: 1; 2009b: 257)

So the Myth now becomes: perception can place us to know things in making us aware of what makes these thing knowable (or recognizable) without there being operative in it those rational capacities which distinguish us from non-rational animals. Perception, when it is working right, makes us aware of how things are. Seeing, for example, or hearing, or smelling, just *is* a form of awareness of how things are—of, that is, things being as they are. It thereby permits us awareness of *what* ways things are. Seeing, and hearing, the pig snuffling, you see, or recognize, that the pig is snuffling. Sniffing, you smell that the *daube* is burning. In these last examples we see relevant ways of standing towards those things towards which we do stand with the fundamental problem solved. The 'myth' is that this can be accomplished without 'those capacities which distinguish us from thoughtless brutes' already operative in perception presenting us with that which so places us.

So the idea now is: the way in which perception makes the world bear *for us* on *what* to think must be through work of our rational capacities (what unthinking brutes lack) in its presenting what it does (in presenting us with 'things to know'). Or, put otherwise, perception *could* make the world bear for us on what to think *only* if those rational capacities were at work *in it* in its presenting perceptually (such as visually) what it does for us to be aware of. Or at least all this is meant to be so if the 'myth', or what McDowell understands by this, really is a myth.

What (thus unmissable) work might be done by these rational capacities? McDowell addresses that question in passages like these:

> The idea is not just that experience yields items—experiences—to which judgements are rational responses. That would be consistent with taking rational capacities to be operative only in responses to experiences, not in experiences themselves . . . But that would not do justice to the role of experience in our acquisition of knowledge . . . it is in experiencing itself that we have things perceptually given to us for knowledge. Avoiding the Myth requires capacities that belong to reason to be operative in experiencing itself, not just in judgements made in response to experience.
>
> (2008: 3; 2009b: 259)

> An object is present to a subject in an intuition whether or not the 'I think' accompanies any of the intuition's content. But any of the content of an intuition must be able to be accompanied by the 'I think'. And for the 'I think' to accompany some of the content of, say, a visual intuition of mine is for me to *judge* that I am visually confronted by an object with such-and-such features.
>
> (2008: 8; 2009b: 265)

Experience thus represents things *as* being thus and so; it remains for thinking to add a force: not bare representing-as, but representing things *to be* that way (if we so respond). *I think* that things are a certain way—such that that pig is snuffling. But, whether I think this or not, experience has already represented the world *as being* such that the pig is snuffling (a feat which might be done with no commitment to whether such is actually the case—as, for example, in the antecedent of a conditional, or a request: 'See to it that that pig is snuffling').

There are two ideas here which need examining. One is that 'capacities that belong to reason' must be involved in experience itself, and not just in response to it. The other is that intuitions have *content*, where this is content susceptible to being accompanied by an 'I think', in which case it, or that instance of so accompanying it, is a judgement. (McDowell means to use 'intuition' roughly as Kant uses 'Anschauung': a particular instance of, as McDowell puts it, 'having in view' (2008: 5) or, perhaps, a viewing. In the (perceptual) experiential case of concern here, I take this to be just perceiving—enjoying, or being afforded, perceptual awareness of. What is given in perception would then be, at least first of all, that of which one enjoyed, or was afforded, perceptual awareness—such as a pig, or some snuffling.)

This second idea is, for the first time here, an idea about the work that 'rational capacities' would have to do in our being given things perceptually. They would have to invest intuitions with content. (This should not be read so as to suggest that there is such a thing as an intuition without content. If not, then rational capacities are (partly) responsible for their being intuitions.) Here, then, we have an application of Kant's Slogan, read so as to do the work on McDowell's problem which he thinks needs doing. Whatever rational capacities provide us with the contents of attitudes or stances, such as judgements—make such contents available to us towards which to stand, *thus* available to our consciousness in thought—now also form our intuitions—our viewings, or havings in view—so that these, too, contain these same contents—I have suggested, in the form of pure representing-as. I will turn presently to the question of *why* one might think such a thing.

Now we also have a reading of McDowell's talk of being given only what one has a capacity to get. If I am perceptually given something to know—if knowledge of it is made available to me perceptually—then to *get* what I am given (thus to know it) is for me to stand in a certain way towards, *inter alia*, something conceptual in the sense of section 2. I stand in a certain way towards some given way *for* things to be—for example, such that a pig is snuffling: I recognize it as a way things are. So for me to get what I am given is for me to draw on, *a fortiori* to enjoy, conceptual capacities. They are at work in the getting. But getting here—recognizing, knowing—is a *response* to what I am given. McDowell's idea is that this is not enough. Those same capacities must also be at work in that case itself of being given, of my having the world perceptually in view, of my being presented with that to which I thus respond. Otherwise I could not have been given the thing to get at all. Eventually we will need to raise the question of why someone might think this. For the moment I work to make that question urgent.

I have led the discussion back to imagery of giving and getting. The ways this imagery might work already carry intimations that there is something wrong with at least this last idea of McDowell's. Consider Uncle Willard. Returning from the fens, he presents me with a stuffed bittern. He has thus made a raft of things available for (my) cognition, most of which I am, as things stand, in no position to get. He offers opportunities which I cannot *yet* exploit. Suppose I am asked whether there are *greater* bitterns in the fens. I have not a clue.

Staring at the stuffed bittern is no help. But now I study bitterns. In time I acquire the ability to tell the lesser from the greater at sight. Now I look at Uncle Willard's bittern and find in it a message for me. It is, plainly, a greater bittern. So there must be greater bitterns in the fens. In one perfectly good sense, I was given something to get when Uncle Willard gave me the stuffed bird. That bird was full of information about the fens (in the only way our mute friends could be). But it takes sophistication to extract these riches from the bird's *Gestalt*. One must know that there is such a thing as a greater bittern, so know of a certain way for things to be: being one. One thus needs some grasp of what it would be for a thing to be one; then, quite a different matter, of how to tell one (here at sight), in particular, from a lesser bittern. Such things came to me only with time. But as soon as they had come, the bittern stood there, as it long had, ready to serve.

Might perception fit this model? Has it not already? Unfortunately, before I could acquire the needed ornithological expertise, Uncle Willard's trophy disappeared—an overly enthusiastic char. I was still to learn that there are both greater and lesser bitterns, much less how to tell the one from the other. Such knowledge was to come, though. When it did, all was revealed to me. I could remember what the stuffed bird looked like—what *perceptual* experience had then given me to know. *Now* I could, at last, recognize what I *saw*, before that char's work, as a case of the instancing, by a certain object's being as it was, of a certain generality, something being a greater bittern. My powers of deduction, and memory of the stuffed bird's provenance, now allow me to conclude that there are greater bitterns in the fens.

McDowell insists (rightly) that perception must provide us with something we have the *capacity* to respond to, rationally, knowledgeably, in taking it to be so (judging, seeing) that such-and-such. This requires, he insists, that our rational capacities—those same capacities at work in 'forming the unity' of a judgement—must be at work in perception's providing us with what it does for us (thus) to respond to. There is a clue to why he insists this in one description above of the work thus done: perception must provide us with something bearing content (a viewing) to which one might attach an 'I think', and *would* thus obtain a judgement. Nothing less would allow for knowledgeable judgement. This gap between what perception must supply and the response thus permitted corresponds exactly to the gap between representing things *as being* some particular way—as might be done without endorsing their so being—and representing things *to be* that way. So, if perception *must* supply the above, that is to say that the most that could be supplied by our ability to *respond* to what we see (and so on) is what fills the space between representing-as and representing-to-be—in one vocabulary, the attaching of a force.

If such is the work our rational capacities must do for us to have something to respond to rationally, a conclusion follows about those capacities by which we are able to take the world to bear on what to think—in Frege's terms, by which we are able (rationally) to pursue the goal truth. These capacities are only able to operate on things shaped like a thought, or at least like what a thought is of, a way for things to be. They can operate only on generalities, only *within* the conceptual (at least while guiding what we judge). Thus it is that these same capacities must operate in perception itself—presumably on something else (though how *that* trick could then be turned remains a mystery).

But, as Frege has shown, this could not be right. A capacity to judge *must* be, *inter alia*, a capacity to relate the conceptual to the *non-conceptual,* to recognize the instancing relation to hold between what it does. Its work *cannot* be confined *within* the conceptual. To take something to be so is to acknowledge the fundamental relation to hold between a denizen of the one realm and a denizen of the other: between things being as they are, on the one hand, and some way *for* things to be on the other. In one place in the relation, something which lacks generality, has no reach; in the other, a generality, something to be instanced. Recognition here draws on acquaintance with both domains. One needs acquaintance with the workings of the relevant generalities. One also needs acquaintance with that particular case which is to do (or not) the instancing—as one does to think at all of that which is the way things are, for example, to think of what Elmer is now doing that *that* is snuffling. Perception's role is precisely to provide this last sort of acquaintance. Filling it with generalities would be no help.

If a capacity to judge were not sensitive to particular cases, and to how, in each, things are, it would not be a capacity to judge at all. If *we* were not sensitive *in our responses* to which particular cases were such as to count as, for example, ones of Elmer snuffling, and which were not, we would not have the capacity to feel, or see, any bearing of the world on the thing for us to think. Then we would not be judging at all. True enough, *logic* (what Frege called the *laws* of truth) deals only with relations within the conceptual. The instancing relation is not one of these. But if our responses to the world are to be rational—so if we are to have a capacity to judge at all—then our rational capacities must extend beyond logic's ambit. Turning McDowell's vision around, they must do so in operation in our *responses* to experience, and not just in our being provided things to respond to.

We can go a step further. One could say about the instancing relation much the same as Frege said of what he held to be the relation of an object falling under a concept: it is the *fundamental* relation to which all relations within the conceptual can be reduced. (See Frege 1892–1895: p. 128) One does not have the conceptual in view at all, has no particular concepts in mind—and so *has* no capacity for such things as judgement—unless one has an adequate grasp on how (enough) denizens of the conceptual reach, thus unless he is able to recognize, well enough, particular cases *as* cases, or not, of enough ways there are for things to be (knows well enough what counts as what)—unless, that is, he can so exploit acquaintance with the particular cases themselves. McDowell loads what we *receive* in experience—what we get to respond to—with the content he does because he confines our rational capacities, or their work in our responses, *within* the conceptual. Frege's point is that doing so robs us of rational capacities *überhaupt*.

It also misconstrues the role of perceptual experience. Perception's role is to provide us acquaintance with terms which stand on one side of the instancing relation—that occupied by the non-conceptual. It is thus that we exercise our capacities to see (tell, recognize) what counts as what. Thus it is that Frege stresses the distinction between seeing as a perceptual accomplishment—seeing-O—and seeing as a function of thought—seeing-T. The perceptual accomplishment is (such as visual) acquaintance with that which is fit to operate on our sensory transducers (for example, to form images on retinas). It is awareness of such things as the pig, an episode of snuffling, the pig snuffling, the pig standing just *there* beneath the oak.

McDowell is concerned to preserve the good idea that sometimes one can *just* see that a pig is snuffling. One need not infer this from, or take it on the evidence of, something *else* experienced. I see the pig, snuffling. My *reason* for taking the pig to be doing this (insofar as we can speak of reasons here) is just his doing it, or that I can *see* (hear) him snuffling. But, as stands out clearly in Frege's picture, the relation between the pig snuffling and the fact that the pig is snuffling is nothing like entailment, not a logical relation. So nor is the move from seeing the pig snuffling to seeing *that* the pig is snuffling anything like an inferential move. Such moves and relations live *within* the conceptual. They are not available for lining up those two distinct domains, the conceptual and the non-conceptual. Recognition, as when one recognizes what is, in fact, the pig snuffling as a case of things being such that the pig is snuffling, is not inference, not even inference with a foot in each domain. Frege does not threaten that good idea which, as McDowell sees, must be preserved here.

If what we see does in fact instance things being such that a pig is snuffling, then just *that* which we are visually aware of is a case of a pig snuffling. But what perception affords is acquaintance with what so counts, thereby opportunity to recognize its doing so—opportunity afforded anyway, whether exploited or not. (And whether the instancing is recognizable or not, as snuffling might not be were some swine catarrh a dead ringer for it.) Again, *that* a pig is snuffling is not located in the environment. Nor is that what is going on there so counts.

A fortiori it is not something *perception* could supply awareness of. Nor is such perception's role. It will do for it to provide *perceptual* awareness of the pig snuffling, thereby affording awareness that the pig is snuffling to those capable of recognizing, to that extent, what it is they see.

Our senses (such as sight) provide us with a view of things engaged in that which in fact instances all that is (visibly, audibly, and so on) instanced in (those) things being as they are—far more than we could ever recognize. We see and hear the snuffling. We thus witness what is, in fact, an historical instance of snuffling. We are not thereby presented with a view *as to* what ways for things to be are instanced by what we see. We are not presented with what we are *as* falling under given generalities. Such is not an object of visual awareness. Nor could it be the way for perception to make the world bear for us on what to think. To *recognize*, identify, the way things are as such that a pig is snuffling, we must be afforded acquaintance with that which *is* so to count, and which might or might not do so, all depending on what would count as something being a pig, and as something snuffling. Not that our *recognizing* what so counts as so counting need change the way anything looks, or looks to us. *The way in which perception opens up the world to us is by affording acquaintance with what falls under genralities*. Without such acquaintance we could not so much as acquiesce (rationally) in a view as to which ways for things to be were instanced by things before us being as they are. We would not have those things to think about at all.

Relations *within* the conceptual—ones holding between given ways for things to be and given others—cannot, on their own, fix how the conceptual relates to something else, the non-conceptual. They cannot decide how it participates in the instancing relation. They cannot fix to what particular cases anything reaches. They fix nothing unless it is already fixed, for enough of their terms, and enough particular cases, to which of these those terms would reach. The reach of the conceptual to the non-conceptual is not fixed by any structure internal to the conceptual. It is not fixed independent of that to which it reaches. Perceptual experience is experience of, affords awareness of, *just* that other side of the relation. It thereby does its job. It allows us to see *that* an oak is before us, or that a pig is snuffling, in seeing the oak, or the snuffling pig. Or it does that for those who know their oaks, or snuffling pigs, when they see (or hear) them.

Some relations within the conceptual are negotiable. Whether *oak* is a genus depends on how the world is, on what it provides so to classify. Perhaps some are non-negotiable, fixed in advance of whatever particular cases the world may dish up. So it would be on some accounts of categories: *no matter what*, something could instance a thing being an oak only if it also instanced those other ways for things to be. Someone, even if not in thrall to Kant's problem, *might* see in this work for rational capacities—capacities whose first home is in thought and judgement: in allowing (for example) visual awareness to provide does provide for us to respond to, these capacities would infuse it with representational content, so that in such experience things were represented as instancing at least *those* most general ways for things to be. Or it might just shape visual experience so as to make their instancing somehow easily recognizable. The uselessness of the first sort of work has already been discussed. As for the second, if there is really no such thing as objects of perceptual awareness *not* instancing these ways for things to be, then it takes no shaping to make this recognizable to one who knows that fact. If it is recognizable at all, it is recognizable no matter what the shape.

4 Unities Revisited

What of the first term in the slogan's comparison? Here the unity of a judgement (or thought) is meant to be formed by some 'function' out of thought-elements ('concepts'). The direction is counter to Frege's core insight that whole thoughts come first. For Frege we can make sense of the idea of a concept, and then isolate some, only in terms of the notion of a thought. As he puts it in 1882:

> I do not think that the formation of concepts can precede judgements, because this presupposes an autonomous existence of concepts, but I think concepts arise through the decomposition of a judgeable content.
>
> (1882: p. 118)

We come to concepts by breaking down thoughts. A thought, for Frege, just is a question of truth, presented, not in interrogative form—the question whether (it is true that) Sid snores—but, as it were, in the form of a supposition—that Sid snores. We come to concepts in carving up a thought's task—making truth (*simpliciter*) turn in a particular way on how things are—into sub-tasks—making truth turn in part on such-and-such. We *have* decomposed (articulated) the thought *only* if the sub-tasks we identify, performed jointly, *are* the thought's whole task. There can be no question of any further factor *unifying* these sub-tasks into the whole task. What a concept does it does *within* a thought. We can understand what it does only in terms of that notion of truth *simpliciter* whose first application is to whole thoughts. Objects *fall under* concepts: concepts are *true of* them. No *true of* without *true* full stop.

When we carve an element out of a thought, we move from that generality intrinsic to *all* thoughts (see above) to a wider generality. We do this in a way which is moving from the generality of a thought to the generality of something not a thought—in the core case here, from a way for *things* to be (catholic reading) to a way for *a thing* to be. We thus move from a reach to one range of particular cases—say, things being such that Sid snores—to a wider class—say, things being such that *something* snores. Where this is a move to what is not a thought (here a concept) it is a move to a wider range of *thoughts*—that Sid snores, that Pia snores, and so on. Moving to a concept, we thus bring the thought from which we abstract it under a given generality. The point about *true of* again: no ranges of thoughts without *thoughts*.

Decomposing the thought that Sid snores, we might thus reach a range of thoughts, each of someone that he snores, and a range, each of Sid. Think of a range as reaching to all the cases anything in it does. Thus the wider generality of the concept than of the thought from which we extract it. Conversely, so thinking, the thought that Sid snores stands at the point where these two ranges intersect. Where each element thus partially identifies the thought's reach, no further unifying work is called for.

What Frege describes is the structure of *being true*, not *holding true*. Whatever the structure of being true, it is not literally inconsistent with that to suppose the structure of holding true to require, for holding this stance—or others—towards a thought, that thought be presented to the holder (whether by himself or something in him) in a way which needs to be constructed out of other material—building blocks of some sort—by some 'unifying function'. Nor is it literally inconsistent with the structure of truth to suppose that such should be so independent of anything as to how our psychology merely happens to be, or of anything to be established by empirical enquiry. The idea of such construction is anyway rife in current *philosophy* of psychology. McDowell's talk of the unifying function as '*operative* in the unity of judgements, in that case *actively exercised*' (my italics) suggests that he *may* have some such thing in mind. But if, through change of topic, such is not quite *inconsistent* with Frege, it is at least hard to see, if thoughts themselves are not so structured, what could make for such a requirement, even if misleading analogies between thinking and talking might make for the appearance of one.

If McDowell and/or Kant is interested in some issue about the structure of *holding true*—an issue in (presumably non-empirical) psychology—what sort of interest might this be? If unifying is called for here, then there is, perhaps, a legitimate question in empirical psychology as to how, for us, the relevant mechanisms work. I think Jerry Fodor thinks of things in this way. But I doubt that either Kant or McDowell does. Between this and the structure of being true, what else is there? 'Transcendental' psychology perhaps? Kant, we are told, was much concerned with questions how things *could* be. How could a thinker, or one of us, stand towards a thought such as to judge it true? A possible answer: he, or we, could not unless we had a faculty in us which constructed such standings-towards-thoughts out of building blocks. To so much as entertain the thought that monkeys fly, say, you, or some faculty in you, would have to construct a presentation of this thought to consciousness out of smaller units.

Such a thesis about holding true is not contradicted, strictly speaking, by anything in the structure of being true. Perhaps it is suggested by thinking of judging as an episode, one of *raising*, and then answering, a question, rather than—as it usually is for Frege—a stance, or posture, towards the world—not an episode gone through, but something maintained. For postures the thesis at least cannot be transcendental. Things *need* not be like that. I will develop this through an analogy with an idea of Frege's. In 1882 Frege continued that passage about the primacy of whole thoughts thus:

> I do not believe that for each judgeable content there is only one manner in which it can be decomposed, or that one of these possible manners can always claim material precedence.
>
> (1882: p. 118)

The idea continued throughout as central to Frege's thought (see, for example, 1892, 1919). A *whole* thought, the idea is, is structur*able* in many different ways. Or at least this is often the case. No-one such structure, he tells us, is *as such*, or for serious (*sachliche*) ends, more fundamental than any other. Perhaps there is an analogy here between a thought and a thinker.

One can draw an analogy here between thoughts and judgers. A thought represents the world as a certain way. A judger at a time represents the world as a certain way. For the thought, that certain way is *a* way for things to be. For the judger, it lies in his finding things as he does: in the bearing he is prepared to find in the world on what the thing for him to do, or think, would be in adopting projects, and in their execution; on how to conduct his (thinking and doing) life. There is what he is prepared to acknowledge as to when the world turns out to be as expected, when not. All this the beginning of a long story, an unfolding of the idea of a thinker holding a *picture* of the world—picturing things as he does, not necessarily equivalent to picturing things as such-and-such way there is for things to be. The analogy would be: this picture of the world, equivalently the posture thus held, is decompos*able* in many different ways into thinking this, that and the other; and in different ways on different occasions and for different purposes. For one thing (to go beyond Frege for a moment), what counts as thinking that, say, Pia drinks *mojitos* on one occasion for saying what she thinks may not do so on another. This idea of a posture decomposing in many ways repays much more elaboration. But its function here is just suggestive. In any case, a posture decomposable in many ways, none with a serious claim to priority 'for *sachliche* ends', cannot be one formed by some fixed set of elements, each itself built up in a particular way from building blocks. Nor could it be that if it is decomposable (for some purposes) into, *inter alia*, thinking, say, that Pia drives a Porsche, that *that* sub-posture, entertaining, or thinking, *that* thought, need be built up out of elements if it is to make good on its claim to be a posture held.

One sign that the analogy is on the right track is our preparedness to recognize the same thought as expressible in different ways. Sid might report, 'Pia's Porsche is in the shop'. Or he might report, 'Pia's ride is being serviced'. In suitable circumstances, at least, we would recognize these as different ways of expressing the same thought. That thought, expressible in either way, could not then be built up in some one way out of given building blocks. Nor could our stances towards it, if these are such as to make either of the above equally recognizable to us as an expression of it. Nor could a picture of the world if, in these circumstances, such picture would not differ in being decomposable as containing what is expressible in one of these ways, but not what is expressible in the other.

Another reason concerns our relation to our perceptual experiences. In seeing, for example, we see, and recognize ourselves as seeing, what we do of how things are. What we thus recognize ourselves as seeing (then having seen) is, in fact, such that things, in so being, thus instantiate countless ways for things to be—more than we shall ever know of. What among these are such that in taking in, visually, what we thus do of how things are, we thus come to take things to be *that* way? For example, I see a greater bittern cross the path ahead and disappear into the brush. I am duly impressed. But I do not know what a greater bittern is, have never heard of one, could not, if asked, finger the *greater* bitterns in a lineup. The *way* I take things to be is in fact a way such that a greater bittern crossed the trail. But does this decide things? Or, again, I am in court. The defence challenges my claim to have seen a greater bittern cross the trail. Did I not really see only its hind quarters, or facing side? Am I quite sure it was not a mechanized stuffed bittern I saw? And so on. Suppose I acquiesce in the defence's suggestions. So now I revise my description of what I saw. Many are the revisions I might choose from, depending on how those suggestions impressed me. I saw an avian profile flitting across my path and dissolving in the brush, for example. But my revised descriptions require the right provocation. I state things according to my belief, as it is and was. But do these descriptions really give the content of judgements I held all along, do they express thoughts towards which all along, thanks to some unifying function, I stood in such relation?

In any case, what I saw and took in does become part of my image of the world, how I picture it, along with all I then take to be so. It guides me in my perceptions, and choices, of the thing to do, and the thing to think, as belief does. Thus it is that I can be stating my long-held belief in giving a description I would never have thought of but for that particular form of provocation in which the defence indulged. That what guides as belief does is thus formed counts, I think, against the idea that what thus guides me decomposes in any unique way into thinking that this, that, and the other; so equally against the idea that the picture needs to be, or could be, built up by some unifying function out of building blocks for thoughts.

But this only gestures at a more principled discussion which I omit here. I only note that the idea of thoughts, or stances towards them, as each built in a particular way of particular blocks is the idea Diderot (the French politician of *Investigations*, §366) expresses thus:

Whatever the order of terms in a language, ancient or modern, the mind of the writer has followed the didactic order of French syntax.

(1751: p. 390)

We say things in French as the mind is forced to consider them no matter what language in which one writes.

(1751: p. 371)

There is a particular way which is the *mind's* way of organizing, structuring, thoughts. Wittgenstein mocks this view, I think, because he was once gripped by it himself. There is no evident reason to think it right.

5 The Second Term

If we follow Frege, no unifying function is called on to *compose* thoughts. Nor, I have suggested, is one called on to compose stances towards them. *Decomposition* is another matter. Logical relations between thoughts are structural relations. So these only appear in decomposing. If all pigs grunt entails that this one does, that can only be because of something in common to those two thoughts—what one might capture in describing both as about pigs grunting. Logic thus requires that thoughts be decomposable; grasping it, plausibly, an ability to decompose them. If it is the same function at work in thinking and seeing, perhaps, then, it is a decomposing function.

Rereading the slogan in this way gives us: the same ability to decompose thoughts which is exercised, sometimes actively, in judging must be operative in decomposing (empirical) *Anschauungen* (for McDowell (and for seeing) viewings, or havings in view, cases of our seeing what we do) if perception is to make the world bear for us on what to think. Our seeing what we do must be decomposed for us by some such function into (*inter alia*), say, our seeing a pig beneath that oak if we are, indeed, really to *see* the pig beneath the oak; if we are to be able to exploit our experience in thereby *recognizing* what we confront as things being such that a pig is beneath an oak. This seems right. What we *see* (O-see) must be such as to permit recognition of things being as they are as a case of there being a pig beneath the oak; must allow us thus to connect the non-conceptual we encounter with that bit of the conceptual. What we are given in receptivity—the non-conceptual, presented in a given way—must *permit* knowledgeable responses (*suitable* work of spontaneity).

But what kind of organizing is this being supposed to require? Once again, there is that organizing work studied in the psychology of perception. Visual processing so works in us that we are visually sensitive to colours, colour boundaries, edges, depth, various particular kinds of motion, and so on. When the instancing of a way for things to be is recognizable by such features, we are, so far as that goes, well placed to do the recognizing (when processing goes well). The rest, if we follow Frege, is up to thought.

No processing, no seeing. Empirical psychology *has* been forthcoming about the details. But there are three things to note. First, what the relevant processing operates on is not (in general, at least) itself an object of visual awareness, not itself part of what we experience visually. What a given such mechanism does is more like operating on, and modifying, some electrochemical signal. Second, what does the operating is, in general, not capacities for thought, but rather dedicated and more or less encapsulated, capacities to process signals of the relevant sort—for example, to fill them in with information (or misinformation) about the location of edges in the scene before the viewer. Third, while we *can* describe what all this processing does as organizing our visual experience for us (in a certain way), at least so far as the uncontentious idea is concerned all this need come to is that it affords us visual awareness of our environment (the scene before us). For example, it allows us to be sensitive to—visually aware of—the presence of edges, so of detachable objects, at certain places in that scene. It provides (when all goes well) no *new* things for us to be *visually* aware of. Or where it does, it is not *thereby* that the world comes to bear for us as it does on what to think and do.

We must be suitably sensitive to the right features of our environment—colours, shapes, and so on. But neither Kant nor McDowell is, I think, interested in the details of what enables this. Or at least that function which is meant to work both in thinking and seeing is not assigned such work. I *think* this is clear at least for Kant. First, Kant's organizing function operates on the *unbestimmte Gegenstand* (undetermined, or indeterminate object) of an empirical *Anschauung*—on what Kant calls an *appearance* (*Erscheinung*). But the object of an (empirical) *Anschauung* is what one *views* in a viewing/having in view. It is thus, unlike the signals on which visual processing works, itself an object of (for example) *visual* awareness. Second, the functions operating in visual processing are not at work in organizing thought. They are dedicated, encapsulated (more or less).

As to the third point, I leave it open whether what we are meant to be offered *visual* awareness of when Kant's function has done its work is any more, or other than, those objects beyond our skin which provoked *Sinnlichkeit* in the first place; whether what we are thus provided to witness, thus to recognize as instancing the being of *ways* they visibly are, is any other than those extradermal *Sinnlichkeit*-provokers, or any other than that of which we judge, sometimes knowledgeably. With a modifier before it—for example, 'empirically'—a 'Yes' should be read as 'No'. If the answer is unqualifiedly 'Yes', it is for *empirical* psychology to identify the work done—doubtfully the study Kant had in mind.

For McDowell, the objects of our visual awareness are to be none other than what is before our eyes, those very *Sinnlichkeit*-provokers. His organizing function is to provide no additional objects of *visual* awareness. He still sees organizing work as needed, so that those provokers can be presented to us *as* instancings of such-and-such generalities, as what count as cases of things being thus and so. Were they not so presented, the idea is, we could not *recognize* them as—*knowingly* take them to be—what they thus are.

Frege shows why *this* cannot be right. For one thing, what we have in view on an occasion instances, in being as it is, *many* more ways for things to be than we could ever get in mind. For many more than *we* could entertain, it does so visibly, recognizably to a thinker equipped to recognize their instancings. It is not as if what we *see* would differ, or as of things would be *visually* presented to us differently, were the ways whose instancings we could recognize other than they are. It is just that which we do see, and to which we are visually sensitive, which instances far more than we will ever know. For Frege, no one way of decomposing a thought can claim priority over another for serious purposes. No one way is most fundamental. Similarly here none of the ways whose instancings we witness in our viewings of things can claim priority as a way the experiencing itself represents things as being (though our particular visual equipment may make it easier to pick out the instancings of some of these ways than of others).

6 Images

In A120 Kant speaks of an 'active power of synthesizing multiplicities' (in an 'appearance'), which he calls the *Einbildungskraft*—the power to imagine, or to form images. Of this he says:

The *Einbildungskraft* must bring the multiplicity of an [empirical] intuition (*Anschauung*) into an image

('Bild').

There need be nothing wrong with this idea. But there are various understandings of it. There is, first, the question whether a *Bild* here is an object of *sensory* awareness, like the image of Ulysses S. Grant now in my wallet, or of thought, or some mixture of these, or neither. Second, there is the question whether *Bilder* are to be things presented to us for us to respond to, or rather themselves responses to something else, or, again, a bit of both, or neither. Third, there is the question how, if at all, these *Bilder* articulate—into things of propositional form—particular ways for things to be—or as the pictorial (a painting, say) articulates, or as the way I remember Burgos looking might articulate, or, again, a mixture of these, or none of them. And are such images articulable exhaustively? Fourth, how is *forming* out of other elements to be understood? Is the image formed *of* them, so that they are part of it? Or are these transformed, or mapped, into elements of some other sort? Finally, are these *Bilder* that of which we judge? Or do they bear for us in some other way on what the thing to judge would be?

We have learned by trying that certain answers to these questions will not do. For example, relevant to Kant's concerns, these images had better not be that *of* which we judge. They had better be, if *images* at all, then images of something other than themselves, where it is *this* of which we judge. To hold otherwise would be a thoroughly virulent form of idealism. If we needed to learn this, then it is one thing Frege taught us. Equally, for familiar reasons, those images had better not be our access to that of which we judge. In that role, they would rather cut us off from the possibility of judging of this.

McDowell posits work of rational capacities in our being presented perceptually with what we are. I think that work can be seen, neutrally, as the formation of images. Such certainly need not be objects of visual awareness. It is not that he posits some *such* objects other than those before our eyes. As he rightly insists, it is precisely that pig snuffling which, when seen, can be reason (our reason) to take a pig to be snuffling. But suppose the images here are organized, provided, *for* us on the presentation, rather than the response, side of experiencing. And suppose they are not objects of visual awareness. We are *given* them to respond to, perhaps to incorporate into the way *we* picture things. Here Frege has another lesson for us. Perception, in supplying such images, would be doing work it is not perception's job to do. Rather than merely affording acquaintance with that which is to be recognized as instancing a way for things to be or not, perception would prejudge issues for us. Such would not help make the world bear for us on what to think. It would merely be telling us what we need to see for ourselves. It would be, if anything, mere distraction. Such images as McDowell has in mind—*contentful* intuitions—might harmlessly, even fruitfully, occur on the response side of the divide. But he insists that this is precisely not were he means to finds them.

9

Desperately Seeking Ψ

> A thought's existence can also be understood to be its being so that the thought can be grasped as that same thought by different thinkers.
>
> Frege 1919a: p. 146

J. M. Hinton begins his essay 'Visual Experiences' (Hinton 1967) by characterizing a particular sort of (would-be) mental state or occurrence, which he dubs, "Ψing'—or, more exactly, a certain sort of would-be statement, Q, which would mention Ψing, were there such a thing. He remarks that it is 'moot' whether there is any such statement—nor, hence, any such thing as the envisaged Ψ. In fact,

> I do not at present see how it can be, or could be, shown that there is such a thing as (Q). Consequently I do not see how it could be shown that there is such a thing as my psi-ing for these and other statements to be about.
>
> (Hinton 1967)

Many, I think Hinton among them, think, stronger, that there is good reason to suppose that there is no such thing as Ψing; and that such can be seen from careful reflection on what it is that we take seeing, and, more broadly, visual experience, to be. Those who so think are often called (even by themselves) *disjunctivists*. Others think otherwise—Tyler Burge, apparently, on both counts. He is, at any rate, against what *he* calls 'disjunctivism'. He thinks this *blatantly* false, moreover at odds with (what should be) known results of science. He writes of disjunctivism:

> It is fairly unusual, at least since the days of Descartes and Newton, for philosophical views to be as directly at odds with scientific knowledge as disjunctivism is.
>
> (2005: 29)

Though, as it turns out, this needs to be taken with a grain of salt.

Other topics—knowledge, belief, for example—leave room for positions of the form of disjunctivism about seeing. These too are called disjunctivism—for example, about (singular) belief. Burge thinks that disjunctivism about belief is mistaken, and on the very same grounds as disjunctivism about seeing.

In this essay I will discuss disjunctivism about seeing and about belief, though I will say much more about belief than about seeing, and discuss seeing only at the end. Following Frege I will try to show that both these disjunctivisms are cogent, motivated positions, and not so much as spoken to by vision, or any other, science. Burge, I will argue, misconceives the the topics of disjunctivism, notably belief, in ways one who followed Frege's lead would not. More broadly, with many others today, Burge misconceives how science (notably physics) *has* spoken to philosophy.

1 Ψ-ing

In Hinton's special case, disjunctivism rejects a certain ingredient in perceptual experience, Ψing. In other cases, a disjunctivism rejects a similar ingredient in some other area of our mental lives. As a first step in understanding disjunctivism, one might ask just what Ψing is.

Hinton inspired at least the term 'disjunctivism'. The disjunction here is between a pair (or more) of cases, for example, one of seeing such-and-such, and one of illusion thereof. Ψing, if there were such a thing, would be something common to both terms. In Hinton's somewhat special case, the one disjunct is seeing a photic flash. There is also such a thing as experiencing a phosphene—a visual experience, not seeing, caused by electrical activity in the brain. Some such experience might be, or seem to its subject, visually just like seeing a photic flash. Seeing the flash might provide nothing by which to tell by sight that one is not experiencing a phosphene. Conversely, experiencing a phosphene, one might be unable to tell by sight that he was not seeing a photic flash. He need be provided visually with nothing by which to tell this. In this sense, if he saw a photic flash, what he experienced would be, visually (for him), *just* like what he would experience in an indefinitely extendible range of possible cases of experiencing a phosphene, and if he were experiencing a phosphene, what he experienced would be, visually (for him), just like what he would experience in an indefinitely extendible range of cases of seeing a photic flash. In this sense, his photic flash admits of perfect illusions—namely, certain phosphenes, and his phosphene (where he experienced one) admits of perfect illusions—namely, certain photic flashes (just as fuzzy print may produce an illusion of blurred vision).

Two initial points about Ψing. First, to make sense of the idea we need to make sense of pairs of an actual case of 'the real thing', for some value of 'real thing'—here, as the case may be, seeing a flash, or experiencing a phosphene—

and a range of cases of perfect illusions thereof, along roughly the lines just sketched. Second, assuming that we have done this, Ψing is to be experiencing something which one would be experiencing either in that case of the real thing, or in any case which was a perfect illusion thereof. A disjunctivism is about seeing where a value of 'real thing' is seeing such-and-such, or, perhaps, where any case of seeing what one there does generates a range of perfect (visual) illusions thereof, as just sketched.

Hinton's position is not meant just to concern photic flashes. It is meant to generalize. Suppose Sid, on *esplanada*, spots Penelope Cruz, lounging on some adjacent rocks. There are (imaginable) body doubles, silicone dummies, holograms, and twins. And there is excess of *orujo* or psilocybin. In those first cases, Sid would be provided, visually, with nothing to go on if he needed to *tell*, by looking, whether it was Penelope or some such ringer. Perhaps that is enough for defining *some* Ψing-like notion. Generally, though, Ψing is meant to be something liable to be present in cases of the second kind as well. A case of the second kind might be, for Sid, just as though he were seeing Penelope. It might so impress him. It is less clear that the idea of it providing no visual cues by which to distinguish it from seeing her makes sense here—one problem for the position which disjunctivism (about seeing) means to reject.

One more note on *perfect illusion*. Sid saw Penelope in a yellow shift. He might experience an illusion of her in a yellow shift—say, her in a beige shift in special light. Not all such would be perfect ringers for his seeing what he did. In the illusion she might be in a *chaise longue*, rather than on the rocks. Or the shift might be from A. Salazar rather than from P. Garcia. Or her hair might be blowing in the wind, rather than at rest. And so on. The problem stands as we add to our list of features the illusion must have: in it, she is in her yellow shift from P. Garcia, sipping a *mojito* languidly. There are many different ways for things to look while she was doing that. To be a perfect illusion of what Sid *sees* in seeing her on the rocks sipping cannot just be to satisfy certain generalities. It should be no less than an illusion of *what he saw*, a ringer for his seeing what he did. His seeing what he did does not reduce to his seeing things being this, that, and the other way.

Sid seeing Penelope on those rocks is just one more case of seeing. But the presumption is that any case of seeing admits of (imaginable) illusions thereof on the model of Sid's case, or of the photic flash. So for any actual case of seeing, one might equally well (or badly) identify a range of perfect illusions thereof, for which one might posit, or refuse to posit, a common feature such as Ψing. Ψing, as Hinton defines it, is specific to photic flash-phosphene pairs. To indicate that I am generalizing that notion, I will write 'Ψ(γ)ing', the γ indicating the particular actual case of seeing (or of illusion, where applicable) which generates the relevant range of perception–illusion pairs.

What we have so far is just that for any such range of pairs, $\Psi(\gamma)$ing is experiencing visually something one would experience in any case within the range. To this Hinton adds three features, which I will call plenitude, determinacy, and illusion-resistance. Plenitude is the idea that $\Psi(\gamma)$ing is not only present in all cases within the range, but present only there; so that to be $\Psi(\gamma)$ing is, *ipso facto*, either to be seeing what one did in the case which generates the range, or to be experiencing a perfect visual illusion thereof.

Determinacy is the idea that $\Psi(\gamma)$ing is experiencing something identifiable (without reference to its presence in that range of cases), thus (in principle) specifiable. It is not just experiencing what one does in all those cases, but moreover, experiencing such-and-such—things being, or looking, such-and-such way there is for things to look. As Hinton says, to say that one $\Psi(\gamma)$ed is to answer the question *what* one experienced visually (in seeing what he did, or being illuded as he was).

Illusion resistance is the idea that, while it is easy to imagine a ringer for seeing Penelope sipping—experiencing a perfect visual illusion thereof—and easy to imagine a ringer for experiencing such an illusion—seeing her sipping—it is difficult to see what it might be for there to be a ringer for doing either the one thing or the other. Since $\Psi(\gamma)$ing (if there is such a thing) is to be what one does precisely in those cases of seeing and illusion thereof, it is equally difficult to see what a ringer for $\Psi(\gamma)$ing might be. Indeed, something seems to speak against this. Suppose there were such a thing. Call it $X(\gamma)$ing. $X(\gamma)$ing would be, in this case, experiencing a perfect visual illusion of either Penelope sipping (as in the initial case), or a perfect visual illusion thereof. But how might a perfect illusion of a perfect illusion of Penelope sipping fail to be a perfect illusion of her sipping, save by being a case of seeing her sipping, and hence, either way, a case of $\Psi(\gamma)$ing, and not just a ringer for it?

So far, disjunctivism about seeing. Disjunctivism about belief would be rejection of some Ψ-like state as an ingredient in our believing the things we do, and/or, perhaps, some parallel common ingredient in the representations we relate to in representing the world to ourselves in the way, or ways, we do. For a Ψ-like ingredient in our believing what we do, we first need to identify some way in which we may be under illusions as to what it is that we believe. So the initial idea, by which Ψ-like common factors are brought into view here, would be that where, say, Sid thinks that Penelope is sipping, there is one or more other thing for him to think such that if circumstances were right, it might *seem* to him that he was thinking just that which he in fact is thinking—he would experience a perfect ringer for so thinking—where, in fact, he would be thinking this other thing; and/or that, if circumstances were right, it would seem to him that he was thinking just that which he in fact is—he would experience a perfect ringer for so thinking—where he was thinking nothing (or no thought) at all. The Ψ-like factor would then be some way of thinking of the world—some way for it to be represented *in* representing it being some given way—which is a way it would be represented both in representing it as the way it was represented in the initial case, and in representing it as one does in all those ringer cases—ones of representing it as being some other way, perhaps some ones of failing to represent it as being any way there is for it to be.

Where there is such a Ψ-like factor to deny, disjunctivism about belief is its denial. Where there is none, disjunctivism can just consist in saying so. More needs to be said to make sense of the idea of a belief and its ringers. My concern here will be with Burge's attempts at saying this. Here Burge, and I, will restrict attention to one sort of thing one might believe, namely, that things are thus and so, where the thought that they are that way is (or is representable as) singular. (As Frege reminds us, the same thought may be decomposable as singular, general or particular (see 1892a: 199–200).) A singular thought is one for which there is an object on which its truth turns *essentially*. More on this in due course.

2 Burge's Target

Is disjunctivism Burge's target? He says this:

> The key disjunctivist claim entailed by naive realism is negative. No specific explanatorily significant state is common between the different perceptions in the three cases: the case of perceiving object a, the case of perceiving contextually indiscernible object b, and the case of having a referential perceptual illusion which is for the perceiver phenomenally indiscernible from the two preceding cases.
>
> (2005: 41)

> Our concern is with disjunctivism's denial of common, explanatorily relevant perceptual state types and perception-based propositional attitude (belief) types, in the three sorts of cases...
>
> (2005: 26)

> It cannot be emphasized too strongly that disjunctivism is not merely the claim that there are mental differences among the three states... Disjunctivism denies that the relevant perceptual experiences have any explanatorily relevant *type* of perceptual state in common. This is the view that I shall criticize.
>
> (2005: 27)

Sid sees Penelope, on the rocks, reclining, in her yellow shift. In the blink of an eye, Penelope is replaced by a silicone dummy Penelope. Sid notices no difference. In another blink, the whole scene disappears, but computers generate the same patterns on his retinas. Here are three cases of the sort Burge has in mind—what I will refer to as a 'stock triple'.

Ψ(γ)ing is a very special sort of perceptual state or episode, one with the particular features just listed. To deny it is not obviously to hold that the perceptual states or episodes in the three terms of a stock triple have *nothing* in common. Indeed, for the case he discusses, Hinton suggests that they do:

> In a way (A v B) does say what my A-ing and my B-ing have in common... It says that my A-ing and my B-ing have in common that one is, what the other merely is like.
>
> (1967: 223)

Thus, *a* perceptual state in common throughout the terms: one of being such that that disjunction holds. Perhaps this is ruled out by what Burge means by 'explanatorily relevant'. We will explore that possibility in due course.

But I think Burge's real beef with disjunctivism about perception (and about belief) lies elsewhere. It is that such disjunctivisms conflict with what he calls 'The Proximality Principle':

> What I firmly reject is the disjunctivist denial that there are fundamental explanatorily relevant perceptual state types that accord with the Proximality Principle.
>
> (2005: 28)

He states that principle as follows:

> On any given occasion, the total antecedent psychological state of the individual and system, the total proximal input together with internal input into the system suffices to produce a given type of perceptual state, assuming no malfunction or interference. Call this the *Proximality Principle*.
>
> (2005: 22)

It is first worth noting that this principle is not really any *result* of science, but rather (so far as it is a good one) some piece of methodology with which the relevant science approaches its topic in the first place. Not that it is a bad principle. As Hinton puts it:

> Well, and indeed it would be strange if, given a certain type of impulse reaching certain structures, what happened next there, or in adjacent structures, was different according to the nature of the remoter cause, the initial stimulus; the mechanically 'observable' effect of the given proximate cause taking after its grandfather, so to speak.
>
> (1973: 75–6)

So for Hinton, as for Burge, for given processing (typed by steps for *a* processor to go through, and input *for* it to receive) there must be some outcome-type such that same processing yields same outcome.

How, though, is disjunctivism meant to run afoul of this? The idea is, in the three terms of a stock triple, the same proximal stimulus (type)—the same pattern of irradiation of the retinas—receives the same visual processing (the same processing of whatever sort it is the task of vision science to identify). So, the idea continues, there must be the same processed product in each case. When the science has explained how that processed product, or end state, would be produced under the circumstances obtaining in each term of the stock triple, its explanatory burden is discharged, or at least its means for explaining whatever it is it does explain have been exhausted. So, Burge reasons, there must be some *one* thing which it does explain throughout the terms, thus some one thing present and to be explained in each term. But the task of vision science, as Burge sees it, is to explain visual experience. So, he thinks, that one thing must be a type of visual experience; moreover, a type typed by what it is that is thus experienced visually. From this we can see what 'explanatory relevance' must come to here. An explanatorily relevant perceptual state is to be, first, a state (or episode) of experiencing such-and-such visually, and, second, that state whose occurrence is explained by given processing of given proximal stimulus, as per above.

If (but only if) this line of thought is right, there is something experienced visually in all terms of a stock triple, moreover something specifiable (what that processing would explain). Moreover, one might think, if one were experiencing that, he would have to be either, say, seeing Penelope sipping, or seeing a perfect ringer for that, or witnessing, or otherwise experiencing, a perfect visual illusion of that. For for him to experience something visually (be visually aware of something) which allowed him to *distinguish* his experience from seeing Penelope sipping, there would need to be further visual processing, or a different proximal stimulus, which, by hypothesis there is not. So it looks like we have something like plenitude, determinacy, and illusion-resistance for this supposed state of visually experiencing. What we do not have, to be sure, is that the specified output could be produced only by *that* processing of *that* proximal stimulus. But we can bracket that for the moment.

On these assumptions what vision science revealed really would be at odds with disjunctivism. We can see that it would be without even knowing the specifics of what it will reveal. Thus Burge's comparison with (supposed) Hegelian astronomy—though what disjunctivism would be at odds with is the methodology of the science, not some result of it. But we can see already that more is assumed here than just that innocuous principle which Hinton enthusiastically endorses. Let us agree that there is some product of processing which is present in each of the three terms of the triple. It is another step to conclude that that something is a state, or episode, of experiencing such-and-such visually. It is in recognizing this as an extra step that Hinton takes Proximality in his stride.

The Proximality Principle (same intradermal aetiology, same product) applies, or *sowieso* applies, only where the notion *proximal* applies. It is automatic only for what has location. It is agreed on all hands that in the area of visual experience there is that to which it does not apply, such as seeing. If Penelope is not sipping, Sid does not see this. Nor is there any other thing which he both sees in seeing her sipping and must still be seeing so long as the intradermal aetiology remains fixed. Given intradermal aetiology does not guarantee *seeing* some one thing. Nor, to be sure, is Sid's seeing her sipping at a location, at least an intradermal one.

Seeing does not fall within the ambit of any genuine requirement of proximality. Now the question is whether *any* visual experience so falls, and if so, whether, moreover, it has the properties which mark $\Psi(\gamma)$ing. Burge supposes that we can prescind from the shackles of the quotidian—those boring facts as to who is where doing what—so as to be left with a *visual experience* which is determinate, a plenum (relative to something there *might* be for one to see) and illusion-resistant, and on which a requirement of proximality gets a grip. But *this* assumption is not part of the methodology of any science. It is a bit of all-too-familiar philosophy, as will emerge.

3 Postures

Disjunctivism sins, Burge tells us, not only *in re* perceptual experience, but also *in re* belief. It denies 'common, explanatorily relevant... perception-based propositional attitude (belief) types'. Here again the issue is whether there are belief states governed by a requirement of proximality, and if so, what sort. Perception and thought stand on different sides of a divide. In perception we encounter, witness, things to which to respond, *inter alia*, in thought. Thought, notably belief, is a response to what we thus confront. One might find it surprising if explanations of *visual* processing required some end state which was a *response* to what was thus visually experienced. Such surprise will prove well placed. But then too, perception's role is to make the world bear for us on what to think and do. Burge would not be the only one to think this to require perception itself to confront us with something already conceptualized—some content for representing, notably a belief, to have. It might seem a short leap from this to the idea that there is—must be—a particular response it thus demands; a particular belief it would (*ceteris paribus*, perhaps) provoke. What inspires this thought, I note, is not some supposed demand of vision science for a given end product of given processing, but rather an idea, whose source lies elsewhere, as to with what perception must confront us.

Following Frege, one would not see the conceptual on the presentation side. And one would diverge from Burge on more points than this. Burge operates with a very particular picture of belief. I think we can only find our way back from that picture to the actual phenomena with an alternative picture in view. Frege offers just what we need. This section will sketch it in nine points. This alternative mandates precisely Burge's target. One might *dispute* Frege's picture. One awaits.

1) Judging (*urtheilen*) is Frege's term for the central case of a truth-evaluable posture. The first point is that judging in his sense (believing, taking to be so) *is* a posture, a way of standing towards things. It is not an *act*, still less one of representing. Sid takes things to be such that Penelope is reclining. He so stands. No *act*, of representing or otherwise, could achieve, or constitute, this. Sid tells Pia that Penelope is reclining. Such is an act of representing. New representing is created in and by thus making it recognizable. A new way for things to be is thus created: things being as represented in that episode. Suppose that, observing her, Sid comes to take Penelope to be reclining. For him to hold that posture is for him to be prepared to acknowledge this as being so—Penelope reclining as among the ways things are. No *act*, of thought or deed, would count as being so prepared. Nor is there any such which could not go missing while he remained so prepared. Believing thus involves no *acts* of reference. Acts belong to belief's expression. If I write myself a note, I make recognizable to myself the representing I have thus done. I do not thus make recognizable *to myself* what I believe. If there were any question about that, *that* question would remain open. An *act* of representing-to-be-so is, Frege says, the *Kundgebung* (announcing) of *Anerkennung* (acknowledgement) of some thought's truth. *Kundgebung* does not create *Anerkennung* to be announced.

2) Believing (taking to be so) is a posture liable to a particular sort of success or failure. One may believe truly or falsely. The posture presumes its own success. It represents itself as a case of taking in how things are. But it also aims at that success in that it presents itself as what would be a failure unless a certain condition were met. To hold it is to acknowledge such liability, or at least to be suitably sensitive to the difference, for it, between such success or failure. Crucially, such a posture is always one for *one* to hold—for any given ones, perhaps another. Human reproduction ensures that our beliefs meet this condition. Given this, *someone's* holding of the

posture is a success (of the indicated kind, thinking truly) just in case *anyone's* holding of it would be. (See 1893: xvi; 1918: 67–9.) To stress a crucial point, someone believes that such-and-such only where that such-and-such is something for *one* to think—only where indefinitely many might agree or dispute as to precisely that. Such is a *sine qua non* for that objectivity Frege insisted on for (what he called) judgement.

3) We come now to Frege's notion of a thought (*Gedanke*). A thought, Frege tells us, is that by which truth is brought into question at all. (See, for example, 1918: 60–1.) But there is no such thing as simply bringing truth into question. For postures, there is no such thing as simply aiming at truth. Truth can be brought into question only by raising some particular question of truth. A posture can aim at truth only in making its success turn in some particular way on how things are. A thought fixes some such way. The thought is *of* things being such-and-such way there is for things to be. Viewed as a thought *that* such-and-such, it presents that way as among the ways things are. (For Frege, so presenting things is still to be distinguished from *committing* to truth.) A thought is a particular way to aim at truth. So, *inter alia*, it identifies a particular posture of believing—one for *one* to hold—in fixing what *its* success turns on. Each thought arbitrates success for some such posture. A thought is the content of a belief, where 'content' has precisely this significance.

If a thought is what brings truth into question at all, then, Frege insists, it is *essentially* invisible, intangible, not perceivable by the senses:

A thought is something not perceivable, and all perceptually observable things are excluded from the domain of that by which truth can come into question at all.

(1918: 61)

An utterance, or some other perceivable thing, might go in for that success just discussed—make itself liable for being true or false (for example, stating truly or falsely). But then there would be an intelligibly contingent question on what its truth was to turn, just how it had exposed itself to success or failure. One can (for the purpose) identify the utterance by (some of) the words that made it up, its speaker, its date, and so on. It is *that* utterance. An utterance's having all those features is compatible with its having *no* content, or, if some, then (near enough) any. If its content is *this* rather than *that*, such remains to be said. And it is so far a contingent matter. It makes sense to ask why its content is such-and-such—what else in its occurrence mandates this rather than something else. Such questions cannot be asked intelligibly of a thought in Frege's sense. A thought is a way for the truth of, for example, an utterance to turn on how things are. Circumstance connects it to any utterance whose content it may be. That a thought's truth turns in a particular way on how things are (if we so speak at all) cannot *depend* on anything else. For its truth to turn on what it does is just for it to be the thought it is. Otherwise it could not be an *answer* to the question what question of truth some given utterance raised. Such, Frege sees, requires a thought *not* to have a perceivable form (say, orthographic, or geometric, or historical) which identifies it as the thought it is. Corollary: for any perceivable form of the expression of a thought, there might be another.

Such invisibility of thoughts separates them, and whatever has that generality intrinsic to them as such, from what lacks such generality—notably, its instances, what falls under it. This is to say that what has that generality is *never* the object of the senses, or of *perceptual* experience. Such will be crucial in what follows. But next to identify the generality in question.

4) It is intrinsic to a thought to have a certain sort of generality. As Frege puts it:

A thought always contains something which reaches beyond the particular case, by means of which it presents this to consciousness as falling under some given generality.
(1882: *Kernsatz* 4)

The success of a posture of believing cannot turn on *all* of how things are. For any given such posture, there must be something *specifiable* on which truth turns. Suppose that Penelope is sunning in her *chaise longue*. Such is a way *for* things to be. Things might be that way while she was being watched by Sid, while she was not; while she wore a yellow shift, while she wore britches and held a riding crop, and so on *ad infinitum*. There is indefinite variation in what might make for a case of things being such that Penelope is sunning. So for things to be as per some given specifiable posture of belief is not simply for things to be as they are, but rather for them to be what they would be in an indefinite range of other circumstances. Such generality is intrinsic to a way for things to be. Equally for a posture, so thought, which represents things as that way. Such is also contained in the idea that a given posture of belief is, *per se*, a posture for *one* to hold.

By contrast there is what a thought presents as falling under some given generality—what Frege calls 'the particular case'. This precisely lacks that generality which marks thoughts and ways for things to be. A thought just *is* what brings particular cases under some given generality. *It*, in being what it is, fixes what instances that generality, what not—what particular cases the generality would reach to. Nothing in a particular case as such brings anything under any generality—fixes what would *count as* anything. Penelope's yellow shift does not fix what it would be for anything else, or even for itself, to instance something being yellow. Nor does any particular case even determine what it would be for something to be a particular case. *It*, in being as it is, does not fix what *a* particular case might be. A thought makes it *recognizable* what would instance things being as per it. For a particular case there is no such thing to recognize.

> 5) Perceptual awareness is *essentially* awareness of the particular case; of things being as they are. Generalities—ways for things to be, thoughts of things so being—are, as Frege insists, *not* possible objects of sensory awareness. To adapt one of his examples (1918: 61) one sees the sun, large and red on the horizon. One sees it sinking into the sea. One sees the red glow it leaves behind. But one does not, in this sense, see *that the sun has set*. That the sun has set is not the sort of thing to form images on retinas. Nor, as opposed to the sunset itself, is it the sort of thing to have location (or even apparent location). Thoughts, again, are not objects of sensory awareness. What has the generality of a thought, or a way for things to be—is *not* perceivable. It is an object of a different sort of awareness. The distinction between generalities of the sort a thought is—what I will call the *conceptual*—and particular cases—what I will call the *non-conceptual*—is intrinsically such that what falls on the first side cannot be an object of perceptual (visual, auditory, tactile) awareness, so that what might be such an object either falls on the second side, or on neither.

This 'invisibility' of thoughts provides an opportunity. One need not see them as structured in anything like the same way an object of the senses might be: either geometrically or acoustically, or syntactically. Frege exploits this opportunity to the full, starting with the idea, stressed throughout his career, that whole thoughts come first, and elements are arrived at by decomposing them. Thoughts are not, as he puts it, constructed out of building blocks. As he wrote to Marty:

> I do not believe that the construction of concepts can precede judgement, because that presupposes an independent existence of concepts, but I think that concepts arise only through the decomposition of judgeable contents.
>
> (1882/1980: 118)

Thoughts are decompos*able*: the same thought may be decomposed in many ways; no one decomposition is privileged *per se*.

A thought, as sketched so far, has a task. It must fix something for a determinate question of truth to turn on. To decompose the thought is to decompose this task into sub-tasks, perhaps performed in some given structured way. For a decomposition to *be* a decomposition just is for those sub-tasks, so performed, to be the performance of the whole task. This is just what decomposition is. Which allows, in principle, for multiple, diverse but equally correct, decompositions of a given thought—but *none* which jointly fail to yield a whole thought back.

6) Some thoughts admit of decompositions on which they are *singular*. For any singular thought, there is some object such that the truth of the thought turns precisely on how *that* object is. Hence, trivially, there is no such thought where there is no such object. Without the object, there is *no* way the thought makes truth turn on how things are. There is no thought which *might* have been singular, but in fact is not.

A whole thought makes truth turn, in a particular way, on how *things* are—on whether they are such-and-such way. 'Things' here bears its catholic reading, as in 'Things have been slow lately': one cannot ask 'Which things?'. In a decomposition of a thought as (once) singular, one element among others—one subtask which, with the others, forms the whole—is making truth turn on the object it does. Frege argues that there are ways of performing such a sub-task: different ways in which some *one* object might be made to play this role in a thought of it that it is thus and so. He calls such a *way* of performing this task a mode of presentation (*Art des Gegebenseins*).

When we express a thought in a sentence, the sentence, as a rule, functions to present that thought as decomposed in a particular way. Different syntactically proper parts of the sentence correspond to different elements in the thought so decomposed. A part of the sentence corresponding to a mode of presentation of an object on the decomposition thus presented would make that expression of a thought whose truth turned essentially on how *that* object is. Where a sentence expresses a thought, for a part of it to refer to an object just is for it to make this contribution. Here, and just here, for *words* to refer to such-and-such is for some element of a thought (on a decomposition) to make that such-and-such that on which that thought's truth turns. There is *that* much coincidence between what words do on the understanding they bear, and what modes of presentation do, where a mode of presentation is a feature of a thought. Even here, nothing requires that about the words by which they are to be understood as referring to that object to coincide with, or *be* the way that object is presented within the thought itself. Nor, within the present conception, is this generally the case. Such depends on further factors, to be mentioned soon. (Frege himself was not always surefooted on this point. See 1906: p. 208.)

So on the notion *mode of presentation* on which *thoughts* might differ in their modes of presentation of an object, something *is* a mode of presentation of an object only as an element of a given thought on a particular decomposition of it as singular. A mode of presentation of an object, on this notion, just *is* an element in a thought: that which makes some object the one on which *its* truth turns. 'Refers', 'reference' and 'mode of presentation' *might* all be used in other ways. When they are, it is incumbent on their user to make clear *what* ways. A mode of presentation on some such other notion is not, or not *per se*, the way an object is presented in a thought as the one on which truth turns, hence by an element of the content of a belief.

> 7) For Frege, a thought is something essentially public: if thinkable by *anyone*, then by indefinitely many. A thought cannot be what Frege calls a 'Vorstellung': something one must be so-and-so to have in mind. Frege's way of conceiving the objectivity of truth makes sense *only* supposing this. Only this gives the right sense (for Frege's purpose) to the idea that anyone thinks truly just where everyone who *so* thought would. 'Der Gedanke' (1918) argues elegantly (see Essay 2) that a thought cannot be a *Vorstellung* (cannot be private). Nothing is more crucial to his picture of belief.

For Frege, a thought marks a point on which thinkers can agree or disagree. It is something whose truth can be (jointly) argued, investigated, discovered. For every such point, its thought, for every such thought, its point. For Frege this and the idea that a thought fixes something on which truth can turn ('brings truth into question at all') are two sides of one idea.

So a thought is identified in one way by how it represents things being—what question of truth it raises—but in another by in what cases two thinkers would be agreeing or disagreeing as to its truth. How is a given thought decomposable? As it would need to be to figure in all such (dis)agreements. Suppose we decompose a thought as singular—for example, as about Penelope, to the effect that she is reclining. So decomposed it contains an element making her the one on whom truth turns. Following Frege (1892a), what element that is is liable to depend on its *way* of making Penelope the one. Such a way is as must be for a question of truth to disputes over which all the right thinkers would be parties. If Sid thinks that Penelope is reclining, that which he thinks presents her in a way (or ways) accessible to all those with whom he thereby agrees or disagrees. Nor could the question who these other might be have the answer, 'No-one'.

On our present notion, a mode of presentation is an element of a thought. There might be other notions, such as ones on which a mode of presentation is a way in which something is presented to *Sid*, a feature of *his* particular psychology. There is the way Penelope is presented to Sid visually as he observes her on *esplanada*—for example, in profile, or half-shadow. Perhaps there is also such a thing as the way she is presented to him in thought: his way of thinking of her as, say, the one he takes to be reclining—though it remains to explain what such a notion is to be. But—the present point—no such notion bears a direct relation to the notion *mode of presentation* where that is a feature of an element of a thought. If one got so far as being able to individuate, or identify, modes of presentation where such things belong to a person at a time, it would be a mistake, for the reason just given, to conflate one of these with the mode of presentation of an object in some thought that thinker thinks. A mode of presentation of an object within a thought must serve a different function. To mistake it with some mode of presentation fixed by someone's individual psychology would be to conflate the psychological with the logical in *just* the way Frege fought against.

8) A thought is what stands at a point of (dis)agreement among an (indefinitely extendible) range of thinkers. So two thoughts to a given effect—say, of someone that she is reclining—differ in their mode of presentation of that someone just where they represent different disputes into which one might enter. Such is a regulative principle of counting thoughts. It can *seem* in tension with another, *perhaps* suggested by Frege. It is that thoughts must count as different where they differ in what Frege calls 'Erkenntniswert'— roughly, in what one knows when he knows that they are true (or false). Frege highlights cases where (as he sees it) difference in ways of presenting some object is what makes thoughts so differ. I will not attempt to unfold this second idea here. I merely note that, whatever the right way of doing this, it must be such as to honour the idea stressed above: the essential publicity (shareability) of thoughts. Nothing is more central to Frege's thought.

9) Sid witnesses Penelope reclining, and thus comes to think that she is reclining. *What* thought does he thus come to relate to believingly? Is this even a good question? Two suppositions might make it so. First, one might suppose that there is just one right way of counting thoughts—one right way of identifying where one thought was expressed or mentioned twice, where two, each once. Second, one might suppose that Sid's *whole* posture towards things—his taking things to be as he does—has *one* correct decomposition into his taking things to be this, that, and the other way there is for things to be—his relating believingly to precisely *such-and-such* collection of thoughts.

By the first supposition, whatever might *ever* call for discerning two thoughts by virtue of difference in *Erkenntniswert* always does so: there are two different thoughts here *tout court*. One might then be moved to distinguish between thoughts *very* finely, by correspondingly fine differences in their modes of presentation of some object. Which is one thing which *has* moved some to seek the nature of a mode of presentation of an object in a thought in the vagaries of individual psychologies. (See Dummett, 1981: chapter 10.) Frege's conception of belief contains a cogent warning against so proceeding. Kripke also so warned (see Kripke 1979). Frege is silent on the first supposition. As to the second, it is at least in the spirit of his insistence on the multiple decomposablitiy of a thought to insist on a parallel multiple decomposability of whole postures.

These last debates I will not enter into here. What I have stressed is that ideas about some intrinsic 'fineness of grain' of thoughts need to be balanced against ideas about their publicity. One must not lose sight of Frege's insistence that what thoughts there are to think, what questions of truth there are to raise, is independent of who, if anyone, thinks or raises them, or under what circumstances. Frege compares a thought with a planet, 'which was already interacting with other planets before anyone had seen it' (1918: 69). He also remarks:

> That which I recognize as true I judge to be true entirely independently of my recognition of its truth, also independently of whether I think of it. It is not part of the truth of a thought that it is thought.
>
> (1918: 74)

In saying what Sid thinks we always choose from among things there are anyway for *one* to think. If there is a range of distinct thoughts, all of Penelope, all that she is is reclining, perhaps many (if any) are ones which count, or would sometimes count, as ones *Sid* thinks in being as he is. It is anyway not reasonable to suppose that *his* way of thinking of Penelope at a time makes some one thought, and its mode of presentation, *the* thing he thinks to that effect. If a mode of presentation of an object is to make a thought available to a range of diverse thinkers, as per above, and *if* a mode of presentation is the sort of thing individuable in terms of given representational features, then one would only expect any such mode to be underdetermined by the psychological history of any one person who may think a thought of which it is a part.

4 An Example

There is the psychology of thinking thoughts, of holding things true; and there is the logical structure of thoughts themselves, for which principles of *being* true. The two, Frege insists, are always to be separated sharply (1884: X). Holding these apart matters to reading Frege himself. For example, in the 'Logik' of 1897 Frege remarks:

It is not necessary that the thought that he is cold be expressed by the one who is cold himself. This can also be done by another, in his designating the cold one by name.

(1897: 146)

In 'Der Gedanke' (1918) Frege tells a more complex story:

Now everyone is presented to himself in a special and primitive way, in which he is presented to no other. If now Dr Lauben thinks that he has been injured, this primitive way in which he is presented to himself probably underlies this. And only Dr Lauben can grasp the thought so determined. But now he wants to tell this to another. He cannot communicate a thought which only he can grasp. If he now says, 'I have been injured', he must use 'I' in a sense which others can also grasp, say, in the sense of 'the one who is speaking to you at this moment', by which he makes use of the accompanying circumstances of his expression of a thought.

(1918: 66)

This second discussion immediately precedes Frege's negative answer to the question whether a thought could be a *Vorstellung*—raise a question of truth available only to so-and-so.

In 1897 there is *the* thought that N is cold which N thinks, and also *expresses* using the first-person pronoun, and which others can also think, and express, for example, in calling N by name. In 1918 there is *a* thought which Dr L thinks, his thinking which is 'underlain' by a way in which he is presented to himself alone. And there is *a* thought which he communicates to others, relying on a certain understanding of 'I' in his mouth. Is there one thought here or two? If there *must* be two, then the thought Dr L. thinks is one one must be *him* to entertain. So then, Frege has changed his mind since 1897—which is odd, since he is about to argue that there could be no such thought.

Frege need not have changed his mind. True, in *some* sense of 'present', each of us is presented to himself in a way he is presented to no other. Plausibly Dr L bases his thinking that he is injured on what he is presented with in being so presented with himself. But what notion of mode of presentation is in play here? First, a psychological one, since it is a question of how Dr L is presented to *himself*, not a question of how he is presented in the internal structure of any given *thought*. Second, it is a notion that occupies the same place along the presentation–response divide as does that notion on which Penelope is presented to Sid visually in a certain way (for example, in profile). Not that the mode here involves some sort of seventh sense. But perceptual modes of presentation present us with the non-conceptual: they gain us access to what *instances* ways for a thing to be, permit recognition of such instancing. They are a source of information. Thus is Dr L's special mode of presentation of himself. It allows him recognition of his being as he is as a case of someone being injured. It does this in affording hi awareness of his injury. Whereas a mode of presentation in thought—a way of thinking of some object as the one in question in some particular case of representing things as thus and so—is no such source of information about the thing in question. It merely helps individuate the question of truth thus raised; locates it within the space of such. That way in which Dr L is presented to himself alone is no *such* guide.

In the sense in which Dr L is presented to himself as no other is, that his being injured is so presented to him tells us nothing about any mode of presentation in any thought he thus comes to think—any more than the fact that Penelope is presented to Sid in profile tells us any such thing about the thoughts he thus comes to think. On the other hand, Frege tells us that Dr L *bases* a thought that he is wounded on what he is thus presented with. What thought that is depends on when someone else would think the same thing.

Who else can think (or dispute) what Dr L does in thus thinking that he is wounded? Who else, for a start, can think of him that he is injured? All those acquainted with him, or with the right event. Anyone who knew who Dr Lauben was, and when the condition was supposed to obtain—can, so far, think just what he does to this effect (though not learn in the same way about the injury). Perhaps, Frege's argument notwithstanding, *something* requires a thought available to Dr L alone; but nothing yet in view.

The literature contains stories to this effect: Dr L, having fallen from the carriage, has forgotten that he is Dr L, but is aware (in that special way) that he is injured. There is something he does not know. This can be put as: 'that he is Dr L'. Decomposing this as an identity thought, it would contain two elements, each making that thought about him. If we follow Frege (1891, 1892a, for example), these different modes of presentation are deployable to say of *what* he was then ignorant. The question again is: When would one thus be thinking him ignorant of this? When would one be thinking a thought in which he is presented first in the first way (identified by 'he' above), then in the second? At most this: that first mode of presentation (signalled by 'he') must make it recognizable that the truth of the identity in question turns on what particular cases instance a certain generality, *being that very thing so-and-so* (where so-and-so is its referent, in fact Dr L), and such recognizability must not presuppose, or depend on, already recognizing that the case in question is one of something's being as it is instancing that generality, *being the very same person as Dr L*. (See Frege 1882b.) No more yet follows.

We are not yet pointed towards an element in a thought which presents Dr L as that on which truth turns in a way recognizable only to one to whom Dr L is presented (on that other notion) as he is only to himself. So far, there is no reason to suppose this. Dr L's special access to himself allows him special means of *settling* certain questions of truth. But it provides, so far, no special *questions* of truth on which only he can take stands. A good thing if we follow Frege, for then there *are* no such questions. So far the fact that Dr Lauben, after the fall, bases his belief that he is injured on information provided him in that special way at best grossly underdetermines to what *thoughts* he thus relates.

Now for communiqués. Sid dials Pia and says, 'Penelope is on *esplanada*'. For there to be such representing is for it to be made recognizable as the representing that it is. Language helps with this. In the circumstances, Sid is to be taken as speaking language both he and Pia understand, and in a familiar way, using expressions in it for what they *are* for in it. Thus, for example, that he said '*esplanada*' makes recognizable that he was speaking of *terrasse*—presumably, in the circumstances, a certain familiar *terrasse*. In the circumstances, his use of 'Penelope' would most reasonably, naturally, be taken as speaking of Cruz, not of his ten-year-old niece Penelope, currently in her boarding school in Lausanne. Similarly, if Dr L announces 'I have been injured', the words he uses, as *thus* used, in *those* circumstances, make it recognizable how he has represented things being. Frege gives an idea of how 'I' might help with this.

Words used on an occasion to express a thought (where one *was* expressed) make it recognizable what thought this was. Just *that* is their function. They do that because, in the circumstances, they bear a certain understanding as to *what* is thus made recognizable. 'I' might work, as Frege suggests, by directing one to the mouth from which it issues. But there are two distinct issues here. There is how the words work to make something recognizable, and there is what is thus made recognizable—that what was expressed was such-and-such. Those factors in the workings of words which allow them to achieve *their* end of the bargain are not automatically elements in the thought thus recognizably expressed. It conflates the psychological with the logical just to assume that some given mode of presentation of a *thought* (in words) just *is* some mode of presentation within that thought. Such *must* be wrong where it makes thoughts unshareable.

The role of words parallels that of visual experience. Penelope is presented to Sid visually in a certain way. His seeing her is occasion for him to think various things about her. *Perhaps* it affords him certain things to think about her which he otherwise could not. Perhaps it allows him to recognize certain ways for truth to turn on how things are. But the way in which *he* happened to come to stand believingly to some such thought cannot decide, on its own, what the nature of that thought is. Similarly, the way words work on an occasion to make a thought's expression recognizable can never be conflated with the way that thoughts' truth turns on how things are. Language use belongs to the psychological, not the logical, when it comes to holding these two things separate. Such space between psychological and logical modes of presentation—the psychology of grasping thoughts, and the logic of being true—is essential if thoughts are to be those points of (dis)agreement which, for Frege, they necessarily are. It is space within which Frege need not have reversed himself in describing Dr Lauben as he did in 1918.

5 Common Factors

Burge's antidisjunctivism rests on a picture of belief very unlike Frege's. As with perception, where it equally departs from Frege, it is contained in the bearing assigned ringers. For Burge, certain constancies throughout a stock triple, built in more or less by definition, impose a certain common factor in (certain) beliefs formed in its terms. Each term of the triple involves some visual experience. The aetiology of the experience in each case is the same proximal (visual) stimulus (type), and the same processing of it. In basing a belief on this experience, the subject represents the world to himself as a certain way. In each term of the triple, as Burge sees things, the subject brings the same representational, so conceptual, capacities to bear on how he does this. These draw on the same pre-existing picture of how things are. In Burge's words,

> The perceptions are formed from type-identical registrations of light rays. The... beliefs... are covered by many of the same psychological principles... They are formed from the same perceptual categories and concepts. They use the same demonstrative singular representational abilities and demonstrative representation types.
>
> (2005: 34–5)

Such constancies, Burge takes it, assure a certain common factor in the beliefs thus formed. Suppose, for example, Sid spots Penelope sipping a *mojito*. He thus comes to take it that she is so engaged. Burge tells us:

> An illusion might occasion... a type-identical belief. A contextually indiscernible duplicate could be substituted, occasioning a... type-identical belief... Type-identical representational contents mark, or type-identify, the same representational state types and abilities... What differs among these... belief states is nothing about their general type.
>
> (2005: 34–5)

Sid sees Penelope, and forms the belief that she is sipping. Had it been a Penelope-ringer (a dummy, say, or a body double), then, unable to detect this, he would have responded (so far as he could tell) just as he did—*hence*, Burge holds, gone into a type-identical belief state; one of holding a type-identical belief. Had he been experiencing a visual illusion 'as of' Penelope sipping, again, 'same response', *ergo* a new type-identical belief.

What types these (supposed) type-identical beliefs? 'Belief' is the form of two different nominalizations. It may speak of a state or condition of believing, a 'belief state'. Or it may speak of something there is to believe—for example, what one comes to believe in coming to think that Penelope is sipping. Henceforth 'belief' (neat) here speaks of something one might think, 'belief state' of a condition of doing so. Burge types belief states by beliefs, or rather types of them. A belief in this second sense represents things as a particular way there is for things to be. A type of belief in this sense is a class of ways to represent things being, united by a common way things would be represented in representing them as any way within the class.

Such a common-factor way of representing which thus types a belief need not itself be a way for things to be—the way some thought represents things being. What types the types Burge is after here will not be that. For no *thought* is in common to what Burge wants to fall into one type. Some thought of Penelope that she is sipping, some thought of one or another ringer that it is sipping, and some other thoughts of as yet unknown nature are all meant to fall into one type by Burge's principles. The common schematic way to represent things being which types things here is, so to speak, a representation a few elements short of a thought (so of some way to represent things being).

At this point the psychological has linked itself to the logical. The psychology of holding true, as supposedly manifest in the stock triple, is meant to have consequences for being true; for the structure of at least some thoughts (questions of truth) towards which one might, and we sometimes do, hold stances. By the reasoning thus far there must be thoughts which are structured so as to type those belief states in the stock triple which, we are told, share a type. How is this link forged?

Could the link be forged by Proximality: same input, same processing, so same type of thing believed? Here the situation is much as with perception. As Burge agrees, Proximality does not apply to belief itself. If the terms of the triple represent same input and same processing, they do not represent—certainly not by Burge's lights—three cases of same thing thought so. For Penelope to be sipping and for a ringer to be are two different ways for things to be. Thinking things the one way is not thinking them the other. So it remains an open question for what *else*, if anything, Proximality does hold. 'It must hold for something if there is to be something for vision science to explain'. Well, *perhaps* so. But first it is not clear why what explains our perceptual capacities should also be burdened with explaining our beliefs. And second, it is not yet required that this something be some identifiable form for thoughts (objects of attitudes) to share—some representation a few items short of a thought. We need to look elsewhere for a rationale for that idea.

The stock triple is meant to exhibit a core phenomenon. Sid watches Penelope sipping a *mojito*. Suppose that a ringer had been substituted for Penelope. Then he would have been watching the ringer sipping. But—such it is to be a ringer—he would—*could*—have noticed no difference. Everything would have seemed to him just as it does. In particular, how, and what, he thought of what he was watching would have seemed just the same to him. Similarly if, surreptitiously, he had been tampered with so that, undetectably for him, his retinal images were no longer products of those distal objects before him—Penelope, her sipping, and so on. If, watching the ringer, he could have thought that he was thinking of Penelope—if he could have so much as entertained that thought—then this ability would, at the same time, be liability to error—an error he would commit, undetectably from his position, if he did think such a thing. (This, I take it, is the point of imagining surreptitious switches in mid-course.) The question for the moment is what consequences this core point is meant to have.

Watching her, Sid thinks of Penelope that she is sipping. Conceivably, there could have been a ringer sipping. Had there been, the idea is, Sid's thinking would seem just the same to him as it in fact does. Nothing in the way it does seem to him makes it recognizable to him, in his present position, watching, as something it would not be were there a ringer. Or nothing currently recognizable about his thinking would make it recognizable (by its absence) that he was not so thinking were there a ringer. Yet the way he is thinking of things differs from the way he would be. In thinking as he did in the hypothetical situation, he *would* be thinking of some ringer that she/it was sipping. He does no such thing as things stand. Burge also supposes (though it is less clear) that as things stand he thinks something of Penelope which he would not be thinking were there a ringer. The way he *is* thinking (as to who is sipping) and the way he *would* be in that hypothetical situation are, in some such sense, ringers for each other.

So what? Here is one thing one might think: if Sid's thinking *would* seem (or would have seemed) just the same to him were there (or had there been) a ringer, then there must be an identifiable way he thinks of things as things stand which is a way he would still be thinking of things in those hypothetical circumstances. Here is another: there must be such a way which, in the counterfactual circumstances, would be his thinking of the ringer that she/it was sipping, but as things stand is not that. And another: there is such a way which, as things stand, is his thinking of Penelope that she is sipping, but in the counterfactual circumstances would not be that. Yet another: that way which would be his thinking of the ringer that she/it was sipping is, in fact, his thinking this of Penelope. One more: that way which is his thinking of

Penelope that she is sipping would be, in the counterfactual circumstances, his thinking this of the ringer.

I have listed these ideas in rough order of dubiety. But I am more concerned here with their utility. None of them, as it stands, reaches beyond the psychological to link this with the logical. The ideas concern Sid's way of thinking of things, or representing, or presenting, things to himself. The ideas are that he has ways of thinking of things which are his thinking things of Penelope, or which would be his thinking things of a ringer were there one, and so on. But so far, *his* ways of thinking of things are just parts of his (current, perhaps transient) psychology. If some of them are, say, his thinking of Penelope that she is sipping, then for him to think in that way is for him to relate (believingly) to some thought or other. So far we know nothing about what thought this might be, or how it might decompose.

The point stands out clearly if we suppose, as we are now to suppose, that there are many thoughts, of Penelope, that she is sipping, each distinguished from all the others by its way of making *her* the one on whom truth necessarily turns. (One *might* dispute this. But for present purposes it serves as common ground.) Such a way for a *thought* to link itself to an object—for that object to be presented within the thought—is known in the trade as a mode of presentation. If Sid has *his* way of thinking of Penelope as the one he takes to be sipping, such is a feature of his psychology. It might be called a mode of presentation too. But now 'mode of presentation' speaks of a psychological notion. Perhaps there are respectable such notions which distinguish different such modes in some well-defined way. But, as we have seen already (Section 4), such notions must be distinguished both from a different sort of psychological notion, concerning channels of information rather than forms of thought, and from that which figures in the logical notion of a thought—what is to be counted by the questions of truth which there are towards which to stand.

On the one hand, Sid's mode of presentation of Penelope, where that is an element in *his* way of thinking of things, must be distinguished from a mode which is, for example, a way for Penelope to be presented visually—say, in right profile and half shadow. On the other, it must be distinguished from those modes of presentation which are elements of thoughts. Here there are two points to keep in mind. First, it is intrinsic to a thought to be shareable. A mode of presentation of an object, such as Penelope, in a thought to the effect, say, that she was brilliant in *Jamón, Jamón*, is something which makes that thought accessible—entertainable, thinkable—in that indefinite variety of different ways in which it is by all the different thinkers, in different circumstances, who can agree or disagree about its truth. It is what indefinitely many different and various individual psychologies might make one thinker or another count as thinking or disputing. It is (thus) not what is identified merely by the individual psychology of some particular thinker who manages to count as so connected to it.

Second, following Frege, we get to the elements of a thought only by decomposing the whole thought—some whole question of truth, distinguished from others by just how it would be settled. For a mode of presentation to be a way some thought presents an object as the one it is tied to in the singular way is for it, in the context of the thought's other elements on that way of decomposing it, to contribute the relevant part of making truth to be settled as, for that question, it is to be—to fix, for example, how it would be settled whether the *right* thing was among the sippers. What how his thinking seems to him on an occasion equips him *then* to recognize as to who was, or was not, the one who must be sipping if things are to be as he thinks does not automatically settle what it would be for someone to be the one on whom truth turns for any thought he thus counts as thinking. Moreover, what Sid is *prepared* to recognize as to when things would be as he thinks, given enough information as to what it is that is so to count or not, is a very different matter from what he would be able to recognize in his present circumstances as they stand.

So no bridge has yet been built. What sorts of further principles might do the building? An idea of this shape may tempt: if, in thinking someone to be sipping, Sid thinks in a certain way as to who it is he thus takes to be sipping—if he presents the one in question to himself in a certain way—then the (or some) thought he thus thinks is one in which that person is presented in that way as the one on whom its truth turns. For such an idea to have applications, we would need a psychological notion of mode of presentation which fixed just what a way for Sid thus to think of Penelope might be, thus what sort of constraint this imposed on the thoughts he might thus count as thinking. In any case, for reasons just given, ideas of this shape are not initially plausible. They await argument.

But there is a more general idea with perhaps deeper appeal (though I think still the wrong way to frame questions of who thinks what). Roughly: where Sid's thinking as he does is his thinking a certain thought, and where his thinking in other circumstances would be for him a ringer for his thinking as he does, but *not* his thinking that thought, there must be a thought he would then think which would be a ringer, for him, for the one he does, and which the one he does would be a ringer for. If Sid thinks that Penelope is sipping, and in those different circumstances would be thinking, not that, but rather, of some ringer, that she was sipping, then there must be a pair of thoughts—one there *is* to the effect that Penelope is sipping, and one there would be to the effect that the ringer is, each a ringer for the other.

What might it be for two thoughts to be ringers for each other, either for someone on an occasion, or just *tout court*? Here is a line of thought. To mistake one thought for another, you must first grasp each. You must grasp each for it to be those thoughts you have in mind. To grasp a thought you must know what question of truth it raises—just how it makes truth turn on how things are. So you must know something which fixes *a* requirement on truth such that the thought is true just where that requirement is met. For two thoughts to be ringers, then, there must be *a* such requirement which each imposes—so that one can *thus* grasp each without yet grasping anything about them which distinguishes one from the other. For that to be so it must be that the common requirement—the one there is to grasp in each case—while there is truth in each case just where it is met, nonetheless leaves a role for things being as they are in deciding, not just *whether* things are as the thought represents them, but also just *what* way the thought represents things being. In the case at hand, for example, for each thought in the pair of mutual ringers, the *right* person must be sipping for that thought to be true. But for each a different person plays that role. Each thought is to be taken as, say, about that person who relates to it in a certain way on a certain occasion for its thinking—for example, as the one to whom the thinker of it would then be attending. Thus it is that one thought in the pair may be about Penelope, the other about some ringer for her, while each remains a ringer for the other.

The idea was: for there to be ringer ways for one to think of things, there must be ringer thoughts—ringer things to think. Unfolding the notion of a ringer thought, we have arrived at a position on which thoughts, and their structures, must be tailored to what a particular thinker, in a particular position in which he thought them, would be able then to recognize as to what it was he thought. The general idea that what one thinks is constrained by what he would be prepared to recognize as to when things would be as he thinks is not without appeal. Here we have a very special version of it. For one thing, 'would be prepared to recognize' has been exchanged in it for 'is able to recognize as things stand, while in his exact current circumstances'. *So read*, that general idea may well bridge the gulf between the psychological and the logical. It may dictate, say, that how Pia is presented in any thought of her which Sid counts as thinking is fixed by what he can *then* recognize as to when someone would be the one in question. *Perhaps* this yields the result upon which Burge insists. To a Fregean eye, though, this special reading of that general idea will seem suspicious.

To complicate matters, this special reading comes coupled in Burge with a particular epistemology. The idea was: as things stand, Sid is unable to distinguish how he is thinking of things from how he would be thinking of things were he watching a ringer and not Penelope. He is unable to because his experience provides him nothing by which to tell the difference. Everything looks *just* as it would (or might) if it were Penelope; but equally just as it would if there were a ringer. If he can suppose himself to be thinking in the one way rather than the other (as he might after a mid-course switch), he would thus expose himself to risk of conceivable error. Such are ringers. What Sid thus lacks, and is not provided as he watches Penelope, is *a* proof that it is she and no ringer. *A* proof would start from things Sid anyway had to go on, without prejudice to whether it was Penelope he saw sipping, and, by some inferential steps, end in the conclusion that it is Penelope, and not a ringer, of whom he thinks. What is not allowed to weigh here is the possibility that where Sid sees Penelope, no ringer in the offing, he *might* have proof without having *a* proof: he might simply recognize Penelope, thus that it is she who he sees. Such epistemology is all too familiar, and most unFregean.

6 The Third Term

Whatever links the psychological to the logical for Burge, whether ideas as above or others, it also leads him to two strange and notable conclusions. The first concerns the third term in a stock triple. The second is that singular thoughts may, and the ones we think must, be hybrids, in a sense of 'hybrid' I will explain in due course. Each is revealing of his understanding of what thinking is. I begin with the third term.

Burge insists that for any stock triple, there is some type of thought (a quasi-thought), such that a thought of that type is thought in each term. Perhaps he thinks this because he thinks that, since Sid's thinking would seem just the same to him in all three terms, there must be, in each, a ringer for that which he thinks in each other; and, perhaps also thinks that only a thought could be a ringer for a thought. But no matter why he thinks this, the question concerns what the relevant thoughts in these three terms might be. A thought that Penelope is sipping might exemplify the type in some such first term. A thought that her twin is sipping might exemplify the type in a related second term. But what could instance the relevant type in a related third term? What might such a type be? Those first two instances of the type decompose as singular. For a thought to do this is for an element in it (so decomposed) to make a particular sort of contribution to when the whole thought would be true: for a certain object, it makes truth turn on whether *that* object is some way. Without the object for which they did this, they would make no such contribution. Without making such a contribution, they would not be *elements* of a decomposition at all, or certainly not of *such* a one. In the third term there is no object for the thought thus to be about. So the relevant thought cannot be of any object that *it* is thus and so. It cannot be singular. So it cannot decompose into, *inter alia*, an element as above, by which, *in that thought*, an object is presented in a given way. What, then, is so according to this supposed thought? In what sense could it be of the same type as these others?

Burge answers cryptically. He writes:

Consider a belief of the form *Franz bought that tomato*. The belief rests on a perception as of a tomato. An illusion might occasion a type-identical perception and a type-identical belief.

(2005: 34)

Suppose that the individual forms a belief of the form *Franz bought that tomato*, where no successful reference is made to any tomato. Then whereas the original belief is true, the subsequent belief is false or truth-valueless.

(2005: 32)

What identifies the thought thought in the third term is an English sentence in italics. To know what thought this identifies, one needs to know how this device is to be understood to operate. This is none too easily seen. An English sentence, when used to express a thought, presents this as decomposed in a particular way. The way it thus presents this thought may then be used to identify a form, or structure, of this thought so decomposed. Italics may be used to show that it is so serving. '*Penelope is sipping*', understood as expressing some thought that Penelope is sipping, might also be used to exemplify that thought's form so decomposed—one, for example, in which an element makes the thought about Penelope. But suppose that a sentence does not express a thought, or we are in the dark as to what that thought might be. Then, *ipso facto*, it presents no thought as decomposed in any way, or if it does, we are in the dark as to what the decomposition might be. Now putting it in italics points to no form for any thought. So it is with Burge's '*Franz bought that tomato*'. The mystery was how any thought could be structured as a singular thought would be, while not being one: how it could contain an element 'of the same type' as what, in a singular thought, made its truth turn on some object, without having its truth *thus* turn on anything. Italics clear up no such mystery.

For something to *be* an element in a thought, if we follow Frege, just is for it to perform a certain function. The whole thought makes truth turn in a certain way on how things are. An element in it, in the context of others with which it *is* an element, does *part* of what the whole thought does. It makes truth turn, in part, on something in how things are—for example, on how Penelope is, or on what instances there are of *something being such as to be sipping*. To see what an element in a given thought might be, we must first see what the whole thought does. If there is an object such that that whole thought makes truth turn specifically on how that object is—more specifically, on whether *it* is thus and so—then the whole thought can be decomposed into an element which performs that part of this job, making truth turn on that object, and how it is. If the whole thought does not make truth turn on things in that way, then it contains no such element. There is no part of what it does for such an element to do. Such a thought *can* contain no mode of presentation of an object. There are no thoughts with modes of presentation of an object which present nothing. Such an *idle* 'element' would not be an element at all.

If being of the same type as the thoughts thought in the first two terms does not involve containing any such element, Burge gives us no idea of what it might be. Nor does he give us any idea what is so according to this supposed thought. Italics do not tell us that. Still, he thinks there is one. One can only speculate on why. I think it is because he conflates the psychological with the logical in a way which parallels a way of confusing the linguistic with the logical. Pia says 'Cheney smokes'. She means Dick, not Lon. She thus expresses a thought, of someone, that he smokes. Her whole utterance 'Cheney smokes' contributes to making it recognizable what thought this is. Her 'Cheney', in particular, helps us to identify that person of whom the thought is that he smokes. If the thought is one in which that person is presented in a particular way as the one, then *perhaps* it also helps make recognizable what way this is. (Though in fact I do not think this is a good way of approaching the relation between words and thoughts.) But suppose it is now discovered that 'Cheney' (Dick, not Lon) was all a media invention (good press, good revenues). So 'Cheney' (Dick, not Lon) does not exist. There would be no such discovery to make unless the name 'Cheney', on relevant occurrences (notably, in Pia's utterance), bore a definite understanding. As it is to be understood, for example, verifying Lon's actual existence would not show that this discovery was only a 'discovery' (media inventions on media inventions). It is our understanding of the name as used by Pia which settles when such a discovery would have been made, when not—when there would be someone of whom she expressed a thought that he smoked.

Does all this show that had 'Dick Cheney' been a media invention, Pia would have expressed a thought, of no-one that he smoked, but which presented the supposed one it represents as smoking in the same way Cheney is presented in the thought Pia in fact expresses, given the sad fact that Cheney is no myth? Hardly. What we need to recall is that while the function of a thought is to identify, or just be, some determinate way for truth to turn on how things are—a particular way of settling a question of truth—the function of words is to make, or help make, the expressions of thoughts (or other acts we do with words) *recognizable* (to us) as the expressions of thoughts they are. The function of words is not to *be, per se*, the expression of such-and-such thought. If Cheney is no myth, then Pia's words perform their function, and in doing so identify that object on which the truth of that thought (the one expressed) turns in the singular way. If Cheney is a (yet undiscovered) myth, then her words fail in that purpose. They fail in this in bearing the understanding they do. They identify no thought as the one expressed, much less some thought with some mode of presentation presenting nothing. Which simply reminds us that if, in some sense of 'sense', 'Cheney', in Pia's mouth, has a sense, that is no reason to suppose that 'the' mode of presentation of Cheney, in 'the' thought she expresses, is at all like that sense's way of making recognizable who it is she is talking about. The (now familiar) social nature of thoughts, as Frege conceives them, precludes any such facile equation.

Now the parallel. Sid's thinking of things as he does does not make the *expression* of thoughts recognizable, since it is not the expression of any thought. But it does make him recognizable, or at least identifies him, as one who stands to particular thoughts in particular ways, notably, holding them true—thinking them. It may, for example, make him recognizable, or make him count, as thinking certain thoughts about Pia. He may thus count as thinking thoughts in which she is presented in certain ways, while not thinking ones in which she is presented in others. But what makes him *recognizable* as thinking what he thus does—*his* understanding, say, as to of whom he thinks that she is sipping—need not be, nor bear any fixed relation to, that in the thoughts he thus counts as thinking which requires it to be *Pia* on whose being thus and so their truth depends. Nor need we think (nonsensically) that that about Sid which identifies certain thoughts as ones he thinks would still have identified something as such where there was no such thing to be thought at all. A temptation to think otherwise is one sign of that conflation of the psychological with the logical which Frege warns against, and to which Burge succumbs.

7 Hybrids

On Burge's view, singular thoughts admit of ringers: *other* singular thoughts which, in the right circumstances, may masquerade as them. What would it be for one singular thought to be a ringer for another? In the cases of concern here, these thoughts would differ from each other in that each thought's truth turned on how a different object was. Now there is the line scouted in Section 5. The ringer would require something for being the one on which its truth turned.

What did, or was, as thus required would, *ipso facto* be the one on which its truth turned. But to grasp this much would be to grasp what there is also to be grasped about the thought it is a ringer for. Precisely so can the one be a *ringer* for the other. So what is required for being the right object cannot simply be: being such-and-such one. For such is not constant across the two cases. So the requirement is one which could have been satisfied by other than what does (or, *were* there the ringer, *can* be satisfied by other than what might have). What object an object must be to be the right one depends on the world (or circumstance) in which this requirement is imposed (so in which there is *that* thought to impose it).

Only Penelope, perhaps, could be the right object as things stand. But had they stood differently, it might have been her twin. The thought which imposes this requirement is (meant to be) a thought of *her* that she is sipping. *It* could not be, or have been, made true by anyone else. But (so as for it to allow for ringers) that in it which makes it so is what could (might) have made a thought one of something, or someone, else. Such is for it to be a *hybrid* in my present sense.

Frege tells us that *any* thought has something general about it: it presents things being as they are as a case of things being something they need not be *just* as they are to be. Penelope is sipping languidly; it might still be sipping if she were doing it avidly. Generality in this sense is instanced by things being as they are (or by something's being as it is). But a thought can also be general in the sense that if certain objects being as they are is things being as they are according to it, different objects being as they were might also have been this. Not all thoughts have this sort of generality. Singular thoughts do not. That is their whole point. To distinguish these two notions of the general, I will call what has this second sort *generic*.

So for thoughts paired with ringers, decomposed as singular, there is their generic way of making an object that one whose being thus and so their truth turns. Then (all going well) there is a unique object which relates to this thought in a particular way, the world being as it is (or if you like, designated thinkings of the thought being as they are). It is *the* object picked out by that generic way of making one the one whose being thus and so counts. Given these two features, there is a non-generic way for things to be, *that* object being thus and so, which is also a way—in fact, the way—things are according to this thought. To grasp this generic way is to grasp, in one way, *when* the thought would be true (though perhaps not how to *tell* whether it is). To grasp the way *and* to recognize the fact of *that* object playing the role just sketched is, *per se*, to identify which thought the thought in question is. Such are hybrids.

As Frege tells us, a generic way for a thing to be is not, as he puts it, a disjunctive name. In his example, it does not follow from the fact that all men are mortal that Cato is. For that we need one more premise: that Cato is a man. The point holds, as he insists, even if that generic way is one such that at most one thing could be it. (See 1914: 230–1). If Penelope is *the* one whose being thus and so makes things such that the last star left is sipping, things might be that way even if Penelope had not existed. That way for things to be does not require there to be *that* way of instancing it. There is this thought: whoever parked across Sid's driveway likes *mojitos*. Penelope is the guilty one. She likes *mojitos*. But that she does is not a way things are according to that thought. That she is the *only* one who so parked hardly converts what is *not* singular—that generic thought—into something which is. A hybrid (would-be) singular thought is true just in case things are a certain generic way: there is something which satisfies its generic requirement for being the one which makes it true or false; and that thing, whatever it may be, is thus and so. Suppose Penelope is as required, as at most one thing can be. How can that circumstance any more conjure the generic into the singular?

Frege insists that the sun (1892b: p. 35), or Mount Blanc (1904: p. 93; 1906: pp. 203–4), cannot be elements of a thought. Seeing why clarifies the present point. In brief, one arrives at elements of a thought by decomposing the *whole* thought. The whole is what he calls a *Sinn*—something general in that sense in which he tells us all thoughts are general. When we decompose a thought we remain at the level of *Sinn*: its intrinsic generality is found also in its parts. The way things are according to the whole thought may be, say, such that Penelope is sipping. Decomposing this as singular, we arrive at an element whose role is to make the thought about Penelope—that is, to make its truth turn on how she, specifically, is. It thus does a proper part of what the whole thought does: making truth turn in a particular way on how things are. *It* effects this; Penelope cannot. Like any *Sinn*, it does this in bringing things under some given generality.

Let us employ a trick Frege suggests in 1882, and often thereafter. Suppose we have an identity statement, say, 'That woman is Rossy de Palma'. We can read the 'is' here as standing for a two-place relation, and then what flanks it as each designating an item which stands in it. But we can also, equally well, regard that 'is' as an 'is' of predication: that woman is that very thing, Rossy de Palma. We can even apply the trick twice if we like, getting something like: whatever is that very thing, that woman, is that very thing, Rossy de Palma, thus rendering what looked like a singular thought in the form of a general one. *Being that very thing, Rossy de Palma* is a way for a thing to be, a concept if you like. It has the generality which all ways for things, or a thing, to be have. That same generality must be found in that mode of presentation of Rossy on our first, equivalent, analysis.

In representing the thought here as a universal generalization we do *not* lose for it its singularity. Being Rossy de Palma is a thing there would not be for an object to do had there not been Rossy. And it is doing what it would take being *her*, and nothing less, to do. So if there is such a concept, something falls under it, and at most one thing could. Such a one place concept thus shares the crucial features of a singular thought. So I will also call such a concept singular. (One might then think of the singular thought as a zero-place singular concept.)

Where lies the generality? Rossy is sometimes sipping, sometimes texting her agent. When she is sipping, her being as she is instances someone sipping. We may put this by saying: she falls under the concept of (someone) sipping. While she is texting her agent, she falls under the concept (someone) texting his agent. Her being as she is is then someone doing that (but perhaps no longer someone sipping). She falls under such concepts transiently: at the moment, but ask again this afternoon. Throughout her being as she is is a case of someone being Rossy. So she falls under that singular concept, someone being Rossy. It is indifferent to falling under that concept whether she is sipping, or whether she is texting. Nor will it be relevant to ask again this afternoon whether she still falls under it (unless this is to ask whether she still exists). So many ways for someone to be are cases of someone being Rossy. Someone texting may be, someone sipping may be, and so on *ad infinitum*, just so long as the one texting, or sipping, is Rossy. Many, in fact, all occasions of Rossy's being as she then is instance someone being Rossy. None instance someone being Penelope; and *vice versa*. Here we find that generality intrinsic to all concepts, from zero to any n places.

A general point applies. No case of something's being thus and so (a sunset, a *mojito*, a balmy day) determines, just in being as it is, what it would be for something to be another case (or even any case) of this. You cannot study a particular sunset, or a particular *mojito*, to discover what it would be for something to be one—what range of variation is permitted. For that you must look somewhere else (as Frege insists, to something non-sensory). The point generalizes to any specified collection of cases. And it holds, in particular, for cases of something being Penelope. It holds, too, for concepts, and objects falling under them (if we so conceive concepts), thus, in particular for the concept of being Penelope, even if, necessarily, only Penelope could be that. Penelope is a creature of our environment, living out an historical career—a life—in, as the Chinese put it, the red dust. Study her as closely as you like (if, improbably, she permits this), and you will not find there how it is that necessarily only she satisfies the concept. You will not find, in studying her, what it would be to satisfy this concept.

The point about the hybrid view is now this. The singular thought—the non-generic way for things to be is: such that *Penelope* is sipping. Whatever the relevant generic way for things to be would be, that, plus the fact of *Penelope* being the one who stands in some specified way to that generic way (thus as other things might have) cannot tell us, on their own, what it would be for something to be this *non*-generic way. *Generality*, so the non-generic sort, does not factor like that. If the generic way does not provide what requires Penelope to be the one, one cannot find what does require this merely in studying Penelope.

The point is about how a singular thought might factor. If the question is what distinguishes one such thought from all others, its being of Penelope, and of her sipping, *might* do that, for all said so far. But it is being *about* Penelope, and not Penelope, which does this. The distinguishing element of the *thought*— that part of making truth turn on what it does—is: making it turn on how Penelope is. *This* Penelope cannot do by herself. Nor could any mere historical fact of her standing towards other things in the world as she does (at given times). Conflating functions of language with functions of thought can, once again, help illusion. If Sid asks 'Who blocked my driveway?', the answer 'The woman sipping the *mojito*' might make recognizable the right singular thought. Those words would have picked out another woman had another one been sitting there. They thus exploit a generic way for a thing to be, banking on there being exactly one thing that is that way. But to say this is not to describe the structure or content of any thought. It is only to describe a way of making some thought recognizable.

8 Ignorance and Error

Frege's conception of truth demands that this be the *Bedeutung* of a thought. Accordingly, it is crucial for him that the relation between *Sinne* and their *Bedeutungen* be many-one. He says, for example,

One might object here that '$2^2 = 4$' and '$2 > 1$' surely say something completely different, express completely different thoughts... One sees from this that identity of *Bedeutung* does not entail identity of thoughts. If we say 'The Evening Star is a planet whose orbital period is smaller than the earth's', we have expressed a different thought than that expressed in the sentence, 'The Morning Star is a planet whose orbital period is smaller than the earth's'; for someone who did not know that the Morning Star is the Evening Star could hold the one true, the other false; and still, the *Bedeutung* of the two sentences must be the same...

(1891: 13–14)

Frege's standard reason for taking the relation *Sinn-Bedeutung* to be many-one concerns ignorance. Where there *is* ignorance, many *Sinne* for one *Bedeutung* allows us to say just what the ignorance is of. Someone might not *know* that the Morning Star is the Evening Star. *What* would he not know? Here we can re-employ that trick from 1882: at least he would not know that that which is that very thing, The Morning Star is also that very thing the Evening Star—that that which falls under one singular concept also falls under another. The content of a mode of presentation of an object is here represented as the content of a certain concept. We must, accordingly, now recognize many singular concepts of a given object. Below I sketch a way of doing that.

Ignorance, as most of us now conceive things, is a very different thing from what concerns Burge: the *conceivability* of ringers, or of whatever errors such ringers would allow for. So one might expect each notion to yield different results when it comes to discriminating senses. Since that summer in Donastia, Sid and Penelope have been fast friends. When he arrives on *esplanada* and sees her sipping, he recognizes her instantly. Though no well-defined notion of an object being presented to *someone* is yet in play, one might expect this encounter to have little impact on how Sid thinks of Penelope as the one of whom he thinks ever so many things, now including the trivial detail that she is currently sipping. Pia, brooding in her darkened flat in Vigo, may think, enviously, that Penelope is now on *esplanada* sipping. There is no difficulty in seeing Sid agreeing with her on this, the two of them thus thinking one thought to the effect that Penelope is sipping—one in which Sid's present visual encounter with Penelope has little role to play.

Suppose there had been a ringer. Then, too, Sid would have thought of Penelope, much as he now does, that she was sipping. He would have been mistaken. But only in so thinking. That visual mode in which the ringer would have been presented to him would play no role in the mode of presentation of Penelope in any thought he thus thought. Sid would also have thought something of the ringer, to the effect that she was sipping. His present experience is *all* of his acquaintance with her/it. *Perhaps* this confers on it some role in the modes of presentation in *some* thoughts of her/it he would thus think. Does this not reveal *some* state of thinking something he is in whether confronting Penelope or the ringer? Before answering I want first to present a way to think of *Sinne*—particularly ones whose *Bedeutung* is an object such as Rossy, or Frege.

It is said that we cannot view ourselves thinking from sideways on. 'One rushes ahead and therefore cannot also observe the rushing' (*Philosophical Investigations*, s§456). There are, no doubt, truths in that. But we can certainly see our neighbour from sideways on. Suppose we want to say what he thinks. The first step is to identify some ways there *are* for things to be. We can then ask which of these are ways he thinks things are. For Penelope now to be sipping is a way for things to be. So perhaps he takes things to be that way. In all judgement, one (as Frege put it) exposes himself to risk of error. If our neighbour takes Penelope to be sipping, he thus exposes himself to risk of error—error he would succumb to if she is not. When we identify a way for things to be, *we* expose ourselves to risk of error—one *we* would succumb to if there is no such way, for example, if 'Penelope' is mere media hype. I stress the 'we'. If we take our neighbour to take things to be some way, where there is no such way, the error is all ours, not his. There is, so far, nothing for him to be wrong about. If for Penelope to be sipping is a way for things to be, it provides *us* with a way of articulating the way he thinks things into his thinking things this, that, and the other way there is to think them. If he thinks Penelope to be sipping, he is not (normally) *thus* in error if 'Penelope' is all hype. If he does think this, she is not all hype; if she is, there is no such thing he thinks.

It is a contingent matter what ways for things to be there are. In February 1848 (I estimate) an event took place which may have been highly contingent—perhaps mere chance. As a result of it we now have Frege to think about. Without it we would not have. So there are countless ways for things to be (such that Frege smoked, for example) which there might not have been. All those ways for things to be which count on Frege for their existence thereby depend on a certain bit of history. Some, perhaps, depend in part on generic history: what could have been someone else's. All depend on whatever history there is in there being that very person, Frege. Such history cannot be *all* generic. Some of it must be, intrinsically, *his*.

If there are many *Sinne* for one *Bedeutung*—Frege, say, or Rossy, or Penelope—we may identify them by refining history further. Frege had a career at Jena. He might not have. He would have been Frege for all that. A certain planet has a career as the first 'star' seen at night. It might not have. There might have been a brighter, or closer, heavenly object. Rossy has a career including a role in which she was unconscious for most of the film. She need not have. But since they did have these careers, these objects are identifiable by their having them. Someone able to identify one of these objects by its having had some one of them may be unable to identify that object by its having had some other. I suppose we are all in that position with respect to any object we can identify. I, for example, can identify Rossy by her having played the role just mentioned, but quickly get stuck after that. So if Rossy also modelled for Prada on a certain occasion, I can be in the position of failing to know that that model was Rossy. Where there are such different ways of identifying an object, we can, accordingly, suppose there to be different *Sinne* with that object as *Bedeutung*, each such *Sinn* requiring a different bit of history for its existence. Perhaps what it thus requires is some generic history—say, that someone, of a certain general appearance once modelled for Prada. But if it is to do the work of making a thought about some individual in particular, it must also require some specific history—that *that* person (the one it presents) did the modelling.

Once again the trick of 1882. For any such *Sinn* (mode of presentation of an object *in a thought*) there is the corresponding singular concept, being that very thing so presented. As with any concept, there is that which it requires for falling under it. What it requires in this case is that what falls under it (thus, more generally, the world) have a certain history. Once again, we can extract from the required history generic elements. If Rossy modelled Prada shifts then someone did. But if the concept is singular, it cannot just require this. There is a certain person one would need be to fall under it, no matter what—that very one with the history in question. History allows concepts of individuals to work like that.

So conceiving *Sinn*, let us review the first two terms of a stock triple. In the first term Sid encounters (his old friend) Penelope, sipping. He thus comes to take things to be a certain way, in particular, *in re* whether she is sipping. He can *see* that she is. There are then those thoughts which count as ones he has come to think (*in re* this matter). To see which, we must ask with whom he would now (dis)agree. There is, for example, Pia in Vigo brooding. He agrees with her. There is, accordingly, a way for things to be which is a way they both take things, thus a thought they both think. For there to be that way the world must have had a certain history. For a start, it must contain Penelope for us to think of. If there are many *Sinne* with her as *Bedeutung*, then more is required by any given such thought there is for Sid and Pia both to think. If we needed to say just *what* history Penelope must have had in order for Sid and Pia to agree as to whether *she* is sipping—to agree on some *one* question to this effect—it would be difficult to find an answer. If we are to distinguish thoughts about her by the different parts of her history by which she is identified, in them, as the one who sips, then there are no doubt many which would count as ones Sid and Pia both think. Conversely, for any one of these, there are many different ways for someone's thinking as he does to make it count as one he thinks. Recall Dr Lauben. There is no reason for these ways Sid and Pia both take things to be to require for their existence that Penelope then be on *esplanada*, or be seen by Sid—episodes in her history which Pia has not encountered.

Now the second term. Here Sid, arriving on *esplanada*, encounters a ringer—say, Penelope's twin. Suppose that he is taken in. This would be for him, mistakenly, to think of *Penelope* that she was sipping. The thoughts he thus relates to are, for the most part, ones he would have been thinking in the first term; for example, answers to questions as to her sipping on which he and Pia agree. None of these requires for its existence that Penelope then be on *esplanada*, or seen by Sid. If it did, there would have been no such thought under the imagined circumstances. Sid also takes the ringer to be sipping. Perhaps he *sees* her to be. There are, then, some thoughts of her that she is sipping, which count as ones Sid thinks. His acquaintance with her, we can suppose, is *only* through this encounter. Perhaps that is reason enough to think that at least some of these thoughts are ones there would not have been—their ways of presenting her ones there would not have been—had she not then been on *esplanada*. For them, it is crucial that *that* bit of history identify her as the one they are about.

Spotting Penelope sipping, does Sid come to think *some* thought as to her sipping which shares *something* in common with some thought he *would* have thought of a ringer, had there been one to think it of? Well, with whom, or what, might he agree or disagree? Sid sits on *esplanada* with his niece Mafalda. Both see Penelope sipping. But though Penelope is Sid's old acquaintance, she is a stranger to Mafalda. *Perhaps* this means, though it need not, that the only thoughts of Penelope Mafalda counts as thinking are ones which require no more history of the world than that Penelope now be sitting, sipping, there. In any event, Sid and Mafalda are certainly in agreement as to whether she is sipping. So, on the assumption, there is a thought Sid counts as thinking which, for its existence, requires no more history of the world than that Penelope then be there sipping. But to require that history is to require a certain generic history: that *someone* be there sipping. Had there been a ringer in Penelope's place, a stranger to both Sid and Mafalda, each would have thought, *inter alia*, a thought which, in requiring for its existence that *that ringer* being there, requires just that generic history.

So there is a commonality between something Sid *does* count as thinking and something he might have. What follows? Spotting Penelope, Sid comes into a state of belief: he takes things to be a certain way, stands towards Penelope's sipping in a certain way. Spotting Penelope, Mafalda also comes into some such state. If there are many different thoughts of Penelope that she is so sipping, then for each to be in the state he/she is thus in is to count as thinking many of these. Since there is something they agree on, for each there is some one of these thoughts which the other also counts as thinking. The belief state, in each case, represents what perception (the spotting of Penelope) has brought about. Such a state is not typed by a form for any given thought to have, so nor by some representational structure a few items short of a thought. So not by some schema which, filled in one way, is a thought about Penelope, filled in otherwise, perhaps a thought about a ringer, or about nothing. The state Sid comes to be in is one of thinking of *Penelope*. Ditto for Mafalda.

The belief states we attain to through perception—for example, standing towards Penelope's sipping as we come to in seeing her so engaged—are not typed by any structure for a thought to have, perhaps a few items short of a thought itself; much less by one which, filled in one way, would be a thought of, say, Penelope, filled in in another a thought of someone else, or of no-one in particular. This parallels Hinton's idea about seeing. The kind of state one is in in being *visually* aware of what he is in seeing a photic flash is not typed by any identifiable thing one is thus visually aware of, still less where what does the typing is awareness a few items short of seeing something, and even less where some instances of what is thus typed—some ways of filling in the schema which does the typing—are seeing a flash, some only experiencing a phosphene. This parallel, to be sure, does not yet show that Hinton is right.

The *generic* history required for the thought Sid and Mafalda share is the world's—our shared environment's. What sat there, then, would be interactive with its surroundings—a particular location in Gijón. It would be, for example, there for *one* to observe. A thought which required *such* history for its existence could not be the third term in a Burgean stock triple (where there is no such history). So far, *its* mode of presentation of Penelope could not contain the sort of common factor Burge posits in his triple. If we follow Frege, such would hold of *any* requirement on a thought's existence, so of any (whole or partial) mode of presentation. For only our shared environment is what *truth* can turn on. (See 1918: 67–9.) For, again, there *is* a thought only where there is what could be agreed to or disputed, so, too, what *would* be agreed to, by indefinitely many, in rational pursuit of the goal truth.

A thought is designed to capture what those who agree on something share. Just as *its* form is not imposed by how any given thinker thinks of things being as according to it, so too it can be grasped, so thought, in thinking in any of many ways of the way things are according to it. One can grasp the thought Dr Lauben thinks in thinking himself injured without the sort of access to his injury he has. Similarly, Sid can grasp how Mafalda thinks of Penelope sipping. He can thus grasp a thought which requires only the history available to her. He thus recognizes when it would be true. To count as thinking P is, grammatically, to be in a state such as so to count. But what P is does not decide just what state a thinker who so counted might be in.

I return to ignorance versus inconceivability of error. Burge focuses on a particular thing Sid could not do. Were he to encounter a ringer on *esplanada*, or were a surreptitious switch made mid-course, he would be unable, as things stood, to detect any difference in how he thought of things. Burge wants such facts to lead us to conclusions as to the natures of the modes of presentation of some object in the thoughts which count as ones Sid then thus thinks. But alongside what Sid cannot do stands what he still can do: what he is equipped, and prepared, to recognize, on suitable encounter. As he views the twin, he cannot tell that he is in fact thinking thoughts of two different people that each is sipping, in one case truly, in the other falsely. But confront him with the facts (for example, let Penelope walk by and whisper in his ear 'Remember Donastia?') and he can recognize exactly what it is that he *was* doing all along.

What matters here—what Sid can do, or what he cannot? For a start, thinking (holding) so is Lutheran: to take something to be so is to see oneself as with no other course; to feel the world so to bear that there is nothing else for *him* to think in pursuing the goal truth—hence (holding true being what it is) nothing else to hold *punkt*. To believe is thus to commit, to adopt a policy: here I *stand* (not *am now standing*). But policies lie in what one is prepared to do, here, *inter alia*, prepared to recognize. Given this, what matters to what Sid thinks is what he *would* recognize, not what he can tell at the moment. In which case the stress (burden) which Burge places on ringers, or the possibility of error, here is simply misplaced. It will later emerge just *how* misplaced.

As Sid confronted the twin he would in fact think thoughts of each of two different people that she is sipping. His thinking would seem to *him* just as it does in his thinking of Penelope. His thinking would be a ringer, to him, for what it is. Burge wants it to follow from this that there is some *thought* Sid would think which, if it existed, would be a ringer for some thought he does think, and would be so because that very same way in which some thought Sid thinks presents Penelope as the one on whom its truth turns might be the way some thought about the twin presents the one on whom its truth turns, with the sole exception that in that counterfactual circumstance what would thus be presented is the twin and not Penelope. No such thing follows from the ways there are for Sid to fail to realize, as things stand, of whom he thinks one thing or another.

The common factor Burge posits in belief is meant to be required by, and for, empirical psychology. It is also, in part, a common factor in that which is believed in a certain range of cases. Whether there is *such* a factor depends in part on what believing something *is*. It is on these last grounds that a disjunctivist would deny the factor.

9 Scepticism

Vision science did not teach us that there may be ringers. *Perhaps* it banks on this. Burge casts them in roles Frege assigns ignorance. Their mere conceivability is meant to show something about the structures of the singular thoughts we in fact think, notably, about their ways of making truth turn on particular individuals—how, for example, some thought Sid thinks in thinking Penelope to be sipping presents her as the one in question. Ignorance is not the same as defencelessness against *conceivable* ringers. Does the use Burge makes of this last yield a viable way of conceiving of *Sinne* with objects as their *Bedeutung*.

Burge assigns ringers two roles. One is to point us towards a sort of common factor there must be throughout certain ranges of thoughts, each of *some* object (though some of different ones), that *it* is thus and so. (For Burge this common factor also points to thoughts only *purportedly* about some object in particular.) The second role is to *distinguish* modes of presentation in different thoughts about some *given* object. This second role figures in passages such as these:

> In accounting for a belief, we must distinguish between belief in a self-identity ... and a substantive claim that might be mistaken, because it involves two logically separable acts of reference (deriving from two perceptions) ... Given that duplicates and illusions could make a belief false—wherever there is a logically distinct act of reference—there is pressure to recognize different representational contents for different applications, even in the case of tracking that is actually successful.
>
> (2005: 34)

> The difference in application-representation occurs if there is a psychologically relevant, logical possibility that the individual might have been mistaken in taking the object to have remained the same.
>
> (2005: 37)

Arriving on *esplanada*, Sid spots Penelope. She is sipping. He takes her to be. He strolls around to the other side of *esplanda* and glances back at her. Still sipping. He so takes things. There is a logical possibility of a mid-stroll switch: a ringer-Penelope in for Penelope, thus a ringer for Penelope sipping. Experience would furnish Sid no means to tell this. Thus, Burge holds, what he does think from the far side must present Penelope differently than what he did think from the near side does.

How is this meant to follow? I think the story can be factored into three stages. **Stage 1:** Here ringers are used to reveal a potential bit of substantial knowledge. Had there been a ringer, Sid would have been ignorant of something; namely, that that very thing which, from the far side, he took to be sipping was not that very thing which, from the near side, he took to be sipping. So, the idea is, *as things stand* there is something substantial for Sid to know: that that one viewed sipping from the near side is that one viewed sipping from the far side. Let us name the one first-mentioned, NSS (for Near-side-sipper), and the one next mentioned, FSS (*mutatis mutandis*). Then the substantial bit of knowledge is that NSS is FSS.

Stage 2: Ignorance and knowledge now safely in the picture, we can run through Frege's line of thought. If it is true, but substantial knowledge, that

NSS is FSS, then 'NSS' and 'FSS' must identify two different modes of presentation within the thought of this identity. It is one thing for a thought to present that regarding which it is singular as NSS, another for it to present this as FSS, even though the same thing, Penelope, is presented both times. Had there been a switch (as per above), Penelope could still have been presented as NSS, but she could not have been presented as FSS. If this last is a mode of presentation of *Penelope*, then there would have been no such mode of presentation of an object at all. So NSS and FSS identify two *different* modes of presentation of Penelope. Each requires her to have had a different bit of history for it to exist. (Symmetrically, presenting her as FSS might have been a way of presenting Penelope as the one on whom truth turns even if there were no such thing as presenting her as NSS.)

Stage 3: So far our topic is thoughts there are to think. Our concern is with *being true* (what questions of truth there *are*). Now we aim for a conclusion as to what thought(s) Sid *does* think from the near and from the far side, watching Penelope sipping. We thus aim to move from facts about being true to a conclusion about the psychology of holding true. The idea is simple, though *ought* to be controversial. The inference is this. Had there been a switch, Sid could not have told that Penelope lacked the history for her to be presented as the one on whom truth turned in the way she might have been had she been seated on the far side. In thinking the ringer to be sipping, he would have been unable to tell that he was not thus thinking of the one (Penelope) he saw from the near side. So what he *does* think from the far side in thinking *Penelope* to be sipping cannot present her as the one in question in a way there would not have been had she lacked this counterfactually-missing history, that which makes her identifiable as NSS. Thus his (actual) stance towards Penelope from the far side *must* be on a different question of truth from that on which he stands from the near side, though both are questions, of Penelope, of whether she is sipping. The thoughts to which he thus stands must differ as would a thought about NSS and one about FSS.

Reverting to the trick of 1882, the idea can be put as follows: what Sid thinks of Penelope from the near side presents the object it is about as falling under a different concept than does what he thinks from the far side. The first presents her as being that very object, NSS; whereas the last presents her as being that very object, FSS. The thoughts in question in each case thus differ in what they require of an object for its being the one they are about: that it be NSS, and that it be FSS respectively. Each thus requires a different specific, and thereby a different generic, bit of history for it to exist at all.

Sid need not have walked for this argument to get a grip. He might have stood frozen, staring. Still, at any moment he might have blinked. Where passing time makes room for a conceivable ringer-switch the argument grips. For how long, then (if it is good) can Sid continue to believe the same thing—or at least stand in the same way towards some one and the same question of truth—some one thing to be thought as to who is sipping? Such questions do not just arise for times. Sid and Mafalda stand shoulder to shoulder, watching Penelope sip. It is logically possible for a mad neuroscientist to have tampered, undetectably, with Mafalda: her retinas no longer register ambient light; she is supplied with proximal stimuli transmitted from a Penleope-ringer in a ringer-situation far away. Had that happened, there would have been a substantial fact of which Sid and Mafalda were both ignorant: that the one who Sid sees to be sipping is not (the) one who so seems to Mafalda. By the above reasoning, there *is*, in fact, a substantial fact for both to know: this last, with 'the', minus the 'not'. So, it seems, Penelope is in fact presented in thought to Mafalda differently than she is to Sid; hence, by the above line, differently in the thought each thinks to the effect that she is sipping. When, if ever, then, could two people think the same thought?

These questions immediately recall Russell. As to time, he answered thus for those singular thoughts *he* thought there could be:

You can keep [thinking it] for about a minute or two... If you argue quickly, you can get some little way before it is finished.

(Russell 1918: p. 203)

Such flows from Russell's conception of what a genuine singular thought would need to be. To begin with, it would need to be about a quite special sort of object: in Frege's terms a *Vorstellung*, something needing a bearer, to whose consciousness it belonged, and brooking no two bearers. Accordingly (as Frege notes), it would need to ascribe to that object a special sort of property—one which only such an object would be eligible for having (though the same vocabulary—such as 'yellow'—might speak of it as also speaks of properties of those denizens, with us, of our shared environment). Russell thus happily answered the second above question with 'Never!' For him, singular thoughts are intrinsically unshareable. All of which flowed, for him, from taking Frege's advice: to find the logical structure of a proposition, ignore the grammar of its natural language formulation, instead ask directly the question under what circumstances it would be true. (In Frege's words, 'Our logic books still always drag much in—for example, subject and predicate—which really doesn't belong in logic' (Frege 1897: 154).)

How far does this first role Burge assigns ringers carry us along, like it or not, down Russell's path? Does it leave us with, if singular thoughts at all, then at best only ones about non-environmental objects—*Vorstellungen* in Frege's sense? Might a thought Sid thinks (of Penelope, that she is sipping) from the far side, and specifically its mode of presentation of the object it is of (Penelope) require for its existence some generic history which one such as Penelope *might* have had—say, that someone have then been *sitting* (there, on that *esplanada*)? Or does the line just scouted rule this supposition out?

Sid, from the far side, *could*, conceivably, have been experiencing a ringer for Penelope, or for experiencing her, or sipping. As he strolled from one side to the other, there could have been a surreptitious switch. Had there been, there would have been something he did not know: that the one he watched sipping from the far side was not the one he had watched sipping from the near side. Representing that ignorance would require two different modes of presentation of an object. The mode of presentation of the object he was watching (from the far side) could not require for its existence that certain bit of history, that object's former presence on the near side. *Idem* any thought that it is part of. By the line just scouted, this means that there *is*, as things stand (Penelope throughout) something substantive for Sid to know or not: that the one he had watched sipping from the near side is the one he watches sipping from the far side. Representing this object of knowledge or ignorance requires a mode of presentation of the one he is watching from the far side which, like that mode of presentation of the imagined ringer, does not require for its existence such a history as that the one it presents was formerly present on the near side. Again, *idem* any thought that it is part of. Following out the line, this fact about the modes of presentation in a thought which represented the knowledge, or ignorance, thus in question filters through to the modes of presentation in thoughts Sid thinks from the far side, as things stand, of Penelope, that she is sipping.

Sitting (there, then) is the sort of history an item like Penelope might have. Such history would, crucially, belong to our common environment. For someone to be sitting is for him to occupy a place in webs of factive meaning. There is what it would mean if he were sitting for how things would be at places throughout our environment. For example, normally his sitting would be visible from an indefinite number of places in its surroundings—if from the near side, for example, then, barring impediments, also from the far side. Webs of factive meaning are not in general *a priori* matters. But if Penelope is now sitting at a certain table, or under a certain umbrella, on that *esplanada*, there is the way someone's then sitting there would interact with the rest of the environment, things being as they then were. What did not thus interact with the environment simply would not be a case of someone *sitting* (whatever else it might then be). Sid, watching Penelope sipping, *could* have been watching a ringer sipping. But the point just made also means this: Sid, watching Penelope sitting, could have been experiencing a ringer for someone *sitting*. If what he sees does not interact with the environment as sitting would, it is not sitting. There is the logical possibility of ringers for so interacting.

Does our scouted line now apply to sitting? By it, a mode of presentation of Penelope, in a thought Sid thinks of her from the far side, cannot require *her* to have a certain history: to have then been sitting. Might it still require that *whoever* it is of be *sitting*? Sid in fact watches Penelope *sitting*. But he could, conceivably, have been watching her, or someone, *ringer*-sitting—so far as he could tell a case of someone sitting, but in fact not that: not interacting with the rest of the environment as a case of sitting (there) then would. Perhaps no such thing was to be seen, or otherwise registered, from the near side, or from anywhere else, as sitting then would have been. Such are the possibilities given proximal stimuli and processing leave open.

Taken in, Sid would have been ignorant of such things. He would have been unable to tell that what he experienced lacked the history to be a case of someone sitting. He would not have known that what he experienced was not anything Mafalda, on the near side, might have. Representing such ignorance would require a mode of presentation of what he experienced (a case of ringer-sitting), so of that which ringer-sat (if something did) which might have existed without any sitting going on.

Now the scouted line takes hold. As things stand, there is a substantive fact Sid *might* fail to know: that the one he watches, and supposes sipping (Penelope) has the place in history required for her/it to be sitting. Saying *what* might be known or not here requires a mode of presentation of Penelope which does not require for its existence that she have such history, so that she be sitting. Finally, by the scouted line, this mode of presentation of her is to be found in those thoughts Sid does think of her, for example, to the effect that she is sipping. So it, and those thoughts she thus thinks, do not require for their existence that she then be sitting (much less at that table, on that *esplanada*).

All that matters about sitting here is that it is an environmental way for an object to be: to be that way is to occupy a suitable place in webs of factive meaning. So the point generalizes. That just-postulated mode of presentation of Penelope cannot require for its existence any history, generic or specific, such that Sid, watching from the far side, could have been experiencing a mere ringer for what had it. So, for any environmental way for a thing to be, it cannot require for its existence a history in which something was that way. A singular thought containing such a mode of presentation thus cannot identify what it is of by that item being any ways there are for an inhabitant of our environment to be. What now separates us from Russell's view that it would have to be a *Vorstellung* in Frege's sense?

Let us shift to the other use Burge makes of ringers: to identify common factors in modes of presentation within thoughts there are and ones there might have been—such as a thought of Penelope that she is sipping, and one there might have been of some ringer had there been such. On Burge's view, such pairs share a common Ψ-like factor: a concept whose satisfaction identifies the one of whom the thought is, given the world in which that thought exists, but which might have identified a different one for some thought there is not, but would have been had the world been different. Such a common factor could only be generic. So a thought in which it is present could require of the world no more than some generic history for it to identify as it does what object it is of. But the question now is whether it could even require that much—whether there is still room for even that much space between Burge and Russell.

We face a dilemma. Frege sets out both sides. On the one side, there is this:

For the word 'red', if it does not indicate a property of things, but is to characterize sense impressions belonging to my consciousness, is applicable only in the domain of my consciousness.

(1918: 67)

If one were to call some *Vorstellung* 'red', he would be using the word in a different sense from that in which it might speak truth of a shift or a beach ball. A *Vorstellung* could not have the sort of property that a shift might. Nor a shift a property that a *Vorstellung* might. For a shift, or whatever, to be red, for Penelope, or whoever, to be *sipping* is always, *per se*, for it to have location in webs of factive meaning; for it to interact with the world as it (or something of its sort) *would*. Its being red, for example, may make it a bad idea to wash it with the whites. If Penelope is sipping, *mojito* is ingested. What is ingested is (*ceteris paribus*) later there to find. So the further course of history *could* reveal the 'sipping' as, for example, mere thespian's art. Similarly for being red. For a shift to be red, for someone to be sipping, is for that item to have a career, its condition's (factive) meaning, which extends beyond what is observable on an occasion. Equally for any other generality under which one of our environmental cohabitants might fall. This is not to say that for any given way for an object to be—being red, say—there is some such career an object must have.

We would like to suppose that Sid can think such things of objects as that they are sipping. For that he would need to think thoughts which presented the object in question as some way such things as Penelope might be; so some way an object would need a worldly career to be. We would like thoughts available to Sid to present an object as, for example, that one now sipping, or in a way requiring some such history for its existence. But now the other horn. Frege expresses it succinctly:

By the step by which I win myself an environment, I expose myself to risk of error.

(1918: 73)

If Sid, seeing Penelope, takes her to be sipping, he is thus exposed to risk of error. For for Penelope to be sipping is for her to have a career richer than what Sid now observes in this sense: conceivably, further history Sid had not observed could mean—show—that she was not sipping (even if things looked that way to Sid). An empty glass rigged to look like a *mojito*. Now a parallel for modes of presentation. Suppose that Sid takes Penelope to be seated. Suppose the thought he thus relates to presents the object in question in a way which exploits the fact that that object is sipping. So what qualifies an object as the one in question is, *inter alia*, its history as (then) sipping. So the thought could not present the object it in fact does as the one sipping unless there were that certain bit of history: the right object's then sipping. (Such is neutral as to whether it is a generic or a specific requirement which makes this so.) Then there is a ringer for an object's meeting this requirement, and thus a ringer, from Sid's position, for thinking a thought which requires it. Sid could have been thinking of a ringer-sipper (whether a different object or not) that it was seated, with no means for distinguishing what he thus thought from what he in fact thinks. The thought he thus thought in the ringer case would share its common Ψ-like factor with the thought he thus thinks. But sipping would not be required for being the one in question in it. So, by Burge's principles, that Ψ-like factor could not require sipping for being what it presents.

I do not think that Burge imagines that any Ψ-like factor he is concerned with would implicate such things as sipping in *its* way of presenting an object. A Ψ-like factor would be part of a *thought*—something there is for one to think. But as Burge links the psychological to the logical, a thought's way of presenting what it presents might rely on features specific to some one particular thinking of that thought. (The problem here is whether such reliance, or Burge's form of it, yields shareable thoughts at all.) So perhaps he thinks of such a way of presenting an object as exploiting such things as its having appeared such-and-such a way to Sid on an occasion (for example, as he gazed from the far side), or having then been related to him spatially so as to be picked out deictically in a certain way. So it is important to note that the argument just run through applies for *any* environmental factor. For an environmental item to be positioned *thus* before one is, just as much as for it to be sipping, for it to have an environmental career. Ditto for it *appearing* positioned, or any other way, as an environmental item might. In any such case, just as for sipping, there may fail to *be* any suitable such career where there seemed to be. Such failure may fail to make any difference in the way the thinker thinks things which is then discernible by him.

So for a thought identified by Burge's method, what distinguishes an object as the one in question, what distinguishes it from what is not in question, cannot be its being any way for an environmental thing to be. Accordingly, what is thus identified cannot be an environmental object. It must be a *Vorstellung* in Frege's sense. But as Frege showed, a thought cannot be a *Vorstellung*. Nor, accordingly, can it be *of* some *Vorstellung* that it is thus and so: its truth cannot turn on whether some *Vorstellung's* being as it is does or does not instance some way for a *Vorstellung* to be. There are no such generalities under which for an *object* (a potential *Bedeutung* of a mode of presentation) to fall. In brief, his point is that what goes for 'red' also goes equally for 'true' (see 1918: 68–9). For the same reason that 'red' would need a different sense as applied to a *Vorstellung*, so, too, 'true' would need a different sense used of a thought of a *Vorstellung*, rather than of some environmental object, that it was thus and so. (Unsurprisingly, given the relation Frege notes between the thought that that shift is red and the thought that it is true that it is.)

Here a new sense for 'true' is, as Frege tells us, a change of topic. Thoughts are what bring *truth* into question at all. What could be 'true' only in some new sense of 'true' would not be a thought at all. (Frege also shows that there can *be* no such new sense for 'true' or any other word.) So, giving ringers the free rein Burge allows them we arrive at (if anything) Ψ-like factors which cut the thoughts containing them off from the world (our cohabited environment) entirely. If such thoughts were about anything in the singular way, it could not be an object with an environmental career. We must thus agree with Russell that a genuine singular thought would need a special sort of object for it to be about. But for the reasons just scouted, this means that with ringers cast in Burge's roles, what we had hoped would be singular thoughts turn out not merely not to be singular, but not to be genuine thoughts at all.

This conclusion assumes Frege to be right about the *essential* publicity of thought. I have omitted his argument. It is remarkable enough if Burge must count on Frege being wrong on *this*. Burge types belief states by representations thus related to. He assigns ringers a certain role in distinguishing the states, and thereby the representations there are thus to relate to. If Frege is right, thoughts—questions of truth—cannot be so counted; so nor ways of standing towards them. Science hardly forces the impossible on us here. Such a role for ringers has a quite other and familiar source.

10 Seeing

Disjunctivism about belief fits with Frege's view of thought. It differs from Burge's in the way it sees someone's stance towards things—his taking things to be as he then does—as decomposing into particular postures of believing one thing or another—taking things to be particular ways there *are* for things to be. At the core of disjunctivism is Frege's idea of the essential shareability of thoughts, and of the essentially environmental nature of those ways things are thus thought to be—so to speak, Frege's argument against the possibility of private language. One particular manifestation of the difference here is, in the case of singular thought, rejection of that hybridism which, as we have seen, Burge finds compulsory. Within Frege's conception, much speaks in favour of disjunctivism. But my aim here has not been to establish it. It is enough for the moment that it is coherent, not to be rejected out of hand, and certainly not at odds with any recent (or ancient) result of science. It is not science's business to show what interests we *must* serve in decomposing postures. Nor, despite his protestations, is it science that moves Burge. He is, rather, moved, as we have seen, by a small, if depressing, set of familiar philosophical ideas.

Postures (such as belief) and perception, I have suggested, lie on two sides of a divide. Perception furnishes thought with things to respond to; postures such as belief are our responses to these. One must be wary of importing morals across this divide. As Frege continually insists, belief and seeing are organized by fundamentally different principles. Still, there is one point of agreement: beliefs are shareable. What Sid believes in taking Penelope to be sipping is measured by in what cases another thinker (or he himself at other times) would be in agreement, or in dispute, with him as to whether things are the way in question. Perception—when it *is* perception, and not merely perceptual experience—is also shareable. What Sid sees is, *per se*, what there is for one to see. I plan now to work this point hard in exploring what visual experience might be in common to the three terms of a Burgean stock triple—in particular, whether there is anything in common resembling $\Psi(\gamma)$.

A few initial points about seeing need to be kept in view. As points about *seeing* these apply, naturally enough, only to the first two terms of a stock triple. Illusions as Burge understands these are another matter. First, seeing is a particular form of awareness of one's surroundings—more specifically, of what, in some suitable sense, is before one's eyes. That form is *visual* awareness. The sense thus exploited (or exercized), sight, affords this. Insofar as there are visual (processing) *systems*, the same may be said of them. Sight *affords* awareness. It puts this on offer. In seeing, the offer is taken up. One then has something to take in (or just to take) as a case of things being thus and so.

Seeing is occasion for exploration, investigation, discovery. One might look closer, or move around to get a better look, so as to discover more about what it is he sees. Or one might keep track of it and see what it will do—another route to such discovery. The key point is that what one sees is, *per se*, what is open to examination, and so *opened* by one's seeing it.

What one sees is precisely what is before his eyes—unless he misses it, or it is occluded, or something of the sort. Modulo such exceptions, the question *what* Sid saw in viewing Penelope in he *chaise longue* is answered by what is before his eyes: if a yellow shift by P. Garcia, then that; if a striped *chaise longue* from Habitat, then that. There is no need for Sid to know that this is what he sees. No need to get inside Sid's skin (or mind) and see how things look as *he* views them to answer this question. Sight's role just is to provide such access to one's environment. Seeing just is a relation to that in these surroundings which thus supplies such answers.

The sorts of things one might see are the sorts thus encountered: a *chaise*, its stripes, Penelope's arm stretching languidly, the *mojito* being lifted to her mouth, the yellow of her shift, and so on. What one sees is *historical*, a temporally located part of the world's unfolding. One does not see what has that generality that marks a thought, what might be instanced by things being as they are. Such belongs to that realm of which Frege says:

What belongs to this agrees with *Vorstellungen* in that it cannot be observed with the senses, but with things in that it needs no bearer.

(1918: 69)

Penelope's arm moving languidly is an event unfolding before Sid's eyes. It is thus something he might see, or miss. Those stripes on the chair are also before his eyes. Ditto for them. That Penelope's arm is moving languidly is not before Sid's eyes. Nor is it dateable (though there is a date at which the arm *was* moving). So it is *not* something Sid can see, where seeing is perceiving. We speak of Sid seeing that Penelope's arm is moving. Frege notes of this:

One can say that, but then does not use the word 'see' in the sense of mere light-sentience, but means by this a thought or judgement connected with it.

(1897: 149)

Sid may see the yellow of Penelope's shift. He thus sees yellow. But what he thus sees is not a generality under which things may fall—being coloured yellow, being such as to be so coloured—but a case of something (here the shift) being such as to instance that generality. What he sees is the yellow of the *shift*, something to be seen only by looking there. One cannot see that case of something being yellow by looking at another shift, or a canary, or flamboyant Porsche. The yellow of Penelope's shift may be cadmium yellow. Another case of something being *so* coloured may still be on the rack, to be seen *there*. Frege's point about the conceptual and what instances it stands.

I have already introduced Frege's idea that the word 'red' (or any other), if it is to apply to a *Vorstellung*, cannot speak of the same thing (or way to be) that it would speak of applied to an environmental object. The key idea is: a *Vorstellung* is precisely what could not interact with an environment. Or, more precisely, its being in some given condition, where that is one a *Vorstellung* might, or might not, be in, could not so interact. I now want to wield that idea again with regard to objects of perceptual experience, and in particular, now, in the case of the third term of a stock triple, such as experiencing, visually, an illusion which is as though Penelope were reclining (or her shift were yellow, and so on). In the cases which make third terms, an illusion is generated by some proximal stimulus, so by retinal images, where these are *not* images of anything impinging on the retinas. Perhaps they are computer-generated. So the experience thus generated is not one of *seeing* Penelope—or anything. It is not as though the illusion is only of her being *yellow*. It would still be visual experience, though 'aware' read as a success term would be a bad fit.

If there *is* an answer to the question *what* Sid experienced visually here, what this is is not found in his surroundings. If Sid sees Penelope's yellow shift, there is an object—the shift—which *is* yellow—moreover, canary. Sid takes in, visually, the historical circumstance of things so being. Some (such as Price 1932: p. 105) used to think that if Sid experiences *an illusion* of yellow, there must be something which is yellow, and which he experiences so being. The idea would be: one can experience yellow (visually) only in experiencing an instancing—a particular case—of something being so coloured. One has no visual experience of generalities. Not a bad idea. Still, neither Burge nor I thinks that there are non-environmental objects whose being as they are just is, *inter alia*, their being yellow. Frege's point which I am exploiting here is that there could not be. So either Sid does not experience yellow in this illusion (though it may well be for him as though he did), or there is something else for his experiencing yellow here to be—something other than experiencing things which, in being as they are, just are a case of something being yellow.

Frege's point applies. Being yellow is an environmental property. To think of something that it is yellow, one needs to win for himself an environment in which that thing is found. For something to be yellow is for it to occupy a particular place in that web of factive meaning which belongs to the environment (*that* environment we all inhabit): that such-and-such was so means that the thing would be yellow, for it to be yellow means such-and-such *in re* the rest of how that environment is. It is only a start on this to say that it is the sort of thing one of us could see if he could but work his way into the right position to observe it. (It might also be that washing it with new jeans would turn it green.) A visual illusion as though one were seeing a yellow shift is not an experience of anything whose being as it is could occupy such places in this web. This is what Frege means when he says that if one were to call a *Vorstellung* yellow he would have to be using 'yellow' in some new sense—in which it applied, if at all, only to *his* Vorstellungen (or perhaps only to that one then).

What, then, of Sid's illusion? It is *for him* 'as of' a yellow shift. For him, such is what it is like. But what it is like for him here is not independent of—is perhaps precisely a matter of—how things *impress* him. Which, in turn, is a matter of his responses, or his responsiveness, the other side of the divide from that to which, in offering awareness, perception offers opportunity to respond. Responsiveness takes up here work done elsewhere, but not here, by the environment itself—the scene before Sid's eyes. It offers compensation, such as it is, for there being no scene relevantly before Sid's eyes.

This much allowed, one may say what he likes as to whether Sid's illusion is experiencing yellow. It would be natural to say not. Then Price's principle can stand, though it invites a modus tolens where he sees a modus ponens. But if we like we can say that for there to be such responsiveness on his part just is for him to experience yellow. The illusion Sid experiences gains him no access to his surroundings, or to the presence or absence of yellow in them. But his *experiencing* it belongs to the environment—its being as it is. His being as he thus is may instance someone experiencing an illusion of a particular kind, such as of something yellow. One might also count the way yellow figures here as something experiencing yellow might be. For present purposes, say what you like about this so long as you see the facts.

Where do we now stand? In the first two terms of a stock triple, Sid's visual experience, provided by the visual processing (vision science's business) that then went on, was visual awareness of *yellow*, in that it was visual awareness of an instance of something being yellow—of something which so counted. He saw a *shift's* yellow—in the first case, Penelope's, in the second, that of some ringer for it. In the third term the experience was no such thing. If its being as though experiencing yellow was Sid's experiencing yellow—if this, too, may so count—still, for all that, Sid's experiencing yellow in this case is (as it is not in the first two) a matter of his posture towards what is happening to him, not just the availability of postures by him towards it.

With which we return to Hinton: what seeing and an illusion thereof have in common is, he says, 'that the one is, what the other is merely like'. We now see how this encapsulates disjunctivism, captures what is *not* in common to the two cases. In the one case (either of the first two terms of a stock triple) there is awareness of yellow in awareness of something whose being as it is is, *per se*, a case of something yellow. In the second (the third term of a stock triple) there is being impressed in a certain way by what is going on visually with one; its being, for him, *like* seeing yellow. In the one case what was experienced is settled by what was there to be experienced (if it was not missed). In the other, it is settled by how the experiencer was impressed. Only in the first is there something whose being as it is *is* its being yellow, so that it is awareness of *that* which is experiencing yellow. There is no object of visual *awareness* present in all cases of the triple with the further features which might make awareness of it $\Psi(\gamma)$ing.

The point turns on some observations of (philosophical) grammar; on how our means for representing, thinking of, perceptual experience work. Such observations are always open to dispute, and, in philosophy, often enough wrong. But vision science has given us no reason to think our concepts do not—or cannot—work that way. And there is a plausible case that they do. Again, there may well be a good sense in which vision science provides us with the same materials for explaining what is going on in each case of the triple. In the first two, it allows us to understand how one of us can be visually sensitive to the sorts of features of the environment we are—to a shift being uniform yellow, say. In the third it may offer an explanation of why things seem to us as they then might. Burge supposes further that in providing these same materials throughout, vision science also demands of us that we find some *one* thing for them to explain throughout, and, moreover, that that one thing must be, throughout, our experiencing such-and-such—some one thing to be experienced visually. I doubt very much that vision science claims this for itself as a result. It is, anyway, an entirely gratuitous assumption.

11 Veils

Burge writes,

I want to remark on one motivation for disjunctivism. The usual motivation is a concern to insure that we make 'direct' perceptual contact with the physical world. The doctrine was originally an over-reaction to veil-of-perception views of the British empiricists.

... On such a view, experience of the physical world is held to be indirect, both in not being the first object of perceptual reference, and in being the product of an epistemically evaluable inference from more fundamental objects of perception.

... The veil-of-perception view is empirically and philosophically a dead position. All present empirical theories of perception and nearly all serious philosophical positions reject it.

(2005: 29–30)

He pleads innocence of commitment to such a veil for the following reason:

Perceptual representation does not produce a 'veil of ideas' because the first objects of perceptual reference are physical entities in the environment. This is a sense in which perceptual representations are directly 'about' the environment: They are *referentially non-derivative*.

(2005: 30)

In the old days some spoke of sense-data, or qualia, where these were, first what we *really*, strictly speaking, perceived, or experienced perceptually, and second, these gained us access to what surrounded us by resembling, or otherwise relating to it. Such views are gauche today, though some still mention qualia. Philosophers now speak instead of (truth-evaluable) *representations* (of things as being thus and so). There is, it is rumoured, a way things are according to perceptual experience. *Things* here, Burge tells us, are what surround us.

It may be comforting to think such things. But I think Burge has forgotten what it is to represent things as some given way. There are two cases. One is simply holding a posture towards the world (felt as forced on one by the weight of things being thus and so). No-one suspects perceptual experience of such things. Perception is a source of information, not a reaction to it. Second, representing-as may be placing messages on offer; making available to one suitably placed and equipped what the representer *has* to offer (or chooses to). Such representing fixes when a particular goal would be reached: representing things being as they are. The way it represents things being is that way which things would then be. For such representing to exist is for it to be recognizable as what it is. It works via something (such as a sentence) recognizable without recognizing any representing going on, but by whose presence one knowledgable in such things can tell this.

If an experience issues, or bears, messages—if such-and-such is the way things are according to it—then something in it must make these recognizable. If the representing is for *us*—not just that of one sub-doxastic mechanism for others—then it is something experienced which must make this recognizable. We can *see* how things are thus represented to be in being so represented to. This something cannot be things *around* us, things seen. Penelope's yellow shift, or her wearing it, may be a signal to Sid to meet her at La Bellota Hermosa at 9 o'clock. But it hardly represents itself to be a yellow shift. In fact, if an experience represented it to be so that Penelope was wearing a yellow shift, what made this representing recognizable would need to be something which would be there to do its work whether Penelope *was* so clad or not—what, so far as it went, *could* be making *false* representing recognizable.

So if experience does the representing Burge supposes, what makes it recognizable must be sought elsewhere than in what is before us. Accordingly, when we have recognized the representing done on an occasion, and concern ourselves with whether this was representing *truly*, we must look beyond what made it recognizable to find what settles the question: that historical circumstance, things being as they are, which, in being a case or not of that generality, the way things were represented being, makes this representing a case of representing truly, or, as it may be, falsely. We must look beyond what makes the representing recognizable to those surroundings themselves which were represented as being some given way, to such things as *Penelope's shift*, and its being as it is. If these were themselves things then experienced, that representing, and this exercise of evaluating it, would be simply idle. Now, though neither sense data nor qualia have yet an *acknowledged* place in this picture, one might well ask what more one could want for a veil between us and that of which (supposedly) perception places *us* to judge.

12 Conclusion

Burge turns the personal psychology of holding true to revealing the structure of being true—those points there are at which for thinkers, such as us, to meet in agreement or dispute. He then gives ringers free rein in fixing a thinker's epistemic standing towards what he thinks—what he can *recognize* this to be. Had he followed Frege he would have done neither. As Frege shows, much, some set out here, speaks against each. It is this that moves disjunctivism about (singular) belief. Perception (seeing) parallels belief at least in this: what there is to see is what there is for *one* to see. Personal psychology cannot tell us what *that* is. Ringers, charged with uncovering things we experience perceptually, instead uncover nothing.[1]

---

[1] Special thanks are extended to Bill Brewer, Matt Boyle, Naomi Eilan, Mark Kalderon, Guy Longworth, Paul Snowdon, and Matt Soteriou.

10

The Preserve of Thinkers

> In a common mediaeval outlook, what we now see as the subject matter of natural science was conceived as filled with meaning, as if all of nature were a book of lessons for us; and it is a mark of intellectual progress that educated people cannot now take that idea seriously, except perhaps in some symbolic role.
>
> John McDowell, *Mind and World* (1994: 71)

> It is as though we had imagined that the essential thing about a living person was his outer form, and so produced a block of wood in this form; and were abashed to see the dead block, which had no similarity to the living being at all.
>
> Wittgenstein, *Philosophical Investigations*, §430

Have we made the progress McDowell speaks of? Science has, no doubt. In philosophy, though, that mediaeval idea may masquerade as science itself. Masquerade only: *nothing*, so not science, suggests messages in nature of the sort found in books. So I will argue. Nature *is* full of messages for us. That red sky at night tells a sailor something. But it is superstition to approach such messages as one would a text or utterance or speech act—though superstition which still tempts some.[1]

What distinguishes the messages in texts or speech acts? First, they are *issued*, produced, conveyed, by some author. (They are also *borne* by, or contained in, the text or act itself.) Representing *can* just be holding a stance or posture towards things, a condition one is in. Representing something to be so, for example (henceforth representing-to-be) can just be *taking* it to be so. I will call such representing *autorepresenting*. Such will be a side issue here. By contrast, the authoring of a message is an episode, a happening. (We can, of course, think of a book's *bearing* of an authored message as a condition it is in.)

---

[1] I am grateful to Mike Martin, Mark Kalderon, Guy Longworth, and Craig French for helping me see where some of the lines here lead.

Second, the episode in question is one of *producing* something. An author of the sorts of messages found in texts and speech acts, *issues* a message, thus assuming responsibility; liability to praise or blame for achieving, or not, those successes or failures at which the message is to be taken to be aimed. Where a book contains *messages*, there is a door at which blame is to be lain.

Third, the kind of representing involved in texts and speech acts is representing-as: it is (*inter alia*) representing things *as being* some way there *is* for things to be. Not all representing-as is representing-to-be. Pia may represent Sid as a ballerina by sketching him in tutu and third position, without suggesting that he is one. Correspondingly, not all the representing found in books is representing-to-be. But all representing-to-be is representing-as. To express the wish that Sid stop snoring, Pia must represent Sid *as* being one who snores, and assign this a certain status: what is wished to become not so. Equally, to represent Sid *to be* one who snores, she must represent him *as* a snorer and assign *this* a certain status: a way things are. (I do not claim that speech acts have unique parsings). So representing-as is a general case of which representing-to-be is a genre. What had the capacity to represent-to-be, thus what had the capacity to represent truly or falsely, would *ipso facto*, more generally, have the capacity to represent-as.

Fourth, *issuing* a message, so bearing one, is *making* it suitably available, its issuing manifest. So for representing of the kind at stake here, the kind books go in for, to be is to be suitably recognizable. Making something recognizable requires suitable means for doing so. Among the means at work in any given case of the representing I am after here is what I will call a *vehicle*. A vehicle is, first, something which is recognizable as what it is—so as occurring, present, or not—independent of whether any representing is going on, or of what messages, if any, it bears. Second, it is such that its production, in the circumstances in which it serves as vehicle, makes recognizable just that recognizing-as done by its author (producer) in producing it. It might, for example, be some English words, or some graphic form they have. If an author may be said to have represented things as being thus and so, or to have assigned that way for things to be a certain status, then his vehicle may be said, on a different reading of the verbs 'represent' and 'assign', to do so too. Pia *said* that Sid snores, her words *say* that he does.

With an eye to the contrast with autorepresenting, I will use the term 'allorepresent' (and its derivatives) for representing which is authored by an author who (which) thus incurs responsibility for its successes and failures, which is representing-as, and which as such that for it to be is for it to be suitably recognizable. I mean this to be read so that both the author and his (its) vehicle can be said to allorepresent, each on his/its proper reading of the verb.

My theses are then: allorepresenting and autorepresenting are the only forms of representing-as, hence of representing to be so; only a thinker, or a thinker's vehicles, can allorepresent. (For a vehicle to represent-as as it does is for it to be the vehicle it is for the thinker, or thinkers, whose vehicle it is.) Hence (bracketing for the moment autorepresenting) only a thinker, in a demanding sense to be spelled out, can engage in representing-as, thus in representing to be so. Some think that what bore content as an authored vehicle does *might,* for all that, be authorless. As noted, I hope to help that idea out of the world.

Allorepresenting contrasts with what I will call *effect-representing*—a relation between one historical circumstance and another. Here one bit of history is what is represented. Another does the representing. That teetering rock represents aeons of wind erosion. Pia's haggard mien represents years of Sid's grunting. Generalizations obtain. Teetering rocks may always represent wind erosion (except where they do not). Effect-representing is far from reserved for thinkers. Whatever happens does it. All it takes is an aetiology. Its role here is as what allorepresenting had better not turn out to be.

Allorepresenting is choosier than effect-representing. Those empty seats in the house may represent (the workings of) poor casting, a hostile press, Sid's paunch (he playing the lead), and so on *ad infinitum*. No need to choose; *a fortiori* no need for the seats to choose. Where there is a case of allorepresenting, there is such a thing as *the* way things were thus represented as being. *Something* must choose what way this is to be. I mention this now, for elaboration later, because it is a point that will matter *very* much.

This essay effect-represents the posing of a question, 'Does perceptual experience have content?' It places that question in a wider context. If having content is indulging in representing-as, and if my thesis holds, then the answer is 'No'. This is not to say that someone who enjoys perceptual experience does not, perhaps inevitably, in doing so thereby autorepresent.

1 Thinkers

The notion of a thinker at work here is Descartes'. Aiming to distinguish *res cogitans* from dumb brutes and refined machines, he offers two marks,

of which the first is that they [machines, brutes] could never use words or other signs, composing them as we do to express their thoughts to others. For one could indeed conceive of a machine being so arranged that it offered words, and even that it offered certain ones about material actions causing certain changes in its organs . . . but not of it arranging them diversely so as to respond to the sense of all that was said in its presence in the way that even the most mentally deficient men can . . . And the second is that, while they did several things as well as, or perhaps better than, any of us, they would infallibly fall short in others, by which one would discover that they did not act through knowledge, but solely by the disposition of their organs.

(1637: p. 92)

'Reason', Hilary Putnam wrote, 'can transcend whatever it can survey' (Putnam 1988: 119). Such is Descartes' idea. Take any implementable theory of how to do such-and-such—a theory with definite predictions as to the thing to do when faced with such a task. A Cartesian thinker is always prepared to recognize ways of performing the task other than those the theory dictates; moreover, to recognize whether such a new way, and not the theory's, would be the thing to do—and whether the task itself is a thing to do. We, but not swallows, can recognize when old ways of building mud nests, or times for building them, are not best. Our sensitivity to the world's bearing on the thing for us to do is, unlike theirs, unbounded in this sense.

Suppose the task is recognition—such as telling pigs at sight. Pigs are recognizable by how they look. No-one thinks, though, that to be a pig just *is* to have that look. Porcine (or ovine) cosmetic surgery is, so far, pointless but hardly inconceivable. Though most of us could not *say* just what it is that makes a pig, for any putative porcine feature, we are sensitive to what would bear on whether what lacked it might, for all that, be a pig (or what had it might not be). Here our capacities transcend whatever reason can survey, as per Putnam's idea.

Keeping up one's end in a conversation is a project, often taxing. Descartes' first mark of a thinker is, thus, a special case of his second. Pia says, 'My Porsche is in the shop'. For Sid to respond to this—with what intelligibly *is* a response— would be for him to say what bears, in some understandable way, and some way he could understandably aim for it to bear, on the Porsche being in the shop (or on Pia's having said so). He might say, for example, 'I hope you like Opels', or 'I'll warn our *taxista*', or 'German over-engineering!', or 'I'd better rent some films', or 'Have you been paid this month yet?', depending on the way this would be understood to link to what Pia said and the links he aims to forge. Renting films may or may not be the thing to do when Porsche-less. Any of indefinitely many things might make it so—because one just *would* not go out without the Porsche, because the films will cover the sound of Pia's weeping, because if you give the mechanics films to watch, perhaps they will actually fix the Porsche, and so on. Moreover, the connection between the Porsche being in the shop and Pia being Porsche-less for the weekend is itself contingent. 'I'd better rent films' might, or might not, be *continuing* the conversation, depending on whether *some* such connection between films and Porsche-lessness is one there might, in the circumstances, intelligibly be, and one Sid might be understood to be making. Sid need not aim to *continue* the conversation. But for him to be an intelligible conversation partner—*equipped* for conversing—he must be sensitive to how the world might work in forging such links, and to their existence or not; to how it might thus bear on the response for him to make. Descartes' point: such sensitivity, for a Cartesian thinker, transcends, in Putnam's sense, whatever reason can survey.

Not all allorepresenting continues a conversation. A weather bulletin does not. Pia telling Sid that the Porsche was in the shop *started* one. So, one might think, not all allorepresenting requires sensitivity to those same factors on which the cogency of a response depends. But for a Cartesian thinker, at least, allorepresenting is always a project, guided by sensitivity to the world's bearing on the thing to do in realizing it—*inter alia*, on *how* to represent things—so to those same considerations which filter *responses* from mere chatter. What Sid says to Pia depends not just on what, as he sees things, a reply might be, but also on what further ends he aims for his allorepresenting to serve—being sympathetic, making light of things, evincing disinterest, suggesting how Pia can make it through the weekend. That Cartesian, theory-transcendent, thinking which guides his perceptions as to what a response would be (and *what* response) works here, too, in his seeing what to do to reach his aims, and, in such matters, what his aims should be. It is thus at work whether it is a question of continuing a conversation or not. *Our* allorepresenting draws, *per se*, on those capacities which mark a Cartesian thinker off from an unthinker.

So far, allorepresenting draws on resources reserved for a Cartesian thinker only insofar as it is in the service of further ends, such as conversing. It has not yet been shown that all allorepresenting must aim so to serve; nor, more importantly, that such resources are drawn on anyway in fixing just *how* things are thus represented being. A first step in this direction is to note that alloreposenting is creative. In saying of a Mondriaan, 'That's Dutch', Sid created a new way for things to be. There was already, thanks to the painting's creation, such a thing as its being Dutch; now, thanks to Sid's performance, there is also such a thing as things being as he thus represented them. Had Mondriaan not so painted, there would not have been that first way; had Sid not so performed, there would not have been that second. The vehicle Sid might have represented otherwise if *used* otherwise. Something in *his* use of it must identify when things would be as *he* thus represented them.

Talk of creativity here *may* seem mere word play. Sid (somehow) *selected* a certain (already existing) way for things to be—for that painting to be Dutch. He represented things as being *that* way. There is, to be sure, the question how he effected *that* selection. An answer might be interesting. But given this much, when (in what cases) things would be as he represented them is decided by when that painting would be Dutch. There is no more to Sid's created way than this. So one might think.

But perhaps not. Signs of more emerge when we ask what it *would* be for a painting to be Dutch. Mondriaan, born in Amersfoort, with Dutch roots dating from before the seventeenth century, moved to Paris and spent much of his working life there. Suppose that he took French citizenship, joined a French collective, and produced the painting, in their signature style, as (an anonymous) part of their grand entrance into art history. Is the painting, then, perhaps, French? Or, conversely, suppose that Mondriaan, born of French expatriates in Amersfoort, had worked there all his life. Is his painting then French or Dutch? Might its style matter to this? Again, were the van Eyck brothers (of South Netherlands) Dutch? Such questions have no flat answers. With the van Eycks, for example, it depends on what you count as being Dutch, or *where* you so count things. But there *may* be unequivocal answers to some parallel questions as to whether things are as Sid represented them in representing the painting as being Dutch. If Mondriaan had come from, and worked in, Ghent, for example, it might (depending on the circumstances of Sid's allorepresenting) be clear that things were then *not* as he had represented them. Given such possibilities, *creating* a way for things to be—as one represented them in some episode of representing—might plausibly draw on such capacities peculiar to a Cartesian thinker as the ability to tailor one's representing to the purposes it is to serve.

The ability to converse contains in it a certain *freedom* in language use, to which Noam Chomsky points:

> A typical example of stimulus control for Skinner would be the response to a piece of music with the utterance Mozart or to a painting with the response Dutch . . . Suppose instead of saying Dutch we had said Clashes with the wallpaper, I thought you liked abstract work, Never saw it before, Tilted, Hanging too low, Beautiful, Hideous, Remember our camping trip last summer?, or whatever else might come into our minds when looking at a picture . . .
>
> (*Language*, 35, no. 1 (1959): 26–58, 52)

What Pia says as Vic shows her his new Mondriaan might be any of indefinitely many things. Her ability to allorepresent is one to respond to such provocations, or any specifiable one, in any of indefinitely many ways. As I hope to make clear, it would be misunderstanding what freedom is involved here if one took it for anything other than the operation of Cartesian thinking—if, for example, one thought of it as merely the ability to produce what was to be one's representing in the absence of what it was to represent.

Descartes' conception of a thinker is not the only one. A simpler one would be: a thinker is whoever, or whatever, thinks things so. Cats and dogs *might* do this, depending on what it is to think something so. I take no stands here. *If* cats and dogs are thinkers in this sense, perhaps for all that they fail Descartes' tests. We would then have a weaker notion. It would remain to decide whether such weaker thinkers might, not just autorepresent, but also allorepresent—*emit* representing-as. But where unthinking representing-as has so far been suggested, it is not the work of such weaker thinkers. I thus leave this issue unresolved.

There is, though, one reason why allorepresenting *might* be a more demanding enterprise than autorepresenting. It is that an allorepresenter is responsible for *which* way things are thus represented being—under which generality things are thus presented as falling—in a way that an autorepresenter is not. One illustration. Thanks to a happy turn of events in the winter of 1848 there is now a range of thoughts to think which there might easily not have been. If Pia thinks that Frege was glabrous, she thinks one of these. If Sid says that Pia thinks that Frege was glabrous, he assumes liability for there being such a thought. Were there not, Sid would thus be wrong as to how things are (as to what Pia thinks). By contrast, Pia assumes no such liability in thinking this. If there really never was a 'Frege', she simply would not have thought what Sid said her to. She would not still have thought that, but mistakenly. Another possibility. If the wild boar were not in rut, things would not be as Pia thinks. Do what you like, and but for that fact Pia's picture of the world would not jibe. But an overly genteel upbringing has left her without the notion *for a beast to be in rut*. Perhaps she might still count as thinking that the wild boar are in rut; but not thanks to *her* ability to identify that as a way she thinks things. Perhaps (for all that matters here) a cat might stand similarly towards a hole's presence in a wall. Such, anyway, are reasons for separating two notions of *thinker* as I have just done.

2 Generality

Effect-representing is a two-place relation, representing-as a three-place one. In effect-representing, one historical circumstance represents another. The presence of those empty seats represents poor casting. (One *type* of circumstance might, as a rule, or invariably, represent another.) By contrast, in representing-as, something, A, represents something else, B, *as* something, C.

What fills the A-place in allorepresenting is either its author, or his (its) vehicle—not circumstances, but that whose being thus and so might be a circumstance. Where allorepresenting is liable to success or failure (as in representing-to-be), it is the author at whose door blame, where fitting, is to be lain. *He* (it) bears the responsibility. Some suggest that authorless vehicles might *bear* messages, so represent-as. It would be obscure where then to lay such blame. It matters, correspondingly, how much it matters that there should be such a place.

What might fill the B-place? In one case *things* which may be represented as being thus and so, on that reading of 'things' which bars the question 'Which ones?' 'Things', taken straight, means: things being as they are. Modified, it may refer to things being as they will be, or were, or would be if . . . Such are cases of what might be represented *as* something. So might *a* thing. Its being as it is is then what is its being, or not, as represented. So to represent a thing as something is to represent its being as it is as something.

What matters most here is what occupies the C-place: that *as* which something is represented being. What fits in this place is a way for things (or for a thing) to be. For Sid to snore, or things *so* being, is a way for things to be, so a way to allorepresent things being, for example, in *saying* so, or asking whether.

Frege identifies a generality inherent in any thought:

A thought always contains something which reaches beyond the particular case, by means of which it presents this to consciousness as falling under some given generality.
(1882: *Kernsatz* 4)

The generality at issue here is not one which distinguishes some thoughts from others, but one belonging to all thoughts. A thought is, for example, that Sid snores. It is thus *of* things being such that Sid snores. It *presents* things so being; and with 'that' attached, their so being *as* enjoying a certain status: as part of how things are. Representing-to-be takes a further step: not merely presenting a given way *as being* a way things are—what would be just more representing-as—but as assuming, or incurring, liability to a particular sort of success or failure, getting it right or wrong. No thought takes this extra step. It cannot *aim* at such success or failure (or anything). The *thought* that pigs swim is not to blame if they do not.

Whence this generality? Following Frege, a thought is what brings truth into question at all, done only by fixing (or being) a particular question of it; a particular point on which *thinkers* might agree or not. One cannot simply aim at truth *tout court*. It must be truth *in re* something. Which is to say: one cannot aim at *everything*. So a question of truth cannot turn on everything. Whether that Mondriaan is Dutch may turn on Mondriaan's parentage, but not on whether Pia was at Hédiard yesterday, or Sid is wearing sandals. It follows that a range of cases—an indefinitely large one—are ones which would, or might, count as things being such that that painting is Dutch—ones with Sid in socks and sandals, ones with him *pieds nus*, and so on *ad infinitum*. A thought (and that way for things to be which it is of), reaches in its own way to particular cases, thus reaching just what it does. *How* it reaches is contained in it being the thought it is. Thus a thought's inherent generality and that of a way for things to be.

Frege puts two pieces in play. Thoughts, so ways for things to be, are one-piece. The other is what he calls 'the particular case'—what a thought presents as falling under some generality. What falls *under* a generality is intrinsically one-off: nothing *else* could be things being as they now are. What makes the particular particular, though, is rather its lack of reach. Nothing in *its* being the case it is identifies *any* question of truth, or what matters to it. The sun is setting slowly over the Douro's mouth. For the sun to be setting slowly is a way for things to be. Things being as they now are is a case of this. Study *that* case as closely as you like, and you will not learn from *it* what matters, and how, to whether *a* particular case would be a case of this or not. For this one must look at just *what* generality is to be instanced. Generalizing, no proper part of a generality's reach determines what further reach it might or might not have. Generalities and particular cases are thus two fundamentally different sorts of things. I will speak of the first, ways for things to be, as *conceptual*, the last, things being as they are, as *non-conceptual*. That core relation between these two domains, being a case of, I will call *instancing*, its converse *reaching to*.

One can *witness*, for example, watch, things being as they are. One does this, for example, in seeing the sun, setting over the Douro's mouth. What is *visible*—the sun, for example—has location. What has location is what *may* interact causally with its surroundings. Such is part of Frege's point in insisting that thoughts cannot be objects of sensory awareness. They are the wrong sorts of things for that. They are equally unfit for causal interaction. It cannot be the causal profile of a way for things to be which makes it occupy the third place in the relation *allorepresenting* for given first and second terms. It *has* no such profile. Allorepresenting cannot be made of effect-representing by any such route.

A given item within the conceptual participates in the instancing relation in a given way. It pairs up in this, in a given way, with the particular cases the world provides (or allows for). *What* determines its participation? Not logic. Logic concerns relations *within* the conceptual; not those between the conceptual and something else. Nor do relations *within* the conceptual, determine this; or at least not without enough facts already given as to enough other terms of those relations reach themselves. What makes *things being such that Sid snores* reach as it does cannot be some law which dictates when to count a particular case as instancing that generality, unless it is already given what particular cases that law reaches.

Nor can it be relations *within* the conceptual which fix how the conceptual as a whole relates to the non-conceptual. A question, 'How, by what, does the conceptual reach to the non-conceptual *überhaupt?*' can only be misbegotten. For a way for things to be to be the one it is is (*inter alia*, perhaps) for it to reach as it does. There is no identifying it as what it is while leaving it open for something *else* to settle where *it* reaches. There is, accordingly no problem of how something else *could* make it reach as it does. So, too, there is no grasping *what* way for things to be a given way is without grasping well enough when something would be a case of it.

Not, though, as though there cannot be *reasons* for and/or against counting a particular case as a case of such-and-such. Quite the contrary. A way for things to be, as Frege argued, is *per se* a way for our shared environment to be. Its instancing (if it were instanced) by things being as they are would thus bear in a particular way on how things would be otherwise. Its instancing would stand at particular places in webs of factive meaning. There is, then, the question how its instancing *would* matter if things being as they are did count as this, and, correspondingly, of how its instancing *ought* to matter, to how things were otherwise. Would it be *right* to count what mattered as its instancing would if *this* so counted as *instancing* this way for things to be? A chrome yellow Porsche would normally look yellow in daylight. Pia's Porsche, though painted chrome yellow, would not so look, for example, because it is covered with baked-on beige mud. Is its being as it is a case of a Porsche being yellow? What would follow if we said 'yes', what if we said 'no'? Is the way its being yellow *would* then bear on things consistent with what it is or might be for a Porsche to be yellow? Such is a topic for rational discussion, in which one who grasped what it was for a Porsche to be yellow would be equipped to engage. To count her Porsche as yellow would be to take one view as to how a yellow Porsche ought to, or might, look in daylight. To refuse so to count it would be to take a competing view. To grasp what (a Porsche) being yellow is is to be positioned to weigh such alternatives properly.

Here Putnam's words apply again: reason transcends whatever it can survey. How *ought* one to expect a Porsche to look if it is yellow? If Pia's Porsche, while painted yellow, does not now look yellow in normal daylight, one cannot expect a theory which generated in advance all the reasons there might be (or might have been) for this. Nor, correlatively, could one expect to say in advance what it would mean (factively) for the Porsche to be yellow if its failure here did, and, again, if it did not, cancel its claim to count as being yellow—as instancing the generality *being a yellow Porsche*. So nor could there (plausibly) be a theory which predicted in advance, when it would be true to what a Porsche's being yellow is, where there was such a failure, to rule in the one way or the other. Which, if right, is to say: there can be no specifiable prosthetic for *our* sense of when to say (when it would be true to say), when not, that a Porsche is yellow. Which is to say: the ability to see this draws essentially on those capacities which mark a Cartesian thinker. Thus, too, for the ability to see when things would be as Sid represented them in representing Pia's Porsche as yellow, so the ability to grasp *what* way his created way—things being as he represented them—is.

An ability to see what would, or might, *count* as a case of something being yellow is very different from a mere ability to detect what are in fact cases of what does so count, as an ability to see what would count as something being a pig differs from an ability to tell a pig at sight. An ability to tell a pig at sight *is* that thanks to the fact that pigs are recognizable by certain visual features—by how they look. But we all recognize that to be a pig is not, certainly not just, to have those features. Not all that grunts is, or need be, porcine; not all that is porcine need grunt. So an ability to tell pigs at sight *is* that only in an hospitable environment. Flood the environment with enough ringers, and it ceases to be an ability at all. An ability to see what would *count* as something being a pig transcends such limits. It is, *inter alia*, an ability to see when we have ringers to deal with. *Such* an ability is what is drawn on in identifying what way Sid represented things being in representing Pia's Porsche as yellow. It is for such abilities, I have suggested, that there is no prosthetic.

An author of allorepresenting is responsible for his creations. Blame for success or failure—for example, for representing things as they are not, or as they ought not to have been—is to be lain at his door. But he can be *blamed* only for what is in his control, for what he/it can be responsive to having done or not. He could, might, have done otherwise; he is *thus* blameworthy for not *having* so done. The point just made is, in brief, only a Cartesian thinker could be thus responsible for having represented things in one way rather than another.

To some this will seem wrong. To their eyes, nature, or some of its creations, though no thinker in any sense, can assume the sort of responsibility for some of its (or their) productions that one does *per se* in allorepresenting; notably the sort of responsibility one does in representing truly or falsely—in making oneself liable for being right or wrong as to how things are. The rough idea is: those creations exist to fulfil a purpose; they assume the responsibility something would in undertaking to fulfil that purpose. What follows, I hope, will demolish that idea.

3 Selecting

Allorepresenting must accomplish a certain task. Something in its doing must select, or identify, some one way for things to be as the way things were thus represented being. I will call this *the selection task*.

To identify a way for things to be is to fix its reach—what would be a case of it. Selecting is thus tracing a path through a cloud. Suppose we think of a space of ways for things to be. A point in that space is, say, things being such that Pia's Porsche is yellow. Now think of a space of particular cases. Take a proper part of it. Restrict it, say, to all the cases there have been so far. Then that point in the space of ways traces a class of paths through this space (if you like, fixes a sub-space). It traces those paths which connect all the particular cases to which it reaches. *Inter alia*, it traces paths through that proper part, all the cases so far. Now take any particular case not in that proper part—say, things being as they will tomorrow. Three classes of ways for things to be trace that same class of paths through the proper part as our initial way does, but differ in what they do when it comes to this novel case. One class are instanced by it. Another are not. A third do not settle whether they are instanced by it or not. In what class is our initial way? The same question arises for any way for things to be which allorepresenting creates, for example, for being as Sid represented things. Where the selection task is accomplished such questions have answers.

What gives them answers in our own case? I now mention, briefly, two sources of material. First, we are retrospectively sensitive to what we do. We have, as one might put it, the capacity to be abashed. Sid can recognize that, as it turned out, things were as he represented them, would not have been had the Porsche been in the garage when it burned, but are all the same even though it is now mud-covered. Answers to the question how he represented things *could* appeal to what he is thus prepared to recognize. There is at least that source of material.

Retrospectively we stand detached from what we have done—not catching ourselves in the act, but now seeing ourselves as other might. The capacity for such detached stances is also exploited in other ways. We, or some of us, may collectively identify some way for things to be independent of it being a way things were represented on any given occasion. There is such a thing as calling Pia's Porsche yellow. We can then ask what we are prepared to recognize anyway, independent of any episode of presenting something as falling under that generality, what we would, or might, count, what not, as a case of things being that way—what *we* would be prepared to call Pia's Porsche being yellow. How much chrome could you add, for example? We are *jointly* sensitive to such things. We can agree or dispute about them. Room is thereby made for the objectivity of judgement; room for a given case's being one one of a Porsche being yellow to be among the ways things *are*. It is unclear how *else* such room might be made.

For Cartesian thinkers allorepresenting is a project, part of, and aimed at serving, further ones. Such is a second source of material which could effect selection. A Cartesian thinker guides his projects by his perceptions of how the world bears on what the thing to do would be—on which projects to execute, and how. His perceptions reflect an unbounded sensitivity to ways the world does, and might, bear on this. So it is, in particular, with his perceptions of *what* to allorepresent, and how. *We* represent with an agenda. Such agenda may include contributing to, or furthering, further projects in particular ways—for example, saying that whose being so would bear in particular ways on how those further projects *are* to be executed. If such is *on* the agenda, and if the representer succeeds in representing things accordingly, he *will* make the contribution. Conversely, if such is (recognizably) on the agenda, and if he *can* be understood as having represented things accordingly—saying what, if so, would have that bearing—then such is reason so to understand him. In what it would be so to understand him there is material which *could*, *if* applied to identifying a way for him to have represented things, effect selection.

I will elaborate this idea later. For the moment I merely illustrate. Guests are coming. As Pia opens the wines to breathe, Sid sets the table. He has forks and spoons in hand, but seems unable to find knives. Noticing this, Pia says, 'There are knives in the third drawer'. Indeed there are. Suppose, though, that the third drawer had contained Pia's art supplies. These include a fair collection of matte knives (roughly, handles mounting razor blades). One *can* understand there being knives in a drawer so that the presence of matte knives counts as things so being. But one might sometimes understand such talk such that such presence, on its own, would not count as things being as thus represented. When I tell you where the knives are, matte knives *need* not count as specimens of what I mean. The *words* Pia used might be understood in either way. But *she* was to be understood as speaking in aid of what Sid is doing—contributing in the way just scouted to his project's execution. Understand *her* in the first way and there is no such bearing. Understand her in the second and there is. Such contributes at least to tracing a path through the cloud of ways for things to be which contains all those which are there being knives in that drawer on *some* understanding of there so being. Whether this *does*, in fact, achieve selection for things being as Pia represented them may remain an open question for the moment.

4 Agreement

We guide our allorepresenting by what *could* achieve selection. But, to borrow Freud's term, we are not always masters in our own house. When, and how, not?

Frege distinguished the psychology of holding true from the logic of *being* true. Similarly one can distinguish the psychology of holding forth as true from the logic of being as represented. In Adelaide, Sid comes in from the backyard and announces, 'The lamb is on the barbie'. Little Tara screams 'Oh, no!', and runs into the backyard, where she finds her doll safe and sound on the table, while smoke rises from the grill. There is something Tara understood Sid to say. That is a psychological fact. There is something Sid meant to say. That is another. There is then the question what Sid did say, how he is, in fact, *to be* understood. That 'to be', like the 'to' in 'the thing to do', removes us from the psychological. Our concern now is with the logic of being as represented. Such a non-psychological question need not have a determinate answer: there was an amusing misunderstanding, and there is an end on it. But it may. Perhaps Sid said what he meant to, and Tara misunderstood. Or perhaps the other way around.

What answers such a non-psychological question? What makes an answer *right*? A starting point: for there to be allorepresenting is for it to be (made) recognizable. How are we to understand this 'recognizable'? Sid's representing might not be recognizable to a monolingual Latvian, nor to a martian, nor a cat. Such hardly matters. His analyst might recognize what he intended. She might recognize this of still more bizarre performances. Such again does not bear on how he ought to be—is to be—understood to have represented things. There are, though, those who *ought* to be able to understand him; those competent enough, and appreciative enough of his circumstances to do so. There may then be what they would have a *right* to expect if then so addressed; how a competent understander who knew what he should have of the circumstances would reasonably have taken Sid to be representing things. So, the idea is, *did* Sid represent things being?

Who are these people? In the example, most Australians, one would suppose, and some of the rest of us (most of us, if initiates in Aussie practice and patois). But what matters is this. You and I (and most Australians, and others) share a sense of what to say in cases like Sid and Tara's. It is a sense which indefinitely many other thinkers—perhaps not all—either share, or could be brought to share through sufficient familiarity with our ways of allorepresenting. Given the *psychological* facts—the actual facts of our agreement in such matters—there is such a thing as what a competent, appreciative audience for Sid's words *would* be; such a way for a thing, or group, to be as *being such an audience*. *That* there is is something we can recognize. Given what it would be to be this, we can also recognize this to be a way for a thing to be which *is* instanced. There are, further, recognizable facts as to how one who was this way would understand Sid, and his representing, were he so addressed. Such (non-psychological) facts would of course be recognizable to one who was the way in question. They are recognizable to us because we are that way.

For *any* allorepresenting there is its audience—the sort of thing equipped and placed to recognize it for what it is. To belong to Sid's audience is to instance the just-mentioned way for a thing to be. In other cases, it would be to instance being competent and appreciative *in re* the representing there occurring. In any case, the audience is, in principle, indefinitely extendible. Sid, as any Cartesian thinker, shares with his audience those retrospective abilities I called a capacity to be abashed. Such can be directed in concert at what Sid has done. *Just* this is what allows for effecting the selection task for his allorepresenting. So it is with a *thinker's* allorepresenting. It should be stressed that *this* way of failing to be master in one's own house, so of relying on others for effecting a selection task, is reserved for Cartesian thinkers. It works where a way the representer ought reasonably to be taken is as doing what a Cartesian thinker *might* be doing (in the circumstances). If the representer is not a Cartesian thinker, then, while mistaking it for one might be *understandable*, he cannot have been to be taken as so performing.

Where allorepresenting *has* an audience (present sense), where there is such a thing as what it would be to belong to it, to belong to the audience is to have sufficient insight into how the representing *is* to be understood, and to have such insight is to belong to it. When it comes to cases the audience is the measure of what insight is here. That there *is* an audience may be manifest in its (extendible) agreement. Just what is the audience's role? Following Frege we may take it as intrinsic to any given way for things to be to reach just as it does. So fix a way and nothing extrinsic to it, so no audience can make *it* reach in one way rather than another. But what way a given way for things to be is is *one* question. What way is such that Sid represented things as that way is another, as is what way *one* speaks of where he speaks of lamb being on the barbie. If an audience provides no answer to the first sort of question, it *does* provide the answer to the second. For a way for things to be to be the way Sid represented things being (in speaking of his barbie) is for it to reach to particular cases just as his audience (in the above sense) would be prepared to recognize his representing (what he did) as reaching.

Any allorepresenting needs its audience, whether thinkers or not. For a Cartesian thinker's representing, the audience is of a certain sort. It *shares* a capacity: one, as I put it, to be abashed. This capacity can be directed collectively at any instance of relevant representing. It issues in acknowledgement of particular cases as thus reached or not (not determined). Just here, in what a thinking audience *would* expect, the crucial step is taken from the psychological to the non-psychological—here from holding forth to being true. What the audience would do, where it is *this* audience, is no longer a psychological generalization, nor a prediction. It is not like a statement about what Sid, or Tara, or the average Australian would do. It is about how *anyone* would respond to Sid if getting things *right*.

Our shared sensitivity to the conceptual performs this step for us. We achieve selection tasks in ways which are the reasonable ones for the sort of representing *we* engage in. *Our* sensitivity to the conceptual, such as it is, cannot be enlisted to perform this step for an unthinker. If there are (parallels to) psychological generalizations to be made about the unthinker's doings, such need not be refractory to us. If there are patterns in its responsiveness to the environment, we need not be blind to these. But what it *would* thus do does not yet take us from the psychological to the logical, as something must if there is to be allorepresenting. Such a step must be taken by the unthinker on its own, or anyway left on its own by us. And the unthinker's mere sensitivity to the presence of yellow, or pigs, in its surroundings, whatever such may be, gives no right to construe any of its responses as episodes of representing something *as being* yellow, or a pig, rather than as simply detecting yellow's, or porcine, presence. They effect no selection from within the cloud in which that class of paths, cases of something being yellow are but an element. The unthinker's responses in its (presumably) hospitable environment give no right to extrapolate from that sub-region of particular cases to the space as a whole. It would be anthropomorphism to construe its responding as it does to pigs as, for example, its *telling* us, or its peers, that a pig is about. If it were to present particular cases as falling under generalities, the fact that *we* would be inclined to call what it is doing detecting pigs, or yellow, gives no right to take *those* generalities to be at all like the ones we thus get in mind.

5 Deference

An unthinker could not take the step from the psychological (or mechanical) to the logical in the way just sketched. The unthinker *could not* be to be recognized as guiding execution of its representing as a Cartesian thinker would or might. Such could not be the right thing to suppose of it. The Cartesian thinker's way of tracing a path through the space of particular cases could not be the unthinker's. But perhaps the unthinker need do no such thing. Perhaps he/it can simply contract the work out, defer the selection task to some other source. One idea along these lines would be: there might be a vehicle, identifiable independent of how it represents things, which *as such* represents things as being some given way; and which, in being the unthinker's vehicle, would make it so that *he/it* so represented things.

Birds build nests but fail Descartes' tests. So, Descartes thought, building nests requires no intelligence. Who would think otherwise? Things *are* otherwise, he thought, when it comes to holding conversations. If not all allorepresenting is holding conversation, perhaps some, like nest-building, is achievable by unthinkers. Something else would do the work for the unthinker that thinking does for us. The above is one idea of what that something else might be: vehicles. These, the idea is, would relieve the unthinker of the burden of selecting on its own. Its incapacity would then not matter.

English sentences *might* seem a model for such vehicles. An English sentence as such represents things as being a given way. It speaks as such of that way. The sentence 'Monkeys fly' speaks of what it does used or not, whether I take it to do so, speak English, exist, or not. If it speaks of monkeys being flyers, then, where I speak English, it would do so in my mouth. If *it* represents things as being a given way then, the idea is, so do I in speaking it. The idea concludes: where I thus so represent things, for things to be as I represented them is just for monkeys to be flyers. If English sentences so work, then, perhaps, so might other things, among which things which would so work produced by (suitable) unthinkers. That English thus models deference is an idea I hope now to dispose of. In its place I hope to put this Fregean idea: the *only* way for a would-be content-bearer to come by the content of a thought, or of an element in one—to contribute to representings-as so as to make them somehow about, say, relevant things being flyers—is for it so to function, or to be for so functioning, in the expressing of thoughts (by thinkers). No other life it might lead could confer such content on it. In other words, the only content-bearers there are (where content is a way of representing-as) are thinkers' vehicles.

The sentence 'Monkeys fly' *does* say that monkeys fly. It speaks of them as flyers. But in what aspect of the verb? Shifting aspects may produce illusion. The aspect in which sentences say, or speak, stands out in other verbs. Robin, showing his cousins from Peoria the Batcave, comes to the Batmobile. Pointing at levers and buttons on the dash, he says 'This one ejects the seats. This one fires the grappling hooks. This one autodials the commissioner'. Levers and buttons lack initiative. It will be a long wait before a lever undertakes a project. Or so we hope. Such does not reflect on what Robin said. That lever is *for* ejecting the seats. It is the thing to pull to eject. If it is in working order, you (new aspect of the verb) will then eject.

Such it is for levers to eject. This contrasts with the verb's reading in 'Don't let little Tarquin near the Batmobile. He always ejects the seats'. It is equally a reading of 'fire' and 'autodial' as above. It is one reading, too, of 'say'. It fits the case where we speak of the sentence 'Monkeys fly' as saying that monkeys fly. That sentence (used neat) is *for* saying that monkeys fly, anyway for speaking of their being flyers. If, on an occasion, you wish to say, in speaking English, that monkeys fly, this sentence is, *ceteris paribus*, just the thing for you. Use it in speaking English, in circumstances in which you would say something, and *ceteris paribus*, such is what you will say, or at least speak of.

If Sid says, or said last Tuesday, that monkeys fly, such *may* be reason to think they do. If the sentence 'Monkeys fly' says that monkeys fly, such cannot be reason so to think. The *sentence*, unlike Sid, is the wrong sort of thing to give such reason. Tarquin always ejects the seats. He last ejected them, just as Robin was leaving the Gotham Diner. The sentence cannot have said last Tuesday that monkeys fly, unless this means that it has not, in the interim, changed meaning. To say, where 'say' has that past tense, is to incur liability to success or failure—to getting things right or wrong—of a sort for which a sentence is ineligible.

For an English sentence to *say* something is for it to have a role in the lives of (some) thinkers. It is for it to be a means for *them* to make certain allorepresenting recognizable to their fellows; thus to execute successfully certain of their projects of representing. There is no hint of an idea here that sentences might lift the burden of effecting selection from a being which *could not*, on its own, find its way through, or select from, the space of possibilities, of ways for things to be, as we do in aiming as we do to represent things as some given way, and in recognizing what we have done as representing with a certain reach. English *eases* a burden for those who *can* perform it, but does not lift it. Sid said that monkeys fly in saying 'Monkeys fly' only if he aimed, or ought to have been taken to be aiming, at saying *that*; only if 'Monkeys fly' was used, or ought to have been taken to be used, for achieving the success which would thus be aimed at. He would not have said so if, as Frege puts it, the necessary seriousness were missing, for example, if he *could* not properly be taken so to have aimed.

English has a syntax. It thus generates an indefinitely large set of vehicles, its sentences, from a smaller set of building blocks by fixed rules. What a sentence says, or speak of, is then fixed by what its blocks do, plus the rules which structure them in it. Some ideas for unthinking representers-as require these to have an indefinitely large set of vehicles they might produce. If perceptual experience represented things as being given ways, for example, it would need to be able to represent things as any of indefinitely many different ones. So then it would need a stock of vehicles built from a smaller set of blocks by some fixed rules. What a vehicle said would thus be fixed by what its blocks contribute to this. Now, it may seem, content may accrue to a vehicle merely by virtue of accruing anyway to its blocks.

But if Frege is right, this analogy breaks down. If a building block is to contribute to representing-as, what has accrued to it anyway, independent of this representing-as, then what has accrued to it anyway must be no less than that of representing-as. In representing-as, truth is made to turn in a particular way on how things are. An element of such representing makes truth so turn, in part, in that way. Being what *so* functions in the context of representing *things* as a certain way—making truth turn, full stop, in that way on how things are—is what a building block would need to be already to function in the imagined way as a building block at all. Representing-as cannot emerge from mere syntactic structuring). Combine what effect-represents the presence of something puce and what effect-represents the presence of a Porsche however you like, and all you get so far is something which effect-represents the presence of something puce, and the presence of a Porsche. What a given vehicle would require for representing some given thing as puce is, *inter alia*, a block which, in context, represent as puce. If it does so in context by virtue of content it has anyway, then that block must already be what functions to *make truth turn,* in part, on how things are. It is difficult to see how any block could have come by this through interactions with the environment which are any less than roles in representing it as being thus and so.

In 1882 Frege wrote:

I do not think that the formation of concepts can precede judgements, because this presupposes an autonomous existence of concepts, but I think concepts arise through the decomposition of a judgeable content.

(1882: p. 118)

Concepts *arise* through decomposing whole thoughts. A thought is true of *things*, where there is no question 'Which?' It is true of things, so true, *tout court*. A (non-zero-place) concept is true *of a* thing. Truth-of, Frege notes, can be understood only in terms of *truth*. For the concept (*a thing*) *being puce* to be true, say, of Ed is for it to be true that Ed is puce. A concept (as here spoken of) is a common feature in a range of thoughts—for example, that Ed is puce, that Pia is puce, that that torus is puce . . . It is *one* way each reaches to particular cases. It fixes a generality under which all such thoughts fall: making truth turn on what is puce. It just *is* a common feature of those thoughts. There is no such feature unless there are such thoughts. Concepts *thus* cannot precede thoughts.

So, too, for speaking of. There is no speaking of a thing as puce except in the context of saying something as to what is or is not puce, or, more broadly, representing things as some way the being which turns somehow or other on things being or not puce. Speaking of a thing as puce (expressing the concept of being puce) is not something which can precede speaking of *things* (catholic reading) as thus and so. So speaking of a thing as being puce, expressing that concept, is something a building block could do only in the context of its role in the expression of whole thoughts. A building block might do that in isolation only in that aspect of 'speak of' in which to do so is to play a role in the expressing of whole thoughts. Speaking of a certain way for *a* thing to be thus cannot precede the expression of whole thoughts. So the accrual of content to building blocks cannot precede the accrual of content to expressions of them. What could not select a thought for a whole vehicle to express—a way for things to be as how *it* represents things being—could not select a way for *a* thing to be as what some building block contributes to such representing.

6 Recognition and Responsibility

Where allorepresenting is a project, making recognizable the representing *done* may involve making recognizable *what* project is thereby executed. If it is one of aiding further projects, or serving further ends, *such* may be what needs making recognizable if it is to be made recognizable *how* things are then represented being. Those further aims and ends would then play a role in achieving selection for the representing done. *How* things were represented being could vary according to what those further aims were. Such would make allorepresenting like conversing and unlike building nests. This section expands that idea.

In speech acts, words are our allies in achieving recognition. We can exploit their meanings to *help* make recognizable how *we* mean to represent things as being. Such departs from the idea of English as a model for deferred selecting. Words are *aids* in achieving recognition. For them to aid as they do need not be for the way we *do* represent things being, when there is such success, just to be the way they do anyway. Their role as aids need not be to be, on their own, the expression of some given thought. Nor need it be fixed by their meanings alone just what thought would be expressed in using them. Such is an idea exploited to great effect in one way by David Kaplan (1989), and in a different way by Cora Diamond (1991). It has appeared here so far in the idea, for example, that there need be no *one* way one speaks of things being in speaking of there being knives in the third drawer. I now add: perhaps the ability to stand towards a vehicle as thus described—to use it to express what need not be just what the vehicle anyway expresses (two different aspects of 'express' here) may be intrinsic to the ability to author representing-as at all.

Words which aid recognition need not do so by virtue of their meanings; nor at all. In a restaurant in Abbeville Pia asks for '*ortalans*'. Of *course* one cannot order *ortalans*, or not in *this* establishment, or in this *salle*, or season. But of course, too, this is not what Pia (an anglophone) meant. The way she is eyeing the *oursins* shows her to mean them. Habituated to tourists, the waiter simply brings Pia her *oursins*. Pia managed to make recognizable what way for things to be she was representing as wished for. She managed to request *oursins*. The sentence 'I would like the *ortalans*' speaks of a different way for things to be. But not every use of it to allorepresent speaks of that way. Even where it does, *that* it does so need not be enough to identify how it represents things as being.

In the restaurant, the waiter arrives with their *plateaux de fruits de mer*—*bulots* for Sid, *oursins* for Pia. But he looks perplexed. Clearly he has forgotten his orders. Seeing this, Sid tells the waiter that Pia ordered the *oursins*. Suppose Pia garbled things, or Sid had done the talking. Are things as Sid thus represented them? If Sid were reporting Pia's progress with speech therapy, or with her pathological shyness (say, to a worried mother), the answer might be 'No'. But here Sid's words are in the service of a further project, placing orders. In contributing to such an enterprise, one is hardly to be held responsible for who did the talking. One *can* understand ordering *oursins* so that who did the talking does not matter. So here, for reasons stated, one *is* so to understand Sid.

To *hold* Sid to have represented things in one way rather than another is to hold him *responsible* for something—here something as to how things are. There is a way things had better be if he is to be let off with discharging responsibilities assumed. For *what* is he reasonably held to account here? Where should his wishes be acceded to, aims honoured, where not? Is he accountable for who did the talking; liable to praise or blame accordingly? Is such reasonably reckoned part of the bargain in the liability he went in for in representing to the waiter as he did? Above, I suppose, the answer is, 'No'. He made clear what message he had to offer. He need be, so is not to be, held responsible for more.

Responsibility gives a reading to that 'ought to be taken' in that step, in section 4, from the psychological to the logical, from holding to being true, the step in the 'way one *did* allorepresent things being is the way one ought to have been taken to have'. There is what Pia is reasonably held responsible for in then lending Sid her Porsche (at least what one should have foreseen). There is the responsibility Sid undertook, *signed on for*, in saying Pia to have ordered *oursins*. Allorepresenting is among a thinker's means for undertaking responsibility. There is then what it is *fair* to hold him to have signed on for in using those means then. How he represented things as being is fixed thereby.

Sid makes recognizable two things about his allorepresenting. First, he is to be taken as representing things being as he does *in* representing them *as* being a certain way, namely, such that Pia ordered the *oursins*. In his execution of his project, the words he used are assigned the task of making *this* recognizable. Second, he is to be taken as representing things as being that way whose instancing would have a certain bearing on the way to execute a certain further project—the perplexed waiter's. He is to be—or asks to be—assigned responsibility accordingly. Perhaps he *could not* be doing both these things jointly. Such is *one* way for it not to be possible to take him as he asks to be. Perhaps one *cannot* understand *ordered oursins* so that whether Pia spoke does not bear on this, or so that whether she did *thus* bears on what the waiter is to do. But suppose we can. Sid ought not to be held to be taking on responsibility he makes *recognizable* that he is not signing on for. One ought not so to rely on him. In which case, these two features of what Sid was to be taken to be doing jointly identify what it would be for things to be that created way, being as he thus represented things. It is that way which reaches to just those cases in which the world is such as to bear as it was to be supposed to bear on what the waiter was to do, where things so being is understandable (*might* count) as Pia having ordered *oursins*. It matters not whether it has another name.

Sid represents things as he does *in* speaking of them as a certain way there is anyway for things to be: such that Pia ordered *oursins*. He speaks on a particular understanding of her having done so. *One* way to picture this would be as filling-in. That way he spoke of, Pia having ordered *oursins*, reaches as such in a certain way. Some range of cases is thus reached. Some other range fails to be. Other cases remain undetermined. What it *is* for Pia to have ordered *oursins* yields as such no verdict where Sid alone spoke to the waiter. The particular understanding on which Sid spoke fills in some undetermined cases: on it some of these are reached, some fail to be reached, by that way he spoke of.

If this is how things are, one might get a further idea. If Sid's work of representing fills in understanding of that way he speaks of, so that *his* representing things as that way reaches differently than that way on its own, then, perhaps, on some occasion his representing simply fails to accomplish any such work. Then things being as he represented them would reach exactly as things being such that Pia ordered *oursins* does on its own. Perhaps an unthinking allorepresenter could represent like that. What Sid thus did contingently would just be, necessarily, its lot.

In what sort of case would Sid have done no such work? One might think: when Sid spoke to the waiter, his talk of Pia ordering had an agenda. Our talk often has much less of one. Suppose Sid simply wrote a postcard to Ed back home: 'Wonderful dinner last night. I ordered *bulots*, Pia ordered *oursins*'. Not much there by way of further purpose to be served. But now, must Pia have done the talking for things to be as Sid wrote? Nothing in his writing this gives one any reason to suppose so. So if she did, things are as Sid said. If Sid spoke for her, things still are. But this *is* a special understanding of Pia having ordered *oursins*. What it is for her to have done so does not, on its own, *decide* whether she needed to do the talking. What it would be for her to have ordered can be understood in either way. A case where no filling in was done would be a rather special one. Perhaps we get closer to it in those rarefied situations where, as philosophers or semanticists, we ask what one *would* call ordering *oursins*, what not—projects of classifying cases (though we seldom get far with them). To direct one's 'Pia ordered *oursins*' so as for it to be understood as contributing to such a project would not be to represent aimlessly, but, on the contrary, to bend one's representing in a very special way to the service of further aims and projects. If such can be done, it is surely available only to one who, by the same token, has a capacity for filling in.

Sid's filling in as he does is the exercise of a capacity. Such is a capacity to direct (orchestrate) his representing so as to achieve representing in some one way rather than another—to fill in in one way rather than another, if such is to be the image. He can direct so as to select. For this he must be sensitive to what there is to aim at—to what would be achieved in directing things in some one way as opposed to others. Thus that he can assume responsibility, be held to account. Still retaining the image, he must also be sensitive to the possibilities for filling in— to when one *can* understand ordering *oursins* in various ways, and *how* one can. For one so equipped, achieving *no* filling in is just directing one's representing in one way rather than others he might. It is just one case among others, the null case, drawing on the same capacities—the null case, a degenerate case if you like.

Sid represents as he does *in* representing things as a certain uncreated way. Sensitivity to the possibilities for filling in the reach of that way is just sensitivity to how that way reaches, an ability to acknowledge *it* for what it is. Such belongs to a capacity to represent things as that way *punkt*, independent of how one represents things in doing so. Even if Sid deployed a vehicle which, as such, speaks of being that way (in the only aspect in which a vehicle could), still, it is not automatic that every use of that vehicle in representing (or attempting to) is a case of representing things as that way. (Recall Pia and *ortalans*.) Sid has a capacity to direct his representing so as to deploy that vehicle for representing, in *his* representing, that which it speaks of. It is thus that he can be credited correctly with representing *in* representing things *as* that way which is the very one of which that vehicle speaks (even, sometimes, when he does not so aim).

The unthinking representer supposed above is *saddled* with its representing. It represents blindly. It is not sensitive to possibilities for filling in a way it represents things being. For, unlike Sid, it is not equipped to acknowledge any way for things to be as the way it is—as required for filling in. As we have seen (Section 3), such equipment is proprietary to Cartesian thinkers. If *it* could represent things as that way some vehicle it produces represents them, that would not be just one special case among others of the ways open to it to direct its representing. At which point the comparison between Sid and this hypothesized unthinker collapses. The unthinker brings nothing to representing, or nothing which has yet emerged, to make its use of any vehicle representing things as being any way, no matter what the vehicle may do as such.

7 Force

Those ways *we* can represent things as being—so those ways we can take things to have been thus represented (whether by us, or by *any* representer)—are such that where we represent things as some such way, it might be any of many things to be as thereby represented. The last section concerned the capacities drawn on in such representing. Its idea can also be put in terms of force. For Sid to have represented Pia as having ordered the *oursins* in the way he did is for him to have assigned that way for things to be a certain status: as to be *counted* as among the ways things are where its being instanced is understood as it would be for certain purposes. Assigning status cannot be just more representing-as. This, too, would await a status. To coin a term, it is doing one's representing-as with *force*—here, in assuming responsibility, vouching for the status thus assigned.

As force is usually conceived it comes in a small range of varieties: assertive, interrogative, imperative, optative, and so on. Things change if, as per above, *in* representing things as some given uncreated way there is for things to be, *one* can represent them as any of indefinitely many different ways. Throughout one would present that way *in* which he so represented things with a certain force. But it would need to be a different force in each case. He would assign *that* way for things to be a status *in re* being among the ways things are. But that status would be, not being a way things are *full stop*, but *counting* as a way things are when you understand things so being in a particular way (in the previous section's image, with a particular permissible filling-in). Force would vary here—even in an assertive, or an imperative, or another case—according to the responsibilities signed on for, as identified, for example, as per the previous section, in terms of projects to be taken as contributed to.

There is thus a selection task for force paralleling that for what way things were represented being. How Sid represented things being *in* saying Pia to have ordered *oursins* is fixed, not just by this being the way he spoke of, but also by with what force this was presented—*how* it was presented as counting as a way things are. An unthinker is as little equipped to effect the task for force on its own account as it is the selection task for ways for things to be.

An unthinker would be *overcome* by allorepresenting, as a Tourette's victim is overcome with blurtings. The expletives are not the sufferer's. The allorepresenting, one might well think, would no more be the unthinker's. Is there some default force such unthinking representing might have? Perhaps it is a 'purely generic' assertive (or imperative, or optative) force. 'Purely generic' here would be abstracting from all particularities of ways of presenting that way for things to be in which the unthinker represented things as it did. The status assigned would be: *a way things are no matter* how *you understand things so being*. The usual way of thinking of such abstraction is in terms of universal quantification: the way things are on *all* understandings of things being it.

The idea here is familiar in philosophy (see Clarke 1972). To paraphrase Clarke, to see whether Pia *really* ordered the *oursins*, we stand back from any mundane, local concerns such as how to tell the waiter what to do, and, purely considering the concept *ordering oursins* as such, and the world as such, ask whether Pia's doings do, or do not, fall under that concept. Whether there *is* such a project of pure inquiry is controversial. As indicated in the last section, *if* there is, it would not be one reached by *abstracting* from all the particular varieties of assertive force we have now seen there to be (all the ways of counting a way for things to be as a way things are). It would just be another particular way of so counting things; one to be applied where very special ends were to be served. And, as we saw in Section 3, classifying things according to the reach of some way as such for things to be anyway draws on the full resources of a Cartesian thinker. So such abstraction, if possible at all, does not relieve the unthinker of a burden. Nor is the burden one the unthinker would have the capacity to discharge.

Perhaps, then, the task of force-selection is performed *for* him/it. We already saw one idea for this: deference to vehicles. We saw already that *that* idea cannot work. So perhaps the work is done by whatever *thrusts* allorepresenting on our unthinker in saddling him/it with (producing or being) some vehicle. Putting things in terms of force, though, brings out a point of Frege's. It is that no *vehicle* as such can impose a force on any representing (a version of the point above that what gives force to representing-as cannot be just more representing-as). To put the point one way, any way for an instance of 'Pia ordered *oursins*' to fail to be an assertion is a way for 'It's true that Pia ordered *oursins*' to fail to be one. When assertive force is absent, 'It's true' will not restore it, nor will 'I assert that', nor any other form of words. *Mutatis mutandis* for any other force. In another version Frege tells us that there is no assertive force 'when the required seriousness is missing'. Seriousness is not conferred by a vehicle. What is in question is the seriousness with which it is produced. A thing cannot produce the necessary seriousness by having representing *thrust* on it. It is the (would-be) *representer* who (which) must be serious. This, as we have seen, the unthinker *cannot* be on its own. This idea of abstraction, and of resulting generic forces, thus leads nowhere.

Might the unthinker then, perhaps, represent things *as* ways they are or not (though not itself thereby representing truly or falsely), while doing so with *no* force? When might a vehicle be produced forcelessly? A rhythm poet, or dadaist, might produce English sentences simply for their sound—the sentence 'Red balls roll', say, simply for the way it rolls off the tongue. Or a graffiti artist might spray such a sentence on garage doors for its elegant shape. Most red balls probably do roll, if not made of glue. *Such* is not what (if anything) makes the poet right. If his interest in sound is pure enough, then while he wrote a sentence which speaks of a way for things to be, he did not thereby engage in any representing-as at all. And if, as we stare at the garage door admiringly, a red ball rolls by, well, what a coincidence! But it is *just* a coincidence. As *some* philosophers have it, in (a) perceptual experience the world is represented to us as a certain way. If we see a pig under an oak, say, then perhaps as such that a pig is beneath an oak. But if this representing is conceived as forceless, then it might equally well represent things as any other way, say, as such that cool waters run deep, or Pia drives a Porsche. Experience's so representing things may *mean* (factively), effect-represent, or indicate, or make likely, that a pig is beneath an oak. But if the representing here is forceless, then it is not through its content that such meaning is effected. It is not as if a reason thus created for thinking a pig beneath an oak might be that experience, or this representing in it, might be *right*. Whether it is right or wrong *cannot* matter here: without force there is no way for it to be either. Representing-as thus cancels out. Representing Porsches as fast would do as well as representing a pig as beneath an oak for nature's signal that a pig is beneath an oak. For what meant in this sense of meaning to represent things *as* the way it means they are would just be a curious accident. Force is part and parcel of the step by which we move from the psychological to the logical, from mere effect-representing, or its relatives, to that *three-place* relation, representing-as.

8 Finding and Presenting

There is finding, or marking, instancings, or *the* instancings, of some given way for things to be; and there is presenting things *as* some given such way. The one thing is not the other. But some might hope for the second to emerge out of the first. This section explores that idea.

An unthinker lacks capacities which, so far, appear essential for allorepresenting; *any* capacity which might permit that leap from the psychological (or its counterparts) to the logical, from the psychology of holding forth, to the logic of being true, with which allorepresenting *per se* engages. How might unthinking representing-as even appear possible? One prominent idea is that allorepresenting might emerge out of (the maintaining of) patterns of effect-representing, aided, perhaps, by the point of maintaining them. The allorepresenting would be by, or in, that in which such patterns were maintained. This section explores that idea.

The simplest patterns are generalizations, the simplest generalizations universal. Those empty seats in the theatre (or their presence) effect-represent casting Sid in the lead role. Empty seats in a theatre might always do that, if Sid got around enough. Or, to complicate things, they might usually, or normally, or (other modifier) do so. So far, it is the presence of those empty seats which does the representing. If allorepresenting emerged here, what would do it? Frege writes:

No-one can be prohibited from adopting any arbitrarily occurring event or object as a sign for whatever.

(1892b: 26)

Empty seats *could* be appropriated as a sign that Sid plays the lead. They would thus be a *vehicle* of representing-as. What would do the appropriating in the allorepresenting that emerged here? Whose vehicle would it be? It is sometimes thought that the question needs no answer; vehicles can get on on their own. We have seen reasons to think that idea leads nowhere. Bracket them for the nonce.

Such simple patterns are no improvement on the individual case. They put nothing in play not already there. Two problems. First, if we read nature's messages well enough—if we know what empty seats would mean (effect-represent), then their sight gives us good reason to suppose that Sid is in the lead. If allorepresenting emerged from their effect-representing, then, recognizing this last, we might also recognize that allorepresenting for what it was. It, too, might give us reason to suppose that Sid is in the lead. But no different, or other, reason than we had simply in recognizing the effect-representing; that we would have had if blind to the allorepresenting thus emerging. *This* allorepresenting of Sid as in the lead is no better reason to take him to be in it than that given by the effect-representing from which it emerged; whereas allorepresenting is the sort of thing, by nature, for giving reason of a new and distinctive sort. With this we have Sid's *word* for it. If, as a rule, when Sid says 'Roses are red' this effect-represents a spent compressor in Pia's Porsche, the reason this gives to think her Porsche thus in need depends on the reasons, if any, to think this case of Sid's speech an exception to the rule. If we have his word for it, the reason this gives depends on the extent to which Sid can be counted on to be speaking sincerely, judiciously, knowledgeably, where the point is not that such things, if they occur, might effect-represent a defective compressor.

If Sid tells Pia that her Porsche needs a new compressor, there are things one might recognize his performance to effect-represent without yet recognizing what allorepresenting thus occurred, or that any did—such as successful speech therapy. That Pia's Porsche needs a new compressor is not one of these. If nature *does* hold such a message in Sid's performance, we would have to be *much* better at reading nature's messages to get this one than we need to be to recognize Sid's allorepresenting for what it was. But if do now recognize it for what it was, then Sid's *word* for it may give us a reason we did not already have. We need only recognize his word as good. He represents himself as having settled the issue. We need not ourselves know how such issues are to be settled (independent of taking someone's word for it). We may nonetheless see *in Sid*—in his integrity, sagacity, and so on—that he is doing what he purports to be doing: giving his word for what he has settled. What we thus see about Sid is not likely to *effect*-represent Pia's Porsche needing a new compressor. But if it is how things are, then the Porsche *is* thus in need.

(A related point. Where there *is* allorepresenting, what it *is* and what *it* effect-represents are absolutely independent. Sid's telling Pia that her Porsche needs a new compressor may effect-represent a checkered (or checker-flagged) past, or a bad hangover—and it may do this regularly, or normally, or usually—without his thereby allorepresenting things as these ways.)

The second problem in brief. In effect-representing Sid in the lead role, those empty seats represented a certain instancing of a certain way for things to be: such that Sid was in the lead. If they did that, they *ipso facto* effect-represented the instancings of countless other ways for things to be—countless co-denizens of clouds within the conceptual that *Sid being in the lead* inhabits. Such would remain so if empty seats *always* effect-represented Sid in the lead—wherever, that is, nature is so arranged. Effect-representing does not perform the selection task. Nor would generalizations of the kind just scouted.

But if allorepresenting has not yet emerged, perhaps we are looking at too simple patterns. Here is another idea. Sometimes we can say: A effect-represents (or *would* effect-represent) B *if all is/were going right*. That needle on the gauge effect-represents the tank's being half full if all is going right. Those hands on the dial (or their present position) effect-represents its being 10 o'clock local time if all is going right (if Sid remembered to reset his watch). Such patterns, if any, are those from which someone *might* think allorepresenting could emerge. I will expand that idea.

There are designs which, if realized, would make for A effect-representing B. A device, or mechanism, or system, or (perhaps) phenomenon may realize such a design. Man, or nature, may provide such devices (and so on). (Examples above.) Sometimes by this design, sometimes, perhaps not, the device produces, on occasion, a certain outcome (or type of outcome), A. The output may be a product—a signal, say, or an effect—or it may be the device's going into a certain state, A (or of type A). When such a device is working as per design (as *any* device is liable, on occasion, not to do), A, as thus produced, effect-represents B (what it was designed to). A would occur *only* if there were B to thank. Such a device may be *for* realizing this design in this sense: but for some need thus to connect A and B, the device would not have been created. I will call such a device a B-detector: where the device produces A as outcome, you can bet on B's occurrence (*if* all went as per design). Bs are historical occurrences, for example, of porcine presence. What the device detects is thus particular *instancings* of things being a certain way, for example, such that a pig is present.

Depending on what it was detecting, a detector might need to exploit compositionality. If, say, it were detecting where animate things were, it would need indefinitely many dedicated outcomes for each of indefinitely many arrays of locations relative to it at which there might be such things for it to detect. Composing outcomes would be called for. For present purposes such changes nothing.

A design might also be for (as I will speak) *locating* (cases of) B: not just for making it so that A, if it occurred, would effect-represent B, but also for making it so that, all working as per design, B, if suitably occurring would be effect-represented by A. So if B is (suitably) occurring, you can bet on A, again all going as per design. Now the hope is, either for detectors, or for locators, that, in detecting, or locating, as the case may be, they will also be representing things as being that way whose instances are thus detected or located.

On one notion of *device*, a device for detecting (or locating) would work in the first instance by responsiveness to *proximal* provocation. It would effect-represent such provocation. If allorepresenting were to emerge from its workings, one might see it as simply representing things as being such that there is such provocation—in this sense simply representing the proximal. But in most cases of interest, the device will be for detecting, or locating, the distal, such as porcine presence. When it works as per design, it will effect-represent those distal things too. And the hope will be that those ways for things to be whose instancings it detects or locates will be the ways it allorepresents things being. What is thus responsive to the distal *in* its responsiveness to the proximal is inherently subject to what would be for it ringers: there might be the right proximal provocation without the wanted distal happenings, and *vice versa*.

Our samples, so far, are man-made; but such devices can be natural. Pigs chew straw, it is said in some parts, when it is about to rain. In perceiving, it is sometimes said, we experience the world being represented (to us) as being thus and so. What of this case? Pia sees the pig before her. Her doing so is thanks, *inter alia*, to there being one. So it effect-represents there being one. *Thus* far all is in place for her to be a pig detector, her seeing a pig being the outcome which would be detection. But it takes no *design* to realize this connection, *a fortiori* not one which works via responsiveness to the proximal. There is no such thing as her seeing a pig failing to effect-represent presence of that pig. So, though I have tried to remain ecumenical on the crucial point here (not to anticipate routes by which *someone* might see representing-as as emerging), Pia's case to be a detector by virtue of her capacity to *see* pigs sits ill with our present notion of a detector—one designed to fit the intuition that *nature* might make representing-as emerge.

Design comes into the picture here when it comes to *locating* cases of porcine presence. What needs explaining is not that when Pia sees a pig there is a pig, but rather that she does such a thing at all. Indeed, Pia (if adequately sighted) is such that, by design, when a pig is before her (and she is looking), all going well, she will see it. Such is no thanks to *her* responses to proximal provocation (though it may depend on some processor's responses). Nor, correlatively, is *this* capacity exposed to ringers: the indicated outcome with no pig before her. Nor to a ringer for *no* pig (hence a pig) which she experiences visually without thereby seeing a pig.

If Pia sees a pig, then, though this does effect-represent porcine presence, such does not bear on the reason she thus gains for taking there to be a pig before her. Her reason gained is not given by the fact of her seeing a pig, but rather by what she sees—a pig before her—which she can recognize as a case of a pig being before her (as being such that a pig *is* before her). As Frege notes, such recognition is a function of thought, not vision. What is gained is reason so to suppose—nothing short of *proof* that there is a pig—which need not consist in *reasons* so to suppose. Such reason gained, considerations of effect-representing could add nothing, could not so much as *be* reason so to suppose. If representing-as emerged from this effect-representing, it would offer *exactly* that much.

Things would be different if for Pia to see the pig is for her to be in, not just that state, but some other visual state—one, say, of being appeared to *thus*—which she could conceivably be in even were there no pig. Then it needs explaining how *this* state in fact effect-represents a pig before her (when it does).

A design is called for; one whose realizing would maintain the right relation (all going well). A design for given proximal responsiveness seems indicated. With *this* state as the indicated outcome Pia fits the model of a pig detector. If allorepresenting ever does emerge out of effect-representing, conditions might now be ripe for this. Such allorepresenting might even have a point. It might give Pia reason to suppose of what *this* state is visual awareness of that *this* time it effect-represents what it ought, porcine presence (though it is hard to see how this could ever be good reason). Reason the more, I suggest, to find this a bad picture of perception. For present purposes, though, I simply mark this as the picture in which the idea of representing-as in perceptual experience *might* look promising.

Back to the general question how representing-as might emerge. What I now want to stress is the distance by which detecting instancings of some way for things to be, or locating *its* instancings, falls short of presenting things as being that way, or placing things under given generalities—as one does in representing-as. Such will bear particularly on the second problem above. A good way into the matter is the following. A detector (or locator) works according to a particular design; a design for detecting whatever it is that it detects. It works via the proximal, and it works in a particular way. A pig detector, for example, may be sensitive in its outcomes to a pig's distinctive snout: whether it produces that outcome which is to effect-represent porcine presence depends on whether it has detected (or done what, for it, ought to be detecting) such a snout. And it detects such snouts by marks of such which, by design, would be proximally accessible to it, once again, all going well. But by what marks, or means, such things as pigs or Porsches, yellow or snores, *are* detectable depends on the environment. Equally for anything else liable to be *detectably* present or not in the sub-lunary world we inhabit. So a condition for a detector, or locator, so much as *being* that is that it work in an environment hospitable to its ways. This point entered the picture already, as we saw, with the very idea of proximity.

You *can* tell a pig by its snout. You can rely on this given how things are. But no-one supposes that to be a pig just *is* to have such a snout. Plastic surgery alone rules that out. To be a pig is not just, and not *per se*, to *look* some particular way. So in the wrong environment (too much cosmetic surgery, for example), a pig-detector which worked by means of snouts simply would not be a *pig* detector. *We* can recognize when it would not be. We can look at its workings, on the one hand, and, on the other, at the reasons for and against counting what *it* would be identifying as pigs (if detecting at all) as *pigs*. We can exercise our capacities for retrospection, capacities to be abashed. An unthinking detector has no such capacities, *cannot* be abashed.

The unthinking detector lacks a capacity we have: sensitivity, case by case, to what bears, or might, and how it might, on whether *that* case is to be counted as one of instancing any given generality—notably, here, that generality whose instancings are to be detected. As noted long ago, such capacities are reserved for Cartesian thinkers. An unthinking detector thus could not be sensitive to what distinguishes *this* way for things to be, such that there is a pig beneath the oak, from countless others, notably, others inhabiting clouds around it. This does not matter to detection, but certainly does to presenting. For presenting things as being such-and-such way, a selection task must be achieved. That way things are presented *as* being must be distinguished, in the presentation, from its fellows within conceptual, notably those overlapping with it through some proper part of the space of particular cases, but diverging from it in other proper parts. Such selecting is beyond the powers of an unthinking detector (or locator). Mere detection does not demand it. Assume the detector/locator in an hospitable environment where he/it always gets things right. If it is representing things as some way it is detecting in this environment, such fixes *something* as to how that way reaches. It reaches to *these* cases. But such is only a proper part of its reach. The unthinking detector/locator has *no* capacity to see when it would have left an hospitable environment or how, or, when it has, what detection then would be. It thus cannot do what any thinking allorepresenter can. Which robs us to our right to suppose that the notion *environment hospitable to its detecting* has a determinate sense or application, that it is so much as fixed what an hospitable environment for *it* would be.

A detector might fail either through migration into hostile territory, or thanks to some one-off ringer. *If* he/it represented things *as* those ways whose cases he/it was thus detecting, such would be cases of representing falsely. But the unthinking representer *cannot* represent itself as in an hospitable environment. It is blind to when *this* would be so. The Porsche detector which blinks each time a Porsche passes, put in the world of knockoff Porsches, can do no more than carry on. Its detection work in no way equips it to approach the question whether it is in a knockoff world. That it is not cannot be how things are according to it. Nor can it be held responsible, where ringers are about, for whether what it blinks to is a *Porsche*. Such thus cannot really be, in such circumstances, how it represents things being. If it represented-as at all, it might just as well be that those instancings to which it continues blinking are just those of the way it represents things being.

Detection buys the unthinker no standing in the realm of allorepresenters, since it does not equip him/it to effect selection. With which the idea of allorepresenting emerging out of detecting, or locating, collapses. What qualifies an unthinker as a detector is not what *could* qualify it as a presenter, or placer, so as allorepresenting-as (as presenting something *as* falling under some generality). Allorepresenting cannot *thus* emerge.

9 Collapse

A pattern which made for detecting (or locating) instancings of some bit of the conceptual would not thereby make for *presenting* anything as falling under any generality. If representing-as emerged from it, so far that representing might as well be anything. Suppose we decided, though, that such representing must represent things *as* some way whose instancings are being detected. We might then try to say: it must represent things as *that* way whose instancings are being detected (or located). If it detects yellow things, the idea is, then it represents things *as* such that there is something yellow. But that move is illegitimate. The detector *detects* in its actual environment, one hospitable to such detection. By our decision it thus identifies a *proper* sub-part of the reach of the way it represents things being. Nothing it does as a detector extrapolates from this sub-reach to the whole reach of that way it represents things. Otherwise put, nothing in the pattern it incorporates determines when it would have moved into a world of ringers (or what a *ringer* for what it was detecting might be). *Thus* is the move just tried on illegitimate.

In its actual environment the detector detects/locates yellow Porsches. It is endowed by design with its distinctive outcome for suitable encounters with them. Now it enters a world full of yellow silicon dummy Porsches. There is something yellow Porsches and such dummies both are. I will call it *being a siliporsh*. In its actual home, it detects and locates yellow Porsches, and it detects and locates yellow siliporshes. In its new home it detects and locates siliporshes, and detects, but no longer locates yellow Porsches. For it, the dummies are ringers for Porsches. Which of the ways whose instancings it was detecting all along (if either) would be the way it represented things *as* being (if it were to do this at all)? If it is to represent things as a way whose instancings it detects, *has* it now encountered ringers for the *relevant* such way? Nothing in its design, or in the patterns whose incorporation this maintains, decides this. Patterns of effect-representing thus cannot perform the selection task for it.

Back to the actual. Our detector produces its assigned outcome on encounter with Pia's yellow Porsche this morning. It produces this outcome again for her Porsche this afternoon. But has it encountered a ringer *this* time? All those cases of an object's being as it was which occurred up to noon today form a sub-region of the space of all particular cases. Pia's Porsche being as it will be this afternoon lies outside that sub-region. Three classes of ways for things to be trace that same path through the sub-region: ones which go on to reach to her Porsche being as it will be this afternoon (being a yellow Porsche among these); those which fail to reach; and those which determine no outcome for this novel case. If you wanted to detect instancings of some way in the second or third class, you might well rely on a detector of the present kind. You might well be prepared to count this case as a one-off ringer, a momentarily inhospitable environment, especially if it were trouble to guard against it. Call this way *being a yellow Porsche★*. Then the present device *is* a yellow Porsche★ detector, on a suitable understanding of *inhospitable*. If some natural function is served by equipping *us* with yellow Porsche detectors (perhaps preservation of the species is furthered by designing females to be attracted to them), that function is served as well (up to insignificant differences, unforeseeable at time of design) by a yellow Porsche★ detector. Up to noon today, the detector has been 'trained up' on cases of both being a yellow Porsche and being a yellow Porsche★, just as up to its entrance in the world of silicon dummies it had been 'trained up' on cases of both being a yellow Porsche and being a yellow siliporsh. Once again, what a detector is detecting could not tell us as what way it represented things if it went in for that at all.

So far we have been supposing that a detector which allorepresented would allorepresent things as some way whose instancings it detected. Why should we? Suppose a weather bureau detects the weather. When the temperature had dropped to 14° it would detect that. Its signal—the outcome reserved for this—might be some bulletin, 'Current temperature 14°'. But it might also just as well be 'Wu's bird's nest soup is legendary', if its first mission is to promote tourist trade and it sees this as currently the best means for that. Or a detector *designed* to detect temperature without wind chill might, in fact, detect temperature with wind chill. Might not such a detector still allorepresent (falsely) temperatures without wind chill, if it did allorepresent at all? A capacity to allorepresent, one would have thought, makes room for such possibilities. Nothing closes them off in our case except our capacities, as thinkers, to recognize what projects we engage in, and their respective successes and failures. What would shut them down in an unthinker's case remains obscure. Anyway, not mere blindness to the options.

Nor should we allow ourselves to be impressed by the fact that *we* think, for example, in terms of Porsches and not siliporshes, or being yellow and not being yellow★. An unthinker's selection task is not thus to be foisted off on us. There is no reason to suppose the unthinker to share *our* sense for what the thing to do, or, specifically, the way to represent things, would be. There is every reason not to. The unthinker has no such sense. Nor, as we are about to see, could any natural function be served by nature's arranging for the unthinker's representing to coincide with what *ours* would be.

Where nature incorporates a design for detection (or location) in one of *its* creations, the purpose thus served—say, furthering procreation—is always found in our actual environment (or that at time of incorporation). It is just part of designing for interaction with an environment that one *cannot* design for immunity to ringers. But nature's purposes are served as well as anything could serve them by designs which are not so immune. If allorepresenting emerged from such design there could not but be the problem just scouted. In one form the problem is what to count as a ringer, or when to count one as having occurred. *Something* whose *instancings* are detected by design is to be the way things are thus represented *as* being. A ringer would be a ringer for *that*. But nothing in the design choses any one such thing. Nor does the purpose such design might serve. That same problem is now familiar in another form. Nature designs for the *actual* environment, thus for a sub-part of the reach of whatever way the instancings of which might thus be detected. For allorepresenting to emerge, a move must be made from this sub-part to a whole reach. But such moves are no concern of nature's at all.

So things stand with the second of our two problems. I return now to the first. I approach it first through this question. If allorepresenting arose out of some pattern of effect-representing, with what *force* would this be done? An unthinker does no *autorepresenting* (I here bracket dogs and cats). Where there is *allorepresenting*, there is what makes it recognizable, its vehicle. Here this is to be some occurrence—some production or its product—which instantiates the pattern, is produced by a design for maintaining it. It is to be, in present terms, what is reserved by design in some detector for signalling detecting of some instancing of the way as which things are thus represented. The problem I will scout now arises from the fact that, to speak a bit loosely, all the information carried by the (supposed) representing is carried already by its vehicle.

The occurrence of this vehicle, like any occurrence, effect-represents all that to which it owes thanks. If all went well—if it was produced by design, and the environment was, even locally, hospitable (no ringers)—then this occurrence effect-represents *inter alia* what the design is a design to detect. On a given understanding of *going well, hospitable, ringer,* and so on, this would be the instancing of some way for things to be. So the occurrence of the vehicle is liable to give reason to think that there was such an instancing. It gives precisely as much reason to think this as there is then reason to think that all went well, surroundings were hospitable, and so on—*conclusive* reason, plain proof, where such things are not in doubt. The *vehicle* itself (properly, its occurrence then) has that much significance. There is, anyway, *this* to be recognized as to what to think and do. So much is recognizable to one blind to the fact that the vehicle is a vehicle of allorepresenting; to what allorepresenting there thus was, or to there having been *any,* so long as he recognizes the vehicle as produced, as it was, by what incorporates such a design—by what would, if working well, and so on, thus maintain that pattern of effect-representing which it is a design for maintaining.

Now suppose allorepresenting to have emerged in this operation of what produced the vehicle (the detector). What reason does this allorepresenting give for thinking and doing? How does *it*, or its occurrence, bear on what the thing to think, or do, would be? If it emerged from the pattern, as per above, then for it to have occurred is for it (or its vehicle) to have been produced in the maintaining, by design, of the relevant pattern—one such that, things going well, and so on, its (or its vehicle's) production would effect-represent the instancing of what is thus effect-represented. It would have occurred on *just* that condition on the *vehicle's* effect-representing such instancing. To recognize it as the representing it is is to recognize it as *just* such a designed production. So its occurrence, if recognized for what it is, gives just the reason to think things the way it represents things being as the vehicle's occurrence itself gives for thinking this. And if it really thus emerges from the pattern, its mere occurrence can give no more.

Whereas it is essential to allorepresenting that *it* (or its occurrence) can bear on the thing to think (or do), give reason to think things one way or another (where they are represented to *be* F, *that* way) which there would not be anyway, without supposing it to have occurred, or which might recognizably be present without recognizing it to have occurred. When it comes to reason-giving, allorepresenting cannot be thus inert. If our yellow Porsche detector did what would here be (emergent) representing there as being a yellow Porsche, what it did, whether that or not, would anyway give as much reason to think there *was* a yellow Porsche as there is to think that all was then going well with it. For its (supposed) allorepresenting to give, and be able to give, precisely and only this much reason is for there to be no representing-as here at all.

Pursuing our question about force is one way to see why. For allorepresenting to have a given force is for it to be taken as aimed at particular successes (and for it to represent itself as a success in some of these). If the force is assertive, there is the success, representing things as they are. If it is imperative, there is the success *obligating* so-and-so. And so on. A force is fixed, and is identified by, the successes thus aimed at. All the more if forces are as multifarious as above suggested. From this perspective, one isolates the force of Sid's words to the waiter only in isolating in what ways what projects would be served if things are as he said. It is by, and according to, its force that given allorepresenting bears as it does, and not in other ways, on questions of the thing to think or do. If Sid had said 'Pia ordered the *oursins*', and continued 'That's what you think, isn't it?', then though he would still have represented Pia *as* having ordered the *oursins*, his doing so would not have borne as it did on what the waiter was to do. The force of an allorepresenting is recognizable in how it bears. Where *it* (or its occurrence) may be taken to bear in one way or another on questions of the thing to think, facts of how it is to be taken may be rich enough to choose some force, from among the panoply of options, as its. For our yellow Porsche detector, its would be allorepresenting (on the present scheme) could have *no* bearing on the thing to think or do. The bearing there would be on such questions if it occurred would be just that which there would be without supposing it to have. In the facts of how its supposed representing is to be taken, then, there can be nothing to choose between one force and another. So it can have none.

If such allorepresenting can have no force, then (as we have already seen in one way) it can have no content either: there can be no such thing as the way it represents things as being. For, again, what content some allorepresenting has cannot matter independent of its force. The Porsche detector might signal Porsche detection in given words, say, 'Porsche ahead'. But that those words mean *Porsche ahead* is irrelevant to their function. The words might as well be 'Pigs whistle'. All that matters is that those words, whatever they are, and whatever they mean, are the detector's response-by-design to the presence of a Porsche, so that if things are going well there will be a Porsche ahead. The words might happen to *speak*, in English, say, of a Porsche being ahead. But for their purpose here they might as well speak of anything else. It thus cannot be that the detector *uses* them to speak of that (to represent things *as* that way). Whatever the words are, they are merely recruited by the detector's design to stand as a synthetic addition to nature's messages. From their occurrence one may (sometimes) conclude that there is a Porsche, as from the pawings in the dust on the trail ahead one may conclude that the wild boar are in rut.

The difficulty with emergent allorepresenting has been, so far, that what is to make this representing recognizable as what it is is *identical* with that in it which gives reason for supposing things as to how things are, or are to be. Whereas allorepresenting is always a source of new and distinctive sorts of bearing on questions what to think or do. It is a source of reasons to think things that an unthinker could not give. In spelling this out a bit, I can reinforce and deepen the points just made.

Suppose that Sid tells us that a Porsche is in the drive. His doing so *might*, by any of countless routes, effect-represent the presence of a Porsche in the drive. (For example, perhaps in his seeing Pia chatting with the countess, by the French doors leading to the garden.) It *could*, but need not, effect-represent his ability to tell a Porsche at sight. Such things may be nice if so. But they are not what makes his representing recognizable. No pattern of effect-representing makes for his representing, nor for it being recognizable. What makes for *his* representing, so for its recognition is independent of any patterns of effect-representing in which such performance may stand (Chomsky's point); which makes room for Sid to achieve recognition through choosing means according to his insight into that audience (to which he belongs) for which (in the sense of Section 4) he allorepresents; according to that audience's shared sense for how such means, deployed then, would be to be taken.

What makes Sid's representing recognizable is thus also independent of that which gives it the bearing it does on what to think and do, which makes it the reason it is for thinking this or that. If Sid represented a Porsche as in the drive, there would be a Porsche in the drive, provided that he was then executing a project of seeing how things *were*, knowing *how* to do so and *when* he would be. Where this condition is recognizably met, his so representing things gives conclusive reason to take a Porsche to be in the drive. More generally (in parallel with that supposed emergent representing-as by a detector), Sid's saying so gives as much reason to think so as there is reason to think the condition met. Notoriously we do not always tell the truth; nor are always able to tell whether we are doing so or not. But being serious (one's project being one of saying how things are) and knowing what one is talking about is something we, sometimes, can *manifestly* do. So, sometimes we can recognize the reason Sid's saying so gives to take there to be a Porsche in the drive in recognizing the reason there is to take him to be thus engaged. Sid's saying so then gives *us* such reason.

For Sid's representing to give the reason it *thus* does for thinking a Porsche in the drive, it need participate in no fixed, specifiable, pattern of effect-representing (a pattern maintained in Sid in some given way). Nor is it in recognizing such a pattern that such reason is recognizable to us as given. We need know nothing of such things. Nor *could* such reason emerge from such participation. So nor could it be such participation which made it recognizable to us as given. Thus is the reason of a distinctive sort, a sort which, by nature, (non-auto) representing-as makes room for.

Sid *can* give us, in his representing, such reason to think things because, and only because, he has the capacity to see when a question, or at least the relevant question, has been *settled*. Such it is to know what one is talking about. An unthinker, a mere detector/locator, is, *a fortiori*, denied any such capacity. For such a capacity transcends any mere design for recognition in *just* the way that the reach of a way for things to be transcends those cases occurring in any given hospitable environment. Sid can tell a pig at sight, as most of the rest of us can. But you *cannot* always tell a pig by looking. A capacity to see when it is settled that it is a pig is a capacity to take such things into account. By the same failing, an unthinker could not separate what makes its allorepresenting recognizable from what makes it the reason-giving that it is; and (thus) could not make that reason-giving of the distinctive sort allowed for by allorepresenting in being what it is. The unthinker's representing-as would thus be idle. It could not add to the reason-giving there would be without it, just in nature's messages. But, for reasons given (above in discussing force), intrinsically idle representing-as would be no representing-as at all. In a different context Wittgenstein said:

Symbols that are dispensable have no meaning. Superfluous symbols signify nothing.
(Waismann 1979: p. 90, his italics)

Such fits the present case exactly. In 1922, telling us that an unneeded sign is meaningless, he offers a reverse side to the coin:

If everything behaved just as though a sign had meaning, it *has* meaning.
(1922: 3.328)

Perhaps those who propose unthinking allorepresenting (or representing-as) think they have found what *does* behave just like the real thing. If so, one might invoke this reverse side of the coin. But above are reasons why they have not.

Allorepresenting is a complex pattern woven into the fabric of our thinking worldly doings. For it to be what it is is for it to serve as it does execution of our projects. Unthinking allorepresenting would detach this pattern from the fabric, patching it into some simpler activity, still recognizable there, perhaps in more primitive form—still allorepresenting. But events, or occurrences, of representing-as are creative: for each, there is a new way for things to be, *things being as thus represented*. Only within that original whole fabric does it makes sense to speak of creating generalities under which for things to fall. Only there could doing so be serving the needs thus to be served. It is precisely there that it makes sense to think of a way of issuing, or holding, messages which relates the issuer/bearer to a term, such as the third term in the relation *allorepresented*, which, belonging to the conceptual, does not *interact* with an environment.

Frege notes that thoughts (so ways for things to be)

are not thoroughly without effects, but their effectiveness is of a wholly other sort than that of things . . . their effects are triggered by the doings of thinkers . . .
(see 1918: p. 77)

Instantiating, thinkers' doings are what it takes to place thoughts in allorepresenting. Instantiating again, perceptual experience is nothing like being represented to.

Appendix to The Preserve of Thinkers

Suppose there were unthinking representing-as. It might involve some vehicle, V, of some unthinker N. Or, perhaps, V might *bear* content—represent things as some way they are, or are not—while nothing's vehicle. V would represent things as being some given way, say, Π. If V decomposed, it might contain a part, P, which represented *a* thing (or some given things) as some given way, Φ. How *would* Π, or Φ, reach to particular cases—for example, to some novel case such as things, or some given thing, being as they, or it, will be tomorrow at 10? What might answer such questions? What answers have been proposed? What follows applies the points of the main text to two sample proposals: Gareth Evans' and Jerry Fodor's.

1 Gareth Evans

Evans begins here:

> In general, we may regard a perceptual experience as an informational state of the subject: it has a certain *content*—the world is represented as a certain way—and hence it permits of a non-derivative classification as *true* or *false*.
>
> (1982: p. 226)

One might have thought perceptual experiences episodes, things one undergoes; episodes of witnessing episodes for that matter. But grant Evans a grain (or block) of salt here. Registering (or *having* registered) what one sees can be a state; a sort often entered. Such a state might count as containing the information registered. Perhaps Evans means to speak of something in this neighbourhood. Evans also speaks of such states as internal, and as accessible to a perceiver in a way to suggest, at least, that these are states, not of the perceiver himself, but rather of some sub-doxastic part of him—perhaps some state or system. Representing by such non-persons, not by the perceiver himself, is what is of interest here.

Evans thinks that, not just sub-doxastic states and systems, but also *photographs* engage in representing-as. In fact, he uses these last to make clear how he thinks representing *within* a perceiver works. He writes:

A certain mechanism produces things which have a certain informational content. I shall suppose for the moment that this content can be specified neutrally, by an open sentence in one or more variables... Thus if we are concerned with a photograph of a red ball on top of a yellow square, then the content of the photograph can be represented in the open sentence,

Red (x) & Ball (x) & Square (y) & Yellow (y) & On Top of (x, y).

The mechanism is a mechanism of information storage, because the properties that figure in the content of its output are (to a degree determined by the accuracy of the mechanism) the properties possessed by the objects which are the input to it.

(1982: pp. 124–5)

The camera produces, perhaps, a Polaroid, or jpeg file. *This*, Evans suggests, represents something *as* a certain way—typically, something photographed. An open sentence identifies a way for a thing (or here a pair of things) to be. It represents neither things, nor any thing, as any way. (For any thing that *is* that way, or not, the open sentence is not about it.) It, then, does not bring us to representing-as, much less representing-to-be; so nor to truth full stop. If the camera *reproduced* well, it does identify, in part, *one* bit of information the photograph (or file) stores—that is, effect-represents: that *some* red ball was on top of *some* yellow square. For identifying this information fully we need the place-holders to take on values. These will be, Evans suggests, those

objects that were the input to the mechanism when the product was produced. Correspondingly, the output is *of* those objects with which we have to compare it in order to judge the accuracy of the mechanism at the time the output was produced.

(1982: p. 125)

If, for example, it is Sid's jack ball on Pia's serviette that was photographed, then that bit of information is that that jack ball is on that serviette. Causal relations between world and camera settles issues here.

Evans takes a further step. He suggests that the photograph *represents* the scene before the camera *as* such that a/that red ball was on a/that yellow serviette. Just here lies the rub. What a camera photographed *is* a causal matter. For a thought (a representation of things *as* a certain way) to make truth turn on how a certain ball or serviette is is for that thought (equivalently, for that representation-as) to decompose in a certain way. There can be a question what objects a thought, or representation-as, refers to only where there is already some representing-as to decompose. If there were, then perhaps (for all we now care) causal relations might answer the questions that would thus arise. This is not to say that causation can put representing-as in the picture in the first place—so that such questions about referents can arise at all. Evans puts it there, not through causation, but rather through a simple flick of the pen.

To see how far the pen-flick leaves us from representing-as we need only consider this. The camera records a bit of history; one (for us) naturally described as Evans did. That description identifies *one* fact thus recorded: a certain red ball was on a certain yellow serviette. But thus to record history is to record *countless* such facts; to store indefinitely much information. That ball, in being red, was also countless other ways there is for a ball to be. It was, for a start, *shmed*, where most cases of something being red—perhaps all so far—are also ones of something being shmed, and *vice versa*, but not all are: there is such a thing as being red but not shmed, and *vice versa*. Being red and being shmed, that is, differ in how they reach to particular cases—a difference which will emerge in novel ones, even if it has not emerged already. They are two items in a cloud of close relatives within a small region of the conceptual. Both are equally close to being shmed*, being shmed**, and so on. Representing-as poses a selection task. It is inherent in selection tasks to face such choices. Where the representing-as is done by one of us, *that* it is often enough provides adequate reason for making short shrift with clouds of the sort just alluded to. But if we are to induct a camera, or photograph, into the *confreries* of representers-as, we have no reason to suppose (and every reason not to) that it is just one of us; thus to be treated accordingly. All paths are open here until something rules some out.

The point emerges in another way when we ask just when the photograph, or file, would have represented falsely—a possibility provided for in the very idea of representing-as; and *not* merely in, or by, recording and storing information. How is this possibility provided here? In Evans' example the camera duly records a red ball on a yellow square. Suppose the square were grey cardboard, turned golden by reflected rays of golden light. Does the photograph thus represent things as other than they are—so falsely? If one of us represented things to be such that a red ball was on a yellow serviette, he *might* do this on an understanding of something being yellow on which that square *was* as thus said to be, or on one on which it was not. One would look to circumstance to decide this. If the camera really did represent the square as being yellow, then the question would arise for it too. If there is *no* question of it doing this on one or another understanding of being yellow—if representing a thing as yellow *on an understanding of this* is just not the sort of thing it might do—then nor is there question of it representing-as at all. Yet nothing in the way the camera works, or worked on an occasion, chooses between such understandings. The photograph *effect*-represents whatever in fact produced it—a yellow serviette, if so it was, a grey square bathed in golden light if *so* it was. There is as yet no room for falsehood. For there is as yet no answer to the question *how* it represented things as being. So there is as yet no representing-as about which to ask this.

Nothing in photography makes for representing-as. Evans misses the problems faced in making for this. He does, though, suggest one more device for doing so:

> For a perceptual state to be ... regarded [as 'representing the world a certain way'] ... it must have a certain motive force on the actions of the subject. This motive force can be countermanded, in the case of more sophisticated organisms ... In the case of such organisms, the internal states which have a content by virtue of their phylogenetically more ancient connections with the motor system also serve as input to the concept-exercising and reasoning system ... [one] can then speak of the information being accessible to the subject ...

(1982: pp. 226–7)

A subject can gain knowledge of his internal informational states in a very simple way... Here is how he can do it. He goes through exactly the same procedure as he would go through if he were trying to make a judgement about how it is at this place now, but excluding any knowledge he has of an extraneous kind.

(1982: p. 227)

Suppose we see before us what, anyway, looks just as a red ball on a yellow square would (or might). Our experience, Evans tells us, is an internal state which represents things as a certain way. For it to represent things as it thus does, he here tells us, is for it to have a certain natural motive force. In our case, for it to have this motive force is (modulo some asterisks) for it to have a certain force on our judging. Again, setting aside 'extraneous' considerations (if any), seeing the above, we would naturally take it that there was, before us, a red ball on a yellow square. To judge is to be prepared to act accordingly. So we would be so prepared. The power thus exercised over our doings is (modulo those asterisks) that motive force which determines the content of the representing-as here. The way we would thus represent things to *ourselves* identifies (again modulo those asterisks) the content which such motive force makes for. It is to be such power of experience over action which is to perform the selection task.

But what bars a photograph from representing-as bars the present idea as well. A photograph is, so to speak, *thick* with information. If it depicts a red ball on a yellow napkin, it equally, by the same token, depicts (*inter alia*) a shmed shmall on a yellow napkin, a red ball on a shmellow shmapkin, and so on *ad infinitum*. Similarly, vision is overflowing with information for us. In seeing a red ball bouncing, I also see, equally, a shmed shmall shmouncing, and so on. As Evans conceives extraneous information, what it might do, if present, would be to give reason *not* to judge that a red ball is bouncing, even if things certainly appear that way. Rule out any such extraneous information. What way *would* one judge things to be on seeing a red ball bouncing (or what looked *just* as this would or might)? What *someone* would judge, if there is to be any such thing as that, must depend not just on what he saw, but on his ability to register the information on offer (and on vagaries of the case on hand, for example, on what he happens to think of). He might judge that a ball was bouncing—if he knows bouncing balls when he sees them (can recognize instancings of *for there to be a ball bouncing*). He might judge that a ball was bouncing★ (a sort of bouncing which requires a particular sort of damping) if he knew what it was for something to be bouncing★. If he comes to know what shmed is, for some version of shmed as per above, then he may come, after the fact, to realize that what he saw was a shmed ball bouncing. And so on.

If 'extraneous information' is just what would provide reason *not* to judge that a red ball is bouncing (thus, nor that a shmed shmall is bouncing★), 'what one would judge if...', if there *is* such a thing, is inadequate for the selection task for perceptual experiences (otherwise known as internal states). It may be a sociological fact that on seeing a red ball bouncing, the first thing that would come to the minds of Evans and those of his sort would be (bracketing extraneous information) to say that a red ball was bouncing, and not, for example, that a shmed ball was bouncing★. But Evans' inclinations are not responsible for *experience's* representing. Vision provides *both* pieces of information. Among the plethora of bits of information it thus provides, it is neutral as to which to judge if it is not to be discounted.

In any case, in Evans' story it is not 'what one would judge' which is meant to perform the selection task, but rather some supposed 'phylogenetically primitive' motor responses naturally triggered by seeing a red ball bounce. The origin of content here is thus meant to be some relation between some unthinking things—our ancestors—and historical episodes of some given sort—perhaps, *inter alia*, encounters by these creatures with red things, or with bouncing. So Sid sees a red ball bouncing. Such would trigger a response in those ancestors. Such triggering has, in them, an aetiology. Should this be past encounters with red things, or shmed things, or bouncing, or bouncing*? But if it is with some one of these, it is *ipso facto* with indefinitely many others—if with red things, then so, too, with shmed things. Phylogeny thus does not harbour an outcome to the selection task. That it comes naturally to *us* (say, Evans and his readers) to *describe* those primitive encounters as with red things rather than shmed things is irrelevant to the called-for selection task.

Let us review. Pia sees a red apple in a bowl. She thus sees what has a natural motive force on her. This motive force is a residue of the motive force it had on some more primitive ancestor—for it is this, Evans tells us, which determines the content of the relevant content-bearing internal state (what Evans takes to be Pia's experience of seeing what she thus does). How might motive force determine the content of an internal state? The idea seems to be something like this. The 'natural' motive force Pia feels corresponds to some way she would naturally take her experience to bear on the thing for her to do—if she did not, for one or another reason, 'countermand', or discount, the inclination, take the experience to be other than it seems in the relevant respect. We might then ask what way Pia would be taking the experience to be in taking it so to bear for her on what to do. An answer might be: things being such that there is a red apple in the bowl. The unthinking primitive ancestor, on whom Pia's state's content depends, cannot, perhaps, *take* an experience to bear for him in a certain way on the thing for him to do. But there is a counterpart to this for him. He can be moved to act as one would in taking the world to bear for him in a certain way on what to do. And we can ask, as with Pia, what way for things to be would make the world such as so to bear for him. The answer might be, for a start, such as for there to be something red before him. Such might be what triggered in him attempts to eat, or fight, the red thing. That there is something red before Pia would then be part of the way *her* experience represented things as being.

But this story does not work. First, if *Pia* takes what she sees to have a certain bearing for her on what to do, and if what would have that bearing was things being Φ, perhaps we can say *her* to represent things as being such that Φ. So, too, for how she *would* take things to bear for her if she did not discount her experience. But we cannot just foist *her* representing on some presumed internal state/perceptual experience as *its* representing. If *it* represented, such would need a different source.

Second, if Pia saw something red, then, for indefinitely many values of 'shmed', she also saw something shmed. If seeing something red had a particular motive force on the ancestor, then so did seeing something shmed for indefinitely many of these values. The red things he saw *were* shmed things for these values. Many things are equally responsible for the postulated motive force, if any are (if there is any such force). No outcome to the selection task is yet in sight. Where Pia saw something red, the *history* she thus witnessed is what no ancestor ever saw. The red thing she saw fails to instance many things instanced by all cases with the relevant motive force on the ancestor, instances many others never then present. Suppose Pia saw a candy-coated green apple, as no ancestor ever did. The apple is red on one understanding of what such might be, not on another. If Pia *thinks* it red (thus not discounting her experience), this might be on either of these understanding, or neither, depending on the course her thinking took on that occasion, all compatibly with not discounting. Even (illegitimately) reading *her* representing back onto that of the supposed state, the selection task remains undone. Whether the candy apple *would have* triggered the response in the ancestor is anyway as may be. For if so, it would have done in being any of indefinitely many different ways.

The only tacks here which even hint at an outcome for the selection task are: either reading the way Pia represented what she saw to herself into the supposed representing done by the *experience*; or reading our natural outsider's descriptions of what she saw—such as something red—into the content of that supposed state. Neither tack is permissible.

2 Jerry Fodor

Fodor begins from a piece of ideology. As he pithily puts it:

If aboutness is real, it must be really something else.

(1987: p. 97)

Ideology plays a crucial role in Fodor's story—lending plausibility to the desperate. Fodor's use of 'represent' and 'representation' also engenders *seeming* plausibility by conflating effect-representing with representing-as. In fact, it is this last which he needs to conjure out of the first. But effect-representing is *au fond* a two-place relation, between one historical circumstance and another. Whereas representing-as is three-place, involving a representer (an agent, a vehicle, a content-bearer), what is represented as something (some bit of history), and what it is represented as (some way for things in general, or for *a* thing, to be). The problem for Fodor is that nothing in effect-representing identifies any such third term.

Fodor offers a *general* way for unthinking representing-as to arise. His specific concern, though, is with what he calls 'mental representations' (henceforth MRs). Their content is, typically, a thought: they represent things as a way there is for things to be. MRs *bear* content as a vehicle does, but need no representer whose vehicle they are. An MR is identified as the item it is by features independent of what content, if any, it bears. There is thus room for a story as to how that MR *came by* just *that* content. But the function of an MR is not, as with a vehicle in allorepresenting, to make for representing in making it recognizable. Nor does it inherit its content from the representer whose vehicle it is.

In Fodor's story, each MR has a constituent structure: there is some given ensemble of elements out of which it is built—structured in some definite way. Such elements (henceforth MREs) are drawn from a larger (fixed) stock. Each element in the stock comes by its content independent of its role in the MRs in which it figures. For it to have the content it does (to make the contribution it does to representing-as) is to be for it to stand in given relations of effect-representing (or generalizations of one kind or another on effect-representing) to given things (in crucial cases at least, to instancings (historical cases) of that way for a thing to be which its presence in an MR makes that MR about).

There is a parallel here to what separated Frege from Lotze. For Lotze, it was (certain) combinations of *Vorstellungen* which were either true or false. A *Vorstellung* was, *inter alia*, what could be an object of *perceptual* awareness. Its contribution to making truth depends on something thus derived from features it acquired in some role, or life, other than that of being an element in a thought (that is, making truth depend on such-and-such). The right way of unifying *Vorstellungen* in a combination was what was to form a thought. For Frege, the sole way to arrive at a thought-element was by decomposing a whole thought. No life outside the thought (on a decomposition) could possibly confer on anything the properties that a thought-element would have.

The point here is not just about *Vorstellungen* in Lotze's sense—anyway, no doubt, suspicious entities. It is a general point about anything that might aspire to representing-as, or to a role in it. So it has a parallel for anything that aspires to express thoughts, and for anything which aspires to be a contribution to such expressions—such as for English sentences. Suppose the sentence 'Penguins waddle' says penguins to be waddlers. Then 'waddle', in it, may contribute to its so doing in speaking of waddling. But, the idea is, for 'waddle' to have this contribution to make can be nothing other than for it to play the role it does in English sentences (in general, perhaps) being, severally, for what they are. Nothing independent of this can make 'waddle' the right sort of thing for such a role—what *would* play it if only inserted in the cited sentence. One way to put the point: to say that 'Penguins waddle' speaks of penguins as waddlers can only be to say (simplifying only a bit) that such is what one would speak of, in speaking English, in using that sentence for what it *is* for in English; *mutatis mutandis* for 'waddle' contributing to the sentence so doing by itself speaking of 'waddling'.

From this perspective, Fodor's strategy, *in re* MREs, lines him up with Lotze. One might well worry. Or not, given Fodor's ideology. But to cases. Fodor's Lotzian strategy is to begin with MREs, to squeeze elements of representing-as out of their effect-representing, and then to build up to full MRs. Once (2008), he recognizes, but fails to be deterred by, the distance there is between effect-representing and representing-as. He raises the question how X might 'represent' Y without representing Y as 'falling under some concept' (being some way there is for Y to be). He finds an answer in what he calls 'Dretskian information'—a correct one, if 'represent' is read as as *effect-represent*:

> X represents Y insofar as X carries information about Y, where 'carries information about...' is read as transparent... In particular... tokens of symbols typically carry all sorts of what I'll call 'Dretskian information'. (Come to think of it, so too does practically everything else.) And 'carries information about...', unlike 'represents as...', is transparent to the substitution of coextensives at the '...' position.
>
> (2008: pp. 179–80)

Those drumlins yonder carry the information that a glacier was once here: if they are, then so was it. As Fodor notes, near enough everything engages in this sort of thing. Not even Fodor thinks you can make representing-as out of *anything*. Why, then, his optimism?

Fodor's original strategy for locating representing-as elsewhere (as of 1987) was to begin with an avowedly defective story and patch it up to evade counter-examples as such arose. Twenty years later (2008) the strategy remains the same, with one exception, to be noted. This mistaken story, the Crude Causal Theory (CCT), goes like this:

> A sufficient condition for 'A's to express A is that it is nomologically necessary that (1) every instance of A causes a token of 'A', and (2) only instances of A cause tokens of 'A'.
>
> (1987: p. 126)

An 'A' might be an MRE. It would then express a thought-element; in the first instance, what would make a thought about being some way there is for a thing to be. What would trigger a token of such an A would be an encounter with an instancing of the way to be in question—for example, with a case of something being red. Relevant retinal images, for example, might set off 'A'-production.

As Fodor notes, the Crude Causal Theory does not work. Among other things, it leaves the selection task unperformed—for reasons already given in discussing Evans. Fodor concentrates on one small aspect of this problem. He meets it with an innovation he dubs 'asymmetric dependence'. This figures in his amendment to the Crude Causal Theory, the Slightly Less Crude Causal Theory (SLCCT):

> For (2) read: 'If non-A's cause 'A's then their doing so is asymmetrically dependent upon A's causing 'A's.' For (1) read: 'All instances of A's cause 'A's when (i) the A's are causally responsible for psychophysical traces to which (ii) the organism stands in a psychophysically optimal relation.'
>
> (1987: p. 126)

The amendment to (1) is meant to discount instances of A sufficiently obscured from 'the organism'. Asymmetric dependence is the key notion in selecting content for an MRE, and remains key in 2008.

Fodor introduces the notion *asymmetric dependence* with this intuitive explanation:

> From a semantic point of view, mistakes have to be *accidents*: if cows aren't in the extension of 'horse', then cows being called horses can't be *required* for 'horse' to mean

what it does. By contrast, however, if 'horse' didn't mean what it does, being mistaken for a horse wouldn't ever get a cow called 'horse'. Put the two together and we have it that the possibility of saying 'that's a horse' falsely presupposes the existence a *semantic setup* saying it truly, but not *vice versa*. Put it in terms of CCT and we have it that the fact that cows cause one to say 'horse' depends on the fact that horses do; but the fact that horses cause one to say 'horse' does *not* depend on the fact that cows do.

So, the causal connection between cows and 'horse' tokenings is, as I shall say, *asymmetrically dependent* upon the causal connections between horses and 'horse' tokenings.

(1987: p. 108)

If 'A's *did* 'express' *being a horse*, they might then be activated, or tokened, where, for example, a cow was mistaken for a horse (or, to the relevant mechanism, a ringer for one), or where it prompted in the mechanism's owner thoughts about (*inter alia*) horses. Such, the idea is, would not count against 'A's expressing *being a horse* (and that only) if asymmetric dependence reigned as per above. Such is the idea, as it continues through to 2008 (see p. 204).

Asymmetric dependence thus comes into play only after a number of other pieces are already in place. Suppose there is a given stock of potential MREs—items *eligible* to bear content of a certain sort (for example, to express 'predicative' elements in thoughts). Suppose there is some determinate set of specifiable choices for what an MRE might express (or 'speak of')—for example, all those ways for a thing to be which *some* English expression speaks of (in English). Then it will not count against a given MRE, E, having a given content (expressing a given way for a thing to be, W) that E is sometimes a response to the instancing of some other way for a thing to be, if that response is asymmetrically dependent on E's history with instancings of W. *If* E expresses either W or W★, then it expresses W if its relevant history with W★ is asymmetrically dependent on its relevant history with W, and not *vice versa*.

This last 'if' highlights an important fact: asymmetric dependence can come into play only after it is supposed that there is *something* it would be for the potential MRE to *have* one or another content; so only *after* it is supposed that there is a way for the selection task to be performed for, or by, such a would-be MRE. It is useless in addressing such prior problems as, for example, those Evans faced. If the question is whether E expresses *being a cow* or *being a shmow,* (most cows so far having *been* shmows, and *vice versa*), asymmetric dependence is inapplicable. E's history with instancings of *being a cow* is (or near enough) its history with *being a shmow*. If E did express being a cow, this coincidence of histories might just be coincidence. But this observation is useless until we first understand how E could express *any* way for things to be at all.

There is, of course, what *will* happen on encounters with cows which are not shmows (or *vice versa*). But that matters only *given* a route from effect-representing to representing-as. It does not itself make for one. Fodor's fondness for asymmetric dependence reflects obliviousness to the work involved in performing the selection task. Like Evans, he mistakes the ways it is natural for us to describe encounters between organism, or mechanism, and world for itself a solution to that task.

As noted, 2008 introduces one ingredient not found in 1988. Here it is:

> Following Loewer and Rey... (who are themselves following the usage of ethologists) I'll say that acquiring a concept is getting *nomologically locked* to the property that the concept expresses.
>
> (1998: p. 125)

> My story says that what doorknobs have in common qua doorknobs is *being the kind of thing that our kind of minds (do or would) lock to from experience with instances of the doorknob stereotype*. (See to be red *just is* to have that property that minds like ours (do or would) lock to in virtue of experiences of typical instances of redness.)
>
> (1998: p, 137)

Does *locking* bridge the gulf between effect-representing and representing-as? There are two ways of understanding it. Read one way, locking is something personal: it is *we* who, in thought, lock onto this or that way for things, or a thing, to be. Read the other way, locking is something *sub*-personal. It is some mechanism or system responsible for producing MREs which locks onto some particular property it encounters in its 'training up', rather than any of the host of rivals it equally, and by the same token, thus encounters.

An ethologist, interested in the *organism*—the duck, the stickleback—would naturally assume the first reading. It comes naturally to us to think in terms of cats, not so much to think in terms of shmats. Something like this must be so if we are to grasp, or come to grasp, what being thus and so (for particular values of 'thus and so') might be at all. What sort of sub-doxastic explanation might there be of our biases in such regards? The outcomes of selection tasks for *our* representing-as do not await an answer.

The first reading, however, is not available to Fodor. For him, MREs are the origin of *all* content. So an MRE cannot inherit the outcome of its selection task from the outcomes of one or another of *ours*. For us to agree as we do on what would count as a case of something being what we have in mind in speaking of cats cannot be, in Fodor's scheme of things, what it is for MRE1739, say, to express *being a cat* rather than *being a shmat*. If MRE1739 (or whatever produces it) is to lock onto *being a cat*, rather than any other near neighbour *in re* instancings, it must be responsible for its own lockings. In Fodor's scheme, some mechanism, or system, which tokens MRE1739s is 'trained up' on encounters with instancings (cases) of a thing being a cat, which, *ipso facto*, are also (on the whole, or always) cases of a thing being a shmat. As Fodor *would* have it, tokenings of MRE1739s thereby come to be responsive to, thereby expressive of, being a cat and not being a shmat. *If* so, this would reflect the fact that the mechanism is so designed as to lock onto being a cat as opposed to those other near neighbours. But what might it be for it to be so designed?

Suppose I build a (light-sensitive) cat-detector: in the visible presence of a cat, it buzzes. The detector *might* be so constructed that if it ever *were* presented with a cat which was not a shmat it would still light up; but would not light up in the reverse case. This may or may not matter to its purpose. Perhaps something similar holds of the mechanism that tokens MRE1739s. But if we further suppose that my device, or the mechanism, *represents* what it responds to *as* being a cat, or, *casu quo*, as being a shmat, how does this fact about its construction matter to which way it thus represents things? It is this last, if anything, which bears on how my device, or the mechanism, locks onto ways for things to be.

An allegory (in which I represent nature, or evolution, my products MRE-producers). I build a pig-detector. It is sensitive to the sounds, or scents, or looks, or feels, and so on, around it—to what might be encountered on normal exposure to a pig, or other fauna. In the nature of the case, my detector, however I thus build it, is exposed to possibilities of ringers. Being a pig is not purely a matter of looks, scents, and so on. So there is always room for there to be a non-pig with the looks and scents (or whatever) to 'fool' my detector. I take reasonable precautions against ringers. So in practice (if I am good enough) we can expect my detector hardly ever, or even never, to be fooled. But precautions can go only so far. One reaches a point where the expense of going further would be too great; or where the risks the detector actually runs are just too small to prompt further refinement. Suppose my detector has a purpose: I want to help others avoid non-cud-chewers. Then reason might dictate that my precautions have gone far enough when the purpose is served: one can in fact rely on it for avoiding non-cud-chewers. In any event, wherever precautions stop, *being a pig* being what it is, my detector will be responsive, not only to pigs, but, equally, to shmigs, shmig*s, and so on, for indefinitely many values of such things. Regardless of what I mean it to detect, it *does* detect all these things. And, by hypothesis, detecting any of them serves my purpose equally well.

If we tried to suppose that my detector not only detects (hence effect-represents) what it does, but also, when activated, represents things *as* some way or other, nothing in its detecting what it did could tell us *what* way this was—whether such that a pig was present, or that a shmig was present, and so on. *I*, of course, may *mean* it to detect pigs, and not shmigs. But if I represent nature, such falls without the allegory. Nature's interests are not served any better in any one of these ways than in any other. My intentions aside, then, there is no case that my detector engages in representing-as at all. One day my detector encounters, for the first time, what is a shmig, but not a pig. It gives its positive response. If it thus represented the thing to be a *pig*, things would not be as represented. If it thus represented the thing to be a shmig, they would. It would serve its purpose as well in either way. Someone *using* it to detect pigs, say, would be just as well off. The detector would give it just as good reason for thinking there was a pig no matter which way it represented things being, and then whether truly or falsely. The reason it gave either way would be just as good, and not a jot better than, the reason there is to think on this occasion that it has so functioned as to be responding to a pig.

My detector is replete with Dretske-information, available to those sufficiently privy to its workings. Their access to the world would be in no way enhanced if, in addition, it engaged in representing-as. It detects, *inter alia*, porcine presence—except when it does not: not just where there are ringers, but where there are glitches, malfunctions, and so on. If there is a glitch, it may register positive where there is, not a pig, but, patently, a cow. Where there is a glitch or malfunction, it is *not* doing what it was designed to do. It was designed to detect (the presence of absence of) something. It is not detecting this. If it was also designed, not just to detect, but further to represent things as (or not as) *some* way whose instancings it was so designed as to detect, it would not be doing that either. If my watch fails to keep time, it simply does not work. It is not thereby *representing* the time, falsely, to be what it is not. My pig-detector may call for a warning: 'Watch out for glitches'. A further warning, 'Watch out for misrepresenting' would call for no further caution.

The allegory's main point generalizes. There is perceptual recognition, and there is conceptual recognition. Perceptual recognition is, for example, recognizing a pig at sight. Conceptual recognition is, for example, recognizing what would count as a thing being a pig as so counting. What it is that is to count, or not, as this may be presented perceptually, or otherwise (for example, by description). A perceptual recognition *device*—for example, my pig detector—embodies some particular way of recognizing pigs. It inevitably exploits facts as to what would distinguish pigs from the other fauna from which, *in fact*, pigs need distinguishing—such things as sheep and cows. Such a device is, *inevitably*, exposed to being fooled by ringers. When this happens, it is because there is something with all the features to which the device is sensitive, but whose being as it is does *not* count as a case of a thing being a pig (or *vice versa*). It takes a conceptual recognition capacity to recognize when this is so. Conceptual recognition capacities thus reach beyond the range of any fixed perceptual recognition capacity (identified, like a conceptual recognition device, by how it works—to what other (visual, auditory, olfactory, and so on) features it is sensitive). Correlatively, there is no reason to expect there to be such a thing as 'the way they work'—some definite, explicit, set of principles which generate just the results, or verdicts, they would yield, or some definite procedures which could be incorporated into a 'conceptual detection device', paralleling perceptual detectors for the issues that conceptual recognition faces.

We enjoy conceptual recognition capacities. We can appreciate just what makes a ringer pig a ringer. It is not just accidental that this goes along in us with an ability to engage in representing-as. Fodor's ideology forces him to suppose that representing-as arises already in the workings of perceptual recognition, so that if you stripped away from us our capacities for conceptual recognition, there would still be representing-as, if, perhaps, not exactly by us, anyway by the information processors literally within our skins. But stripping away *such* capacities would leave us, *eo ipso*, without the capacity to recognize any case of representing-as for the representing that it thus was. The above shows some of why *such* representing-as would be pointless, superfluous; thus *how* representing-as is a substantial further step beyond effect-representing. As with superfluous symbols, superfluous repesenting-as can simply be omitted. *This* fact makes the selection task unperformable for it. Why think otherwise? Why, for example, should enabling *perceptual* recognition require representing-as? So far, no more than prejudice.

11

That Object of Obscure Desire

> Seeing is not a form of knowing.
>
> H. A. Prichard, 'The Sense-Datum Fallacy', pp. 208, 213

> That the sun has risen is no object which emits rays which arrive in my eyes.
>
> Frege, 'Der Gedanke', p. 61

The object of the desire is the sense datum. It is not so much the object, but the desire—its enduring capacity to charm—that is obscure. Thompson Clarke offers a diagnosis of that charm. On the way to it he illuminates a number of other things—most notably knowledge, and, more generally, the occasion-sensitivity of thought. But his diagnosis of the allure of sense data misfires. Not that I know a better one (unless, like the common cold, different aetiologies for different victims). But there are lessons in the misfire.

1 Prologue

Prichard's words are a motto for what follows, but not as he meant them. What Prichard had in mind was this. First, what one sees is mind-dependent. Colours and shapes, or colours with shapes, are his suggestion. Second, what is mind-dependent is not the sort of thing one can know things about. To know is, *per se*, to take in how things are *independent* of your responses to them. So, as to which ways mind-dependent things are (just in being as experienced) there is nothing to know. There *are* no (response-independent) ways for such things to be. There are no generalities under which for them to fall (again, independent of one's responses to them). On the second point Prichard aligns himself with Frege. I align myself with both.

The first point is utterly fantastic. Here Prichard departs from Frege, who writes:

Vorstellungen cannot be seen or touched, nor smelled, nor tasted, nor heard.
(1918: p. 67)

Vorstellungen, on Frege's notion of them, just are mind-dependent things, among which those which Prichard has in mind (if such exist). We *have* them; we do not perceive them. Perceiving—seeing, hearing, and so on—is a relation to, a form, or family of forms, of awareness of, that environment which we all cohabit, and which, for Frege, is unlocked for us by our capacity for thought, specifically for judgement. That seeing is *per se* a relation to the environment is a point Frege was clear on at a time when few others were—certainly not Prichard. Nor does Clarke's account of the road to sense data reckon fully with this. I side with Frege here.

So, though I take over Prichard's words, I do not take over the thought he uses them to express. What I have in mind is this. To judge something (take it to be so) is *always* (as Frege puts it) to expose oneself to risk. It is to make oneself *liable* to be in error: for whatever might be judged, there are always ways for one to have been wrong; ones such that *were* things that way, one would not have noticed. To *know* is to see what rules out there in fact *being* any such risk. still, whatever one might know is what admits of ringers. It may well *be* that the cat is out. But where this is so it is also so that it *could have* been *just* as though the cat were out when it was not. Seeing, too, similarly admits of ringers. Where you *see* the cat, there *could* have been something (a *very* good synthetic simulacrum, or just a different cat) whose presence in the room looked (from your perspective) *just* as the cat's actual presence does. But such possibilities for ringers matter very differently in the two cases.

Frege makes a related ontological point. The cat is sitting in the corner on the mat. (Where else?) From that location it can reflect light which forms images on your retinas. (It can also impregnate the mat with flea eggs, or worse.) The cat, its presence, the episodes which make up its biography, all belong to the environment. *That* the cat is on the mat does not. It is neither on, nor under, the mat, nor even anywhere in Middlesex. Insofar as causation is a local affair, it cannot causally act or interact. It cannot impregnate mats with larvae. For the cat to be on the mat is a way for things to be. It is a way to represent things *as* being. For it to be a way things *are* is for things being as they are to stand in a particular way to that way of representing them.

Seeing and knowing are both success verbs. If you know that it is raining, then it is raining. If you see rain, there is rain. Both are forms of *awareness* of how things are. But the successes in each case are very different. Knowing is taking in the way things stand with regard to some particular way to represent them being. It thus involves one with thought. Seeing is simply a form of awareness of, acquaintance with, that which so relates. Sight presents us with what, in knowing, we thus respond to. From this follow the differences just discussed. I use Prichard's words, not as he did, but rather so as to capture this difference.

Just this difference grounds the difference between the bearing of ringers on seeing and on knowing. To be stuck in a tailback on the A1, all that is required is that there *be* a suitably located tailback, and that one be suitably in it. To be startled by the horn of the impatient driver behind you, all that is needed is a suitably engendered and located startling honk. That there is a ringer for being in a tailback, or for being startled by a *horn* has not the slightest bearing on whether you were actually so stuck or startled. If you hear the driver behind you hurling expletives the pattern holds. There is no doubt a way for it to be just as though you were hearing this while you are not—for example, because there is no such thing to hear. Again, that things *could* have been so has no bearing on whether you *are* hearing expletives or not. Equally for seeing. Perhaps there is a perfect ringer for the cat lying on the mat. That things *could* be so has no bearing on whether what you see is, in fact, the cat. A possibility of ringers does not impeach a claim to see or hear, whereas it *may* impeach a claim to know. If you *might* just be imagining those expletives, then you do not know that they are being hurled, for all of which, if they *are* being hurled, then that is what you hear. That simple point does yeoman work in what follows. One *could* think ringers matter in a different way to what we see—an idea to be explored.

That seeing is *per se* awareness of how things (around us) are—a way of relating to an *environment*—is not an open question. Which leaves open, so far as it goes, whether we ever see opaque objects, or even *see* at all. So, as Frege notes, there is no *open* question as to whether we see *Vorstellungen* in his sense— things which do not belong to our environment. What there *might* be, for all said so far, are open questions as to what might be experienced visually. Such sets bounds to the ambitions of any cogent enquiry into what it is we see. Clarke *may* not quite see the matter this way.

Prichard, among many, does not. He thinks there *is* a cogent investigation which leads us out of this world to locate those things which are (strictly speaking) seen. He writes:

> It goes without saying that anyone who has not been, so to say, sophisticated by philosophical questioning, if he is asked what he sees or touches, answers in effect, 'chairs and tables, boats going downstream', and so forth... This answer also expresses what is implied in the everyday attitude of mind of those who are philosophers... It need hardly be said that this view, much as we would all like to be able to vindicate it, will not stand examination.
>
> (1950a: pp. 52–3)

In his day Prichard stood here with the majority. What Clarke calls 'The Sense Data Inquiry' is an investigation of just the above sort—a sort I have just suggested we can really make no sense of. That it comes so naturally to suppose otherwise calls for explanation. Clarke's is beautiful and elegant. But he does not spell out the details. His parallel diagnoses of two other phenomena work; his unworked-out diagnosis of the allure of sense data will prove not to.

2 A Problem Posed

Of Clarke's three published articles, the two post-dissertation were one on knowledge (1972) and one on seeing (1965). Each of these assigns a major role to a phenomenon which I call occasion-sensitivity. In his thesis Clarke refers to it as a 'non-rule-like-dimension'. But these roles are strikingly different.

Before considering the difference it is best to say what occasion-sensitivity is. It begins with ways for things, or a thing, to be. For such a way to be occasion-sensitive is for it to admit of understandings. For example, being such as to be sitting on a sofa, or such as to be watching *The Avenging Angel*, is a way for a thing to be. For such a way to admit of understandings is for there to be various things which *might* count, and again might not, as a case of something being the way in question: what it is for a thing to be that way, so far as this goes, leaves it open to count (some) instances of a thing being as it is either as a case of a thing being that way, or as not. For example, so much reclining, or fidgeting, or doing yoga poses, might, or again might not, be counted as *sitting* on the sofa, consistent with what sitting on a sofa is as such. That much banter with Sid, or dozing off, might or might not count as *watching* the Buñuel film. So many interruptions might or might not count as showing it.

The term 'occasion-sensitivity' is meant to capture the idea that where a way for a thing (or things) to be makes such room for understandings, there can be occasions on which it would be *correct* to count a particular case in one way (such as a case of sitting on the sofa) rather than the other, and also occasions when the opposite would be the correct thing to do. If Sid has been banned from sitting on the sofa and is now positioned there, the fact that his slump is at best a poor example of sitting may well fail to get him off the hook. But if his mother frets about his posture, it may be disingenuous to assure her that now he is *sitting* on the couch. Some words speak of ways for things, or a thing, to be, or a family of them—as 'saw___' speaks of (someone, or something) seeing something. They are occasion-sensitive if what they speak of is.

'The Legacy of Scepticism' (1972; henceforth 'Legacy') is a proof that at least some of our concepts *must* be occasion-sensitive, and, accordingly, that we must be occasion-sensitive thinkers—as, perhaps, any thinker must. (Clarke's term here is 'thinkers of non-standard type', 'standard type' being his term for concepts which, occasion-insensitively, apply to things or not.) In particular, one could not think about knowledge coherently except in an occasion-sensitive way. Without occasion-sensitivity, the concept of knowledge would simply lack coherent conditions on application. Nothing would count as knowing, or failing to know, anything. The concept would collapse. Without occasion-sensitivity, it would not be the case that we know nothing. *Nothing* would be the case as to what we know or not. Philosophical scepticism would not be vindicated. It would be as incoherent as anything else one could say about knowledge.

Clarke's argument is an ingenious adaptation of an idea also found in Prichard (this time discussing knowledge and professing only to be transmitting Cook Wilson's view):

[W]e can only be uncertain of one thing because we are certain of something else, and therefore to maintain as the sceptic does that we are uncertain of everything is impossible.

(1950b: 86)

Prichard depicts the collapse of the concept, were this maxim unenforceable, as follows:

Of Descartes' reasons for doubting the truth of various thoughts, obviously the most important is the thought that God, or some demon, might have made our intelligence defective. But if Descartes really had this thought in the process of doubting, as he said he did, it is difficult to see why he did not at once stop the process at that point. For once we have that thought we shall think that any thought we subsequently attain, whether it be about or own existence or anything else, may be defective and so not possibly knowledge.

(1950b: 79)

Such gives the right feel of the kind of collapse Clarke unearths. His case is that the collapse is avoidable *only* if knowledge is occasion-sensitive. I think his case cogent, but will not argue this here.

In 'Seeing Surfaces and Seeing Physical Objects' (1965; henceforth 'Surfaces') occasion-sensitivity plays a very different role. Here it is a device for preserving features we would all acknowledge seeing to have. Perhaps it is mandatory for preserving them. It is, anyway, arguably present. But if we were to suppose seeing not to have those features, the concept of seeing would not collapse.

Talk of seeing would not thereby be rendered *incoherent*. If what Clarke calls 'the surface inquiry' really yielded correct results, it would turn out that all we ever see, in the case of opaque solids, are their (facing) surfaces. That would be a surprise. But at least (if the rot stops there) there might still be determinate facts as to the things we have seen and the things we have not. So whereas the sceptical inquiry (the parallel to the surface inquiry in the case of knowledge) is proof that our thinking *must* be occasion-sensitive (at least sometimes), with respect to the surface inquiry occasion sensitivity is only a device on offer for avoiding unwanted results.

Both in 'Legacy' and in 'Surfaces' occasion-sensitivity functions to defuse a certain line of thought. In 'Surfaces', if that line is not defused, we must reject a raft of things we would have supposed true. We would have made a surprise discovery, not thanks to science, or closer attention to what was actually before our eyes on various occasions, but rather through philosophical reflection—what just *might* be philosophical sleight of hand. Someone might say, 'The detective entered the room, and seeing a tomato on the sideboard realized at once that he was in the home of a philosopher'. We would all regard that as (possibly) true. If the surface inquiry is correct it is not. What the detective saw was not actually the *tomato*. But then life does hold surprises. If the sceptical enquiry really worked (and if it leads where Clarke and I think it does), then the result is not a surprise discovery that we do not know all the things we thought we did, but rather the still more disconcerting discovery that there is nothing to say about knowledge at all. The evils occasion-sensitivity spares us thus differ in kind in the two cases.

The surface inquiry, or any other, *would* reduce seeing to an incoherent notion if it led, not to the result that all we see are surfaces, but rather, still further, to the result that what we see is not part of the environment at all. For, since seeing *is* awareness of one's environment—of what, in being as it is, may be a case of things being such-and-such way—the result would thus be that there is really no such thing as seeing. If we were then to have anything to talk about in speaking of people seeing things, seeing would *have* to be occasion-sensitive. But, as the name suggests, this is not where the surface inquiry leads.

Why this disparity in ambition between 'Legacy' and 'Surfaces'? Several answers are possible. One is that, in 'Surfaces', for simplicity's sake, Clarke considered only part of an enquiry: the enquiry in 'Surfaces' could be extended to lead us out of the environment and force us to retreat to something non-environmental as the proper objects of seeing; it is just that, for sake of exposition, Clarke omitted so extending the enquiry. Another is that while the surface enquiry cannot be extended so as thus to force us out of the environment, some other parallel enquiry can be produced, and would do this, unless it were defused in a way we can somehow read off from Clarke's defusing of the surface inquiry. Such, I think, is how Clarke views the matter. In either of these cases, there is a valid case that seeing *must* be an occasion-sensitive notion on pain of collapse. Knowing and seeing would then be parallel in this respect. Or there is a third possibility: that no such way of forcing us to retreat from the environment exists; that, though seeing may *be* occasion-sensitive, there is no way in which, through ignoring this, ringers for what we see (or for our seeing it) come to threaten the notion with *collapse*. If seeing thus differs from knowing, such might reflect those deeper differences, already hinted at, in what it is that each relates us to.

3 The Sense Datum

The previous section suggested two roles that the surface enquiry might play in saddling us with sense data. First, it might be an initial proper part of some enquiry which, in full, so saddles us. Second, it might model, more clearly since more simply, the form of some distinct enquiry which so saddles us. First, then, can the surface inquiry be so extended? The answer: perhaps it can be extended, but not to sense-data if, with Prichard, we take these to be things without our shared environment.

Clarke's surface enquiry leaves us with the conclusion that, in the case of opaque solids, what we see is at most their facing surfaces. To extend the argument would be to apply the same considerations over again to reach the conclusion that what we see is, at most, not even that. We get to surfaces on roughly these lines. Consider someone looking at a tomato. Now ask yourself the question how much of the tomato behind the facing surface he sees—whether, for example, he sees the tomato's insides or backside. The answer to such questions is, inevitably, 'No'. If he does not see those parts of the tomato, then the conclusion is meant to be that the most he sees of the tomato is what remains: the facing surface.

To push this line further we might ask just how thick a surface would be. (Mark Kalderon tells me that Leonardo da Vinci, among others, pushed it in this way. So inspired, I call the enquiry thus extended *the da Vinci enquiry*.) Suppose we think of the surface of the tomato as part of the tomato in a sense in which this means that the surface is made up of molecules. So it has some thickness. Ignoring what is *physically* possible, let us ask just how thick the seen surface is. For any (opaque) positive thickness, one can in imagination (still ignoring physical possibility) divide the surface into two opaque rings, inner and outer, each of half that thickness. Asked whether one sees the inner ring, one would need to answer 'No'. So the seen surface can have no thickness. So it cannot be made of molecules. In a sense, then, it is really no part of the tomato at all.

The original surface enquiry relies on an idea on these lines: what one sees of the tomato is the tomato minus those identifiable parts one does not see (notably, the insides and the back side). One could also think of the operative principle this way: what one sees when he looks at the tomato is just what he would see if those parts he does not see were not there—that is, if he were looking at a certain sort of ringer. He would see just the same whether he were facing the tomato or such a ringer. Thus involving ringers brings the da Vinci enquiry into closer parallel with the sceptical enquiry into knowledge. Now we might try amending the da Vinci enquiry. Suppose that, instead of that tomato, there had been some ringer on the sideboard—perhaps a wax tomato, or just another tomato. Ringers are, by definition, indistinguishable (by, or on, sight) from the real thing—not just by some viewer, but full stop. There *is* nothing visible by which to distinguish them. So our viewer would see no such thing. So (the idea would go) he sees nothing, in viewing that tomato, that he would not also see in viewing the ringer. Since the ringer and the tomato share no parts, he sees, as things stand, no part of the tomato. It does not yet follow that he *does* see something non-environmental, nor even that he sees nothing environmental. Perhaps, though, we have been moved in that direction.

Now, though, the enquiry takes a quite different form. It is an *argument*—something Clarke wants his enquiries not to be. (Rather, they are to be working one's way into a position where he just *sees*, or seems to see, the fact the desired conclusion states.) Now there is a crucial move from the (true) thought that the viewer sees nothing by which to distinguish the tomato from the ringer to the thought that he sees nothing, in viewing the tomato, that he would not see in viewing the ringer. Why buy that move? One cannot just *see*—in Clarke's terms, have visibly before one's eyes—that *this* is so. Here things really do depend on just what sort of concept seeing (objects) is—on its rule-like, rather than non-rule-like dimension. Moreover, if, as seems, you need not know what you are seeing to be seeing it, then the fact that you could not tell whether the surface you see is a tomato's or a wax ringer's hardly suggests that what you *see* could not just be the one thing or the other. The surface enquiry turned on no such inference. What does so turn is no mere extension of it.

The da Vinci enquiry minus emendation yields the conclusion that what one sees of the tomato, if anything, is something with no thickness. This alone does not drive us to conclude that one sees something which might still be there were the tomato not; much less to look for objects of *perception* which are not part of our environment at all. One can, for example, think of the tomato as inhabiting a spatial shell (closed surface) in which it forges its career. The shell would travel with it. It would be deformable, as a cat's, or a squash ball's, shape is. It would not be made of molecules. Any time-slice of it would be made of points—in the space we all cohabit. It would not be something non-environmental. If the *da Vinci* were sound, what one would see in viewing an opaque object might be the facing part of such a shell.

Or one *could* view such a shell as spatially fixed, filled at one moment by the tomato, at another moment by nothing, or by something else, or part of something else. Suitably occupied, *it* might be visible. A shell so thought of is still a part of space, the locus of visible things. So thinking, what one sees when he views a tomato really is no part of the tomato, nothing essentially present when the tomato is. But it is still part of *space*, a part of that environment in which things which reflect light form images on retinas, are thus *visible* (to *one* who is sighted). We are still not led out of the environment. We can take such shells to be the things we see while still following Frege in taking *Vorstellungen* to be had, not seen, without thereby falling into contradiction. There is still no call for sense data (if these are *Vorstellungen*) to fill the role of what is seen.

But *are* sense data *Vorstellungen* in Frege's sense—things which need a bearer (to be which is to belong to some particular thinker's consciousness) and which brook no two bearers? Frege tells us that you and I may stand shoulder to shoulder viewing the same tree, and yet, if we have visual *Vorstellungen*, have different ones. You and I can stand shoulder to shoulder viewing the same (occupied) spatial shell. We need not be seeing different ones. Does this matter to whether spatial shells are sense data? It does, so that sense data are not where any extended surface enquiry leads, if sense data meet any of the following conditions:

1 They are immune to ringers. It could not be just as though you were seeing (or experiencing visually) the sense datum (or data) you now are while you were *not* experiencing it, but rather some ringer for it (something visually indistinguishable from it). Sense data have no such ringers.
2 (Correlatively) the sense datum (or data) you experience visually now is/ are what you would be experiencing visually no matter how things were at least in your extradermal environment. What sense datum (or data) you see (or have) is independent of how things are there. (Such is the price of *not* admitting of ringers.)
3 Correlatively, sense data are not things for *one* to see (or experience visually). Their career is *entirely* fixed by how things are for their haver, *now*. They are what you experience visually now in a sense in which to experience *thus* one would need to be you.

Condition 1 is what makes sense data argument/enquiry-stoppers. If amended da Vinci were sound, then whatever A was, it could not be what you *see* (or directly experience visually) if there were some B such that things would have looked *just* the same had it been B and not A that you viewed. If sense data admitted of ringers, amended da Vinci would thus rule them out as what was seen. So for such an enquiry to lead to sense data, 1 must hold of them. Conditions 2 and 3, I think, follow upon this. But any one of these would do to remove sense data from the environment.

Our present concern is not to settle whether there *are* sense data, but to see what can be learned from the search for them as to the different sorts of relations to the world that seeing and knowing are. Nowadays few own up to belief in sense data. It may still be that more than just these posit objects of perceptual experience which meet at least some of conditions 1–3. There may be more than one way to make seeing disappear.

4 The Role of the Surface Inquiry

Neither 'Legacy' nor 'Surfaces' makes Clarke's own attitude towards the surface inquiry clear. In his thesis he is more explicit. The surface enquiry relates to sense data in the second of the two ways so far suggested. It is to be a simpler model for a form of enquiry which is also exemplified, in different instantiations, both by what he calls 'the hallucination enquiry'; that is, the sceptical enquiry into knowledge and 'the sense-data enquiry'—what is meant to land us with that sight-destroying conclusion just scouted. In the thesis, he says:

> I believe the sense-data inquiry is too complex to tackle head-on. In this chapter I shall study it *indirectly* by studying a far simpler inquiry which is a microcosm of the sense data inquiry.
>
> (1962: 52, ch. 2)

The sense-datum enquiry is thus supposed to have a certain form, which it shares with the surface inquiry, and also, Clarke elsewhere tells us, with the sceptical inquiry. Later in the thesis Clarke outlines that form, the elements in it filled in with their values within the surface inquiry:

> The maze of the sense-data inquiry should be easier to traverse, however, if we are forearmed with a blue-print of what its general interlocking elements probably are. These elements are the following: seeing is a *unit* concept. The *rules* of ordinary language, applied in the *philosophical* case, from which the *non-rule-like dimension* responsible for criteria of relevancy/irrelevancy is absent, conditionally dictate the basic philosophical

inquiries. The philosopher's *assumption* that ordinary language is, in this kind of case, fully meaningful implies that these inquiries are to be performed together with the *mental act* which, because Seeing is a *unit* concept, moves Seeing down, before our eyes, to surfaces (or, in the sense-data inquiry, to colours-in-certain-shapes). Finally, the *generalization* ... seemingly makes surfaces (and sense data) into independent entities.

(1962: 229–30, ch. 4)

What *form* of inquiry is set out here? In the surface enquiry what occupies the first place in that structure is the idea that seeing is a unit concept. Clark suggests that that place holds the same occupant in the sense datum enquiry, though that enquiry remains to be specified. In the sceptical enquiry that first place must be occupied by something else. For seeing to be a unit concept is for it to exhibit a particular sort of occasion-sensitivity—variation across Clarke's 'non-rule-like' dimension. On different occasions for asking what N saw (on some fixed occasion), different things are to be understood as to what would count as seeing such-and-such. In the sceptical enquiry, which Clarke does set out, it is another sort of variation across such a dimension—a variation in understandings of knowledge—which occupies that same place in the structure. That *form* common to all these enquiries is thus that the concept (or way for things to be) as to whose instancings the enquiry asks has a particular sort of occasion-sensitivity—susceptibility to understandings—which is crucial to what the answer would be (if any) to the questions the enquiry tries to pose.

The second element is that certain 'rules of ordinary language' apply to the relevant concept. Strictly speaking, rules of language cannot apply to a concept. But perhaps there are rules which apply to any expression which expresses a given concept. A distinction of Frege's can help, I think, in understanding what Clarke has in mind here by a rule. Frege distinguishes between what has generality of a particular sort—call this a generality—and what does not—what he refers to as a particular case—but is what might instance such generalities. He writes:

A thought always contains something which reaches beyond the particular case to present it to consciousness as falling under some given generality.

(1882: p. 189)

A thought, in Frege's sense, just is a particular way to make truth turn on how things are. It is *of* things as being a certain way there is for things to be. It makes truth hang on things being that way. Ways for things to be are thus the first locus of the sort of generality in question. For it to be determinate how truth is to turn on how things are is for there to be indefinitely many (possible) cases of instancing that generality (if any), and indefinitely many ways of failing to (if any). If Pia is drinking absinthe, that might be the way things are while Sid fiddles, or while he does a slow burn. Such are two ways for things to be such as to fit that generality. By contrast, what does the instancing—things being as they are—is the wrong sort of thing itself to be instanced. It does nothing to fix what truth *is to* turn on. Perhaps Pia is drinking in a murky corner. Her doing what she thus does does nothing to determine what would count as someone drinking absinthe, or being in a murky corner—what would be a case of that, what not; and equally for any other generality. No instance of a generality fixes how it reaches. Nor does any proper part of the range of its instances.

Two distinct sorts of things are thus in play: things with a certain generality—ways for things to be—and particular instances of things, or a thing, being some given such way. A way for things to be thus participates in two distinct sorts of relations: relations with other ways for things to be—relations *within* the domain of generalities in this sense of the term—and relations *between* some such generality and particular cases, the fundamental relation of this second kind being *instancing* (or its converse, call it *reaching to*). Sipping absinthe is sipping something alcoholic (first type). What Pia is doing is sipping absinthe (second type). Clarke's rules of language govern relations of the first type. If it is yellow then it is not blue. Variation along his non-rule-like dimension is variation, from occasion to occasion for counting something as a case of something, in which particular cases then count as instancing the generality in question.

We come now to the philosophical case, the third element in the form. Here the philosopher actually carries out the relevant enquiry. In the course of it he finds himself reaching conclusions, making judgements as to, for example, whether Sid (really) saw Pia's yellow Porsche. He thus applies the relevant concept—seeing, say—to a (usually imagined) particular case. He applies it as it then seems it does apply. For the case to be *philosophical* is for the non-rule-like dimension to be out of play. Circumstance selects no particular value of the variable along the relevant dimension; fixes no particular *sometimes*-called-for understanding as to what, for example, seeing a Porsche might be. Still, while conducting the enquiry, the philosopher feels no such lack. It is for him as though a definite understanding of the concept *is* fixed—all the understanding one might wish, or enough to decide how the relevant concept must apply.

The variable in the non-rule-like element thus concerns that inter-domain relation, instancing. Where it takes on no value of the sort occasions fix—where no choices are made between those different understandings the relevant generality (seeing X, knowing X) can bear, it remains accordingly unfixed what bears this relation to that generality—despite an impression the philosopher might have to the contrary.

Were there no occasion-sensitivity, there would be no non-rule-like dimension to mishandle, no such thing to be alert to. But since there is, blindness to it can be fatal. If what Pia is doing (reclining languidly) would sometimes not count as *sitting* on a sofa, then, noticing this, and supposing that in matters of what counts as what, what is sometimes so must always be, it can come to seem mandatory to think that actually sitting is a much rarer phenomenon than, before philosophical reflection, one would have supposed. Clarke, in the cases he does work out—seeing, knowing—does more to make the philosopher's position poignant, to show how what one would sometimes say seems forced on the philosopher as what he then must say. But this catches the form of the wages of ignoring occasion-sensitivity. Clarke has brought the nature of this peril well into view.

A philosophical case, then, is to be one in which an occasion is called on to fix some occasion-specific understanding of a concept under investigation, but fails to fix any such. The concept alone does not fix, for the relevant particular case (or cases) whether it is to count as instanced by them. Rules of *language* (relations *within* the domain of generalities) may remain in force in the philosopher's circumstances. *They* need not vary across any relevant range of occasions for applying them. But nor do they alone fix what stands to what in the instancing relation. The philosopher, blind to occasion-sensitivity, supposes otherwise. For him, rules of language, by themselves, must fix what words are true of. The truth on that assumption, Clarke argues, *would* be that Sid see at most the front surface of the tomato.

There is a fourth element in Clarke's form, which he calls 'generalization'. The philosopher considers a particular case—say, Sid facing a tomato. He comes to his conclusion about Sid. He then generalizes: if the most Sid sees is a facing surface, and if Sid is in as good a position for seeing more as one could ever be, then the most *anyone* ever sees of an opaque object is its facing surface. There is no occasion-sensitivity—variation across occasions for answering a question as to what someone sees—so there is also no variation across occasions for seeing (or missing) things.

In the case of the surface inquiry, the occasion-sensitivity being ignored is contained in the idea that seeing is a unit concept. What matters in that idea can be put as follows. (Here and henceforth I depart somewhat from Clarke's way of setting things out. But the operative idea remains the same.) A determinate (fully meaningful) question 'What did N see?' is asked against the background of a (determinate enough) space of options. The correct answer to that question, if there is one, is the best option among these. As one might put it, the content of a correct answer—when there is one—is always of the form 'This, rather than any of those'. What the relevant space is depends on (conversely, identifies) what the question is; which (normally) depends, further, on the circumstances of its posing. So, for example, the detective enters and looks at the sideboard. What does he see? Possible answers: a tomato, a lemon, a cherimoya, nothing (it was all a blur, went by too fast, there was a lot of dry ice between him and the sideboard, just at that moment he got hit on the head). If there were a tomato on the sideboard, in plain sight, clearly illuminated, then, *ceteris paribus*, 'A tomato' is the right answer to that question. In other circumstances, there might have been a different question. 'What was on the sideboard?' 'A tomato'. 'Are you sure?' 'But you know this was a philosopher's study. Philosophers are always up to tricks with half tomatoes. Did you really see the whole tomato, or only a facing half?' 'Well, now that you mention all that, I suppose I only saw the facing half'.

So the relevant occasion-sensitivity here consists in this. There are different questions to pose in asking what N saw on occasion O. These differ in that each is to be understood as asked against a different background—with a different space of possible answers. Their correct answers may differ accordingly. A question what N saw on O, posed on a given occasion for the posing, may, in the circumstances, be to be understood as asked against some given such background. As circumstances of the posing may differ, so, too, will the question asked. Such a question *will* be to be understood as asked against some such background if a question was successfully posed at all. But there is no guarantee of such success. For this, circumstances must do their work. Nothing ensures that wherever one tries to pose such a question, circumstances will be up to the job.

When the philosopher tries to ask what N saw, his circumstances are not up to the job. Among the different understandings the question what N saw might bear, they choose no-one in particular. They do not fix with what seeing the tomato is to be contrasted. Moreover, even if they did some such selecting, the most they would achieve is fixing what it would be true to say in *those* circumstances—what would *then* count as seeing such-and-such. One would get the philosopher's result only in supposing that what it is *sometimes* true to say as to what the detective saw on entering the philosopher's study—what might sometimes count (or fail to count) as seeing a tomato—is what it would always be true to say as to this; what it would *really* be, *per se*, to see a tomato. Which is just to suppose that there is no occasion-sensitivity in the notion *see*, or none of the kind Clarke points to; which at best begs a question.

For the sceptical enquiry the idea again will be that there is a diversity of things to ask, here in asking whether N knows that P, for given N and P; various things knowing that P might be understood to be, each on *some* occasion. Relevant differences might start from this idea: a doubt must earn its spurs. A doubt is a way for it not to be the case that P, perhaps, in pointed cases, even while so seeming. For example, a way for there not to be tomatoes in the bin is for there to be tomato-like persimmons. A doubt so understood may, or may not, make it *doubtful* whether P—count as a way P might not, in fact, be so. Such is liable to vary from one occasion to another of asking what N knows. In given circumstances for so asking, it may or may not count as so that there might be persimmons in that bin. Only where it does so count might failure to settle it impeach N's claim to know that P. Or so it is if the notion *know* is occasion-sensitive.

If the notion *know* so behaves, what might vary along a non-rule-like dimension is thus what it would be for a doubt to have earned its spurs, and accordingly which doubts have done so. With this comes that pattern found in the surface inquiry. The possibility of persimmons would *sometimes* matter as per above. A philosopher, noticing this, and blind to occasion-sensitivity, could do no other than suppose this always to matter. *Mutatis mutandis* for other doubts. At which point knowing comes to seem an entirely unattainable ideal. At which point, too, Prichard's maxim collapses and with it the concept of knowing *überhaupt*.

So the surface inquiry is, indeed, a model for a sceptical inquiry into knowledge just as Clarke says. It does bring out the structure of that inquiry. I think it also helps defang it. But now what about sense data? Here we need a particular kind of non-rule-like dimension; a variation across occasions in what seeing something, V, is to be understood to be. Specifically, within this range of variation there would have to be occasions on which what would count as seeing V rules out seeing *any* part of an opaque object, or its shell or envelope on either of the above understandings of this; anything that might be before the eyes. Noticing what we would thus *sometimes* say, the philosopher might, in the way thus scouted, conclude that we *never* see anything before the eyes. But with this, the road to sense data would be only half traversed. So far, the terminus of this (imagined) enquiry might just be: no-one ever sees anything. Such would be a kind of collapse of the concept. What still must be added in a sense-datum enquiry is something, not before the eyes, which in fact, in the imagined circumstances, counts as something one *does* see.

The sought-for enquiry runs into trouble enough meeting the first of these two demands. With the second it faces a fundamental obstacle. For there is now a significant departure from the pattern of the other two cases. The surface enquiry leads us to a conclusion as to the most one *ever* counts as seeing when viewing a tomato full face, where this would at least be a true conclusion as to what one could truly be said to have seen on at least *some* occasions for saying this. One *would* sometimes say (truly) that the most N saw of the fruit before him was its facing surface (for example, so he has no basis for thinking it is a tomato and not a persimmon). *Just* this is what provides us with something on which Clarke's step of generalization might operate. Similarly for knowing. There can be circumstances in which one *would* say that N cannot really know it is a tomato if he has not cut it open, or squeezed it. But, as Frege notes, a sense datum is not even a candidate for being seen. It *cannot* bear that sort of relation to us. Nor (accordingly) are there purposes for which it would count as true that the most N saw in viewing the tomato was a thing of a sort not liable to be before anyone's eyes at all. On what then, is one to generalize? If someone did not see the tomato, what he still might have done for all that is see its facing half. Such are alternatives to choose between in identifying what it is he saw. A sense datum is never such an alternative. The notion *see* admits of no *such* understandings.

The variation across occasions relevant to the surface enquiry is in the possibly correct answers to a question posed on them as to what N saw, where, throughout that variation one thing which remains constant is that *all* possible answers cite something environmental, before the eyes. No such variation (mishandled) could drive a sense-datum enquiry. Such an enquiry (if there is one) must thus fit a different pattern from that exemplified by the surface enquiry. It must drive us out of our environment by appeal to *something* other than what we had anyway always been prepared to recognize as so.

5 All Those Colours

If there *is* a sense-datum enquiry, what in it varies across a non-rule-like dimension so as to *seem* to force sense-data on us—something whose absence would actually do so? At each stage in the surface enquiry we are faced with a choice: Did N see A, or rather at most B—the tomato, or at most the front half? At each stage, it is the B option which *seems* mandated, and would be were seeing not occasion-sensitive along lines Clarke suggests. A sense-datum enquiry, were there one, would also offer us a choice for what we see— ultimately, a tomato or a sense datum. What resources might it have to force, or seem to force, our hand? In any case, an entirely different sort from what a surface enquiry relies on.

Clarke sometimes describes the sense datum enquiry as a *continuation* of the surface enquiry. Its conclusion would be, he thinks, that what we see are items with colour and shape, not in, nor parts of anything in, space. He never sets out the enquiry. But he gives hints. In one place he comes (speculatively) nearer to saying what it is whose non-rule-like dimension, mishandled, lands us with sense data. That place is an appendix to his thesis where he is comparing his own view with that of Roderick Firth. He says:

> There must be a proposition in the sense data inquiry which, like the above proposition in the surface inquiry, has to be *true* if the common sense beliefs are fully meaningful, and which is not properly meaningful unless accompanied by distinguishing. I think this proposition may be the assertion that there could be an hallucinatory experience which looked and felt just the same as the present veridical experience.
>
> (1962: 259)

'Distinguishing' is marking off 'units', or, more generally, fixing with what a possible answer to the question asked as to what was seen might contrast. For the surface enquiry's questions, this is properly done in an occasion-sensitive way. *Mutatis mutandis* for any sense datum enquiry. Where the need for this is ignored, we are landed, in the one case, with surfaces, in the other with sense data. It is not entirely clear what Clarke thinks is relevantly occasion-sensitive in the assertion he cites—whether that sensitivity is contained in that 'there *could* be', or rather in the notion of looking and feeling *just the same*. Perhaps it is the two working jointly. In chapter 2 of the thesis (p. 97) he says,

> In the surface inquiry a mental act is required if we are to attend 'properly' to the how much fact. In the sense data inquiry I think a mental act is an essential ingredient if we are to take in 'properly' the fact that hallucinatory experiences can look just like real ones.

So, it seems, all turns on how one understands *being capable of looking just like real ones*. Missing the occasion sensitive in how this is to be understood is to be what saddles us with sense data.

For an enquiry to be what Clarke has in mind here it must be what, if valid, would land us with sense data as the most we ever (really) see, and be what *would* be valid were it not for the relevant occasion-sensitivity. For it to be valid in the sense that matters here is for it to force our hand in making a certain choice—here, a choice between seeing something which is part of our (shared) environment, and seeing something which is not—as a sense datum would not be. The fact which would thus force our hands if taken in improperly—ignoring the occasion-sensitivity of some notion applied in it—is to be one of things being capable of looking just the same to one while there is nothing relevant before his eyes as they would were there a relevant something there.

There are problems enough in understanding the relevant notion of looking just like the real thing. If it bears any coherent understanding, then no doubt it bears many, so understanding it is an occasion-sensitive affair. But is there *any* understanding on which what does the looking even *seems* (if only to a philosopher's eye) both mandated as what is *seen*, and not part of the (shared) environment? Is there any (sometimes) possible understanding which, but for occasion-sensitivity, *would* be mandated for the philosopher, and then (hence) universally—one on which we can just *see* that sense data are what we see?

One reason for thinking that no enquiry could do for sense data what the surface enquiry does for surfaces has been given already. For sense data, the relevant choice would be between seeing a tomato (or some bit of it) and seeing a sense datum—between something we *do* ordinarily count as seeing, and—unlike the surface enquiry—something which (for Frege's reasons among others) we never do, or could, count as seen. The choice is between the tomato and changing our understanding, along the *rule-like* dimension, of to what seeing might be a relation.

With ringers, here hallucinations, in the picture, there is a further reason. With the pig in full view before him, Sid may yet not qualify as *knowing* there is a pig before him either because of *his* capacities for distinguishing pigs from other things, or, if ringers might be good enough, because pigs are simply not distinguishable from other things by sight. Here is a fact which, if taken in improperly, may land us with *scepticism*. But that a ringer might look *just like* a pig (or so look to Sid) does not even begin to touch a claim that what Sid *saw* (whether he knew it or not) was a pig. You need not *know* what you are seeing. Glancing at the next table, you need not know yourself to have *seen* Rachel Weisz in the Lansdowne.

Such is central to what makes knowing and seeing two fundamentally different sorts of relations to the world. Knowing is coordinating the conceptual with the historical—what is instanced with what does the instancing. It is awareness of the *fact* of, for example, what is before one's eyes falling under a given generality—for a thing to be a pig, say. It is a success always liable to threat, or undermining, by failure of that fact to hold—in fact, being the success it is, by the very possibility of such undermining, if such a possibility there really is. Without occasion-sensitivity, a notion of such success would be incoherent. It would collide with Frege's point that to judge is *intrinsically* to expose oneself to liability to error.

Seeing, by contrast, is merely a form of acquaintance, or affording acquaintance, with that which is to do the instancing. It places one in a position to take *that*—things being as they are before one—as a case, or not, of, for example, a thing being a pig. If what is before you *is*, in fact, a pig, then, for all that there might *not* have been that before you, it is still *that* whose acquaintance you have made; that which you are thus positioned to take to be a case of a thing being a pig, that which you will be right or wrong about in so representing it to yourself. The possibility of hallucinations—that there *could have* been one—thus has no bearing on what, in fact, you saw. Such makes hallucinations unpromising for generating a sense-datum enquiry.

Clarke supposes that a sense datum enquiry will appeal to hallucinations. Must it? Viewing a wax tomato, one confronts a ringer for *a tomato*. The ringer is *before* him, *looking* as it does. Hallucinating a tomato may be, perhaps, a ringer for seeing one. Such does not make it *of* what is a ringer for a tomato. Nor is there clear sense to be made of *that* idea. Emended da Vinci appeals only to ringers which may be before the eyes. Is there a way in which hallucinations yield impetus towards sense data which such environmental ringers do not? Emended da Vinci, to be sure, leads us off that track on which Clarke wants to keep us. With it we leave the pattern of the surface enquiry. We descend into argument, or grammar-defying assumption. The problem is now with seeing's 'rule-like' dimension. Are hallucinations means for staying on Clarke's designated path?

In emended da Vinci Sid stares at a tomato on the sideboard. We are struck with the thought that there *could* have been a wax ringer there. Had there been, Sid *could* not have told the difference. But why should he have been able to? To repeat, seeing a tomato does not require *knowing* it to be such. There might seem to be this reason. Ringers being ringers, seeing what he does gives Sid nothing by which a ringer might be told from what he sees (or *vice versa*). This *could* be put: what he sees is *just the same as*, or stronger yet, *just*, what he would see were there a ringer. Such are (sometimes) natural enough things to say; *true* if properly understood. But whatever Sid does see, and would see were there a ringer, cannot be any part of the tomato. So, it seems, if *what* he sees is just the same, ringer or not, then what he sees viewing the tomato cannot be any part of it, or of any bit of the environment. It must be something *not* before the eyes. *If* this is still enquiry in Clarke's sense, and not argument, then perhaps, on closer inspection, it instances that form the surface enquiry is meant to exemplify. But hallucinations play no role in bringing us to this point.

How, though, ought one understand *just the same as* here? Pia makes fake Rolexes. Showing her handiwork to a peripatetic merchant she might say, 'You see nothing here you would not see were it a real one'. If the merchant can point to something—'Rolex' is in the wrong font—then Pia is refuted. If there is no such thing to cite, she is right. Similarly for the tomato. What Sid sees is *not* what he would see if he were viewing a wax ringer if, say, the wax ringer would look waxier, or more orangeish, or scab-free. It is built into the notion of a ringer that no such thing is so. What Sid would see in either case is something reddish, something roundish, and so on.

Sid sees *something* red. He would have seen *something* red had it been wax. The same thing? Viewing the tomato, Sid sees *a case of* something being red, an instancing, by what is before him, of a certain way for a thing to be—for a thing to be red. He would see *that*—that is, an instancing of *that* way for a thing to be were it a wax ringer. For Sid to see just the same as he would see were he viewing a wax ringer, on the understanding on which this is what he does, is just (or no more than) for him to see—witness—visible instancings of all the same ways for a thing visibly to be. The instancings he happens to witness are *by*, and in, what is visibly before him being as it visibly is. Were there a ringer, he would not be witnessing *those* instancings, but rather instancings by what then would have been before him. The case for sense data thus collapses at this point, by virtue of a mishandled rule-like dimension. Mishandling of non-rule-like dimensions need not be an issue.

A misunderstanding of *see the same* is thus defused; along with it a false impression of seeing something ultra-worldly. Hallucinations played no role in this misunderstanding. But nor did we arrive at a sense-datum enquiry. Might appeal to hallucinations allow us to avoid the pitfalls just cited? In fact this seems only to make matters worse. For in hallucinating one does not witness the instancing by anything of anything. There is nothing in hallucination to engage in instancing. Sherwin-Williams makes paint. Their motto: 'Sherwin-Williams covers the earth'. The crucial point has thus been hit: colours spread. An instancing of that way for a thing to be, for it to be red, takes up space. Hallucinating a tomato may be a ringer for seeing one. If so, for one so hallucinating it is just as though he were seeing a tomato (or ringer therefore). But hallucinating a tomato is not experiencing something which takes up space. (If one hallucinates a tomato on the (actual) sideboard, one may *hallucinate* it taking up a given portion of space. Such makes for no tomato in that space, or at least none one thus experiences.) So it is not experiencing, certainly not visually, something red, nor (*a fortiori*) something which is a ringer for a tomato. (If it was that little red pill that caused the hallucination, hallucinating may be experiencing the red pill. But not visually.)

To drive a sense-datum enquiry one needs a seeming fact to the effect that what Sid sees viewing the tomato is (just) what he might see, or experience visually, were he hallucinating. But such is simply not so. Where Sid hallucinates a tomato it may be for him just as though he were seeing a tomato; just as though he were witnessing instancings by what was before him of such ways for things to be as *being a tomato* or *being red*. But its being *as though* one were witnessing such things is not witnessing them. For Sid to witness instancings, for example, in seeing, is for him to witness instancings by *what is before him*, or suitably related to him in the environment. As Frege shows, such are the only sorts of instancings there are. *Hallucinating* may be a ringer for seeing. But this does not make it the witnessing, or experiencing, of ringers for the sorts of things that might be seen—ringers in the sense that they *do* instance all those ways for things to be which one could see to be instanced in things looking as they do. If the possibility of hallucinations seems to suggest sense data where the mere mundane possibility of a ringer for a tomato would not, this can only be because one has misidentified what the ringer is in an hallucination: not something which is *what* is hallucinated, but simply the hallucinating.

It would be nice if occasion-sensitivity were the only barrier to sense data, as I think it is the only barrier to scepticism. It would be nice if the concept of seeing, like that of knowing, would simply collapse without it. But I cannot see how this is so. Rather, it seems, the road to sense data is blocked simply by minding one's grammar—by attention to what there is to see along the *rule*-like dimension, to use Clarke's term. This leaves us with precisely that problem to which Clarke offers such a nice solution on the assumption that the sense datum enquiry does follow the pattern of the surface enquiry. Why should the idea of sense data have such a strong and enduring hold on our imagination? Why should it have seemed to so many completely compelling, however unpalatable? Unlike Clarke, I have no answer. For some it may be mere inattention to (ordinary, school-book) grammar. For others it may have been a desperate attempt to save *knowledge* from the sceptic (on which more anon).

In a different context, Wittgenstein writes:

The greatest danger here is wanting to observe oneself.

(1982b: §459)

A philosopher's investigations are best conducted in the third person. The first is liable to mislead. Thus can things go wrong. Sid tells Pia that there are tomatoes in the kitchen. Pia then points out that there *could* be persimmons there, and that some types of these, in some states of ripeness, look much like tomatoes; too much so for Sid to tell the difference on a causal glance. Sid takes the point and then retracts. 'Alright', he admits, 'so perhaps all I really saw was some roughly ovoid reddish fruit'. Such *might* be taken for a result as to what one really sees. Moreover, a general idea *might* be seen as in operation here. Pia impeaches Sid's right to claim he *knows* there are tomatoes in the kitchen. And (paradoxically) what impeaches that now seems also to impeach his claim to have seen any. (One might say, reasonably, 'If he *can* claim to have seen them, then he can claim to know'.)

It only needs noting that there are two reasons one may need to retract a claim. If the claim is that P, then it needs retracting if P is not so. But to assert something is to represent oneself as having taken in, settled, its being so. If it turns out that, for all you know, it might not be so, then you were in no position to make the claim, should not have, and should not, make it, thus must retract—*whether or not* the claim is, in fact, true. If Pia's considerations are good, then Sid had no right to claim that he saw tomatoes in the kitchen. He had better move on to (in the circumstances) 'weaker' claims which he may still have a right to make. *He had* better leave open whether, he *saw* tomatoes or not. Hence there is no result here as to what he saw. He cannot claim to know because he cannot *claim* to have seen. But all that is beside the point—as it should be, as per the point of departure of this essay.

6 Seeing and Knowing

It is important to Clarke that his three enquiries are not *arguments*. In the surface enquiry we consider Sid staring at a tomato. A certain fact then occurs to us: Sid cannot see the insides or the backside (and so on). We focus on what Sid thus cannot see. We then just *see* the fact, or 'fact', that the most Sid can see is the front surface. It is not as if we first need to be convinced of some principle of the form 'One sees A only if...', and then, having come to accept it, manage, with its aid, to deduce the conclusion that the most Sid sees is the front surface. The conclusion is, Clarke tells us, 'right before our eyes'. Perhaps a rough parallel is this. We look at the large flexible plastic shell filled with little pellets. We cannot recognize it as a chair. But then we observe people using it. We see *how* one sits in it. And we immediately see it as a chair. Not that it follows from some principle about chairs that this is what it must be. Our ability to recognize what counts as a chair as so counting is enough. Similarly for the sceptical enquiry. We consider Sid standing towards the tomato as he does, with all the capacities he in fact has for settling whether something is a tomato or not. Then some sceptical possibility occurs to us. We think of some ringer for the situation Sid in fact is in, there staring at the tomato. We focus on this. It then occurs to us (or seems to) that, for all Sid can tell, he in fact *might* be in the ringer situation. We now see—just as we see the bean bag chair to be a chair—that this cannot *really* be knowing that there is a chair. I think Clarke is right about these first two enquiries.

In stressing that they are not *arguments* Clarke calls our attention to an important feature of these cases. But the road to sense data is not like that. There is no way of landing us with them without getting us to accept some principle linking seeing to something else. Given the principle, we can see it to *follow* that, with a tomato in plain sight, the most one could *see*, strictly speaking, is, if anything, a sense datum. Here we deal in argument. The most likely source of such a something else to link to seeing is epistemology, specifically, some notion such as knowing, telling, or having proof. Perhaps some such links have at least initial plausibility.

Clarke himself suggests that the road to sense data may be paved with some connection between seeing and knowing. He says, for example:

Traditional epistemology has shown that if empirical knowledge must be independent of the non-rule-like dimension, then we are confined to a world of sense data.

(1962: 246)

The image of confinement here needs to be unpacked. But it is clear *what* it is here which is meant so to confine us. If empirical knowledge must be independent of the non-rule-like dimension, then, Clarke argues, the sceptical enquiry is valid. Knowledge thus disappears (not because we have none, but because there is no such thing as knowing or not). What we want to see now is how this brings down seeing with it.

One might seek a link in an epistemic role which seeing is designed to play. Abstractly put, the mission of seeing is to make the world bear *for us* on— sometimes to *settle*—what the thing to do (or think) would be. If a tomato is the sort of thing one might see, for example, then at least sometimes it should be a (true) answer to the question how one knows there is a tomato before him that he *sees* it. Put otherwise, at least sometimes seeing the tomato should settle the issue for someone whether there is a tomato before him. Seeing it should not inevitably leave over some task of inferring the presence of a tomato from other premises of one sort or another. Of course, seeing is not always having proof. You cannot always tell a tomato at sight. The requirement is only that *sometimes* you can truly be said to have done so. If seeing Rachel Weisz is the sort of thing that *one* can do (her income may depend on this), then knowing that Rachel Weisz is dining because he *sees* her doing so is the sort of thing that *one* can do.

Weak as this requirement may be, if the sceptical enquiry is valid, it is surely not met. You cannot know that Rachel Weisz is present because you see her if you can never know that Rachel Weisz is present *überhaupt*. Such would defeat the purpose of seeing. It would not be entirely implausible to take it to defeat seeing *tout court*. Such *might* be the end of the story. The concept of seeing has collapsed. Visual experience, if such is still recognized, must just go looking for other descriptions. Sense data are not yet in the picture.

But one *might* then try a different tack. The thing about Rachel Weisz is that she admits of ringers. That is why, if the sceptical enquiry is valid, you can never know whether she is there. *If* there were items which did not admit of ringers, the *sceptical* enquiry would not thus defeat a claim to know one was experiencing them; so nor, by the above line, a claim to *be* experiencing them visually. Prichard's sense data fit this bill. He rightly takes it to follow that these are *not* what you can know things about, since there are no such things to *know*. But suppose someone missed this point. He might then *posit* sense data, as a) objects of visual *perception*, hence *sight*, b) objects which may *seem* to be various ways (such as red), and c) objects such that if one *seemed* to be a case of, for example, something being red, then it would be—ringer-proof *in re* being the various ways they may be, whatever these are. Failing to heed Frege, or Prichard, or others, he would then think: at this point, the reach of scepticism stops. We know less than we thought, perhaps, but still something.

Our philosopher might then continue. Sometimes one *seems* to see what seems to be, say, red. By the sense-datum enquiry/argument, we know this cannot be anything in the (our) environment. But (the thought is) one cannot *seem* to be seeing *something* without there being something one thus sees. For, by the above, a sense datum would be such a something. For there to be seeming-to-see is all that is required for there to be such a thing.

No more need be said about such lines of thought than that there is nothing such that for it to seem to be, or to be such-and-such, is for it to be, or be that such-and-such. There is *nothing* which is proof against ringers for it, or for its being thus and so. As Frege wrote, 'By the step by which I win myself an environment I expose myself to risk of error' (1918: p. 73). And, as he argued, the environment is all there is to judge about. When we leave the environment we move to *Vorstellungen* in his sense. And such *Vorstellungen* are *never* things one whose being as they are *truth* (of a thought or judgement) might turn. I omit Frege's elegant argument, which I have discussed elsewhere (Essay 2, for example).

The sceptical enquiry leaves us with nothing *other than* sense data—if *even* that—towards which to enjoy empirical cognitive success. Such is one understanding of confinement. Frege offers another. Near the end of 'Der Gedanke' he writes:

> Sense impressions are certainly a necessary *element* of perception, and these are part of an inner world...These alone do not open an outer world for us...Having sense impressions is not yet seeing things...What must still be added is something non-sensory. And it is just this which opens the outer world to us; for without this non-sensory thing we would remain confined in an inner world.
>
> (1918: p. 75)

A propositional attitude, such as taking something to be so, relates one to two absolutely different sorts of things: to a way for things to be—what has that sort of generality intrinsic to a thought; and to what instances such generalities, while lacking generality itself—the particular case, things being as they are. The attitude represents some way for things to be as instanced (pleonastically, by things being as they are). Perception is a form of acquaintance with things which can be represented as being thus and so; with particular cases (of things being as they are); acquaintance which permits taking just *that* to be a case of one or another way there is to represent things being. But to take something to be a case of such-and-such, one also needs acquaintance with that such-and-such—for that way to represent things being, familiarity with its way of reaching to the particular case. Such, Frege points out, is familiarity with something *not* an object of sensory awareness, not liable to be before the eyes, or in the environment at all—something like *that* the sun has set, by contrast with, for example, the setting sun. It is just the capacity for such sensitivities—a capacity for *thought*—whose absence, Frege tells us, would lock us in an inner world, a world of *Vorstellungen*.

If such capacity for thought went missing, perceptual capacities—sight, hearing, and so on—need not thereby fail to keep up their part of the bargain.

They might still provide an acquaintance with the world that *would* allow for recognizing instancings—cases of things being thus and so—were thought equipped to do its part. One lacking the capacity might still see the tomato, mid-career from vine to compost. The sight might have its impact on him. *Such sights might have* their *(regular) impact.* But there would be no generality he could see his experiencing as he does as falling under. He could not, thus, take it to be experiencing a *case* of something being a *tomato* (or, wrongly, a case of something being a persimmon). He would not see how the way a thing was mattered to its being (or not) a tomato; would not see *that* way of making truth turn on how things are. So he would not see this way in which what he experienced mattered to how things are. His experience would not thus bear for him in that way on how things were; nor make the world bear for him in that way on how to treat it. For the person lacking the capacity Frege signals as going missing here would be for him to fail to see such things for *any* generality what he experienced happened to fall under.

One would have to have *been* Sid for it to have been *that* experiencing he then underwent or enjoyed—for it to have been *that* case of someone experiencing something. So Sid's experiencing as, or what, he did on a particular occasion—insofar as this belonged to his consciousness (see Hinton 1973)—is his having a *Vorstellung* in the meaning of the act. We need not banish *Vorstellungen*. Sid, a thinker, recognizes his (such as visual) experiencing as falling under various generalities, for example, as a case of *someone* seeing a persimmon. He can thus appreciate seeing the things he does as sharing something in common with his fellows—hence his seeing the persimmon as a success to be shared by others with different visual endowments, in a range of other cases of someone having a *Vorstellung*. Without the capacity for thought, such things would be unrecognizable to him. Recognition, in fact, would not be in the cards for him *überhaupt*. Experience would not be for him as though it instanced generalities. His having *Vorstellungen* would be *just* that. Such is one thing it might be to be locked in a world of them.

Such is not to posit new objects of Sid's perceptual awareness. Sid's experiencing is presented to him, among other ways, in a way in which each of us is presented to himself alone—whether what he experiences is a tomato, or the wind blowing his hair, or annoyance at Pia's long-windedness. He may have *Vorstellungen* in experiencing what there is, in fact, for *one* to experience. The *tomato* is not presented to him in a way available to him alone, even if his experiencing it *is* so presented to him (as the consequences of his squeezing it too enthusiastically may also be). Experiencing *seeing* a tomato in a way available to him alone need not be *seeing* anything other than things there for all to see, or experiencing *these* things in any way not available to all.

One can be right or wrong only as to ways one might *think* things to be. One can only think things to be ways whose reach he might know. If the sceptical enquiry is sound, there is no knowledge. So there is no thought. At which point, perhaps, Clarke's confinement imagery and Frege's merge.

7 Conclusion

In 'Legacy' and 'Surfaces' occasion-sensitivity plays two quite different roles. In 'Legacy' the idea of knowing something collapses without it. It is a *sine que non* for there being such an idea. Hence (since we have such an idea) we are occasion-sensitive thinkers. In 'Surfaces', without occasion-sensitivity we get some strange results. One might argue, in Moorean fashion: these results are manifestly wrong; therefore thinking is occasion-sensitive. Still, without occasion-sensitivity seeing does not *collapse*. So the non-rule-like dimension operates differently in each of Clarke's three enquiries. Our question was how.

In the surface enquiry, ignoring occasion-sensitivity seems to mandate a particular point along that dimension itself; a particular understanding which is one seeing *might* bear. If we focus on the case where seeing the tomato is opposed to seeing half of it, or the facing surface, and so on, then, reflecting on the options reminds us that, of course, we do not see the backside, nor the insides, and so on, so the answer must be—at most—the facing surface. (Perhaps da Vinci might push us further.) Such *is* an understanding of the question; something which *might*, on an occasion, count as what was seen.

By contrast, in the case of the sceptical enquiry, ignoring that dimension leads us off of it altogether, to something which is *not* a possible understanding of knowing. Without occasion-sensitivity, it appears mandated that when it comes to knowing that P, *no* coherent way for it to have been so that not P can fail to count as a doubt which must be disposed of, somehow, if there is to be knowledge. The 'understanding' of knowing we thus arrive at is not just one we never do have, but not one anything could possibly bear. It is, as Clarke shows, incoherent. The result is that the concept of knowledge collapses. The sceptic does not win. There is nothing to be said, either as to what we know, or as to what we do not. Note where the enquiry does *not* lead us. It does not lead to the conclusion that whereas one would have thought that objects of knowledge were such things as that P, that Q, and so on, they are really 'that P★', 'that Q★', and so on, where these are some somehow less ambitious objects of knowledge, inherently less susceptible to sceptical undermining. Some philosopher might believe such a thing. But it would take extra premises to argue it. And then we would have an argument, not an enquiry in Clarke's sense.

One might imagine that a sense-datum enquiry could follow the pattern of the sceptical, rather than the surface, enquiry. Here ignoring some form of occasion-sensitivity (perhaps in one of the notions Clarke suggests, perhaps in others) could, as with knowledge, move us out of the non-rule-like dimension entirely, to something which, though it seemed the only thing seeing could possibly be, corresponded to *no* understanding we would ever have, on any occasion, of what seeing might be. If there were a sense-datum enquiry, it would *have to* thus lead us to no place along the non-rule-like dimension, since there is no understanding of *seeing* on which a sense datum might be what one saw. Then, too, if there were such an enquiry, the result it would lead to would be, as with knowledge, that there is really no such thing as seeing. It would make the concept collapse. To reinstate seeing as a relation to such things as sense data would take extra premises—this, too, paralleling knowledge. Here, too, the would-be sense datum enquiry would cease to be an enquiry in Clarke's sense.

But then, there does not seem to be a sense-datum enquiry which gets even so far as leading us out of the non-rule-following dimension. Seeing is not vulnerable to ringers in ways that knowledge is. I have tried to explain that difference in terms of something more fundamental: the distinction Frege draws between the historical and the conceptual—that between what is instanced and what does the instancing. Knowing is success in an enterprise of fitting the historical to the conceptual; insight into how what does the instancing *does* mesh with what gets instanced. As such, it is vulnerable to ringers in ways that seeing—which only provides one side of that relation to respond to—is not.

Clarke ends 'Legacy' with the remark:

It's a pleasant surprise when skepticism, which has always given us plenty to think about, gives us something new to ponder.

(1972: 768)

What scepticism, examined closely, gives us to ponder is the role of occasion-sensitivity in our thought. Investigating sense data leads us to something Frege gave us to ponder: the fundamental difference in kind between what instances and what does the instancing. Ignoring this is, on its own, a main source of philosophical confusion.

I would be gratified if occasion-sensitivity were the key to disarming all the problems Clarke addresses. But it is not. Some missteps transgress against Frege's historical/conceptual distinction—that more fundamental ground in which occasion-sensitivity may grow. *Instancing* is the point at which there may be more than one way of going on.[1]

---

[1] Mike Martin and Mark Kalderon have helped me greatly in clarifying whatever I have arrived at on the above issues.

12

While Under the Influence

> And thus, too, for that whose form presents it as a statement, there is always still the question whether it really contains an assertion. And this question is to be answered in the negative when the requisite seriousness is absent.
>
> Frege 1918: p. 63

> Here we must be careful not to think in traditional psychological categories. Such as simply parsing experience into seeing and thinking; or something similar.
>
> Wittgenstein 1982: §542

Belief is a demanding attitude. It imposes one sort of discipline, as represented at the most general level, but not exhausted, by what Frege called the laws of truth. It imposes another by the requirement (argued elegantly by Frege) that its objects—*what* is believed, thoughts in Frege's terminology—must be something which an open-ended range of thinkers *could* believe, doubt, disbelieve, and so on. It is intrinsic to a belief to be shareable. A corollary to this is that it is only *of* what is part of an environment—a habitat accessible, open to, an open-ended range of thinkers—that there could *be* things to be believed (truly or falsely, not just believed-in). Belief is also demanding in another sense: where it occurs at all, it presents itself as what one is *compelled* to; as forced on one by something, under whose influence one thus is. To see one's hand as thus forced is to *be* under the influence of something. To be under such influence, I will suggest, is to access—be presented to—oneself in a special way; one in which (as Frege put it) each of us is presented to himself alone. It is to be presented to oneself as a believer. And, I will suggest, to be so presented to oneself is to *be* a believer. Belief thus exemplifies a special sort of way of standing towards oneself. If it *exemplifies*, one might ask after the other examples. I will conclude by scouting, briefly, the possible scope of this way of standing. But all that follows is just preliminary probing in an area left to future work.

Moore's Paradox, so called, is a good entrée into the special form of access I have in mind. It is not really a paradox. It is more an anomaly in need of explanation. I will call it 'Moore's anomaly'. Its present interest, I will suggest, is that it is only explainable by supposing that in belief we do stand to ourselves in that special way I will set out below. I will suggest this, then move on to a more general characterization of the way, and consequences, for what is so presented to us.

Thoughts, as Frege argues, are *intrinsically* shareable. He argues this in arguing that no thought could be a *Vorstellung*, in his sense of 'Vorstellung' (see 1918: pp. 67–8). In essence this means: a thought cannot need a bearer—some thinker but for whose entertaining of, or having, it it would not exist—and it must allow two thinkers of it, or for any given thinkers of it, more. The corollary then becomes: no thought's truth can turn *essentially*, for some *Vorstellung*, on how that *Vorstellung* is, all the less, on whether it is thus and so. There are no 'thus-and-so's for a *Vorstellung* to be. As Frege himself is quick to stress, this does not rule *Vorstellungen* out of our inner lives. There is, for one thing, a trick, in evidence in Frege's own example: pain. For me to experience pain (for me to feel it) is for me to experience (feel) *my* pain, which again expands into: me experiencing my being in pain. On the one hand, only I can feel *that* episode of pain. For me to feel it is for that pain to be presented to me in a way it could be presented *only* to me. So in feeling pain I have a *Vorstellung* in the meaning of the act. But for the pain to be so presented to me is just for *me* to be presented to myself—my being in pain to be presented to me—in a way each of us is presented to himself alone. So now the other hand. *My being* in pain is not a *Vorstellung*. It belongs to our cohabited environment. You, and others, can experience it too. You can experience just that, if not in the way I do. Truth is thus made to turn on what is accessible to many (if to any), as truth always must. Where I stand towards, or am presented to, myself in a way only *I* could manage, things must work like this if there is to be a question of truth at all—if I am genuinely to stand towards, or be presented with, my being thus and so. Such is Frege's message for philosophy of mind. Here belief seems to follow suit. The believing which I encounter while under the influence—while believing that P—that particular instance of it—is *my* believing that P. So my encountering that believing, and its being presented to me as it is, is also my encountering a certain bit of environmental history, my believing that P. Only I could have that believing presented to me as it thus is. But you need not be me to encounter the environmental episode which is also thus presented to me. Whether *that* episode instances some given generality—notably, whether it is one of someone believing such-and-such—does not (cannot) turn on whether some *Vorstellung* is thus and so.

The question is then how, in the case of belief (or in any case fitting the above pattern) what is presented to me in that way only I could manage relates to that which you need *not* be me to encounter—the pain to my being in pain, the believing as only I encounter it to my believing such-and-such. Dr Lauben's injury (see Frege 1918: p. 65) is presented to him in a way each of us is presented to himself alone. So too (see Wittgenstein 1958: p. 66) Ludwig is presented to himself in a way each of us is presented to himself alone in being presented with the wind blowing his hair. This does not make belief, or pain, *much* like being injured or having wind-blown hair. For one thing, whether Dr Lauben's gash is deep or shallow is independent of how anyone—even Dr Lauben—*responds* to what he is presented with. Whether it is excruciating promises to be otherwise in this respect. So too may whether he *believes* that it is deep. These last cases thus offer something else to take over *some* work reserved in the first sort for the environment alone. For another, hallucinating the wind blowing your hair is, while improbable, an unproblematic idea as such. Whereas it is difficult to make sense of the idea of hallucinating *believing*, for example, that *Chez Fred* has changed its menu. Someone might be presented, in a way he is presented to himself alone, with a ringer for the wind blowing his hair. It is at best difficult to imagine one being presented with a ringer for his believing that *Chez Fred* has changed the menu—especially in some way he is presented to himself alone. I think this points to a crucial feature of that channel, what I will call its creative nature. But only later will I explain that use of 'creative'.

The data admit a spin which can make it seem all too easy to imagine ringers for me for my believing that *Chez Fred* has changed the menu. Such, I will suggest, is the wrong spin. Section 3 discusses this.

1 The Anomaly

First, a distinction. There is representing things *as* being such-and-such way; and there is representing them *to* be that way. The first is a wider category than the second. If, for example, I represent things to be such that if Sid still snores, then Pia will leave, then in doing so I *eo ipso* represent things *as* being such that Sid still snores. I represent things *being* that way as the condition on which Pia will leave. But I do not represent things *to be* that way. On that I remain (officially) neutral. When I represent things *to be* such that Sid still snores, I assign that way a certain status: being a way things are. In that conditional above I assigned that way a different status, the one just mentioned. There are countless statuses I might assign that way in representing things *as* so being, each a way of representing-as without representing-to-be. (The 'things' in 'way for things to be' here bears catholic reading: there is no question which things.)

While we are on the topic, such *assigning* a way for things to be a status cannot be just more representing-as—for example, representing it *as* having that status. The way's having this status could *also* be assigned any of many statuses. If we think of a thought as, grammatically, the thought *that* such-and-such, then the thought, so thought of, presents *that such-and-such*—that way *for* things to be—*as* being a way things are. But it does not commit to it so being. Thoughts—abstractions as they are—cannot commit. A thought thus cannot represent-to-be. If assigning a status were just more representing-as, a thought *could* assign statuses. But the *thought* that for Sid to snore is among the ways things are is just more representing-as. It can be the object of a wish, or antecedent of a conditional, just as well as any other thought. So, to borrow a phrase from Frege, if we represent a way for things to be as having such-and-such status, the game (here *assigning* status) can just begin anew. Such is the point of distinguishing between *content*—the way things are represented *as* being—and force—whatever that new element is where status is assigned. The boundary between the two may be moveable, but the distinction is one we need. It still remains, of course, to say what force comes to.

These preliminaries are worth delaying the proceedings over because they will be of the greatest importance for understanding Moore's anomaly, and, thereby, that form of access to oneself which I mean to investigate here. Now for the anomaly. It starts from this idea: a way for things to be—a specifiable way they *might* intelligibly be—is a way they might be represented *to* be. Normally, anyone who grasped what it would be for things to be that way *could* represent things so to be. Roughly this is one thing intrinsic to that objectivity which Frege insisted on for thoughts. Moore points to an exception. Most of us suppose there are, or might be, some things we take to be so which are not so. Each of us grasps what it would be for him to take something to be so which is not, or for there to be something so which he does not take to be. Such happens often enough. As a rule, then, for a way for things to be—say, such that it is cherry season—we can grasp what it would be for it to be cherry season while we thought it was not, or for it not to be while we thought it was—two perfectly possible ways for things to be. Each of us can represent things to *have been* that way, or to be a way things *will* be at some future date. But we cannot (unproblematically, at least) represent such things to be a way things *are*. Such is the anomaly. It calls for explanation. How *can* it be that there is a perfectly possible way for things to be, which anyone other than me could perfectly easily represent to be a way things are, but which I cannot (or not unproblematically)? *Mutatis mutandis* for you.

Representing things as being a certain way might be a case of thinking something. Or it might be a case of saying something. Thinking is fundamental here. If it were saying, then it should be that while *I* cannot (unproblematically) say of myself that I think that, while it is cherry season, I do not think it is, *you* should be able to say this of me. But saying it of me is, in fact, equally as problematic for you as for me. You say, 'He thinks that, while it is cherry season, he does not think so'. But the problem is, how can someone think *that*? What would count as doing so? Without answers to those questions, we cannot see what to understand you as having said of me. Still, the situation is strange. You can unproblematically think of me that, while it is cherry season, I do not think so. I cannot. Why the difference?

2 Filling the Space

Moore's anomaly shows in stating it what an explanation of it would have to look like. There is no difficulty in one merely representing things as being those (for him) anomalous perfectly possible ways. The difficulty is only in representing things *to be* those ways. So the explanation must lie in the space between representing-as and representing-to-be. It must be that, in the vexed cases, *nothing* lies in that space: whatever would be needed for filling in the space, there is no such thing as that in the particular cases to which Moore points.

Where this space *is* filled, it is filled by *force*: for a speech act, the force with which representing is *produced*, offered; for an attitude, the force with which the attitude is held. Force, I have suggested, can be understood as the assigning of a status. For a speech act, I think, such assigning can be understood in terms of assumption of responsibility; of liability to successes or failures, to praise or blame, of certain specific kinds. For the present this is as may be. For an attitude to assign a way for things to be some given status would be for that way to *enjoy* that status in the doings, and/or thinking, of its holder.

For belief, perhaps the simplest way to think of this is, to borrow a Kantian image: the way enjoys that status in one's attaching an 'I think' to the *thought* of things as that way. It is for one to make that way of thinking of things *his* way of thinking: part of how he thinks of how the world bears on what to do (or, more specifically, to think). The point of that image here—that attaching an 'I think'—emerges in the way in which to believe something—to hold a view as to its being cherry season, or there being a Porsche in the drive—is, at the same time, to hold a view of, or stance towards, oneself—again such view or stance *not* consisting in mere representing-as. Equally, to be *presented* with the view one has from his position *in re* it being cherry season, or there being a Porsche in the drive, is to be presented with a view of oneself. Two different notions of a view in holding, and in being presented with one. Which raises a question to which I return at the end of this section.

Such assigning of a status—such a holding of a stance, at the same time towards a way for things to be and towards oneself—can be viewed from two sides—to borrow another pair of images, from the side of introduction (assuming of the stance) and elimination (the stance in operation). I begin with an introduction. Here perhaps the most striking feature of belief: one cannot *choose* what to believe—or at least in believing one cannot so see himself. Pia might tell Sid, 'I prefer not to believe that you would do such a thing'. But if as she sees herself such preferences are not already irrelevant—if it is not anyway decided what she *must* think as to Sid's having done it—then the condition she is in is *ipso facto* neither believing that he did nor that he did not. In belief one sees the world as having so impressed itself on him that his hand is forced—to borrow yet another fitting image (this time from David Wiggins), in the matter at hand there is nothing else for him to think. Stare at Pia's Porsche in the drive and *try* to believe there is no Porsche. The very suggestion makes no sense. The Porsche's presence convinces you, or (if you are firmly enough into fantasy) does not. Either way, there is no fixing things up by trying.

To believe is to be under the sway, or influence, of something: (one's encountering of) things being as they are. To be under such influence is to *feel* it—to feel compelled to think as one thus does. One might think of belief in this respect as Lutheran: one so stands towards things, unable to do other. But such felt compulsion must be of a special kind. To understand the kind is to understand how fitting an image 'the only thing to think' is. It must be what one is presented with—that which, in belief, one recognizes, or misidentifies, as a case of things being thus and so—which one sees as doing the compelling, and not anything proprietary to one's particular way of responding to this. It must not be *psychological* compulsion that one sees himself as under. If Sid sees himself as so longing for Pia that he would take *any* Porsche for hers, and, while so seeing himself, feels overcome with an irresistible urge to take that Porsche in the drive for hers, such, again, simply is not thinking that *Pia's* Porsche is in the drive.

What other sort of compulsion might there be? To judge, or, in present terms, believe, is, Frege tells us, to pursue the goal truth. Suppose you see a Porsche in the drive and know one when you see it. Then, (*ceteris paribus*) for you, to think otherwise than that there is a Porsche in the drive would simply not be pursuing the goal truth. For you, then, in this position, thinking otherwise would not be thinking-so (believing) at all. So thinking is *thus* ruled out for you. Such is thus the way one must see himself—the sort of compulsion he must see himself as under—to be believing that there is a

Porsche, *or* that there is not one, or that the question is still *sub judice*. Feeling rational force is, of course, unlike feeling centrifugal force on a carnival ride, or the force of the gale impeding one's headway. There is no bodily sensation of rational compulsion. Nor would any psychological tugs or temptings fill the bill here, though feeling, or finding, oneself with nothing else to think manifests itself psychologically, for example, in those feelings of bad faith one would suffer in saying other than what one is compelled to think.

Turning to elimination, Frege's idea also connects believing with pursuit. Believing that Sid snores is pursuing the goal truth *in re* whether Sid snores. To believe that Sid snores is, moreover, to shape one's general pursuit of truth accordingly. Pursuing truth differs from mere attraction to views which happen to be correct as *rushing* forward differs from moving forward at a rapid pace. One *holds* himself in pursuit. In matters of truth, one holds his forming, and holding, of views to a certain standard. In rushing forward one *maintains* momentum. In pursuing truth one maintains due respect for, and gives due respect to, the mattering of what matters, and the not-mattering of what does not. Believing that P, in its elimination guise, is guiding one's pursuit of truth— thus of *any* goal—accordingly; accepting that P as *the* guide (so far as it goes) to the thing to do or think. To believe that P is, where one sees P's being so as what *would* bear in a certain way on whether Q (or whether to do Q), to take the world thus to *bear* on whether Q, or to do Q. Belief is, *per se*, what so eliminates.

To believe that Porsches are fast is to see oneself as (rationally) compelled (by the world) to pursue the goal truth accordingly. Is to *see* oneself as so compelled to *be* so compelled? Is to *be* so compelled to *feel* this? If I think that it is cherry season, I may just be misinformed, or not know the signs of cherry season, or how to tell whether it is. In that case, I may think that it is cherry season while the world does not in fact make that the thing for *one* to think in pursuit of the goal truth. But the benighted must pursue truth benightedly. If I am (mistakenly) quite sure that Meireles would not be drinking *espumante* had cherry season not begun (in fact, he is only drinking it because, for him, the statute of limitations has just expired), then, unless his *now* drinking it disabuses me of this view, *I* can do no other than think the cherry season to have started. *One* could do better. But for one in my benighted position, that it is cherry season is the only thing for one to think. Conversely, all the signs may be that it is cherry season, so that anyone with an ounce of sense would so think. But if I do not see these signs as forcing *my* hand, *my* pursuit of the goal truth does not yet require *my* thinking that it is. Being and feeling thus merge here.

I introduce the next point via a comparison. For me to feel pain is for me to experience *my* being in pain. I am thus presented with that very thing which might also be presented to others, but here in a way available to me alone. I *can* also experience my being in pain in ways available to others—for example, by watching my grimaces in a mirror. One *could* say: I then also experience my pain in these ways. Now, where the one thinking it is cherry season is *me*, that thinking of this is presented to me (among other ways) in a way accessible to me alone. It is so presented to me in that attaching of the 'I think' which I thus realize. This, too, might be presented to me in other ways as well. I may stand back and observe my eagerness to reach Resende.

Suppose that I now see myself as others see me—observe myself believing what I do as others might—while under the influence of that which forces a particular course from me in pursuit of the goal truth. I thus observe myself being under the influence. I might be watching a video of myself. I *need* not even recognize it as a video of me. I might see what, seen in another, would make me take that other for one who thought that it was cherry season (or who did not). But suppose that, while thus seeing myself, I see myself otherwise in that way I am presented to myself alone. Watching the picture of myself, I would say, 'There is the very picture of a man who thinks it is cherry season'. But while doing that I do not see myself with nothing else but that to think. Presented to myself as one is in feeling rational compulsion, I see thinking that it is cherry season as what, for me, would not be pursuing the goal truth. For me to see myself as in such a position just is, despite the video, what counts as my *not* thinking that it is cherry season. Given what it is to think something, my special form of access to my believing—that access I enjoy just in attaching that 'I think' to that way for things to be (such that it is cherry season) plays, and must play, such a special role in settling what it is I think. Only then can thinking-so *be* pursuing the goal truth. I do not mean to overestimate that role. But it is at least this. The modesty in this claim will emerge in the next section.

I cannot, while seeing nothing else for me to think, treat the question as open whether so to think. Nor can I treat the question as closed without believing. That I can suspend belief and reconsider is beside the present point. So while I see myself in such position, there is no further question as to whether I thus think the thing in question—a question that might go one way or the other, depending on further considerations of some kind, presented in ways one need not be me to enjoy. My *seeing* nothing else for me to think, my thus attaching an 'I think' to some way for things to be, fills in that space in belief between representing-as and representing-to-be. My so seeing myself is my *having* nothing else to think. So it just *is* my believing things to be the way in question. My view of myself thinking as I do is in this way decisive. If I so see myself, the question *what* to think (*in re* whether it is cherry season), is settled for me. Further considerations cannot *decide* it for me in one way or the other. Thus the ineptness (noted by Wittgenstein) of reasoning, 'I believe it, and I am reliable, so it is (probably) the thing to think (I'll believe it)'. (See, for example, 1980: §§ 482–3.) Thus it is that my seeing nothing else for me to think, as my thinking that it is cherry season, cannot be what settles for me whether it is cherry season.

Where experience *mediates* between our attitudes and their objects, where it works to make our attitudes *responsive*, sensitive, to how things are, the rule is that things factor as follows: there is, on the one hand, that with which we are presented for responding to; and there is, on the other, our responses. So it is in perception. I see the pig wallowing; I *recognize* it as a pig wallowing, thus think it that. As already mentioned, the word 'view', in use above, has a place on both sides of this distinction. There is the thirty-fifth view of Mt Fuji, from a certain piece of shoreline. Then there is the dim view I take of pedagogues. Such double useage runs through the vocabulary used here for spelling out that attaching of the 'I think' to a way for things to be which I am presenting as, in the case of belief, filling that space between representing-as and representing-to-be. In thinking that Pia drives a Porsche, I am presented with myself in a certain condition—with nothing else to think. Is it *I* who am doing the presenting? Or am I presented with this by other means? Again, I see, or find, myself having nothing else to think. 'See' is here, anyway, not (literally) a *perceptual* verb. But is this seeing mere seeing-as (as Sid may be alone in seeing himself as a great wit)? Or is it, like the perceptual seeing, a success-verb, so that one *sees* himself only in conditions he is in fact in? 'Feel', too, has double uses. Feeling injured by Pia's snub, or feeling compelled not to let her remark pass, is different from feeling the spilled soup seeping through one's trousers. It is a stance rather than a sensation (here, as of something warm and wet).

On what side of this distinction does feeling, or seeing, stand where it is seeing *oneself* with nothing else to think, feeling (rationally) pressed into shaping one's pursuit of truth in such-and-such way? Is this being *presented* with something to respond to? Or is it a *response* to what we are presented with— what foists compulsion on us? Does one feel pressure of the world's weight in that sense of 'feel' in which one feels a foot pressing against his beneath the table? Or does one feel compelled so to pursue truth as he may feel compelled to return Pia's snub, *according* this a status as the thing for him to do? A reasonable question, so far ducked. At this point we might recall that remark of Wittgenstein's (*Last Writings*, §542). Perhaps we have here reached a point where we must abandon such traditional categories as presentation and response (or, as Wittgenstein puts it, of thinking and seeing)—categories into one of which seeing a pig before one, and into the other of which seeing *that* it is a pig so neatly and exclusively fit. Here 'see', 'feel', and so on, bear either reading, or both. It remains to be seen just where and how widely Wittgenstein's idea applies. Belief, though, presents a clear case. Hence, I suggest, Wittgenstein's interest in Moore's anomaly.

In fact, here such verbs *demand* elements of both readings. On the one hand, belief just is pursuit of truth. But it can be that only where one feels his stance as forced on him, his course as set, by pressure from without. It must be (in his view of things), what is thus external, independent of the idiosyncratic in his makeup, which leaves him nothing else to think. The Porsche in the drive, and not his wish for one, must be (at least as he views things) what forces his hand *in re* a Porsche being present. So there is feeling in the sense of feeling something pressing on one. On the other, there is that 'I think' attaching to belief: to belief that P is to make that P part of one's thinking as to how things are. So one must feel where feeling is pure response, feeling as thinking in a certain way as to the thing for him to do. To believe that P is to accord the world the status of bearing for one on questions of the thing to do (or think) as it would if P. There are the caveats. A believer is one *sufficiently* responsive, sensitive, to the demands of pursuing truth—to the course in fact forced on him by the pressure from without. But, if the above is right, for such a being, to feel as though pressed into a course just is to be so pressed—even when one seems to feel pressure there is not. On the elimination side, one may accord the world a status while blind to *some* features of what such status would entail.

In any event Moore's anomaly is now explainable. As we saw, the trouble must be that in such a case there is no such thing as making the relevant representing-as into representing-to-be. Sid can certainly represent things *as being* such that, while it *was* cherry season, he thought it was not. If that is how things were, he might think, he would be missing out. But he cannot take it to be *so* that, while it is cherry season, he thinks it isn't. Trouble arises for him in filling in that space. He would, to begin with, have to stand towards that first conjunct in a way which was *attaching* that 'I think'. He would thus have to see himself as with nothing else to think, as with hands thus tied in pursuing truth. Thinking that it is cherry season must be what he sees as required for him to be thinking (*in re* that matter) at all. Then and only then is he *thinking* the first conjunct.

Now, to think the second conjunct he must (trivially) see himself as not thinking it is cherry season. But he so sees himself only in seeing himself as not compelled so think—in fact as compelled to think otherwise (even if otherwise is just that the question remains open). To believe, to repeat, is to see *oneself* in a particular way. What he cannot do here is to see himself as seeing himself as with hands untied—so it is with the one he thus observes—while, at the same time, for his part, seeing his hands as tied. There is no *such* separating oneself from himself.

Believing the anomalous conjunction, though—according *it* the status as part of *his* thinking as to the thing to do (and think)—requires seeing himself in both these ways at once. Just this is what would fill the space between representing-as and representing-to-be when it came to taking such a conjunction *to be so*. But, when spelled out, there is clearly no such thing as that. Moore's anomaly is thus explained in just the form we knew at the start such explanation must take. Still, there is a perspective from which this explanation can seem wrong. I turn to that next.

3 Blindness

The connections drawn so far between believing that P and seeing oneself as set out above account for Moore's anomaly—*if* they exist. But there have been worries as to whether they really can exist, generated largely, I think, by the possibility of blindness to one's thinking as he does—to missing facts as to (as it may sometimes be put) what it is one 'really' thinks. But such possibilities, I will now suggest, are compatible with those connections drawn in the present idea of believing such-and-such as attaching an 'I think' to it.

The opportunity for blindness lies in the fact that believing is a *state*, or, otherwise put, an *interval* notion: it is the sort of thing that has an onset, perhaps an extinction; or at least it is continuous between given intervals. It thus presents the epistemic perils of any interval notion. At any point, or in any small enough interval, one may take himself (just as he may take another) to be within an interval of the relevant sort—here to believe—when he is not: the right things are not so of any large enough interval surrounding the occasion of his so taking himself. For the moment, it may be to him just as though he were in an interval of the relevant sort, while he is not. Equally conversely: he may take himself not to be within any relevant interval—so it seems at the point, or in the sub-interval—while he in fact *is* in such an interval—does, in fact, believe. So, in this way, one may not believe something while failing to see that he does not, or believe something while failing to see that he does. That intervals, so far as they go, allow for such situations does not by itself mean that they are possible. Something else about belief in particular may rule them out. But a great deal of effort has been spent in recent times in arguing that such possibilities are not ruled out—I think with some success. So I will take them not to be ruled out *tout court*.

What problems would this make for the present idea of believing as attaching an 'I think'? The core idea here would be this: if I fail to see that I believe that P, then I fail to feel the relevant compulsion so to think, or so to shape my thinking in pursuit of truth. I do not accord *that P* the relevant status in my thinking, make it relevantly mine. I do not attach to it that 'I think' scouted above—while, for all that, I do believe that P. Conversely, where I fail to see that I do not believe that P, it seems to me, at least, that I *do* thus attach the relevant 'I think'—that I am compelled to think no other. And, I have suggested, its being for me just as though I am rationally compelled is my being so compelled (however benightedly I may thus be pursuing truth). Then, too, if I am aware that belief allows for such possibilities, I may always suspect myself to be in such a situation, wherever it seems to me just as though I have, or have not, attached a relevant 'I think'. So—it *seems*—believing that P and attaching the relevant 'I think' to it are entirely independent.

An example may help keep us on track here. Mine will not be particularly convincing. But it will illustrate the structure of the idea. Sid would tell anyone if asked—with all the sincerity he ever musters—that Pia is an expert driver. He even tells himself this, with conviction, from time to time. Yet somehow Sid always seems to find reasons to avoid riding with her, or, when they do travel together, always arranges somehow for it to be he who drives. When this is pointed out to him, reflecting on what accounts for it, he comes to see that, really, he does not think that Pia is much of a driver; he was only fooling himself in conjuring that sincerity with which he once said otherwise. (The scales are fallen from his eyes.)

As I have portrayed things, the root of the problem lies in the nature of intervals, or interval phenomena. The possibilities these make for extend *very* widely; which shows that they are not always *problems*. I stand at the stop watching my bus approach. I *take* myself to see the bus approaching. But approaches occur over intervals. It is conceivable that, as I so take myself, the 'bus' disappears into thin air. I have seen no bus approaching if I have seen only what might have been (but was not) one momentary stage of this. Or I witness, or so I think, dinner being served. But as I take my first bite the whole thing disappears. Such are logical possibilities. But they do not rule out seeing the bus pull up to my stop, or witnessing dinner being served. Similarly, that I *might*, on occasion, be blind to how things (really) stand with me *in re* belief does not rule out that I should sometimes just see what it is that I believe ('see' here not a perceptual verb).

But dissolutions of our apparent problems with the idea of the 'I think' do not lie in this direction. For the epistemology that thus goes with interval phenomena, just as that which goes with the presence of opaque objects— aubergines, say—is necessarily occasion-sensitive. Sometimes I may count as simply seeing a penguin before me, and thereby *knowing that* a penguin is before me. But sometimes I would not so count. Sometimes a 'penguin' really *might* be a ringer. What penguins are makes room for this. Similarly with serving dinner. Similarly with belief from a third person perspective. Sometimes we can just *see* that Sid still believes that his wallet is in his pocket as he reaches for it to pay the check (we having just watched it artfully being lifted therefrom). But sometimes that momentary slice of Sid's life proves misleading when set in a larger interval. (His 'reach' was a signal for the police to move in.) So we really saw no such thing as his so believing. So it would be from a first-person perspective if, as per above, Sid really could believe that P while feeling his hand not forced in that direction, or *vice versa*. So the epistemology which generally fits intervals and moments or sub-intervals must not fit the relation between believing that P and such attaching to it of an 'I think'.

The first thing to observe here is that, while believing that P is an interval phenomenon, so is the relevant attaching of an 'I think'. Or at least this is so if believing that P is attaching such an 'I think'. What is needed, if believing and attaching the 'I think' are connected as per the last section is that in any given case the two intervals must be co-extensive. That is, the vicissitudes of Sid's thinking that penguins waddle, or that Pia's Porsche is in the drive across any interval in which he does so think must also be those of his attaching the relevant 'I think'—of his feeling compelled, in the relevant way, so to shape his pursuit of the goal truth. So, for example, Sid's blindness to his not believing that Pia is an expert driver must also be blindness to his (relevantly) seeing himself as *not* bound to think none other than that she is. And his seeing himself as bound to think none other than that she *is* an expert driver—insofar as that is how he sees himself—must be co-extensive with his *thinking* that she is. But, in the case sketched, how can *all* this be so? Must not Sid either see himself as relevantly bound to think that Pia is an expert driver, or not so bound?

To see what it might be for things to be like that, we need to keep in view the occasion-sensitivity of belief. Such is a special case of an entirely general phenomenon. Here is a philosophically less sensitive case. As we enter *Chez Fred* in Beaujeu, we observe a waiter setting a plate of *salade de museau* in front of Pia. Did Pia really order *salade de museau*? Well, what do you mean by *ordering*? Tongue-tied, she asked Sid to speak for her. But yes, *museau* is what she wanted. Ordering *could* be understood in a way on which it is something Pia thus did; or, again, in a way such on which it is something she did not. So the answer to the question is liable to depend on the point of, or occasion for, asking it. Absent point or circumstance, the best answer is, perhaps, 'Yes and no'—a form of response which, in most cases, is rightly understood as: *you could say yes, and you could say no, all depending on how you understand* ordering. Thus a thumbnail sketch of occasion-sensitivity in general.

Now substitute believing for ordering. One sort of case which then comes to mind is this. As Sid is putting dinner into the oven, Pia telephones to say that she will be home late—an extra person was needed for dinner with the speaker. Sid turns off the oven, opens a beer, and settles in front of the television. He has no doubts as to Pia's fidelity, nor hence, as to her doing what she just said. As the two teams are coming out onto the pitch, though, he is suddenly gripped by agonizing scepticism. Pia's story now seems to him a mere cover. Images of her trysting with Vic upstairs at La Bellota Hermosa now fill his mind, driving out all other thought. All of which rages unabated until stopped by a whistle. The game starts, Sid's scepticism melts away. At half time, enjoying the new steamy commercial for shampoo, he looks back and laughs (or wonders) at his momentary *folie*. Now, in that interval between the teams' entrance and the whistle, did Sid believe that Pia was (as they put it in Brussels) playing comedy with him? Here, too, a 'Yes and no' answer may well seem the right one.

The particular cases so far on offer may or may not be convincing. But they point to a general framework within which to cast our present problem. Sid is prepared to say, to others, and to himself, unhesitatingly and with conviction, that Pia is a skilled driver. Such is, grammatically, a state he is in throughout a certain (reasonably extended) interval. He also, regularly, and more than just accidentally, manages to arrange not to be a passenger in a car that Pia is driving. Being one of whom such may be expected is also a state he is in over an extended, and overlapping, interval. That first state (or some state it partly constitutes) is something which may (and would) sometimes (for some purposes, or occasions) count as a person believing that Pia is a skilled driver. Such is one understanding of what believing such a thing might be. That second state (or again some state responsible for it) is what might (and sometimes would) count as a person *not* believing that Pia is a skilled driver. These two states do not compose (at least for Sid). Sid is not in any state which would ever count as believing that Pia is, and furthermore, is not, a skilled driver (if there is any such logically defective state to be in at all). So, where, or when, the first state counts as his believing that Pia is a skilled driver, the second state does not count as his (also, further) not so believing, and *vice versa*. But sometimes, for some purposes, on some occasions, his being as he is in being in the first state does count as his so believing; sometimes (for some purposes, on some occasions), his being as he is in being in the second state counts as his *not* so believing. (On pain of contradicting ourselves, we can never count him as both believing and not believing anything.)

Now the idea of believing as attaching an 'I think' to things being some way for things to be is free to operate. If attaching that 'I think' is constitutive of believing—as I have argued that it is—then, for any interval which sometimes counts as Sid believing that P, that very interval also sometimes counts as Sid attaching that 'I think': wherever it counts as the one thing it counts as the other. For any interval which sometimes counts as his not believing that very thing, P, that very interval also sometimes counts as his not attaching that 'I think'. What sometimes counts as his making that P part of *his* thinking as to how things are (his being as he is throughout some relevant interval) sometimes counts as his not so doing. Of course, it never counts as both at once. He never counts as both attaching and not attaching that 'I think', just as he never counts as both *thinking* and not thinking that P. Now let Sid's mental life be the hell it no doubt is—let it be unbearably convoluted, full of inconsistencies, straining the limits of coherence—and for all that it poses no threat to the work of the first three sections above. One does not make it into a counter-example to that by making it all the harder for him (or anyone close to him) to bear.

4 Pyrrhonian Attitudes

The Pyrrhonians eschewed belief. Nonetheless they saw the need to guide conduct in a way that was responsive, somehow, to the way things are. So they proposed an attitude, called (roughly) *acquiescence in appearance*. Such attitude, the idea was, has the content of a belief. Its object, *what* one could acquiesce in—for example, that a Porsche approaches—was, they held, what could also be the content of a belief. And it was action-guiding in roughly the way a belief would be: if you held that attitude *in re* approaching Porsche, and if the thing for you to do if a Porsche approached would be to mount the curb, you would then see mounting the curb as the thing for you to do. But the attitude was not belief. One reason, according to them, is that, unlike belief, in holding it one did not expose himself to risk of error. As they put it, if it appeared to me that a Porsche approached, and none did, still, things so appeared to me. Ergo, I was not wrong. One need not agree with the Pyrrhonians that belief is thus dispensable, nor that if it were dispensed with there might be that remainder, 'acquiescence', which they supposed. But it is an interesting idea that there can be attitudes towards what *might* be objects of belief, which would guide conduct in much the same way belief would, but which, for all that, are not belief. I will call such attitudes *Pyrrhonian*.

That attitude towards oneself which, in belief, makes representing-as representing-to-be is Pyrrhonian in this sense. For me to hold it (towards P) is for me to see myself as with nothing else to think (but that P), to find my hand forced. It is thus to see myself as occupying that position vis-a-vis things which *is* believing that P. So I thus see myself as thinking that P, that very thing which someone else may *think* me to do. And I guide myself (near enough) accordingly: the thing for me to do or think is, as I see it, what it would be if I thought that P. But since thus seeing myself as with nothing to think *is* occupying that position, this attitude towards myself cannot be *thinking* that I think that P, understanding thinking as a truth-evaluable attitude. My holding it is too close to its object—that which it is towards—for it to have that objectivity which truth demands. A truth, as Frege (nearly) put it, does not become true in being *held*, or even seen to be, true (see 1918: p. 69). Our finding ourselves believers, at least where it is *attaching* that 'I think', is what fills the space between representing-as and representing-to-be. If it fills the space, the space is thus filled. There is belief. *Thus* is the attitude Pyrrhonian. It is for this that I have spoken above, a bit cagily, of our *finding ourselves*, or *seeing ourselves as*, choiceless, or with hand forced, rather than of our judging, or believing, ourselves so to be.

Frege's conception of judging carves out a territory for Pyrrhonian attitudes. The territory is marked in one way *via* Frege's notion of a *Vorstellung*. A *thought* is, or fixes, a question of truth. A question of truth cannot have a bearer. There is no-one must one be to grasp it, or (thus) to see *how* it makes truth turn on how things are; so nor to see how it participates in the instancing relation—what, in a particular case, would make it, or make it not, a case of things being as per the thought, how a particular case's being as it is would matter to this. So seeing such things cannot require an acquaintance with particular cases which one would need to be so-and-so to have. So a *Vorstellung*'s being as it is cannot be what makes a particular case relevantly what it is. (Though we could allow, in counterflow, that for some particular case to be what it is just is, by *fiat*, for some *Vorstellung* to be thus and so.)

So marking the territory does not rule *Vorstellungen* out of existence, nor prohibit responses to them, nor ones which take objects of propositional form. Nor even (as we have just seen) with ones towards objects towards which someone *could* take a truth-evaluable attitude. But a response to a *Vorstellung* need not aim at any success which might be truth, and *cannot* so aim without making its success or failure turn in some determinate way on how the environment is. If I have a splitting headache there is an episode (particular case) of pain you would need to be me to feel. So I have a *Vorstellung* in Frege's sense. To borrow from Thomas Nagel, that episode is awful (or so I find). Such may be my *response* to what is a *Vorstellung*. But for the headache to *be* awful, or, if Nagel is right, for it to be *painful*, just is for me so to respond. My response is thus not a *judgement* (in Frege's sense), of some determinate *Vorstellung*, that its being as it is instances some way for a *Vorstellung* to be—it being awful, or painful. My responding as I do is an environmental circumstance. Hence, by the connections thus drawn, my being in pain may be an environmental circumstance. By Frege's point it *must* be if there is to be such a circumstance at all. My being as I am is a particular case which one might judge to fall under (instance) various generalities. If one being in pain is thus an environmental circumstance, it is thereby a generality my being as I am may be judged to instance. But only then is it a way I may be judged to be. And, by the above, so judging is *not* what I do when, responding to what is going on with me by finding it awful, or painful.

There are roles for responses to *Vorstellungen* which only a Pyrrhonian attitude could play, thus reasons for taking some such responses to be Pyrrhonian. One sort of role is: such a response might be creative, constitutive. For example, there may be—and be good reason for there to be—no, or little, gap between my *finding* my head to be splitting (in the sense of the metaphor) and its being so. For one to have a splitting headache may *be* for it to be a certain sort of awful for him. Such might show itself in a sort of immunity to ringers. Where correctness turns on the environment ringers are *ipso facto* in the cards. If Dr Lauben thinks he is suffering concussion, or eye strain, then, no matter how good a diagnostician he is, there is such a thing as what could not be distinguished by him from concussion, but is not that. By contrast, it is none too easy to see what a perfect illusion of a splitting headache might be. But constitutive roles could have more complex structures. Perhaps, for example, what Sid really thinks is fixed, not necessarily by what he *would* now say, but by what he is prepared to recognize (at the end of analysis if need be) as the truth about him.

Vorstellungen provide one way of marking out a territory. But there is a way which, viewed one way, is more fundamental. It is contained in Frege's remark.

If man could not think and take for the object of his thinking something of which he was not the bearer, he would have an inner world all right, but not an environment. But can such thinking not rest on a mistake? . . . Indeed! With the step by which I win myself an environment I expose myself to risk of error.

(1918: p. 73)

An environmental circumstance is *embedded* in its environment. There is a way its obtaining would matter to how else things were, conversely, a way in which other ways things are matter to whether it obtains. It is, so to speak, embedded in networks of factive meaning. For a question of truth to turn on whether some such circumstance obtains is for it to turn on whether there is anything embedded as the obtaining of that circumstance would be. Whether a Porsche's (or Pia's) being yellow would attract the wrong kind of man is not decided by the *idea* of a yellow Porsche—merely by what might *count* as a Porsche's being yellow. But if, all considered, Pia's Porsche's being yellow would attract the wrong kind of man, then if her Porsche does no such thing, it is not yellow. The open-endedness of webs of factive meaning does not rule out that one should just see, by looking at it on some occasion, that Pia's Porsche is yellow; that seeing for oneself may be *proof*. Exposing oneself to risk of error, in the sense needed here, need not mean being in any actual danger of it. But it does mean that, for anything having proof might be, there is always room in conceptual space for ringers for this; for unforeseen, but decisive, considerations against so regarding one's having what he does.

Frege makes his remark having argued already that questions of truth arise only where they turn on the (our) environment, thus only for attitudes towards what is embedded in an environment. So the point of the remark is that they arise only for attitudes in which one exposes himself to risk of error in the present sense. It is part of the notion of proof that if I have proof I cannot be wrong. So if seeing for myself is having proof that Pia drives a yellow Porsche— as it may be so far as we know—then if I have seen for myself I cannot be wrong. But suppose the attitude I hold is one *for me* to hold which I could not be holding falsely; such that my holding it rules out my holding it in error— something my taking Pia to drive a yellow Porsche is not. What Frege tells us is that the only way for there to be an attitude which is thus not susceptible to falsehood is for it to be susceptible to *neither* truth nor falsehood.

Vorstellungen, tied as they are to their bearer's consciousness, are not environmentally embedded. So for an attitude to be purely towards them, to turn on nothing more than their being as they are, is one way for an attitude to be immune to falsity. Whether things are as represented *in re Vorstellungen* turns on nothing environmental, or nothing independent of their being so represented. So, within the present framework, it turns on nothing.

Where I see myself as a believer as I do in attaching that 'I think' to, say, it being cherry season, it is natural to trace absence of liability to be seeing falsely to another source. The believing is, of course, *my* believing. So, *inter alia*, it is *presented* to me in a way you would need to be me to be presented to. You may feel compulsion to think that very thing which I thus do (that it is cherry season). But only *I* can feel that instance of the exertion of (rational) compulsion which I thus do. Only I so relate to *my* being so compelled. So, one could say, in so standing towards myself I have a *Vorstellung*. One could try to make that out as a source here of immunity to going wrong which is compatible with getting something *right*.

But immunity to error may also lie in a creative role assigned a response to what is happening to one—to the impression the world then makes—here to the role of *according* a status to a way for things to be as part of one's *own* thinking as to the thing to do or think. Seeing myself as I do in according that statues with hand forced—with nothing else for me to think—*fills* the space between representing-as and representing-to-be. So for me so to see myself is for me to *be* a believer. Or, more cautiously, where I count as so seeing myself I *ipso facto* also count as a believer. Which is why, though my so seeing myself is *judging*, for example, *that it is cherry season*, it is not *judging* that I so think. I do not *believe* myself to be doing this; I am doing it. Such is a way of incorporating Frege's point about objectivity. *What* I see—the object of my response here—is not something there to see independent of my seeing it it, so not an object of judgement *for me*. In an image of Wittgenstein's, I am rushing forward so cannot observe myself rushing forward. (*Investigations*, §456). Indeed not: *observing* is not what I am doing in standing towards myself as I thus do.

Wittgenstein treated believing, as I do here, as an *example* of something. It emerges now as an example of a way for one to be in which a Pyrrhonian attitude is present as an element, and thus plays a certain role. Believing that Pia drives a Porsche is an objective, truth-evaluable attitude. But taking it involves taking an attitude towards oneself which is not *believing* that one believes, but subscribing in a different way to that being how things are. Now the thing about examples is that one can ask after the others. That is the last topic I will consider here.

5 Scope

The contrast drawn between seeing oneself as a believer in attaching an 'I think', and *believing* that one is a believer, is reminiscent in some ways of that between intending to go to Pia's party and *believing* that, resolutions to avoid it notwithstanding, one will (in the end) succumb to temptation. In both cases, that one will go to the party is the way things are according to him. Intending and believing here guide action similarly. If I really believe that I will go, just as if I intend to go, civility requires me to decline Vic's invitation to join him at La Bellota Hermosa. But if I change my mind, I did not intend falsely, whereas if I resist temptation then I did believe falsely. Intending does not implicate one with its object in the same way as belief. Perhaps, then, intending too is, or involves, Pyrrhonian attitudes.

On the way to introducing his notion of a *Vorstellung* Frege gives a list of things which 'belong to an inner world'. These include 'sense-impressions', creations of our imagination (imaginings, images), sensations, feelings, moods, inclinations, wishes, and decisions. Excluding decisions, he brings the rest under the rubric 'Vorstellung'. Perhaps it would be better put to say that *in* having a feeling—say, feeling strongly about Porsche drivers, or feeling moved by Pia's plight, one encounters, or experiences, or has, *Vorstellungen*. In any event, the role of *Vorstellung* in such things *may* signal a constitutive role there for Pyrrhonian attitudes.

Wittgenstein interested himself in Moore's anomaly in a series of late manuscripts (around 1946–49), always in the context of a discussion of a wider swathe of mental life—such as hope, fear, grief. His swathe overlaps considerably with Frege's examples of an 'inner world'. But the bulk of discussion in these manuscripts centres on a family (or perhaps several families) of phenomena which he brings under the rubrics 'seeing-as' and 'seeing aspects'. Frege would have placed some of these under the rubric, 'Schöpfungen einer Einbildungskraft' (creations of a power of imagining). Some of these are, or are in part, *perceptual* phenomena (the Necker cube, for example). The status of some—perhaps the ones which interested Wittgenstein most—is unclear. In this connection he says the following:

Here we must be careful not to think in traditional psychological categories. Such as simply parsing experience into seeing and thinking; or something similar.
(*Last Writings*, II: §542)

There is a natural line between, as one might call it, receptivity and spontaneity, or presentation—being presented in experience with things to respond to—and response—responding to them. Seeing (where not seeing-that) is presentation. It affords *visual* awareness of what is before one's eyes—of that pig wallowing, say. Thinking something so is a response to being (or having been) presented with what we were. One can respond to the sight of the pig wallowing in taking, perhaps recognizing, there to be a pig wallowing, or that pig to be. Wittgenstein suggests here that some psychological phenomena, and indeed some experiences, do not fall neatly on the one side or the other; that things do not always divide into the categories thus on offer. I have suggested above that belief itself is, or involves, such a case. As such it illustrates one way in which such a case may arise: through the presence of a Pyrrhonian attitude in a creative role. Imagination can provide others. Suppose Pia is imagining lying on hot sand on a hot day, the heat of the sand penetrating her beach towel and causing all her muscles to relax. Was the sand white or yellow? Was there the sound of surf, or seagulls? Were the seagulls wheeling and diving? It is her story; she gets to tell it. (Within limits of coherence), for the imagined sand to be white just is for her to see things that way. Some of what Wittgenstein calls 'seeing aspects' may be like that. Perhaps, too, *some* of perceptual experience is. Such are topics Wittgenstein thought worth investigating, as so might we.

The categories into which such things might not fit neatly are, as he states them, seeing and thinking. As this underlines, he is not suggesting that seeing and thinking themselves do not fit into those categories presentation and response. But then, not all visual experience is seeing. And not all the experiences which concern him are so much as plainly visual or plainly not—though *one* thing I think he hoped to achieve by study of such more recherché phenomena was a better understanding of the relation of seeing to visual experiences which are not that. Perhaps, for example, the role of Pyrrhonian attitudes in seeing aspects where this is *not* a visual phenomenon can point to a role for them in seeing-as where this *is* visual.

By circuitous route we thus arrive at an area ripe for an investigation which, Mosaically, I will not now enter. One reason for interest in the topic is the particular way in which the fact that not all perceptual experience is *perceiving* has seemed to some to be impressive. What someone saw is bounded by what there was, anyway, to be seen. It is then reduced by what was obscured, or beyond the visual acuity of the observer, or not attended to or registered. What someone experienced visually is not confined within these bounds, nor thus determined. In which orientation he saw the Necker cube, whether it looked to him blurry, or seemed to jump around, are matters to be decided in some other way. The temptation is to take this second category of visual experience, rather than the scene before the eyes, as the base case which gets narrowed down, restricted—perhaps by aetiology—into seeing. When I see the tissue box before me, there is anyway, the idea runs, such a thing as the way things then *look* to me, the way experience is, visually, anyway, tissue box or not; with the right causal history (or whatever), things so looking to me will just be my seeing the box.

But suppose now that Pyrrhonian attitudes play some constitutive, creative, role in visual experiences of the second kind. Such would be for some of the work done in fixing *what* was experienced visually, where that is a matter of what was *seen*, to be taken over by such attitudes—by such things as my experience having impressed me as it did. If there is that difference between seeing and other visual experiencing, then it might seem surprising if those two sets of concepts—*perceiving*, and experiencing visually as, or what one does—to line up as they would if, succumbing to temptation, we took the second category as the base case of which, as per above suggestion, seeing forms a proper part. For one thing, how my visual experience *impresses* me—for the cube to *impress* me as jumping, or for it to be *for me* as though it did—is not plausibly a product, or *purely* a product, of *visual* processing (something one might think of as more or less encapsulated). Here thinking demands its due. Whereas the arbiter of what is seen is what there *is* to see, in (mere) looking as though it is how one is impressed. Hinton's image thus read: The first, witnessing, is what *undergoing* the second seems like to one.

If *looking to me as though* (or *as A would*) involves Pyrrhonian attitudes in the way sketched, the idea of visual experiencing as a wider domain, to be narrowed down by aetiology involves a questionable assumption—to wit, that there is such a thing as *the* way things looked to me when I saw the tissue box. Attitudes may take over some of the work done by what was there to be seen in the case of certain visual experiencing. But there is no reason to suppose that they can do all that the scene before the viewer does, notably, *in re* determinacy. Compare their role in story-telling, such as writing *policiers*, and in imagining, such as Pia daydreaming of strolling on the sands of Ancão. Moreover, if Pyrrhonian attitudes are thus involved constitutively in such visual experiencing, such may dampen the hopes one might have of such experiencing, or its occurrence, reducing to the neurophysiological in ways which *might* have seemed in the cards if visual processing were encapsulated enough. But in all this I merely scout, without prejudging, prospects.

There is a tendency, perhaps Kant-inspired, to read material drawn from, and belonging to, thinking into *all* visual experience, thus all seeing. Succumbing to it, seeing a pig may appear as, *inter alia*, having the pig presented to one *as a pig*, just as seeing the window frame as a swastika, or a cloud as a sheep, is (*if* it is) being presented with the frame *as* a swastika, and so on. Those who think this way see motives for it: were things not so presented, I would be helpless to recognize the pig as a pig. Frege showed why they are wrong to think this. But such is a topic for elsewhere. In any case, though the categories seeing/thinking cannot be imposed neatly on all *Schöpfungen der Einbildungskraft*, still, testing the proper bounds of Pyrrhonian attitudes *may* show that those categories cannot be eroded so as to allow for *such* participation of thought in seeing. Wittgenstein never suggested otherwise.

I hope to have done two things in the above. First, to show how Frege's conception of objectivity provides a useful framework for questions about subjectivity; how he thus contributes significantly to our study, not just of The Mind, but of our minds. Second, to introduce a topic for investigation: the role of Pyrrhonian attitudes in mental life. And now, the better course of valour, for one with so much of the projected work undone, is to pause here.

Bibliography

Anscombe, G. E. M. (1965). 'The Intentionality of Sensation: A Grammatical Feature', in *The Collected Philosophical Papers of G. E. Anscombe, vol. II: Metaphysics and the Philosophy of Mind*. Oxford: Blackwell, 1981: pp. 2–20.
Austin, J. L. (1962). *Sense and Sensibilia*. Oxford: Oxford University Press.
Ayer, A. J. (1940). *The Foundations of Empirical Knowledge*. London: Macmillan.
Burge, Tyler (2005). 'Disjunctivism and Perceptual Psychology', *Philosophical Topics*, 33, no. 1 (Spring 2005): 1–78.
Byrne, A. and Logue, H. (2008). 'Either/Or: Disjunctivism for Dummies', in *Disjunctivism: Perception, Action, Knowledge*, ed. Adrian Haddock and Fiona Macpherson. Oxford: Oxford University Press.
Chomsky, Noam (1959). 'Review of B. F. Skinner's *Verbal Behavior*', *Language*, 35, no. 1 (1959): 26–58.
Clarke, Thompson (1962). 'The Nature of Traditional Epistemology', thesis submitted for the degree of Doctor of Philosophy, Harvard University.
—— (1965). 'Seeing Surfaces and Seeing Physical Objects', in *Philosophy in America*, ed. M. Black and W. P. Alston. Ithaca, NY: Cornell University Press.
—— (1972). 'The Legacy of Scepticism', *The Journal of Philosophy*, 69, pp. 98–113, no. 20: 754–69.
Crane, Tim (1998). 'Intentionality as the Mark of the Mental', *Contemporary Issues in the Philosophy of Mind*, ed. A. O'Hear. Cambridge: Cambridge University Press: pp. 1–17.
Davidson, Donald (1983). 'A Coherence Theory of Truth and Knowledge'; reprinted in his *Subjective, Intersubjective, Objective*. Oxford: Oxford University Press, 2001.
Davies, M. (1992). 'Perceptual Content and Local Supervenience', *Proceedings of the Aristotelian Society*, 66: 21–45.
Descartes, René (1637). *Discours de la Méthode*, Paris: Flammarion, 2000.
—— (1641). 'Meditations on First Philosophy', in *Selections From Descartes' Philosophical Writings*, ed. G. E. M. Anscombe and P. T. Geach. London: Nelson, 1954.
—— (1644). 'Principles of Philosophy', in *Selections From Descartes' Philosophical Writings*, ed. G. E. M. Anscombe and P. T. Geach. London: Nelson, 1954.
Diamond, Cora (1981). 'Wright's Wittgenstein', *The Philosophical Quarterly*, 31: 352–66; reprinted in *The Realistic Spirit*. Cambridge, MA: MIT Press: pp. 205–24.
—— (1991). 'Frege Against Fuzz', in *The Realistic Spirit*. Cambridge, MA: MIT Press: pp. 145–78.
Diderot, Denis (1751). 'Lettre sur les Sourds et Muets', in *Oeuvres complètes de Diderot*, vol. 1. Paris: Garnier Frères, 1875.
Dummett, Michael (1981). *The Interpretation of Frege's Philosophy*. London, Duckworth.
—— (1991). 'Frege's Kernsätze zur Logik', in *Frege and Other Philosophers*. Oxford: Oxford University Press: pp. 65–78.

Evans, Gareth (1982). *The Varieties of Reference*. Oxford: Oxford University Press.
Fodor, Jerry (1987). *Psychosemantics*. Cambridge, MA: MIT Press.
—— (1998). *Concepts*. Oxford: Oxford University Press.
—— (2008). *LOT 2*. Oxford: Oxford University Press.
Frege, Gottlob (1882). Letter to Anton Marty; reprinted in *Gottlob Freges Briefwechsel*, Hamburg: Felix Meiner, 1980: pp. 117–19.
—— (1882?). '17 Kernsätze zur Logik', *Nachgelassene Schriften*, ed. H. Hermes, F. Kambartel, and F. Kaulbach. Hamburg: Felix Meiner, 1983: pp. 189–90.
—— (1884). *Die Grundlagen Der Arithmetik*, Breslau: Wilhelm Koebner Verlag, 1884.
—— (1891). "Ueber Funktion und Begriff", lecture to the Jenaischen Geselschaft für Medezin und Naturwissenschaft, reprinted in G. Patzig, ed., *Funktion, Begriff, Bedeutung*, Göttingen: Van den Hoek und Ruprescht, 1962, pp. 17–39.
—— (1892a). 'Ueber Begriff und Gegenstand', *Vierteljahrsschrift für wissenschaftliche Philosophie*, 16: pp. 192–205.
—— (1892b). 'Ueber Sinn und Bedeutung', *Zeitschrift für Philosophie und philosophische Kritik*, 100: pp. 25–50.
—— (1892–1895). 'Ausfuhrungen über Sinn und Bedeutung', in *Nachgelassene Schriften*, ed. H. Hermes, F. Kambartel, and F. Kaulbach. Hamburg: Felix Meiner, 1983: pp. 128–36.
—— (1893). *Grundgesetze der Arithmetik*, vol. 1. Jena: Hermann Pohle.
—— (1897). 'Logik', in *Nachgelassene Schriften*, ed. H. Hermes, F. Kambartel, and F. Kaulbach. Hamburg: Felix Meiner, 1983: pp. 137–63.
—— (1904). Letter to Russell, 13 November 1904; reprinted in *Gottlob Freges Briefwechsel*: Hamburg: Felix Meiner, 1980: pp. 91–6.
—— (1906). 'Einleitung in die Logik', in *Nachgelassene Schriften*, ed. H. Hermes, F. Kambartel, and F. Kaulbach. Hamburg: Felix Meiner, 1983: pp. 201–12.
—— (1914). "Logik in der Mathematik", *Nachgelassene* Shriften, 1983, pp. 219–70.
—— (1918). 'Der Gedanke', *Beiträge zur Philosophie des deutschen Idealismus*, 2: pp. 58–77.
—— (1919a). "Die Verneinung", *Beiträge zur deutschen Idealismus*, 1, 1918–1919, pp. 143–57.
—— (1919b). 'Aufzeichnungen für Ludwig Darmstaedter', in *Nachgelassene Schriften*, ed. H. Hermes, F. Kambartel, and F. Kaulbach. Hamburg: Felix Meiner, 1983: pp. 273–7.
Harman, G. (1990). 'The Intrinsic Quality of Experience', *Philosophical Perspectives*, 4: 31–52.
Hinton, J. M. (1967). 'Visual Experiences', *Mind*, NS 76, no. 302: 217–27.
—— (1973). *Experiences*. Oxford: Oxford University Press.
Kant, Immanuel (1781/1789). *Kritik der reinen Vernunft*. Frankfurt am Main: Insel, 1956.
Kaplan, David (1989). 'Demonstratives', in *Themes From Kaplan*, ed. J. Almog et al. Oxford: Oxford University Press: pp. 481–563.
Kripke, Saul (1979). 'A Puzzle About Belief', in *Meaning and Use*, ed. A. Margalit. Dordrecht: D. Reidel: pp. 239–83.
Leibniz, Gottfried (1765). *Nouveaux Essais sur l'entendement humain*, ed. Jacques Brunschvig. Paris: Flammarion, 1966.
McDowell, J. (1984). 'De Re Senses', in *Meaning, Knowledge, and Reality*. Cambridge, MA: Harvard University Press: pp. 214–27.

—— (1986). 'Singular Thought and the Extent of Inner Space', in *Subject, Thought, and Context*, ed. J. McDowell and P. Pettit. Oxford: Oxford University Press; reprinted in *Meaning, Knowledge, and Reality*, Oxford: Oxford University Press, 1998: pp. 228–59.

—— (1991). 'Intentionality *De Re*', in *Meaning, Knowledge, and Reality*. Cambridge, MA: Harvard University Press: pp. 260–74.

—— (1994). *Mind and World*. Cambridge, MA: Harvard University Press.

—— (1998). 'Having the World in View: Sellars, Kant, and Intentionality' (The Woodbridge Lectures), *The Journal of Philosophy*, 95, no. 9: 438–9.

—— (2008). 'Avoiding the Myth of the Given', J. Lindgaard, ed., *John McDowell: Experience, Norm, and Nature*: Oxford: Wiley-Blackwell, 2008, pp. 1–14. Reprinted in McDowell 2009b.

—— (2009a). 'What Myth', in *The Engaged Intellect*. Cambridge, MA: Harvard University Press: pp. 308–23.

—— (2009b). *Having the World in View*. Cambridge, MA: Harvard University Press, 2009.

McGinn, C. (1982). *The Character of Mind*. Oxford: Oxford University Press.

—— (1991). *The Problem of Consciousness*. Oxford: Blackwell.

Peacocke, C. (1992). *A Study of Concepts*. Cambridge, MA: MIT Press, 1992.

—— (2001). 'Does Perception Have a Nonconceptual Content?', The Journal of Philosophy, vol. 98, no. 5. (May, 2001), pp. 239–64.

Price, H. H. (1932). *Perception*. London: Methuen: p. 125.

Prichard, H. A. (1909). *Kant's Theory of Knowledge*. Oxford: Clarendon Press.

—— (1938). 'The Sense-Datum Fallacy', *Proceedings of the Aristotelian Society*, 17: 1–18; reprinted in *Knowledge and Perception*. Oxford: Oxford University Press, 1950.

—— (1950a). 'Perception', in *Knowledge and Perception* (essays and lectures). Oxford: Oxford University Press: pp. 52–68.

—— (1950b). 'History of the Theory of Knowledge: Descartes' Meditations', in *Knowledge and Perception* (essays and lectures). Oxford: Oxford University Press: pp. 71–103.

Putnam, Hilary (1977). 'Models and Reality', Presidential Address to the Association for Symbolic Logic, 1977; reprinted in *Realism and Reason: Philosophical Papers, vol. 3*. Cambridge: Cambridge University Press, 1983.

—— (1988). *Representation and Reality*. Cambridge, MA: Harvard University Press.

—— (1999). *The Threefold Cord*. New York: Columbia University Press.

Russell, Bertrand (1918). 'Lectures on Logical Atomism', in *Logic and Knowledge*, ed. R. C. Marsh. London: Allen and Unwin, 1988: pp. 177–281.

Searle, J. (1983). *Intentionality*. Cambridge: Cambridge University Press.

Travis, C. (1997). 'Pragmatics', in *A Companion to the Philosophy of Language*, ed. Crispin Wright and Bob Hale. Oxford: Blackwell: pp. 87-107; reprinted in Travis (2008).

—— (2004). 'The Twilight of Empiricism', *Proceedings of the Aristotelian Society*, vol. 104, part III (February 2004), pp. 245–70. Reprinted in *Objectivity and the Parochial*.

—— (2006). *Thought's Footing*. Oxford: Oxford University Press.

—— (2008), *Occasion-Sensitivity: Selected Essays*, Oxford: Oxford University Press.

Travis, C. (2011). 'Thought's Social Nature', *The European Journal of Philosophy*, 19, no. 4: pp. 585–606; reprinted in Travis, *Objectivity and the Parochial*. Oxford: Oxford University Press: pp. 301–24.

Tye, M. (1995). *Ten Problems of Consciousness*. Cambridge, MA: MIT Press.

Waismann, Friedrich (1979). *Wittgenstein: Conversations with the Vienna Circle*. Oxford: Blackwell.

Wittgenstein, Ludwig (1922). *Tractatus Logico-Philosophicus*. London: Routledge and Kegan Paul.

——(1953). *Philosophical Investigations*. Oxford: Blackwell.

Wittgenstein, Ludwig (1958). *The Blue and Brown Books*. Oxford: Blackwell.

——(1969). *On Certainty*. Oxford: Blackwell.

——(1980). *Remarks On The Philosophy of Psychology*, vol. 1. Oxford: Blackwell.

——(1982a). *Remarks on the Philosophy of Psychology*, vol. 2. Oxford: Blackwell.

——(1982b). *Last Writings*, I. Oxford: Blackwell, 1982.

Index

acquaintance
  with the non-conceptual, with the conceptual (comparison) 7–10, 247–50, 387
  with the non-conceptual 72, 95, 99, 155, 174, 258, 365–6, 381, 387–8
allorepresentation 26–8, 29, 30, 49, 314–51, 358
  is creative 267, 317, 351
Anerkennung 105, 108, 128–31, 176, 214–15, 267, *see also* recognition, two notions
Anscombe, G. M. 51, 102, 201–216
appear, see looks
appearance
  Pyrrhonian 86, 405
  Kant 229, 256, 257
apperception 108–10
articulation
  of Kantian *Bilder* 257
  of the way things are into ways things are 131–2, 136, 195
  of thought into elements, *see* Frege, on the context principle; Frege, on multiple decomposibility
aspect (linguistic) 329–32, 335
aspect (visual) *see* surfaces; Wittgenstein on aspect-seeing
Austin, J. L. 2, 29–31, 41, 111, 128, 144, 153, 182, 203, 210
autorepresentation 26–58, 313–19, 347
Ayer, A. J. 102, 112–15, 201–17

belief
  and disjunctivism 259–312
  -formation 194–5
  Lutheran 129, 297, 311, 391, 396–405
  presumes its own succes 267
  and Pyrrhonism, *see* Pyrrhonian attitudes
  and sensation 141–2
  and sharibility, *see* Frege, on the intrinsic shareability of thought
  state/interval notion 401–5
Burge, T. 259–312
Brentano 220, 222

Carnap, R. 1–2
Chomsky, N. 318, 349

Clarke, T. 21, 168–73, 337, 364–90
committed representing, *see* representing to be
concepts
  as functions, *see* Frege, on concepts
  as of ways for things to be 18, 93, 124–5, 184–5, 205
conceptual recognition capacity 121, 185–7, 189, 191, 197, 239–40, 316, 363, *see also* reason, transcends what it can survey
conceptual/historical distinction 1–8, 13–22, 71–2, 93–117, 123, 124–43, 149–51, 157, 187–97, 232, 236–41, 247–55, 269, 275, 288, 307, 320–2, 347, 374, 387, 390
conceptual/non-conceptual, *see* conceptual/historical distinction
contain
  as element 14, 66–8
  as aura 15
  fixing 4–6
  essentially 220–1
Cook-Wilson, J. 59, 180, 368
Crane, T. 220–2

Davidson, D. 122, 132, 140–3, 234
Davies, M. 23–5
Da Vinci inquiry 370–82, 389
Descartes, R. 30, 86, 115, 144, 152–5, 260, 315–19, 329, 368
Diamond, C. 184–5, 196, 332
Diderot, D. 254
disjunctivism 9–13, 59–89, 259–312
Dummett, M. 15, 180–1, 184–5, 273,
  effect-representating (factive meaning) 24, 31–2, 34, 39, 43, 44, 63, 91, 152–4, 162–3, 190, 211, 301–3, 308, 315–22, 331–51, 353–63, 407–8

Einbildungskraft 257, 410, 412
environment, *see* exposure to risk of error; Frege on the instrinsic shareability of thought
Erkennung see recognition (two notions); *Anerkennung*
Evans, G. 21, 147–66, 175, 192–96, 352–7, 360
exposure to risk of error 60–2, 66, 68, 70, 75–6, 90, 92, 94, 141, 200, 212–13, 292–3, 303–4, 365, 381, 387, 405–9, *see also* Frege, on the intrinsic shareability of thought

face value of perception 24–8, 45–9, 58
factive meaning, *see* effect-representing
Feigl, H. 1–2
Fodor, J. 21, 181, 251, 357–63
Frege, G.
  on concepts 5, 7, 18, 19, 93–5, 126, 204–5
  on the context-principle 4, 15–17, 208, 223–4, 242, 250, 254, 270, 282, 289, 330–2, 358
  on decomposing a thought as singular or general 14–15, 263, 271, 284–5, 287, 289
  on *Erkenntniswert* 273
  on the fundamental logical relation 93, 149, 153, 188–90, 195, 237, 247, 390
  on the generality of thought, *see* conceptual/historical distinction
  on idealism 85, 112, 231, 257
  on intentions 339
  on the laws of truth 7–8, 74–5, 140–1, 247, 392
  on modes of presentation 18, 199–200, 221, 271–305
  on multiple decomposibility 4–8, 14–19, 223, 242, 250–6, 263, 270–4, 282–9, 291, 331, 353, 358, *see also* Frege, on the context-principle
  on psychologism 251, 273, 274–5, 326, 406
  on uncommitted representation 27, 337, 391, 393–4, *see also* representation-as; representing-to-be
  on sense-impressions 233–5, 387
  on thought's integration into the world 351
  on that thought is intrinsically shareable (*Vorstellungen*) 15–17, 62, 70, 78–9, 82–3, 85, 87, 89, 91, 92, 96–9, 115, 143, 154, 176, 212, 214, 226–30, 234–5, 259, 272, 274–5, 300, 302–9, 322, 358, 365–6, 372, 387–8, 391–2, 406–10, *see also* exposure to risk of error
  on that what is visible is not thinkable and vice versa 7, 40, 41, 44, 49, 89, 123–4, 150, 191, 238–9, 268–70, 289–90, 307, 342, 364–5
Feyerabend, P. 185
Freud, L. 108, 325
fundamental question of perception 3, 153, 189, 224–5, 242–3

generality of thought, *see* historical/conceptual distinction
generic generality introduced 288–97
the Given, myth of 139–43, 242–50

hallucination 81, 106, 380–3, 393
Harman, G. 23, 48–58
Hinton, J. M. 9, 79, 259–312, 388

idealism, *see* Frege, on idealism
ideas, *see* Frege, on the intrinsic shareability of thought
illusion 33
  argument from 180
  Müller-Lyer 33, 36, *see also* ringer
indicate (relation) 28, 32–4, 43–4, 46–7, 52–4; *see also* effect-representating
instance (relation) see reach (relation)
intensionality 200–11, 217–18, 221
'I think' 246, 395–409

judgement, *see* representing-to-be

Kant, I. 16, 20, 193, 223–34, 251–2, 255–8, 395, 412
Kaplan, D. 332
Kripke, S. 274

Leibniz, G. W. 11, 108–10, 156
looks 26, 28–9, 106, 226
  hybrid 45–8
  and shifted use 100–3, 111–16
  thinkable 39–45, 77–8, 80, 157, 160, 222
  visual 34–9, 51, 148, 167, 170, 284
Lotze, H. 15–17, 358

McDowell, J. 24–6, 33, 45–8, 80, 85–6, 119–23, 127, 132, 139–43, 156, 193–7, 199, 224–5, 242–58, 313
McGinn, C. 23
mediation, *see* veil of ideas
Moore's paradox (anomaly) 21, 391–410

Nagel, T. 406
naming 210, 217–18
non-conceptual content 151, 156–63, 164

occasion-sensitivity 30, 36, 43, 130–9, 168–73, 367–90, 402–5

parochial 225
particular case see historical/conceptual
Peacocke, C. 23–4, 155–65, 171, 192–6
perceptual recognition capacity 50, 186, 239–40, 255, 363, *see also* conceptual recognition capacity
phenomenal character 2, 23, 60, 78, 116, 311–12

picture
  mental 9, 59
  perceivable 124, 257, 318
  of the world 252–4, 257–8
Price, H. H. 308–9
Prichard, H. A. 145–6, 179–80, 227–9, 233–4, 240, 364–8, 370, 378, 386
private thought, *see* Frege, on the intrinsic shareability of thought
propositional form (*that things are thus and so*) 6, 40, 122, 134, 156, 257, 406
propositional element/structure 67–8, 121–2 127, 130, 270, 274–5, 279, 285, 291, 300
the Proximity Principle 264–6
psychologism 273–87, 299, 304, 312, 326–8, 333, 338–9, *see also* Frege, on psychologism
psychology 24, 50, 87, 185–7, 190, 230, 239, 242, 251, 255–6, 297
Putnam, H. 21, 132, 178, 181–7, 189–91, 195–6, 316–17, 322
Pyrrhonian attitudes 182–3, 193, 405–12; *see also* scepticism, ancient

qualia, *see* phenomenal states
Quine, W. V. O. 142, 204–5

rational
  animals 158–9, 182, 194, 197, 243
  relations/structure 3, 8, 118–43, 183, 195–7, 243–50; *see also* Frege, on the fundamental logical relation
reach (relation) 6, 93–5, 149, 187–8, 237–8, 249, 251, 269, 320–2, 324, 327, 374–5; *see also* conceptual/historical
realism
  empirical (Kant) 231
  internal 132, 178
reason
  structure of, *see* rational relations/structure
  transcends what it can survey 316–17, 322, 323
recognition (two notions) 105, 128, 130, 214, *see also* Anerkennung
recognizability of content 2, 314, 326–7, 332–4, 347–51, 358, *see also* veil of ideas
recurrability 63–4, 69–70, 75–6
representing-as
  only for a thinker 315, 329
  poses a selection task 323–8, 336–7, 344–6, 353–63
  three-place relation 2–6, 27, 319–20, 338, 357
representing-to-be 4, 26–8, 152, 166–8, 244–6, 267–8, 314, 320, 336–8, 348–51, 393–401, 409
resemble, *see* looks, visible

ringers 10, 45–7, 77, 79, 81–2, 84, 168, 235, 260–3, 263–5, 278–84, 287–8, 292, 294–305, 308–9, 312, 323, 342, 344, 345–7, 360, 362–3, 365–6, 370–3, 381–3, 385–7, 390, 393, 403, 407–8; *see also* scepticism, modern
Russell, B. 60, 199, 300, 302, 303, 305

scepticism
  Ancient 86–7, *see also* Pyrrhonian attitudes
  modern 235, 297–305, 368–90, *see also* ringers
Searle, J. 23
seeing
  a success verb 8, 365
  unit concept 374–6
  what is not there 201–6, 220
Sellars, W. 119–20
sensations 63, 86, 89, 90, 108, 141–2, 227–31, 234, 241, 409–10
  in contrast to rational compulsion 397, 399
  pain 87–8, 96–7, 111, 392–3, 397–8, 407
sense data 60, 77, 235, 312, 364–90
sensibility (*Sinnlichkeit*), receptivity 123, 142–3, 227–33, 255–6, 243, 410, *see also* conceptual/historical
shifted use 100–3 (introduced), 113–5
sideways on, *see* Wittgenstein, on sideways on
sight affords awareness 11–13, 30–1, 79–80, 133, 145, 148–50, 175–7, 179, 195, 231, 248–9, 255, 258, 306, 381, 410
singular/general thought 14–15, 59, 72, 74, 218, 263, 271–2, 284–5, 287–91, 297, 300, 302, 305, 306
Sinn 289, 291–4, 298
Stuff Happens Model 9, 146–7, 151–63, 172, 175
sub-doxastic states 2, 80–1, 108–10, 311, 353, 361
sub-personal states, *see* sub-doxastic states
surfaces 168–71, 368–82

things being as they are, *see* conceptual-historical
truth-evaluable attitudes 6, 25, 27, 41, 60–2, 71, 73, 75–6, 84–6, 120, 128, 141, 151–2, 155–7, 160, 182, 187–8, 192, 211, 215, 222, 267, 311, 406–7, 409
Tye, M. 23

unity of thought/content 223–33, 242, 246, 250–4, 358

veil of ideas 8, 30–3, 54–7, 310–12, *see also* recognizability of content
vehicle for representations, *see* recognizability of content

Vorstellung
   history of 115–17
   Frege, *see* Frege, on the intrinsic shareability of thought
   Kant 16, 223, 228–34
   Lotze 15–17, 358

way for things to be, *see* concepts, of ways for things to be
Wiggins, D. 396
Wittgenstein, L.
   on aspect-seeing 13, 99, 101, 410
   on conceptual capacities 184–5
   on the difficulty of beginning at the beginning 178–9
   on essential structure 122, 127, 254
   on inner pictures 59
   on insubstantial a priori 225
   on intentionality 217
   on I-thoughts 110–13, 393, 399
   on judgments of inner sense 86, 90
   on meaning 91
   on Ockham's razor 351
   on other minds 178
   on outer form 313
   on presentation and response 391, 399–400, 410–12
   on properties as ingredients of things 133–4
   on sideways on 292, 384, 409
   on the tendency to do philosophy as if it were science 144, 177